Women in the World
of Frederick Douglass

Women in the World of Frederick Douglass

LEIGH FOUGHT

OXFORD
UNIVERSITY PRESS

OXFORD

UNIVERSITY PRESS

Oxford University Press is a department of the University of Oxford. It furthers the University's objective of excellence in research, scholarship, and education by publishing worldwide. Oxford is a registered trade mark of Oxford University Press in the UK and certain other countries.

Published in the United States of America by Oxford University Press
198 Madison Avenue, New York, NY 10016, United States of America.

Library of Congress Cataloging-in-Publication Data
Names: Fought, Leigh, 1967– author.
Title: Women in the world of Frederick Douglass / Leigh Fought.
Description: New York, NY : Oxford University Press, 2017. | Includes index.
Identifiers: LCCN 2016042212 (print) | LCCN 2016045837 (ebook) |
ISBN 9780199782376 (hardback) | ISBN 9780199782611 (Updf) |
ISBN 9780190627287 (Epub)
Subjects: LCSH: Douglass, Frederick, 1818–1895—Relations with women. |
African American abolitionists—Biography.
Classification: LCC E449.D75 F68 2017 (print) | LCC E449.D75 (ebook) |
DDC 973.8092 [B]—dc23
LC record available at https://lccn.loc.gov/2016042212

1 3 5 7 9 8 6 4 2
Printed by Edwards Brothers Malloy, United States of America

For the men of my world:
Louis, Karl, Keith, Jake, Bradley,
and, most of all,
Doug

CONTENTS

ACKNOWLEDGMENTS

Although the writing of a book often takes place in solitude, books themselves do not go from an idea to an object in a reader's hand without the collaboration and influence of multitudes. In thanking my multitude, I must also tell the story of how *Women in the World of Frederick Douglass* came to fruition. The seed of this book was planted during my time as an associate editor at the Frederick Douglass Papers in the early 2000s at Indiana University–Purdue University at Indianapolis. I was very happy to have worked there because I became a better researcher and found myself embroiled in the life of one of history's most fascinating characters. Mark Emerson, Rachael Drenovsky, Candy Hudziak, and Diane Barnes spent many hours with me mining and opining upon the details of Douglass's life for the first correspondence volume, while Robin Condon saw the project to completion. During those years, I had envisioned this book as a series of biographical chapters focused on particular women. "Nah, no one is interested in them," my friend Babu Srinivasan told me. "Make it about the thing that connects them all." Babu counseled me through my first book, and he is also one of the smartest people anyone could ever want to know, with the *Jeopardy!* credentials to prove it. I listened. His suggestion to reconceptualize the book made it far more interesting to far more people.

Then, I took a few detours. The way back to Douglass wandered through the blogosphere. There, my pseudonymous avatar met many wonderful scholars also exploring the creative freedom that comes with adopting a slightly different persona than allowed in their usual lives. They formed a community of intellectual possibility that allowed me not only to articulate the idea for this book, but to also see it as something other people might actually want to read. For that, I will always value Historiann, Digger, Feminist Avatar, Belle, Ink, Bittersweet Girl, RPS77, Claire, Susan in comments, Squadratomagico, FeMOMist, GayProf, Notorious PhD, and others whom I am certain to have forgotten in name if not in spirit.

When I finally found the gumption to write a proposal and submit it to someone with clout, Susan Ferber at Oxford University Press seized it. She did not mind my frantic call when I nearly missed our first appointment due to the DC Metro's business as usual, and the contract that she offered gave the project legitimacy when I was applying for funding and jobs. She has been more than patient as my job changes, moves, and health delayed progress and the research revealed a much more complex story than I originally anticipated. Her comments forced this to be a better book, and she will be remembered among the great editors of our time. Her colleagues behind the scenes at Oxford University Press have also made this volume come to life beautifully.

Susan also chose some fantastic external evaluators for both the proposal and manuscript. Two remained anonymous, although their comments were useful and supportive. Catherine Clinton, who read the proposal, is a model of generosity. As I have admired her career since I first read *Plantation Mistress* back in graduate school, so she has helped mine from my first book, to the comments that she made on papers I gave at a Frederick Douglass conference in 2005 and a British American Nineteenth Century Historians conference in 2009, to writing for my tenure. I only wish I could be as grand as her one day. I would have guessed that Nancy Hewitt had read the full manuscript if she had not revealed herself because no one knows so much about the lovely Amy Post as she. Nancy gave incredible suggestions that helped me reshape three frustrating chapters into something much more coherent and, indeed, intelligent than they otherwise might have been.

The National Endowment for the Humanities Summer Research Stipend allowed me to research for weeks in the Post and Porter Family Papers in Rochester, the Rochester Ladies' Antislavery Society Papers in Ann Arbor, the Amy Kirby Post Papers at Swarthmore, and the Walter O. Evans Collection in Savannah. Vice President Paula Matusky and Nancy Newell in the grants office at Montgomery College in Takoma Park, Maryland, where I worked at the time, officially nominated me for the award. Then Dean J. Barron Boyd orchestrated my move to Le Moyne College in Syracuse, New York, where the Research and Development Committee, chaired by Julie Olin-Ammentorp, helped defray the costs of photographic images.

Having earned a library science degree and worked as an archivist myself during one of those professional detours, I have a great appreciation for the work, procedures, and nuisances encountered by those who make collections available to researchers. I wish I could name everyone who brought me yet another box or folder, or who answered another in a series of obtuse questions. Wayne Stevens, who handles Interlibrary Loan for faculty at Le Moyne College, could find Amelia Earhart if I put in a request. Lori Birrell, Melinda Wallington, and their staff in the Rare Books and Manuscripts Collections in the Rush Rhees

Library at the University of Rochester have created a wonderful online exhibit of the Amy and Isaac Post Papers and still remember my work there with enthusiasm. Eric Frazier helped me through the Antislavery Collection at the Boston Public Library and spoke with me about becoming an archivist when the seed of this book had not yet germinated. He reappeared when I contacted the Library of Congress about images. Marilyn Nolte of the Friends of Mt. Hope was more than generous with information and records about the Douglass burial site, in spite of my initial, inexcusable snappishness. The librarians at the Jagiellonian Library in Krakow, Poland, had great patience with an American who did not understand the monetary conversion figures and willingly scanned almost an entire series from the Varnhagen von Ense Collection. My gratitude also goes to the staffs at the Clements Library at the University of Michigan in Ann Arbor, Mt. Holyoke College Archives in Massachusetts, the Bird Library in Syracuse, the Lynn Museum and Historical Society, the Library of Congress, the National Archives, the Talbot County Historical Society, the Talbot County Public Library, the Maryland Historical Society, the Massachusetts Historical Society, the Onondaga Historical Society, the town clerk's office in Honeoye, the Moorland-Spingarn Research Center at Howard University, the American Antiquarian Society, the Archives of American Art, Colgate University and its database of the American Missionary Association Archives, the Hall of Records Commission at the Maryland State Archives, the Houghton Library at Harvard University, the Nebraska State Historical Society, Smith College Special Collections, and the Butler Library at Columbia University.

A special debt of gratitude goes to Dr. Walter O. Evans, who is so generous with his spectacular collection of Douglass material that will ultimately reshape the way that scholars address the Douglass children. His curiosity about the Douglasses and perspectives on the family forced me to explore and articulate several ideas about the home life in an upwardly mobile black family. His wife Linda and he permitted me to mine the scrapbooks and papers in their well-appointed dining room for a week, a most satisfying research experience. I also thank Stan Deaton of the Georgia Historical Society, who made the introduction.

Then, of course, there are all of the people who took the time to read part or all of this manuscript. The Binghamton Early American History workshop accepted Chapter 2, the first one that I completed, and their comments and questions helped me see the questions that many readers would have. Josh Canale, who later became a colleague at Le Moyne, pointed out that I had buried the key quote, "I shouldered one part of our baggage and Anna took up the other," from Douglass's *Narrative*. "That, right there, is the story," he said, and he was right. Donald R. Wright and Alan Gallay could always find the parts that I myself knew were weak but suggest ways to make them stronger. Richard J.M. Blackett probably thought he was done with me when I graduated with my PhD, but he proved that he is an adviser for life, read the whole thing, and flattered me by asking me to read parts of his work. Diane Sommerville and the late, brilliant Stephanie Camp offered great suggestions on the early chapters. Stacey Robertson, Gary Kornblith, and Carol Lasser read middle sections, and Gary and Carol allowed me access to their research on black Oberlin in order to give context to Rosetta's time there. I have admired Carol's work since I first read "The Sororal Model of Nineteenth-Century Female Friendships" in graduate school, and whenever I went searching for an article about abolitionist women, hers always ended up being the exact one that I needed, and she always had the right insight into the questions that I ask.

The first time that I heard that David Blight was writing a biography of Douglass, not long after I had received the contract for my own book, I thought my whole project was doomed before it began. Thoroughly intimidated, I stalked him around a snack table, trying to get a word in between the many people who flocked around him. When I finally got the nerve up to squeak out an introduction and explanation of my own work, we realized that we were writing entirely different types of stories. Ever since, he has won my devotion with his generosity and command of Douglass's life. He has read chapters, exchanged research, written for my tenure, and invited me to speak to his class at Yale. He also made possible the translation of Ottilie Assing's correspondence to her sister Ludmilla and to Sylvester Rosa Koehler. His sympathy animates Douglass in ways that I can only hope to shadow, and I'm stunned that he has any interest in what I might have to say. Some of the most incredible conversations that I have had in my life have been with David, nerding out over Frederick Douglass.

Many others have also contributed to the creation of this book, whether they know it or not, often by merely tolerating my incessant chatter about Douglass and the women. These include people who commented or asked questions on papers that I delivered at meetings of the Association of Documentary Editing, the Southern Historical Association, the Society of Historians of the Early American Republic, and conferences held at Howard University in 2005 and St. John Fisher College in 2013. Le Moyne College, Montgomery College, University College-Dublin, and Queens University in Belfast all invited me to give talks, which turned out full audiences. The British American Nineteenth Century Historians have the most polite meetings, filling the room and engaging in lively debate despite morning slots on the last day of the conference. National Endowment for the Humanities Institutes in Jackson, Mississippi, and Savannah, Georgia, produced more than their fair share of discussion, surpassed only by the seminar on slave rebellions in the Atlantic World held at Johns Hopkins in Baltimore in the summer of 2009. The Frederick Douglass National Historic Park, Women's Rights National Historic Park, Seneca Falls Convention Days committee, and the Onondaga County Civil War Round Table all invited me to give talks on my work, despite not yet having a product to sell, which showed me both the commitment of local historians and that audiences outside of the academic world are very interested in some of the same questions that I have about the way people lived, loved, and coped in the past.

"Exploring the Lives of Anna Douglass through History and Poetry," sponsored by the Villanova History and English departments in 2013, brought my research together with the poems of Nzadi Keita of Ursinus College. Her beautiful imagining of the interior life of Anna made me jealous of her skill and her craft, which allow her to go into the spaces between the documents forbidden to historians. The dinner conversation with her and the other faculty at Villanova enhance my own understanding of the questions that Anna faced and her reasons for making certain decisions. In particular, I would not have picked up the importance for her of Douglass's decision not to become a minister without their insight.

Colleagues, staff, and students at Montgomery College and Le Moyne have also encouraged and just as often endured my Douglass fascination. Particular sympathy must go to Karl Smith and Lesley Casey, who shared an office suite with me at Montgomery College, and the Department of History at Le Moyne College, as well as anyone on the fourth floor of Reilly Hall. The committee that chose *Narrative of the Life of Frederick Douglass* for Le Moyne's Common Core reading for the 2014–2016 school years deserves many cheers. Thanks to them, David Lloyd, Carolyn Bashaw, and Bruce Erickson's COR 100 class now know quite a lot more than they anticipated about women in the life of Frederick Douglass. Students in my classes at Montgomery and Le Moyne colleges now know that I was not just making this book up. Many who made observations may find their influence in these pages from time to time.

Thanks also go to Ann Ryan, who suggested that I look at the relationship of Margaret Fuller and Ralph Waldo Emerson for comparison; Pat Keane, for all-round Keane-ness; the Pub Committee, just because; Elizabeth Pryor and Sowande Mustakeem, whose Facebook posts expand my mind; Dwight Watson, who made me aware of questions that I could not have articulated when we first met in 1995 but whose presence is felt throughout this book; Margaret Washington, who adores the charming William C. Nell and whose work on Sojourner Truth illuminated parts of Anna's life; John Muller, who knows more about Douglass in DC and the neighborhood around Cedar Hill than I thought possible, who pointed me toward the black women whom Douglass worked with there, and who is a meticulous researcher; Celeste-Marie Bernier, for her unflagging enthusiasm; Frank Fee for respecting Julia Griffiths for herself and sharing his work with me; Kenneth Morris, for his joy in discovering anything about his ancestor and his activism against slavery as it exists today; Joyce Jennings, Julie Bondanza, and Frances Haxton, who kept me sane; Manisha Sinha, who crushes on abolitionists with the best of them; AJ Aiseirithe, who does not shy away from pointing out racism in the woman's movement, and who found the great Henry Highland Garnet quote to Maria Weston Chapman; Beverly Tomek, for her love of the women abolitionists of Philadelphia; Angela Murphy, for her affection for the Loguens and Syracuse; everyone who responded to the call for a Kurrent translator; and Heike Polster and Katerina Schmidt for their wonderful translations and perspectives on Ottilie Assing, shaming me in my prejudices against her by highlighting the reasons that Douglass found her engaging.

I have a t-shirt from the Flannery O'Connor house that says "Anyone who has survived his childhood has enough information about life to last him the rest of his days." That is certainly true of my family, and our peculiarities have afforded me sympathy with those like the Douglasses, who disappoint one another, fight with one another, support one another, and love one another in equal parts. My parents, Louis and Glenna Fought, have often despaired of my eclectic path, much as the Douglasses did with their own children, but no one is more thrilled by my success than they are. My aunt, Catherine McKenzie, is my rock. My brothers and sisters-in-law, Karl, Keith, Dorit, and Sharon, may not be sure what I do for a living exactly, but seem a little bit impressed by it. My nephews Jake and Bradley probably think this book is a myth on par with the Loch Ness Monster, but they are nonetheless happy to show me that they are familiar with "Funky Fresh Freddy Doug." Niece Claire deserves mention simply because she is determined and cute.

Douglas Egerton belongs in every paragraph of these acknowledgments. At that NEH summer seminar on slave rebellions, he sat across from me at dinner and, as a matter of polite conversation, asked, "So what do you research?" "Are you sure you want to know?" I warned, "because I can talk about it for a long time." He shrugged gamely and said, "Sure." He has been hearing about it every day since. *Women in the World of Frederick Douglass* could not have happened without Doug, a historian who has written two books and begun a third in the time that I have written this one. He urged me to write the initial proposal and send it to Susan Ferber. He then brought me with him on his Fulbright to Ireland, liberating me from a crushing teaching load so I could focus on this project for a year. We have read each other's work, shared our research, and discussed ideas, books, and anything else incessantly for seven years. His amazing daughters, Kearney and Hannah, say that we are alike in "a lot of really scary ways," exclaiming "oh my god I'm so glad you two found each other" at each bit of evidence that he and I are the same kind of nerd. His unflagging confidence in me as a scholar and a worthy person makes me stronger. My admiration for him as a historian and a man knows no bounds, and my life is bigger for knowing him than I ever thought possible. He is my great adventure that has paralleled the joy of writing this book and will continue long after.

Women in the World
of Frederick Douglass

Introduction

"I belong to the women," declared Frederick Douglass at the mid-point of his life.[1] More so for him than for any other prominent man of his time, this was true. His race, his enslaved status, his ability to read, his self-emancipation, his success as a speaker and newspaper editor, the way he lived every aspect of his life in opposition to racism, his understanding of equality between the sexes, his intellectual development, and even the very documents that later generations use to reconstruct his life—like this book itself—all emerged from the world of women. At key points in his life women ensured that he realized his ambitions; and, in some instances, no man could have played the same type of role in his resistance to racism. Nevertheless, aside from platitudes, they have not found their way into the telling of his life in any way that would reflect their influence.

Most remember Frederick Douglass as the important black man of his time. His life spanned almost the entirety of the nineteenth century and included some of its most important movements, people, and events, and his accomplishments startled even his contemporaries. "I was born in Tuckahoe" began his first autobiography, naming the remote area in Talbot County, Maryland, where he was born into slavery in 1818. He grew up there and in Baltimore, but escaped at the age of twenty. In 1842, he began lecturing for the American Anti-Slavery Society headed by William Lloyd Garrison, embarking on a career that took him to Ireland, Scotland, and England. There abolitionists purchased his freedom and raised the funds to allow him to start an antislavery newspaper in Rochester, New York, which he published under three successive titles, the *North Star*, *Frederick Douglass' Paper*, and *Douglass' Monthly*, between 1847 and 1864. During the Civil War era, he agitated for the emancipation of slaves, the recruitment of black soldiers, and African American citizenship, including the right of black men to vote. His expansive view of suffrage also extended to women, and he attended one of the earliest woman's rights conventions, held at Seneca Falls, New York. After the war, he edited the *New National Era* in Washington, DC, where he had moved in 1872. As he became embroiled in Republican Party politics in order to ensure the protection of African American rights, he held a series of public offices that included a position on a diplomatic mission to Santo Domingo, US Marshal of the District of Columbia, Recorder of Deeds of the District of Columbia, and US diplomat to the Republic of Haiti. He traveled to Britain three times during his lifetime and took the Grand Tour of Europe at the age of seventy. He published his life story three times, first as *Narrative of the Life of Frederick Douglass* in 1845, then as *My Bondage and My Freedom* in 1855, and finally as *Life and Times of Frederick Douglass*, which appeared in three editions in 1881, 1882, and 1892. He married twice. Anna Murray, a free black woman he met in Baltimore, had helped him escape and bore him five children, Rosetta, Lewis, Frederick Jr., Charles, and Annie. After Anna's death, Helen Pitts, a white woman, became his wife, and as his childless widow, she preserved his papers and his home for posterity after his death in 1895.

This biographical summary touches upon the major moments of his career as provided by Douglass in his autobiographies in which he intended to expose the plight of African Americans through the lens of his own experience. Although he acknowledged individual women at key moments, he also obscured the degree to which they, at every turn, proved integral to his advancement and protest against racism. His biographers, closely hewing to Douglass's narrative, pushed women further to the margins, relegating them to standard roles and platitudes about importance without demonstrating their contributions or expressing curiosity about their motivations. One explanation for this problem lies in the ways that each generation of historians builds upon previous generations' work. The earliest biographies of Douglass, published in the late nineteenth and early twentieth centuries, tended to celebrate him as an exemplary black man. Coming from an era not too far removed from Douglass's own, these writers conformed to the practice of shielding women from public view, while also assuming that women lived wholly in a private sphere that they considered off-limits. Douglass's mother, Harriet Bailey; grandmother Betsey Bailey; cousins; and two slave mistresses, Lucretia and Sophia Auld, made brief and sometimes unnamed appearances as part of his life under slavery. Rosetta seldom played a part, but the daughters of great men are often overlooked. His wives, Anna Murray and Helen Pitts, received mention, but in the respectable manner of a wedding announcement and usually with the comment that one was black and the other white. Biographers included woman's rights leaders because Douglass considered himself a "woman's rights man," but more as an aside. In all, the evidence that an undercurrent of female activity ran just beneath the surface of his work was not explored because the idea that women's work should be invisible held sway.[2]

Later generations of biographers both of Douglass and of other figures became more interested in the interplay of the various facets of their subjects' professional and personal lives. They incorporated topics once considered private, increasing the numbers of pages devoted to parents, wives, and children. Meanwhile, women's historians began to challenge the notions that women occupied wholly private spaces and that their lives and work had to be shielded from public view. As a result, the roles of the women who were close to Douglass became more visible to historians. Yet biographers have struggled to say much more about women, because the paucity of documentation has always plagued historians of those marginalized or behind the scenes. Thomas Jefferson, for instance, seemed unable to leave a thought unrecorded, yet little information remains from which to piece together the life of his wife, Martha Wayles Skelton, or of Sally Hemings, the mother of his enslaved children. Biographers using their antecedents as their main sources found themselves rehashing the same material about women. This often led to something that should be christened "source drift" because, as each author attempted to add something original with each retelling, small artistic liberties gradually accumulated to tell a story quite different than what the evidence indicated.[3]

The presumption seemed to be that little more could be said about certain figures unless heretofore unknown documents surfaced. Instead, the questions that biographers asked about their subjects' lives demanded a refocus if they hoped for any fresh insight, especially with someone like Douglass, who lived such a long life engaged in elemental questions about race, democracy, and the ideal of "America." This refocus required asking different questions of existing evidence and searching for answers in different documents. As a result, some intriguing books have emerged that have added nuance to well-trod stories, especially when authors have turned to the women who surrounded these figures. After all, great men often appear quite differently from the perspective of their wives.[4]

Frederick Douglass's life cried out for such a treatment. Not only was he involved in the woman's rights movement, but little of the rich body of scholarship about the importance of women to the antislavery crusade, the woman's rights movement, black families in slavery and freedom, and about gender had penetrated later treatments of his life. An exception was Dickson J. Preston's *Young Frederick Douglass: The Maryland Years* (1980), which grounded Douglass's autobiographies and thus the lives of his grandmother, mother, sisters, cousins, and slave mistresses in evidence beyond his autobiographies, thereby raising new questions about the world of his childhood. At the same time, much speculation about Douglass's sexuality has crept into interpretations of his adult life, with assumptions based on sexual behavior in the late twentieth and early twenty-first centuries serving in the place of evidence. Two examples of this phenomenon were William McFeely's *Frederick Douglass* (1991), and Maria Diedrich's *Love across Color Lines: Ottilie Assing and Frederick Douglass* (1999). The shadow of both hangs over any work on Douglass.[5]

To the credit of McFeely and Diedrich, both attempted to incorporate Douglass's public and personal lives into one narrative, no easy feat. McFeely, however, had difficulty understanding women as agents in their interactions with Douglass, often attributing to them little more than emotional motivation and failing to demonstrate their importance to Douglass. Diedrich had more success in taking women seriously as actors in Douglass's life because she proceeded with the premise of a private, even secret, relationship. As a result, she approached her subject from an entirely different direction than those biographers who used his career as their framework. This allowed her to make greater strides in portraying Douglass's life as an integrated whole rather than two separate halves lived in public and in private. Her access to a cache of letters that offered an outsider's view into the Douglass home gave her work the advantage of new and unplumbed documentation. Unfortunately, her use of those letters, often to the exclusion of further research and in the face of contradictory evidence, suffered from an unquestioning insistence upon an erotic affair that she never proved existed and that frequently flew in the face of material realities. Her interpretation, along with the willingness of audiences to believe that Douglass was sexually promiscuous, looms over any discussion of his interactions with women. Rather than hamper this book's narrative by addressing the conclusions of McFeely, Diedrich, or other scholars in the text, discrepancies between the evidence and other works appear in the notes.[6]

The artistic term "negative space"—the space around an object—seemed to be the best method to use in addressing questions about the role of women in Douglass's life and the role of his in theirs. The negative space, in this case, is the feminine space. Focusing on the women who surrounded him illuminated nuances in his activism and his perceptions of human rights, race, gender, and himself. In relief, the motivations of individual women, each of whom has a back story of her own, became clear. Although of lesser stature than Douglass, they saw themselves as engaged in the same questions. Like him, they had their own ambitions and navigated restrictions placed on them because of the body and circumstances into which they were born. With a few exceptions, he and they sympathized with one another and understood themselves as collaborators rather than as potential competitors, as occasionally became the case with his male colleagues. Honing in on this feminine space revealed three intersecting themes.

First, family was of paramount importance to Douglass and a necessary component of his politics. His first autobiography, *Narrative of the Life of Frederick Douglass,* began with a family shattered by slavery and ended with the foundation of a new one in freedom. His two subsequent autobiographies retained this organization in the sections relating to the early years of his life, even as he expanded both the section and the volume. In nineteenth-century America, not only did

Figure I.1 Just as he lived his life as an open contradiction of racist stereotypes of African Americans, Frederick Douglass commissioned profile portraits as a means of countering depictions of Africans and African Americans in contemporary scientific literature on phrenology. "Profile, Frederick Douglass," c. 1858, daguerreotype, 2005.27.42, unknown photographer. Gift of Hallmark Cards, Inc., Nelson Gallery Foundation, Nelson-Atkins Museum of Art.

masters commonly break apart families, but stereotypes of African Americans also depicted them as incapable of forming and maintaining the emotional bonds of marriage and parenthood. Seizing the right to marry, have children, protect the integrity of a family, and raise the next generation to lead a better life was both a personal desire and a political statement in opposition to racism. Much of the Douglasses' adoption of middle-class norms of behavior and comportment also fell into this category. Yet, Frederick could not have accomplished this without Anna. She was not simply any wife. She was a woman who, despite having been born free, faced limited opportunities for marriage and children. Like her husband, she too lived in a society that devalued her, even in the circles of her husband's antislavery colleagues. Their children also carried with them the obligation of internalizing and projecting the image of obedient and resourceful offspring who would help improve the lot of African Americans, a responsibility that they continued long after both parents' deaths and passed to their own children. Thus, accusations of marital infidelity leveled against Douglass by rumormongers, anti-abolitionists, and abolitionists alike all must be understood within this context of cultural hostility toward black families and stereotypes about the sexuality and morality of African Americans.[7]

Furthermore, charges of adultery focused only on Douglass's associations with white women, a second theme of this feminine space. There is no escaping the fact that he spent much time in the company of white women and that he exuded a charisma that was attractive to them. At the same time, both Douglass's white associates and subsequent historians deemed Anna so physically and intellectually unattractive that they questioned his fidelity to her on those grounds alone. That cruel assessment avoided addressing the importance of the Douglass marriage, the fact that his friendships with black women did not elicit the same charges of impropriety, and the traits that Douglass himself found beautiful. He seemed most at home in the company of women, and those women were most often white because they comprised the majority of women in the middle-class, activist world in which he moved and because they had greater access to the resources that he needed. During his childhood in the South, his slave mistresses provided him with food, clothing, and an introduction to literacy. In the North of his adulthood, white women ran the fundraising and publicity machines that fueled the abolitionist movement, they introduced him to the world of literature and ideas that he craved, and they brought him into the middle class to which he and his family aspired. While much of this was true of middle-class black women, who were fewer in number but among Douglass's allies, their understanding of the antislavery movement as a civil rights movement with a broader agenda placed them in a different relationship to his specific needs. Moreover, because of their shared race, charges of infidelity would not tap into white anxieties about racial mixing that existed even in the abolitionist movement. Accusing Frederick of committing adultery with white women served a much more powerful purpose to enemies hoping to discredit him among both abolitionists and anti-abolitionists.[8]

Yet, as with Anna and their family, Douglass's friendships with white women were also a form of protest. When he was a child, white woman such as his mistress Sophia Auld could offer him affection because his age classified him as subordinate and nonthreatening. As he grew into a powerfully built man, well fed by those mistresses, white society deemed him a physical and sexual danger to white women. Unless he assumed a servile position, any interaction with a white woman placed both parties in jeopardy, and the bulk of ire was aimed at him. At the beginning of his career, he suffered beatings and public derision for accompanying them in public, his business partnership with an Englishwoman was attacked by his former abolitionist allies, and white woman suffragists invoked the image of rapacious black men in opposing the Fifteenth Amendment that enfranchised only males. Later on, his second marriage to a white woman brought down throngs of criticism, and at the end of his life he worked with Ida B. Wells to call attention to the false accusations of rape against black men that lay behind lynching. Fully aware of the peril, he continued to accompany these women, to work with them, and to count them among his close friends. In doing so, he transgressed conventions surrounding not only friendships between the sexes but also the particular configuration of an equal friendship between black men and white women.

A third theme concerned the control of boundaries between public and private life, an issue that has resonated across the centuries. Privacy was a privilege not granted to the Douglasses as African Americans. Masters and employers claimed access to all aspects of black people's lives and bodies as a means of total control. For Anna, as for all black women, association of female public life and black women's sexuality with prostitution meant that a private life offered her protection. When Frederick's celebrity grew, he and Anna found that they had to repulse those who might pry into their lives and make judgments about the Douglasses' marriage and family that would be used to discredit him personally and African Americans generally. Private time also allowed Frederick the space to think, read, and write. Therefore, the Douglasses claimed such space for themselves as a right, and much of the responsibility of maintaining it fell to Anna. Her household work upheld the face that their family displayed to the outside world by presenting a well-ordered home, dispensing with unwanted guests, and raising their children to uphold the image of respectability necessary for combating racial prejudice. The Douglasses' public performance of an upstanding middle-class black family created a private space in which they could live without prejudice or judgment. Furthermore, Frederick and Anna controlled the extent to which different individuals had access to that space, and their marital friction resulted partly from differences of opinion as to who should be granted admission.

While the Douglasses insisted on the right to shield their family life from the world, Frederick's friendships with white women were characterized by defiant transparency. Incensed at the hypocrisy of prohibitions on interracial relationships, Douglass chose to invert the practice of white sexual exploitation that had led to his own birth. Whereas interracial interactions such as his parents' involved some combination of clandestine, nonconsensual, abusive, and extralegal behavior on the margins of society, his friendships with white women played out in public with the collaboration of a partner who came armed with social respectability and, when he married Helen Pitts, gained the sanction of law. No evidence exists to suggest that any of these associations other than his second marriage became sexual. Indeed, Douglass threw accusations of infidelity back upon the accuser, always demanding public testimony that never surfaced. The sin lay in the failure to imagine that a black man and a white woman could have anything more in common than carnal desire or that a black man could honor his familial and marital bonds to a black wife.

Douglass and his female colleagues understood the rules that applied to them along the intersections of race, gender, and class. More than speak out, they engaged in a demonstration that required them to live in opposition to restrictions. The women did not simply play the role of helpmeet to the Great Man in this; they saw themselves as partners in a type of protest that only had meaning because of their gender and race in relation to his gender and race. Only a black woman could be his partner in challenging attacks on black families. Only white women could be his partners in challenging the particular charged color line between black men and white women. Their middle-class status, or aspirations to such, armed them with a respectability that would not allow class prejudices to discredit them. They were not just the women behind the man. They worked together to live out an ideal of racial equality in the face of constant attack.

In his third autobiography, *Life and Times of Frederick Douglass*, he famously insisted that "when the true history of the anti-slavery cause shall be written, woman will occupy a large space in its pages; for the cause of the slave has been peculiarly woman's cause." The same should be said of him, for a true history of Frederick Douglass requires that women occupy a large space, from beginning to end.[9]

1

"A True Mother's Heart"

She was born in Talbot County, on the Eastern Shore of Maryland, in 1792. Her son, Frederick, introduced her to the world as Harriet, "the daughter of Isaac and Betsey Bailey, both colored and quite dark." Darkness permeated his memories of her skin color, the moments when she curled up with him to sleep, and his comprehension of her life. When Harriet died in 1825, at the age of thirty-two, he recalled, "I received the tidings of her death with much the same emotions I should have probably felt at the death of a stranger" and "with no strong emotions of sorrow for her, and with very little regret for myself on account of her loss." Sophia Auld was also born in Talbot County, in 1797. Harriet's son first encountered her as "a white face beaming with the most kindly emotions," something he had "never seen before." In 1826, she hired the six-year-old slave to work; instead, he remembered being treated "as she supposed one human being ought to treat another." For a short while, at least, he "learned to regard her as something more akin to a mother, than a slaveholding mistress." This period of affection, too, was doomed. The precocious little boy became a suspicious intruder in Sophia's eyes, someone she had to monitor, control, and limit.[1]

Thus did the childhood of Frederick Douglass twist its way through the perverted intimacies of slavery. Black mothers could neither care for nor protect their enslaved children. White mistresses could become "almost a mother" to their property. Small children, through their own wits, manipulated anyone who would respond to get their basic needs met, and accepted pity, with all of its condescension, as a substitute for affection. Even then, they could not depend on kindness from anyone for any extended period of time. As an adult, Douglass described, explained, and condemned the world created by slavery, and his audiences could glimpse the ways that world had shaped his growth. Yet the child Frederick Bailey saw only its fragments. As Frederick Douglass, he constructed a narrative from those fragments for the specific purpose of attacking slavery and for a white audience still struggling with their own racial prejudices. As Frederick Bailey, he lived the experience with less of a thesis than his autobiographies indicated. Slavery permeated and mutated his conception of the world, the formation of his identity, and his relationships to other individuals, especially women.

Any comprehensive understanding of Frederick Douglass must start with the conditions that created the man, and those conditions included not only slavery, or even slavery on Maryland's Eastern Shore and in Baltimore, but also the people who affected Douglass's interaction with that world. In his childhood, both enslaved women and mistresses shaped his immediate experience. Operating within the hierarchy of power created by the slave system, some with more power than others, those women acted as mediators between Frederick Bailey the little boy and the institution of slavery. Their circumstances not only affected the material conditions of Frederick's daily life but also taught him his earliest lessons about race, slavery, gender, and the interaction of all three. Their stories explain his upbringing in ways that he himself could not or would not let himself know.[2]

From the beginning, Douglass decried the ways that slaveholders assaulted black families and stripped them of their history. He himself knew little of his past beyond his grandmother and possible grandfather, and his brief life within the slave community that included his family left him unable to glean anything from the oral traditions that they could impart. Arguably, Douglass's ignorance of his past had no bearing on his life beyond his general sense of loss and its place in his critique of slavery. Yet inquiry into his family history fills in the parts of his story that he did not include in his autobiographies, especially about the women who shaped his early experience, and suggests with more precision the contours of the world into which he was born.[3]

Had he been able to trace his maternal family tree, Douglass would have found a line of women stretching back to the mid-eighteenth century, to the Chesapeake Bay farm of Richard Skinner. There, in January 1746, his great-grandmother, Jenny, was born into a slave kin that included two, twenty-year-old women named Sue and Selah, an elderly black man named Bale, and six other children. A second infant joined this family a month after Jenny's birth.[4] Richard Skinner's death in 1746 occasioned an inventory of household property, including the slaves, and called for the appraisal and division of Jenny's family. As moveable property, slave families and communities faced upheaval in the aftermath of any major change in their master's family; but Jenny's appeared to escape some of the worst consequences of Skinner's death. All but the oldest children remained the property of his widow, Katherine, and because the oldest children were inherited by Skinner's minor-aged children, they were able to remain with their own families for a few more years, at least.

Two years after Richard's death, Katherine married Hugh Rice, who took over the Skinner farm and its slaves as his own. When Katherine died, sometime

Figure 1.1 No images of Harriet Bailey, her mother, or her sisters existed, but Douglass considered this illustration of Rameses a strong likeness of his mother as he remembered her. By seeing her face in that of an Egyptian ruler, he symbolically gave himself a family tree that stretched back to one of the oldest known civilizations on the African continent. "Head of Ramses," James Cowles Prichard. *The Natural History of Man* (London, 1843), 157.

before 1769, Hugh inherited all of her property, including the slaves, and brought them with him to his marriage to Ann Sutton Skinner. Ann was the widow of one of Katherine's sons from her marriage to Richard Skinner. Her inheritance and, therefore, the property that she brought to her marriage to Rice, included slaves once owned by Skinner. Thus, when Hugh and Ann married, they reunited the enslaved community that had been separated by Richard Skinner's death twenty-three years earlier. When Ann became a widow again in 1781, she inherited all of Hugh's property, which led to another inventory of Jenny's extended family. Jenny, who was now thirty-five, appeared in this 1781 census with Sue, now in her sixties, and Bale, now around eighty, as well as with four other adults from her own generation and seven from the next. Few certainties attached themselves to Jenny's life, but among them was the knowledge that those seven children included her daughter Betsey, Frederick Douglass's grandmother.[5]

Jenny gave birth to Betsey in May 1774. Jenny may or may not have had two older children, Hester and Harry, born in 1760 and 1762, respectively. Likewise, she may have had a fourth child, also named Jenny, born in 1776. The connection of all four children to one another and of all of them but Betsey to Jenny is yet another uncertainty about their lives. The master controlled the records, and the records reflected slaves value as property, not the bonds of blood and affection, but a woman's ability to reproduce sometimes allowed her connection to a particular infant to slip into notations, as did Jenny's to Betsey. As for their children's fathers, as Douglass later observed, they were "literally abolished in slave law and slave practice."[6] Betsey's may have numbered among the other men of Jenny's generation living on the Skinner-Rice farm; but if those men were Jenny's cousins or siblings, then Betsey's father could have been any of a number of white or black men: her master, a local white man, a free black man, or another slave on another plantation. Only their contemporaries knew the identity of all of Douglass's male ancestors.

For the first twenty-three years of her life, Betsey grew up on the Rice farm with her daughter Jenny, a privilege not extended to her grandson, Frederick. The Rices most likely followed the eighteenth-century trend in Talbot County by converting the farm from tobacco to grain production. With twelve slaves on the farm through the latter part of the eighteenth century, half of them children, all hands took to the fields for much of the day. The exception was probably Sue, who lived into her sixties, and perhaps Selah, who did not. Based on age alone, Skinner and Rice may have designated Sue as more productive in caring for the children, releasing the younger mothers to work in the field. Betsey, then, likely spent her first years under the supervision of Sue or Selah, joining the other women alongside the men in the field around age nine. As Betsey grew, Sue, Jenny, perhaps Selah, Doll, and newcomer Sarah taught the girl fishing, gardening, and net-sewing, which they used to supplement their diets and which Betsey later developed into lucrative skills. According to her grandson Frederick, Betsey's fish nets were "in great demand" throughout the neighborhood, and he insisted that she "was also somewhat famous for her good fortune in taking the fishes" and in her methods of improving a sweet potato crop.[7]

Farming, fishing, and net-making, however, were not the main sources of her status in the slave community. Frederick recalled Betsey as someone who commanded high respect in that later stage of life, "far higher than is the lot of most colored persons in the slave states," which stemmed from her work as "a nurse" or midwife. With knowledge and power to guide new lives into the world, midwives were revered among both the black and the white communities in the late eighteenth and early nineteenth century. An experienced midwife who attended the births of more than one generation of families became a living genealogist and family historian, linking generations over time. She also enjoyed relative freedom of movement, usually denied to rural slaves, especially women. Because husbands and wives were owned by different masters, kin were hired to different parts of the countryside, or separated by the inheritances and marriages of white families, slaves relied on those with mobility to pass along messages between visits, making a midwife one of the most important purveyors of information in the community. Even as the masters controlled the physical proximity of enslaved family members to one another, a midwife could bind families together by passing along their news. A midwife's expertise extended beyond childbirth to all aspects of healthcare and lore, and even a touch of clandestine conjuring. Enslaved midwives often assumed the role of "granny," watching the babies during the day, and, in a rural neighborhood, they acted as the doctor for slave and free alike, providing services for which their masters could charge others. As they became more valuable to their masters, they might receive rewards, such as a cabin away from an overseer's direct supervision, which gave them the privilege of privacy, and the claim to cash earnings enjoyed by Betsey in later years.[8]

As with any profession, both the training and reputation of a midwife took time to develop, and novices entered long apprenticeships to wiser, more experienced women. More often than not, mothers or grandmothers educated their daughters in the craft. If the women of the Skinner-Rice farm followed this pattern, then Betsey learned her trade at Jenny's side. Jenny just as likely learned her skills from Selah or Sue, who had probably cared for the children on the Skinner farm. Although most midwives' careers often began later in life, often around the time of menopause, this did not appear to have been true in Betsey's case. If she had learned from Jenny or Sue, then Betsey's training ended in 1797, when she was twenty-three and circumstances took her away from her mother to the far side of Talbot County. By age thirty-five, still bearing children of her own, she was in demand as a midwife, attending eleven confinements in 1809 and nine in 1810. Thus, Douglass's passing mention of his grandmother as a "nurse" concealed a body of experience and a line of skilled, revered women who were entrusted with the lives and histories of their neighborhoods. Indeed, any favor shown to Betsey's grandson by her white masters and mistresses resulted from the respect that they accorded her rather than anything exceptional discerned in Frederick. He himself acknowledged that fact, writing, "This high reputation was full of advantage to her, and to the children around her."[9]

Describing Betsey's life once she became a grandmother, however, gets ahead of the story. While she was still in her apprenticeship for delivering children, she herself began bearing them. In January 1790, at age sixteen, Betsey gave birth to her first child, a daughter named Milly. A second daughter, Harriet, followed two years later, on February 28, 1792. After a gap of seven years, Betsey went on to have ten more children, between 1799 and 1820. Two of Betsey's grandsons, Frederick and his brother Perry, identified Isaac Bailey as the father of their mother, Harriet, by calling him their grandfather. Although Isaac was recognized as Betsey's husband long before Frederick and Perry came along, and although he served in the role of a grandfather to Frederick and Perry and father to Harriet, he may not have been the natural father of Milly or Harriet.[10]

Isaac Bailey, a free black sawyer, does not appear in records until 1798, the year after Betsey had left her mother as part of Ann Skinner's dowry. Ann Skinner, step-daughter of Hugh Rice, daughter of his second wife Ann [Sutton Skinner] Rice, and granddaughter of Richard and Katherine Rice, married Aaron Anthony in January 1797. Their first son, Andrew, arrived the next month. Ann brought not only this impending heir to the marriage, but also the slaves Betsy Bailey, her two daughters, Betsey's cousin (or brother) Phil, his wife Emblem and their children, Bale and Katy (sometimes called Cate). Ann's new husband worked as lead overseer of the plantations and farms belonging to Edward Lloyd, one of the wealthiest planters of the county and a state representative. The Anthonys lived in an outbuilding on the main Lloyd plantation, Wye House, but Aaron Anthony also owned Holme Hill Farm on Tuckahoe Creek on the far side of the county. Initially, the Anthonys' slaves joined their master at Wye House, but shortly thereafter Betsey and her daughters were moved to Holme Hill. About the same time, in 1798, Aaron began hiring "Isaac Baley, free negrow," a sawyer who lived in the vicinity of Holme Hill and the nearby town Hillsboro. Isaac, in turn, hired and trained Betsey's cousin (or nephew) Bale. The next year, on October 28, 1799, Betsey gave birth to her third child, Jenny, named to honor the mother whom Betsey was forced to leave.[11]

Eight more siblings followed Jenny: Betty on October 19, 1801; Sarah on February 7, 1804; Maryann in April 1806; Stephen in 1808; Hester (sometimes called Esther or Easter) in August 1810; Augustus in 1812; Cate in early to mid-1815; Priscilla in August 1816; and Henry in February 1820, when his mother was forty-five. An average of 25.55 months separated the babies. This regularity and spacing of Betsey's pregnancies followed the pattern of rural families in which both parents lived together, without separations or the loss of a spouse that would produce larger gaps between children. This suggests that Betsey's eight younger children had the same father. Similarly, the thirteen months between Milly and Harriet suggest that they, too, shared a father. Stillbirths and miscarriages might explain the seven years between Harriet and Jenny, just as menopause could explain the large gap between their youngest brother and sister. It is more likely that the father of Betsey's first two children had died or left the county sometime between 1792 and 1797, then she married Isaac between 1797 and 1799, and he became the father of her eight younger children.[12]

Douglass mentioned Isaac only in passing in his autobiographies, saying that his grandfather was dark-skinned and free, that he lived with Betsey as part of a "family," and that he numbered among the "old settlers in the neighborhood" along Tuckahoe Creek. Douglass's sharp focus on his grandmother eclipses Isaac to the point that he refers to his aunts and mother as "the daughters of my grandmother," not of both Betsey and Isaac. Several possibilities might explain this depiction, but the most likely is that Douglass had no more information about Isaac than that which he passed along. Frederick knew his grandfather only for the first six years of life. As a sawyer working at various jobs away from his wife's cabin, where the children lived, Isaac may have appeared there only at night, leaving at dawn, becoming a fleeting presence in a little boy's memory. For Betsey, however, Isaac was her life's companion, living with her at least until Frederick left her cabin in 1824 or as late as her death around 1845.[13]

Sometime before 1820, when their observant grandson Frederick arrived into their care, Betsey and Isaac moved into a small house set apart from the other outbuildings on Holme Hill. Frederick remembered the structure as being "a log hut, or cabin, built of clay, wood, and straw," with one room and a loft. The dwelling sat on a lot flanked by Tuckahoe Creek to the east and a road to the west, both running north past the main farmhouse to the crossroad town, Hillsboro. In his old age, when he was much older than his grandmother had been during the time he knew her, Frederick wondered if Betsey had been placed so far from the other slaves "because she was too old for field service, or because she had so faithfully discharged the duties of her station in early life." He noted, however, that living apart was a "high privilege" and that Betsey "esteemed it a great good fortune to live there," where she enjoyed autonomy removed from the daily scrutiny of master or overseer and the freedom to make decisions about the farm's production. There, she kept her garden, made her nets, and spent long portions of each day fishing in the creek. She and Isaac each brought in enough in payments to purchase pork, meal, wheat, and, at least once, beef. Betsey presumably continued to provide healthcare for the neighborhood, and, of course, she became the "granny," taking care of the almost yearly additions to her extended family.[14]

Douglass described the children living with Betsey in the cabin as "not her own, but her grandchildren—the children of her daughters," but this was not entirely accurate. Betsey gave birth to twelve children over a span of thirty years, meaning that she was still bearing her younger children when the elder ones began having children of their own. In 1806, when Betsey was a mere thirty-two years old, she became a mother for the sixth time, while also becoming a grandmother for the first time. Focusing only on Frederick's line of the family: in 1813, Harriet, Frederick's mother and Betsey's second daughter, gave birth to her first child, Perry, only a year after the birth of her own brother Augustus, who was Betsey's ninth child. Harriet's second child, Sarah, arrived in 1814, a year before Harriet's sister Cate was born. Harriet's third child, Eliza, was the same age as Harriet's youngest sister, Priscilla, both born in 1816. Harriet's most famous son, Frederick, born in 1818, was two years older than both his youngest uncle, Henry, and his younger sister Kitty, both born in 1820. During this same stretch of years, Harriet's sisters gave birth to eight of Harriet's nieces and nephews. By the time Betsey saw the end of her own childbearing years, she already had thirteen grandchildren. She supervised all of them, along with her own children, during their early childhoods, and there were up to nine small children in her cabin at any given point before 1826.[15]

According to her grandson, Betsey "took delight in having them [the children] around her, and in attending to their few wants." If their wants were few, however, their needs were many and beyond their comprehension at the time. Betsey provided the children an environment in which they began to learn ways to survive slavery. She taught them to fish and farm, so they could learn to supplement their meager diets and, as she did, trade their surpluses. Frederick followed her example, turning his hand to fishing with a pin and string, but he also picked up enough detail about her gardening methods to suggest that he could copy her. Her cabin protected the children from immediate contact with the master, but she made them understand their position as slaves. As Frederick remembered, she was the person who "conveyed to my mind a sense of my entire dependence on the will of *somebody* I had never seen." She spoke of the all-powerful Anthony "with fear and shuddering" to ensure that the children felt the same. Better they learn to fear a bogey-man and check themselves in Anthony's presence than to wander into a beating because she had protected their innocence too much. She also gave affection, something Frederick sorely lacked in subsequent years.[16]

Betsey, however, was forced to play a role in a more insidious arrangement. Douglass remembered that "in the part of Maryland from which I ran away," masters separated mothers from their children "before the child has reached its twelfth month." The master "hired out" the mother "on some farm a considerable distance off," and "the child is placed under the care of an old woman, too old for field labor." Frederick held his own childhood up as proof, having been moved first from the mother he did not remember, then from his grandmother, and finally to Baltimore, going farther away from family and home each time. This description accords with his master's management of the Lloyd slaves. Aaron Anthony downgraded new mothers for the first year of their infants' lives, allowing them to nurse the babies. Beginning the next year, the children spent the entire day under the care of older women whom Anthony had designated as "past work." Sometime between the child's ninth and twelfth years, he or she went into the fields to work or was sent elsewhere to learn a trade. With his own slaves, who lived on the far side of Talbot County from himself, Anthony seems to have added another step. When the child was between five and seven years old, he removed the girl or boy from the older woman to his own household for observation or, in Douglass's estimation, as "a method of obliterating" their ties to Betsey. Then, after a few years, he sent them into the fields or into a trade.[17]

If all went according to Anthony's usual pattern of slave management, Frederick's process of separation probably began around March 1820, when his sister Kitty was born. On her arrival, Frederick would have moved from his mother's side to Betsey's cabin. Two years later, in October 1822, when their sister Arianna was born, Kitty joined him there. Arianna followed in 1824 or 1825, after Harriet had given birth to another little girl, also called Harriet. Now that Frederick was approximately six or seven years old, Anthony ordered Betsey to carry the boy to Wye House. At the time, Frederick had probably never seen his older brother, Perry, who would have been separated from his mother in about 1814, and then taken from Betsey's house around the time of Frederick's birth, in 1818. The same went for his sister Sarah, who would have left their mother in 1816, when younger sister Eliza was born. Eliza would have joined her at their grandmother's cabin at the time of Frederick's birth in 1818. Sarah then left Betsey's cabin just as Frederick moved in, and Eliza departed when Frederick was only four. By the morning in 1824 when Betsey, "yet a woman of power and spirit," adjusted the "ample and graceful folds of her newly-ironed bandana turban," took her grandson Frederick by the hand, and led him off to Wye House, she had made the journey at least eight times before. Little wonder that she, "with the reserve and solemnity of a priestess," would not meet his eyes, steeling herself against her own loss, or that she granted herself the last pleasure of "toting" him, until he felt himself too much the little man and wanted to walk. She had learned to slip away, escaping an emotional scene but leaving another child to feel, as this one later wrote, "not only grieved at parting—as I supposed forever—with my grandmother—but indignant that a trick had been played upon me in a matter so serious."[18]

Removed from his grandmother's cabin and his extended family so early, Frederick did not understand that some of the children under Betsey's supervision were her own, and he may have missed other details about life in the cabin as well. Not only did Betsey have the babies and toddlers about her, she also had some of her older daughters. On January 9, 1820, a census-taker arrived at the cabin on Tuckahoe Creek and named Isaac Bailey as head of household. Seeing the rough dwelling, inhabited by African Americans, without a Big House or white supervisor in sight, he probably assumed that Isaac's free status extended to the rest of the occupants. They included three boys and six girls under the age of fourteen, three young women between the ages of fourteen and twenty-four, a woman aged between twenty-six and forty-four, and a man over age forty-five. The older adults were Isaac and Betsey, who was nine months swollen with her last child. Of the children, Frederick had probably not yet arrived but would in the coming months. The youngest boys were more likely his cousins, six-year-old

Tom and the one-year-olds Isaac and Stephen. The youngest girls may have included two of Betsey's daughters, four-year-old Priscilla and ten-year-old Hester, as well as Milly's daughters, nine-year-old Betty, eight-year-old Margaret, and four-year-old Henny; Harriet's two daughters, six-year-old Sarah and four-year-old Eliza; and Jenny's youngest, two-year-old Mary. Of these eight girls, the least likely to have lived in the cabin in 1820 were Hester, young Betty, and Margaret, all being of an age to have moved to Wye House. Of those three, Hester did end up at Wye House by 1824, but it is more likely that the two younger girls left in 1820 because their mother was Milly. Betsey's daughters were probably the three young women in the cabin: fourteen-year-old Maryann, nineteen-year-old Betty, and twenty-one-year-old Jenny.[19]

In other words, probably because of her status as a midwife, Betsey Bailey had the privilege of keeping all but her two oldest daughters with her for much longer than her own daughters would be able to keep their own children. Jenny and Betty seem to have had a degree of the same luck, presuming that they were in fact living in the cabin, not just visiting, on the day of the census. Jenny, after all, had been hired out to Elinor Maloney (variant spellings include Melony and Malony) until November of that year, and Hester went on to assist her cousin Katy at Wye House a few years later. Yet Jenny and Betty had only very small children in 1820. Not only did the extent to which they saw these children during the day depend on their work assignments but nothing could guarantee that the children would not move to Wye House and beyond as they grew. Furthermore, whereas their mother lived with her husband, Jenny and Betty appear to have had "abroad marriages"—that is, their husbands resided elsewhere. Indeed, 1820 may have been the last time that so many of Betsey's family were gathered together in the same place. Over the next ten years, the family was separated by work assignments, death, escape, sale, and divisions of their masters' estates.[20]

Betsey's oldest daughters, Milly and Harriet, did not live with their mother or their children after their teen years. Although they had stayed with Betsey after she moved from the Skinner-Rice plantation to Anthony's farms, Anthony had begun hiring them out by 1808. At sixteen, Harriet went to work with her sister Milly at the farm of Nathan Maloney. The next year, Anthony sent the sisters to work for Athel Stewart (also spelled Stuart or Steward) for a year. Two years later, in 1811, Harriet went with her sixteen-year-old cousin Tom to work for John Nabb. A year later, she and Tom moved to the home of John Maloney, the husband of Anthony's much older sister, Elinor. When John died in 1813, Elinor kept Harriet, but she replaced Tom with Harriet's sister Jenny at the beginning of 1814. The two sisters stayed with Elinor until the end of 1817, when they were both seven months pregnant. Elinor retained Jenny and Jenny's baby, Mary, for another two years; but Harriet moved on. Her son Frederick believed that her next assignment was at Anthony's Holme Hill farm, where she was under the supervision of the tenant overseer, Perry W. Stewart.[21]

Frederick assumed that Harriet was a "field hand," and she could very well have worked in the fields. The farms of both Nathan Maloney and Athel Stewart required additional labor during the peak seasons, and when Anthony sent Tom and Harriet to work together at the Nabb and Maloney homes, he charged the same rate for both, suggesting that they did similar types of work. Yet, when women were hired out, it was often for housework. Except for six months in 1808, which came during the harvest season, Anthony tended to hire out Harriet for the full year, not just for the busier parts of the agricultural cycle. Furthermore, the items that Anthony purchased from the people to whom he hired out Harriet indicate that farming was not their primary occupation. Nabb, though he sold beef on occasion, more often provided Anthony with trousers, jackets, coats, and other items of clothing. The Maloneys sold Anthony peach brandy, and the occasional gallon of cider. Sewing and distilling being among women's skills, and one of the employers being an aging widow, Harriet was probably brought on to perform domestic services instead of or in addition to field labor.[22]

If Harriet worked in the house, it could have accounted for her son's claim that she was literate. Douglass himself found the feat stunning. "The achievements of my mother, considering the place and circumstances, were very extraordinary," he rightly marveled, noting that "she was the *only* one of all the slaves and colored people in Tuckahoe who enjoyed that advantage." Frederick, of course, never observed his mother reading, and, he carefully explained, "I learned, after my mother's death, that she could read," couching the information in a rumor without a source. This rumor served to establish that Douglass's intellectual prowess originated with "the native genius of my sable, unprotected, and uncultivated *mother*," not his purported white ancestry. His use of the rumor as propaganda did not mean that he had fabricated the information, any more than his telling proved it.[23]

Instead, the importance of Harriet's literacy lies in its meaning for her. As a field hand on a remote farm, Harriet would have had few opportunities to receive reading lessons. As a domestic, however, the needs and values of her mistress could have provided her with one. The wives of Nathan Maloney, Nabb, and Stewart could each have ventured to educate Harriet, but Elinor Maloney appears to be the most likely teacher. As a Methodist in her fifties, Elinor was of an age and a denomination uncomfortable with slavery during the early decades of the republic and thus inclined to attend to slaves' spiritual lives by teaching them to read the Bible. After 1813, the widow Maloney lived without the daily threat of a husband's admonition against teaching a slave to read, something that would be faced later by another Methodist who taught Harriet's son to read.

Elinor might also have required a slave to have some nominal understanding of written instructions to carry out her daily chores. Furthermore, during the years Harriet worked for Elinor, Elinor hired a teacher for the young white women in the house, from whom Harriet could have surreptitiously acquired instruction. If Harriet could read, then Elinor Maloney's house was most likely place where she could have acquired the skill. Many years later, Harriet's son identified literacy with liberation of both mind and body. He wrote that reading "enabled me to utter my thoughts, and to meet the arguments brought forward to sustain slavery"; reading also allowed him to forge a pass when he and his compatriots attempted to escape in 1836. In attributing literacy to his literary interpretation of Harriet, he thereby granted her ambition for freedom. Harriet may have longed for liberty, and she may have had nominal reading skill, but, for her, literacy did not mean liberation from slavery.[24]

In the spring of 1812, not long after she had begun working for the Maloneys, Harriet conceived the first of her seven children. Perry arrived in January 1813. By giving birth at age twenty-one, Harriet fell well within the average of her enslaved contemporaries, but this was late in comparison to her mother and sisters, who started families as early as age fifteen. Before Perry passed his first birthday, Harriet conceived her next child, Sarah, who was born in August 1814. Her third child, Eliza, arrived in March 1816. She conceived Frederick, the fourth child, while she still worked for Elinor Maloney. According to Frederick, Harriet gave birth to him in her mother's cabin, probably delivered by Betsey herself. Two years later, in March 1820, Harriet's fifth child, Kitty, joined them. Arianna followed in October 1822. Last came baby Harriet, born between July 1823 and early 1826. Although large enough gaps exist between her youngest children to admit the possibility of a miscarriage among the last three and a stillbirth between the last two, on average, Harriet had a child every two years over fourteen years. This is the one certainty about her childbearing and was a typical fertility rate for slaves during the first decades of the nineteenth century. Yet her consistency suggests that, contrary to later assumptions, Frederick and his siblings had the same father.[25]

Douglass's uncertainty and ambivalence about his father crept into the different versions that appeared in his autobiographies. His most explicit statement on the matter appeared in his first autobiography. "My father was a white man," he wrote in 1845 in *Narrative of the Life of Frederick Douglass*. "He was admitted to be such by all I ever heard speak of my parentage." He titillated readers by writing, "The opinion was also whispered that my master was my father," but prevaricated by adding, "of the correctness of their opinion, I know nothing." A decade later, in *My Bondage and My Freedom*, he distanced himself from the claim, writing that his father may have been "nearly white." As to the rumor that his master was his father, he reiterated, "it was only a whisper, and I cannot say that I ever gave it credence." In fact, he added, "I now have reason to think he was not." In *Life and Times of Frederick Douglass*, written at the end of his life, he dismissed the discussion with the matter-of-fact statement, "Of my father I know nothing." The issue of his particular paternity was not so much the public point as exposing the sexual hypocrisy embedded in the legacy of slavery.[26]

Even as he distanced himself from the specific relation to his own master, Douglass continued to employ his alleged mixed parentage to attack the sexual exploitation of enslaved women, opposition to interracial marriage, and scientific racism. His reticence only perpetuated the assumption that Aaron Anthony was his father. He further confused the matter of his paternity by portraying himself as having grown up isolated from the context of his siblings, something that perplexed even his own children, who did not seem to understand their connection to Perry when the brothers were reunited after the Civil War. For these reasons, most biographers assume that Frederick and his siblings did not share the same father, and that blood ties with his master led to his seemingly favored treatment. Following Douglass's lead, they addressed the question of fatherhood only in relation to Douglass and Anthony, not in relation to the rest of the family, particularly the person most affected by the answer, Harriet. For her, the father of her children was a central character in her life. Investigation into his identity may not provide definitive answers, but it does highlight the choices faced by women in Harriet's situation and suggest explanations for her behavior toward her son.[27]

Assuming that Harriet's children all had the same father, that father must have been a man with whom Harriet had regular contact for the twelve to fourteen years between the conceptions of Perry in 1812 and little Harriet between 1822 and 1825. Assuming also that he was white, the most obvious candidates are those for whom she worked, John Maloney, Perry Stewart, and her master Aaron Anthony. John Maloney died just before Perry's birth, which means that he could not have fathered the subsequent children. Perry Stewart died in 1821, which eliminates him as the father of the younger children. The same holds true for the other overseers at Holme Hill farm or anywhere else she may have worked between 1818 and 1825. The same does not hold true, of course, for any of the young men in the families of those men. Maloney's household included no white men other than himself, but Stewart's did. Stewart had been in business with Anthony since the early 1800s, offering the potential for some connection to have formed between one of Stewart's sons and one of Anthony's slaves. Wherever Harriet went, however, it was Aaron Anthony who had the most consistent access to her body and power over her life. Not only was he her master, but she worked for Anthony's widowed sister when she became pregnant with her first three children, and Harriet presumably was working on his farm when she became pregnant with the rest.[28]

If Anthony did father Harriet's children, then it was because Harriet had neither the power nor the right to refuse him. Rape threatened all enslaved women, and the coercive methods employed by the masters often varied. Harriet Jacobs, in her autobiographical *Incidents in the Life of a Slave Girl*, described masters bribing, beating, and threatening their enslaved women with sale to coerce them into having sex. Anthony's behavior toward Harriet's sisters suggests what his tactics may have been. In his autobiographies, Douglass told a terrifying story of his Aunt Hester, Harriet's younger sister. Douglass could not fix a date for this event, but he recalled that it took place during his two years at Wye House, when Hester was between fourteen and sixteen years old. As Douglass told the story, Hester had begun a courtship with Edward "Ned" Roberts, one of Edward Lloyd's slaves, but Anthony forbade Hester to see Edward. When Hester defied his order, Anthony beat her to a bloody pulp because, as contemporaries, historians, and Douglass all pointed out, Anthony had clearly intended to use Hester as his own, exclusive concubine, denying her the choice of a husband and intending to beat her into submission. "When the motives of this brutal castigation are considered," Douglass pointed out in 1855, "language has no power to convey a just sense of its awful criminality." In 1882, he added that Anthony's motives were "as abhorrent as they were contemptible" and robbed his victim of any means "of the honourable perpetuation of the race."[29]

The savagery inflicted on Hester occurred around the time Harriet gave birth to her last child and fell fatally ill. Hester's beating suggests that with his wife dead since 1818, no discernible plans to remarry, and his black mistress dying or dead, Anthony turned to one of Harriet's sisters as her replacement. Douglass did not speculate about his mother's sexual treatment at the hands of their master. His inclusion of the story of Hester's fate, however, served not only as a graphic example of both the physical and sexual violence that was common under slavery but also as a way of shifting what he would not discuss about his mother's experience onto her sister. In Douglass's telling, by accepting a violent beating rather than submitting, Hester had virtuously defended her chastity and thereby countered the prevailing stereotype of promiscuous black women. His own existence was evidence that his mother had failed in this regard. He left out the detail that in 1826 Hester, too, had a child.[30]

The proximity of Hester's story to Douglass's discussion of his father in the autobiographies leaves the reader to infer that Harriet had been raped, a perception reinforced by the assumption that Douglass had a different father than Harriet's other children and that the rape that produced him was a singular incident. The regularity at which Harriet gave birth, however, could imply a degree of resignation. Always threatened with sexual exploitation, under certain circumstances, enslaved women exercised slivers of autonomy when the opportunity arose. The Hemings women in Virginia, for example, leveraged their masters' exploitation to gain benefits for themselves, their children, and their extended families. The Hemings, however, were unique cases. At best, other women could maneuver themselves away from their aggressors, as did Harriet Jacobs, who took the path of a lesser evil by choosing a white man who could defend her from her predatory master. He was not the man she preferred, but he was also her choice in a situation that seemed to offer her no other, and he promised her the reward of emancipating their children in exchange. Nevertheless, when he abandoned her and kept their children enslaved, she had no recourse. Many more women could not secure their children's freedom or extract any concessions from their masters. Like the women enslaved by James Henry Hammond, who notoriously purchased a young mother and her adolescent daughter for his own sexual gratification, and those described throughout the narratives of former slaves, they were raped repeatedly and gave birth to the children of their masters with no expectation of reward. If Harriet was Anthony's concubine, perhaps she had some small modicum of privilege that gave weight to her later threats to report her cousin Katy to their master for starving her son Frederick; but little else suggested that she received anything resembling compensation for any repeated assault on her body.[31]

In addition to the sexual violence inflicted by their masters, many raped women and their offspring faced the wrath of the master's white wives and children, who could be just as vicious and cruel as any white man. "Women—white women, I mean—are idols at the south," Douglass wrote of them, "and if these *idols* but nod, or lift a finger, woe to the poor victim: kicks, cuffs and stripes are sure to follow." Worse yet, mistresses demanded that their half-white slaves be sold, a command that could also be issued by other white family members. Douglass illustrated the phenomena by telling of the jealousy that the white son of Edward Lloyd exhibited toward the son of Lloyd and an enslaved woman. The two young men so resembled one another that the white brother abused the enslaved brother, ultimately sending him to the auction block. The reactions of the mistresses and white family members, therefore, profoundly shaped the world of their enslaved nieces, nephews, half-brothers, half-sisters. The black woman, in addition to being the victim of rape, usually received the brunt of the white women's wrath as the mother of the master's children.[32]

If Anthony took Harriet as his concubine, it seems that he kept her far from his wife, Ann, while Ann was alive. After all, Ann lived on the west side of Talbot County, and Harriet lived on the far eastern side, and there was little reason for either to breach the distance. Ann's death in the year of Frederick's birth, and before his older brother Perry would have arrived in the Anthony kitchen, eliminated her as a threat to Harriet and her children. Anthony's white daughter, Lucretia, must have had some inkling of her father's motives for beating Hester, but Lucretia would have had contact with Harriet only on the few times that

Harriet visited the Anthony house, and thus probably knew little or nothing of any sexual connection between her father and Harriet. Lucretia's contact with Harriet's children also seems minimal. The enslaved children lived under the supervision of the cook, Katy, and Lucretia only extended her attention to Frederick through his own machinations.[33]

Elinor Maloney, on the other hand, had hired Harriet during Harriet's four pregnancies and must have suspected the identity of the father. If the father of Harriet's children was her brother, Elinor could deny his involvement, proselytize against his interactions with Harriet, or focus her attention on Harriet herself. Any reaction could have led to Harriet's removal at the end of 1817. The state of Harriet's womb, however, seems unrelated to her departure. By January 1817, both Jenny and Harriet were equally far along in their pregnancies, but Elinor kept Jenny on through 1818. Jenny was considered to be married to another slave, Noah, and her situation was therefore morally acceptable, unlike Harriet's. Yet, the child Harriet was expecting would be her fourth while in Elinor's employ. With her daughter and granddaughter under her roof and as the moral guardian of the household, it seems unlikely that Elinor would have tolerated the debauchery of her married brother bedding an enslaved woman in her own home for so long a period of time. Harriet's departure may have simply reflected Elinor's preference for having only one nursing mother in her home instead of two.[34]

Anthony's power over Harriet as her master and his consistent access to her body throughout her childbearing years make him a plausible candidate for father of her children. Yet, other men may have filled this role, men whom Harriet may have chosen for her own reasons, whether affection or, like Jacobs, protection. For instance, Harriet's oldest son, Perry, took the surname Downs later in his life. Perry lived in Talbot and Caroline counties until 1860, when he and his family were sold to Texas. Until that time, he had been the slave of the descendants of Aaron Anthony, who had also inherited Perry's sisters Sarah, Kitty, and Arianna, along with their grandmother Betsey, the repository of family history. One of those Anthony descendants remembered him as "Uncle Perry," indicating that he spent a portion of his time in or around the household. Perry, then, had ample opportunity to learn more about his ancestry than his brother Frederick did, and his choice of surname might indicate a tie of kinship. A free black man, Daniel Downs, lived in Caroline County between at least 1810 and 1816, and rented property from Aaron Anthony. Charles Downs and Ben Downs, both free blacks, lived in Caroline County during the same time period, as did a white man, Henry Downs. Perry also mentioned an "uncle harry Dons" in a letter to Frederick in 1867, possibly referring to Betsey's youngest son, Henry. Downs, then, may have been another name in their kinship network. Nothing, of course, indicates that any of the older Downs men fathered any of Harriet's children, but this line of reasoning opens the possibility that, given Harriet's later age when she gave birth to Perry and the consistency of her fertility, her experience may have differed markedly from the one that her son Frederick pieced together based on much less information.[35]

After all, within the question of paternity lies a set of contingencies that might offer other explanations for Harriet's near-total absence from her son's memories of his childhood. Douglass rationalized her absence by describing masters who stripped enslaved women of their children early, "to hinder the development of the child's affection toward its mother," and who then did not allow those mothers to visit those children. Anthony's management of his slaves fit this pattern, hindering Harriet's ability to mother her children by removing them from her care once they were weaned. Likewise, Harriet's employers and overseers controlled her mobility. As a result, the few times she managed to see her son were, in her son's telling, acts of heroism. "The pains she took, and the toil she endured, to see me," he wrote of the twelve-mile trek from Holme Hill to Wye House, "tells me that a true mother's heart was hers, and that slavery had difficulty in paralyzing it with unmotherly indifference." In the autobiographies, her valor culminated in a visit that he identified as her final one. After a day on which the Wye House cook, his cousin Aunt Katy, had pledged to "starve the life out of" Frederick, Harriet swooped in, rescued her son and railed against Katy with "fiery indignation." Then she wrapped him in her "strong, protecting arms" and ensured that he had a sweet feast on a "large ginger cake." He later recalled that as he sat on her knee, devouring the treat, "I learned the fact, that I was not only a child, but *somebody's* child."[36]

Douglass and his audiences discerned in these glimpses of Harriet a "true mother's heart." In the absence of more evidence Douglass constructed an image of her that could satisfy both his own longing for a loving mother and his audiences, who needed to be convinced that enslaved mothers could, in fact, love their children. In portraying his mother as so devoted, however, Douglass glossed over a detail. "I do not remember to have seen my mother at my grandmother's at any time," he recounted. "I remember her only in her visits to me at Col. Lloyd's plantation, and in the kitchen of my old master." The distinction is important. Harriet walked twenty-four miles round trip to visit Frederick at Wye House, but Frederick did not remember her walking the single mile or less to the lot neighboring Holme Hill when he lived there with Betsey. Several factors might account for this. When Frederick first described his mother's visits, he relied solely upon his memory of events taking place over twenty years earlier and covering a period of approximately three or four years, but when he was less than seven years old. With the exception of the story that involved a third party, Aunt Katy, his other memories may have blended locations. Furthermore, he consistently described their meetings as occurring at bedtime, which probably came earlier when he lived at Betsey's cabin and which may have meant that Harriet arrived after he was asleep. Indeed, Harriet herself could have petitioned Anthony to assign her to Holme Hill to be closer to her youngest children once she realized that they would only be with her for a year. If she visited all her children as assiduously as she did Frederick, then her limited free time, her employers' restrictions on her freedom of movement, her cycle of pregnancy and breastfeeding, and the necessity of walking twenty-four miles round trip to see the older children conspired to ensure that she saw each only the same "four or five times" that she saw Frederick.[37]

Yet motherhood contained intricate and contradictory emotions for enslaved women. Douglass initially suspected ulterior motives when he wrote that masters separated mothers from children "to blunt and destroy the natural affection of the mother for the child." In his experience, "This is the inevitable result." These suppositions were as harsh as the nostalgic ones were generous, and, in searching for explanations, neither type quite comprehended the complex emotions Harriet would have experienced. Year after year, from 1813 until 1825, she bore children whom she could seldom see after they left her breast. By the time Frederick came along in 1818, she understood that he, too, would be taken from her. She may have steeled herself against her impending loss even as she developed an irreversible attachment to the baby she carried in and fed from her body. Then separation recurred every time she saw each child. The episode in Katy's kitchen may have proved Harriet's love for Frederick; but for Harriet, the incident only underscored the abuse her children faced every day and her utter lack of power to defend them. If her children were the products of rape, they may have reminded Harriet of those violations, further confusing her emotions, and leaving her with a powerful ambivalence that drew her to them and also repelled her. Love could be humiliating and agonizing under slavery and left Harriet, and every other woman, to endure in ways that felt neither noble nor heroic. Her own sister, Jenny, for instance, ran north to find freedom with her husband Noah in 1825, but they left behind their two children, whom Anthony sold south a month later.[38]

Harriet's death came the same year. Her son could only place it as occurring "when I was about seven years old, on one of my master's farms, near Lee's Mill." She died after an "illness," most likely from the puerperal fever she suffered following the birth of her last daughter, Harriet, around 1825. Lee's Mill sat on Tuckahoe Creek, within sight of Betsey's cabin, so Harriet may have spent her final hours in the care of her mother. Betsey had buried five of Harriet's brothers and sisters a decade earlier. If she closed Harriet's eyes that final time, she may have had some small comfort in thinking that her daughter's suffering had ended. As for Frederick, he recalled that "she was gone long before I knew any thing about it."[39]

At the time of Harriet's death, Frederick had been living in the kitchen of the Anthony home at Wye House for approximately a year. As an adult, he described the transition from his grandmother's cabin to the Anthony kitchen as a hard lesson in the realities of slavery, one in which violence and abuse did not always lead to sympathy and camaraderie but, instead, to yet more violence and abuse. "The whip is all in all," he observed; it had a power so envied that "slaves, as well as slaveholders, use it with an unsparing hand." In Douglass's telling, his cousin, the cook Katy, exemplified that philosophy among the slaves. He remembered Katy with such words as "the sable virago," "ambitious, ill-tempered," and "fiendish." He depicted her as controlling the distribution of the Anthony slaves' provisions and overseeing the children, and taking to her assignments with an iron fist. She starved all the children, but others more than her own. She told Frederick that it "served [him] right" for mixing with *dem Lloyd niggers*" when he ran to her, bleeding profusely from what must have been a serious facial wound inflicted by "a sharp piece of cinder, fused with iron, from the old blacksmith's forge," thrown at him by another slave. When Katy was hired out to a man whom she did not like, she made her displeasure so evident that the man sent her back to her master. She even assaulted her own son with a knife. For these reasons, Katy received little sympathy or understanding from anyone in Douglass's audiences.[40]

Katy's personality may have indeed left much to desire, but, considering her position in the Anthony household, she had to navigate a thorny set of relationships. Her reputation as a "first rate cook" and for being "really very industrious" gave her charge of the kitchen and the status that went with such a position. Like her equally skilled cousin (or aunt) Betsey, she oversaw the other "ten or a dozen" children whom Frederick joined on his arrival, both her own and their cousins. Unlike Betsey, Katy did not enjoy relative privacy and distance from her master on a cabin on a distant lot. She lived under the constant supervision of the Anthonys, and her orders seem to have included keeping her crowd of children separate from the Lloyd slaves, away from the Lloyd house, and from under the feet of her master's family. She also extended Betsey's lessons of fear to the reality of violent punishment.[41]

Katy learned to ensure her own well-being by ingratiating herself to her master's family, even if it was only an act. Douglass remembered that "she had a strong hold on old master" and was "greatly favored," though Anthony's great-granddaughter, also named Harriet, insisted that the other "old servants" did not recall Katy as Douglass did. Katy appeared to use her master's perception of her good nature to her benefit. Douglass noted that in contrast to his mother, her contemporary, Katy "was the only mother who was permitted to retain her children around her." Later, in the 1830s, she was hired out to a home that she did not like. She exhibited to her employer the temperament she had revealed to Frederick and was reassigned back to the master's house that she seemed to prefer. Furthermore, Douglass did not single her out as a slave who was made cruel by the system, but placed her in the context of other slaves who, like "everybody, in the south," wanted "the privilege of whipping somebody else." Katy, then, wielded what little power she could grasp to take care of herself.[42]

Douglass contrasted Katy with his own mother and grandmother but also with their mistress, Anthony's daughter, Lucretia Auld. While Katy had dismissed his bleeding facial wound inflicted by the Lloyd slave boy as "good for me," Lucretia drew him into her parlor and, he remembered, "washed the blood from my head and face, fetched her own balsam bottles, and with the balsam wetted a nice piece of white linen, and bound up my head." Lucretia's ministrations recalled the image of his "good nurse" grandmother. Frederick drew a similar comparison between Lucretia and his mother when Lucretia, not quite so avenging an angel as Harriet, also filled the belly that Katy kept empty. Singing in

Figure 1.2 As a child, Frederick Bailey lived with his "Aunt" Katy, Aunt Hester, and other siblings and cousins in the small kitchen attached to the home of Aaron Anthony, known as the Captain's House, on the Wye House estate. The savage beating of Hester and Frederick's last encounter with his mother took place there. He remembered singing outside of the window of the main house when he was hungry in order to persuade his mistress, Lucretia Auld, to give him a piece of bread. "Wye House, Captain's House," May 1936: Frederick D. Nichols, "Wye House, Captain's House, Bruffs Island Road, Tunis Mills, Talbot County, MD." Photograph. Historic American Buildings Survey, National Parks Service, Dept. of Interior, May 1936. Library of Congress, Prints and Photographs Division (HABS, MD, 21-EATO.V, 2B-2).

the yard to ward off hunger pangs Frederick captured Lucretia's attention, and he received the reward of bread and butter. He learned to position himself near her window to repeat the incident and met with success each time. In that respect, Lucretia, though she "pitied me, if she did not love me" and whose "interest was never very marked," served as substitute for an absent mother and grandmother, counteracting the meager sustenance provided by Katy, the cook who should have fed him.[43]

Frederick, however, had lived through this period as an abused, hungry child. He had a child's myopic focus on his own conditions and no knowledge of the remote Lucretia's role in the operation of the household or much direct experience of Katy's. As a result, when he later recalled these events for his audiences, he did not show any of these women interacting with one another. He did not say, for instance, whether Lucretia nursed Hester, who served as Katy's assistant in the kitchen, when Hester received the sexually charged beating from Lucretia's father. Nor did he say whether Katy bound the wounds or told Hester that she had deserved the punishment, or both. He did not mention whether a healer, such as his grandmother, had been called in to attend to Hester by Lucretia or Anthony. He never described Lucretia as issuing instructions to Katy. Indeed, he portrayed no relationship between Katy and Lucretia at all, leaving his readers to assume that Lucretia was ultimately powerless and thus absolved of culpability in the violence perpetrated under her roof. Yet, Katy, in his telling an abusive mother figure, was the slave of a benevolent mother figure, Lucretia.

Lucretia had learned to be a slave mistress from birth. Her father was a slave-owner, and her mother, Ann, was the daughter of slave masters and had managed household slaves until her death in 1818. After Ann's death, Lucretia presumably took over the management of the slaves; but, being only fourteen at the time, she may have relied on her aunts or on the expertise of Katy, which would explain Katy's influence. In 1823, when she was nineteen, Lucretia married Thomas Auld, the son of ship builders and seamen, and captain of the Lloyd schooner *Sally Anne*. The couple remained in the Anthony house, where Lucretia was mistress. Although she was distinctly of a less distinguished class than the Lloyds, for whom her father worked, she grew up embedded in the planter class, well aware of slave management and mastery. She exhibited none of the discomfort or lack of familiarity with the social codes governing the interaction between slaves and masters that her sister-in-law, Sophia, later did with Frederick. Furthermore, if her responsibilities resembled those of other mistresses of her standing, then she oversaw and delegated tasks such as cooking and cleaning to slaves and supervised the household economy through the purchase and distribution of food, clothing, and other material.[44]

Thus, while Douglass lay the blame for his abuse at Katy's feet, the seemingly kind Lucretia bore her own share of guilt for his treatment, and Katy's behavior must be understood in the context of her position as the main enforcer of Lucretia's policies regarding the children in her charge, much like that of a slave driver. If Katy gave the children meager rations, she presumably apportioned them from those given to her by her mistress. If they froze from their lack of clothing or blankets, that was because Katy had received none to distribute. If Lucretia adopted the same management practice as her father, who always backed up his overseers, regardless of the injustice or disproportional severity of their punishments, then Katy abused the children with the knowledge that her master and mistress condoned her behavior. In this way, like Betsey bringing the children to the Anthony house, Katy occupied an involuntary position in which she imposed the law of the master. Douglass could later understand, if not forgive, Katy for her complicity in the slave system, in the same way that he forgave the betrayal by his grandmother and abandonment by his mother. Indeed, he explained Katy's behavior as a result of her mastery by Anthony, who ultimately controlled the purse strings, but omitted Lucretia's position in the hierarchy between the master and the household slave. Lucretia, however, had the power to intervene on behalf of Frederick and the other children. Katy did not.

As mistress, Lucretia may have had some influence on her father's decision to send Frederick to Baltimore in 1826, thereby removing him from the scene of his abuse. She also presented him with his first pair of trousers for the journey, yet another contrast to the scanty kitchen garb he usually wore that he blamed on Katy, as well as a sign that he was no longer a small child. Still, Douglass himself never pointed to any specific instance in which Lucretia knowingly protected him from Katy or anyone else. The bandaged wounds came with no reprimand for Katy's neglect or punishment for the guilty attacker, and the treats of bread and butter came as payment for his entertainment rather than a redress of the meager kitchen rations. Even Frederick's good fortune in receiving a coveted assignment in Baltimore resulted from a convergence of other circumstances, not the least of which was timing. Frederick had reached the age at which other enslaved children under Anthony's supervision went into the fields or a trade. If he had not gone to Baltimore, Frederick would have likely been sent to one of Anthony's farms or hired to someone in the county, as his brothers, sisters, and other Anthony slaves were. Thus, Frederick's removal from Katy's dubious care was imminent rather than an intervention. Furthermore, of the children among the Anthony slaves, Frederick seemed most qualified for the task at hand.

The journey to the city came at the request of Lucretia's sister-in-law, Sophia Auld, wife of Thomas Auld's brother Hugh. Sophia needed household help in tending her two-year-old son, Tommy, "to prevent his getting in the way of carriages, and to keep him out of harm's way generally" as well as "to run errands." "In fact," Douglass later wrote, "it was to 'little Tommy,' rather than to his parents, that old master had made a present of me." Sophia wanted a servant to watch over her son because she was expecting her second child in November 1826. She had no other household help and would have to go through the process of advertising and interviewing for the position in Baltimore; but the wife of her husband's brother had access to a pool of children who might prove an excellent attendant for her toddler while the infant occupied her time. Frederick had called attention to himself with his singing at Lucretia's window, so the request for a child's companion might automatically have brought him to mind because he might amuse a small child like Tommy. Furthermore, Frederick had already spent time as a personal servant to the older Daniel Lloyd, son of Edward Lloyd, and had observed the etiquette and bearing expected of slaves in white homes, where a "sort of black aristocracy" exhibited "graceful agility and captivating address" and could "anticipate and supply, wants before they are sufficiently formed to be announced by word or sign." Frederick was the answer to Sophia's request, and, in March 1826, he found himself aboard a schooner, headed for the big city.[45]

Changes in the Anthony family also may have prompted Lucretia to send Frederick to work elsewhere. In January, before Frederick's departure, another man had assumed Aaron Anthony's responsibilities at Wye House. Thomas Auld also left Lloyd's employ to open a store in Hillsboro, not far from Betsey's cabin and Anthony's farm. By October, the whole household had moved there, and Lucretia was expecting a baby by the end of the year. Then, Aaron Anthony died in November, leaving his three heirs to carve up his estate in a process that shocked Frederick in its "open contempt" for the Bailey kin, degrading them by ranking them with the livestock "in the same scale of social existence." Frederick returned to Talbot County for the experience of receiving a dollar value and seeing attorneys placing similar prices on the members of his family, their "personality swallowed up in the sordid idea of property." The proceedings, he remembered, gave "new insight into the unnatural power to which I was subjected."[46]

Lucretia would have received Frederick in the final settlement of her father's estate, but she had died shortly after the birth of her first child, Arianna Amanda Auld, in late 1826 or early 1827. Frederick probably saw her for the last time when he was being assessed for her possession. Instead, Frederick became the property of her heir, Thomas Auld, who also inherited Frederick's sisters Eliza and the baby Harriet, who died sometime during 1827, along with his aunt Milly and Hester, Milly's three children Tom, Nancy, and Henny, and Hester's unnamed infant. Betsey stayed in her cabin, now the property of Andrew Anthony, who also assumed ownership of her daughter Betty, Betty's son Stephen, Frederick's sisters Sarah, Kitty, and Arianna, and his brother Perry. Betsey may have had the privilege of retaining her own cabin until her death, but within the space of two years, she had buried her daughter Harriet and seen another daughter sold south along with three grandchildren, and she could only hope that a third had reached freedom. The Anthonys and Auld shuffled the rest of Betsey's children and grandchildren around two counties, uncertain fates looming, while her grandson Frederick sailed back to Baltimore, only returning to her decades later, after her cabin and her grave had disappeared. By then, he had immortalized her in his autobiographies as a weapon against slavery.[47]

Meanwhile, in Baltimore, Sophia Auld drew Frederick close, shocking him by behaving, in his words, "entirely unlike any other white woman I had ever seen." When Douglass later explained his attachment to his first mistress, Lucretia, he wrote, "In a family where there was so much that was harsh, cold and indifferent, the slightest word or look of kindness passed, with me, for its full value." Sophia Auld offered him more than the illusion of affection by welcoming him into her family as if he were a fosterling or an adopted son. Like many of the other women for whom he had affection, she fed him, serving "good bread and mush." Then she dressed him in "good, clean clothes" that he had lacked on the plantation. She introduced him to her toddler, Tommy, bidding the older boy to watch over the younger and the younger to be kind to his keeper. She solicited his needs with "sundry little questions." When she sat Tommy on her shrinking lap, she pulled Frederick to her side where, he believed, she "made me something like his half-brother in her affections" and tried, with "the caressing stroke of her gentle hand, to convince him that, though *motherless*, he was not *friendless*." She seemed to genuinely consider him "a child, like any other child," not a "pig" and not "*property*," and she filled the void left by the absence of his mother and separation from his grandmother.[48]

Sophia's initial interest in his welfare had a profound impact upon his development. In her presence, he found he could look her in the eyes and carry himself with dignity. "The crouching servility, usually so acceptable a quality in a slave, did not answer when manifested towards her," he wrote. "Her favor was not gained by it; she seemed to be disturbed by it."[49] The intimacy and trust that she nurtured with Frederick made him unafraid to approach her. Thus, when she read aloud from the Bible, piquing his curiosity in such a "*mystery*," he felt no compunction about asking her for lessons. "Without hesitation, the dear woman began task," he recalled, "and very soon, by her assistance, I was master of the alphabet, and could spell words of three or four letters." Self-respect and a love of letters were lessons not easily forgotten.[50]

These early sessions continued perhaps a year or more, long enough for Frederick to acquire skills he could build on later, and ended at the command of Hugh Auld. After being treated to a presentation of Frederick's new skills, Hugh flew into a rage and, as Douglass recounted, "unfolded to her the true philosophy of slavery, and the peculiar rules necessary to be observed by masters and mistresses, in the management of their human chattel." The rules, if not the law of

Maryland, forbade literacy because it made a slave "disconsolate and unhappy" with his condition, able to forge passes to run away, and entirely "unfit." So devastating a diatribe against his newfound love, Douglass later remembered, actually had the effect of becoming "the first decidedly anti-slavery lecture to which it had been my lot to listen." Hugh had no idea that his words, meant to discourage Sophia, had exposed the subversive power of literacy and inspired Frederick, not only to continue his lessons, but to become a teacher himself. As for Sophia, the object of the harangue, she, too, proved an apt pupil. "She finally became even more violent in her opposition to my learning to read, than was her husband himself," recounted Douglass. She continued to feed him, to clothe him and otherwise take care of him; but she refused to further Frederick's education or even allow him in a room alone with books or newspapers. She had adopted her husband's philosophy wholly and, by extension, that of the slaveholder.[51]

Douglass attributed Sophia's naiveté about slave management to her background as an artisan. "She was by trade a weaver," he wrote of her life before marriage, "and by constant application to her business, she had been in a good degree preserved from the blighting and dehumanizing effects of slavery." Her family, the Keithleys, lived in St. Michaels in Talbot County, her birthplace. All, including her father Richard, lived in households engaged in some type of manufacturing. In St. Michaels, that manufacturing probably included some aspect of shipbuilding, as it did with their neighbors, the Aulds. Yet, the household headed by Nancy Keithley included only women and boys between 1790 and 1820, suggesting another sort of manufacturing that could have included weaving. In either case, both Sophia's parents and her husband were artisans, and not of the planter class or seemingly aspiring to the planter class, as were the Anthonys and Thomas Auld. If she grew up among artisans, then she may also have grown up around apprentices. While not free, apprentices were also not property and would one day become full and equal artisans themselves, which may have colored Sophia's attitude toward Frederick.[52]

Sophia, however, was probably not as "simple" about slavery as Frederick or her husband believed. If she had no experience of being a slave's mistress, she did live in a society in which she could not escape awareness of slavery, race, and the attendant social codes. She grew up in Talbot County, just as Frederick and Hugh had. Her neighbors in Fells Point owned slaves, and Austin Woolfolk's slave coffles departed for the Mississippi River at the foot of the street on which she lived. Yet, Sophia's perception differed from her husband's and from Frederick's expectations. Both she and her husband had grown up in St. Michaels, on a peninsula of Talbot County, where the typical slave holdings were much smaller than those of Wye House. For three years, between 1833 and 1836, Frederick returned there, where he was hired out to farms on which the masters owned no more than three slaves, and the wealthiest man owned fewer than twenty.

Sophia's parents, Hester Coburn and Richard Keithley, appear not to have owned any slaves. Her husband, a shipbuilder, had married into a nonslaveholding family, and neither came from slaveholders nor expressed any aspiration to own slaves. Hugh's behavior toward his wife and Frederick, however, indicated that he would gladly use the labor of slaves and fully accepted the rights of masters over bondsmen. Sophia did not, but lack of familiarity with the daily reinforcement of racial codes in her household did not fully explain Sophia's heresy in her behavior toward the slave child entrusted to her supervision.[53]

Sophia seemed "remarkably pious" to Frederick, who remembered that she was "frequent in her attendance of public worship, much given to reading the bible, and to chanting hymns of praise, when alone." He noted that outside her home, she spread charitable benevolence with "bread for the hungry, clothes for the naked, and comfort for every mourner that came within her reach." Her motivation lay in her understanding of her place in the world, and her world was ordered by her religious devotion, which, as with Elinor Maloney, took the shape of Methodism. Like many denominations born in the waves of religious revivals of the late eighteenth and early nineteenth century, the Methodists accepted that all people, even those they considered otherwise inferior to themselves, could attain spiritual equality and salvation in the kingdom of God, if not on earth or even in their denomination. While white Methodists accepted the centrality of literacy, specifically for the purpose of reading the Bible, in their own attainment of God's grace, that conviction broke down in discussions of slave conversions. Masters could accept their duty to save and protect slave souls, but church missions to slaves failed when the missionaries met with masters' abject refusal to allow their slaves to read. Literacy took conversion one step too far, and the church avoided setting policy in order to placate the sectional differences of their members. Yet, even as the church backed away from teaching slaves to read, individuals, particularly women, often did not.[54]

When Frederick arrived at her door, Sophia saw him not merely as another of God's creatures but as a fellow human soul and a child—physically small if the amount of bullying he received was any indication—entrusted to her care. Furthermore, he had asked to read, not understanding the difference between one book and another, but she probably took him to mean that he wanted to read the particular book in her hand, the Bible. If the path to salvation ran through the words of the Bible, and if she was responsible for this child's spiritual wellbeing, then, in the eyes of her God, she could not refuse. From her point of view, Frederick had not simply asked her to read. He had asked her to save his soul.

Sophia had her duty to God and to the child in her house, but she also had her duty to her husband. Christianity and nineteenth-century society expected a wife to be obedient to her husband. Although marriage grew out of common principles, when the values of husband and wife differed, a wife was expected to conform to those of her spouse. If Sophia assumed that her husband would, at the very least, tacitly support her work with Frederick as something akin to missionary work and part of her feminine role as caretaker of the household's morality, then she was mistaken. Hugh's opposition to her lessons for Frederick placed her duties to God and to Hugh in direct conflict.

Douglass imagined Sophia's moral struggle. "In ceasing to instruct me," he explained, "she must begin to justify herself *to* herself; and, once consenting to take sides in such a debate, she was riveted to her position." He observed that, in subsequent years, Sophia's minister visited her in concern over her falling involvement with the church. Her growing household, expanded by four children during the years Frederick knew the family, certainly hindered any active participation in her congregation. Yet, if Sophia had been as devout as Douglass indicated, and if she honestly did believe that Frederick's lessons constituted a religious education, then she may have also had a crisis of faith, especially if she had consulted her minister and he had counseled her to obey Hugh against her conscience. As Douglass portrayed her, Sophia's furious reversal suggested that she struggled as much to convince herself that Hugh was correct as to prove to him that she had acquiesced to his demand. She had accepted the role of slave mistress, if not a slave owner, and abandoned her initial belief in salvation through literacy, assuaging her guilt by permitting Frederick to seek religious instruction in the black community of Fells Point.[55]

With three more additions to the Auld household and, for assistance, only a fifteen-year-old boy who required policing lest he be found reading, Sophia requested more servants. Again, the Fells Point Aulds contacted the Talbot County Aulds, now living in St. Michaels, for another slave to hire. Thomas Auld and his new wife, Rowena, sent Henny, Frederick's cousin and the daughter of Milly. In Douglass's telling, the period of time that Henny lived with the Aulds is compressed into the year 1833, but she may have been there since 1830, or she may have replaced another young slave woman between the ages of ten and twenty-three who lived with them in that year. In either case, Henny probably did not receive the same welcome that Frederick had. She was two years older than her cousin, making her a teenager when she arrived in Fells Point, and she had a misshapen hand, the product of a severe burn she had suffered as a child. According to Douglass, the Aulds were not happy with Henny and asked for another young woman instead.[56]

Douglass explained Henny's disability as the source of the Auld's dissatisfaction, which resulted in a "bitter and irreconcilable" dispute between the Auld brothers. Thomas Auld had three other able-bodied women working in his home in St. Michaels and, with the exception of Frederick, who was the youngest, Auld had hired all of the men out for field labor. Perceived as unable or insufficient to perform either type of work to the satisfaction of Thomas, Henny became the dispensable slave in Thomas's household, one whom he could relinquish to his brother's family. The Baltimore Aulds, however, shared the perception that Henny was incapable and returned her to St. Michaels. After a brief few months there, during which Thomas beat Henny savagely, she was sent back to Baltimore to work for Thomas's sister, Sarah Cline. According to Douglass, Henny also dissatisfied the Clines, and the Aulds "set her adrift to take care of herself."[57]

Frederick's evaluation of Henny's condition in his autobiography supported his attack on slave masters, but provided little insight into Henny's own assessment of her options. Throughout her history with these masters, the young woman may very well have been incapable of the work demanded of her, thereby incurring the wrath of a master who was unable to make her profitable. That was the story that Douglass told. Yet, slaves also occasionally used their own disabilities to negotiate favorable work assignments, weighing the punishment for malingering against whatever benefits they sought. Henny may have faced beatings from Thomas Auld in St. Michaels, but she also lived at the Aulds with her Aunt Priscilla and cousin Eliza, both her age, as well as networks of friends and kin. On her first assignment to Baltimore, she had Frederick for companionship, but he alone could not replace the support that she had received from her kinswomen, especially as he began to turn to young black men for company. On her assignment with the Clines, she was alone. As a result, she may have used the perception of her incompetence to ensure that she remained precisely where she wished. If she was, in fact, emancipated or cast out of the Hugh Auld and Cline homes as her cousin supposed, Henny may have considered that liberation rather than dejection, especially if she could rely upon kinship networks or could support herself regardless of disability.[58]

When Hugh Auld returned Henny to his brother, Thomas exacted his punishment by taking Frederick, too. But if Henny had contrived her return, Frederick did not welcome his own. The change was "another shock to my nerves," he recalled. When he had first departed Talbot County at age eight, he was a small, bullied, hungry child. His strategy for material and emotional survival drew him to women who were willing to grant him an approximation of the affection he had lost when he was severed from his mother and grandmother. His brief return that year caused him to weep at the prospect of losing his connection to Sophia Auld. Seven years later, he mourned the loss, not of a mother figure, but of a community. "My attachments were not outside of our family," he wrote. His chosen network included the people whom he taught to read, the starving, white boys who traded bread for reading lessons while urging him to free himself, and his spiritual guide "Father" or "Uncle" Charles Lawson. In Baltimore, his was a kinship based on shared class, intellectual interest, and spiritual study in which he held a position as both a student and a leader. Furthermore, after seven years of good meals and growth, he returned "a big boy." At fifteen, he was actually a man, literate, aware of ideas like abolition, and used to the autonomous corners that city life had permitted.[59]

His arrival in the St. Michaels household also upset the balance of relationships in the Auld home. There, Frederick and Henny joined their aunt Priscilla and Frederick's sister Eliza. Douglass estimated that Priscilla's "road was less rough." He did not elaborate on the reasons, but as the cook she earned some prestige in the house. Eliza assisted Priscilla and became Frederick's "stubborn and defiant" companion. Henny, Priscilla, and Eliza had all been born in 1816, making them two years older than Frederick and thus adult. Indeed, Eliza was already married to Peter Mitchell, a free black man, and spent at least part of 1833 pregnant with their first child. Of the white family, the men included Thomas Auld and Auld's youngest brother, twenty-year-old Hadaway. Seven-year-old Amanda, daughter of Thomas and Lucretia, was the only child in the household. The mistress was Thomas's second wife, twenty-one-year-old Rowena, who was five months pregnant.[60]

Like Frederick's former mistress, Lucretia, Rowena had been born into slaveholding, with her father, William Hambleton, owning a farm with ten slaves. When Lucretia was his mistress, however, the child Frederick was ignorant of the operations of the Auld home and kept away from the white family. He found a way to appeal to Lucretia as only a child could. Now unable and unwilling to delight his mistress, Frederick saw Rowena's hand in enforcing the hierarchy clearly and portrayed her more like a typical slave mistress than her predecessors. He recalled that Rowena "possessed the ability to make him [Thomas] as cruel as herself," instructing her husband to command his chattel and requiring that they address "Captain Auld" as "Master Auld" in recognition of his position over them. She and Thomas were converted Methodists, kneeling together to pray even as they kept and starved their slaves, and were, in Douglass's estimation, "a well-matched pair." The upwardly mobile captain cared more for profit than the people in his house, making him "stingy," and the experienced lady of the slaveholding class demanded obedience and locked food away from her slaves, making her "cruel." Meanwhile, the family in the kitchen went hungry and resorted to "appropriating" food where they could find it.[61]

Comrades in defiance, Douglass remembered that he and Eliza had proved "inapt scholars" in obeying Rowena. Eliza also had a role in Frederick's operation of a clandestine Sabbath school in St. Michaels. Eliza's husband, Peter Mitchell, and his brother James, both free, had been working with a white Quaker, Nathan Wilson, to begin a Sunday school for African Americans. They approached Frederick to become the teacher, knowing from Eliza that he had some experience in black churches in Baltimore. Unfortunately, Thomas Auld and other slave owners broke up the first meeting. Frederick himself was sent to the slavebreaker Edward Covey for his role in the school, but Peter and Eliza had plans to purchase her freedom as well as that of the child she was expecting, which Auld could leverage to coerce her obedience and dissuade Peter from involving himself in any plans for another school.[62]

Eliza was one of the few black women complicit in Frederick's rebellion, part of a support network that led him ultimately to freedom. Yet he buried many of these women in the narrative of his autobiographies. As an able-bodied man he gradually spent more time at work assignments that excluded women. In Baltimore, he noted that, "I was much in the shipyard—Master Hugh's and that of Durgan & Bailey" before 1833, and then he trained as a caulker after his attempt to escape in 1836, when Thomas Auld sent him back to Baltimore. During the intervening years in Talbot County, his sentence at Covey's farm in 1834, and his subsequent sixteen months at William Freeland's farm placed him in the fields, working side by side with only men. Both at reading lessons he led there and at the earlier Sabbath school organized by the Mitchells and Wilson, Douglass mentioned tutoring only children and men. Only men participated in his first escape attempt, in 1836. His spiritual guides, Lawson and Sandy Jenkins, were both men, and his church affiliations segregated Bible study by gender. The East Baltimore Mental Improvement Society debating group in Baltimore included only men; and his description of his final escape in 1838 included only parts played by men. Thus, he gave the impression that he lived in an almost entirely masculine world throughout his teen years. That was not the case.[63]

The reason for his exclusion of women lay in the audiences for his autobiographies. Douglass recounted his life to appeal to white readers, who could only sympathize with victimized black characters. Even among the abolitionists, his first patrons encouraged him to describe atrocities. Thus, when Douglass depicted many of the enslaved women, both in and out of his family, he depicted them as victims. He described in graphic detail the beatings of his cousin Henny, his aunt Hester, his Fells Point neighbors Henrietta and Mary, the "impudent" Nellie Kellum, and the Reverend Daniel Weeden's slave Ceal. Sexual exploitation shaded some of this treatment, not only with Hester and the gossip that his master was his father, but also in his description of Covey's cook, Caroline, purchased as a "breeder," and in the near-naked state of dress of the enslaved children. As he bluntly wrote, "The slave-woman is at the mercy of the fathers, sons or brothers of her master. The thoughtful will know the rest." Mothers, like Harriet, lost their children. Grandmothers, like Betsey, turned over their grandchildren to the harsh realities of slave life. Others, like Katy, meanly doled out already small rations to feed her own children at the expense of their cousins.[64]

These gruesome scenes appealed to the sympathies of his sometimes voyeuristic white audience. Douglass, however, did not reduce all of them to one dimension. Their agency in maneuvering through the slave system emerged through his crafting of their stories. In his own family, Hester continued to see her paramour, even after Anthony beat her. His aunt Jenny and her husband escaped north. Nellie Kellum, the light-skinned wife of a favored slave on the Lloyds' sloop, believed herself exempt from beating and fought back when the overseer, William Sevier, tried to bind her for a whipping. Her three children attacked him as well. "There were numerous bloody marks on Mr. Sevier's face," Douglass remembered. "The imprints of Nelly's fingers were visible, and I was glad to see them." Even afterward, Douglass recalled, "she continued to denounce the overseer, and to call him every vile name." Her story foreshadowed his own more successful resistance at Covey's. There, as he and Covey engaged in their epic battle, Caroline passed through the yard, and Covey demanded she help subdue Frederick. "She was a powerful woman," Douglass remembered, "and could have mastered me very easily, exhausted as I now was." She refused, despite the punishment she could expect to receive later. Even in small ways, women assisted him. Mary, the Hambleton cook, always fed Frederick when he allowed one of the Aulds' horses to escape to the Hambleton estate so he could follow to retrieve it, and Sandy Jenkins's unnamed wife prepared him a meal late at night when he found himself trapped between Covey's cruelty and an unsympathetic Auld. These black women had replaced Katy's insensitivity and the patronizing benevolence of Lucretia and Sophia, sustaining him in his resistance.[65]

Douglass wrote to expose the depravity of slavery, and only included the experiences of women that supported his argument. Thus, he omitted the enslaved women living on the Freeland plantation, or those in St. Michaels and Baltimore. The lives of free blacks also lay outside his scope, and all but Sandy's wife, whom he did not name in his first two autobiographies and eliminated from his third, were enslaved women. His depiction of life in Baltimore left his readers imagining a city devoid of all but three black women, two slaves, and the third only mentioned after she had departed Maryland. Yet, women made up one half of the free black population in the city. Although an increasing number of them worked as domestics after 1830, others worked as artisans, as craftsmen, and in factories, and even maids and laundresses populated the streets and markets in their weekly routines and as they attended church on Sundays. Frederick's daughter Rosetta later told of meeting an older woman, an "old friend of my parents of those early days, who as a free woman was enabled with others to make my father's life easier while he was a slave in that city." One story mentions a group of women working in the Fells Point market who served as contacts for slaves wishing to escape. Douglass's omissions protected his subjects from recrimination but also from his audience's prejudices. Free black women, however much they participated in his community and populated his world, had to be shielded from scrutiny to protect both his and their respectability. Having no place in his critique of slavery, they could remain unmolested by the prying eyes of the public, including critics with harmful intentions. Meanwhile, black men became the public face of the black community as leaders and organizers.[66]

Douglass grew into one of those leaders, but he emerged from a world in which women delineated many borders. Because fathers were all but erased by the laws of slavery and the records of slaveholder, his family traced its ancestry through his mother, grandmother, and great-grandmother—Harriet, Betsey, and Jenny. As property, he also traced his provenance through women, passing from one white family to another through the marriages of Ann Skinner and Lucretia Auld, each woman making her husband a slave owner, and they and all white women every bit as capable of beating, maiming, and killing as any overseer.[67] As a child, he also passed through the hands of women, from the un-remembered years with his mother to his grandmother Betsey to Aunt Katy, and also among the Auld wives, Lucretia, Sophia, and Rowena. In these intertwined lines of white and black women, Frederick gravitated toward those who offered any hint of kindness, which meant food and intellectual stimulation. As he grew, he found himself more often among peers, both male and female, almost all African American, and he assumed the role of a man in his community, even as his masters considered him a boy. He no longer needed a mother figure, he needed a partner. He found that partner among those free black women who were hidden from his audience, a place where she preferred to stay.

|| 2 ||

Anna Murray, Mrs. Frederick Douglass, 1810–1848

Anna Murray was born on the Eastern Shore, Caroline County, Maryland, on an unknown day in an unknown year. Indeed, "unknown" described much about Anna's life. "As is the condition of most wives," her daughter Rosetta reflected many decades later, Anna's "identity became merged into that of the husband." She perplexed her contemporaries and subsequent generations by refusing to behave in a manner expected of the wife of Frederick Douglass; and while her much-noted illiteracy might explain the absence of the usual windows into a woman's life, such as letters or diaries, her silence seems more an act of will in which she kept herself carefully hidden from prying eyes. Anna did not record her thoughts for posterity, nor did she trust those who might pass along her confidences. Those privy to her inner life kept her secrets. As a result, most of the existing depictions of Anna resort to formula or cliché in their attempts to explain the woman who knew Frederick Douglass the most intimately through forty-four years of the most dramatic changes of both his life and the nineteenth century. Her husband's biographers have puzzled over the attraction of a man with intellectual aspirations to a woman who appeared to have little desire to read. Many have drawn direct and ungenerous comparisons between Anna and the educated white women with whom Frederick worked. Others shoehorned her into a model of activism more fitting for a romance of the Underground Railroad than consonant with the material conditions of her life. Her daughter, however, identified the problem in understanding Anna. "She could not be known all at once," Rosetta reflected. "She had to be studied." To do so requires sifting evidence from those unsubstantiated interpretations, and then reconstructing Anna's as a life separate from but intersecting with her husband's.[1]

Anna told her children that she had been born on Maryland's Eastern Shore in Denton, the Caroline County seat, east of Talbot County. She knew both her parents, Mary and Bambarra Murray, and claimed that her mother had been freed shortly before Anna's birth. Rosetta recounted that Anna, "the eighth child," had "escaped by the short period of one month the fate of her older brothers and sisters," making her "the first free child." Yet, no record ever pinned down her birth year. Rosetta's memoir, city directories, Anna's death certificate, and state and federal censuses all place her birth at anywhere between 1804 and 1825, a significant span of time.[2] The extreme ends of that span seem unlikely. Anna's birth before 1810 might place her outside of Frederick's peer group and thus exclude her from consideration as a wife. The same holds true for the 1825 date because that would have made her thirteen years old at the time of her marriage.[3] She told Rosetta that she had moved to Baltimore at age seventeen and lived there for approximately nine years before marrying Frederick. By that estimation, Anna was twenty-six when she married in 1838, and thus born in 1812. Yet, she may have miscalculated by a few years; the first family for whom she worked did not arrive in the United States until mid-1832. Had she found a position in that family immediately upon their arrival in the city, then Anna would have lived in Baltimore for only six years before her marriage, putting her birth in 1815 and her age at twenty-three when she wed Frederick. In any case, 1810 to 1815 seems to be the most plausible window for Anna's birth and for Mary Murray's emancipation.[4]

Anna described little of her upbringing on the Eastern Shore to her children, offering only enough information to satisfy their curiosity, leaving out crucial details that later generations might trace in records. For instance, her father's name, Bambarra, might suggest that he came from a group of people by that name living in western Africa or that he had a father, grandfather, or great-grandfather who either was, or, given the haphazard assignment of African ethnicities by Europeans, was classified as a Bambara. Whatever associations the name had for Anna's family, if any, they stayed within the family.[5] Nor did Anna and Rosetta clarify Bambarra's status after Mary's emancipation, and they provided no specifics about the Murrays' enslavement, including the name of their master or the type of work that they did for him. Anna's free status depended on her mother's, so Bambarra could have remained a slave after his wife became free. He might also have had a different master, been freed earlier, or purchased Mary's freedom just in time to save their next child from slavery. The fate of the seven older children—whether they died in slavery, gained freedom along with their mother, ran away, or remained slaves until the institution was ended—did not survive the retelling. This was not a part of her life that Anna kept alive for her children, but she, too, was a victim of slavery. The institution surrounded the free Murrays, embedding them in the system through ties to children, siblings, and cousins and threatening them with the same separations and violence as those suffered by Frederick's family in the neighboring county.[6]

Slavery circumscribed Murray's life in other ways, too, tainting her future prospects for work and marriage. In Caroline County, the ready availability of forced labor depressed wages and employment opportunities for women. If she sought work as a domestic, she would encounter masters who either owned or hired slaves for that purpose. If she turned to field labor, she would find herself competing with men, enslaved and free, black and white. So, sometime between 1827 and 1832, Murray headed to Baltimore. Even there, she would have entered a city teeming with other free women, black as well as white, working-class, and immigrant all scrambling for the same jobs. During the decade between 1810 and 1820, the free black population in the city doubled through migration from rural areas and as a result of individual manumissions. The numbers continued to increase at a rate of 10 percent a decade over the next thirty years, and over half of that free black population entered domestic service, answering newspaper ads seeking "good plain cooks" and women "acquainted with housework." Childcare usually entered the equation and, occasionally, laundry. Some employers specified a preference for slaves, some for white "girls," some for black. One promised "liberal wages." All wanted good references.[7]

Although Anna may have taken in laundry at first, she told Rosetta that she found work in a "French family by the name of Montell" and then, later, in "a family by the name of Wells living on S. Caroline Street." The French creole Montells hailed from the Bahamas, where Francis Montell had been a merchant and a master of twenty-five slaves. Perhaps sensing impending economic upheaval as the British Parliament debated West Indian emancipation, Montell sold his slaves in early 1832 and, with his wife Elizabeth and their eight children, immigrated to Baltimore. There, he and his son Charles opened a shop on the Inner Harbor at Smith's Wharf, the same place where seven-year-old Frederick Bailey, fresh from Talbot County, had disembarked from the sloop *Sally Lloyd* in 1826. The Montell family lived farther east, on Pratt Street, just west of Gough. A few blocks away lived the Wells family, just south of the intersection of Gough and Caroline streets. Peter Wells had started his working life as a shipbuilder, a decade and a half earlier, living on Aliceanna Street, the same street where Frederick had lived during his first few months with the Aulds. In the 1820s, Wells married and turned to civil service, working for the post office in the 1820s and 1830s. By 1833, he and his family had moved to South High Street, nearer to Pratt Street and the Montells, before settling on Caroline, on the northern edge of Fells Point, in 1835.[8]

Simply because they employed a servant, these two families identified themselves as middle class, although the Montells, having once owned many slaves and employing two domestics, probably considered themselves better off than the Wellses. Indeed, less than a decade after Murray had left Baltimore, a neighbor in Rochester noted Anna's "very aristocratic ideas" and speculated that "her training had evidently been in Southern families of high standing." Yet, even with only two servants, the Montells probably hired Anna for "good plain cooking" and "housework," and the mistress or misses of the house might have worked alongside her in addition to issuing instructions. Murray had likely learned those two specialized and laborious skills from her mother back in Caroline County. Cooking involved extensive preparation, building and maintaining the fire, stoking a bake oven, pickling, and otherwise readying food for storage. Many decades later, the English abolitionist Julia Griffiths and the Douglasses' Rochester neighbor Jane Marsh Parker both fondly recalled Anna's "Maryland biscuits," a type particular to the Eastern Shore. Murray had probably baked many of them for the Montells and Welles. In the city, she could purchase manufactured butter, butchered meat, produce, and candles or other lighting at the local market, shopping either on her own or with her mistress. Two of her children remembered Anna as "the banker" of the family; so, just as her husband had learned to read, she must have picked up math. That suggests that she acquired knowledge with the same agility as her husband and that her employer entrusted her with a degree of financial responsibility.[9]

Taking care of the house took up much of her time, too. Throughout her later life, Murray was universally declared by observers to be a clean and neat housekeeper. At first glance, such comments may seem condescending, as if Anna had no other redeeming qualities, and tinged with racist assumptions about African American hygiene. But in the early nineteenth century, homes were appallingly filthy by the standards of later generations. The connection between cleanliness and good health was not yet widely understood, and the conditions outdoors made polished floors and dust-free surfaces nearly impossible. As the century progressed, however, clean bodies and clean homes indicated status and morality, and the housekeeping literature for whites and African Americans stressed cleanliness as a middle-class virtue. As a servant in middle-class homes, Murray held the filth of Baltimore's streets at bay. Her ability to keep the house and her person clean and neat allowed her employers to project an image of order and social standing. In performing her job well, Murray also elevated herself above the stereotypes of slovenliness that plagued women of her race and class. She may have secured her employment in these households because of her skills, but she maintained her position by absorbing and adopting middle-class norms of presentation and deportment.[10]

That Murray moved from one position to another and from one neighbor to another indicated her desirability as a servant. Living so near the Montells, the Welles may have observed or gathered information about her abilities, and they would have known how to weigh the Montells' reference. It is clear Anna satisfied the Welles since they kept her on for five years, or longer, and she at least tolerated them for that period. Indeed, Rosetta later believed that "an attachment sprang up between her [Murray] and the members of that household [the Welles], the memory of which gave her pleasure to recall." Yet "attachment" between an employee and employer in so intimate an arrangement as domestic service always included a clear hierarchy, the potential for violence, and the awareness that one party served the other. When the servant was black, whether slave or free, the inequalities of class and roles were even more pronounced. Although Murray may have, either in retrospect or at the time, felt an attachment to the family she served, she may also have cultivated what her daughter experienced as "a certain reserve," one "that forbade any very near approach to her." Her white contemporaries and historians later attributed that reserve to Anna's discomfort with the educated white people who visited her husband in subsequent decades. "Discomfort," however, seems an inaccurate description, especially if it was used to imply intellectual deficiency. Murray had grown up in a slave society, worked in close quarters in white homes, and lived in a busy, rapidly growing city that was dense with slaves, free blacks, whites, slave traders, and opportunists. For self-protection, she perfected a stoic mask.[11]

If Murray's "aristocratic ideas" and "certain reserve" developed in response to the experiences of her formative years, then other aspects of those years may also have influenced her later decisions and behavior. As always, slavery defined the world in which she lived, as is seen in her narrow escape from bondage by the good fortune of her mother's emancipation, the part of her family that may have remained enslaved in Caroline County, and the man she chose to marry. She competed with hired slaves for jobs. She worked for a family that had recently been part of the slaveholding class in a slave society. At her other employers' home, she either replaced or joined an enslaved woman whom the Wellses had either hired or owned. Trader Austin Woolfolk drove his slave coffles to the docks at the end of Caroline Street, and the Strawberry Alley Methodist Episcopal Church, located around the corner from the Wellses' home, ministered to slaves and free blacks alike. Murray also faced a future in which she might marry a slave, if she were permitted to marry at all. While her free status meant that her children would be free, they could never be secure in their father's ability to participate in the support and life of the family. Free though she was, she could not escape the ways in which slavery and its attendant prejudice infected the world of all African Americans.

Furthermore, through her employment, Murray both observed and maintained the trappings of the urban middle class. Having come from rural poverty and seen the ravages of urban destitution around her, she could not help but notice a marked difference between the lives of poor families and middle-class families. Her employers did not have to manufacture as much of their food and clothing as did poor, rural families. They could purchase more and better food and textiles than urban poor families could. They could hire her to relieve their workload. They could afford to educate their children and offer them a better future, instead of sending them immediately to work. They lived in cleaner houses and enjoyed better health, despite epidemics. Daily, too, she witnessed the indignities that the poor, especially poor African Americans, had to endure but that the middle class could escape. She may have wanted these things in and of themselves, but she may also have wanted them as a means to a better life and the respectability that many African Americans struggled so hard to attain. While she might have identified as working class, she lived within the middle class on less precarious footing than her own family had.[12]

Murray, then, probably had ambitions. She told her daughter that by the time she left the South she had "been able to save the greater part of her earnings." She gave Rosetta a small inventory of the things she had acquired: "a feather bed with pillows, bed linen, dishes, knives, forks and spoons, besides a well filled trunk of wearing apparel for herself," as well as another featherbed, which she sold in September 1838. Murray remembered and kept these items, until a fire destroyed them in 1872, indicating they held great importance for her, not only as "souvenirs" from the early years of her marriage and of her material contribution to the partnership, but also as symbols of her own work and youthful hopes for her future. She may have been proud and thankful that she had a secure position with acceptable wages in a family that treated her well; but she probably also dreamed that all of her hard work could one day make her a mistress in her own house rather than a servant in another.[13]

From her vantage as a young woman, in 1837, Murray might have considered the options available to her for the future. Her marketable skills kept her a servant rather than a proprietor, although some women parlayed their skill in the kitchen into a cookshop business. She had limited opportunities for marriage since black women outnumbered black men in the city. An enslaved husband presented problems because of the constant negotiation with the threats of his master. A free husband engaged in a trade as a caulker or barber had more promise, but most faced the vagaries of the general labor market, and many men sailed away as mariners. Regardless of her husband's status, she would probably always work both outside and inside her home; but, because so many other black women did the same, she would have felt no stigma in this, and the wages she earned benefitted her own family. Still, until Frederick became a suitor, Anna could expect to continue as she was, single and without children, saving her money for an as yet undefined future, and working in service.[14]

Murray did not tell her daughter the story of meeting Frederick or of their courtship. Rosetta's circumspect description—"Anna Murray, to whom he had given his heart"—took her father's point of view and was vague enough to suggest that she did not know how her parents had met. In the absence of evidence, most Douglass biographers have assumed that Anna met Frederick through the East Baltimore Mental Improvement Society, an organization of free black men who agreed to allow the enslaved Douglass to participate in their debates. This version has become accepted as fact, despite Frederick, Anna, and Rosetta giving no indication that it was the case. Rosetta wrote about a "little circle of free people—a circle a little more exclusive than some others," where "Frederick Bailey was welcome." She did not specify, however, whether she was describing simply a group of friends or an organization giving itself a formal title; and, while she described her mother's sympathy for her father, she did not include Anna among the members of this circle. Given that Rosetta's account of her mother's life was addressed to an African American woman's club dedicated to racial uplift, and that she strained to portray her mother as involved in abolitionist activism, she hardly omitted her mother's participation in this society by accident.[15]

All other allusions to the East Baltimore Mental Improvement Society point to an all-male membership, and there is no mention of any formal social gatherings. The Young Men's Mental Improvement Society, a group of free blacks "for the Discussion of Moral and Philosophical Questions of All Kinds," that had been organized by 1838, may have been the same as the East Baltimore Mental Improvement Society. If so, the name indicates an all-male membership, and Frederick himself recollected that its members were "young men" and "young caulkers" who "could read, write and cipher." Indeed, decades later, in 1870, Douglass received a letter from an old friend from the Baltimore days, William E. Lloyd, who recalled a time when "D Keeth, E. Cummins J Jackson and others of the old Stock" such as John Locks and James Mingo, met together to debate in "the old frame House in Happy Alley." Daniel Keith, Enoch Cummins, John or James Jackson, and James Mingo, all free black laborers and caulkers in Baltimore during the 1830s, had most likely formed the group of "young men" who "had high notions about mental improvement." Furthermore, with a handful of noted exceptions, women shunned public speaking and any other type of public activity that might label them immoral, which precluded participating in a debating society. Women tended to dominate charitable, fundraising, and organizing committees; however, nothing suggests that this group of men had a woman's auxiliary or held socials, dances, or any of the other activities historians have credited them with. These working men used their few free hours to groom themselves as their community's leaders.[16]

Murray, however, knew the men whom Lloyd mentioned, as Lloyd indicated when he lamented that, in 1870, he "would have been so glad to have seen Her [Anna] However John Locks told me That She Said She had not forgotten me." Fells Point was a small geographic area, with narrow streets and small houses, but African Americans created their own gathering places, such as the market on Broadway; homes, such as James Mingo's; and the Strawberry Alley church, another place Anna could have met Frederick. Decades later, at her funeral, the eulogizing minister proclaimed that "She is said to have first met Mr. Douglass at church in their native State." He clearly knew nothing of Anna and less of

Frederick, claiming the two professed Methodists were Baptists. Still, Anna lived on the next block over from Strawberry Alley, and Frederick had friends connected to the church, if he was not himself part of the congregation, making meeting at a Sunday service or Bible study probable.[17]

Another potential meeting of Anna and Frederick could have occurred in the summer of 1838. Frederick had convinced Hugh Auld to allow him to find his own work and live away from the Auld household so long as he paid his own expenses, including three dollars each week to Auld himself. "I bent myself on the work of making money," he wrote and, hoping to save for an escape, "I was ready to work at night as well as day." He took odd jobs when caulking provided uneven work. Five years later, in March 1843, after he had escaped and begun lecturing for the American Anti-Slavery Society, a southern woman attending one of his speeches recognized him. Abolitionist Anne Warren Weston, who was in attendance, reported that the woman remembered Douglass's "master was a Mr. Merriman who had a son at E. M. D. Wells school at the time," adding that Douglass's "real name was Edward" and "that he was considered a very valuable servant." Later in the evening, when Douglass was confronted with this bit of news, Weston observed that he "started as though he had been shot." Frederick confirmed parts of the story, and Weston's sister, Maria Weston Chapman, told Anne that "Douglass has made some arrangement with his master though he says nothing about it." She probably referred to his quasi-free summer in 1838.[18]

Frederick, who had a history of taking care of children, may have found a position that involved walking a child to school, and several people with the phonetically similar name Merryman lived and worked in Baltimore in that year. Three had addresses on the eastern side of the city, near Fells Point, where an E. M. P. Wells ran a school on Caroline Street. Elizabeth Wells also lived on Caroline Street. Both the school and Elizabeth Wells's home lay a short distance from Peter Wells's home. These coincidences suggest that the southern woman in Weston's story had unveiled a detail of Frederick's life. Furthermore, if Frederick did take a job that involved walking the young Merryman boy to the Wells school, then perhaps he met Anna as she went about her day at the Peter Wells home, located a few buildings down. Of course, Anna and Frederick may have already known one another, and, if so, she could just as likely have used her influence to gain Frederick a position with the Merrymans.[19]

Whatever the specifics of their meeting, the connections mentioned by William Lloyd and the geography of Anna's and Frederick's employment and residence in Fells Point, as well as their connection to the Strawberry Alley church, sketch an outline of their social circle in Baltimore composed of working-class, free blacks. Despite the admitted elitism of the free blacks of any class in Baltimore, this group welcomed Frederick. His and Anna's association with the Strawberry Alley church, in particular, and Methodism, in general, indicated a sense of community responsibility and morality based in self-reliance and self-sufficiency, which, in turn, led them to aspire to the middle class even when their income kept them firmly in the working class. All of these factors placed Frederick and Anna on common ground in the ways they lived and envisioned their lives. That common ground became the foundation for their union.[20]

Most of Douglass's biographers prefer a more romantic story. They conclude that Anna and Frederick married because they fell in love. Love naturally led to a wedding, and the wedding could only take place in the North in order to satisfy Frederick, leading Anna to urge him to escape. That narrative, however, says more about a later century's notion of matrimony than about the reasons these two people joined their lives together. Mutual attraction was probably a consideration. According to their daughter, both possessed several similar personality traits. Anna had a sense of humor that Rosetta described as "grim," an outlook also evident in Frederick's noted sarcasm. Like him, Anna had a gift for righteous anger and a distaste for hypocrisy, or what her daughter called "shams." Still, whatever their subjective attraction to one another, this marriage and its significance to both parties lay in the context of working-class marriages and African American life in Baltimore in 1838.[21]

Anna and Frederick wed on the cusp of historical changes in the institution of matrimony, and their union exhibited elements of both prior and later ideals of family. In the eighteenth century marriage was an economic partnership entered into for survival and household production. The wealth, skills, and social connections that the spouses brought to the marriage far outweighed any romantic attraction. Ideally, a mutual affinity accompanied those more important qualities and deep affection would grow in time; but to marry for love alone was dangerous. People primarily married for practical reasons, not emotional ones, and children added to the household economy as much as their age permitted. Only the privileged could afford the luxury of marrying for love. For working people throughout the nineteenth century and beyond, marriage remained akin to a business contract to which both parties brought a set of abilities and expectations of the other that would enable them to create a harmonious and solvent household. The marriage of Anna and Frederick fell into the latter category. Anna, with years of experience as a housekeeper, could run a household. Frederick, with a marketable skill in the second-highest-paid trade in the shipbuilding industry, could provide for that household. Both saved their wages, an important practice in a city in which much of the working class and black population lived in debt and one indicating that both had ambitions for the future. In these respects, they were a good match, and their shared values probably led them to predict that the years would deepen their affection.[22]

Yet the law would not recognize their marriage any more than it did those between two enslaved partners. Frederick had to receive permission from his master to marry, and as a couple they faced the same threat of family disruption that any family of slaves did. On the Eastern Shore, both Frederick and Anna had witnessed the assaults on the integrity of their own families. In Baltimore, the coffles of Austin Woolfolk's human cargo marching to the wharves at the end of Caroline and Philpot, at the intersection of the streets where Anna and Frederick each lived, kept the specter of the slave trade ever present. Even then, Frederick's masters did not have to resort to sale to threaten his marriage, because other factors loomed. Anna would have to continue to work after their wedding, even if Frederick could convince Auld to allow him to keep part of his wages. The two might never live together if she remained employed as a live-in domestic or if Hugh Auld insisted that Frederick reside in the Auld house without her. If the Aulds permitted Frederick and Anna the freedom to live in the same household, they could also alter the arrangement at any moment by hiring him out elsewhere or calling him back to St. Michaels, both of which had happened in Frederick's past.[23]

Children would complicate matters further. As a mother, Anna would have difficulty maintaining her position as a live-in housekeeper. Even if she remained in domestic work but lived in her own home, she would have to find someone to look after her child. As a slave father, Frederick would have to rely on the benevolence of his master to allow him to contribute to the well-being of his family or, reminiscent of his own mother, visit them. Their children, though free because of Anna's status, lived with the possibility of kidnapping and the loss of their father at any moment, not to mention the shadow of abject poverty. In Baltimore, Anna's future with Frederick more likely than not saw her heading the household and raising her children alone. With upward of 20 percent of households in the neighborhoods around the Wellses' home headed by women, she had plenty of examples of the difficulty of that life. If she had as much ambition for her own future as Frederick did for his, then the prospect of marriage to him in Baltimore probably invoked more ambivalence than hope.

For couples such as Anna and Frederick, forming a family was the privilege of whites and a fortunate few free African Americans. To seize that privilege for themselves was an act of subversion, and nearly impossible as long as they stayed in Baltimore. In this context, Frederick's escape was not simply an act of self-emancipation; nor was Anna's assistance simply a sign of her love and devotion to her husband. Their flight north was a joint venture undertaken to create a life in which they could have a chance to thrive and protect the integrity of their family to the fullest extent of their abilities. Together, they rejected the racism that both included and radiated from slavery.

As if to underscore the limits on their futures in Baltimore, in August 1838, Hugh Auld revoked Frederick's privilege of living on his own. Frederick could take no more. Throughout Sunday, August 12, 1838, he debated his options, settling upon Monday, September 3, as the day of his escape. "I now had three weeks during which to prepare for my journey," he remembered. If he and Anna had spoken of marriage before this time, then Frederick's plan sealed the decision. Rosetta later indicated that her father had included her mother in the scheme from near the beginning. "Having been able to save the greater part of her earnings," Rosetta explained, Anna "was willing to share with the man she loved that he might gain the freedom he yearned to possess." In the autobiographies, Frederick omitted Anna from the story of his flight until she arrived in New York, situating her as a partner in his life as a free man. When Anna spoke to her children of her marriage, however, she saw her partnership with Frederick and, by extension, their family life, as originating in the mutual efforts of preparing for Frederick's escape and their life together.[24]

Frederick described his trepidation as he made his escape from Fells Point to the relative safety of David Ruggles's reading room in New York, the center of the city's black abolitionist community. Back in Baltimore Anna, too, surely felt uneasy. She lived under the supervision of her employers, the Wellses, which would make her preparations difficult if they suspected that she planned to marry a slave who had just escaped. If they discovered that she had aided a runaway, they could fire her without a reference; or, she could be arrested or fined for aiding a fugitive. She had no way of knowing how long news from Frederick might take to arrive. He could be kidnapped, retaken, or killed. He could abandon her and their plans. For nearly ten days, in September 1838, she waited. Then, his message came, and she, too, made a hasty if less clandestine departure, severing her ties to family and community in Baltimore in order to protect her new family and community in the North.[25]

Anna and Frederick's wedding took place at Ruggles's Manhattan home the day after Anna's arrival in New York. The bride wore a new plum-colored silk dress. The groom joked that in his "homeless, houseless, and helpless condition," he seemed an unpromising husband. Frederick's initial account of the wedding ceremony emphasized the importance of the proceedings, containing more detail than any of his other descriptions of their life together. A minister officiated, and Ruggles, the boarding house matron, Mrs. Joseph Michaels, and "two or three others" witnessed the proceedings. In the text of the *Narrative*, Frederick transcribed "an exact copy" of the minister's statement verifying their marriage:

This may certify, that I joined together in holy matrimony Frederick Johnson and Anna Murray, as man and wife, in the presence of Mr. David Ruggles and Mrs. Michaels.

JAMES W. C. PENNINGTON.

New York, Sept. 15, 1838.

The careful rendering of the certificate, the names of the witnesses, the presence of a respectably married female witness, and Pennington's name and his known status as an ordained minister all testified to the legitimacy of the union. Furthermore, Frederick's description of the wedding, and thus the start of their family life together, came at the end of *Narrative*, a tale that began with the illegitimacy of Frederick's own birth, a discussion of the rape of black women, and the recurring theme of destruction wrought upon slave families. In later versions of the story, he reminded his readers that Pennington, himself a former slave, was "then a well-known and respected" minister, adding that, knowing the couple's poverty, Pennington "seemed well pleased with our thanks" in lieu of a fee. The marriage of Frederick and Anna was defiantly legal, sanctified, and documented, and it took place with the support of black activists.[26]

Unlike white New Yorkers when they married, both of the newlyweds acquired a new last name. Traditionally, slaves did not have last names, and free wives took the surname of their husbands. Frederick had abandoned his family name, Bailey, for the alias of Johnson during his journey to freedom, and Anna had left behind Murray for Johnson upon their marriage. Within days of the wedding, they abandoned Johnson for Douglass. Frederick wrote of choosing Douglass as a practical decision, hiding him from slave-catchers and distinguishing him from the many other Johnsons in their new city. The choice seemed to be solely his, symbolizing his new life as a free man; but he and Anna took the name Douglass together, refashioning themselves as free partners. So, too, did Frederick depict the beginning of their marriage as a partnership. After the wedding ceremony, he recounted, "I shouldered one part of our baggage, and Anna took up the other." Anna, he knew, would now "share the burdens of life with me." Everything between them in the subsequent forty-four years flowed from the importance of both the legitimacy of their marriage and their separate perceptions of that partnership.[27]

After collecting their baggage, the newlyweds set out for their first home in freedom, New Bedford. This southeastern Massachusetts port thrived on whaling and shipbuilding and, in many ways, resembled Baltimore, with the notable exception that slaves lived in Baltimore while former slaves lived in New Bedford. As a result, the city contained a strong antislavery element, much of it based in the black community. Organizations and institutions for African Americans had emerged throughout the 1830s, including a small number of private black schools, the African Christian Society, and the African Methodist Episcopal Zion church. All drew different classes of African Americans together, from the growing numbers of black mariners who roomed in boarding houses run by black men, to artisans such as the blacksmith Lewis Temple, to established black families such as that of Ruth Cuffe, daughter of Paul Cuffe, who had been the wealthiest black merchant in the country in the earlier part

Figure 2.1 Anna Douglass sat for this portrait several years after her marriage to Frederick. National Park Service, Frederick Douglass National Historic Site, Washington, DC, Anna Douglass, [n.d.], FRDO 246.

of the century. Ruth Cuffe's husband, the Reverend Henry Johnson, had organized New Bedford's African Methodist Episcopal Zion church, and Shadrach Howard, one of her sons from another marriage, became a leader in the abolition movement. The tendrils of Ruggles's activist networks ran to this community, so he sent Frederick and Anna to Nathan Johnson, who had much experience harboring and helping the newly self-emancipated.[28]

Johnson, along with others, had created an activist community in New Bedford that became adept at hiding former slaves and their families and working against the myriad issues facing free blacks in the North. As Frederick soon learned, a society absent of slavery did not mean a society absent of racism. Jeremiah Sanderson, who soon became the Douglasses' friend, characterized the racial attitude as one of "caste." Public transportation was segregated, which leaders such as Ruggles, Sanderson, and Douglass himself challenged in the early 1840s. Churches and schools maintained the appearance of integration, but inside African Americans encountered "negro pews" and open disdain for anyone crossing the color line. Young black men faced harassment on the street and unfair treatment in the courts. Black mariners could not guarantee that they would return home, not only

Figure 2.2 Five years after his marriage to Anna Murray, Frederick Douglass sat for this portrait in Syracuse, during his first tour through New York State in 1843. Frederick Douglass, c. 1845. Unknown photographer. Daguerreotype. Onondaga Historical Association, 321 Montgomery Street, Syracuse, NY 13202.

because of the usual dangers of a seaman's life, but also because they faced kidnapping, and because of the Negro Seaman's Acts, passed throughout the southern states in the 1820s, which incarcerated free black seaman for the duration of their ship's stay in port. For protection, African Americans in New Bedford organized against all forms of racial discrimination, including enslavement.[29]

In addition to the abolitionism inherent to the city's black churches and Society of Friends, more popularly known as Quakers, integrated antislavery societies multiplied, reflecting a multiplicity of strategies and ideologies. The New Bedford

Union Society was the first, followed by the New Bedford Female Union Society, the Bristol County Anti-Slavery Society, the New Bedford Anti-Slavery Society, the Anti-Slavery Society of New Bedford, the New England Non-Resistance Society, and the Wilberforce Debating Society. Antislavery lecturers spoke at the New Bedford Lyceum or, when they were barred from the Lyceum premises, elsewhere. Agents sold the *Liberator* and the *National Anti-Slavery Standard*, and David Walker's *Appeal* made the rounds of the taverns, boarding houses, and other places in which interested readers and listeners gathered. Individuals involved in these societies included African American activists, such as the Johnsons, both William and Nathan, and Sanderson, as well as wealthy white businessmen and professionals, such as William Rotch and Rodney French. One of the leading white women of the movement was Deborah Weston, sister to both Anne Warren Weston, who wrote of Frederick walking the Merryman child to the Wells school, and the formidable Maria Weston Chapman, secretary of the American Anti-Slavery Society and sometime editor of the *National Anti-Slavery Standard*. Untold numbers of fugitive slaves populated the city's streets, homes, boarding houses, and wharves, where, on several occasions, abolitionists had shown a commitment to preventing their return to slavery. In other words, Ruggles pointed Frederick and Anna toward New Bedford because the city offered as much protection as a fugitive slave's family could hope to find. A self-emancipated person could disappear into New Bedford and slip out just as easily, always with a modicum of protection.[30]

Furthermore, in New Bedford the Douglasses found an existing community to replace the network they had left behind in Baltimore. In the autobiographies, Frederick remembered that his plans to escape had evoked "the painful sensation of being about to separate from a circle of honest and warm-hearted friends." As another fugitive, Anthony Burns, later discovered, any communication with friends and loved ones in the South could lead to discovery and capture, something Frederick had risked in writing to Anna after his escape, making continuing those connections unwise. Frederick estimated that "thousands would escape from slavery who now remain there, but for the strong cords of affection that bind them to their families, relatives and friends." Anna, too, had left connections and family behind, with no expectation of ever seeing them again. Like her husband, she must have mourned this loss. Yet comfort could be found in New Bedford, among people with similar concerns, who aided the newcomers.[31]

Frederick, barred from practicing his trade by white caulkers, took work as a "common laborer on the wharves," where he "sawed wood, shoveled coal, dug cellars, moved rubbish from back-yards, worked on the wharves, loaded and unloaded vessels, and scoured their cabins." Anna, he wrote, went "to live at service," working again as a live-in domestic, meaning that they spent their first few months of marriage apart. They were not entirely separated from one another, however. That winter she quit her position because, Frederick delicately explained, she "was unable to work." She, in fact, was expecting their first baby. By this time, the couple had moved from the rooms they occupied on the second story of Nathan Johnson's home to two rooms in a house on Elm Street. Rosetta later identified this house "overlooking Buzzard's Bay" as "my birth place," where she began life on June 24, 1839. Sixteen months later, on October 9, 1840, Lewis Henry joined the family. To earn wages, Anna began taking in laundry. Like many black women who turned to that backbreaking work, Anna may have found that the job at least left her free from the direct supervision she had endured as a live-in domestic. She could contribute to her household income while remaining in her own home and supervising her own children. Despite their poverty in those early days, Anna maintained her standard of housekeeping, and Rosetta remembered that, "Father frequently spoke of the neatly set table with its snowy white cloth—coarse tho' it was." On an 1890 visit to the house, Rosetta, wondering at her father's ability to summon memories of the life he and Anna had shared there fifty years earlier, noticed that "every detail as to the early housekeeping was gone over, it was indelibly impressed upon his mind, even to the hanging of a towel on a particular nail."[32]

The specificity with which Frederick described this first home and the particulars Rosetta gleaned from her parents' stories indicated that Anna and Frederick infused those years with great importance. "I have frequently listened to the rehearsal of those early days of endeavor," Rosetta remembered after both of her parents had died, "the wife at the wash board, the husband with saw, buck and axe." Frederick, too, referred to Anna as "truly a helpmeet." Anna may have felt satisfied knowing that she kept her own household and raised her own children, not those of a white woman. Earning wages, too, bought her a negotiating position in the marriage, as it did for other working-class women. Meanwhile, Frederick expressed the powerful feeling of making "nine dollars a month" and knowing that "no master Hugh stood ready at the end of the week to seize my hard earnings." He portrayed himself as the epitome of black, masculine, self-reliance, but that self-reliance included the ability to support his family, and the self-reliance of the family depended upon both his and Anna's work.[33]

The Douglasses also moved into the life of black New Bedford. Frederick related his own development, marveling that he "was now living in a new world, and was wide awake to its advantages." He continued his self-education, attended meetings of black citizens, registered to vote, and developed a public life that engaged his intellect. Continuing the work he had begun in the East Baltimore Mental Improvement Society, he joined the Wilberforce Debating Society and spoke at the African Christian Church against emigration to Liberia. By his own admission, he had "backslidden" in his religious life, unable to bear the hypocrisy of institutions that professed Christianity while also tolerating, when not outright committing, the sin of slaveholding. Yet he could not deny his powerful faith. After encountering racial prejudice in several of New Bedford's churches, he found his way to the meetings of the African Methodist Episcopal Zion group led by William Henry Johnson, himself self-emancipated and self-educated, in the rooms of a Second Street schoolhouse. "I was soon made a class-leader," Frederick recounted, "and a local preacher among them."[34] He seemed on the path to becoming a minister.

This was an important development for Anna, too. As his wife, Anna would become a leader as well, serving as an assistant to her husband, heading charitable organizations, and working with women whose experiences were similar to her own. Some of them might also have fugitive husbands or be fugitive slaves themselves. Some might lack reading skills. Some would work while raising families. Some might rely on the support of the community in facing racial oppression or personal misfortune. All would appreciate her housekeeping, would want better education for their children, and would understand her reserved bearing as dignified. In other words, they would appreciate her strengths, and she could sympathize with them as they would with her. She would have status within this community, wielding moral authority and commanding respect.[35]

Even in a black church, however, denominational consent to slavery alienated Frederick. "I could not see it my duty to remain with that body," he wrote of his African Methodist Episcopal congregation. He retained his faith and the language of evangelism, but he soon became a sharp critic of all churches as institutions and of their cowardice in opposing slavery. Instead, after encountering the abolitionist newspaper the *Liberator* during his first winter in New Bedford, he became, by his own admission, a "hero worshipper" of William Lloyd Garrison. Undergoing a type of conversion experience, he "took right hold of the cause." His appearance at an 1841 Nantucket meeting of the American Anti-Slavery Society, where he captured the attention of its leaders, expanded his experience beyond the smaller venues in New Bedford. His audiences grew when he entered the lecture circuit, first for the Rhode Island Anti-Slavery Society and then for the American Anti-Slavery Society. There is no evidence to suggest that Anna had a problem with this activity initially. She too grew up amid slavery and, presumably, had family still under its yoke, and Frederick's improved standing enhanced theirs within their community. Nevertheless, this shift from religion to abolition, from prominence in a black community to apprenticeship in integrated but predominantly white organizations, and from work that brought Frederick home each night to work that took him away for weeks, months, and years on end dramatically altered the conditions and terms of the Douglass marriage only four years after their wedding.[36]

This transformation led to another move northward, in autumn 1842, when they left the port town of New Bedford for the manufacturing enclave of Lynn.

Just north of Boston, Lynn appeared less than welcoming to a young black family. After the 1837 depression, wages there had steadily declined, while in the 1840s and 1850s Irish immigration rose. The organized white working class turned their hostility toward the abolitionist movement, believing that those energies might better be spent protecting northern "wage slaves" against cheap immigrant labor and exploitative management. Nevertheless, the Lynn Anti-Slavery Society and Lynn Ladies' Anti-Slavery Society had earned their reputation as relentless advocates, while the Ladies' Society petitioned against the Massachusetts antimiscegenation laws and routinely canvassed the city. Lynn's abolitionists, however, were overwhelmingly white. In neighboring Salem, Sarah Parker Remond and her brother Charles Lenox Remond, who would soon be an influence on Frederick, led the black community in opposing both slavery and segregation, but similar organization was less visible in Lynn. Indeed, Remond being the most popular black abolitionist at the time, the American Anti-Slavery Society may have hoped that Frederick would provide a focal point for greater activism in Lynn. The move there, however, took Anna away from a black community and thrust her into a new, predominantly white one at a time when she would probably have preferred to rely upon familiar faces. As her family grew, her husband left home for longer periods of time, and her role as his wife grew more complicated in ways that neither could have anticipated when they joined their lives together.[37]

Between 1842 and 1848, Frederick traveled throughout New England, the northwest, and overseas on exhausting and often dangerous tours. Anti-abolitionist mobs, throwing stones and wielding clubs, plagued many meetings. After an attack in Pendleton, Indiana, in 1843, Frederick returned to Anna with a poorly set broken hand. Each tour threatened to end tragically, leaving Anna to support their family alone. Already, instead of taking in laundry to supplement her husband's paltry income, she had begun taking in piecework, sewing the tops of shoes to soles for local shoe factories. Frederick's longest absence occurred between 1845 and 1847, when he traveled to Ireland, Scotland, and England, extending his stay for several months after Anna had anticipated his return in 1846. The tour followed the publication of his first autobiography, *Narrative of the Life of Frederick Douglass, a Slave*, in 1845, and the details that he included in this work, intended to verify what he was saying in speeches about his experience as a slave, exposed him to the risk of recapture. While he lectured in England, the Auld brothers made their intention to do so public. Anna then faced the prospect of seeing her husband sold South or uprooting her family yet again by moving to Britain. British abolitionists stepped in and purchased Frederick's freedom, but at some cost to his credibility among the Boston-based abolitionists, who were opposed to this practice. Meanwhile, *Narrative* and the fame that accompanied her husband's rise led to scrutiny of their home and family.[38]

Abolitionist women used their activism to satisfy their curiosity about the functioning of the Douglass's African American household. As she would have if Frederick had become a minister, Anna had joined one of the organizations supporting her husband's cause. Rosetta later wrote that her mother was "a recognized co-worker in the Anti-Slavery Societies of Lynn and Boston, and no circle was felt to be complete without her presence." Rosetta was a small child at the time, and her memory of the period was probably dim, but she believed that Anna attended weekly meetings of the Lynn society, served on a committee to provide refreshments, and "put aside the earnings from a certain number of shoes that she had bound as her donation to the Anti-Slavery cause." The society's members seemed aware of the material difficulties facing Anna, and Rosetta was insistent that "it became the custom of the ladies of the Lynn society each to take her turn in assisting mother in her household duties on the morning of the day that the sewing circle met so as to be sure of her meeting with them." Rosetta interpreted this aid as growing out of the benevolent and hardworking spirit of the New England abolitionists. Given their differences in race, class, and background, however, the relationship between Anna and the other ladies was probably more complicated.[39]

Although the members of the Lynn Anti-Slavery Society and the Lynn Ladies' Anti-Slavery Society formed a tight circle of extended family and neighbors who could welcome Anna, the women of these societies, many in their twenties in 1842, had few children. Anna, on the other hand, already had two toddlers and an infant when she arrived in the city. She had given birth to Frederick Jr., on March 3, 1842, when Lewis was seventeen months and Rosetta nearly three years old. A fourth child, Charles Remond, arrived two years later, on October 21, 1844. Even among the most avid abolitionist women, small children interfered with their activism. Both Angelina Grimké and Abby Kelley Foster, who tried to continue their speaking careers after marriage, found that family life frustrated their work. Elizabeth Cady Stanton consistently annoyed Susan B. Anthony as Stanton's growing family took her from the work of their movement. The indefatigable Lucretia Mott slowed in the early years of her family life; and after marrying, William Lloyd Garrison's wife, Helen, succumbed to the demands of her household. Only the older members of the Lynn Ladies' society might have understood the difficulties Anna faced.[40]

Yet none of the Lynn abolitionist women held jobs outside of the home. Anna's piecework for the shoe factories both complicated her ability to participate in antislavery work and heightened her status as an outsider. Middle-class women in the movement faced criticism from their upper-class comrades when they sought paid work, and even the working women considered benevolent work the only appropriate way to earn wages. Benevolence workers cast working-class women like Anna as the deserving poor, objects of charity. The

offer to help with Anna's housework on meeting days may have seemed a kindness if it was extended as part of a larger communal support network in which
they all helped one another with chores. If they extended this support only to
Anna, or if they tried to direct the housework rather than follow her instructions,
then Anna may have perceived their behavior as patronizing and intrusive.[41]

Anna probably also faced the unexamined racial prejudice of the white
women, often indistinguishable from their elitism. Her husband had already
encountered this in his allies, observing, "In their eagerness, sometimes, to
show their contempt for the feeling [of racism] they proved that they had not
entirely recovered from it." He illustrated by telling the story of a white man who
declared that he was not afraid of black men, leaving Frederick to wonder, "And
why should you be?" They also constrained him by encouraging him to speak of
little beyond his personal experience as a slave. They paid him and other black
speakers less than white speakers, and they privately described Frederick and the
black abolitionist Charles Lenox Remond as "talented and glorious specimens
of 'fallen' humanity as they are still are but unregenerate men." Frederick was,
according to some, "not suitable to be trusted alone" and "likely to be influenced
by the great temptations this country [England] and especially that of money."[42]

White abolitionists also privately revealed their prejudices against Anna to
one another. Irish activist Isabel Jennings, who had never met Anna, defended
Frederick against allegations of sexual impropriety while abroad by writing "had
Mrs. D. been a well educated woman and in all respects a companion for him
he could not have avoided more entirely any of the confidential accusations."
Although Jennings defended Frederick, she implied that Anna was not a suitable
wife for him. Similarly, J. B. Estlin, an English abolitionist, speculated, "My fear is
that often associating so much with white women of education & refined tastes
and manners, he will feel a 'craving void' when he returns to his own family."
As these patrons insulted Frederick with their assumption that he lacked self-
control, they also condemned Anna as too base and uncultured to be a companion for Frederick, their specimen of black potential.[43]

The main characteristic that led some people to assume that Anna was a poor
match for Frederick was her inability to read, which first came to others' attention during these years. African Americans in the nineteenth century, particular
those like the Douglasses aspiring to the middle class, almost universally considered education and literacy an important means of individual and racial empow-
erment. Black organizations and black conventions called for more and better
schools for African American children, including the integration of the schools
in segregated systems. Where schools did not exist, black churches and self-help
societies filled the gap. Frederick himself considered reading and writing central
to his manhood, intelligence, and liberation. That his wife did not read seemed
incongruous.[44]

In explaining her mother's illiteracy, Rosetta pointed out that "an opportunity for a knowledge of books had been denied to her." Anna's youth in Caroline County and her young adulthood in Baltimore had kept her working for a significant portion of the week and in an environment hostile to black education. After her marriage, Rosetta explained, "increasing family and household duties" kept Anna from lessons. Yet, learning to read could not have been easy for Anna. Whereas her husband had begun as a child, Anna would have had to start as an adult in Lynn, New Bedford, or even Baltimore. She faced a painstaking process requiring hours of practice that she did not have, even as her children grew older. Outside the networks in the black community, she would have had to expend money that her family did not have to employ a private tutor.[45]

Anna's situation resembled that of Josiah Henson, a former slave from Maryland, when his young son confronted him about his illiteracy. "If I had any pride in me at the moment," he confessed, his son's inquiry "took it all out of me pretty quick." When the boy offered to teach his father, Henson admitted that "it is hard to describe the conflicting feelings within me at such a proposition from such a quarter" because "it was no slight mortification to think of being instructed by a child of twelve years old." In Lynn, not only were the Douglass children far too young to read themselves, but the Douglasses also worried about getting them a decent education when they reached school age. By the time the children were able to read, the Douglasses could afford to hire an adult tutor for Anna, which could have spared Anna the same embarrassment experienced by Henson. Nevertheless, Anna's ambivalence toward reading lessons emerged in an incident described by their neighbor in Rochester, Jane Marsh. She remembered, " 'For Frederick's sake,' " Anna "consented, rather reluctantly, to have a teacher in the house for herself as well as the children." In other words, an educated white woman entered Anna's house and placed her in the same position as a child. Whether or not the teacher spoke to Anna as if she were stupid or childlike, the subversion of Anna's authority in her own home and in front of her children infantilized her in a way that was not repeated. She did not consent to submit herself to lessons again.[46]

Even as Rosetta excused her mother's illiteracy, she added that Anna "was able to read a little." Rosetta may have been attempting to protect her mother from judgment, but her words inadvertently revealed the differing levels and definitions of literacy. In the antebellum era, a person who could read, or read and write, just enough to function in certain situations would be considered "literate." Even by that modest definition, African Americans suffered low rates of literacy. Functional reading ability also described a qualitatively different concept of literacy than that of the educated people in Frederick's milieu and Rosetta's audience, for whom reading and writing formed an integral part of their lives. If Anna could "read a little," then she fell into the former category, able to recognize just enough words to navigate her daily life. Otherwise, she communicated with her itinerant husband through the literate people who lived with her, such as Rosetta and Harriet Bailey, a young, black woman who stayed with the Douglasses from 1844 to 1847. As with other nineteenth-century families who read aloud to one another, Anna kept abreast of news by having others read to her and, perhaps, like Josiah Henson, developed a strong ability to remember information. She had already learned to adapt to the world without reading and, unlike her husband, probably did not consider literacy crucial to her sense of self.[47]

In this way, Anna resembled Harriet Tubman or Sojourner Truth, who crossed paths with the Douglasses from time to time. Neither woman learned to read, and both defined themselves through actions rather than written words. Truth, like Anna, had encountered some limited opportunities for education, but she did not pursue them, despite her extraordinary aptitude for language. She identified herself as a minister, defined her relationship to the world and to God through the spoken word, and considered an ability to discern character equally important to the ability to decipher letters. Although Anna avoided the public world that Truth pursued, she, too, understood herself through other means. She grounded her identity in caring for her family and her home. "She was a person who strived to *live* a Christian life instead of *talking* it," Rosetta remarked, and Anna's maintenance of her home throughout her life demonstrated that she had devoted herself to the "cult of domesticity" as a privilege that she could not have enjoyed had the Douglasses stayed in Baltimore. In doing so, she defined herself as an effective helpmeet to her husband, propelling her family into the middle class. Literacy for herself paled in comparison to her pride in ensuring the well-being of her family and its future by contributing to the household income or acting as family "banker."[48]

Contrary to the conventional wisdom, Anna's illiteracy did not exempt her from advising Frederick or participating in the intellectual life of their family. When Frederick described Sojourner Truth, he uncharitably characterized her as "uncultured" and lacking "refinement" and "elegance," but he also praised her "strange compound of wit and wisdom" and her "flint-like common sense." That sketch resembled Rosetta's depiction of her mother, whose expressions "might provoke a smile" but who "had large discernment as to the character of those who came around her." According to their abolitionist friend Lucy Colman, Susan B. Anthony allegedly estimated that Frederick "had a great deal of uncommon sense, but his wife had more than her share of common sense." Many of Frederick's biographers leave the impression that the Douglasses hardly spoke to one another, particularly after he returned from England, but letters clearly refute that communication between them ceased. He appreciated discussing whatever he had read with those around him and, at least during the early years, within the confines of the two rooms in New Bedford and the "small cottage" in Lynn, Anna was his closest company. Rosetta insisted that her father kept Anna informed on the progress of the abolition movement at her request, and described Anna as "a good listener, making comments on passing events, which were well worth consideration."[49]

Nevertheless, given Frederick's concern with the image he projected and his commitment to the written word, Anna's continued illiteracy could have been a point of frustration or contention between them. Their disagreement over the matter may have retrenched both positions, with Anna asserting herself within the marriage by demanding that he accept her as the woman he wed. Still, any such conflict may have continued even if she had learned to read because their difference lay not in literacy but in the relationship that literacy would create. Anna was a woman of strong opinions. Rosetta remembered that "her no meant no," and Frederick noted her "powers of speech" in advising him of his faults. Rosetta also believed that Anna's judgment of character was "very fortunate in the protection of father's interests, especially in the early days of his public life." Whether Frederick liked what she had to say or not, Anna's observations probably helped him navigate the sometimes rigid ideological world of the abolitionists in Massachusetts. Yet, as his world broadened through travel and literature, Frederick's yearning for intellectual companionship lay in his desire to discuss what he had read. Anna did not have to read Shakespeare, Dumas, or Dickens herself to engage their ideas because others read aloud to her, but she seemed to have little interest in that world. This was not an issue when they first married because Frederick had not yet discovered his own passion for these authors. By the time he returned from England, however, though their commitment to their family continued to bind them, friction emerged in their relationship based on their different interests outside of the cares of their household.[50]

Still, Anna was not anti-intellectual. She supported the education of her children, which played a key role in improving the prospects of Rosetta, Lewis, Charles, and Frederick Jr., and which involved some personal sacrifice. For a working-class family, sending children to school meant sacrificing the child's wages to invest in the child's future prospects, and families often forfeited their daughters' education to promote their sons', who had more opportunities to see a return on the investment. As the Douglass family continued to struggle their way into the middle class, Rosetta, by 1845, had reached school age. Without question, she would go to school; but as liberal as Massachusetts schools had historically been, they were not welcoming of black students, and a private school was beyond the Douglasses' economic means. With fewer than 300 African American residents, Lynn had neither enough black children for its white population to agree to a separate school nor a desire to integrate the existing schools, which meant that the Douglasses had to look elsewhere. New Bedford and Salem had the only integrated classrooms in the state, but Frederick had given up the New Bedford option for his children when he moved them to Lynn, and a commute to Salem would have been too long for a young girl, although she could have stayed with the Remond family. Instead, the Douglasses sent Rosetta to Albany, New York, to be educated by the white, Quaker, abolitionist sisters Abigail and Lydia Mott.[51]

Frederick had met the Motts and their friend Abby Kelley in 1842, during his first tour through Albany. They had a reputation for lodging fugitive slaves and itinerant abolitionists, so Frederick could trust that his daughter was in sympathetic hands and would be steeped in abolitionist ideology and practice daily. Although the Albany schools were somewhat friendlier to integration than those in Massachusetts, it appears that Abigail, a former teacher, taught Rosetta in the Mott house. Furthermore, the proscriptive literature of the day advised ambitious mothers, both black and white, to raise their daughters to become accomplished housewives even as they sent them to school. The Mott sisters most likely did not neglect the domestic side of Rosetta's upbringing. One of Rosetta's contemporaries insisted that she had sewn a shirt as a present for her father during her time with the Motts. From approximately age six to age nine, Anna saw her parents perhaps once, when her father returned from Britain and took Anna to Albany to visit. She did not see her brothers nor live with her family again until they moved to Rochester in 1848. At age nine, three years was a significant percentage of her life to have spent away from home.[52]

The loss of her child, even if it had been for that child's own good, may have grieved Anna; but Rosetta also left at an age when she could have become useful to her mother, even if only after she had finished her schoolwork. Sending Rosetta away also seemed contrary to an article "FEMALE EDUCATION" that Frederick published in his newspaper in February 1848, a month after he and Anna had visited Rosetta at the Motts'. The piece "told of a father who would 'apprentice' his daughters 'to their excellent mother, that they may learn the art of improving their time, and be fitted to become, like her, wives, mothers, heads of families, and useful members of society.'" The story chastised the type of woman of whom her husband would say "if my girls are to have any chance of growing up good for anything, they must be sent out of the way of their mother's example." If the article came from Douglass's pen, not that of John Dick, his Scottish printer, and if it also reflected his feelings three years earlier, then his sending Rosetta away could be read as an implied judgment on Anna. Frederick could trust his wife to raise their daughter to become a good housewife, but he would have seen Anna's academic shortcomings as her flaw. Anna herself probably felt no shame about this part of her life, but she also would not have wanted anyone to try to make her feel ashamed. Still, if she intended for her children to grow up with greater security than she had experienced, formal education was one area in which she could do little to help them Sacrificing her desire to keep her daughter with her by sending Rosetta to the Motts meant that Rosetta could acquire the sort of refinement and education that would ensure that she would never have to clean other people's homes, take in other people's laundry, or bind shoes for pennies a piece as Anna had. Furthermore, the choice of two abolitionist Quakers assured that Rosetta would be insulated from the harsh racial prejudice that permeated even the integrated schools while also being inculcated in abolitionist ideology. Nevertheless, Anna lived in an uneasy space that included her ambition for her child, her awareness of her own limited ability to propel Rosetta forward, and the perception by her husband and perhaps others that she needed "improvement" in this one respect, at least.[53]

Had they remained in New Bedford and had Frederick pursued the ministry, Anna would have lived as a respected member of a black, working-class community in which her inability to read would not have been unusual and in which she could have taken lessons with other adult learners. The relocation to Lynn had altered circumstances, placing the Douglasses in an integrated community fraught with racial and class differences that challenged their every encounter and made them objects of curiosity. Although Frederick had always envisioned integration as the solution to injustice and inequality, African Americans often preferred to form their own black organizations, in which they could both lead and ensure that their demands took precedence. Frederick worked closely with Charles Lenox Remond, William C. Nell, Jeremiah Sanderson, and other black men and women who had not become antislavery celebrities but who collectively opposed racial segregation and discrimination in the North and slavery in the South. These men probably stopped by the Douglass house as they passed through town, paying their respects to Anna, and Sanderson appeared to have kept an eye on the family during Frederick's absences. Anna was also acquainted with Nell, a charming young man who worked on the *Liberator*.

Then, in the fall of 1844, Frederick returned from a tour with a young woman in tow. The family called her Harriet Bailey and pretended that she was Frederick's younger sister of the same name, whom he had not seen since her infancy. The name that this woman's mother had given her, however, was Ruth Cox. Earlier in 1844, Ruth had escaped from slavery in Easton, Maryland, to avoid being sold in the liquidation of her master's estate. She had made her way to a community of Quakers in West Chester, Pennsylvania, where Frederick had met her at an antislavery meeting.[54] The Douglasses enfolded her into the family, the children calling her "Aunt Harriet" and Frederick and Anna considering her their "sister." She proved to be a boon to Anna, drawing on her experience in her master's town house to help in the Douglass household, but without threatening Anna's authority. She offered familiarity, not simply in terms of race and class, but also as an adult southern woman bringing familiar mannerisms, customs, and even news from the Eastern Shore. Indeed, Frederick could have relied on Harriet's and Anna's memories of places and events when he sat down to compose his *Narrative*. Having learned to read and write, Harriet served as scribe and intermediary between Frederick and Anna, reading Frederick's letters to his wife and writing Anna's replies in return. If Anna could, in fact, "read a little," Harriet, as a peer, may have instructed her. When he was considering staying in England, Frederick's appeals to Harriet to explain his position fully to Anna suggest that he also relied upon Harriet to advocate for him; and Anna probably expected the same, leaving Bailey to negotiate with both of them to find amicable solutions to their differences. "Your devotion to my little boys," Frederick wrote to Harriet, and "your attention to Dear Anna, has made you doubly Dear to me. I will not forget you."[55]

Figure 2.3 Ruth Cox Adams went by the name Harriet Bailey while she lived with the Douglasses, from 1844 until her marriage in 1847. The fugitive from Maryland was a friend to both Anna and Frederick, who considered her their sister. Adams became involved with a militant vigilance organization in Springfield during the 1850s, immigrated to Haiti during the Civil War, and spent the last decade of her life in Nebraska. "Ruth Cox Adams," RG544D.PH. Photo Component of Adams-Douglass-Vanderzee-McWilliams Families Collection, Nebraska State Historical Society.

Frederick also relaxed with Harriet. He made fun of his "low spirits," confiding that "my under lip hung like that of a mother less colt [and] I looked so ugly that I hated to see myself in a glass. There was no living for me. I was so snappish I would have kicked my grand 'dada'!" Then, he became more familiar, using dialect that he would have never used in letters to white abolitionists. "I was in a terrible mood—'dats a fac!" he wrote, "ole missus is you got any ting for poor nigger to eat!!!" He relied on Harriet to forgive him his self-pity, and observed, "You would have been so kind to me. You would not have looked cross at me. I know you would not." In fact, he anticipated that she would comfort him, certain that "instead of looking cross at me, you would have with your own Dear sisterly hand smoothed, and stroked down my feverish forehead—and spoken so kindly as to make me forget my sadness." This message, taken with a later exchange in which Frederick did not gracefully accept the news of Harriet's engagement, could easily be read as a romantic attachment, at least on Frederick's part. Yet Anna did not seem to interpret the relationship in that way, and she urged Harriet to maintain her friendship with Frederick after the two had quarreled. Frederick valued Harriet for both her connection to the past and her counsel in the present. In another state of melancholy following the criticism of the purchase of his freedom, and as he considered the course of his future in America, he wrote, "I wish to mercy I could see you and talk with—I could soon relieve my mind—but I am too far a way." Anna, too, loved Harriet. In later years, anticipating a visit from Harriet, she let her know, "I wish you would come two very much for I want see you about as bad as you want to see me." Although as a child Rosetta did not meet Bailey, letters suggest that they later became acquainted and that Rosetta understood that her mother and this "aunt" shared a deep affection for one another.[56]

Bailey lived with the Douglasses until her marriage to Perry F. Adams in November 1847, after Frederick had returned from England. She and her husband moved to Springfield, Massachusetts, where their involvement in abolitionism over the next twenty years took turns into militancy and emigration. Harriet and Frederick ceased their correspondence, but Anna seems to have maintained a network of women between Rochester and Springfield that passed along news between herself and Harriet and included at least five other women, Charlotte Murray, Emily, Emma, Emeline, and Louisa. Emma and Emeline may have been the same person, but Charlotte Murray was Anna's sister from Maryland, approximately five years her junior, who lived with the Douglasses for some time. Emma, Anna, Harriet, and perhaps Charlotte, also knew Maria Anna Adams, who was the wife of Springfield barber Bennett Adams and had escaped with her children from slavery in Talbot County around the same time that Harriet had. This coterie of friends provided Anna with familiarity and support in ways that the Lynn Ladies' Anti-Slavery Society could not. If, as Rosetta put it, her mother's household work freed Frederick "in every possible way" from worrying about "all the management of the home as it increased in size and in its appointments," then these women collectively supplied the domestic support that enabled Frederick to pursue abolition while they also recogned Anna as the mistress of her home. This formed the core of the Douglass partnership in which he provided for the family that she managed.[57]

During these years Anna became more independent in the running of the Douglass household, especially while Frederick toured England. By the time he returned to Lynn, in April 1847, after nearly two years away, Anna let him know that she "had not allowed herself to expect me [Frederick] *much*, for fear of being disappointed." Earlier anticipation of his arrival had ended in frustration. She had first expected him in July 1846, when his companion James Buffum returned with William Lloyd Garrison and the Hutchinson family of antislavery singers. Although sales of Frederick's *Narrative* covered his travel expenses, he had little money left over to send home and Anna would have to struggle to maintain the household beyond August of that year. When Frederick did not arrive home in July, the earliest she could next expect to see him was in November. Instead, in September, he notified her that he planned to extend his stay until spring. "It will cause her some pain," Frederick predicted as he passed along the news to Isabel Jennings, adding, "disappointment is the common lot of all." He may have made a more impassioned plea for understanding to Anna, and he begged Bailey to read his letter to "Dear Anna over and over again until she fully understands its contents." He reassured the three women that book sales and the advice of Garrison and leading British abolitionist George Thompson that the moment presented "a most favorable opportunity for remodeling the Antislavery feeling of this country" had caused the delay.[58]

When Frederick finally did return to their doorstep, Anna was "exceedingly happy to have me once more at home." For his part, he reveled in the joy "to be among those whose welfare and happiness depend so much upon myself." He not only now had legal freedom, purchased through the efforts of English abolitionists, but also had received a substantial donation that would allow him to start his own newspaper. He envisioned a future of financial and ideological independence that would allow him to return home at the end of each day, an idea that likely appealed to Anna, too. Then, he learned that his allies had no intention of permitting him to pursue that dream, and he found himself back on the lecture circuit. Just as her husband returned to her from England, Anna lost him to yet another antislavery tour. By then, she did not have her daughter with her, and Harriet had moved to Springfield. Whatever support network she had cultivated since arriving in Lynn disappeared soon after with another relocation.[59]

Frederick had encountered intense opposition to his plans to start a newspaper in Massachusetts, and his investigation into prospects in Ohio found the same. Amy Post in Rochester, New York, however, paved the way for the Douglasses to move to that city in 1848. Rosetta called the move to Rochester, "the greatest trial, perhaps, that mother was called upon to endure, after parting from her Baltimore friend several years before." The relocation was more than simply a move; Frederick's ideological development had opened fissures between himself and his old allies that had ramifications for his family. His adoption of new antislavery strategies involved the use of tactics that divided him from former friends, some of whom Anna liked, and exposed his family to increased public scrutiny. The Douglasses had joined together in pursuit of a family and life that almost every aspect of American society had conspired to deny them. They succeeded in marrying, having children, and keeping their family together as a unit, and their personal subversion of attacks on black families had become part of a full rebellion against racism. They continued their efforts to uphold an impenetrable barrier of respectability, but Anna often found herself at odds with Frederick as he pursued competing tactics in his personal politics.[60]

|| 3 ||

"The Cause of the Slave Has Been Peculiarly Woman's Cause," 1841–1847

Douglass began his ascent in the national abolitionist movement on August 12, 1841, at a meeting of the Massachusetts Anti-Slavery Society on Nantucket. Experienced in speaking to black audiences, Douglass now stood before members of an unfamiliar, integrated organization to testify about his life in slavery. In another speech, only two months later, he confessed to having felt "greatly embarrassed when I attempted to address an audience of white people," because, "I am not used to speak to them." He was not, however, unused to addressing "promiscuous" audiences that included both men and women. In his congregations and improvised schools, black women sat beside men. In antislavery meetings, however, the integration of races along with sexes presented dangers. Douglass came from a background in which, despite often intimate living arrangements, black people hid their experiences from white people. Self-preservation lay in the creating the illusion of complicity in the unequal social order. White women, who feared or infantilized black men, presented another layer of danger. He himself had only been treated kindly by Lucretia and Sophia Auld because he was a child. As he grew up, he discovered that white mistresses could be just as capricious as masters. Even in the North, the proximity of a black man to a white woman raised the specter of amalgamation, universally interpreted as a direct challenge to white supremacy. Thus, when standing before black and white men and women, revealing his life as a black man under slavery, Douglass said that "it makes me tremble to do so."[1]

Later generations easily forget that Douglass did not emerge onto the activist scene with his ideas about ending slavery or about woman's rights fully formed. As he himself reflected, his initial encounters with abolitionism had been at a distance, first from nebulous rumors in Baltimore that mysterious people elsewhere wanted to end slavery, then through the black community in New Bedford and as a subscriber to the *Liberator*. After his appearance in Nantucket, when he was only twenty-two and the father of two children, his compelling combination of theatricality, intellectual force, and testimony led to further engagements by both the Massachusetts and the Rhode Island societies over the next four years. He toured not only in New England but also twice through New York State, twice into Pennsylvania, and once through Ohio and Indiana, and he attended the yearly meetings of the American Anti-Slavery Society in New York City. His lecturing culminated with the publication of his first autobiography, in 1845, followed by his first international tour of Ireland, Scotland, and England in the employ of the AAS, from August 1845 to April 1847.

Douglass's biographers have focused on his ideology; his friendships and rivalries with other, usually male, abolitionists; and his drive for self-reliance during those years. Women periodically entered as supporting characters, with only vague references to their influence on Douglass's development. Their role at each step of his advancement through the antislavery movement has been diminished, leaving the impression that he occupied an almost entirely masculine world. As Douglass's ambition led him to envision himself as the black Garrison, able to support his family while also improving the conditions of his race, the system that sustained all professional antislavery activists became crucial to his success. Women created and maintained much of that system; and lifelong features of his ideology, including his integrationist principles, engagement with the rhetoric of racial mixing, and awareness of gender politics emerged from this feminine world of antislavery during the first six years of his activism.[2]

If speaking before a mixed-race antislavery crowd seemed daunting to a neophyte Douglass, the world outside antislavery circles gave any abolitionist reason to quake. Despite the middle-class origins or aspirations of many of the antislavery activists, opposition to the peculiar institution placed its proponents on the fringes of American opinion. Abolitionist meetings also drew opponents, who frequently physically assaulted speakers and otherwise tried to disrupt the gatherings, and the potential for violence was amplified when women or African Americans were in attendance. Barely a year into his speaking career, Douglass attempted to subdue an outbreak of violence at a public meeting in Boston's Faneuil Hall, during which, according to reports, "two colored ladies had their bonnets and shawls torn off them," a description suggestive of molestation. White women at these meetings could gamble that male chivalry and white masculinity might restrain mobs but even that privilege did not keep rowdies from assaulting racially integrated women's meetings in Boston in 1835 and Philadelphia in 1838.[3]

Most of the women whom Douglass met during these years pursued racial integration in order to erase the prejudices of whites against blacks. The Boston Female Anti-Slavery Society had included black members from its inception, in 1833, and they joined their sister society in Philadelphia by actively seeking black delegates and the participation of black women's benevolent societies in the women's antislavery conventions held in 1837 and 1838. At an 1838 meeting of the Philadelphia Female Anti-Slavery Society, black and white women from both societies linked arms to protect the black women from being singled out by a rioting mob that ultimately burned down the hall in which they met. White abolitionist women extended the same type of solidarity to Douglass. The Weston sisters of Weymouth refused to be seen with one of their allegedly abolitionist neighbors because he would only allow Douglass to ride on the outside of his carriage; and when Douglass was thrown out of the dining room on a steamboat in Pennsylvania, two women also departed in protest. Across the country, women took him in to their homes as a guest on equal terms with his traveling companions, giving him shelter in their houses and feeding him at the same tables with their families. This was occurring at a time when Charles Lenox Remond, the most popular black abolitionist before Douglass, would slip off to an antislavery meeting ahead of his white hosts to save them the embarrassment of walking with a black man in public.[4]

The black and white women who were attacked while advocating integration seldom received sympathy or protection from the authorities. Most of the public believed that they were courting degradation by moving beyond the boundaries of "woman's sphere," a place to which few considered black women entitled in the first place. According to dominant ideas about women that had emerged in the preceding decades, women were domestic creatures who should submit to mechanisms of power, and whose sphere of authority lay only within a male-dominated household. The reality of most women's lives subverted this doctrine. Like contentious nations, women of all classes negotiated the borders between the world inside the home and the public world of men outside, pressing themselves into the service of their churches, the poor, partisan politics, and religious organizations. Some middle-class women drew on their education, their piety, and what they argued was their moral duty to "civilize" the unruly working classes. In doing so, they carved a space in public or civic life that enlarged the boundaries of the domestic, female sphere. Antislavery women tested the limits of acceptable behavior more than any others.[5]

None of this was unfamiliar to Douglass. Even as he admitted his own unquestioning adherence to the doctrine of separate spheres in his youth, he moved through a world in which black women spent considerable time outside of the home, shouldered as much of the economic burden of supporting their families as their husbands, and often suffered public acts of violence. Indeed, much of his portrayal of enslaved women in his autobiographies was an attack on the ways that slavery prevented bondswomen from enjoying the privileges of domesticity, unsexing them in all but their reproductive capacities. Meanwhile, the

black women's societies in both Baltimore and New Bedford did not differ markedly from the female antislavery societies that he encountered in that their members banded together and expanded their sphere of influence by extending their
caretaking roles outside their families to the society at large. Women's organizations quite often played a supportive role to larger organizations that, although
not explicitly defined by gender, were dominated by men. The black women's
organizations, however, drew the ire of the white population simply because
they were part of the segrated black community. Anti-abolitionists targeted the
integrated women's antislavery organizations because they took aim at white supremacy and private property, two beliefs held sacred by white Americans, which
made this expansion of their sphere unacceptable to anti-abolitionists and their
persons no longer entitled to the protection of white men.[6]

As Douglass himself admitted, even abolitionists felt challenged by the extent of women's participation in the infrastructure of the movement. In 1840,
as Douglass toiled to support his family and become a leader in his black community, female delegates from American antislavery societies found themselves barred from the meeting floor of the World Anti-Slavery Conference in
London. Similar prejudices against women and the attitudes about their proper
role contributed to divisions within the AAS. In 1841, when the AAS elected
Abby Kelley to its executive board, an opposing faction broke away and formed
the American and Foreign Anti-Slavery Society (AFAS), often called the "New
Organization." The two societies diverged on many issues; in particular, the
AFAS did not accept women in leadership positions except in the ladies' aux-
iliaries, whereas the "Old Organization," the AAS, included women in all roles.
Still, even in the AAS, some men balked at the prospect of having too many
women in top positions. Ohio abolitionist Abraham Brooke, for instance, complained that the men in the West had "something of a horror of the Gyneocracy
which would be constituted by having Miss [Abby] Kelley in the field and Mrs.
[Maria Weston] Chapman in the council." Undaunted, women on both sides of
the divide continued to play important roles in their organizations. They exerted
their opinions and often defied the umbrella societies to form coalitions of the
differing factions. Douglass himself would soon learn that even without official
positions, women wielded a great deal of influence.[7]

When he began lecturing for societies affiliated with the Old Organization,
Douglass witnessed women who brazenly called attention to themselves. This
alone would not have shocked him because he had seen women attending camp
meetings and church services. What made the women at his antislavery engagements so remarkable was their clear intent to effect political change by publicly
expressing an opinion even in the face of violence. Not always as outspoken and
visible as the indomitable Sojourner Truth, whom Douglass had met on a visit
to the Northampton water-cure spa of David Ruggles, they nonetheless made

themselves known. At one meeting in Faneuil Hall, the women present simply "waived their handkerchiefs and clapped their hands, in applauding the various speakers," calling attention to themselves in support of abolition despite the intimidating crowd. At other meetings of AAS-affiliated societies in New England, Douglass worked with women who held official positions in the organization. Further west and in England, the women Douglass encountered tended to work in separate, all-female organizations, but he could not deny their influence on the larger movement. In short, wherever Douglass went, women served beside him in authoritative roles and expressed their strongly held convictions in both female-only and gender-integrated organizations. Their competence wore down the last vestige of any feeling he may have had about the "indelicacy of woman's taking part in politics."[8]

Most of these women did not become famous for their work, yet their names survive because they allowed them to be published in newspapers and city directories, at a time when the names of respectable women appeared in print only when they married and died. Others allowed their names to go on record by writing for the antislavery press. Sarah Mapps Douglass (no relation to Frederick), Rebecca Fenwick Bell, Sarah Ennals, and Sarah Forten Purvis all wrote for the *Liberator,* while Lydia Maria Child distinguished herself by both publishing an early antislavery tract and editing the *National Anti-Slavery Standard.* The women in the Lynn Ladies' Anti-Slavery Society boldly signed their names to petitions to the Massachusetts state legislature but also marched door-to-door in the town to persuade others to do so. One of their most daring efforts involved a petition for the repeal of the state's prohibition on mixed-race marriages. In 1841, Douglass praised their canvassing, saying, "My first knowledge of the abolition movement was through petitions." He reassured his audience that "These petitions delight the hearts of the slaves" because "they rejoice to know that something is going on in their favor."[9]

Corresponding secretaries coordinated these drives and were most often women in integrated organizations. They frequently solicited potential donors, speakers, and newspaper subscribers, and bonded the networks of activists across geographic divides. The most effective of these was Maria Weston Chapman, a founding member of the Boston Female Anti-Slavery Society, who also held offices in the Massachusetts Anti-Slavery Society and the American Anti-Slavery Society. Chapman, educated in England and a former school teacher and principal, brought both her overseas connections and commanding presence to bear in her antislavery work, and drew in three of her sisters, Caroline, Anne, and Deborah. When her husband, Henry, a well-to-do Boston merchant, died in 1842, he allegedly told her on his deathbed that he left her to the movement. He also left her a nice inheritance, which meant she continued to have servants and leisure and could therefore to devote her time to the cause.

Her English friend, the author and activist Harriet Martineau, pointed out the juxtaposition of Chapman's feminine appearance with the force of her personality. As Chapman prepared to face an anti-abolitionist mob in 1835, Martineau marveled that her friend's "aspect, meant by nature to be soft and winning only" was in fact "vivified by courage, and so strengthened by conviction, as to appear the very embodiment of heroism."[10]

During the 1838 anti-abolitionist attack that left the Philadelphia Anti-Slavery Society's Pennsylvania Hall in ashes, rowdies targeted the women's meeting, leaving Chapman hospitalized for post-traumatic stress. Afterward, Chapman focused her energy on literary and administrative pursuits. She poured her sentiments into an antislavery novel and three antislavery songbooks and coauthored a book with Unitarian minister and abolitionist Samuel J. May. Chapman's most ambitious literary achievement, however, was the *Liberty Bell*. Each volume of this annual gift book contained a collection of essays, poems, and stories by both American and foreign abolitionist celebrities, including Douglass, and consistently sold well at the annual antislavery fair in Boston and abroad. The book strengthened the international connections Chapman had forged as corresponding secretary and enhanced the popularity of the antislavery bazaar, her crowning achievement.[11]

That annual fair served as the main fundraising effort by the Boston Female Anti-Slavery Society for the AAS. Under Chapman's supervision from 1835, it earned between $1,000 and $4,000 annually for the next twenty-three years. The proceeds paid for speakers, covered the costs of conventions, and supplemented flagging profits of the *National Anti-Slavery Standard* and the *Liberator*. The fair also gave focus and purpose to many local antislavery women, connecting them to one another and to the national society, and sustaining the movement in years of waning interest. Local societies put their domestic talents to work creating "articles" or handicrafts such as aprons, baby blankets, pot-holders, and decorative items to sell at their own fairs and to donate to the Boston fair, infusing women's work with moral and political importance by sustaining the movement financially. Between her secretarial offices, her solicitations of pieces for the *Liberty Bell*, and her organization of donations to the fair, Chapman guided both ideology and behavior within the AAS by controlling the flow of finances, information, and access to the Garrisonian press. Although she had cared for her ill husband during the first two years that Douglass worked as an abolitionist, she returned in full force after Henry's death, and Douglass thereafter felt her influence even if he was not always aware of it.[12]

Most of the women Douglass met in these early days worked in local societies and in administrative positions. Abby Kelley, however, lectured, something Douglass had not yet encountered. She distilled, in one seemingly demure dynamo, all of the characteristics he had observed in other antislavery women.

Although Kelley was raised as a Quaker opposed to slavery, she began her most active work when she joined the Lynn Ladies' Anti-Slavery Society while teaching in the city in 1836. As the society's corresponding secretary, she urged it to pursue the petitioning campaigns. Her speaking career began in earnest at the ill-fated Philadelphia convention in 1838, where the ensuing riot only strengthened her resolve. She braved a harrowing first year of touring in Connecticut, where the citizens proved less than welcoming of abolitionists or women speakers on the subject, and her name became synonymous with disreputable womanhood. Nevertheless, she was much in demand among sympathizers, and a particular favorite among the women. By 1840, the New York State abolitionists were begging her to consider moving westward because "your services can be no where so well spent & to so good advantage as in Western New York." She answered their call in 1842, and then moved farther west to Ohio in 1844.[13]

In August 1841, when she met Douglass, Kelley was one of the few female antislavery lecturers on the circuit. Maria Stewart, the first female antislavery

Figure 3.1 Abby Kelley was among the first abolitionists who traveled with Douglass when he began lecturing at the end of 1841. Abby Kelley Foster, Photomechanical, halftone, unknown photographer, n.d. Portraits of American Abolitionists. Photograph number 81.248. Massachusetts Historical Society.

speaker, who had chastised black men for being too timid in their opposition to slavery, had retired years earlier. Sarah and Angelina Grimké, who had inspired Kelley, took a break from touring after Angelina's wedding to Theodore Weld and the birth of their first child. The venerable Lucretia Mott did not meet Douglass until May 1842, at the annual AAS convention in New York City, and worked with him only intermittently thereafter. Sojourner Truth, Sarah Parker Remond, and Frances Harper had not yet begun their careers. Yet, even when more women took to the lecture circuit, often at Kelley's urging, they always made up a unique group. Kelley was also singular in that Douglass spent a great deal of time with her during these formative years of his abolition career. His association with most other antislavery women took place over many months of meetings and only for the duration of those meetings, with some socializing in between. He and Kelley, however, toured with one another for weeks at a time. In November and December 1841, not long after their introduction, they lectured together in Rhode Island. They reunited in New York from August to October in 1842, again in August 1843, and at various other venues during the interim and after. Throughout, Kelley proved herself unlike any woman Douglass had met before, especially any white woman.[14]

They must have been impressive on stage together: Kelley with "her youth and simple Quaker beauty combined with her wonderful earnestness, her large knowledge and great logical power" and Douglass with his "keen withering satire," "soul-shrivelling sarcasm" and the force of his physical presence. Individually, each challenged stereotypes simply in their bearing. As a pair, they excited the most dangerous images of black men and white women. In their first two months touring together, along with lecture partners Stephen S. Foster and Parker Pillsbury, the crowds called Douglass "nigger" and crudely shouted for Kelley by her first name or branded her "Jezebel" and "nigger bitch." Together they all suffered these verbal missiles, rotten eggs, feces, and brickbats, often pursued by men brandishing clubs.[15]

The pejoratives of those detractors, along with taunt of a group of Albany boys, who pointed to two black men and shouted "there is Abby Kelley's race," were attempts to insult her by implying that she was black. Rather than allow herself to be intimidated, she embraced her association with African Americans, parrying the invective by declaring that she wished she were, in fact, "colored." Following a speech by Douglass in which he implicitly lumped together all slaves as men, she reminded him "that his mother and sister were still in the hand of the outragers." Identifying herself with the enslaved women, she proclaimed that "it was therefore fit that she, a woman, stood there by his side, and bear her testimony in favor of the cause." Such flourishes had their problems. Kelley had few other black aquaintances, much less any nuanced understanding of the lives of enslaved women. Still, she intended to erase the distinction between herself and

African Americans, thereby suggesting that the virtues attached to her whiteness could also be attached to blackness.[16]

In 1842, Lydia and Abigail Mott warned Kelley, "*Caution* as you are travelling about with Fred Douglas." The Motts did not mean to suggest that Douglass presented a danger. The threat lay in the hostility Kelley and Douglass roused by appearing in public as equals. A year later, Paulina Wright, an activist in Utica, whose home served as Kelley's Central New York base, felt the sensation such a pairing provoked, lamenting that "there is scarcely a woman in the city that will speak to me because we went to the [Niagara] Falls with [Charles] Remond." The "poor 'toads,'" to whom Wright felt superior, "are really making a worse fuss about that than any thing else." Douglass, Kelley, Wright, and Remond risked social ostracism, or worse, for transgressing the etiquette of segregation. Yet, they did so as a demonstration of racial equality, and the particular association of a black man and a white woman added another subversive dimension, as it raised the specter of race-mixing.[17]

Kelley's dynamism impressed Douglass from the beginning of his speaking career, but he also became part of her efforts to revitalize flagging interest in abolition. Leaving New England, with its well-entrenched antislavery societies, they moved to New York State, where economic and demographic changes had caused enthusiasm to taper off. Those who remained committed to reform found themselves in the distinct minority, with their resources drained. Even after a year of work there, Kelley confessed to Maria Weston Chapman, "Between you and me, the Western Society is merely a name and the Central New York Society would be if I weren't here." Nevertheless, between his first visit to New York in 1842 and his second in 1843, both the Western and Central New York societies came into existence through Kelley's endorsement. Receiving local support from Amy Post in Rochester and Paulina Wright in Utica, the societies drew members from the regions surrounding both cities and from the family and religious networks of Quakers in towns in between. Where few or no societies had existed in 1842, more appeared in 1843.[18]

For four years, Douglass traveled among capable women. From the multitudes diligently sewing articles for antislavery fairs to officers at gender-integrated meetings to leaders such as Abby Kelley and Maria Weston Chapman, Douglass saw women's monumental efforts of organization. He noted their vast fundraising network that ensured ongoing awareness of the ways that slavery degraded African Americans, especially women, not to mention American morality and justice. He engaged with various principles and tactics against racism. He observed the coalitions that western abolitionists with diverging principles formed, to the chagrin of the more doctrinaire eastern abolitionists. He witnessed, too, the personal risks the women took to demonstrate black humanity when they could more easily have retreated into respectable domesticity. At the same time, he contemplated the importance of a man like himself, with a compelling experience, presence, and perspective, in representing black people in America. His trip to Britain placed him in a new context, allowing his vision for his own future and that of African Americans to evolve.

On August 16, 1845, Douglass departed for Britain aboard the *Cambria*, arriving in Liverpool twelve days later. From there, he and his companion James Buffum, a white abolitionist neighbor from Lynn, traveled to Ireland, carrying a letter of introduction from Maria Weston Chapman to Richard D. Webb in Dublin. Webb and his wife, Hannah Waring Webb, formed the core of the Irish community of abolitionists. They coordinated the efforts of abolitionists in Belfast and Cork and worked with societies in Edinburgh, Glasgow, and Newcastle-upon-Tyne, all bound by networks of kin as much as shared reform interests. Richard Webb, a printer by trade, planned to issue a new edition of Douglass's *Narrative*. He and Chapman had already corresponded for nearly a decade, and the two matched one another in their quick and unvarnished expression of opinions. In her role as foreign corresponding secretary of the Boston Female Anti-Slavery Society and the organizer of its fair, Chapman also kept in contact with the other societies. Through these connections she monitored American speakers as they traveled through Britain, and she wanted to keep a particular eye on Douglass.[19]

"He has the wisdom of a serpent," Chapman cautioned Webb, before Douglass had even departed for Britain. While there, she hoped that Douglass would follow "the example of Garrison, [Wendell] Phillips, and [Edmund] Quincy, who have been a thousand times offered all the kingdoms of popularity" yet refused to compromise their principles. "Warn Douglass, by the example of Remond," she instructed Webb, "of the ill effect it has on a man's respectability to be aiming at any thing for himself in the prosecution of a philanthropic enterprise." She believed that because "the cause has been nothing but gain to him in a worldly point of view," Douglass would easily succumb to "the temptation to get into his own head (as we call being drunk with vanity)" and abandon the American Anti-Slavery Society if promised "personal help and success." Webb praised the former slave as an "example of the triumph over difficulties" and possessed of "many of the characteristics of the man of genius." Chapman disagreed. Douglass was "all that a strong mind in a strong body can make him without genius," she responded, prevaricating that "a cunning so great as his almost amounts to genius."[20]

Nevertheless, Webb had stoked Chapman's apprehensions. Whereas he characterized Buffum as "openhearted, transparent, unselfish, kindly & reliable in an uncommon degree," he believed Douglass was "touchy, huffish, haughty, & I think selfish" as well as "uneven and unreliable." Webb insisted that Douglass "seems to me to be full of suspicion and jealousy, and the unrestrained exercise of his tendency to ridicule others." Furthermore, "he cannot take a hint

Figure 3.2 Maria Weston Chapman in approximately 1846, when she first sensed that Douglass was becoming too independent for the leadership of the American Anti-Slavery Society to control. "Maria Weston Chapman," c.1846, Cab.G.3.29. Unknown photographer. Print Department, Boston Public Library.

without resenting it." The Irishman also found the former slave's sense of humor off-putting. "His habit of talking in half jests, half earnest," Webb confided to Chapman, "leaves it very difficult for even those who relish a joke very well, to know whether he is in jest or earnest," and as a result "destroys confidence almost as effectually as habitual falsehood." As a result, he worried about "the mischief they [Douglass's character traits] might do to the cause."[21] Douglass, Chapman agreed, "is not transparent."[22]

Douglass, for his part, had already run afoul of Chapman, back in 1843, in what he called "my first offence against our Anti-Slavery Israel." At a convention in Syracuse, New York, one of his lecturing partners, John A. Collins, had become inspired by a movement against private property and had raised the proposition that "to recognize property in the soil is worse than to inslave a man." Douglass and Charles Remond, the other black abolitionist on the tour, objected. They believed that "the antislavery cause had been wantonly assailed" and concluded that Collins should resign as an agent for the Massachusetts Anti-Slavery Society or cease using its platform to promote other causes. "Collins became angry and they became angry," Kelley explained to Chapman. "Both said what they would not in cold blood." Although she insisted that all three "are rather to be pitied than blamed," she ultimately agreed with Douglass and Remond. Chapman, however, issued a "sharp reprimand" to Douglass, in which he perceived that she seemed more concerned about "my insubordination to my superiors" and "the use which the [opposition] liberty party papers would make of my seeming rebellion against the commanders of our Anti-Slavery Army" than about Collins's misappropriation of the meeting.[23]

Chapman's reprimand, aimed at the two black men on the tour, took on greater significance later that month at the Colored Citizens Convention, when she used the *Liberator* to single out the black minister Henry Highland Garnet for his defense of both slave insurrections and the Liberty Party, an organization she despised. "All colored men are not abolitionists," she declared. "The same evil influences are at work to tempt the selfish heart beating beneath a colored bosom," she warned, "that are potent to hold the fearful white man in thralldom." She contrasted Garnet to "those men of color who *are* abolitionist" and then openly doubted that he meant what he had said in an address to the convention.[24] "I can think on the subject of human rights without 'counsel,'" Garnet fired back, defending his capacity to reason for himself. "I was born in slavery," he reminded Chapman. "It, therefore, astonished me to think that you should desire to sink me again to the condition of a *slave*, by forcing me to think just as you do."[25]

Chapman also excoriated Garnet for his support of the Liberty Party, and suspicion of Liberty Party influence lay behind some of her denigration of Douglass. The party had been formed in 1840 by those frustrated with the glacial pace of the AAS's Garrisonian strategy. Named for their ideological leader William Lloyd Garrison, Garrisonians blamed the cause and perpetuation of slavery on human moral failing. Like any sin, slavery could only end through a national conversion experience, much like those of the second Great Awakening religious revivals in the 1830s. They focused on grass-roots organizing and disseminating information about the horrors of slavery. They condemned churches and, after 1842, the US Constitution and government, because all three condoned slavery and required compromise with slaveholding constituents, thus making even those opposed to slavery complicit in its existence. Garrisonians encouraged moral Americans to withdraw from churches, refrain from voting or holding political office, and advocate for disunion. They also controlled the leadership of the American Anti-Slavery Society after the 1840 division.

Liberty Party supporters, on the other hand, considered slavery a legal and political institution that could be dismantled through laws and amendments to the Constitution. After their effort to exert electoral pressure on the existing Whig and Democratic parties had failed, they had formed their own in order to elect antislavery men to local, state, and national government, who would ultimately outvote and overwhelm pro-slavery legislators. In states west of New England, American Anti-Slavery Society and Liberty Party organizations formed coalitions to pursue their ends, which often extended to local concerns about racially discriminatory laws and aid to fugitive slaves. Closer to Boston, however, the AAS leadership, sometimes known as the "Boston Clique," permitted less tactical and ideological latitude. They believed that any alliance undermined the ultimate goal of ending racial discrimination. Given the ensuing bitterness, outsiders could be forgiven for thinking that the two factions considered each other greater enemies to freedom than slave masters were.[26]

Douglass initially opposed the Liberty Party. In early 1842, he explained that he could not trust the organization because "it disposes men to rely entirely on political, and not on moral action" and so did not require the sacrifices made by Garrisonians. After his tours through New York and the West, however, he tempered his assessment. In February 1844, when he asked the Massachusetts Anti-Slavery Society to explain its instructions "to make the liberty party as such a special object of attack," he informed them that "candor compels me to confess, I am not a suitable person to be engaged in your service." In clarifying his position, he wrote to the *Liberator* that "if it [the Liberty Party] could live, let it; if it would die, let us have as little to say or do about it as possible." In other words, he concluded, "*let it alone.*" He elsewhere noted that "the slaveholder," "the Whigs & Democrats," and "some abolitionists" all hated the Liberty Party, "but the slave loved the Liberty Party." Therefore, he concluded, "for his part he must say that he loved the Liberty Party!" In response, stalwarts of the AAS began to question Douglass's loyalty. In March 1844, Chapman predicted that Douglass and others would "eventually open their eyes, or go to 3d party altogether." That October, after touring with Douglass in New England, Kelley confided to Chapman that "some of our force is not suitable to be trusted alone." Douglass came under particular suspicion because "all he does will be collected by" the Liberty Party. Not only would he refuse to join his colleagues in condemning the Liberty Party as "pro-slavery," but his failure to do so, coupled with his disputes with AAS leaders, could be used by the Liberty Party to discredit the Garrisonians.[27]

As Douglass toured Britain, his softening toward political abolition took on greater significance to the Boston Clique, particularly Chapman. In monarchical

Britain, power flowed from the top down, from the central government in Parliament outward to the colonies, and Members of Parliament theoretically did not represent particular constituencies but the empire as a whole. British abolitionists did not have to persuade the entire nation to turn against slavery, just key parliamentary figures. As a result, they based their antislavery movement in London and referred to its leading organization, the Anti-Slavery Society, as the "London Committee." Their success in ending British involvement in the transatlantic slave trade and in emancipating slaves in the Caribbean appealed to abolitionists in the States, who intended to end slavery by political means. After West Indian Emancipation in 1834, however, many British abolitionists changed tactics. They used British influence in transnational institutions, such as in churches or in trade, to pressure other slaveholding nations toward emancipation. This new strategy more closely resembled the Garrisonian methods of organization.

The British Garrisonians and the Anti-Slavery Society, called the British and Foreign Anti-Slavery Society after 1839, attempted to avoid the vicious rivalries of their American counterparts. Local politics and conditions influenced the composition and interests of each abolitionist organization, and often the fight for resources was not among abolitionists but among multiple reform movements. For instance, Cork, Ireland, bore the brunt of the migration from the western counties suffering from the potato blight and famine that began just as Douglass arrived there. In 1847, the organizer of western Ireland's donations to the annual Boston fair, Isabel Jennings, apologized for her region's paltry donations. "All sorts of benevolent societies are every day increasing" to meet the influx of destitute migrants, she explained. Each society begged for aid, yet "misery in the masses seems not to diminish." Throughout Britain, the ravages of unregulated industrialization presented similar situations that affected the British population more immediately than slavery but that also led to alliances among reform movements. As a result, at each stop on his tour, Douglass moved through activist circles configured in ways that permitted different combinations of ideas and strategies.[28]

Meanwhile, he discovered Chapman's correspondence to Webb outlining her mistrust. "You betray a want of confidence in me as a man, and an abolitionist," he charged her. He was, in the words of his companion James Buffum, "quite *sensitive*" to her use of his poverty as a point of weakness. "As Mr. Buffum *was rich—and I poor,*" Douglass perceived that Chapman believed that "while there was little danger but what Mr. Buffum would stand firm, I might be bought up" by the British and Foreign Anti-Slavery Society. This particularly galled him at a time when white speakers received higher pay than black speakers, and because, Douglass noted, most of his income in Britain came from the sale of the *Narrative*. Chapman had also insisted that the Irish edition of the *Narrative* contain a call for the Boston fair, partly to ensure that Douglass did not neglect advocating for the AAS as he promoted his book. Racial undercurrents buoyed these insults. Douglass may have believed that Buffum's wealth exempted him from suspicion, but Buffum was also white. Chapman also held up three white men as good examples for Douglass to follow, using Remond, a black man, a fellow Garrisonian, and Douglass's personal friend, as a cautionary tale of weakness, pride, and greed. Douglass did not point out the racial distinction, but he recalled Garnet's response to Chapman when he invoked an image of slavery in describing her management style, "If you wish to drive me from the Anti-slavery society," he warned, "put me under overseer ship and the work is done."[29]

As Douglass received reminders of the prejudices that he faced in America, in Ireland he began to notice a most profound experience. "I find myself not treated as a *color*, but as a *man*," he marveled, "not as a thing, but as a child of the common Father of us all." On stage, in print, in his demeanor, and in his life, he demanded dignity and respect that transcended race. "Trampled, reviled and maltreated as I have been by white people During the most of my life," he wrote to Cork mayor Richard Dowden Richard, echoing his early apprehension in front of white audiences, "[I was] early taught to regard myself, their divinely appointed prey, and ever looking upon such as my natural eneimeis." Yet in Ireland for only three months, he continued, "you may readily emagine the grateful emotions that thrill my heart when I meet with facts—forever dispelling the darkness of such infurnal doctrines." He thanked Dowden and his hosts, the Jenningses, from whom "flowed much of the light, life and warmth of humanity." "Everything is so different here from what I am accustomed to in the United States," he wrote to Amy Post, in Rochester, who had become a confidante. "My color instead of being a barrier to social equality is not thought of as such." He worried that "it will unfit me for the proslavery kicks and cuffs at home." Nevertheless, he hoped that "it may enable me to indure the more easily knowing from experience that the spirit which induces them is only the results of the infernal system of slavery." He had always demanded recognition of his equality. Now he received it.[30]

Women coaxed him toward this epiphany. After Douglass and Buffum had arrived in Dublin at the end of August 1845, Hannah Webb's sister, Maria Waring, escorted the men to Wexford and Waterford without incident. Buffum and Douglass continued on to Cork, where they lodged with the Jennings family, and while Buffum made only a brief visit , Douglass remained for three weeks. Webb described the Jenningses as "three brothers and five sisters, who are brimming over with good nature, courtesy, hospitality, and philanthropy." They were also members of the Church of England, temperance advocates, and merchants of non-alcoholic beverages. Isabel Jennings served as the secretary to the Cork Ladies' Anti-Slavery Society, whose members included her sisters, Mary, Jane,

Charlotte, and Helen, and sister-in-law, Ann. Isabel and Frederick in particular got along. Shortly after his arrival, she wrote, "He feels like a friend long
[shared] and I think before he goes we will quite understand one another." After
four years of regular correspondence with him, she felt able to say, "I feel that
I could write to him as to a brother." Webb reported that this "most intelligent
& delightful families of ladies" had "jaunted about—walked & promenaded"
Douglass through the city. Isabel insisted that she and her sisters "could find no
fault in him," and "in private he is greatly to be liked." Indeed, Jennings possessed
a more nuanced understanding of the frustration that Webb characterized as
"moodiness." "I always found that he could bear to have fault found with him,"
she observed, "if it were not taken for granted that he *must* be wrong." Douglass
was no stranger to the company of white women, but the striking aspect of these
encounters lay in the absence of violent retribution. He repeated similar scenes
with Eliza and Jane Wigham in Edinburgh, Elizabeth Pease in Darlington, Ellen
and Anna Richardson in Newcastle, Mary Estlin in Bristol, and Julia and Eliza
Griffiths in London. At no time did the sight of a black man among white women
provoke physical attacks.[31]

Douglass's depiction of a society free from racism was idyllic, subjective, and
very profound, and lay in sharp relief to Chapman's suspicion and reminders of
the ways that slavery continued to poison his life. The Reverend Thomas Smyth
provided the latter. As Douglass moved from Ireland to Scotland, the Garrisonian
campaign focused on donations from the American South to the Scottish Free
Church, a predominantly Presbyterian organization. Smyth, a Presbyterian minister who had emigrated from Belfast to South Carolina twenty-five years earlier,
served as a liaison for American churches. In the summer of 1846, he delivered donations from American churches that included money from the South.
Abolitionists objected to gifts from slaveholders, pointing out the injustice of
using the oppression of one group to relieve that of another. Douglass particularly loathed the hypocrisy and began a campaign to "Send Back the Money,"
leading the chant at antislavery meetings and causing many otherwise indifferent Free Church followers to question their connections with slaveholders. "I
think the result will be that *the money of slaveholders will have to go back*," Buffum
predicted.[32]

Smyth had not heard of Douglass until his voyage to Ireland in 1846, and
the influence that a former slave wielded against the Free Church shocked him.
Both began making pointed references to one another in public. Douglass referred to Smyth as the "Rev'd Manstealer," while Smyth insisted that "a deliberate scheme was laid to entrap me in a legal snare because I refused to meet or
be introduced to him, or publicly debate with him." In retaliation, Smyth began
a rumor that Douglass was seen leaving a brothel in Manchester, England. He
himself had not actually observed Douglass there, he admitted, but he had

heard the story from friends who urged him to defend himself by making the gossip public.[33]

Brothels did, after all, meet a demand, and patrons included many middle-class men. Drawing public attention to a particular man's visits, however, slandered his virtue. Smyth and his associates hoped to discredit Douglass and either expose the abolitionists as hypocrites or force them to eject Douglass. By aiming his charges at the single black abolitionist and former slave lecturing in Britain at the time, Smyth probably intended to incite fears of black male sexuality and miscegenation. He did not have to explicitly state that Douglass presented a sexual menace; he merely had to associate Douglass with sex in order to suggest that this powerful force within the abolitionist movement might actually pose a danger to one of his most potent constituencies, the many white women who flocked to his aid. If nothing else, the women might be disgusted at Douglass's betrayal of his wife.

As the New York Tribune pointed out in reporting the story, "In South Carolina, if the negro had ventured to address R. Mr. Smyth, he might have been asked 'Whose boy are you?' and rewarded for his impertinence by sixty lashes well laid on." In Ireland, however, the Tribune continued, Douglass "took the manly and fearless" route by hiring attorneys and demanding an apology. Smyth quickly backed away from the rumor. "I beg to express my sincere regret," he apologized, "I am quite satisfied that the statements that I incautiously made, on the report of third parties, were unfounded." The third parties, incidentally, did not step forward to corroborate Smyth's charges. Although he was not a citizen of Britain and was still legally considered property in the United States, with Smyth's retraction, the legal system had worked in Douglass's favor. Smyth's ploy to agitate anxiety had failed. At worst, the stress of the incident, compounded by his discovery of Chapman's mistrust at the same time, had caused Douglass to behave less than politely to some of his friends, for which he profoundly apologized.[34]

Smyth may not have caused white abolitionists to shun Douglass as a mythic, oversexed black man, but his instinct to play upon the potent brew of sexuality and race was not entirely misplaced. Douglass attracted women and others took note. "You can hardly imagine how he is noticed," wrote Bristol abolitionist J. B. Estlin, "petted I may say by ladies." Estlin judged that "some of them really a little exceed the bounds of propriety, or delicacy, as far as appearances are concerned." Jennings, too, wrote of "one or two [women] who were rather absurd in their over attentions" toward Douglass in Cork. In Belfast, Mary Ireland described the "intense interest [that] has been excited by the oratory of Frederick Douglass," and she was "convinced there is scarcely a lady in Belfast who would not be anxious to join in any means calculated to promote the enfranchisement of the deeply injured Africans." Richard Webb eyed such attention with suspicion, deciding that most of the women found their antislavery sentiment only through "a strong romantic personal interest" in the charismatic African American. Webb also suggested a reason Smyth's tactics did not work. He insisted that racial taboo could not constrain women's attention "in a country where the prejudice against colour is looked upon as a thing only to be laughed at."[35]

Webb made light of Douglass's magnetism where Smyth had attempted to alarm. Yet, both understood that Douglass's race played a role in his appeal. Obviously, his importance lay in his testimony as a former slave, a distinctly African American experience, and many in his British audience had not seen another black person, much less a slave, before Douglass. He delighted them by defying their preconceived notions. One woman even lamented that he was not "full blood black for I fear your pro-slavery people will attribute his pre-eminent abilities to the white blood that is in his veins." He also brought charisma and theatricality to his presentation, riveting them and animating their sympathies. "The Satire, the Pathos, then the true sublimity of this great Douglass, & his rich deep tones of voice were almost miraculous," gushed one London lady. Jennings pondered the "expression of great suffering at times on his countenance," which, combined with his stories of his life as a slave and the scar above his nose evidencing childhood abuse, led Jennings to muse that his melancholy "only renders him more interesting."[36]

Whatever the women's attraction to Douglass, however, no one condemned him for drawing this attention, and he took care to avoid provoking scandal. In Jennings's account, the women behaved foolishly and Douglass behaved like a perfect gentleman. In the face of flattery, she reported, he "evidenced the highest regard for his wife and children," and she thought that "he could not have avoided more entirely any of the confidential conversations which some persons like to have with young ladies when the latter are willing." Webb, too, directed his disgust on this particular matter toward the frivolity of the fans rather than at Douglass. Indeed, the person who received the worst condemnation, albeit indirectly, was Anna. "I wonder how he will be able to bear the sight of his wife," wondered Webb, "after all the petting he gets from beautiful, elegant, and accomplished women."[37]

Few in Britain knew much about Anna. Jennings and Webb perhaps received more information than most because Douglass had stayed with them for so long, and, at least to Jennings, he had revealed that Anna could not read. In the United States, Anna's dark skin may have aggravated many prejudices in regard to her intellect and beauty, even among other African Americans. In Britain, however, few knew much about her color beyond that she was not mixed race. By contrasting her with the "beautiful" white women in Ireland, Webb may have implied that her racial features automatically made Anna unlovely, but his addition of "elegant and accomplished" pointed more toward her lack of the formal refinements middle-class women learned. Jennings's judgment, too, focused on Anna's lack of education. Their critique of Anna, sight unseen, sprang less from racial bias than class. Anna's inability to read marked her as working class, a category that carried greater stigma in Britain, where discriminatory policies targeted the poor or Irish Catholics. That made her an object of charity rather than admiration. Indeed, Mary Estlin suggested that Bristol abolitionists had "low expectations" for Douglass, when they knew no more of him than his writing, in which he disclosed that he had first earned his way through manual labor. "He far exceeds the picturing we had formed," Estlin extolled after meeting him, "both in outer and inner graces, intellectual power culture and eloquence." They observed that Frederick shared their values and, for all intents and purposes, concluded that he was one of them. As Sheffield abolitionist Mary Brady put it, Douglass presented himself as a "gentleman having been, in his travel in England & Scotland, run into the best society." Of Anna they knew little, and the "low expectations" they had initially had for her husband were probably even lower for her. She, in their minds, was not quite the suitable mate for her polished husband, no matter how much he expressed his respect for her.[38]

For Frederick, Anna's inability to read seems not to have presented as much of a practical problem in communication as might be assumed. Instead, the sticking point between the two lay in the uncertainty of their future. The danger of Douglass's return to slavery had followed him since his escape in 1838 and grew alongside his popularity. The Fugitive Slave Clause of the Constitution and the Fugitive Slave Law of 1793 protected Thomas Auld's claim to Douglass, rendering his self-emancipation through escape moot in an American court of law, should Auld find him. That probability increased as Douglass described his life in slavery with greater specificity, culminating with the *Narrative,* in which he named the precise location of his enslavement and his masters. His journey to Britain had removed him from Auld's grip, and the English *Somerset* case of 1772 had effectively emancipated all slaves who entered the country. Yet, legal freedom in Britain only made him an exile from a nation that still considered him property. This troubling fact emerged through 1846 and caused him to examine his attachment to the United States.

By the end of 1845, Douglass's book had made its way to the border states, and Philadelphia abolitionist Mary Grew noted that it was "doing a good work" in Maryland. In December, one of Edward Covey's former neighbors, A. C. C. Thompson, took to the pages of the *Delaware Republican* to defend the slaveholders of Maryland against Douglass's depiction. The Auld brothers and their wives did not appreciate being cast as the villains, and one wrote a vindication of the family. Douglass acknowledged their displeasure, suspecting that "my old master is in a state of mind quite favorable to an attempt at re-capture." By the time he made that statement, however, Hugh Auld of Baltimore had become his new master, having purchased Douglass from Thomas Auld of St. Michaels for $100 in October 1845.

By March 1846, the news of the transaction had reached the American abolitionist press, along with the rumor that Hugh planned to retake his property. His motive was not financial, Douglass believed, but "to feed his [Auld's] revenge."[39]

In May, just as he learned of this news, British abolitionists in London hit upon the idea to raise the cost of bringing the Douglass family to England. They immediately collected, by his estimation, "between £80 and £90" to which donors soon added enough to total $500. "So I rest in the hope of soon being joined by my family," he rejoiced, "in a land where they will not be constantly harassed by the apprehension that some foul imp of a slaveholder may lay his infernal clutch upon me, and tear me from their mists." It was not clear whether he envisioned a visit of indeterminate length or was taking the first step toward immigration, although he suggested the former by jesting, "Master Hugh must bear the loss of my service *one* year longer, and it may be, I shall remain absent *two*."[40]

Back in Lynn, Anna and Harriet Bailey faced their own dangers. If Frederick envisioned slave-catchers lying in wait for his return by watching his family, he must also have worried that this would put at risk the young "sister" bearing his enslaved family's name and living in their home. Frederick probably had considered this, as well as her value to the cause if she shared her own story of enslavement in the family of late US congressman John Leeds Kerr. "What do you think of coming to this country[?]," he asked her in July. Anna, on the other hand, was facing a fine of $500 each for harboring both Frederick and Harriet should Auld or Kerr's heirs choose to press the case. More importantly, the fears of a forcibly divided family that she had outrun when she left Maryland had caught up with her, and immigration to England brought its own anxieties. Anna had uprooted herself from a community twice in eight years, each move taking her farther from her own family and into ever more unfamiliar territory. England loomed more alien still, and she would be alone. In Lynn, at least she had Harriet and the Lynn Ladies' Anti-Slavery Society for support and companionship. Harriet, meanwhile, had become engaged and would not be going to England, a disappointment to Frederick as much as it probably was to Anna. Frederick would not be a companion, either, as he had been in New Bedford, having proved himself an itinerant minister of abolition and appearing to remain so for the foreseeable future. She probably wanted answers to some specific questions before she agreed to expatriation.[41]

Some familial negotiation appeared to ensue. Frederick probably notified Anna of the proposition in May, perhaps in the letter that he had enclosed for her with the one in which he invited Harriet to England, and about the same time that he wrote about the donation in a column for the *Liberator*. Since mail traveled for at least a month, Anna would have received the letter in June, around the time that the *Liberator* column appeared in print, and hers would have found Frederick in July. He then wrote to Anna directly as well as to Jeremiah Sanderson, an abolitionist colleague from New Bedford. "You will see both [letters]," he explained to Bailey, "and both of them I want you to read over and over again until Dear Anna shall fully understand their contents." As with the earlier May letter, in which he gave similar instructions, his words might suggest that he thought Anna a bit simple-minded. Yet in July 1846, he sat in an English hotel, facing Smyth's charges, Chapman's mistrust, and the very real possibility that he might be returned to slavery. He had quite a bit to reassure her about, in addition to persuading her to move to England, and she appeared not to have immediately answered in the affirmative about relocation. He desperately wanted to make sure that she understood his argument and perhaps quiet her apprehension, which he could do better in her presence. He turned to Harriet to plead his case in his stead. The problem, again, lay not with Anna, but with the vast ocean between them that hindered subtleties of communication.[42]

As Frederick awaited Anna's response in late July, he contemplated exile and return. "What has become of old Massachusetts?" he wrote to his old comrade, William A. White. "I have nearly lost all confidence in her honesty fidelity and love of liberty." Safe in England, however, he missed home and family. "I long to see a face which I have seen in America," he lamented. "William do you think it would be safe for me to come home this fall?" Recalling the unsuccessful recapture of another fugitive slave, George Latimer, only four years earlier, he wondered, "Would Master Hugh stand much chance in Mass.? Think he could take me from the Old Bay State?" Others worried, too. "I trust his friends in America will not promote his return," Mary Brady of Sheffield hoped, "without good ground to be satisfied that his doing so is safe."[43]

Then he met the Richardsons. On August 3, 1846, Douglass arrived in Newcastle, greeted by Ellen Richardson, "a clever lady, remarkable for her devotion to every good work"; Ellen's sister-in-law Anna; Anna's cousin Ann; and Ellen's cousins, the sisters Eliza Nicholson and Jane Carr. Anna and Ellen were Quakers by faith and teachers by profession, primarily instructing disadvantaged girls. All of the women had been involved with antislavery since the 1830s and had extended familial connections to the Jenningses in Cork, the Wighams in Edinburgh, and the Smeals in Glasgow, who each had welcomed Douglass. When the Richardsons learned that Douglass faced the dilemma of returning to slavery in America or living indefinitely in Britain, possibly without his family, they decided that the simplest solution was to pay the price of his freedom. Accordingly, they engaged agents who contacted Hugh Auld's agents. Auld set the price at £150, the equivalent of $711.44, and agreed to "furnish such papers as shall render him entirely and for ever free as soon as the money is paid." Through October, the women raised £70, and Jane Carr's brother-in-law collected the difference at an Edinburgh meeting at the month's end. Auld, having realized a substantial return on his investment, signed the manumission papers on December 5, 1846, and filed them seven days later. Douglass began 1847 as a legally free man.[44]

Figure 3.3 Eliza Wigham, Mary Estlin, and Jane Wigham, three British abolitionists, worked with the American Anti-Slavery Society to aid Douglass during his first tour of Britain. Estlin coordinated efforts out of Bristol and corresponded with Maria Weston Chapman. The Wighams worked out of Edinburgh and helped to raise the price of Douglass's freedom. "Eliza Wigham, Mary A. Estlin, and Jane Wigham," c. 1840–1860. Cab.G.3.118. Unknown photographer. Print Department, Boston Public Library.

To the Richardsons and the other donors, the exchange seemed a reasonable means of preventing a horrible injustice, and was in keeping with the history of British abolition. The 1833 West Indian Emancipation Bill, which went into effect on August 1, 1834, provided £20 million sterling in compensation to slaveholders. The Richardsons and their colleagues fell into the less-Garrisonian camp of British abolitionists and thus had no qualms about the transaction. Those of a more Garrisonian mind, in the words of Catherine Paton of Glasgow, thought "it compromising of principle, a recognition of the right of property in a man" and, according to Esther Sturge in London, "a compromise of the great principle that all men have a right to be free." Although the British abolitionists tended to deemphasize their divisions, the matter of Douglass's freedom revealed fissures. Mary Welsh in Edinburgh insisted, "Some of us have been very much grieved at Anna Richardson getting that money collected to purchase Frederick Douglas's ransom," and Sturge and her circle would contribute neither funds nor letters on the Richardsons' behalf, although, she reassured, "we do not feel the less interested in his [Douglass's] welfare."[45]

In America, the Garrisonian press also condemned the deal. "It was unwise and unnecessary," declared the *National Anti-Slavery Standard*, a sentiment echoed by the nonabolitionist *Boston Chronotype*. The *Pennsylvania Freeman* printed a resolution from a meeting in Oxford, Pennsylvania, that the purchase of slaves' freedom "directly encourages and tends to enlarge the outrageous system of Slavery." The authors speculated that Auld would only use the price of Douglass's freedom "in the purchase and rearing of other slaves for the market." Henry C. Wright turned directly to Douglass, couching his criticism as "advice." "You will be shorn of your strength—you will sink in your own estimation," Wright charged, "if you accept that detestable certificate of your freedom, the blasphemous forgery, that accursed Bill of Sale of your body and soul; or, even by silence, acknowledge its validity." Douglass would, Wright insisted, be unmanned. Ironically, the one Garrisonian who did not condemn the transaction was William Lloyd Garrison himself. At the Edinburgh meeting in October 1846, Garrison declared that he "seconded with all his heart the motion of the ransom of Douglass from bondage." He acknowledged that he was contradicting his own ideology, but in Douglass's case, "he would submit to be robbed [of Auld's price] that one so loved should go free."[46]

Douglass understood the Garrisonian objections, but he was the person who would have to return to an unconscionable condition, and his family would have to suffer for it. He considered "my liberty of more value than one hundred and fifty pounds sterling" and the "happiness and repose of my family" worth "more than paltry gold." Thus, he wrote, "I could not see either a violation of the laws of morality, or those of economy, in the transaction." American law supported Auld and Auld intended to re-enslave him, which would leave Anna and his four children in severely reduced circumstances. Recognizing the authority of the law over him did not mean that he condoned it; the price was paid "not to establish my *natural right* to freedom, but to release me from all legal liabilities to slavery." For all that his nation's institutions seemed to deny his claim to citizenship, "My sphere of usefulness is in the United States; my public and domestic duties are there; and there it seems my *duty* to go." Having legal freedom made his duties easier. Whereas some white Garrisonians may have thought that Douglass's return to slavery would serve as a powerful rallying point for the ambivalent or apathetic, theirs was a privileged position with consequences they would never face. Nonetheless, such apostasy only made the truly adamant, such as Maria Weston Chapman, warier, and she continued to ply her sources for information on Douglass.[47]

Douglass probably learned of his liberation from Auld's clutches in January, after he had returned to the north of England. In Carlisle at the beginning of 1847, he visited two of the architects of his legal freedom, Jane Carr and

Eliza Nicholson. They and others had hatched a plan to continue fundraising in order to provide Douglass with an independent income that would allow him to devote his time to antislavery work. He believed the idea not the best course, potentially alienating American abolitionists and draining funds collected for the relief of Irish famine victims, which had engaged the Jenningses since his departure from Cork. Reflecting on the past and coming years, he instead revealed his ambition to operate an abolitionist newspaper. For some time, he had been adding journalism to his repertoire, sending regular columns to the *Liberator* from overseas. Those missives captured the attention of Horace Greeley, who asked him to write a column for the *New York Tribune*. He had also witnessed the effect of his *Narrative* on larger audiences, long before they had met him. Away from home for most of the past five years, absent for major family decisions, and suffering a physical toll from the constant travel and oration, he longed for a more sedentary life, but one that did not require him to abandon his influence on the antislavery movement. As observed by Jane Wigham of Edinburgh, whose father had issued the call for donations to round out the price of Douglass's freedom, Douglass had "an honest wish to provide for his own family—while he is also pleading for the whole family of man." Editing a newspaper seemed the ideal solution. With Carr as treasurer and Mary Estlin, Mary Brady, and the Richardsons among the other coordinators, a campaign began to purchase a "Steam Printing Press."[48]

Those other coordinators included Mary Howitt, editor with her husband William of the literary periodical *Howitt's Journal*. She had met Douglass in 1846 while writing a biographical sketch of Garrison and deemed the African American "one of the most interesting men I ever saw."[49] She soon found that she had two assistants to help her fundraise, the sisters Julia and Eliza Griffiths. Douglass recollected that the Griffiths sisters had escorted him about London and the English countryside, "to see and enjoy sights curious in works of art, as well as natural beauty" and being "to me devoted friends in a strange land." Julia, however, remembered that they had first met Douglass at a party held in honor of his last night in London. Decades later, she asked Frederick if he remembered that "Eliza pinned that white camellia in your coat?" She was still amused that "naughty 'brother Frederick,' never rested 'till he knocked off the beautiful white flower leaving only the green leaves on." Mary Carpenter's aunt had attended the event, as well. "It was a glorious meeting," she proclaimed, gushing, "The Satire, the Pathos, then the true sublimity of this great Douglass, & his rich deep tones of voice were almost miraculous."[50]

Equally affected, Julia Griffiths soon appeared to have taken charge of Mary Howitt's collections as well as begun her own campaign to gather books to send to her new friend, a set that likely formed the beginning of his personal library.

Until then, neither sister was well known among antislavery activists in England, and Douglass's description of them as "taking a lively interest in the cause of emancipation" only after their meeting suggests that abolition had not previously occupied their time, although their uncle Joseph Griffiths, and brother, Thomas Powis Griffiths, belonged to the BFAS. In Douglass, Julia seemed to have found her vocation, and her efforts on his behalf soon earned her a reputation among more established abolitionists as "an enthusiastic friend of Douglass" and "Douglass's devoted friend." They little knew what a force she would become.[51]

On April 4, 1847, Douglass boarded the *Cambria* to begin his voyage home. When he had arrived in Ireland nineteen months earlier, Richard Webb had noted that Douglass "was little noticed except by a few beyond our own circle." Now important people "contend for his company and make him quite a lion." In Bristol, Mary Carpenter suggested that "he is perhaps more generally appreciated than Mr. Garrison," whom everyone continued to admire, of course. Mary Estlin observed that, in gathering donations to the Boston fair, "it makes nearly all the difference between zeal & indifference in different towns whether FD or Mr. Garrison has lectured there." This did not escape Douglass, who early in his tour confessed to Amy Post that her friendship meant more to him because "you loved and treated me as a brother before the world knew me as it now does." He now had acquaintances throughout the British Isles who, in the words of Mary Brady, "have become deeply attached to him & feel an intense interest in his welfare." Just as they had obtained his legal freedom, they would provide him with the means to establish economic and intellectual independence. Indeed, on his return voyage, after Cunard line agents had relegated Douglass to steerage despite his first-class ticket, Estlin reported the wish among many "to seize the opening for collecting a substantial testimonial of British sense of this injustice." Furthermore, they saw no conflict between his wish to earn a living and to advocate for his race and willingly helped him along the way. Douglass had become a transatlantic antislavery celebrity, legally free, and possessing the means to become an independent proprietor and activist.[52]

As the British women noted, Douglass always expressed his desire to support his family, a responsibility he had long embraced, and his family could not be separated from his activism. After almost two years apart and possibly fewer than ten letters from one to the other, Frederick and Anna finally faced one another. She had married a caulker, a man who toiled for wages in obscurity and who had ambitions to become a minister. In his absence, she had been sole manager of the house, and he had become, in the words of their daughter, her "honored guest." Now, she found herself with a husband feted in four countries and embarking upon his own business. If his paper became successful, the Douglass family could anticipate a more comfortable life, one in which they could secure an education for their children, apprentice their sons in trades, and set their daughter Rosetta on a path that might not entail domestic service. At the same time, they faced greater scrutiny and judgment, already seen in others' assessment of Anna but also in the suspicions that Frederick had become vain and "that he thinks that his services are worth more than any one else," according to American Anti-Slavery Society board member Edmund Quincy.[53]

Ever since his days of escaping mobs with Abby Kelley, he had become cognizant of the vital importance of women in perpetuating the antislavery movement and he would draw on them in the future. Yet, because he demanded the right to associate with them, and because they were predominantly white, they became a means for critics to discredit him. Douglass had hardly returned to the country when the Albany and New York *Switch* published "NIGGERS AND NASTINESS," in which the writer portrayed Douglass walking "cheek by jowl" with a white woman in Albany and castigated a white woman for her "depravity of taste" in allowing Douglass to stay in a room adjoining hers on a Hudson River boat, insinuating that the door between the rooms remained unlocked. These assaults directed at him also implicitly encompassed Anna and his family by suggesting marital infidelity, stoking suspicions of black male hypersexuality and the very presumption of African Americans' inability to develop loving, nuclear families. They also came from anti-abolitionists. As Douglass made good on the American Anti-Slavery Society leadership's fears of his growing independence, he found them willing to deploy the same types of insinuations and intrusions. He no longer trembled before audiences of white people, nor feigned to tremble. He knew their fear and refused to be intimidated.[54]

4

"The Pecuniary Burdens," 1847–1853

By November 1853, William Lloyd Garrison had decided that Frederick Douglass "has had one of the worst advisers in his printing-office whose influence over him has not only caused much unhappiness in his own household, but perniciously biased his own judgment." Characterizing this adviser as "active, facile, mischievous," Garrison, in the pages of the *Liberator*, proclaimed that she "has never had any sympathy with the AAS, but would doubtless rejoice to see it become extinct."[1] This adviser was the Englishwoman Julia Griffiths, business manager of *Frederick Douglass' Paper* and secretary of the Rochester Ladies' Anti-Slavery Society and Sewing Circle, who had until shortly before Garrison's outburst lived in the Douglass household. Garrison, defining abolition exclusively as the ideology espoused by the AAS, insisted that Griffiths's antipathy extended to the entire movement and that she had used her wiles to lure Douglass away from the true path, allowing "the pro-slavery Philistines to ascertain the secret of his strength, cut off his locks, and rejoice over his downfall."[2] Although many of Garrison's supporters agreed with his general conclusion, several criticized him for invoking the image of a miserable Douglass marriage and hinting at an untoward liaison. Garrison demurred that the "allusions was not meant unkindly, nor intended to imply any thing immoral." His audience, however, could not help assuming otherwise when his accusations formed part of a commentary on an article from the *National Anti-Slavery Standard*, reprinted in the *Liberator*, charging Douglass with falling under the spell of a "Jezebel."[3] Garrison concurred by painting a portrait of Douglass "slumbering in the lap of a prejudiced, sectarian Delilah."[4]

This was not the first time Douglass's enemies had attempted to connect the black abolitionist with interracial debauchery, but earlier insinuations had come from anti-abolitionists feeding the imaginations of like minds. They had no credibility with antislavery activists; they did not include Douglass's family, nor did they question his commitment to abolition. Garrison, on the other hand, swayed opinion within the movement. For six years, he had watched Douglass go from being his protégé in the AAS to having such financial autonomy that he could develop his own, divergent ideology. Douglass had established a news-paper against the wishes of the society's leadership and without their sponsor-ship in 1847, and throughout the 1850s, he gained organizational support and increased his subscription base independently of their influence. In the wake of the Fugitive Slave Law, these developments were inseparable from Douglass's drift toward the more pragmatic brand of abolition popular in his new home in Western New York and led him to alliances with members of the Liberty Party. Garrison and his cohort in Boston had seldom credited Douglass with having the sincerity or ability to form independent opinions, so they searched for a villain to blame for his betrayal of their ideals. Foreign, assertive, talkative, fearless of her reputation, and disliked by almost everyone except Douglass, Julia Griffiths provided an excellent scapegoat; and the vehemence of Garrison's attack only underscored her importance to Douglass's self-sufficiency.[5]

The confrontation had gathered force ever since Douglass had proposed his idea for a new newspaper to the executive board of the AAS in 1847. He later recalled that, on his return voyage from England, legally free and backed by dona-tions from British abolitionists, he had pictured a glorious future in which "I saw myself wielding my pen as well as my voice in the great work of renovating the public mind."[6] He realized only later that it had been naive to expect the board to throw their resources behind his effort. Instead, explained Massachusetts aboli-tionist Samuel May, "the move was not a judicious one for him."[7] The newspaper business was risky, especially if the paper promoted abolition or if the propri-etor was African American. Antislavery newspapers required not only subscrib-ers and advertisers but also the institutional support of organized antislavery societies to remain solvent. Even then, poverty and failure haunted the editors. Douglass himself admitted, less than a decade later, that "could all the perplexity, anxiety, and trouble attending it, have been clearly foreseen, I might have shrunk from the undertaking."[8]

At the time, he had no idea that the AAS was already struggling to operate the *National Anti-Slavery Standard* and aid the *Anti-Slavery Bugle,* the *Liberator,* and the *Pennsylvania Freeman.* During the seventeen months that Douglass had spent overseas, Maria Weston Chapman, corresponding secretary of the AAS, and Sydney Howard Gay, editor of the *Standard,* had barely succeeded in a six-month campaign to make the paper self-sustaining by adding five thousand subscrib-ers.[9] Farther west, Abby Kelley had her own work with the *Bugle,* based out-side Cleveland in Salem, Ohio. The editors, Jane Elizabeth "Lizzie" Hitchcock Jones and her husband Benjamin, believed that they would be forced to resign when they could no longer stand the stress of managing the paper, lecturing, writing books to supplement their paltry income, and, for Lizzie, also caring for their home and an infant.[10] Even Garrison complained about unpaid bills.[11] The AAS board warned Douglass that they had no money or resources to spare for a new paper, particularly one that they considered superfluous competition and that would pull their prize lecturer from the field. Douglass abandoned his plans, fearing that his failure might "contribute another proof of the mental deficiencies of my race."[12] Instead, from August to October of 1847, he returned to the lecture circuit on an AAS tour with Garrison through New England, Pennsylvania, Ohio, and New York, once more leaving behind his family and facing harassment from anti-abolitionist mobs.

Journalism continued to intrigue Douglass nonetheless. Chafing at slights to his literary ability, he rose to the challenge of writing two columns each week for the *Standard* at a flat rate of between $100 and $150 a year.[13] The board hoped the arrangement would satisfy Douglass's ambition, but he encountered resistance over the issue of compensation. Treasurer Edmund Quincy chafed when Douglass bargained for higher pay, complaining, "These niggers, like kings, are kittle cattle to shoe behind," meaning that Douglass was imperious and untrustworthy. Quincy conceded to the pay because "it is better worthwhile to pay him $20 or $30 more than his letters are worth than to put him in a huff, & perhaps sell them to the [Washington, DC, National] Era or the Chronotype."[14] Douglass had also taken on writing assignments for the *Ram's Horn*, a new African-American-owned-and-operated paper based in New York City. His first column appeared hardly a month after his return to the United States.[15]

Douglass and Thomas van Rensselaer, the editor of the *Ram's Horn* and a former slave, discussed future business arrangements, as well. Douglass firmly believed that black voices should feature prominently in the antislavery literature both as representative businessmen and in speaking from their own experience. Before leaving for England, he had been under the impression "that there was not a single Printing Press in the United States under the control and management of colored persons," and those that had once existed had failed.[16] He later discovered that was not the case. After abandoning his own plans, he began to investigate ways in which he could support the four other black-operated papers in existence.[17] In August, just as the antislavery tour arrived in Pittsburgh, Douglass asked the *Standard*'s editor, Sydney Howard Gay, to investigate van Rensselaer's account books as he considered, in his words, "a proposed alliance" in which he would become "a third party" investor in the *Ram's Horn*.[18] At the same time, he also met Martin R. Delany, who joined him on the tour.[19] Delany had edited the *Mystery* in Pittsburgh since 1843. It, too, survived precariously, and Delany had been forced to turn its management over to a board.[20]

A few weeks later, Douglass's engagements took him to Salem, where Samuel Brooke published the *Anti-Slavery Bugle*. Since it was the only Garrisonian paper in the West, the AAS and its relatively new counterpart the Western Anti-Slavery Society had scrambled to offer it assistance. The *Bugle*, however, was not the official paper of either organization, and was instead run by a publishing committee headed by Brooke. Brooke had sunk over $500 into the paper to keep it afloat and, in 1847, was facing the impending departure of editors Hitchcock and Jones. At this point in the tour, Garrison fell deathly ill, leaving Douglass to continue alone and allowing him to meet with others uncensored. If the Boston clique had rejected Douglass's proposal as a potential burden and competition, others saw him, his fame, and the financing he brought from England as a possible savior.[21]

On September 17, only a week after Douglass had met with Brooke, the *Bugle* announced, "Frederick Douglass proposes to publish in Cleveland, Ohio, a Weekly Anti-Slavery Paper." Douglass had abandoned his talks with van Rensselaer and returned to his original plan to start his own journal, to be named the *North Star*. He soon signed Delany as a corresponding editor and Brooke as an agent. The antislavery network between Ohio and Boston buzzed with distress. Samuel May predicted that "'The North Star,' will probably swallow up several others—the A.S. Bugle and *Ram's Horn* (N. York) etc."[22] Hitchcock worried that "the days of the Bugle are numbered." Her mentor and confidante, Abby Kelley, now Abby Kelley Foster, believed that "two antislavery papers can hardly be sustained in that section of the West." Given Douglass's popularity and symbolic appeal, combined with the crumbling state of the Ohio paper, she feared "that Douglass's will supplant the Bugle." Moreover, she declared, "I, for one, am not willing to trust the anti-slavery cause in the West, to the management of Douglass and Sam'l Brook," confessing, "I always have been and still am fearful of Douglass; and as for Sam'l I would as soon trust a jack o'lantern."[23] At the urging of both Foster and Hitchcock, the Western Anti-Slavery Society moved quickly to take full control of the *Bugle* in October.[24] If Douglass and Brooke had intended to merge the two papers, then this development ended that plan. Douglass had to search elsewhere for a base of operation where he would not interfere with the *Bugle* in Ohio, the *Liberator* in Boston, the *Ram's Horn* and *National Anti-Slavery Standard* in New York City, and Philadelphia's *Pennsylvania Freeman*.

As he pressed ahead, Douglass learned that his putative allies "draw quaint pictures of starvation and predict that I am soon to be victimized."[25] Samuel May opined that, "I think he mistakes his vocation and will regret his course." Chapman insisted, "I regret it for his own sake." Foster saw the move as a failure of character, declaring, "The manner of Douglass' proceeding in this manner was not quite honorable to say the least" because "he never consulted any of the active and responsible abolitionists in the West."[26] Garrison blamed Samuel Brooke for leading his protégé astray and insisted that Douglass possessed a "Strange want of forecast and judgement!" Indeed, many could not separate Douglass's failure to ask Garrison's permission to pursue his latest newspaper plan from what they perceived as his coldness toward Garrison during his illness in Cleveland. Garrison, too, could not understand the reason that he had not received any inquiries about his health from Douglass during his convalescence or the reason that Douglass had "never opened his lips on the subject [of the *North Star*], nor asked my advice in any particular whatever." Douglass, of course, already knew that they had underestimated his ambition. He had nothing more to discuss with Garrison on the matter after the first rejection of his plan.[27] When the Cleveland scheme fell apart, he turned to friends in Rochester, where Amy Post had been hoping for an opportunity to work with him in revitalizing local abolitionism.

Like almost everyone else in the booming city of Rochester in the 1830s and 1840s, Amy Post and her husband Isaac were newcomers. Both hailed from old Long Island families in Jericho and Westbury, but the ready availability of land and burgeoning transportation revolution had drawn them to Central New York in the 1820s and then to Rochester in 1836. They had hoped to continue farming, as they had done on Long Island, but instead Isaac opened the Post, Colman, and Willis drugstore downtown because the city offered better opportunities for merchants. The speed of canal and then railroad travel allowed them to maintain their extensive family connections on Long Island, while the marriages of younger family members, such as Amy's sister Sarah and Isaac's daughter Mary, expanded their networks in the region. These became important links as Amy immersed herself in the organizations formed by the women of the city.[28]

Reform among urban, middle-class women followed the wave of revivals that had begun with Charles Grandison Finney's meetings in 1831 and earned the entire region a reputation as the "Burned-Over District." The Posts had arrived in Rochester at the tail end of the movement, and evangelism tended to be a strictly Protestant phenomenon. Still, Amy Post's spiritual convictions fit with the evangelist zeal for moral perfection and worldly change, and her home sat right in the middle of a variety of reform networks. Although her plain, unadorned dress and simple chignon bespoke her origins in the Society of Friends, she and her husband had always gravitated toward the vanguard of that sect. When Elias Hicks, a member of Amy's Jericho meeting and a distant relation, criticized the denomination's drift from their original reliance on "inner light," Amy and Isaac had followed him out of the orthodox meetings and into new Hicksite meetings. They found many others like themselves in Western New York, including the McClintocks of Waterloo, near Seneca Falls. Amy's own inner light insisted that she sympathize with the downtrodden, chief among them the slaves. In 1837, Post signed an antislavery petition for the first time, putting her name alongside those of non-Friends. In doing so, she doubly defied her Genesee Yearly Meeting, engaging in both political action and association with outsiders, which sparked an investigation of her the following year. Post, however, never let anyone dictate her associations, regardless of religious affiliation or race. By 1845,

Figure 4.1 Amy Post was the corresponding secretary of the Western New York Anti-Slavery Society in Rochester. She befriended Douglass on his first visit to the city in 1843, proved instrumental in providing institutional support for the *North Star*, escorted him to the Seneca Falls Woman's Rights convention in 1848, and aided many fugitives from slavery. "Amy Post," n.d., Unknown photographer. Amy and Isaac Post Family Papers, Dept. of Rare Books, Special Collections, and Preservation, Rush Rhees Library, University of Rochester.

she, Isaac, and others in their extended family had become so deeply involved in antislavery work that they could no longer adhere to the Society's dictates, and they separated themselves from their meeting.[29]

In the context of their meeting's position on public activism, their boldest antislavery act was the founding of the Western New York Anti-Slavery Society (WNYAS) when Abby Kelley, also a former Quaker, had visited the city in 1842.

Amy served as the organization's corresponding secretary, the position Maria Weston Chapman held in the AAS. Post, however, worked on a much smaller scale, with far fewer resources, and had a very different leadership style. Where Chapman commanded, Post built consensus. Like her Boston counterpart, Post drew on networks of family, Friends, and reforming women throughout the city and state to organize an annual fair. However, she was operating with a deficit of experience and a broader spectrum of antislavery ideologies. New York was a stronghold of the Liberty Party, and the American Society's ideological warfare against that party alienated many of its affiliates, including the WNYAS. Indeed, the Western New York Society lost a significant number of experienced and con-nected members for just that reason.

Nevertheless, most abolitionists recognized that Post was the person to contact when organizing in the region, and African Americans turned to her as someone who did not overcompensate to prove herself free from prejudice. Abigail Mott had directed Abby Kelley to Post when Kelley ventured west, and Mary McClintock referred Elizabeth Gay, wife of the New York abolitionist and *National Anti-Slavery Standard* editor, to Post when seeking aid for a fair. Both Harriet Jacobs and Sojourner Truth relied on her as someone who passed no judgment on their sexual history or femininity and promoted their public careers.[30] William C. Nell, Garrison's printer, wrote Post chatty and teasing let-ters of deep friendship and affection.[31] Douglass valued Post for treating him like a brother, embracing him like kin. For Post, abolition meant a total end to injus-tice and to racism, and it began with the imperfect individual fighting sin within themselves. No matter how small, every victory must be considered in this light.

Larger victories, however, required reaching larger audiences. Despite the best efforts of advocates like the Posts, activism had fallen off in Western New York for a variety of reasons, from the 1837 economic crisis to differences between po-litical and Garrisonian abolitionists.[32] By 1846, contributions to antislavery fairs had declined in Western New York, and Post lamented to Chapman, "No man has ever been amongst us who in our opinion is qualified for usefulness in the antislavery field."[33] Post suggested that the American Anti-Slavery Society spare Douglass when he returned from Europe and allow the Rochester society to use part of the proceeds from their fair to pay his fee. They hoped his charismatic speeches would reignite the antislavery sentiment, which would then pay off in increased subscriptions to antislavery papers, donations to the antislavery fair, and active opposition to slavery. Post had already persuaded Douglass to ask the British societies to donate handiwork to the Rochester fair directly, in addition to the one in Boston.[34] Nothing came of Post's proposal to Chapman at the time; but when Douglass found a new place to settle his paper, the New York group was there to welcome him. His first edition rolled off the press on December 3, 1847, and the Western New York Anti-Slavery Society was ready to promote it.[35]

Unlike the relationship between the *National Anti-Slavery Standard* and the AAS, or the new arrangement between the *Anti-Slavery Bugle* and the Western Anti-Slavery Society, the *North Star* did not serve as the official newspaper of the WNYAS. Douglass retained full independence from the organization, but each supported the other. At this point, Douglass was advocating the same antislavery tactics of moral suasion and disunion as the American, Western, and Western New York Anti-Slavery Societies. He made clear in the inaugural issue that his ambition came not from any ideological difference, but because "he who has *endured the cruel pangs of Slavery* is the man to *advocate Liberty*." He considered warnings of failure "a reason for OUR earnestly endeavoring to succeed," because "our race must be vindicated from the embarrassing imputations resulting from former non-success."[36] Other black abolitionists stepped in to help. In addition to Delany's columns, the most prominent black men in the country contributed pieces to the paper during its years of existence, or worked as agents.[37] Douglass also saw his paper as a means of training and offering opportunities to young black men in the printing trade. William C. Nell, for instance, became frustrated at being overlooked for advancement at the *Liberator* and joined Douglass as the *Star*'s publisher.[38] He brought with him nearly two decades of experience in activism, journalism, and publishing.

The *North Star*, therefore, made an important and compelling contribution to American newspaper publishing; but the internal politics of the antislavery movement and competition over fundraising soon fed a rivalry that compromised the paper's existence. Factions competed not only for the minds of antislavery sympathizers but also for the limited number of antislavery dollars raised through subscriptions, donations, and bazaars. The problem became evident shortly after the *Star* went into print. The women of Rochester held their annual antislavery fair with the intention of using the proceeds to help the paper. They hoped to tap other New York organizations for aid in the future, but when Douglass visited West Winfield, New York, he discovered that Maria Weston Chapman had "exacted a promise" from the society that "the proceeds of the [West Winfield] fair should go to the support of the National Antislavery Standard."[39] A subtle struggle over the largesse of the fairs, and by extension the focus and intent of the movement, ensued.

As Post organized the next year's fair, she appealed directly to Chapman's sister, Anne Warren Weston, for donations of the annual collection of abolitionist literature, the *Liberty Bell*, as well as "any other books or articles."[40] Weston replied that the Boston fair had been organized for the "one specific purpose" of supporting the AAS. Post, Weston insisted, had failed to mention "to what particular purpose your funds are to be devoted." She alluded to a circular that Post had sent to the "warm friends of Frederick Douglass, and of Emancipation,"[41] which, Weston believed, indicated that Post had no intention of aiding the American Society. Therefore, Weston could "withdraw *neither goods nor funds*" for Post.[42] Just before the January 1850 fair, Post issued another plea, writing that "we still *need* your sympathy and cooperation or I should not ask for it," but to no avail.[43] Post and the Western New York Society could expect no assistance from that quarter. For the Weston sisters, the movement and the American Society were one and the same, the constituent fairs should support the American Society, and it would aid those organizations in turn. Douglass and his paper were, in their opinion, ancillary to the main thrust of the abolition movement at best and, at worst, dangerous, self-interested competition.

Overseas, too, antislavery societies felt the tension between their desire to support the *North Star* and the demands made by the Weston sisters. Maria Weston Chapman appeared to have questioned Isabel Jennings's loyalty to the American Society when Jennings took up collections in Cork for Post's fair as well as for Chapman's. Jennings assured the Boston maven that the Massachusetts fair had received the greater share. Still, she reminded Chapman, the famine had taken its toll on benevolent societies in Cork, and Douglass and the Rochester society had just as much right to have a fair as Boston.[44] Likewise, the ladies of both the Manchester and the Edinburgh societies divided their donations between Boston and Rochester, while the Belfast group sent most of theirs to the latter. John Estlin in Bristol complained that "Some of F.D.'s friends here are indefatiguable in efforts to support it [the *North Star*] and the Rochester Bazaar."[45] Richard D. Webb, writing from his roost in Dublin, predicted that Douglass "will be likely to get a large share of what is sent" to America.[46] Fair organizers particularly coveted these foreign donations of handicrafts, such as paintings, lace, and needlework, because they tended to sell quickly and at higher prices. As one visitor to the 1849 Rochester fair observed, "had it not been for the large amount of contributions from the Old World, the display, in some measure, would have been shorn of its beauty."[47] Samuel May, in thanking an English supporter, said simply, "Without the British & Irish aid, very little could be done."[48]

Observing Douglass's progress, Samuel May fretted that "the Anti-slavery warfare is a severe one, very nervous still to the few upon whose shoulders the pecuniary burdens fall mainly."[49] Quite understandably, the competition presented by the *Star* and the WNYAS vexed Chapman, Webb, and others in the AAS who had recently worked so hard to save the *Bugle* and the *Standard*, and had yet to clear the former's debt. Of course, if Douglass failed, they could then recoup their temporary losses while shaking their heads in sympathy. They could not appear to be actively aiding that failure, but they carefully monitored Douglass's progress and insinuated to interested parties that his enterprise would not last long. John Estlin, for instance, asked May, "What is likely to be the fate of the North Star" and "is it beneficial to the cause to encourage it?"[50] May replied that he had heard from "from several sources altogether reliable" that Douglass had only collected 1500 of the 2000 subscribers required to maintain the paper.[51] This was an improvement from the 1200 subscribers that Douglass had collected seven months earlier, but the pace of increase seemed insufficient to May.[52] He advised Estlin that donations to the Rochester fair would be wasted because they were meant "only to sustain a paper which cannot long live" and therefore "seems like a dividing & consequent weakening of our strength."[53] Chapman's replies to similar inquiries left her correspondents with a sense of the *North Star*'s imminent demise, as well.[54]

Often the framing of the situation took the form of personal attacks on Douglass's integrity. Abby Kelley Foster, who confessed again that she "always feared" Douglass, suspected that he planned to pilfer *Standard* subscribers in New York. Chapman had already expressed her own apprehension of Douglass's motives while he was in Ireland, and she continued to depict Douglass's newspaper as a vanity project diametrically opposed to abolition. She attempted to interfere with collections overseas by writing to Mary Howitt, who had been among those gathering donations for Douglass and the Rochester fair in England, to say that she "regretted that he [Douglass] should have so many personal presents from England as it was much taken from the Cause."[55] She implied that a former slave's personal success as an editor discounted his activism because he had built that success on the base of an established movement. Webb, too, insisted, "It is not to Douglass's credit that he should have used his influence in this way for his own benefit."[56]

Webb dismissed the ideological commitment of most of the women who amassed donations to aid Douglass, insisting that they failed to "understand the American Anti-slavery cause, or appreciate its importance apart from its romantic & personal interest." Still, he was convinced that he had found evidence of more nefarious subterfuge. The source of Chapman's troubles lay with Maria Webb and Anna Richardson, he believed, both of whom had spearheaded the controversial purchase of Douglass's legal freedom. He described the two women as "great anti-Garrisonians and pro-Liberty Party partisans."[57] In other words, he implied that either these factions had manipulated Douglass or Douglass had defected. The popularity of the Liberty Party in New York could only have aggravated their suspicions. Either way, both Chapman and Webb maintained that Douglass was using abolitionists' donations to enrich himself at the expense of the AAS.

Even those who were more sympathetic to Douglass believed that his inexperience would lead to the downfall of the *North Star*. On hearing about the poor state of the paper from Chapman, one British abolitionist confessed concern that Douglass "might not have sufficient *business habits* to manage so important an undertaking."[58] May, too, had worried from the start: "He has no *experience* in editing, nor in business affairs."[59] They did not exaggerate. Lewis Tappan had approached Garrison with trepidation when investing in the *Liberator* in 1830, by which time Garrison had worked in printing for nearly a decade.[60] Douglass had collected subscriptions for other publications and had negotiated for his wages as a caulker and general laborer, but he not managed so much as his own household accounts, much less a large and sprawling enterprise, nor did he know anything about the printing process. For just that reason, he had hired Nell, who served as publisher for the first six months of operation. When Nell returned to Boston in mid-1848, Scots printer John Dick replaced him.[61] Douglass may not have had experience himself, but he knew to surround himself with those who did and to learn from them.

By autumn 1848, Douglass grew leerier of the American Society leadership when Julia Griffiths supplied him with information confirming his suspicions that Chapman actively worked against him. While Griffiths helped Mary Howitt gather donations for Douglass and Post, Howitt received a letter from Chapman. Chapman attempted to dissuade Howitt from sending donations to Rochester, insisting that Douglass "was a selfish person fighting only for his own hand."[62] Howitt shared the letter with Griffiths, who immediately wrote to Douglass about the situation. He was not pleased and sent a letter in which he confronted Chapman. She hurriedly replied, contending that she had been misunderstood. Douglass told others that her assurances "made him more easy in his mind." Chapman, however, did not change her opinion, and Douglass, May reported, continued to lodge "'complaints' against the Abolitionists of Massachusetts."[63] Mystified and hurt, Douglass could not understand the lack of faith in his venture by the very people who once urged him "to consecrate his time and talents to the promotion of the anti-slavery enterprise" and hailed him as "one of the most efficient advocates of the slave population."[64]

As predicted, the *North Star* drifted into a crisis during its first eighteen months. Throughout 1848, the number of subscribers appeared to grow steadily. Yet, where Samuel May saw an initial boom of subscriptions that would probably peak at 2000 subscribers Douglass saw steady growth that might improve were it not for the opposition of Chapman and others. At least that was the face he put on in public, sending positive reports about his progress to Post and the Western New York Society. In May 1848, he used his journey to the annual Anti-Slavery Convention in New York City as an opportunity to do a lecture tour, and wrote to Post that he had obtained "more than 20 subscribers" in about a week. His consistently large audiences promised more.[65] The woman's rights convention in Seneca Falls that July, which he attended with Post, provided him with another opportunity to gather subscribers.[66] Still, despite Douglass's assurances through the following spring that his "success here [in New York] has been far greater that I had any idea it would be," and that he, at least, "shall not despair of the North Star yet," the very fact that he mentioned despair betrayed his concern.[67]

Indeed, Abby Kelley Foster related some gossip that Douglass was very much in a crisis as he wrote those words. According to her sources, when Douglass stopped in Albany on his way to the 1848 antislavery convention, he confessed to the Mott sisters that the paper's mounting debt might force him to turn it over to the *National Anti-Slavery Standard*.[68] A few years later, even he admitted that "the first two years of the 'Star' spent the whole two thousand dollars sent to me from England" and "stript me of all but a very valuable experience in manageing money in connexions with a newspaper."[69] Unfortunately, he entrusted very few in American antislavery circles with the true state of affairs, having to keep investors interested with one hand, while fending off disaster with the other.

The investors back in Rochester were not fooled. Amy and Isaac Post, Isaac's partner and fellow businessman Edmund Willis, and William Hallowell, all leaders in the Western New York Society, suspected that the paper had fallen deeply in arrears with its creditors. In September 1849, they requested an investigation of the books, and according to Isaac, "would have done so long ago had they have known for a *certainty* they would not have been thought officious." Willis told Isaac that he thought the paper might owe only $400 and that it could be saved without Douglass being "saddled with a Debt that he cannot easily get rid of." The sum, although worrisome, did not trouble them so much as a more fundamental problem. They were positive that Douglass had no idea how to run a business, and they could not understand his reticence in asking for their help. "I dont see how FD can tell how he stands without a regular look over to see how things stand," wondered Isaac.[70] They had risked the Western New York Society's resources and jeopardized their relationship with the AAS, and they wanted some sort of return. Yet they could not be certain how to proceed unless they examined the accounts. Amy Post received the unenviable charge of writing to Douglass, who was on tour, to propose the idea of auditing Douglass's books and forming a committee to take charge of the paper's accounts.

As Isaac predicted, Douglass took offense. The Posts, Hallowell, and Willis believed themselves to be offering expertise to an inexperienced businessman while also protecting their investment, but Douglass felt they were trying to take over. As he understood the proposal, the Western New York Society had voted to discontinue "any further donations to the Star until I put the economical concerns of the paper under the charge of a committee." Amy Post's involvement particularly hurt. He told her that she should be the "last person" to support a plan that, he believed, would be "degrading to me as a man." Her assertion that she had the power in the society to compel him to comply deepened his disappointment. "And while I should be glad to have a committee who would kindly see that the Books of the concern are honestly and properly kept," he conceded, "I can never consent to give up the entire control to persons who are not responsible for the debts of the concern." To do so would, he believed, end up "making me a mere cipher in my own affairs."[71]

Post could not help but think that the source of the trouble lay in Douglass's "incompetency and frequent absence from home." In fact, Douglass had been away from Rochester for most of the year, including almost all of September, when she had written to him.[72] Still, that Douglass had understood her to mean that "any other than *thy ownself*" should run the *North Star* or that the Western New York Society suspected him of some sort of fraud astonished her.[73] Yet, for Douglass, any suggestion of his ineptitude, much less a takeover of the paper, recalled the American Society's wariness of his motives. He kept constant guard for any hint that he had anything but complete control over his own enterprise. Anything less would only confirm prejudice not just about his fitness for business but that of all black men. Nevertheless, he could not escape the fact that the paper was failing. In the end, Douglass consented to the formation of a committee to "superintend the financial and economical concerns of" the paper, to "have the full rights to examine into the affairs of the paper," and to "restore confidence where there may be distrust."[74] In the autumn, all parties appeared to have agreed to allow John Dick to oversee the paper and began directing all business correspondence to him. In January 1850, however, Julia Griffiths stepped in. The committee was never mentioned again.

Since their parting in London in April 1847, Griffiths had become Douglass's leading English advocate. By that summer, she estimated that £400 had already been raised and anticipated collecting as much as £500, a significant sum given that the price of his freedom in British currency, £150, equaled $711.44 in US dollars.[75] She collected books for his library and articles to donate to Amy Post's fair. She even collaborated with her brother, Thomas, to compose a song in Douglass's honor, presumably to raise funds through the sale of the sheet music.[76] She also kept Douglass abreast of developments such as Chapman's interference. By the time she and her sister embarked for an American tour in early 1849, John Estlin in Bristol had written her off as someone "identifying Antislavery with him [Douglass] alone"[77] while having "no ideas upon the subject beyond rendering herself useful to Douglass."[78] He, many of his British associates, and the AAS leadership tended to view Griffiths as, at best, an enamored fan or, at worst, a mischief-maker. They underestimated her abilities, diminished her commitment to abolition, and dismissed the sincerity of friendship between the black American man and the white English woman.

The Griffiths sisters had planned their American tour as a means of improving their understanding of the abolition movement and strengthening the transatlantic ties between England and Western New York. They initially intended to stay six months, envisioning an itinerary that included attending the antislavery conventions in New York City and visiting the the American Anti-Slavery

Society office in Boston and the black communities of Canada West. At the ages of thirty-six and twenty-six, respectively, neither Julia nor Eliza possessed husbands or children. The hardships of their father's two bankruptcies, in the 1820s and 1830s, no longer plagued them, and they could finance their sojourn as well as many other emergencies along the way. They arrived in New York as free and unencumbered as any woman could hope to be in 1849.[79]

When Richard Webb learned that "the Griffiths are going to visit Douglass," he was not mistaken in wondering, "Will this create a sensation in Rochester?"[80] The appearance of the trio certainly seemed calculated to provoke. Douglass, tall, dignified, and, thanks to Anna's efforts, impeccably but conservatively dressed, defied the popular depiction of black men as subservient, sinister, or ostentatious. He commanded attention on stage and, in a sense, was seldom off-stage. Julia was older than her companions and described as "ordinary-looking," which may have said more about others' expectations than her actual beauty.[81] If she dressed extravagantly, "flounced & jeweled a good deal," by the Boston standards of the Westons, then she projected a flamboyance heightened by her ability, in the words of the Posts' son, to "talk about anything at any time and as long as any body will hear her."[82] With Julia on one of Douglass's arms and the young, round-faced Eliza on the other, their triptych clamored for attention.

The commotion had started well before they reached Rochester. On May 5, only three days after their arrival, Douglass appeared at the Franklin Hotel to escort them to a series of antislavery meetings, and the hotel management refused to seat them in the dining room. People on the street approached them with "the hand clinched, head shaking, teeth grating, hysteric yells and horrid imprecation," and "a distortion of countenance, a red a furious look about the cheek, a singular turn up of the nose, and a '*lower me!*' expression of the eyes," wherever they went in the city.[83] Aboard the riverboat *Alida*, on their way from New York to Albany, the trio received "savage looks" and felt the "pent-up wrath" of other passengers, while "a feverish excitement revealed itself among them in 'low and muttering accents'" that, Douglass suggested, were sexual and obscene. When they entered the dining room for lunch, "an ominous silence prevailed." A steward asked Douglass to leave. Douglass, as he did in railroad cars, stayed firmly in his seat. The white passengers moved away from their table and waited for him to be forcibly removed. When the captain and clerk joined the steward, to the applause of the other passengers, the Griffithses joined Douglass as he left the room. The steward later told Douglass that he could be served only as their servant. In another, slightly different version of the story, recounted by Samuel May, "Miss G. Openly spoke her mind to the Captain & the passengers," and chastised them "for their base prejudices & their unmanly & insulting behavior to herself and her sister as well as to F.D." Similar accounts told of the sisters chastising the passengers and threatening to send the story to the British press.[84]

Figure 4.2 Frederick Douglass during the years in which he began publishing the *North Star*, attended the woman's rights convention in Seneca Falls, and began to diverge from the views of his early abolitionist allies, who focused their criticism of him on his work with Julia Griffiths. "Frederick Douglass," Unidentified artist, c. 1850 after c. 1847 daguerreotype, Sixth plate Daguerreotype. National Portrait Gallery, Smithsonian Institution.

Shortly thereafter, a Boston newspaper—"a *low, paltry*, newspaper" said May, "but one which has extensive circulation"— attacked the trio "in the most grossly *indecent* manner." May also reported that "a coarse wood-cut was paraded representing them as contending with each other for the caresses, etc. of the 'Nigger Douglass,' whose face and attitude also were of the same filthy cast."[85] Even Anne Warren Weston, who had little kind to say about Douglass or the Griffithses at this point, disapproved of the way that Julia was "grossly insulted on account of going around with Douglass."[86] The furor continued at the following year's convention. As Douglass and the sisters strolled along the Battery awaiting the arrival of their steamer, a group of men surrounded them. While "assailing us with all sorts of coarse and filthy language," Douglass wrote, "two of them finally struck the ladies on the head, while another attacked me." Douglass fended the men off, but one returned to slug him in the face before they could reach the safety of their vessel.[87]

As it turned out, Webb had been prescient about the reaction in Rochester. "The appearance upon the Main Street of Frederick Douglass with one of these ladies on either arm seriously threatened the order of the town for awhile," recalled Jane Marsh, adding that "threats were openly made of what would be done if such aggressive demonstration of race-mixture were persisted in."[88] One of Douglass's white clerks at the *North Star*, William Oliver, who was himself chastised for working at a black business, remembered that the Griffiths sisters "lived in the family of Mr. Douglass, causing much criticism."[89] Isaac Post recounted a tale heard from an acquaintance, Isaac Gibbs, "who made himself quite merry about F. walking locked arms" with the Griffithses. According to Post, when Gibbs encountered them on a stroll to the train depot, "F. drew his arm from the connexion very gently" before arriving at their destination and Gibbs "appeared to think F. was quite willing to not be seen walking in this manner just at that time." Yet few others noted any such reticence on Douglass's part.[90]

Throughout the latter half of 1849, as Frederick, Eliza, and Julia faced disparagement, ostracism, and outright violence from all quarters, they in no way altered their behavior to accommodate public outrage. During the incident on the *Alida*, Julia had confronted the perpetrators about their prejudice; and Marsh remembered that, despite the scandalized chatter about town, "Frederick Douglass kept his head high as ever, the ladies filling the role of possible martyrs unflinchingly."[91] Amy Post, often condemned for socializing with African Americans, praised the sisters' behavior as explicitly activist, writing that "Julia & Eliza Griffiths are seting us a glorious example on this department of our A S work."[92] Douglass had already survived years of abuse for associating with white people, especially women, and constructed his refusal to recognize color lines as an inherent part of his manhood. "My conduct was governed by what I deemed was becoming a MAN," he wrote of the *Alida* incident, "without once considering my color."[93] Women, on the other hand, took social risks in following suit. Sympathetic reports described the Griffithses as "ladies." Douglass, too, emphasized their respectability, describing them as "two ladies, elegantly attired, educated, and of the most approved manners, faultless in appearance and position." In praising their "fidelity to principle, and indifference to a corrupt and brutal public opinion," he valorized their ability to use that respectability in pursuit of justice, a privilege of middle- and upper-class white women. He advised other activists to fight racial prejudice by doing the same, "to act as though it did not exist, and to associate with their fellow creatures irrespective of all complexional differences." As for himself and the Griffithses, "we have marked out this path for ourselves, and we mean to pursue it at all hazards."[94] In other words, if their friendship was going to inflame such violent outrage, enforcing the separation between black men and white women, then they would protest that particular color line by refusing to be intimidated.

The Griffithses' first months in America coincided with the exchanges between Douglass and the Western New York Society investors over the state of the *North Star*. Julia was probably aware of the situation. She appeared to be the one person, presumably aside from Anna Douglass, in whom Frederick had confided his difficulties from the start. In April 1848, four months into the paper's production, he wrote to her to express his "warmest thanks for the unfaltering interest in which you continue to take in my humble welfare." Then, in a rare moment of candor, he confessed his honest assessment of the prospects of the *North Star*. "I can seldom bring myself to say that I have undertaken more than I have the ability to perform," he admitted, but "I fear I have miscalculated in regard to the amount of support which would be extended to my enterprise," adding that "things have not turned out at all as I expected."[95] He may have calibrated this description to elicit sympathy and assistance, and his optimism and confidence had re-emerged by the end of the letter, but this self-doubt and vulnerability appeared nowhere else, other than in the scene at the Motts' described by Abby Kelley Foster.

The sisters had initially intended to return home in the autumn, around the time the proposal for the financial oversight committee arose. By September, however, they had become involved with the Western New York Society and were marshaling their energies behind Amy Post as she planned the annual Rochester fair.[96] If Douglass had not already included them in the discussions about the paper's finances, they could not have escaped learning the details as they joined in the fundraising and because they were boarding with the Douglasses. They could also witness some of the day-to-day operations of the paper.

Throughout the fall, John Dick, whose official title was publisher, received all correspondence on the paper's "business matters" as plans for the financial oversight committee moved forward. Yet his daily work went beyond that of his official title. Douglass continued to spend a significant amount of time on the road lecturing to build his subscriber list and simply to earn an income since the paper certainly did not provide one. On the road for much of November and December, he left Dick to attend to editorial matters in addition to his printing and new financial responsibilities.[97] If this arrangement was going to continue, there would have to be more help in the office. Otherwise, as Amy Post noted, the paper suffered.

Then, at the beginning of the new year, Douglass announced that he "had taken the management of the business affairs of the paper upon his own hands." The method of bookkeeping and the handwriting in the ledgers changed, however, as Julia Griffiths assumed charge of accounting.[98] She also handled subscriptions, fundraising, and correspondence, much to the chagrin of people who expected to have direct access to Frederick, and eventually contributed a literary column.[99] The fortunes of the paper began to turn.

Griffiths was clearly no amateur when she began working for Douglass.[100] Her father, Thomas Griffiths, had at various times engaged in the publishing, book-selling, and the stationer's trade, which involved printing, copying, and paper sales. When she first appeared on the antislavery scene, she cultivated connections in the literary world, and was mentioned most often in association with Mary Howitt, of *Howitt's Journal*. She also approached the publishers Charles Gilpin and Robert and William Chambers for donations.[101] She seemed to have a solid education, perhaps above average for young women of her era, and most considered her quite clever. A female correspondent for the *Anti-Slavery Bugle* described her as "educated" and "accomplished" with the aura of having come from "a superior position in England."[102] Isaac Post noticed that though she was "older than I expected," she was "talented beyond common," echoing Frederick's early praise of her as "very talented."[103] Post also commended her copyediting, while James McCune Smith, the black abolitionist physician who wrote the introduction to Frederick's second autobiography, noted her "high literary abilities."[104] Her work for the paper testified to her literary background.

Julia clearly had a head for business, too. As the oldest child in her family, she had younger sisters who could have taken her place at home, while she helped in her father's work. Thomas Griffiths's two bankruptcies, one when Julia was old enough to be involved in his shop, likely also familiarized her with the vagaries of capitalism.[105] Her bookkeeping indicates more familiarity with better practices than had previously been seen at the office, and her efficiency did not go unnoticed. When Douglass entered negotiations to absorb the Liberty Party's paper into the *North Star*, in 1851, he recommended, "the money matters of the paper might well be left to the care of my industrious and vigilant friend and co-worker Julia Griffiths" because "had she had the management of my books at the commencement I feel sure that I should have had double the number of subscribers I now have."[106] In other words, Griffiths had demonstrated the types of skills and experience that might be useful to a struggling neophyte. His need for someone trustworthy with solid business acumen matched her own for meaningful work.

A series of shifts took place alongside Griffiths's management of the paper. In February, Douglass criticized Amy Post's fair as both a financial and a moral failure. Later in the year, Griffiths began to organize a separate fair.[107] In keeping with her connection to the politically oriented British and Foreign Anti-Slavery

Society, Griffiths approached such wealthy and influential sympathizers as Whig Congressman William Henry Seward and Liberty Party men Salmon P. Chase and Gerrit Smith.[108] Douglass had also begun a re-evaluation of his abolition-ist strategies through debates with Smith and Griffiths.[109] In mid-1851, the *North Star* merged with the Syracuse-based Liberty Party paper and received the backing of Smith; but the title of the new incarnation, *Frederick Douglass' Paper*, denoted the source of control.[110] At the same time, Griffiths organized a new women's antislavery society, drawing on women associated with the Liberty Party but who had no affiliation with the Western New York Society. The new venture had already been branded a "'bigoted New Organizations' friend" by the American Society leaders, and Griffiths's cultivation of Liberty Party sympa-thizers did nothing to make the hard-core Garrisonians feel any more affinity for her or allay their suspicion of Douglass.[111] Meanwhile, the 1850 Fugitive Slave Act had transformed all debates about slavery and its end, influencing many of Douglass's and Griffiths's decisions.

Saving the paper, however, was the first order of business. Griffiths's primary concern lay in the slow and mercurial task of expanding the subscription list, made more difficult as Douglass's abolitionist strategies and alliances fluctuated through 1850 and 1851. His Boston rivals had already noted that, by 1849, he had approached the 2,000 subscribers necessary for the paper's survival. By May 1851, the last month of the *North Star* as such, Douglass credited Griffiths with pulling the paper out of debt, which also allowed him to pay off the mortgage on his home.[112] The incorporation of Liberty Party positions in 1851 might have further increased circulation, but Griffiths noted that "a number of Liberty Party People have returned their papers" because of Douglass's former association with the Garrisonians.[113] In turn, association with Smith and the Liberty Party tactics alienated Garrisonian subscribers. "Frederick anticipated the falling off of a large number," Griffiths reported to Smith in December of that year, but she herself hoped that "surely not more than one hundred subscribers will secede on account of Frederick's change of opinion."[114] During 1852, she assured Smith, "Our list of subscribers increases."[115] In later years, Douglass insisted that she had doubled the number of subscribers to 4,000.[116]

Because Griffiths handled the business operations of the paper, she became the focus of animosity for those frustrated with Douglass and the paper's poli-cies on unpaid accounts. According to one, "The North Star is sometimes sent to friends who do not take the paper in hope that they may see fit to subscribe to it."[117] The practice did not sit well with some of the recipients, who suspected a swindle. Deborah Weston recounted the case of her sister, Maria Weston Chapman, whose papers continued to arrive at the American Anti-Slavery Society office after she had asked that the subscription be suspended during her European tour. Attributing the continuation to Griffiths, Weston advised appealing directly to Douglass himself.[118] Anne Warren Weston described instances in which others had attempted to cancel subscriptions and found that "this is a difficult matter to accomplish." She did not blame Douglass, suspecting instead that "it is Miss Griffiths who takes the entire management of matters, no matter how much a paper may be stopped continues to send it."[119] If the Westons found Griffiths unethical, her system had its logic; and she did not seem willfully unscrupulous. She argued that she did not expect Chapman to pay the bill for unwanted papers. Instead, knowing that Chapman's unclaimed papers were given away to interested parties who might become subscribers, she considered the uncompensated copies an investment.

Although Griffiths happily mailed complimentary copies to potential subscribers, she had little patience for delinquent existing subscribers. To Gerrit Smith, with whom she began conferring in 1851, she wondered "whether to cut them off *at once*; to notify them individually, or to put a notice in the Paper."[120] She settled on the latter, printing reminders to "PAY UP! PAY UP!! PAY UP!!!"[121] Although the initials appended to the notice were "F.D.," the use of multiple emphases resembled the insistent style of "J.G.," who employed exclamation points, underlines, and double underlines with abandon. At the same time, she wanted paying customers to be fully acknowledged, writing to Smith that she "was much angered to find Mr. Birney credited for $1 instead of $2—It will be rectified this week."[122] "Industrious and vigelent," as Douglass described her, she worked toward ensuring that the paper sustained itself through subscribers. Success in that direction attracted investors.

The primary investor was, of course, Smith. When Smith had approached Douglass with the plan to merge the Liberty Party's paper with Douglass's, he had offered to subsidize the new endeavor with monthly donations for two years. Smith had also contributed enough at the outset to allow Douglass to purchase a new press and type, which cut down on the cost of hiring an outside printer, a necessity after his first printing press proved inadequate.[123] As business manager of the paper and someone sympathetic to political abolition herself, Griffiths found in Smith a powerful ally in lending the paper credibility as she courted a new base of customers and in floating the paper through fallow seasons.

From the outset, Griffiths did not hesitate to use Smith's influence to extend the paper's circulation. Douglass intended to keep Smith's financial interest in the paper quiet for a time, worried that his enemies would accuse him of allowing Smith to purchase his ideological development; but Griffiths worked around her friend and asked Smith to endorse the paper openly. "Would not a word from *you* prove useful?" she suggested, believing that an item from him would bring back those dubious Liberty Party subscribers.[124] Smith agreed, hoping, "My commendation of 'Fred Douglass Paper' in that Letter will do more good than an article from my pen in his Paper."[125] He also issued a circular promoting the paper, and Griffiths sent copies to England with a visiting friend in order to increase subscribers among Smith's British admirers.[126]

She and Smith also negotiated his contributions to the paper, much as a fund-raiser might with a donor or a chief financial officer with shareholders. Their correspondence revealed both this relationship and the condition of the paper. "We have promises and good wishes from many quarters, but *very little money* has come in," she wrote to him two months into the new paper's run. The shortfall meant that she required "pecuniary aid to meet the incoming bills."[127] Two hundred dollars would meet their needs at that time, she assured. In November, she again asked for a specific sum, but assured Smith, "we only owe $100 for paper." She again asked for another $100 in February 1852, another in May, and another later in the year.[128] Between mid-1851 and mid-1852, Smith gave upward of $1000 toward the maintenance of the paper at Griffiths's request. Douglass, for his part, initially seemed slightly embarrassed by her boldness. After the first advance, just as *Frederick Douglass' Paper* began publication, he apologized to Smith because "although the money is needed I regret that you should have been called upon this early" and that Griffiths had "acted in the matter without consulting me."[129] Douglass, aggressive in writing and on stage, had not yet translated that audacity into his business, while Griffiths took these matters into her own hands. He apologized for their need, but did not apologize for Griffiths again.

Griffiths did not ask for these additional sums as new donations. Instead, she considered them advances on Smith's promised monthly contributions. "I should not have presumed to ask," she explained to him in an early appeal of July 1851, "but the urgency of the case was great; and the business is *far* better serviceable *now* than it would be in three or four months time."[130] Again in August, she noted that Smith had "kindly advanced three hundred dollars"; and, although she was "ashamed to ask for more," she again did "not hesitate to say that two hundred dollars, at this time, would prove far more serviceable than by & bye."[131] At another point, she described Smith as having "kindly proposed to give in the year in *six months*" a sum of $600, which he also had paid to her early. These pleas had as much to do with the unsynchronized cycles of debits and credits to the paper accounts as they did with the overall income, or lack thereof, for the paper. She hoped to keep these "paid up pretty closely" and, presumably, paid off in full in time.[132] Subscribers, on the other hand, proved consistently inconsistent, with payments fluctuating from month to month in conjunction with the agricultural cycle. As Griffiths assured him in August, "After harvest the money always comes in more freely."[133] Thus, with bills due every month, but payments arriving sporadically, advances from Smith allowed her to make up the shortfall in the leaner months and to avoid an accumulation of interest.

Griffiths also hastened to note that her requests had become less necessary over time. In December 1851, six months into the run of *Douglass' Paper* and after crops came in, she made no request and wrote, "Financially dear Sir we are doing pretty well, your last kind favor remains untouched."[134] Even as she asked for the February 1852 "munificent donation," she noted, "It is three months, my dear Sir, since I sent my last petition on the subject: which is, I trust, a strong evidence that our incomings have greatly increased since the new Paper was started."[135] Smith and Griffiths in tandem, then, served the function that the WNYAS's committee had hoped to meet for the *North Star* or that the AAS did for the *National Anti-Slavery Standard* or, more aptly, the *Liberator*.

Still, subscriptions and Smith's donations in 1851 and 1852 could not sustain the paper. At one point, Griffiths experimented with raising a "sustention" fund from their wealthiest subscribers, but the most effective methods appeared to be those already established by Maria Weston Chapman, particularly the annual antislavery fair. Unfortunately, the Western New York Anti-Slavery Society fair's receipts indicated diminishing returns. In the February 1, 1850, issue of the *North Star*, Douglass had praised the fair's "few devoted friends in this city," who had "been laboring industriously to make it a successful effort," but ultimately proclaimed the fair "a failure." "A large part" of the two hundred dollars realized by the fair, he noted, "will be consumed in defraying the expenses attendant upon holding it." Just below this item, in implicit contrast, he reported the "three thousand three hundred dollars" raised by the Boston fair.[136]

His evaluation naturally hurt Amy Post, the organizer of the fair. Although it pained her to do so, she took public issue in "so discouraging an account" of the Rochester fair, a sentiment echoed in private by her friend, Elizabeth McClintock of Waterloo, who, with her mother, felt that "Douglass has not spoken of it exactly as he should have done." Both the McClintocks and Post granted that the fair did not raise quite the desired amount. Still, Post declared, "we would not dispise even the sum of one hundred dollars, but rejoice to have it to add to other hundreds that have been raised and used in the cause in the past year." She also pointed to the symbolic success of having "one hundred people, of all classes and colours sat down to one table, and the most perfect decorum and order prevailed." Even as she conceded that "this is a poor market," she did not appreciate the unfavorable report because "it is very bad policy for a person to destroy the influence and character of his friends at home." In other words, a poor notice by Douglass about the fair insulted those already working for his benefit and discouraged future support. Douglass understood her argument and replied that he had intended "to give credit to our few Dear friends who have labored faithfully to make the fair successful."[137] By giving an unsatisfactory review, however, he had also hoped "to do justice to the absent by making them know the truth with respect to the result."[138] Shaming "the absent," Douglass argued, might nudge them to attend future fairs.

Griffiths, however, identified a more profound problem that had plagued Post since 1848. Post supported Douglass, but she ultimately worked for an affiliate of the Garrisonian AAS. In central and Western New York, Liberty Party advocates outnumbered Garrisonians. Attempts by the two factions to work together had waxed and waned over the years, and many had abandoned the Western New York Society. As a result, its fair did not have a large base of support. The bulk of the smaller profits went to the American Society, and Douglass's paper received only modest donations. Griffiths attempted to circumvent the problem by planning a separate fair for the sole benefit of the paper, hoping to attract a cross-section of abolitionists united in their admiration of Douglass.

When she contacted women in existing antislavery networks to implement this plan, however, she discovered its limits. Mary Springstead, who organized contributions from Cazenovia, New York, wrote to Post in confusion when she received requests from both Griffiths and Post. Uncertain as to whether Griffiths had formed a competing organization, Springstead explained that she did "not feel able to work for both societies, providing there be two." The problem was not so much ideological as practical. "There are but few who contribute any thing toward helping *me* in this effort," she protested.[139] A year later, when Douglass's drift toward political abolition began alienating the predominantly Garrisonian Western New York Society, Griffiths changed tactics.

"I am just forming an anti-Slavery sewing circle here [in Rochester]," she informed Smith. "It will, I trust be influential, permanent, & efficient."[140] Douglass, too, let Smith know that "a Female Antislavery Society has been formed in Rochester from which I am expecting much aid."[141] If Griffiths could not rely entirely on the WNYAS, whose fair in any case was not producing the desired monetary results, and if the AAS and its networks presented more impediments than assistance toward her ends, then she would have to create a new society more sympathetic to her purpose. Jesting that "I am no 'woman's rights'" and in spite of not being "a public speaker," she "managed in a *pallor* to talk myself hoarse *on slavery* & antislavery" and thereby tap into a group of abolitionists lying dormant in the city.[142]

William C. Nell, back in Boston since July 1849, criticized the women of the new Rochester Ladies' Anti-Slavery Society and Sewing Circle for having been "Griffithised."[143] He implied that, like the Englishwomen so handily dismissed by John Estlin and Richard Webb, the new society's members were easily manipulated because they had no informed convictions about antislavery. Nell underestimated the group to whom Griffiths appealed. The women who joined the society brought with them a wealth of reform and organizing experience from their days as members of the defunct Female Anti-Slavery Society, the Rochester Orphan Asylum Association, the Rochester Female Charitable Society, and the Home for Friendless and Virtuous Females. Some had even

Figure 4.3 No known image of Julia Griffiths exists, but she attended the Fugitive Slave Law Convention in Cazenovia, New York, where Ezra Greenleaf Weld, brother to abolitionist Theodore Weld, took this daguerreotype. The identified women pictured include the Edmonson sisters, who had escaped from slavery. They stand on either side of Gerrit Smith, who appears at center with an upraised arm. Secretary Anne V. Adams sits at the table to the right of Douglass. Other women at the meeting included Angelina Grimké Weld, Mary Springstead, Caroline Brown, Mrs. F. Rice, Phebe Hathaway, and Louisa Burnett. "Fugitive Slave Law Convention, Cazenovia, New York," August 22, 1850, Ezra Greenleaf Weld, Daguerreotype, 1/6 plate image, J. Paul Getty Museum.

belonged to the Western New York Anti-Slavery Society before the Garrisonian hostility toward churches pushed them away.[144] Many, such as Maria and Susan Porter, had husbands, fathers, or brothers who were Liberty Party members, which put them on the outskirts of Garrisonian reformers. The Liberty Party, however, with its focus on electoral politics, did not try to mobilize women as vigorously as the Garrisonians had.[145] Others had an equal interest in helping Douglass without having to choose between the Liberty Party and the AAS. Still others liked that the direct, organizational support of fugitives was a key activity of their work. The new society provided them all with independent ideological space in which to oppose slavery.

The Rochester Ladies' Society officially claimed nonpartisan autonomy, refusing to position itself as ancillary to the American Antislavery Society, the Liberty Party, or the American and Foreign Antislavery Society. In the first report, it announced that its sole purpose was "the diffusion of Anti-Slavery Sentiments by means of the Press and the Lecturer; to the relief of the suffering Fugitive, and for such other Anti-Slavery objects as may present themselves."[146] As models, they looked to the societies in "Dublin, Belfast, and Cincinnati," which, despite considering themselves essentially Garrisonian, had "taken their stand on 'independent ground, and are prepared to welcome straightforward anti-slavery advocacy, without reference to its coming from Garrisonian or Liberty Party.'"[147] Indeed, throughout the ten years of their existence, their greatest aid went to former slaves who fled to Canada in growing numbers after 1850, paying for railroad tickets, clothing, the occasional night of lodging, and even funeral expenses.[148]

Despite this insistence on neutrality, however, the very language of the Rochester Ladies' constitution placed them in direct opposition to one of the central tenets of Garrisonian abolition. "The national Constitution was adopted by the *people* of the United States to establish *Justice*, provide for the *common Defense*, insure *Domestic Tranquility*, and secure to themselves and posterity the blessing *Liberty*," they argued, and "the perpetuity of Slavery in these United States, depriving one portion of the people of the inestimable blessings of Liberty, is a gross violation of Justice, and greatly endangers the Domestic Tranquility." They would "do what we may that Slavery may be abolished, and that the blessing of Liberty may be secured to all the people of this favored land," but accepted the US Constitution as a tool for ending slavery rather than an instrument condoning slavery.[149] Furthermore, they consistently and, with few exceptions, solely supported *Frederick Douglass' Paper*, which hard-line Garrisonians deemed an anathema. While Griffiths insisted that "Bigotry precludes many of the *old* friends from joining us,"[150] in the minds of the leadership of those most closely aligned with Garrisonianism, the Rochester Ladies' Anti-Slavery and Sewing Circle had delineated themselves as false abolitionists. Amy Post, whom Griffiths hoped would bring her considerable expertise and connections to the new society, chose not to join.

Perhaps to Post's chagrin, Griffiths's organization proved much more effective at fundraising. Post had always lamented that her city proved "a poor market" because of its smaller size and competition from the fundraising efforts of the Syracuse abolitionists, led by the Reverend Jermain Loguen and his wife Caroline, to aid fugitive slaves.[151] Rochester fairs never brought in the thousands of dollars that Douglass had reported of the Boston fair in 1851, but the Rochester Ladies' Circle realized more than the $200 that the Western New York Society's, under Post's direction, had raised that same year. The proceeds of the Rochester Ladies' Circle steadily increased from $408.00 in 1852 to $565.00 in 1855. During those years, they donated a yearly average of $282.03 to *Frederick Douglass' Paper*. The success of the fairs drew on many sources, including the items made by the women of Western and Central New York Anti-Slavery Societies, the donated refreshments, the various speakers, and the *Autographs for Freedom* gift book edited by Griffiths and Anna M. C. Barnes, modeled on Chapman's *Liberty Bell*.[152] Still, through her overseas connections, Griffiths herself was probably responsible for the most profitable contribution. As she later observed to Barnes, "it is invariably the case that people like to purchase articles sent from a distance—& made in *foreign lands*."[153] At the 1852 Rochester Ladies' fair, "foreign goods" brought in $144.02. By 1855, English and Irish goods provided over half of the profits from the fair, being sold for a total of $365.39. Griffiths provided the crucial link between Western New York and donors overseas.[154]

Even Griffiths's critics noted the fair's success. Nell, who remained within the Garrisonian fold as Douglass drifted away, seemed both irritated and astonished at Griffiths's fundraising abilities. Reiterating the old complaint about Douglass's avarice, he wrote to Amy Post that he had "no doubt that F.D. with J.G.s—*contingent* and other Friends will make money by his present position."[155] That is, they would personally profit rather than use the proceeds to support the abolitionist cause. He mourned that "the tired and faithful band of Women" led by Post had been "so *outrageously* superceded by the disaffected."[156] "I never can get reconciled to it," he declared.[157] Although he insisted that he would not "wish to prevent it from doing what good it may," he also regretted "that such victories should perch upon such banners is hard to be endured."[158] Post probably agreed. In Rochester, a less radical and more pragmatic brand of antislavery prevailed, helped along by the figure of a charismatic former slave and the experience of a host of abolitionist women on both sides of the Atlantic, drawn together by Julia Griffiths. She had succeeded where Post continued to struggle.

Griffiths's success enabled Douglass's success. His continued touring indicated that the paper did not, as the suspicious among the American Society feared, make him wealthy; but wealth had never been the point. Ideological and financial independence, raising a black voice out of slavery to testify to an international audience, providing a forum for other black voices and training for young black men, proving the abilities of his race, and supporting his family had. His ability to continue these efforts rested on the survival of the paper, and its endurance through the decade formed the basis of his credibility and influence in subsequent decades. Julia Griffiths was the source of that endurance, which made her dangerous to those who felt betrayed by his defection. If the leadership of the AAS had hoped that the competition would end after the initial novelty of Douglass's venture wore off or after he drifted toward political abolition, then the survival of the paper dashed their hopes.

The survival of the paper did, in fact, afford Douglass ideological independence. As the Garrisonians suspected, need could also have driven some of his decisions. After all, if more support could come from the Liberty Party, then adopting their tactics might seem prudent. Yet, his change of heart came after the passage of the Fugitive Slave Act, which made ending slavery even more urgent. The Garrisonian moral revolution had not come, but slave-catchers had. Breaking their power by ending the institution might be a halfway measure, but to enslaved African Americans, it was everything. As Douglass wrote in 1855 in regard to the Garrisonian refusal to exercise the franchise, "to abstain from voting, was to refuse to exercise a legitimate and powerful means for abolition of slavery."[159] While he never warmed to churches as institutions of morality, he could not deny the morality of the abolitionists who attended them. Griffiths's influence on his intellectual development could not be denied, either. Coming as she did from a monarchical society still struggling with questions of equality but ultimately able to use Parliament's power to end slavery, she may have urged Douglass to recognize the powerful tools in his own hands. He could follow her example and that of the many white women who used their respectability and the privilege of their color to challenge racism by using his own rare privilege of suffrage to challenge slavery. Life in Western New York had broken him out of the tight circle of those closest to Garrison, where he had met different views of antislavery only in rigorous if not acrimonious debate, and allowed him to explore multiple means of obtaining the end of racism and slavery.

Whatever the causes, by 1853, Douglass's philosophy of abolition put him at odds with the most prominent Garrisonians. Fueled by feelings of personal betrayal, their debates became merciless. At one point, Douglass accused his former friends and partners Charles Remond and William Nell of being race traitors, while Nell questioned Douglass's ability to think for himself because he had refused to "shake off those evil elbow influences which have thus far so much controlled him."[160] For Nell and even Amy Post, Douglass's soul was at stake. For others, he was a viable competitor for publicity, funds, and ideological allegience. For everyone, Griffiths was key. A strike against Griffiths might undermine Douglass and eliminate her. An attack that excited racial and gender stereotypes and anxieties about amalgamation, even among abolitionists, and called into question his respectability could discredit Douglass entirely.

Garrison struck. The trollop in Douglass's office had seduced him away from his Garrisonian ideals, friends, and wife, and Douglass had proved too weak, unintelligent, and foolish to resist. So ran the implication in the pages of the *Liberator*. Garrison, however, made a misstep. By including the phrase, "caused much unhappiness in his own household," he had dragged Anna and the children into the fray and exposed the complicated inner workings of the Douglass family to public comment.[161]

5

"I Wont Have Her in My House," 1848–1858

"It is not true," Anna Douglass responded, "that the presence of a certain person in the office of Frederick Douglass causes unhappiness in his family." William Lloyd Garrison, to whom she addressed her letter, complied with her request to "please insert this in your next paper," but he doubted her sincerity, pointing out that the missive was "evasive in its language." He insisted, "It is not possible that Mrs. D. means deliberately to affirm, that there has been no unhappiness created in her family."[1] Susan B. Anthony and Amy Post also questioned Anna's authorship. Post, "who happened to call" at the Douglass home at "about the time it was being concocted by Frederic & Julia," told Anthony that Anna had declared that she "would *never* sign a paper that said, *Julia had not made her trouble.*" Indeed, according to Post and Anthony, Anna believed that Garrison was right about Julia's influence over Frederick and that it was "*Julia* who has made Frederic hate all his old friends." Anthony reported that Post had said that Anna had said, "I *don't* care anything about her [Griffiths] being in the *Office*—but I wont have her in my house." Anthony also swore to Garrison that "there are many, many of the friends here who stand ready to affirm to the truth of your statement."[2] Acting on this information, Garrison published a column reiterating that, despite being ancillary to his quarrel with Douglass, his accusation of improper relations between Frederick and Julia was "strictly true, and we could bring a score of unimpeachable witnesses in Rochester to prove it."[3]

For Douglass, the heart of the matter lay not simply in the content of Garrison's charges but in his line of attack. Garrison, thundered Douglass, "has seen fit to invade my household, despise the sacredness of my home, break through the just limits of public controversy, and has sought to blast me in the name of my family."[4] The alleged "unhappiness" in his household was a subject "wholly foreign to the present controversy" between himself and the Garrisonians, and he would "refuse to answer in this place, or in any public journal, unless required to do so by some proper and competent tribunal, known to the laws of the land."[5]

In freedom, Douglass had claimed, among others, the right to free association regardless of race or gender and the right to protect the integrity of his family. Slavery had denied him both in the South, and even in the North systemic racism called them into question.[6]

His exercise of both rights, however, did not always fit neatly together. His partner in defying the color line in 1849 had become, four years later, the "Jezebel" and "Delilah" whom his critics had charged with leading him into infidelity, ideologically and, by implication, otherwise. The gossips drew on white women's attraction to Douglass, the existing animosity toward Griffiths, archetypes of extramarital affairs, and stereotypes of oversexed black men to create a simplistic public narrative designed to discredit Douglass not only as an abolitionist but also as a respectable and moral man. Yet, Anna's terse precision, as Garrison detected, suggested that the rumors contained a grain of truth, even if they had not been reported with complexity or accuracy. Julia had not only catalyzed the breech between Douglass and the AAS leadership, but also triggered a more complicated dispute between Frederick and Anna that suggested the two had different understandings of their marriage and of Frederick's responsibilities as the head of their family.

In later decades, the Douglasses crafted an image of their history in which activism and family life were inseparable; and this image originated in Frederick's defense of the North Star. His decisions about the paper consistently took into consideration his family, because both the paper and his family constituted a broad struggle against racism. Conversely, any attack that threatened the circulation of the paper also threatened his home. Over a half-century later, the Douglass children told family stories in which all members participated in the paper's production with little separation of abolition and family life, and they often interpreted their mother's work in the home as implicitly activist. For instance, Frederick took his sons in as apprentices at the paper, an idea Rosetta insisted had originated with their mother. Both she and her brother Lewis depicted themselves as sacrificing a day of school each week in order to prepare and deliver the papers, while Anna ensured a special meal awaited them at the end of the day. The children also underscored their mother's aid to fugitive slaves and her labor in New Bedford and Lynn when the Douglass family still struggled in the working class.[7]

Yet, in depicting the family life after they moved to Rochester, they tended to de-emphasize anything that might connect the Douglasses with the working class, which usually meant hiding much about their mother's life. They mentioned neither her taking in boarders during their first years in Rochester nor the additions to the family, such as Harriet Bailey, who lived with them in Lynn as their aunt, or Charlotte Murray, their mother's sister. The "four other boys," African American children whom the Douglasses had "taken into our family," apprenticed in the office, and were mentioned in both Rosetta's and her brother Charles's memoirs, but this was to highlight their parents' personal contributions to racial uplift and their mother's maternal nature, not to describe the sort of extended family of the working class that required collective effort for survival. Whether these other occupants of the house did not impress themselves on the memory of young children or the children intentionally omitted them, Rosetta, Lewis, and Charles constructed an idealized domestic image of their home as a sanctuary and the nuclear family as collectively fighting oppression. Even Frederick hid the complexities of the household in his public depictions of himself. As Charles, the last survivor of the Douglass children, summarized in 1917, "We were a happy family in this work for the enslaved of our race." Although these stories were not strictly accurate, they reflected values that the Douglass parents had passed along to their children and suggested the ways that the Douglass family intended to be perceived.[8]

Perception became more important and more difficult as Frederick's celebrity grew, especially when the household behind the image proved more intricate. Anna and Frederick had aspired to self-reliance, upward mobility, the privacy of their own home, and a family, and their move to Rochester in 1848 brought them closer to that middle-class ideal than they probably could have imagined a mere decade earlier. Yet, their home often included a variety of occupants who might serve as weak points for critical intrusion. When Frederick's old allies scrutinized his progress, searching for ways to discredit him, and when other well-known people passing through town dropped in to see him, the whole Douglass family came under observation.

The Douglass home and its residents represented the tensions between the ideal of middle-class domestic privacy and the dangers of intrusion owing to the public nature of Frederick's work. Jane Marsh Parker, who had lived next door to the Douglasses as a child, remembered the house on Alexander Street, situated in a residential neighborhood on the east side of the city, as being "two-story brick, of about nine rooms, on a large lot about one hundred feet in width." If the building followed vernacular architectural trends of the 1830s and 1840s, a visitor would have entered through a front hall and proceeded into a formal parlor for guests. Beyond the parlor lay a dining room and, sometimes, a less formal sitting room used by the family and open to boarders or dinner guests. A kitchen with an open hearth or stove for cooking and perhaps a rough precursor to a mudroom lay at the back of the house, entered only by family, servants, and delivery men. The back yard served as a work area containing the water pump and privy, and sometimes a garden or livestock, such as chickens. Only family, servants, and overnight guests or boarders entered the bedrooms on the upper floors. According to Parker, Frederick appropriated one of the bedrooms for an office, insisting upon a separate space away from the public areas of the house in order to work at home. Overall, the floor plan progressed from formal rooms intended for public use to spaces reserved for family, servants, and people who were on more intimate terms with the household. In late autumn 1851, the Douglasses moved to a house at the end of South Street. Griffiths described the new location as lying "a mile & three quarters from the office—and quite out of the city," surrounded by "an acre of land." The bucolic setting, made more so by a neighboring nursery and the Mount Hope Cemetery, followed middle-class trends toward cultivating a romanticized natural setting for their homes amid the filth of industrialization and to further separate work life from home life. By moving to the new location, the Douglasses implicitly demanded greater privacy for their family, separating themselves from neighbors and discouraging visits by passersby, while exerting greater control over their public presentation.[9]

Figure 5.1 The house on Alexander Street in Rochester, photographed in the early twentieth century, is purported to have been the first owned by the Douglasses. They lived here from 1848 until 1851, when they moved to a larger home on South Street on the outskirts of the city. The home on South Street burned down in 1871, and the Alexander Street house did not survive the years after this photograph was taken. *Rochester Images*: "[Frederick Douglass home on Alexander Street]," c. 1920–1940? (e.g. rpf02425), Local History Division, Rochester Public Library.

Frederick and Anna had grown up in a world in which slaves and free domestics purloined moments of solitude from masters who constantly monitored their behavior. Their private world was, to some degree, abstract, a place into which they retreated mentally more often than physically. Frederick guarded his interior life, even when seeming to reveal himself before an audience, controlling the type and shape of the information he conveyed. Anna would not volunteer much about herself, and even Rosetta remembered her as reticent. She grounded herself in her home, her kitchen, and her own intensely personal sense of self. For both Douglasses, a physical private space, like marriage and family, signified their freedom, citizenship, upward mobility, and ability to protect themselves and their family.[10]

The reunion of the nuclear Douglass family might have strengthened this sense of privacy, family, and protection. Frederick had spent the first few months in Rochester alone, but early in 1848, Anna brought Lewis, Charles, and Frederick Jr., now seven, five, and three, respectively, to their new home. Eight-year-old Rosetta joined them from Albany in the spring, living with her parents for the first time in approximately three years.[11] A new baby, Annie, joined them in March 1849. Yet, the Douglass family expanded to include others not born into it. After Harriet Bailey married and departed the household, in November 1847, Charlotte Murray, Anna's younger sister, took her place, living there between 1850 and 1855.[12] William and Jeremiah Perkins, thirteen-year-old apprentices at the paper, also joined the household around the middle of the decade.[13] Although the Douglass children excluded most of these additions to the household in their later public reminiscences, the family appeared to absorb them as extended or "fictive" kin at the time.

Still, the household was not precisely an oasis of familial domesticity. By the end of 1849, as many as twelve people lived in the Douglasses' nine rooms, reflecting the intricate social relationships that Frederick had introduced through his work and creating more labor for Anna. William C. Nell, who left his position as the printer of Garrison's *Liberator* to help Douglass, may have been among them, although his fond memories of the Posts suggest that he instead stayed at their Sophia Street home. John Dick, the printer from London, moved into the house around the time the paper began production. Phebe Thayer, an abolitionist and cousin of Amy Post, served as governess to the Douglass children for about a year beginning in September 1848, and Nell hinted that Dick and Thayer had something of an attraction for one another during that time. The household swelled again with the addition of Julia and Eliza Griffiths after May 1849. While all these people lived in the Douglass home, they occupied a middle ground between the intimacy of the family and the world outside.[14]

That outside world increasingly came to the Douglasses' house, too. With perhaps a touch of exaggeration, Parker recalled that "we had only to watch

his front door to see many famous men and women." The visit of Swedish author Fredericka Bremer, accompanied by the poet Robert Lowell, particularly impressed her. Bremer herself wrote of the occasion in *Homes of the New
World: Impressions of America* (1853), in which she gushed over Frederick's
"light mulatto" complexion, "unusually handsome exterior," and "beautiful eyes
filled with a dark fire." She also heaped praise on a white governess, most likely
Julia Griffiths, whose fortitude allowed her to withstand the prejudice against a
white woman living in a black family. Griffiths, in turn, praised Bremer for her
willingness to visit the home of a black family. Publicity, especially for an international audience such as Bremer's, could only help Douglass's career and cause.[15]

Yet, with publicity came judgment. Until Julia Griffiths began receiving a
greater share of attention, Anna bore the brunt of prejudice from even the most
well-intentioned guests. Bremer, for instance, noted Anna's "good expression,"
but implicitly contrasted her "very dark, stout, and plain" appearance with her
husband's resemblance to "an Arab chief," adding that "his little daughter, Rosetta,
takes after her mother." If Anna could, as Parker observed, "read character with
marvelous accuracy" and, as Rosetta depicted, possessed a "large discernment
as to the character of those who came around her," she may have intuited these
slights. Rosetta remembered noticing that her mother "became more distrustful"
and felt a "rampant" racism and "lack of cordiality" in Rochester.[16] On the last
point, Rosetta's perceptions of her mother's experience were entwined with her
own. During their first two years in Rochester, Rosetta was barred from a private
girls' school, and then all black students in the city's schools learned that they
would have to attend the "colored school" held in a leaky church basement. Until
the school system was desegregated, the Douglasses hired Phebe Thayer, a relation of the Posts, to tutor the children at home.[17]

The presence of the governess in the house, though beneficial to Rosetta and
the growing boys, exposed Anna's illiteracy to critical eyes. Certainly, Rosetta
and Parker both felt they had to excuse Anna's inability to read to later generations when they penned reminiscences of her. Both offered the plausible imped-
iment of Anna's daily workload, noting that she did not have servants and took
on all of the household labor herself. Neither Lewis nor Charles mentioned their
mother's illiteracy at all, focusing instead on her domestic partnership with their
father. Nevertheless, these efforts seemed defensive. Anna had embraced a traditional role as helpmeet, but Frederick's rising profile as a self-made man and
the family's improving socioeconomic status placed certain middle-class expectations on Anna that she match her husband in all pursuits.[18]

Anna's illiteracy, however, had consequences for her family, especially for her
daughter. With Frederick away most of the time, someone had to read to Anna
and write her correspondence, to keep her connected to her husband and distant
friends or relations, such as Harriet Adams (formerly Bailey). More often than

not, Rosetta became that person, both because she was the eldest child and be-cause, as a daughter, her parents expected her to attend her mother. In that sense, too, Anna's inability to read served a function for her in relation to her husband and children. If she and Frederick intended to propel their offspring into a more secure socioeconomic class than the one in which they began, and if she did not or could not embrace many of the trappings of that class as her husband did, then she faced a future in which her children would become strangers to her. They were growing up in a world alien to her, in which they might be ashamed of her, and in which she might have little purpose. If she could not read, and if one of her family must always remain nearby, then her illiteracy served to bind her family to her and ensure they did not abandon her.

Anna exerted significant influence within her home in other ways, as well. She, like Frederick, had grown up in a slave society in which necessity made marriages more egalitarian, a situation that did not change when they moved into the black working class in freedom. Just as Frederick had depicted them shouldering their luggage equally after the wedding, their life together began on equal footing. Indeed, that he deferred to her wishes when she refused to move to England indefinitely—that he consulted her in the first place—indicated that this was more than a literary trope. Having provided funds to set up and main-tain their household, not to mention running it in Frederick's absences, Anna probably expected nothing less. In Rochester, the boarders fell within her do-mestic domain and were a way for her to earn income for the family, and she served in her husband's stead in the day-to-day operations of the household and its relations to the world while he continued to tour. Therefore, she had reason to exercise her prerogative. Rosetta indicated the extent to which Anna was, in fact, in charge in the household, when she characterized her father as "mother's hon-ored guest," for whom "homecomings were events worthy of extra notice, and caused renewed activity." Because middle-class conventions required a male-dominated household, however, Rosetta elided this usurpation of Frederick's role as head by interpreting her mother's command as antislavery activism, be-cause it freed her husband to devote all his time to abolition by "relieving him of the management of the home as it increased in size and in its appointments."[19]

Along those lines, Anna's role also seemed to include placing barriers between her home and the outside world. Marsh, from her perch next door, observed that Anna acted as "a wholesome check of her husband's proneness to being imposed upon." Frederick appeared to have used his home study as a place to write, read, and develop his ideas for speeches. If accurate, then Marsh's observation indi-cated that Anna played a part in this work by ensuring that he enjoyed solitude. This task encompassed not only outside visitors, but also children and boarders, requiring Anna to manage the use of space within the house, monitoring who was allowed into which rooms and negotiating with her guests and her husband.

This may have sometimes placed her at odds with Frederick, because many guests were deeply involved in his work, and she may have seen their presence as intruding upon his time with his family. As with Garrison, the sticking point proved to be Julia Griffiths. Griffiths complicated the family dynamic because she was saving the newspaper and therefore ensuring the means of the family's survival, but her lodging in their home made the Douglass family vunerable to attack.[20]

The problem began to develop in 1850, when Julia became a vested part of the paper as its business manager at the same time that the Douglass household lost several members. "Cupid sometimes acts capriciously," remarked Nell when he heard that John Dick's affections had turned from Phebe Thayer to Eliza Griffiths. Dick and Eliza married in June and moved to Philadelphia, leaving Julia the sole boarder. This vaguely improper arrangement did not escape notice. "Where is Miss 'Julia Griffiths?'" queried Betsey Mix Cowles, Abby Kelley Foster's protégé in Ohio, a sentiment echoed in Nell's wondering "if *Miss Julia Griffiths* will follow the footsteps of her illustrious predecessor and take to herself a Husband." By March 1851, John Estlin in England alluded to "injudiciousness" concerning Griffiths and Douglass, but his circumspection left Isabel Jennings to wonder if he referred to "anti-slavery matters or matters more nearly related to F. D." That same month, when the English abolitionist George Thompson passed through Rochester, he noticed "great uneasiness felt on account of the peculiar relationship of a certain English lady to a certain distinguished orator and editor of this city." Rochester had been the meeting place of spirits from the other world since the Fox sisters began hearing rappings in 1848, and even the supernatural world weighed in. "They replied that *the lady was in her right place*," joked Thompson to Anne Warren Weston. He and Weston, like Douglass and Griffiths themselves, granted no credibility to Spiritualism.[21]

That year, 1851, proved particularly tumultuous in other ways. Douglass began reconsidering his position on slavery and the Constitution, then merged the *North Star* with the Liberty Party paper, while Griffiths founded the Rochester Ladies' Anti-Slavery Society. Their association with wealthy philanthropist Gerrit Smith made them even more suspicious to the AAS leadership. Douglass suspected that he was "to be made a particular object of attack," and that "the war will be waged not against opinions but *motives*." Well aware that "insinuations have already been thrown out and will be again," he could not have ignored the reality that Griffiths would become part of them. Griffiths herself admitted that the new iteration of the paper "has thinned our subscription list considerably," making its immediate future uncertain.[22]

Enforcement of the Fugitive Slave Law also began that year, with consequences in Rochester. In September, while the Douglasses were still living on Alexander Street, three men appeared at the door. "They proved to

Figure 5.2 A depiction of the *North Star* office from later in the century showing the typesetting, press, and folding tables. "Frederick Douglass' old post office," c. 1893, Photomechanical reproduction, Picture file, Local History Division, Rochester Public Library.

be '*William Parker*' himself and two others engaged in the *Christiana affair*," Griffiths told Gerrit Smith, referring to an incident on the southern border of Pennsylvania in which Parker led a group in resisting the return of the other two men to slavery. The fugitives spent the next nine hours in the care of Anna while Griffiths and Jermain Loguen, an African Methodist Episcopal minister from Syracuse, secured them passage on an English ship bound for Canada. A few weeks later, on October 1, Loguen, now a target after participating in the rescue of Jerry Henry in Syracuse, followed them. Within a few days, an anonymous source wrote to warn Griffiths of plans to kidnap Douglass, who was attending out-of-town engagements at the time, and she persuaded the Porter family to raise a vigilance committee. Douglass was no longer legally a fugitive, but no African American felt safe, and anyone aiding freedom-seekers faced a federal fine and imprisonment. The entire Douglass household was at risk.[23]

The health of the household suffered, too. Sickness constantly plagued families as a matter of course in the nineteenth century, but the Douglasses seemed particularly affected in 1851. Julia informed Gerrit Smith that from June to August, "we have not had sickness out of the house for a single day." Both she and Frederick fell ill in September when William Parker arrived after the Christiana incident. Headaches popped up from time to time, and throat pain in particular plagued Frederick as a consequence of speaking to large audiences in an age without amplification. Julia, however, confessed to Smith that she was "inclined to believe that grievous anxiety for his paper has much to do with it."[24]

She became particularly alarmed by Frederick's mental state. In November, after two events in defiance of the Fugitive Slave Law, one threat directed at Douglass, in the midst of a household move, and facing the paper's continuing economic instability, Frederick returned from lecturing in Rhode Island exhausted and harried. Julia watched him for several days with growing concern that "the immense anxiety (pecuniary and family) is beginning to affect our dear friend Frederick's mind." She noticed his agitation as "he did not remain ten minutes in posture" one evening and "asked over and over again" about the state of the paper's finances after receiving a large bill. The next morning, she worried at his "strange" appearance, as well as an "unusually strange" letter he had composed to "a friend." She appealed "in a great agony of mind" to Gerrit and Ann Smith, frightened because Frederick "seemed to *lose his balance of mind*, & was not himself—to my thinking."[25]

Julia understood that many elements of Frederick's life contributed to his anxiety, but she placed some blame on his family. She had already hinted about "home trials," which she had discussed with the Smiths when she visited Peterboro earlier in the spring, and her concern about Frederick in November included her frustration that "none about the house noticed any thing especial" and that "the *quiet & repose* he *so much* needs are very difficult for him to attain in his domestic circle." Even after they moved to South Street, she worried that "Frederick's head is not equal to much noise:—and, indeed, his trials are *severe*." That "domestic circle," by this time, had shrunk to only the family and Julia, but the family included five growing children, aged thirteen, twelve, nine, seven, and three, and only Anna's sister, Charlotte, to help. In the nineteenth century, children were to be seen and not heard, but even on days when they were particularly well-behaved, the children could not help but make noise, and they may have expected some attention from their father when he returned from the office.[26]

The real "trials," however, most likely emerged in that space between the home and the workplace, where public and private merged and marital conflicts erupted. Julia occupied that space and, in the process, had assumed a caretaking role that transcended the division between Frederick's office and home. All day, she worked with him in at the paper, and in the evening they returned home, retreating into his study to share a writing table while working on speeches and editorials. They shared an intellectual companionship through their work, activism, and love of literature, which began with her first gift to him of books in 1847, but their camaraderie shut out the rest of the family. This intimacy slipped into a letter that Julia wrote to Amy Post while "sitting in the parlour" one evening in October 1851. "Frederick is rather merrily playing the violin & *singing*, by turns," she told Post, "which will show you that he is in good spirits." She paused her writing to ask Douglass if she should pass along his love. "*Decidedly*," he replied, "my *decided* love to Mr. & Mrs. Post." A moment later she informed Post that "Frederick has begun to *read aloud*—& is asking my opinion of what he reads—so, dear friend, I must say adieu, at once." In the nineteenth century, correspondents usually ended their letters by including the well-wishes of all in the room. In her note to Post, Griffiths offered Douglass's affection but made no mention of Anna, Charlotte, or any other inhabitant of the house. The tableau included only herself and Douglass.[27]

If Susan Anthony's account, in 1853, of Anna's reaction to the gossip about her husband and Julia was accurate, then the precision of Anna's objections about Julia—"'I *don't* care anything about her being in the *Office*—but I wont have her in my house'"—suggests Anna's opinions of this arrangement. To a certain extent, Anna tolerated Julia because Julia had been the salvation of the newspaper and all that it represented for the Douglasses and abolition, and she held the mortgage on their home until 1853. The family, therefore, owed quite a bit to the Englishwoman. Yet, as an intrinsic part of Frederick's work life who also lived in his home, Julia took him away from his family in the evenings when Anna could have reasonably expected his time to herself. Whereas Frederick and Anna had once ended their days together in the kitchen of their two rented rooms, presumably talking of their past, their future, their children, and the consequences of Frederick speaking against slavery, now Julia supplanted Anna for part of that time and in a separate space. If, in 1848, Frederick had in Anna "truly a helpmeet," after 1849, he had two.[28]

The bond between editor and assistant was not lost on others, who interpreted its meaning in ways most useful to themselves. As long as Julia and Frederick lived in the good graces of the Garrisonian faction, their friendship had proved useful in confronting fears of amalgamation. In the climate of what Samuel May called "antislavery warfare," however, they became notorious. The curiosity and "uneasiness" that began in late 1850 and early 1851 coincided not only with the departure of Eliza and John Dick but also with Julia's increasing success in stabilizing the *North Star*. Isabel Jennings inadvertently drew a line between the two when she followed her wariness of rumors spread by John Estlin by pointing out that Julia had "cleared off 700 dollars of debt from the North Star." Meanwhile, the local "uneasiness" reported by George Thompson in 1851 increased through the year as Frederick endorsed political abolition and merged his paper with that of the Liberty Party while Julia helped form the Rochester Ladies' Anti-Slavery Society.[29]

Attention shifted from Julia to the Douglass household in 1852. In March, Maria Weston Chapman insisted that Frederick "was never trustworthy" and should not be counted an abolitionist, especially because of "his disreputable connection with that wretched English woman who has brought so much trouble into his family & disgrace upon himself." Chapman had never before exhibited any interest in Douglass's family. Her sister, Anne Warren Weston, elaborated. "Much to the anger of Mrs. Douglass," she wrote, "Miss Griffiths persists in living in Douglass' family ruling all affairs, & of course *creating* great scandal of all sorts." She then painted what she believed to be a shocking portrait in which, "every morning his [Frederick's] chaise was brought to his door & he & Miss Griffiths got in & rode to his office 2 miles to the city of Rochester where they spent the day, returning to the house at night." Living in Boston, Weston herself did not witness any of these proceedings.[30]

Julia had noticed the strain felt by Frederick during these years, but Frederick also saw its effects on Julia. In February 1852, he thanked Ann Smith, Gerrit's wife, for visiting her. "Poor Julia," he wrote to Gerrit, "the sun light of a sympathizing face is as cordial was delighted." In September, Julia was contemplating "re-visiting England," partly for her health and partly to ensure donations for the fair; but she did so reluctantly as many signs "seem to indicate *this to be my post.*" Sarah Hallowell Willis, Amy Post's sister, noted that some seemed "to rejoice at Julia's removal greatly." By January, however, Julia had changed her mind. Willis suggested that Frederick had played a role in the decision when she wondered "if F. no longer 'behave[s]' so beautifully about it [Julia's leaving]?" Julia herself admitted to Smith, "I like my occupation exceedingly" in Rochester. Others mused about Anna's reaction. Like Weston, Willis suspected anger, wondering "how soon she [Anna] could send J[ulia] to Australia." Willis wished that Anna would "express some wholesome truths," and lamented that Anna would not be able to "control herself to do it properly." Not only was she familiar with Anna herself, but the "home trials" mentioned by Julia during the preceding years indicated a grain of truth in these suspicions.[31]

Instead of returning to England, Griffiths, in November 1852, moved out of the Douglass house and into the home of Maria Weddle. Like Griffiths, Weddle and her merchant husband, Thomas, were English, having immigrated fifteen years earlier. Also like Griffiths, she held office in the Rochester Ladies' Anti-Slavery Society. Weddle's seven children ranged in age from two to twenty-three, with a gap of a decade between the fifth and sixth. The oldest daughter and her three teenaged sisters, along with an Irish servant, could take care of household chores, and they probably helped prepare for fairs even if they were not also members of the antislavery society. The Weddles also lived closer to other members of the society and to downtown. As much as Griffiths liked Douglass's companionship, she lived in a world populated by other concerns and other people besides him, and her new residence proved more convenient for carrying out all aspects of her work and provided a familiar expatriate experience as well.[32]

If Griffiths had also calculated her move to silence the critics, she failed. As 1853 opened, Samuel Porter felt the need to inform Douglass that Rochester

was "full of scandalous reports" about the two. Douglass fumed. Until the accus-
ers "shall put those 'reports' into a definite shape—and present a responsible
person to back them," he retorted, "it will be time enough for me to attempt to
refute them." Still, in spite of himself, he did mount a defense. "When she was in
my family, I was necessarily much in her society, our walking and riding together
was natural," he explained. "Now we are separate and only meet at my office at
business hours and for business purposes." Lest Porter, or anyone else, imagine
shenanigans there, Douglass elaborated that "we are open to the observation of
my printers and to the public from ten o'clock or earlier in the morning until four
o'clock in the afternoon."[33]

His main argument, however, had little to do with either confirming or denying the purity of their behavior. "Miss Griffiths is a free woman," he pointed out,
and "I am a husband and a father and withal a citizen,—honorably, and to the
best of my ability, endeavoring to discharge the duties of this three fold relation."
He detected in the gossip a coercion similar to that directed at him by the anti-
abolitionists who had published "Niggers and Nastiness" and the crude wood-
cuts, or who had ejected him from dining rooms when he was in the company
of white women, including Griffiths. On those occasions, Douglass identified
"the American chimera called 'public opinion'" as the main culprit in the violation of his claim to "all the rights, privileges and dignity, which belong to human
nature." The Rochester rumors contained the same message of social control
by judging his civil rights to be less important than the sensibilities of society.
"Individuals have rights not less than Society," he explained to Porter. "I am as
little disposed to admit any unjust claims which any individual may set up in the
name of Society." In other words, for Douglass, the controversy lay not in behavior but in the right to privacy and free association.[34]

Therein lay the difficulty. Porter himself may not have actually suspected
Douglass and Griffiths of anything indecent. He, the women in his family who
worked with Griffiths in the Rochester Ladies' Society, and the Posts were all
deeply religious and middle class and would therefore not have continued to
associate with Douglass or Griffiths if they had suspected anything immoral
going on between them. Instead, the appearance of impropriety and its threat
to the antislavery movement concerned Porter. After Weston had detailed the
daily routine of Douglass and Griffiths, she insisted that "all *this*, apart from everything else, injures the cause in Rochester & alienates a class of the people."
Precisely because part of the abolitionists' legitimacy lay in their status as morally upstanding members of the middle class, they wanted to protect the recti-
tude of the antislavery image, rather than provide ammunition for their worst
opponents.[35]

This same reasoning may have contributed to the "home trials" of the
Douglasses, as well. Although Anna and Frederick probably had a far more

egalitarian marriage than either might have liked to let on, they projected the image of an irreproachable, upstanding family, with Frederick as the entrepreneur and breadwinner, Anna the frugal housewife, and the children attending school, learning trades, and entering college. Even those absorbed into the family embarked on this path as Charlotte Murray prepared for vocational school in 1854, and William and Jeremiah entered apprenticeships at the paper. Jane Marsh, their Alexander Street neighbor, believed that "the children were raised to self-helpfulness and systematic industry." She knew firsthand that Anna "had severe notions of the proprieties and duties of life" and "disapproved, decidedly, of the idle, pleasure-taking ways of the other little girls in the neighborhood, and she did not hesitate to correct their lapses in good manners." Rosetta knew even better, remembering that her parents "were rigid as to the matter of obedience," a hallmark of nineteenth-century, middle-class childrearing.[36]

Julia's presence in the home and her friendship with Frederick, however, called the decorum of the Douglass household into question. Only three years earlier, in 1850, the disintegration of William Wells Brown's marriage, which had involved accusations of abuse and infidelity, had played out in the pages of abolitionist newspapers. The Douglasses would not have wanted yet another domestic dispute in a black family to be used against their race. Nevertheless, Frederick continued to insist on maintaining his association with Julia because he seemed to genuinely enjoy her company and to value her contributions. Opposition to her presence seemed to make him more determined to assert his freedom of association, much as he had argued for the necessity of transgressing racial segregation. When she moved out of the house, he framed the departure as her choice, explaining that she "of her own free will preferred to live with another family," rather than as a concession to pressure.[37]

Anna probably saw the situation differently. As a wife and mother, the task of upholding the morality of their home fell to her, and she likely felt entitled to deference on the matter, particularly since it involved the perception of the family. Frederick had already indicated that he expected not only the appearance of a male-dominated family but also the reality. His reaction to Harriet Bailey's engagement in 1846, for instance, suggested that he saw himself as a benevolent patriarch. Her decision not to consult him had left him perplexed— he accused her of "not treating me as a sister ought to treat a brother"—and culminated in his ejecting her from the house. The 1855 revision of Narrative eliminated the description of the marriage as one that he and Anna had entered into as equals. Anna, however, indicated that she had not followed him entirely down this path of a strictly patriarchal family and used the power she accumulated in the marriage to assert her own expectations of her husband. In 1857, Frederick described his returns from touring in somewhat different terms than his daughter had. He observed that, despite Anna's many physical ailments, "she still seems able to use with great ease and fluency her powers of speech," and she turned these powers on him. "Before I am at home a week or two longer," he complained, "I shall have pretty fully learned in how many points there is need of improvement in my temper and disposition as a husband, and father, the head of a family!" In private, Anna had no problem challenging Frederick's authority when he had performed his role poorly by her standards; such confrontations indicated that the Douglasses negotiated, and sometimes fought over, the terms of their marriage. By 1852, Julia was one of those terms. For Anna, Frederick's pursuit of his freedom to associate with white women threatened the family and their marriage both in image and practice, making them vulnerable in ways that they could ill afford.[38]

The crisis came in August 1853 with a particularly bitter confrontation between Douglass on the one hand, and Garrison, William Nell, Robert Purvis, and Charles Remond on the other. Hostility escalated through the autumn, focusing predominantly on Douglass's acceptance of political abolition, and nearly a decade of suppressed frustration on both sides intensified the vehemence to a degree that perplexed the readers of the *Liberator* and *Frederick Douglass' Paper*. Unwilling to credit Douglass with sincerity or independence and hoping to discredit him even among his supporters, the Garrisonians targeted Griffiths as the nefarious source of his ideological apostasy. In September, the *National Anti-Slavery Standard*, now edited by Oliver Johnson, referred to her as a "Jezebel," a loaded term connoting religious and sexual infidelity that was not lost on readers. Like Thomas Smyth's innuendo about Douglass in the Manchester brothel, as well as other anti-abolitionists since, Johnson fanned anxieties about interracial sex, the allegedly insatiable sexual appetites of black men, and the immorality of a key abolitionist figure, in order to render him politically impotent. In November, purporting to explain Douglass's animosity toward his former allies, Garrison took the imagery further, portraying Douglass as Sampson resting his head in Delilah's lap, a euphemism meant to lead his readers to infer that Douglass and Griffiths were having sex, presumably under the same roof as Douglass's wife, children, sister-in-law, and the young newspaper apprentices who lived with them. Yet, despite Susan B. Anthony's insistence that "many of the friends" in Rochester "stand ready to affirm the truth" of Garrison's charges, no one came forward with evidence, nor could they bring themselves to detail the shocking arrangement even in their personal correspondence. Lucy Colman, for instance, visiting Boston from Rochester, encountered Anthony's rumors. She immediately informed Amy Post that she had heard "something of F Douglass too *Devilish*, for me to write," and promised to tell the whole "*fiendish art*" to Post in person.[39]

Because Garrison had expanded the scope of his attack to the family, readers probably wondered about Anna's reaction; and someone in the Douglass household seemed to believe that the situation called for a public statement from her. According to Anthony, Frederick and Julia "concocted" Anna's letter to Garrison, then coerced her signature. By Amy Post's report, Anna "would not sign a paper that said, *Julia had not made her trouble.*" The letter that appeared over the name "Mrs. Douglass" was, as Garrison commented, "evasive in its language," referring to "a certain person in the office" instead of in the home of Frederick Douglass. Furthermore, Garrison's observation of misery in the home "had reference to the past," while Anna's letter was written in present tense. Both Garrison and Anthony skirted around the issue of Anna's agency, limited though it was; but, whatever her resistance, she took care to sign a document that adhered to a verifiable version of events. She probably did object to Julia living in the Douglass home. Yet, at the time of the incident, Julia no longer lived there. Julia, therefore, no longer served as a source of discord in the home. Her work in Frederick's office, on the other hand, lay outside of Anna's purview and was not her problem, or not entirely.[40]

Jane Marsh Parker remembered Anna as a woman whose "greatest discontent was when his [Frederick's] admirers persisted in dragging her into notice," and every action of her life indicated that she did not seek attention.[41] Jane Swisshelm, editor of the antislavery Pittsburgh *Saturday Visiter* seemed to be one of the few people who could sympathize with Anna's position in that regard. "How can any man," she demanded, "professing to know anything of the common courtesies of life, dare drag a woman before the public as the enemy of her own husband, and persist in holding her in such position, despite her protest?" Harriet Beecher Stowe also scolded Garrison for his "unfortunate" and "unjustifiable" focus on the Douglass family. Both women implicitly absolved Frederick of any responsibility in the controversy, and Frederick himself considered the inner workings of his home, his marriage, and his friendships a matter "wholly foreign to the present controversy." For Swisshelm, Stowe, and Frederick, the guilty parties were Garrison and the gossips who supported him. They had turned the Douglass family into a public spectacle and used social pressure to dictate a black man's relationships. Anna, on the other hand, could point to culprits on all sides. Garrison had thrust her into public view, but Julia and Frederick had created the conditions that exposed her family and herself to unwelcome outsiders, and they continued to do so even when warned about rumors.[42]

Whereas Julia acted as a companion for Frederick, for Anna, she was probably little more than a boarder. While Anna may not have liked her, she seemed to do her best to hide that fact from the Englishwoman, who in later years remembered Anna without malice.[43] Instead, the main quarrel appeared to lie between Anna and her husband. He, as head of the household, had brought in a guest, spent time with that guest, called public attention to the family through his behavior with that guest, and then requested that she agree to the publication of a letter in which she denied the speculation about her family because of that guest. If she had become used to commanding the household in his absence, then Frederick had challenged that command and done so in a way that she could have interpreted as abdicating his responsibility of protecting the family. If that sense, Frederick had betrayed Anna not sexually but over the terms of their marriage.

Anthony's version of Anna's denial, although self-serving, suggested another element of the struggle between the Douglasses. Anna had allegedly insisted to Post that "*Garrison is right—it is Julia* who has made Frederic hate all his old friends." With her husband, Anna had learned of antislavery "principles, measures, and spirit" through the *Liberator*. Over the next decade, however, her husband's travels had exposed him to multiple strategies, leading him toward methods that were anathema to the American Antislavery Society. Anna, on the other hand, lived her daily life among Garrisonians. She and her sister, Charlotte, remained friends with Nell and Harriet and John Jacobs, and Anthony indicated that Anna and Amy Post shared confidences to some degree. The only evidence of Anna's direct participation in abolitionist organizations placed her at meetings of the Lynn Ladies' Anti-Slavery Society and of the "Ladies of the Western New York Antislavery Society" held at her Alexander Street house, both Garrisonian groups. As a whole, black women in Massachusetts, where she had first encountered abolition, gravitated toward Garrisonianism because its methods empowered those who could not vote and who had strength only in moral force and numbers. Anna, then, may well have remained a Garrisonian.[44]

Furthermore, much of Douglass's ideological evolution began after Julia's arrival. The gossip that Frederick and Julia excited could have made Anna more hostile to anything connected to Julia, including her brand of antislavery ideology or her antislavery organization, which had so diminished that of Anna's friend, Amy Post. Her absence from any abolitionist activities in Rochester, which her children elided by portraying her as "one of the first agents on the Underground Railroad," might be explained by the work of maintaining a large household far from the centers of that activity in Rochester, while raising five children of her own as well as two others. Yet, if she had Garrisonian sympathies, then she would have had little desire to join the Rochester Ladies' Society; neither could she openly defy her husband by joining the Western New York Society. As Frederick's fame grew, to receive the endorsement of his wife might have been a coup for either society, but she denied both. Nor did she become involved in the small black community of Rochester. Keeping a model home and raising successful children remained her realm, contribution, and statement.[45]

Furor over Frederick and Julia subsided for a time in 1854. In February and March, Julia joined Gerrit Smith, now a congressman, in Washington, DC, reporting her observations of the nation's capital for *Frederick Douglass' Paper*. In June, she traveled to Canada West, bringing aid to former slave Emily Edmonson for black expatriates suffering from famine. Yet, speculation did not entirely disappear. From Boston, Nell observed that "there are enough disaffected ones who speak freely" about the Douglasses' home life. Although he swore that he himself "seldom say much," he had no problem repeating stories that depicted "Mrs. D as being unhappy," something "a great many people thus believe," and passing along "certain *facts*" that he had heard from Post. Nell, very much hurt by Douglass's attacks, still sympathized with his old friend by adding, "I am of the opinion that *Mr* D is not very happy." The "disaffected" did not, however, interfere with the success of the Rochester Ladies' annual fair, its ability to attract speakers, or Julia's success in soliciting donations for the paper's sustention. Nell found himself marveling at the "magic and potency" that "seems embodied in J. G." and her victories in organizing abolitionists in the region.[46]

Then, around 1854, the Weddles moved away from Rochester, leaving Griffiths without a home. With plans to return to England the following summer, she moved back to the Douglass house in the interim. Amy Post, who generally avoided confrontation, intervened to forestall another controversy. She described the encounter to her cousin, Sarah Thayer, and Thayer's reaction indicated that neither Douglass appreciated Post's concern any more than Frederick had Samuel Porter's two years earlier. "*Never* was I so much astonished at such a return for such unbounded exertion for his interest and happiness," Thayer exclaimed. "*Anna* I was not at all surprised at her conduct as she is so impetuous," she declared, but as for Frederick, his "friendship has thus turned to such base impudence." The racism that Frederick had detected among Garrisonians and that Anna had experienced in Rochester emerged, too, not only in Thayer's characterization of Anna as an angry black woman but also in her interpretation of Frederick as arrogant. Thayer declared, "I am ashamed that he is a colored man—I wish he could be *colored white*, and then let him act the *Nabob* if he wishes," and confessed that, "I could but exclaim aloud when I read your encounter and the result but dare not say a word as I knew the reply would be 'that is the Nigger of it.'"[47]

Post did not necessarily share all Thayer's opinions, but Thayer's vehemence indicated that Frederick and Anna's response had wounded Post. Over the years, the Posts, Frederick, and Griffiths had disagreed over many subjects connected to religion and antislavery. Neither Frederick nor Julia took the Posts' Spiritualism seriously. Frederick had called the one séance he attended "silly" and so offended Isaac Post, a Spiritualist medium, that Douglass later apologized for his disrespect. Amy Post refused to join the Rochester Ladies' Anti-Slavery Society, only to watch it become more successful than her own. Then, he had abandoned the Western New York Anti-Slavery Society, which had supported him in his early years owing to her influence, and pursued an abolitionist strategy with which she could not agree. In the process, he had insulted her friend, William Nell.

All along, they had tried to agree that "we are all subjects—parts of a great *whole*—in the hands of a Supreme power—and you and I have decided that that power is *Good.*" After having brought her concerns about Griffiths's return to the Douglass house and receiving a rebuff from both Douglasses, Post very well may have concluded with Thayer that "if they can live happy upon such promises, let them have it, the Lord keeps us from the like." Post kept her distance from the couple for the next five years.[48]

Griffiths's return to England on June 16, 1855, continued her transatlantic activism and writing career. Carrying the proof sheets for Douglass's revised autobiography, *My Bondage and My Freedom*, she went in search of a printer in Scotland or England. Then, she planned to travel about the country to raise funds for Douglass's paper and the Rochester Ladies' Anti-Slavery Society. Throughout, she dispatched "Letters from the Old World," a column of travelogues and antislavery reports for *Frederick Douglass' Paper*. Arriving in Liverpool on a "dreary and dismal" July 14, she journeyed to London, where she turned down an invitation to visit Paris with a friend in order to pursue her real business in England.[49]

She began her work by reconnecting with old associates and cultivating influential new ones, starting with the publishers William and Mary Howitt. She also met with Anthony Ashley-Cooper, Seventh Earl of Shaftesbury, Richard Cobden, and John Bright, important reformers and parliamentarians whom Douglass had impressed nearly a decade earlier. She received an invitation to sit in the Ladies' Gallery in the House of Commons, where she noted the heavy brass grating separating the "*elevated*" gallery from the floor that "spoke as plainly as gratings ever did speak, that by great favor alone were the ladies admitted to that hallowed sanctuary." Later, she met with the reverends Thomas Binney and John Campbell, the latter of whom had helped raise funds to bring Anna Douglass and the children to England in 1846 when Frederick's return to America might have sent him back into slavery. Campbell also edited the *British Banner*, a pro-abolitionist journal, and when Griffiths learned that "he always looks over every column of every number of *Frederick Douglass Paper*," she prevailed on him to publish *My Bondage and My Freedom*. She rounded out her visit by calling on Americans visiting England, such as Elihu Burritt and Samuel Ringgold Ward, who in turn had recommended the Earl of Shaftesbury as "*the English Gerrit Smith.*" Thus began the work of strengthening non-Garrisonian antislavery sympathies and networks within England, and she did this with people who had access to both the press and halls of political power.[50]

Griffiths's efforts continued as she traveled north to Scotland. She stayed with the Sturgeses, who had hosted Douglass years earlier when he was in Birmingham. She then traveled on to Leicester, Nottingham, Derby, and Manchester through August and September, finally arriving in Glasgow at the end of the month, only to be felled by the influenza after "two hours of earnest conversation with the Ladies' Anti-Slavery Society, on the 4th inst., in a very damp atmosphere." The Garrisonian network, meanwhile, buzzed with distress. Mary Estlin painted a picture of doom, with the Carpenters in Newcastle organizing fairs to support the Rochester society, Douglass sympathizers in Glasgow circulating his speeches, Maria Webb "propping up Douglass & undermining the faithful" in Dublin, and even George Thompson favorably reviewing the American edition of *My Bondage and My Freedom*, published in August. Estlin lamented that "the Cause here never was so destitute of watchers or so much in need of them." Once Griffiths had arrived in England, "thrusting F.D. & herself on true as well as superficial abolitionists," she would "sweep over the field paving the way for F.D.s triumphant reception next year if he follows the sale of his book by a visit to Gr. Britain." Parker Pillsbury, a noted Garrisonian on tour in Scotland for the American Anti-Slavery Society, chafed at the positive advance publicity that Douglass's autobiography received in the British press and at Griffiths's access to both that press and the influential members of the British and Foreign Anti-Slavery Society. Worried about the "mischief which that bad woman might accomplish" amid the forces who already supported Douglass, Samuel May urged the American Anti-Slavery Society to keep Pillsbury abroad to watch over Griffiths. Although Pillsbury had planned to return to America before winter, he readily complied.[51]

As she had in Rochester, Griffiths tapped into a particular antislavery sentiment among people who did not understand the infighting of the American antislavery activists, felt uncomfortable with the Garrisonians' stand against religious organizations, and found compelling reasons to support both a former slave turned editor and the Rochester Ladies' Society's mission to help fugitive slaves. The top-down model of British abolition that had ended slavery in the British West Indies, and that Griffiths herself advocated, had helped her to rally political abolitionists in Western New York. Now she could demonstrate to Britons, Scots, and Irish that some organizations in the United States were of a like mind, and she could offer them a person and an antislavery society to support. Furthermore, she provided symbols indicating a return on their investment through the continuation of Douglass's paper and reports about the numbers of fugitives aided by the Rochester Ladies' Anti-Slavery Society. Her job became easier because, whereas many in the United States had found her personality grating or exhausting, she did not appear to annoy the British organizations. In fact, when Pillsbury explained to the British activists who complained about his attacks on Griffiths and Douglass that they did the same to him, he found that he "could not make any body here believe that she would call the devil himself an infidel." She also inspired women to found fifteen new antislavery societies, reviving the same zeal for abolition that Douglass had inspired a decade earlier and expanding the base of subscribers for his paper and the donations to the Rochester Ladies' fair.[52]

By December 1855, Pillsbury predicted that "the *Juliad* should be near clos-ing"—using his nickname for Griffiths' campaign—and took heart in the lack of news about her in the preceding month. He learned his mistake two weeks later. Griffiths had mobilized Yorkshire and also persuaded Campbell to publish Douglass's autobiography. To counteract this success, Pillsbury attempted to ex-cite sexual innuendo once again, calling Griffiths a "Jezebel," repeating a story that Anna Richardson would not receive Griffiths, and describing a meeting in which "Julia was the only Lady present." Others, however, returned to the charge that Griffiths and Douglass had less interest in abolition than their own profit. They delved into the Douglasses' private finances for proof. In February 1856, Richard Webb began circulating an argument that, because Griffiths held the mortgage on the Douglass house, her activism was actually an effort to ensure a return on her investment. Any funds raised to aid Douglass, he argued, essen-tially went to Griffiths, who had no real concern about the plight of slaves or the good of humanity. "She is trying to secure herself from harm by saving F.D. from bankruptcy," Webb insisted.[53]

Griffiths did, of course, hold the mortgage to the Douglass house at one time. In August 1849, when the future of the *North Star* had appeared so dire, Eliza Griffiths had loaned Frederick $1000 to stabilize the business, using the house as collateral. When Eliza married John Dick in 1851, they signed the mortgage over to Julia. Julia declared the loan paid in full two years later, in March 1853, not long after she had moved to the Weddles' home and a few months before the *National Anti-Slavery Standard* and Garrison began their attacks. "The Dep. Clerk certifies that he finds no mortgage from F.D. to J.G. 'since the 29 Aug 1849,' " Samuel May reported to Webb in 1858, after a two-year-long title search, "and that there is no other record of any mortgage or discharge to be found since the said Aug. 29, 1849." Just as Garrison had parsed words in the aftermath of his charges about their relationship, May pouted that Griffiths "*has had* a con-siderable pecuniary stake in F.D.'s business success," in the past if not in the pres-ent. Griffiths's ally, Russell Carpenter, defended her right to invest wherever she chose without public comment. Maria Weston Chapman, however, wanted to pursue the case with "legal counsel" to prove that since Douglass had become fully independent of the Garrisonians, he and Griffiths had attempted "to injure the cause by getting a living out of it & living out of it to injure it."[54]

Griffiths left the field of organization in any case, but not antislavery activism as a whole and not through the efforts of Webb, May, or Pillsbury. Amy Post had heard rumors that Griffiths was ill in mid-1857, causing William C. Nell to ponder, "If she does not recover = the loss of her services will be signal and heavy to F.D." Within a year, she suffered from what she later described as "nervous fever," a disorder generally associated with exhaustion, and took an eleven-week break at a spa town in 1858. The greatest change in her life that affected her activism, however, came on March 18, 1859, when she married the Rev. Henry Only Crofts, a Methodist minister and widower of five years with three daughters. Elizabeth, called "Lizzie," the oldest of the daughters and eighteen at the time of her father's remarriage to Griffiths, became a companion to her step-mother; but Saley and Martha at ages eight and four, respectively, needed parenting. Griffiths—now Mrs. Crofts—could no longer travel as she had for so many years. Nevertheless, emulating such women as Amy Post and Maria Weston Chapman, she relied on the assistance of Lizzie and a servant as she coordinated the British support for Douglass and the Rochester Ladies' Anti-Slavery Society from her home.[55]

While Griffiths kept Douglass and his cause before a British audience, back in Rochester the potential for a new foreign audience, and yet more household complications, appeared at the Douglasses' door. Since her migration to the United States in 1852, Ottilie Assing had worked as an American correspondent for the German journal *Morgenblatt für Gebildete Leser* (*Morning Paper for Educated Readers*), providing travelogues and sketches of life in the United States, which she used as a basis to to critique German politics and society. She had attended a meeting of the American Anti-Slavery Society in 1854, and had left sympathetic but uninspired. She extolled Wendell Phillips alone, granted faint praise to Robert Purvis, dismissed Abby Kelley Foster as the "comic interlude," and, since she seemed to have departed before the meeting ended, entirely left out of her account the final speaker, William Lloyd Garrison. Instead, in her rambles about New York City, she observed the condition of African Americans and identified a problem that emancipation alone could not eliminate. Turning to her white acquaintances, she inquired about the poverty in which most black New Yorkers lived. "It is a proven fact that in their abilities they are far below white people" came the reply, along with the insistence that "they would have been better off if they had remained in slavery." Assing did not accept this answer. Part Jewish through her father, the German woman understood something about prejudice. "The free North, although not tolerating slavery," she concluded, "has done and continues to do everything in its power to prevent the further development of the African race by erecting a wall of prejudice separating whites and blacks." She intended to pursue this story in order to prove this hypothesis.[56]

Assing, of course, had other motives. She had spent the years between 1852 and 1855 eking out a living. Indeed, throughout her career, she often found herself unable to wholly support herself with her pen. Her articles appeared only sporadically in the *Morgenblatt* during the 1850s. She may have submitted more, but only an average of eight a year saw print between 1852 and 1865, when the paper closed, and only five of her pieces appeared in 1853, and four in 1854. To earn her living, she turned to tutoring, teaching music, selling her paintings, tinting daguerreotypes, and sewing. If she hoped to make a name for herself, she had to find a saleable topic that could become her unique province. The plight of African Americans, which she realized other German writers had ignored, seemed to be an open beat.[57]

Unfortunately, she knew few Americans much less black Americans. She probably learned of one of her first subjects, the Reverend J. W. C. Pennington, because he was a pillar of the black community in Manhattan and because he had received an honorary degree from the University of Heidelberg in 1849. Even then, she observed, "I would not have had the opportunity to meet Pennington had I not plucked up my courage and introduced myself unceremoniously as the 'correspondent' of Mr. Cotta's *Morgenblatt*." She spent several evenings with the Pennington family, and translated a section of Pennington's autobiography, *The Fugitive Blacksmith*, for her column. In return, Pennington could provide Assing with a wealth of information, seated as he was in the middle of the New York black community and the remnants of David Ruggles's abolitionist network. Pennington also knew Douglass, having married Frederick to Anna. Assing may have also considered James McCune Smith as another subject. Smith had studied medicine in Glasgow and now practiced in Manhattan. He had become a friend and ally of Douglass through the black convention movement, and Douglass remembered that Smith had introduced him to Assing at an antislavery meeting in New York, probably in 1856. She secured an invitation to visit him and, on a journey to the western part of the state, stopped in Rochester to interview him.[58]

At that first extended meeting at Douglass's house, Assing recalled that "we touched on a wide variety of things—large and small, general and personal—in the course of our conversation, and everywhere I encountered understanding and sympathy." Assing also presented to Douglass an idea that he had no means of pursuing and had perhaps never before considered. She could introduce him to a German-speaking audience and thereby extend his message on the European continent and among the German immigrant population who opposed slavery. To this point, most of Douglass's transatlantic activism had been limited to English speakers, the sole exception being the 1848 French translation of his *Narrative*. That development most likely came as a result of Maria Weston Chapman's connections, no longer available to him. Douglass, in return, provided Assing with further contacts in the abolition movement and greater insight into the condition of African Americans, thereby improving her chances of being published in Germany. Through him she met at least one of militant abolitionist John Brown's associates in 1857, and Brown's son in 1859. In 1859, too, Douglass introduced her to Gerrit Smith, who introduced her to Sarah Grimké, to Dr. Harriet Hunt, and to his daughter, the originator of the Bloomer costume, Elizabeth Smith Miller. Douglass probably also directed her to a community of former slaves in Canada, which she visited in 1857, and instructed her to attend more than just the American Anti-Slavery Society meetings during the next annual abolitionist conventions in New York City if she wanted a fuller picture of the movement than her experience in 1854 had provided.[59]

No mere mercenary exchange, Assing and Douglass found an "understanding and sympathy" that emerged from their similar political and intellectual interests. Assing, although not technically a refugee herself, had grown up among the Young Germans, a group of republican intellectuals who had participated in the Revolutions of 1848. Assing's parents, Rosa Maria Varnhagen and David Assing (formerly Assur), as well as her aunt and uncle, Rahel Levin and Karl Varnhagen von Ense, had many friends and associates in the movement in Hamburg and Berlin. In direct opposition to the autocratic governments of the German states, these intellectuals had demanded freedom of speech and artistic expression, religious freedom and the emancipation of Jews, the equality of women, and greater political participation. After the German governments brutally suppressed the movements through 1848 and 1849, they and other revolutionaries fled to the United States. Although Assing had lived in Hamburg when the Prussian army seized the city, she herself had not participated in the popular politics nor expressed more than a passing interest in the subject. Nevertheless, her upbringing and education had shaped her understanding of social justice, and she moved among German expatriates who believed that America offered more fertile ground for their ideology even as it suffered from significant hypocrisy, nowhere more evident than in the treatment of immigrants and African Americans.[60]

Douglass, too, loathed hypocrisy. Like the German immigrants, of which Rochester had many, his criticism of slavery, racial prejudice, and American complicity in both came from his loyalty to republican ideals. His disgust resulted not simply from American failure to perfect those ideals in practice but also from active suppression of those who tried. The global democratic revolution envisioned by German immigrants such as Assing meshed with Douglass's own demand for racial democratic revolution. Furthermore, the Garrisonians' religiosity and aversion to violence and politics failed to entice secular, even atheist, European liberals and radicals to join them. Like Douglass, they understood that the Garrisonians' retreat from the political process was a privilege afforded only to those who had been admitted to the process in the first place. Douglass's incorporation of political abolition and his belief that rebellion was a rational response to slavery fit well with men and women who had openly resisted a government that violently suppressed political liberty.[61]

Assing's and Douglass's sympathy with one another went beyond politics, too. Douglass loved books and ideas, and possessed a voracious appetite for learning. Educated and intelligent people populated his world, but the primary focus of their friendships lay in antislavery politics. During the years that Griffiths had lived with the Douglasses, she had just as willingly spent her evenings discussing books with Frederick as she did the end of slavery or the operation of the newspaper, although antislavery, too, was her driving passion. After she left, Rosetta had the potential to replace her, but her parents' expectations of her divided her loyalties between them and she could not fully step into the role as her father's companion. Moreover, in her teen years, she could not be expected to have the intellectual background of foreign women old enough to be her mother. Douglass could teach her, but her world was his creation. Assing, on the other hand, noticed that, although abolition occupied most of Douglass's time, "he is far too wide-ranging as not to engage other worthy causes with energy." Her own knowledge of German philosophy and literature, to which he had little or no access, was reminiscent of Griffiths, who had shared with him English books and ideas. She could feed his curiosity with ideas, news, and culture from the Continent. As with Griffiths, a friendship emerged from this meeting of minds.[62]

Yet, even more, they may have recognized a similar yearning in one another. Douglass had spent his life demanding respect for his individual humanity and in pursuing self-reliance. Assing, too, had pursued independence for much of her adult life. Orphaned at age twenty-three, alienated from her uncle and sister by twenty-four, and suicidal by twenty-five, she had neither the prospects nor the desire to marry, one avenue of escape from a desperately unhappy household. Instead, she took what little fortune she had and pursued autonomy. She could rely on her education to secure employment as a governess, a job that she later likened to slavery, but she lost all the money she had invested in a theater run by actor Jean-Baptiste Baison, whom she adored and whose household she managed. By 1851, she had built a small portfolio of theater reviews, to which she added a biography of Baison, and using the influence of her mother's close friend and her parents' reputation, she secured the *Morgenblatt* position that led her to America in pursuit of personal and intellectual freedom. Her earliest columns fit into the genre of travel writing; and, indeed, she had stopped to meet Douglass while on a *Sommerwanderungen* (summer wandering) that took her from New York City to Howe's Cavern, west of Albany, to Niagara Falls. Yet, like other German women who wrote in this style, she used her observations to critique her former home and explore a new one, often as a means of creating a new identity, much as Douglass had been doing since his own journey to New York eighteen years earlier.[63]

After their first meeting in 1856, which could not have lasted more than a week given Douglass's crowded speaking schedule, Assing continued on her own itinerary and then returned to her lodgings in Hoboken, New Jersey. She wrote columns about her summer travels, including the interview with Douglass, and began to translate *My Bondage and My Freedom* into German. She returned two years later for a longer visit, lasting over a month, setting a precedent that continued with a handful of interludes until 1881. She grew to claim his home as not only her primary vacation retreat but as her own, and she convinced her landlords to allow Douglass to take a room for a night or two when he passed through the New York area.

In Hoboken, Assing introduced Frederick to a circle of intellectuals who, as German immigrants, were wholly unlike most of the other people with whom he associated. They responded to him differently than white Americans did and their lives were not shaped by activism. With them, he could be an intellectual who was a black man, rather than an intellectual despite being a black man, as many white Americans saw him. Douglass had sought that sort of experience when he attended literary societies and lyceum lectures and in his travels to Europe. Moreover, they brought ideas from the European continent that were not necessarily common to the Anglo-centric circles in which he typically sought art and literature. Their isolation from his usual society allowed him to trust Assing to keep his family life away from gossips and political rivals. Overall, the unique experience that she brought him, the intellectual stimulation, and the vision of himself reflected in her eyes offered him a mental rejuvenation. Having spent most of her life among and writing for Germans, she found in him a person who could expand her understanding of the United States and the particular battles of American republicanism.[64] Fortunately, her visits to the Douglasses did not attract the same intrusive attention that those of Griffiths had. Much of this had to do with Assing's lack of curiosity about the antislavery movement as a whole. She was wholly uninterested in activism in Rochester, eventually treating her summers there as either vacations or months in which she dedicated herself to Douglass alone. Any influence that she might have in helping his career was among German speakers both in the United States and abroad, an audience that the Garrisonians had not considered. She did not participate in fundraising or the operation of his paper, nor did she seduce him into antislavery apostasy, all the sources of the animosity toward Griffiths. She in no way emerged as a threat, or even a consideration, to any abolitionists in the way Griffiths had.

Her visits to the Douglass home, however, were themselves intrusions. Over the years Anna grew openly hostile to the German woman and let her husband know that she did not want this particular visitor in her home. If Ottilie's attitude toward Anna, as displayed in her letters, was any indication, Anna had good reason to resent her. Ottilie seldom demonstrated respect for her hostess, dehumanizing Anna in all her descriptions. She reduced Anna to her color, "completely black," from the beginning, and throughout their acquaintance referred to her as "ignorant and uneducated," a "stupid old hag," and a "real monster" or "creature." Even her description of "feeding" Anna presents suggested that she saw the mistress of the Douglass household as an intractable child. For all her love of the escape the Douglass home provided her each summer, Ottilie seemed unaware of the people who made those summers so carefree, referring to them only in caustic asides and seldom inquiring about their well-being. Nor, for all her purported interest in African Americans and civil rights, did she seem at all curious about the Douglasses' experiences as a black family rising in American society.[65]

Like Griffiths, Assing drew Frederick away from his family and into discussions about atheism, Goethe, Dickens, and politics. Unlike Griffiths, she in no visible way contributed to the operation of the household, nor did she seem to notice its other members. Griffiths had worked in Frederick's office, and her antislavery organization helped to support Frederick, his family, and abolition. Assing, on the other hand, never fulfilled her potential. Her feature about Douglass never saw print, nor did any of her subsequent columns about him that year, although the *Morgenblatt* published ten of her pieces in 1856, as many as in the preceding two years combined. She finished the translation in 1857, but neither her appeal to her uncle Varnhagen nor Douglass's to Assing's sister, Ludmilla, both of whom had connections in the Berlin literary world, yielded immediate results. *Sklaverei und Freiheit* (*Slavery and Freedom*, the German title of *My Bondage and My Freedom*) did not see print until 1860, when Douglass's role in the Harpers Ferry raid and the American sectional crisis may have made the volume more saleable. Assing never attracted the wealth or organizational support that Griffiths did in the same period.[66] After 1865, when the *Morgenblatt* ceased publication, Assing's ability to help Douglass through her writing evaporated, and she relied more on his influence and her own positioning of herself as his special friend and intellectual guide to maintain her identity as an expert on American racial affairs. From Anna's perspective, then, Ottilie served no discernible function in her house except to "bewitch" Frederick away from his familial responsibilities while treating his family as inconveniences in their own home. As he had done with Griffiths, Frederick ignored his wife and allowed Assing access to his life and that of his family, regardless of the effect on them. In response, Anna erected a border, granting that the head of the household could allow Assing into the home, but the white woman could never be part of the family.

Julia Griffiths had engendered a marital disagreement over the extent to which a particular guest was welcomed into their home and the danger that guest presented to the family by exposing it to criticism and attack. Frederick's insistence on his right to have that guest in his home, despite the danger, placed his image as the head of a respectable black family at odds with his demand for his individual right to association. The resulting conflict with his wife uncovered fundamental differences in the ways that he and Anna viewed their marriage and themselves as individuals in their family. Ottilie Assing's presence in their home intensified, prolonged, and repeated the same conflict throughout the 1860s and 1870s.

|| 6 ||

The Woman's Rights Man and His Daughter, 1848–1861

Frederick Douglass insisted that Elizabeth Cady Stanton introduced him to the concept of woman's rights. Hardly a month into his career as an antislavery lecturer, Douglass was accosted by a young, visibly pregnant Stanton after an 1841 meeting of the Boston Female Anti-Slavery Society. Stanton, he recalled, went to great "pains of setting before me, in a very strong light, the wrongs and injustices" of "woman's exclusion from the right choice in the selection of the persons who should frame the laws, and thus shape the destiny of all the people, irrespective of sex." He confessed that he resorted to "the common talk of 'woman's sphere,'" initially because he had heretofore found little reason to think deeply about his notions of "'custom,' 'natural division of duties,'" and the "'indelicacy of woman's taking part in politics.'" Stanton, too, remembered her first meeting with the "African Prince" who was fully "conscious of his dignity and power, grand in his physical proportions, majestic in his wrath." Yet, she made no mention of their discussion of woman's rights. Instead, in *The History of Woman Suffrage*, she and Susan B. Anthony described him as first learning of their cause seven years later, at the 1848 Seneca Falls meeting that they immortalized as the origins of the woman's rights movement. In Stanton's version, Douglass, perhaps the only African American at the convention, proved to be crucial to the inclusion of suffrage in its resolutions. These two accounts, both written in 1881, were not necessarily inaccurate, but events of the intervening decades had shaped their telling. Whereas Douglass placed his awakening within the context of black civil rights, Stanton portrayed him as the representative of black civil rights in a movement for equality between men and women. In the gap between their interpretations lay the inherent tensions among a white-led antislavery movement, a male-dominated black civil rights movement, and a women's movement largely controlled by white women.[1]

Through the 1850s, a discrete movement for woman's rights grew out of the antislavery movement and alongside a revitalized black convention movement, with each holding separate annual conventions as well as local and state ones. Yet, while most woman's rights advocates were abolitionists and many supported black civil rights, the sentiment was not necessarily mutual at all times. The Fugitive Slave Law of 1850 galvanized the antislavery movement, diversifying its tactics and increasing its militancy, but as the decade progressed, the uneasy coalition among the camps became more apparent. Each attempted to separate black civil rights from woman's rights, and proposals that might combine agendas only led to accusations that such resolutions would threaten the whole endeavor. In word and deed, Douglass worked to cross the divide, an increasingly difficult proposition over the decade. Meanwhile, at home, Frederick and Anna brought up a family of three boys and two girls. Although his ideology would likely have developed along similar lines because his lifelong emphasis on race encompassed the social and economic improvement of the status of black women as well as men, raising daughters personalized the experience for him. Rosetta and her little sister Annie, born in 1849, grew up alongside the women's movement, reared by a mother who had been in domestic service and a father who had witnessed the degradation heaped upon enslaved women. Giving all of their children a better life would be a struggle for the Douglasses, but raising two daughters in a world that offered black girls little required special investment, extracted particular demands, and illustrated the impossibility of separating the two movements for African American women. Rosetta in particular lived with the responsibility of fulfilling her parents' expectation that she would become a representative black woman, challenging the limitations on her gender while not challenging black men in a movement for civil rights.

By the time of the Seneca Falls convention, Douglass had already made his opinion on the matter known. He had extensive experience with women's capabilities under slavery, in freedom, and in the implicitly political activity of abolition. The masthead of the *North Star*, a project that fully reflected his ideas as editor and proprietor, proclaimed "Right is of no sex—Truth is of no color," from its first issue in December 1847, and consistently included articles calling for the improved status of women.[2] Thus, a group of women planning "A Convention to discuss the Social, Civil, and Religious Condition of women" in Seneca Falls the following July saw him as a natural ally. When two of the primary organizers, Elizabeth McClintock and Lucretia Mott, invited him to attend and publicize the event, Douglass responded, "To be sure I will do myself the pleasure of accepting" and ran their notice of the "Woman's Rights Convention" in the July 14 issue of the *North Star*. Afterward, he published the proceedings. His presence as a black man reinforced the connection between the emancipation of slaves and woman's rights while he, in turn, could gather more subscribers and support for his fledgling paper. Amy Post, secretary of the Western New York Anti-Slavery Society that sponsored the *North Star*, knew most of the women organizing the meeting through her Quaker and kin connections, so she became his escort and guide. The two, along with Post's husband, Isaac, collected subscribers and drafted agents who gathered more in their home communities.[3]

Although husbands and wives arrived at the gathering together, Anna Douglass did not join Frederick and the Posts. She attended few of his speeches, so her absence was not unusual. Despite the activist women and Frederick's understanding of domesticity as confining and the basis of women's exclusion from public activity, Anna appeared to embrace domesticity as a privilege. She seemed to view her husband's career as supporting their household but distinct from her own marital role as keeper of the home and caretaker of the family. Although she may not have known that she was pregnant with her last child, she was busy settling her family into their new home on Alexander Street after the move from Lynn to Rochester only a few months earlier.[4]

The meeting covered a range of issues—women's education, access to the professions, access to the pulpit, rights within marriage, and working women's wage inequality—all of which would remain part of the long-term woman's rights agenda. The most controversial issue, however, proved to be voting rights for women. Later generations often remembered suffrage as the leading issue because Stanton gave the most complete description of the meeting, and the proposed resolution "urging the women of the country to secure to themselves the elective franchise" was her own. As she recalled in later years, both her husband Henry and, to her surprise, Lucretia Mott warned her not to press the issue. "Now you make the whole thing ridiculous," Stanton recalled her husband exclaiming, while she despaired that "Lucretia Mott said the same thing, and all the committee who were interested in getting up the meeting were opposed to this resolution." She pinned her hopes on Douglass.[5]

"I presented my resolution," Stanton remembered, "then hurried to his side, and whispered in his ear what I wanted said." Yet even so skilled an orator as Douglass could not match her enthusiasm, and voting was an issue about which he had some ambivalence at that point. "He didn't speak quite fast enough for me," she insisted, "nor say all I wanted said, and the first thing I knew I was on my feet defending the resolution." They succeeded in winning over a crucial majority to include suffrage in the woman's rights platform, and Stanton later praised Douglass as the "one man to stand with her."[6] When the Seneca Falls meeting spawned a larger meeting in Rochester two weeks later, Douglass alone among the men defended women's right to the franchise. According to Stanton, he answered the opposition in "a long, argumentative, and eloquent appeal, for the complete equality of woman in all the rights that belong to any human soul," adding that "the true basis of rights was the capacity of individuals; and as for himself, he should not dare claim a right that he would not concede to woman."[7]

Figure 6.1 Elizabeth Cady Stanton with her sons, Daniel and Henry, at the time of the Seneca Falls Woman's Rights Convention. Stanton credited Douglass with supporting her measure for woman suffrage at that meeting, while Douglass insisted that she had introduced him to the concept of woman's rights when they first met six years earlier. "[Elizabeth Cady Stanton, halftone reproduction of 1848 photo with her sons, Daniel and Henry]," Unknown photographer, Elizabeth Cady Stanton Papers, Library of Congress.

The Seneca Falls and Rochester woman's rights conventions took place only a month before a Colored Men's Convention in Cleveland. This was the first such national meeting to be held in nearly a decade, and like the early conventions, it served as a means of formulating agendas for action and spawning groups to pursue particular campaigns. They organized not only to end slavery but also to fight the racial prejudice in the North that barred them from education, employment, and political power, the same types of issues that had brought the women together at Seneca Falls and Rochester. Acutely aware of the ways that slavery and racial discrimination erased privileges of gender difference, however, men at the black conventions intended to assert their manhood by emphasizing their roles as leaders of African American communities. Black women occupied supporting positions, much as they did in black churches and antislavery societies. Yet, in strictly abolitionist organizations, both black and white women interpreted women's influence as going beyond committee work, petitioning, and fundraising to include roles as speakers and officeholders. Black men's conventions resisted this shift. Women who attended most of these conventions did so because they had a vested interest in the issues, but traditionally they did not openly debate, propose resolutions, or vote. If they did so, then they exposed the men to accusations of emasculation and themselves to charges of immorality.[8]

Nevertheless, in 1848, the two woman's rights conventions opened the possibility for a broader critique of power and exclusion in American society that some black men believed could be part of their own movement. At the Rochester convention, three presumably white men insisted that the "woman's sphere was home," but Douglass and William C. Nell, printer for the *North Star* at the time, demanded "the emancipation of women from all the artificial disabilities, imposed by false custom, creeds and codes."[9] At the same meeting, Rebecca Sanford, a white woman whom Elizabeth Cady Stanton and Susan B. Anthony recalled as "a young bride in her travelling dress," called for "the rights of property, the rights of exercising the elective franchise, and the other rights claimed." The audience applauded her impromptu speech. She and her husband, "a delighted, nay, reverential listener" by Stanton and Anthony's description, had been on their way west when they heard about the convention and stopped in the city. Douglass and Nell seem to have persuaded Sanford to accompany them to Cleveland, for she appeared at the black men's convention there. As president of the meeting, Douglass ensured that she received a hearing. After her remarks, the men thanked her, and then debated a resolution on the matter. The opposition insisted that the convention had already passed a similar statement covering all "colored persons" and pointed out that "they considered *women persons.*" Douglass stepped in to offer a modification to include an explicit statement that "persons" included women. That he had to do so said much about their assumptions when they used universalizing language. The convention signaled approval "with three cheers for woman's rights."[10]

Douglass returned home from Cleveland to a reminder that cheering, debate, and resolutions were not enough to ensure that black girls receive equal treatment. After their three-year separation, Rosetta had joined her family in Rochester in time for the 1848 school year. The question of racial integration in New York State lay in the hands of local school districts, which enforced racial policies erratically. When the Douglasses were living in Lynn, a city not inclined to educate its black residents, the Mott sisters in Albany had educated Rosetta privately. Rochester largely maintained segregated schools, placating black taxpayers by operating a single public black school. Still, Public School No. 15, which stood on Alexander Street across from the Douglass home, accepted Lewis, Frederick Jr., and Charles. Frederick Sr. and Anna, however, decided to send Rosetta to the private Tracy Female Institute (also known as the Seward Female Seminary or Seward School) down Alexander Street from their house. There, she could both be educated and learn some of the refinements necessary to be considered a young lady. Principal Lucillia Tracy, whom Douglass had heard was "an abolitionist—a woman of religious principles and integrity," assured him that his daughter's skin color would not present a problem. Yet, when he returned from the Cleveland convention, Rosetta tearfully confessed to him, "Miss Tracy does not allow me to go into the room with the other scholars because I am colored."[11]

Anna, who had deferred action until her husband got home, insisted that Frederick remove Rosetta from the school immediately. Frederick instead chose to confront the injustice. Facing a livid Douglass, Tracy explained that, while she herself had no problem with a black pupil, the school's trustees had objected to Rosetta's admission. She had tried a compromise by letting Rosetta stay enrolled but keeping her in a separate room, doing her lessons by herself. Tracy hoped that Rosetta's presence and performance would erode the trustees' prejudice and that they would eventually allow her back into the classroom with the others. Douglass would have none of that. He threatened to withdraw Rosetta, along with her tuition. If he did not directly state that he would publicize the school's treatment of his daughter, his status as an editor made the implication clear. Tracy tried to forestall that disaster by asking the students if they objected to Rosetta's presence. "To the credit of the young ladies," Douglass noted, the girls welcomed Rosetta as a classmate, shouting for her to sit "By me, by me, by me." Tracy then sent the children home with instructions to ask their parents' permission to admit Rosetta, warning that a single objection would expel her. Horatio G. Warner, the editor of the Rochester *Courier*, was that one. Rosetta went home.[12]

Rosetta could not have escaped racial prejudice before this point in her life, but her parents had attempted to keep her insulated from any direct attacks. They had lived in a black community in New Bedford for the first three years of her life and among abolitionists in Lynn. Then, they sent her to live with two active antislavery Quakers in Albany. At school in Rochester, however, the hatred normally heaped upon her father was aimed directly at her, and Frederick decided to make his daughter's case a matter of public debate. Echoing his defense of the purchase of his freedom only two years earlier, Douglass explained that "if this were a private affair, only affecting myself and my family, I should possibly allow it to pass without attracting public attention to it." Instead, Warner's objection to Rosetta was "a deliberate attempt to degrade and injure" not just his daughter but also "a large class of persons, whose rights and feeling have been the common sport of yourself, and such persons as yourself." The story, ignored in the Rochester papers, was covered by others, including the *Christian Contributor* and the *British Banner*. Indeed, in Britain, activists sent "a little package of sweetmeats to the little girls who believed so rightly in Rosetta's cause." Rosetta, meanwhile, learned her first lesson in being representative of her race.[13]

Rosetta moved to the public school, which her father pronounced "quite as respectable, and *equally* christian to the one from which she was excluded," because they had "gladly welcomed" her, and "no one is offended." The sentiment did not last. Frederick Jr. remembered that, in 1849, "the colored children were sent home on account of their color." A Committee on Colored Schools convened in September 1849 to demand integration. The issue had particular urgency because the Rochester Board of Education was planning to move the black school to the cellar of the Zion Church, a space opponents described as "situated on a low spot without a drain" and without "proper light and ventilation," rendering it a *"cold, damp, and gloomy"* place that "would subject the children to constant colds and injure their constitutions for ever." "If we yield willingly to this encroachment," Douglass editorialized, "perhaps the next demand will require us to live in a certain part of the city." The committee resolved that "we will not send our children to the basement," and Douglass declared, *"in no emergency,"* will we send a child of ours to the miserable cellar under Zion Church." In the meantime, he hired Phebe Thayer, a Quaker relative of Amy Post, to tutor his children at home. In 1850, Public School No. 15 quietly allowed eleven African American students, including the Douglass children, to attend integrated classes. When the Douglasses moved to South Street the next year, the school serving that district admitted them without incident; but the city's schools did not officially integrate until 1857.[14]

Rosetta's case may have contributed to efforts to desegregate Rochester's public schools, but the controversy began with her expulsion from a private school for girls. The Douglasses sent their sons to the public school that also accepted girls, but, at a time when Frederick's finances at the paper were faltering and the family could ill afford the expense, they placed her alone in the private academy. At some point, they also paid for a piano and lessons, instruction that carried the middle-class marker of accomplishment for a young woman. Their investment in Rosetta's education indicated the special difficulties a black family faced in preparing a daughter for a better life.[15]

While Frederick himself adored pursuing knowledge for its own sake, for the majority of African Americans, including his own children, he more often promoted "a practical English education." By this, he meant schooling that would allow them to "learn how to make a good living" rather than "learn Latin and Greek," the basis of a classical, college education. Yet, even a practical education could be difficult. Resolutions at black civil rights conventions called not only for the establishment of vocational schools but also for skilled black laborers to train young black men. This was among the explicit reasons that Douglass believed that the *North Star* was necessary to the future of African Americans. As early as the summer of 1850, he took his sons Lewis and Frederick Jr. into the shop to learn printing. Rosetta later recollected that this had happened at their mother's insistence, so the plan was something that both parents agreed on. Frederick Jr. attested that he only went to school until age twelve, at which point he began working full-time in his father's office and "completed my trade at the age of sixteen." Charles remembered that he had started working during summers and delivering papers at age ten, but stayed in school full-time until he was fifteen. This work engaged them in antislavery activism and the collective support of the family, as well as set them on a path to become printers in their own right.[16]

Douglass extended this plan to women by consistently supporting institutions aimed at educating young black women. In 1853 and 1854, he headed the planning board for an American Industrial School in Erie, Pennsylvania, that would teach "literature" and "handicraft" to develop students' intellect and earning ability. While the skills learned by the students would be determined by gender, admission did not privilege boys over girls and "a prominent principle of conduct will be to aid in providing for the female sex, methods and means of enjoying an independent and honorable livelihood." Douglass, along with Gerrit Smith, William H. and Frances W. Seward, and Samuel May, acted as a reference for the Rockland Female Institute in Nyack, New York, a school with preparatory, academic, and collegiate departments. *Frederick Douglass' Paper* carried ads and endorsements for Myrtilla Miner's school for black young women in Washington, the New York Central College in McGrawville that was "open to all persons, of both sexes, of good moral character," and the Monroe Academy in Henrietta, New York, that accepted female students.[17]

Furthermore, at an 1853 Rochester woman's rights convention, he signed a petition that raised the question, "how shall we open for Woman's energies new spheres of well-remunerated industry?" By employing them without prejudice seemed to be his answer. At the same meeting, he also called attention to "two young women assistants in the County Clerk's office, also young women going into printing-offices to set type," and the next year, he chastised Horace Greeley for failing to employ women in his "composition rooms." Thus Rosetta, alongside Julia Griffiths, entered the business side of publishing at the paper's office. In November 1853, James McCune Smith, who corresponded as "Communipaw" for *Frederick Douglass' Paper*, reported seeing "Miss R.D. just budding into womanhood, laboring with pen in hand, by the side of our earnest and most efficient English benefactress." Like her brothers, Rosetta supported the family business, but her work also took place within the context of her father's support of training young black women.[18]

Douglass published McCune Smith's notice in the midst of his acrimonious exchange with William Lloyd Garrison over that "efficient English benefactress," and both he and "Communipaw" may have hoped to highlight the smooth operation of the office and the family engagement in Douglass's enterprise as an antidote to the alleged "unhappiness" in the Douglass home. Rosetta, in particular, worked with Griffiths and, by her own later admissions, always intended to please her father. At the same time, her mother seemed quite displeased at the entire situation surrounding Griffiths, who took Frederick away from his family and drew the Douglasses into the public eye. Whereas Anna probably, in theory, wanted her daughter to help her father in his business, become educated, and live a more secure life than her own had been as a younger woman, she also did not want her daughter to abandon her or devalue the life that Anna represented. This complicated the relationship between mother and daughter.[19]

"I think my position in the family rather a singular one," Rosetta told her father some years later, "or rather I feel it to be so for I wish to be all you would have me be and I wish also to do something to make mother happy." Doing so, she pointed out, might be less challenging "if both were interested in the same pursuits." She had identified the key point of disconnection between her parents as well as the central tension in her childhood. Her parents had embraced the doctrine of separate spheres in their marriage, partly as an aspiration for upward mobility, partly from circumstance, and partly from temperament. Anna ruled the home while Frederick conquered the public world of civil rights activism. Rosetta's role was between a type of womanhood that her mother embodied through domesticity and a new type of womanhood represented by the educated women who became her father's most valued female associates through their work outside of the home.[20]

Perhaps the strain in her family and in activist circles that was centered on Griffiths became too much, or maybe Rosetta felt superfluous at the paper with Griffiths as manager, but she seemed to have hoped for an independent life beyond her father's office. As the debates at woman's rights conventions highlighted, women found few occupations open to them, and even fewer admitted black women. Teaching, although paying less for women than men, offered one means of respectable employment and, in the context of black civil rights, activist engagement. At the time, states did not require teachers to possess a college degree or to train at a Normal School as long as they could pass a local qualifying exam. Nevertheless, in 1854, fifteen-year-old Rosetta departed for the Oberlin College Preparatory Department. Her enrollment in a program meant to prepare her for entrance into the college suggested that she either intended to make herself more competitive as an applicant for teaching positions, especially if she hoped to break color barriers for teachers in integrated schools, or that she had aspirations beyond the classroom. Just as importantly, the Douglasses invested in their daughter's desire for intellectual improvement.[21]

At the time, Oberlin was the only higher educational institution to admit students regardless of race or gender. The school had a strong abolitionist ethos, and Douglass knew many of its alumni, black and white, male and female, through his activism. Nevertheless, African American women comprised a small number of the already small black and female populations of the school. In the first thirty years that black students were admitted, their population never exceeded 5 percent of the student body, and the total number of women attending during that entire span of time was 140. Rosetta, then, formed part of a tiny, elite cadre from the moment that she set foot on campus.[22] Yet she stayed at Oberlin for only a year. She afterward made no reference to her experiences there and never updated the college alumni on her life's progress. While her great-granddaughter and William Oliver, one of her father's printers, remembered her as "well educated," only one of her father's earliest biographers, James M. Gregory, her brothers, and her obituary mentioned that she had attended the college. Whatever the cause of her abbreviated education, the family's reticence in discussing this episode in Rosetta's life indicated ambivalence about the matter and suggested that the circumstances were either more complicated than they cared to detail or simply too unimportant for comment. Still, a single year in a preparatory school made her more educated than the majority of her black women contemporaries.[23]

Back in Rochester, Rosetta found plenty to do. By the mid-1850s, Anna had begun to suffer from neuralgia, an often debilitating condition resulting from inflamed or damaged facial nerves that could cause spasms or paralysis. Charlotte Murray, Anna's sister and companion, had married and moved into her own home, leaving Anna without her help. The Douglasses had taken in Jeremiah Perkins and William, the two young black men around the ages of Frederick Jr. and Lewis, who apprenticed at Douglass's paper. This meant that, including Rosetta, the household contained six young people under the age of sixteen. Rosetta could be of great service to her mother, especially with the schoolwork of the two youngest, ten-year-old Charles and six-year-old Annie. Lewis, in fact, later believed she would make a "severe" schoolmarm.[24]

The home on South Street was also without Julia Griffiths, whose departure overlapped with Rosetta's return. Griffiths's absence in all likelihood changed the dynamic in the Douglass family, although beginning in 1858, the summer visits of Ottilie Assing became a new source of tension. Rosetta, however, filled the gap at the office left by Griffiths's departure, sorting correspondence, keeping the books, and taking dictation or copying her father's letters and speeches. She avoided the factional disputes among abolitionists by not joining any antislavery society, but she worked with the Rochester Ladies' Anti-Slavery Society to purchase railroad tickets for fugitives on their way to Niagara or to provide them with clothing, food, medical care, and, on one occasion, a funeral. When the fugitives stayed the night, Rosetta's work shifted from supplying their travel needs to helping her mother as hostess. In 1858, she took part in a campaign to prevent the execution of black convict Ira Stroud, working with Susan B. Anthony and Amy Post. Rosetta also traveled with her father to his speaking engagements. In all, she appeared to take on the role normally occupied by the wives of politicians and dignitaries, similar to that of the daughters of William Seward and Salmon P. Chase.[25]

Although Rosetta had in some respects replaced Griffiths, her relationship to abolitionism differed in key ways. Julia's dedication to Frederick had taken place within the context of a movement whereby providing aid to Frederick bolstered abolitionism, as did her mobilization of antislavery women and fundraising. Separated from her family by an ocean and without a husband or children, Julia had no competing loyalties. Rosetta, on the other hand, had learned antislavery as an extension of her family life and a natural outgrowth of her parents' ethic of lived abolition. The sacrifices her parents made for her education, her participation in their father's work at an early age, her father's absences throughout her childhood, Julia Griffiths's residence in their home, and the family's aid to fugitive slaves all reinforced this perspective. In viewing her family as the site of activism, Rosetta followed Anna's model and avoided the conflicts that might arise if she joined one of Rochester's two antislavery societies. Merging filial duty, antislavery work, and domesticity, she oscillated between helping her father at the office and her mother in the house.

As Rosetta navigated her parents' needs, opportunities for her own education, and employment, and the double discrimination faced by black women, her father continued in the fight to remove the institutional barriers that threatened both his sons and his daughters. In 1853, Rochester hosted the national convention of African Americans in early July, and the New York State woman's rights convention in late November. Douglass attended both, as did James McCune Smith and the Reverend Jermain Loguen of Syracuse, a self-emancipated minister who later turned his full attention to aiding fugitive slaves. All three advocated an immediate end to slavery, an expansion of black civil rights including suffrage, and equal rights for women. Attendees at both meetings may have included Julia Griffiths, Amy Post, and Rosetta, as well as many of the local women abolitionists connected to both Post and Griffiths. The 1853 Rochester conventions were perhaps the closest the two movements could come to creating a coalition, but even then key differences revealed fissures that later impeded cooperation, particularly as the context of their common interest in antislavery shifted.[26]

The participants of both conventions asserted themselves as American citizens in common with their presumed audience of white men. "We do not ask for woman's political, civil, industrial, and social equality with man, in the spirit of antagonism," the women pledged, "or with the wish to produce separate interests between the sexes." Likewise, the black men did not "address you as enemies, (although the recipients of innumerable wrongs;) but in the spirit of patriotic good will." Both conventions underscored the fact that their constituents already shouldered many of the responsibilities of citizenship. The black men pointed out that they were "supporters of the State, subject to its laws, interested in its welfare, liable to be called upon to defend it in time of war, contributors to its wealth in time of peace," while the women argued that, as property owners, they should either be exempt from taxation or directly represented in government. Both groups insisted that they be included in jury service, and the women went a step further by insisting that male judges not preside over divorce cases. Both demanded suffrage, drawing on the concept of government by consent, but political exclusion aggravated deeper economic and social problems. The women insisted on "an equally free access with men, to the highest means of mental, moral, and physical culture," an idea that resonated with the black men who, "having the same physical, moral, mental, and spiritual wants common to other members of the human family," desired "the same means which are granted and secured to others, to supply those wants." In both instances, these included better education and employment opportunities, to which the women added equal pay for equal work.[27]

At the same time, the women, predominantly white, gave no sense that their citizenship was ever in question. Their entitlement blinded them to the concerns of free black women, whom they never explicitly addressed in their agenda. Woman suffrage or equal education meant little for African American women in New York if the property restrictions placed on black men extended to them or if racial segregation barred them from schools. White woman's rights activists also did not acknowledge the black men's campaign to remove that property restriction two years later even as they themselves sought an expansion of married women's property rights. Black men, on the other hand, understood that "It may, and it will, probably be disputed that we are citizens." Anticipating denunciation, they felt that they had to establish a case for their own inclusion. They pointed to a shared language, religion, and common past with white Americans, and they excerpted laws and court decisions demonstrating that "by the principles of the Declaration of Independence," "by the meaning of the United States Constitution," "by the facts of history, and the admissions of American Statesmen," "by the hardships and trials endured," and "by the courage and fidelity displayed by our ancestors in defending the liberties and in achieving the independence of our land" African Americans were citizens. Four years later, the Supreme Court would decide otherwise.[28]

Prerogatives of men and expectations about women also shaped their agendas. The women framed their arguments for inclusion as matters of individual development and survival as well as contributors to society as a whole. They approached their audience in a spirit of cooperation, pointing out that "the onward progress of society and the highest aspirations of the human race, demand that woman should everywhere be recognized as the co-equal and co-sovereign of man." The men's convention instead portrayed themselves as contenders in the free market on equal footing with white men who "can need no arbitrary protection from open and equal competition." In doing so, they asserted themselves as equal to white men who questioned black men's intelligence and feared their physicality. Douglass's presentation of himself in his autobiographies as intellectually voracious, physically powerful in defending himself, entrepreneurial, and morally capable of supporting a family illustrated a larger struggle by black men to affirm themselves as American men.[29]

The way that the women framed themselves as engaged in a cooperative effort emerged from the same ideas about "woman's sphere" that affected the men's perception of women in their own organization. "Separate spheres" or "woman's sphere" meant many different things to different people. For many reformers the idea of a "woman's sphere" did not necessarily mean a geographic location in the home and in private, but rather a biologically determined set of roles and responsibilities in which women provided support and influence. The source of debate lay in the definition of "influence." Woman's rights advocates, both black and white, advanced women as individual citizens, not necessarily separate from communities but as "co-equals" within them, different from men but entitled to full, direct influence on the laws of the community and the nation. The men at the black conventions included women "in all our efforts to elevate and to improve our condition as a people" and announced that "we invite the co-operation of woman, regarding her, in all moral, as well as in other relations of life, the God-given helpmeet of man," but the leadership role in their communities was a masculine one.[30]

That assumption did not go unchallenged. Douglass was among the men who pressed to include women as delegates and speakers. He boasted to Gerrit Smith that the men at the 1853 Rochester convention had not "made a fuss" over the seating of Mary Jeffrey as a representative for Geneva. A year later, however, at a New York State Council of black men, a "quite interesting speech on 'Woman's Rights'" by Jermain Loguen met with objections that the issue was "irrelevant to the business of the Council." At an 1855 state convention in Troy, the men would not accept Barbary Anna Steward's credentials, insisting that "this is not a Woman's Rights Convention." At the October Philadelphia meeting, although Rachel Cliff and Elizabeth Armstrong were among the delegates, there were objections to Mary Ann Shadd serving as a corresponding secretary. Douglass, along with Charles Remond, defended Shadd, and he gave Steward a platform at the "Meeting of Colored Citizens of Rochester" only a few days after she had been rejected as a delegate in Troy. Yet, neither Shadd nor Steward attended those conventions to speak explicitly on the rights of women, as Sanford had in Cleveland in 1848. Shadd intended to advance emigration and Steward, based on her address to the Rochester audience, had prepared "a very interesting address on the Rights and Wrongs of her suffering people." Whereas the men in 1848 had responded to Sanford's speech on woman's rights with cheers, they now regarded the very presence of Shadd and Steward as representatives, entitled to propose, debate, and vote on resolutions, as an implicit statement on woman's rights and, therefore, a distraction.[31]

By the middle of the decade, Douglass too had capitulated to the dominant attitude, separating the concerns of African Americans from those of women, without consideration of the particular position of women who were African American. Addressing the Rochester Ladies' Anti-Slavery Society in January 1855, he suggested that the 1840 schism of the American Anti-Slavery Society was over the right of women to participate fully in the organization and "thus was a grand philanthropic movement rent asunder by a side issue" when women could have "nobly" agreed that "the battle of Woman's Rights should be fought on its own grounds." This was a reversal of his 1848 interpretation of those events, in which he had laid blame on those who left the society, "lest by giving their influence in that direction they might possibly be giving countenance to the dangerous heresy that woman, in respect to rights, stands on an equal footing with man." Douglass himself had defended Shadd and Steward that same year. Yet, at least on the latter point, he did not so much contradict himself as make a distinction between a movement to change laws as they affected women and women's right to have a direct and public role in the black conventions. The former could divide the black men's convention, blunting their ability to fight racial discrimination, while the latter enhanced the convention's forces.[32]

Douglass also proved unwilling to challenge the decision of the majority and even defended them when they voted to exclude women. In 1854, when someone pointed out the hypocrisy of a man who defended woman's rights addressing gatherings that forbade women to speak, he replied that "men and women may honestly and innocently differ as to the wisdom and propriety of woman's speaking in public," because "woman is not excluded from the public platform in a spirit of hate." In other words, the exclusion of women from a venue was a matter of differing opinions while the exclusion of black men was a matter of right and wrong. As the decade advanced, women were welcome to attend the black conventions, fundraise in their auxiliary organizations, and support the male leadership, but their right to represent their communities in the place of men was up for debate and ultimately voted down with the acquiescence of allies like Douglass.[33]

Woman's rights conventions, on the other hand, placed no race or gender restrictions on participation and leadership. Black women such as Sojourner Truth and Sarah Parker Remond found that abolitionist white women were more open to black voices than black men's conventions were to women's. Nevertheless, race was as contentious an issue at the woman's rights conventions as gender was at the black men's. Just as the men had feared turning the 1855 convention into a "Woman's Rights" meeting, some white women criticized woman's rights conventions for including issues of race. "In a Women's Rights Convention, the question of color had no right to a hearing," objected Jane Swisshelm, editor of the antislavery Pittsburgh *Saturday Visiter*, in reporting the 1850 Worcester convention. In a response that Douglass printed in the *North Star*, Parker Pillsbury pointed out the obvious fact that some women were also black, thus race did have a place in discussions of woman's rights, and the exclusion of race might account for the lack of enthusiasm for the movement among African Americans. Indeed, in practice, no black women presided over a woman's rights convention and few held office.[34]

Like Swisshelm, Lucy Stone separated race from gender when advocating for woman's rights. Scheduled to speak on the latter in Philadelphia in 1854, she discovered that the venue excluded African Americans when her black friends were denied entrance. The owner of the building told her that he "would close the hall rather than allow colored people there." She spoke to the audience anyway, believing that she could call attention to the problem by informing them of the policy at the end of her lecture. "The woman does not deserve her rights, who is willing to secure them by trampling upon, or ignoring those of any other," she assured her critics, adding "that any future lectures of mine would be in a hall open to humanity without distinction of races." Douglass did not accept her reasoning. "When she learned that colored people were to be excluded," he retorted, Stone "should have felt herself excluded." Her unwillingness to make that sacrifice, however, was because "she did not go there to speak for the slave— only for woman." In this case, he believed, the cause of woman advanced at the expense of African Americans. He castigated her again, five years later, for courting the favor of Senator Stephen A. Douglas, whom Douglass described as "notorious for holding women in bondage, and for defending the sovereign mob in any of our territories to buy and sell women on the auction block" and "for his contempt for Woman's Rights." She had not only betrayed the cause that had elevated her in doing so, Douglass argued, but also black women held in slavery.[35]

The two women who emerged as leaders of the woman's rights movement and whom later generations commonly associated with Douglass exhibited similar racial ignorance, sometimes directed at Douglass himself. Elizabeth Cady

Stanton tended to elide her class and race prejudices, making insensitive statements because they fit a persuasive argument. In 1854, for example, she objected to laws in which women "are classed with idiots, lunatics, and negroes." Douglass chided her for her assumed claim of "superiority over negroes," reminding her that African Americans "don't like now-a-days to be classed with 'idiots and lunatic,' more than do our fair sisters." Susan B. Anthony's aversion to Douglass stemmed just as much from personal animosity and abolitionist factionalism as unexamined racial prejudice. In her first statements about him, written in an 1848 letter to her mother before she had even met Douglass, she joked that someone had told her that "he never saw a man so wrapped up in a nigger as Father is in Douglas[s]." Through November 1853, as his breach with Garrison came to a head, Douglass worked with both Stanton and Anthony on a state convention and petition drive to bring a woman's rights resolution to the state legislature. Anthony, however, appeared to have used the opportunity to work with Douglass more closely than usual to gather information for Garrison. Her friendship with Amy Post, who was still a friend of the Douglasses and who also worked on this campaign, allowed her access to stories of Douglass's home life, as well. On December 13, she sent gossip to the *Liberator*'s editor for him to use in discrediting Douglass and she intimated to Lucy Stone that "Douglas[s] is uncovering what has long been lurking beneath a smooth exterior."[36]

The subsequent explosion in the newspapers over Douglass, Griffiths, his antislavery independence, and his family's right to privacy poisoned his relationships with many of the woman's rights activists in the American Anti-Slavery Society. As late as 1860, Lucretia Mott worried that "England will be led astray further by that Julia Griffiths & Fredk. Douglass," and warned her sister, "We have some arrogant colored people among us who are damaging our cause as far as they have influence." Although he publicized most of these conventions, printed some proceedings, and continued to print or reprint editorials on woman's rights, Douglass attended only two of the national conventions in the antebellum era, one in Worcester in 1850 and one in New York City in 1858, and three local or state conventions, including Seneca Falls and Rochester in 1848 and Rochester again in 1853. Three of these took place before his break with the Garrisonians.[37]

Douglass might not have attended the 1858 convention at all but for its convenient scheduling. Held for the first time during the annual May "Anniversaries Week" of reform conferences, the National Woman's Rights meeting took place amid others that Douglass attended. His uncharacteristically brief speech there suggests that he merely expected to watch the proceedings, but someone noticed him and "loud calls were made for 'Douglass.'" Reiterating his sympathy with women's "call for freedom," he told the audience that "the rights of women to freedom and to equality with man" were based "upon the same

Figure 6.2 Susan B. Anthony at around the time she met Douglass. Although popular history, aided by *The History of Woman Suffrage*, has remembered them as friends, the two had a much more complicated relationship, fraught with conflict. "Susan B. Anthony," c. 1850. Unknown photographer. Photograph number 81.19, Portraits of American Abolitionists, Massachusetts Historical Society.

grounds on which he advocated the right of the slave to freedom and equality with the white race" and that "a woman could do anything a man could do, and by so doing could assimilate herself to man." In the end, the reporting of Douglass's speech left him seeming to speak only for the sake of saying something and that he was the only speaker to be called for by the audience.[38] The following year, his address to the Shiloh Church about abolitionist Judge William Jay was scheduled at the same time as the women's convention. The year after, tragic events kept him at home, and then the Civil War preempted concerns about woman's rights and turned all abolitionist energy toward the eradication of slavery. Until then, the animosity between Douglass and the Garrisonians, who dominated the woman's rights conventions, had kept him away from their meetings, and his absence during that time severed one of the direct links between the woman's rights and black civil rights movements outside of abolition.[39]

Douglass's scarred relationships with the Garrisonians only partly explained his tangential connection to the woman's rights movement by the late 1850s. The onslaught of pro-slavery legislation beginning with the 1850 Fugitive Slave Act; the 1854 Kansas-Nebraska Act, which extended slavery into western territories; and the 1857 *Dred Scott* decision sent a distinct message to African Americans that they had no place in national life as anything other than property. Backlash against these laws led to the rise of the Republican Party in 1854. While this new party opposed the spread of slavery, it often found its harshest critics among abolitionists who condemned Republicans for opposing the extension of slavery into western territories rather than the eradication of the institution as a whole. Like the majority of the men at black conventions, Republicans welcomed women in adjunct roles, which made them more sympathetic to women's political activity than the Democrats. Nevertheless, they did not include any woman's rights propositions in their platform. Militant antislavery also grew during the 1850s, but it, too, fell under the province of men. Even John Brown relegated his wife, daughters, and daughters-in-law to supporting roles.[40]

Militancy also came with a price, paid by the women behind the scenes. The Douglasses' association with John Brown made that clear. Brown had fascinated Frederick from their first meeting at Brown's Springfield home in 1847. "His wife believed in him," Douglass remarked, "and his children observed him with reverence." The Brown family's frugality, "Spartan" living conditions, lack of servants, plain meals "such as a man might relish after following the plow all day," and even their religiosity impressed Douglass. He praised the way that the whole household "implied stern truth, solid purpose, and rigid economy" in the service of Brown's antislavery crusade. Douglass praised what seemed to be the egalitarianism in the family; but the Browns clearly lived a patriarchal model that fit with his own description of himself as believing in " 'custom,' 'natural division of duties.' "[41]

Brown's militant antislavery enthralled Douglass. "My utterances became more and more tinged by the color of this man's strong opinions," he recalled, separating him from the Garrisonian nonresistance to which he still cleaved at the time. The Douglasses' old confidante, Harriet Adams, and her husband, Perry, living in Springfield at the time, were also drawn to Brown. After the Fugitive Slave Law placed Harriet and their children in danger, they joined the League of Gileadites, a vigilance committee of self-emancipated slaves and their families. With Brown's endorsement, they vowed to defend themselves from slave-catchers with violence if necessary. In New York, Douglass opened his home to Brown, and the South Street house served as a way station between Brown's East Coast backers and his western excursions, while Douglass helped Brown find financing for his plans.[42]

Between 1854 and 1859, Brown passed through the Douglass home repeatedly, once staying for as long as two months as he planned the Harpers Ferry raid. He recruited their handyman, former slave Shields Green, while Charles and Frederick Jr. picked up his mail from the Rochester post office and ran his errands. Anna, young Annie, and Rosetta cooked and cleaned for him during his visits and played hostess at a gathering on his final night in Rochester. According to Charles, the hardened fifty-nine-year-old Brown struck up an unlikely friendship with ten-year-old Annie. "He had become very fond of her," Charles remembered, "and she of him." Brown would have had a daughter about Annie's age, had the child not died in infancy. All members of Brown's family understood that they played a role in his plans whether, like his sons, they fought on the front lines or, like his wife, daughters-in-law, and daughters, they played supporting roles behind the scenes. Therefore, Brown probably considered Anna, Rosetta, and the other children integral parts of his network during the Kansas and Harpers Ferry campaigns.[43]

The government and popular opinion certainly saw them that way. When Brown's raid on Harpers Ferry failed spectacularly, in October 1859, the entire Douglass household fell under suspicion. Charles remembered that US marshals were assigned "to watch Douglass' movements, his home, his sons, and all others who came and went forth from the house." Although Gerrit Smith, who had backed Brown's raid, assured Douglass that Rochester's citizens would never allow his arrest, Charles and Annie, the only two Douglass children still in school, experienced so much harassment from the white students that their mother withdrew them. If Rosetta was still teaching in Rochester, she was probably forced to resign, with little hope of returning to the classroom there or elsewhere for the foreseeable future. Charles ultimately fled the city, joining English immigrant Thomas Pierson's family of seven children at their farm in Lockport. Frederick Jr., Lewis, and Rosetta stayed in Rochester to keep the newspaper going. All the while they faced the loss of Frederick, their home, and their property should he be arrested and convicted of playing a part in the raid.[44]

Frederick was giving a speech in Philadelphia when the battle began in western Virginia. Over the course of several hours, he learned of its collapse, Brown's capture, and his own implication in the plan to use a federal arsenal to arm slaves in a massive rebellion. With the help of a sympathetic telegraph operator and his host, black caterer Thomas Dorsey, Douglass escaped to New York City. Fearful that the authorities might be watching the depots, he sought refuge across the river at Clara Marks's boarding house in Hoboken, where Ottilie Assing lived. For at least a year, Douglass had enjoyed the hospitality of Assing's circle of German intellectuals, but his association with the group was not widely known and thus authorities would not immediately search for him there, as they would have had he fled to James McCune Smith's home or another haven in Manhattan. Marks, Assing, and "Mr. Johnson," another boarder, helped Douglass send a telegraph to Rochester, instructing Lewis to "secure all the important papers in my high desk," meaning for his son to destroy any evidence that connected the family to Brown. Then, Assing and Johnson hired a carriage and escorted Douglass to Patterson, New Jersey, a safer point of departure. From there, he caught a train home to Rochester. After bidding his family goodbye, he crossed the border to Canada that night. Looking back years later and knowing that this was the last time that all of the Douglasses would be together, Charles mourned that they had become "a dismembered family."[45]

Frederick's flight restored his friendship with Amy Post. "I am so sorry," she lamented, "we have *lost* five years of *beautiful, joyous, friendship.*" She and fellow Rochester abolitionist Lucy Colman begged him to stay close to home to protect his property in case of seizure. He refused, pointing out that his home was not in danger unless he was caught, and that going back to Rochester would certainly lead to his capture. Meanwhile, he explained to Post, "I can not consent to an inactive exile." He had already planned a trip to England in late 1859, for which Maria Porter had given him $100 on behalf of the Rochester Ladies' Anti-Slavery Society. The plan now proved prescient. To avoid the immediate threat of extradition from New York to Virginia, and to avoid the major US ports of departure for England, he departed from Canada aboard the *Nova Scotian* over a month after he had begun his flight.[46] Arriving in Liverpool on November 24, he went directly to the home of Julia Griffiths Crofts. "I found my old friend Julia quite glad of course to see me," he wrote to Post, and, "of equal importance, her husband, too." Crofts called on her network to ensure that Douglass spent the next two months speaking throughout the Midlands, northern England, and Scotland. Although his mail from America was sent to the home of other abolitionist friends, he told Post that the Crofts house was "my main home" in England. Post regretted her quarrel with Julia, as well. "Tell her there is much which we have known, to make us love each other," she begged Douglass. "The rest should be forgotten."[47]

Back in Rochester, the family carried on under a shadow of suspicion. Lewis, Frederick Jr., and Rosetta helped substitute editor Abram Pryne keep the paper going, while Charles remained at the Pierson farm. By December, Annie had begun attending school with a large number of children of German immigrants, probably at one of the two private institutions created by the German community. While the Germans were not active abolitionists, they supported antislavery, and John Brown had hardly shocked this group of immigrants who had fled government oppression after the 1848 revolutions in their home country. They had no problem accepting the daughter of one of his associates in their midst, and Annie informed her father, "The Ge[r]man children like me very much." She bragged that she was first in her class, having "gone a head of them and they have been there longer than me too." Rosetta reported to their father that Annie "is the favorite of her German teacher" who praised her as "the best scholar he has" and that "she writes daily in her English writing book and intends to astonish you with her advance in penmanship."[48]

Even as the danger of her father's capture dissipated, Rosetta remembered the period after his departure as "the Winter of the John Brown Raid with all its sorrows." Frederick was living in exile and would be for the immediate and foreseeable future, and Rochester had proved itself to be less than sympathetic to Brown supporters. Rosetta, expecting a "full house" for a memorial meeting in Corinthian Hall, reported that "between two and three hundred assembled," which she declared "a mean audience for Rochester." The Douglasses may have also felt a frisson of survivor's guilt, having been so close to Brown's plans. Brown had attempted to persuade Frederick to accompany him to Harpers Ferry, telling him, "'I will defend you with my life.'" Frederick declined to join him, and then turned to Shields Green, the Douglasses' handyman and a former slave, to implore him to return to Rochester. Green replied, "I b'leve I'll go wid de ole man." He mounted the scaffold two weeks after Brown. The whole family mourned their deaths. When Brown was sentenced, Annie cried, "That hard hearted man said he must die," then raged that "They took him in an open field and about a half mile from the Jail and hung him." According to her brother Charles, Brown's death was "a heavy blow" to his little sister, and that "to think of his being hung appaled her." Rosetta lamented, "the Virginia hyenas have murdered our Hero." Although Frederick had left them to face an uncertain future, he could easily have stood beside Green and become yet another in a long history of black men on the gallows.[49]

Then, Annie fell ill. Her condition worsened, "baffl[ing] the skill of physicians and friends." Nine days before her eleventh birthday, she succumbed to "brain congestion." Her brother Charles believed that she simply "pined away" after Brown's execution. Indeed, this became the standard story among Douglass family friends. Her obituary noted that she was "sadly distressed by the dreadful termination of the 'Harper's Ferry Tragedy,' and feared greatly for the safety of her father," speculating that these feelings had "much to do with her death." At her funeral, the Reverend Jonathan Edwards of Rochester's Plymouth Congregational Church connected her death to the raid, and an acquaintance remembered that the illustrated newspapers of the day had "so excited the child, that she drooped and died." Sally Holley, Frederick's fellow Rochester antislavery lecturer, insisted that "poor, dear, little Anna grieved herself to death with fright and terror over her father's flight to England, to escape the fate of old John Brown." Only ten years old, Annie was too young to engage in activism and not yet old enough to join her brothers and sister in distributing the paper. Unable to place her in the context of family abolitionism, family and friends gave her death political significance by linking it to Brown's.[50]

Annie could not have helped but be disturbed by her proximity to two men who met so tragic an end in so bloody an affair, as well as by the threat to her father and his subsequent exile. Unfortunately, hers was an all-too-common nineteenth-century diagnosis that could have meant any condition, such as meningitis, that inflamed the brain tissue. Her funeral took place on March 16, 1860, in the family home. Escorted by approximately thirty-five carriages and more mourners on foot, her body was carried to nearby Mount Hope Cemetery, where she had formerly enjoyed strolls with her father. The Douglasses had made no provisions for a death in the family, so the Porters offered to have her interred with theirs. For at least a month after the funeral, Anna was still "not very well" and "quite feeble though about the house." To Rosetta fell the task of responding to condolence letters, although she confessed to being "neglectful" because "I have to get up considerable energy to write lately." She told the old family friend, Harriet Adams, "I am now left alone being the only sister again." With the baby of the family gone, a brother living elsewhere, her father absent, and her mother inconsolable, Rosetta confessed that "my loneliness at times I cannot describe."[51]

Annie went to her grave without her father knowing of his loss. On the day of her death, he was with the Croftses, reviewing the success of a recent fair and preparing speeches. Four days after her funeral, he traveled to Glasgow, where he spoke during the last week of March. When he finally received his mail from home, his daughter had been dead for over three weeks. Crofts witnessed his first reaction to the news and for years afterward recalled his grief. In the letter that he immediately dispatched, Rosetta detected no "composure of mind." Disregarding all caution, he left for home as soon as he could. Arriving in Portland, Maine, he met Lydia Dennett, an abolitionist who had been his acquaintance since 1842, who helped him return quietly to Rochester by skirting through Canada. He walked through the door at South Street in April, just about the time Rosetta expected his next letter from England. In July, the Douglasses purchased a plot for their family in Mount Hope Cemetery, where they reinterred Annie.[52]

The summer after Annie's death presented several possible scenarios crucial to the emotional lives of the Douglass family, and especially to Anna's and Frederick's marriage. Harriet Adams and her daughter, Matilda, who was the same age as Annie, planned to visit that summer, reuniting her with the Douglasses for the first time since 1848. "Please come," Anna begged. Rosetta reassured Harriet that, in spite of the mourning household or perhaps because of it, "your presence would be so welcome." Harriet shared a background and history with the Douglasses. She had also known John Brown, and she had suffered the death of her own youngest a few years earlier. July, instead, brought Ottilie Assing. She complicated the Douglass household in ways that may not have comforted all members of the family. In all her depictions of her visits to the Douglasses, she described their home as her retreat from the summer humidity of New Jersey and a place where she enjoyed intellectual companionship with Frederick. As early as 1859, Rosetta relayed to her father that Ottilie was "sighing for summer still" because "it is only then that she enjoys herself." He must have appreciated her company because he continued to invite her back, in spite of Anna's clear objections.[53] Assing always thought herself a model guest, but her contempt for Anna was never far from the surface and she poured it into her letters to other friends. Except in caustic asides, Assing seldom noted the people who made her carefree vacation possible, and she more often sent regards to the pets than to the family in her letters. In 1860, the two women had only known one another for three years, and had interacted for only two summers. Over the coming years, they never warmed to one another, and little suggested that they had ever regarded one another with anything but formal cordiality. Unlike Adams, she did not have the affection of both Anna and Frederick.[54]

These two houseguests, one invited by Anna and Rosetta and the other by Frederick, offer insight into the ways that the married couple defined themselves. Anna's desire for Harriet's company showed an affinity with their past, a time in which she and Frederick had a shared companion in their home. Harriet connected Anna to the black working class, a black history, and the kinship of a black community and its lived politics. With Ottilie, Frederick looked toward an implicitly white, European intellectual history, a middle-class status, a transcendence of race, an engagement with republican politics, and work as a balm for suffering. Anna and Ottilie became antagonists; but these two sets of values were neither mutually exclusive nor necessarily hostile, and the tendency of each spouse toward one did not mean rejection of the other. Anna was not anti-intellectual, nor did Frederick repudiate his past, the black working class, or his experience as a black man. Still, each spouse had an individual identity rooted in different aspects of their life together. Within the shared narrative of their family history, they each created their own discrete storylines. If both Assing and Adams had visited the summer after Annie's death, Frederick and Anna would each have had a friend who could relieve Rosetta of the emotional strain of mediating between the two spouses. Assing, however, seemed to be the only visitor, welcomed by Frederick, leaving Rosetta to make up the emotional difference for her mother.[55]

Douglass and Assing had much to discuss that summer, with the 1860 presidential election dividing parties and the nation. As Douglass received news of Annie's death, the Democratic convention in Charleston fell apart because, as Assing reported to her German audience, "This formerly powerful party is internally so unstable and divided into so many factions." She observed that "it was the slavery question that again was the cause of the dissention." By the end of the summer, two Democratic candidates, both odious to Douglass, and a third party of former Whigs were running. Douglass declared that "This political organization [the Democrats] is now hopelessly divided and broken up." He rejoiced that "Babylon has fallen" because "the vital element of the party has been hatred of Negroes and love of spoils." Meanwhile, in May, the ever-strengthening Republican Party, opposed to the extension of slavery into western territories but of varying opinions about the status of both free and enslaved African Americans, convened in Chicago. Everyone who considered themselves antislavery awaited the outcome with anticipation.[56]

"While we should be glad to co-operate with a party fully committed to the doctrine of 'All rights to all men,'" Douglass announced on the conclusion of the Republican Party convention, "in the absence of all hope of rearing up the standard of such a party for the coming campaign, we can but desire the success of the Republican candidates." Assing certainly did, predicting to her German audience that "there is reason to hope that the year 1861 will see the first Republican president installed in the White House." She preferred William Seward of Auburn, New York, the presumed frontrunner, who had a reputation as the most antislavery of the potential nominees; but Douglass had lost respect him when the former senator backed away from that position after Harpers Ferry. He preferred Charles Sumner, the antislavery senator from Massachusetts, whom South Carolina representative Preston Brooks had beat into a coma four years earlier after Sumner had condemned the "slaveocracy" in his speech "Crime against Kansas." "His sacred blood has stained the Senate floor," Douglass declared. He compared the Bay State senator to the leaders of England's movement against the transatlantic slave trade. Assing's powers of persuasion could not overcome Douglass's ambivalence about the party, and neither Sumner nor Seward won the nomination. Instead, the Republicans chose a dark horse, a Free Soil Whig from Illinois whom both Assing and Douglass considered a capitulation to less radical elements in the party.[57]

"I cannot support Lincoln," Douglass told Gerrit Smith, the perennial candidate for the barely extant Liberty Party. At the suggestion of Elizabeth Cady Stanton, who broke with her Republican husband, Henry, he toyed with endorsing an abolitionist party formed by Stephen S. Foster. Foster's wife, Douglass's first lecturing partner and nemesis Abby Kelley, could not bring herself to support her husband entering formal politics. Nor could Susan B. Anthony, who claimed that Stephen Foster was *"repeating the Liberty Party Experiment,"* although she did hope that Douglass would join Foster, "for he stands so isolated alone now." The question of Republican antislavery sentiment notwithstanding, the significance of the election remained clear. The outrage that poured onto the Republicans from the pro-slavery factions led Douglass and other abolitionists to wonder if, despite its appearance as the lesser of an array of evils, a Republican victory might have significant consequences for the future of slavery.[58]

Yet, excluded from citizenship by the loathed 1857 *Dred Scott* decision and from suffrage by state restrictions, few free African Americans outside of New England could vote. As the presidential election progressed, an equally important referendum to eliminate New York State's $250 property qualification for black male suffrage moved onto the ballot in November. As much as Douglass hoped that this initiative would pass, he also knew that "neither Republicans nor Abolitionists seem to care much for it." In November, Republican "Wide-Awake" clubs paraded throughout the North to celebrate Lincoln's victory, but white voters had defeated the proposal. "The moral effect of this defeat of justice and equality," Douglass wrote with disgust, "will be to fix more deeply in the public mind the popular contempt and scorn with which the rights and feelings of colored citizens are regarded, and invite their brutal manifestations wherever the colored man appears." One manifestation of that brutality disrupted a December meeting in Boston's Tremont Temple, where Douglass spoke on the anniversary of John Brown's execution.[59]

By the spring, Douglass struggled to find any reason to hope for the future of African Americans in the nation. Threats of disunion had grown into action in South Carolina, and the Senate contemplated proposed constitutional amendments that would protect slavery so as to forestall the secession movement. Lincoln kept publicly silent, leaving Douglass to wonder if the best option might be to let the South go. "If only we had an abolition President to hold these men in the Union," he lamented, then that man would "execute that part of the Constitution which is in favor of liberty" and enforce an antislavery interpretation. Assing agreed with Douglass, echoing his anticipation that disunion would protect fugitive slaves by offering them asylum and genuine freedom. Douglass grew ever more frustrated by the president-elect's seeming inaction as the states of the lower South voted to leave the nation. "It remains to be seen whether the Federal Government is really able to do more than hand over some John Brown to be hanged, suppress a slave insurrection, or catch a runaway slave," he spat, "whether it is powerless for liberty, and only powerful for slavery." With racism so prevalent in the North, he also suspected that were the federal government to put down the insurrection with armed force, northern soldiers would join the other side.[60]

In this period of despair, James Redpath, the Scottish agent of the Haitian Bureau of Emigration, offered Douglass free passage to visit the island. Douglass had always opposed emigration as the solution to racial discrimination in the United States. White-sponsored organizations, such as the American Colonization Society, made no pretense about their desire to purge the nation of African descendants, but black-led organizations, such as those encouraging relocation to Haiti, gained some support. Redpath had been courting Douglass, who printed several articles about the bureau in his paper. In April 1861, Douglass and Rosetta made plans for the journey. He may have also suggested to Assing that, with her interest in republicanism and people of African descent, she seize the opportunity to see a black nation in action.[61]

Assing told her German readers that she had planned to make the voyage, "but like a bolt of lightning" broke the news of Fort Sumter's fall into rebel hands. Douglass, for all of his prevarication about Lincoln and the Republicans, noted South Carolina's strategic blunder in attacking federal property. "Our rulers were ready enough to sacrifice the Negro to the Union so long as there was any hope of saving the Union by that means," he explained. Now, he rejoiced, southern rebels "have exposed the throat of slavery to the keen knife of liberty, and have given a chance to all the righteous forces of the nation to deal a death-blow to the monster evil of the nineteenth century." Douglass stayed in the United States with the intention of doing all he could to ensure that the arc of war bent toward emancipation. Yet, while he railed that a slaveholder "is a rebel against manhood, womanhood and brotherhood," his prescription beyond emancipation was black male military service and his rhetoric shaped the struggle as one that would prove an honorable black masculinity. Abolitionist women who agreed with him, including his daughter Rosetta, were left to ponder their place in the national crisis.[62]

7

Principle and Expediency, 1861–1870

Douglass believed war could strike the death blow to slavery, but so long as "Mr. Lincoln in his war proclamation assures the man stealers and pirates of the Cotton Confederacy that he shall not war upon their '*property*,'" as runaways were returned to their masters and black men were turned away by recruiters, then African Americans "must fight against the North as well as the South." African Americans had to first fight the US government, forcing it to turn the war into one of liberation as part of a larger conflict demanding the recognition of black citizenship. Although Douglass later insisted that "the cause of the slave has been peculiarly woman's cause," this grander battle had little room for women. Some, like Susan B. Anthony, had no use for the war in the first place, believing it "humiliating" that abolitionists like herself would be forced into "the political world—one of *expediency* not principle." More agreed with Elizabeth Cady Stanton, who, Anthony grumbled, "says it is impossible for her to think or speak on anything but the War." Most white women could navigate the conflicts between patriotism, idealism, and pragmatism by continuing their antislavery activism or carving out roles for themselves in connection with the war. Black men and women, such as the Douglass children, showed more ambivalence toward a conflict that provided them with no role or guarantee of improved status.[1]

The Douglass household felt the marginal status of African Americans from the beginning of the conflict. As their father's frustration with the war effort raged in his editorials and speeches, the Douglass sons found themselves with little to do. Although Douglass had expanded the newspaper in June 1858, launching *Douglass' Monthly* for his overseas audience while also continuing to publish the weekly *Frederick Douglass' Paper*, by 1860 subscriptions for the latter had fallen drastically. He was forced to admit to his main patron Gerrit Smith that he saw no alternative "but to let the paper go down." *Frederick Douglass' Paper* folded in August, leaving twenty-year-old Lewis and eighteen-year-old Frederick Jr. with a drastically reduced workload and the family with one less source of income. The two brothers opened a grocery store, but the enterprise did not last much longer than a year. Sixteen-year-old Charles, meanwhile, remained on the Pierson farm outside Lockport, where he had fled after John Brown's raid. The rejection of black men from military service may have spared the family the prospect of losing a son so soon after Annie's death, but the young men surely felt the same national insult to their manhood that their father did as they endured the indignity of sitting out the fight and the uncertainty that the great events of the day would ever transform them into recognized citizens of the nation.[2]

Rosetta, who turned twenty-two in June 1861, also found herself on the sidelines. Whereas the men in her family saw the military as the main avenue for participation, women's exclusion from service led Rosetta to carve out another role for herself. Like her father and Susan B. Anthony, many abolitionists found themselves conflicted about ways to advance the cause during wartime. Many, such as the Rochester Ladies' Anti-Slavery Society, continued to raise funds for fugitive aid and speakers. Then, in May 1861, General Benjamin Butler began to declare the slaves who arrived at Union lines to be free as "contraband" of war. The organizational effort then turned to aid for the thousands of men, women, and children who arrived with little more than the clothes on their back, seeking the freedom that they believed the war would bring. In major cities, such as Philadelphia, Boston, and New York, black women formed contraband relief associations. Rosetta, who had never involved herself very deeply in Rochester organizations, perhaps wanted to find her own way to contribute both to the cause and to her family. She may have also hoped to experience a world beyond Rochester after the visit to Haiti was thwarted. Her father admired independent women like Julia Griffiths, Ottilie Assing, various abolitionist women, and her own mother in her youth, and he emphasized individualism and self-help in his writings and speeches. Always proud of her father, she both absorbed his message and intended to please him. In January 1862, Rosetta accompanied Douglass to Philadelphia, where he placed her in the care of Thomas Dorsey, one of the city's black elite, who had helped him elude authorities after the Harpers Ferry raid.[3]

Rosetta probably hoped to secure a position in E. D. Basset's school, which her father had praised during his visit to the city. Basset employed stalwarts of black Philadelphia activism, including the mother-and-daughter team Sarah Mapps and Grace Douglass (no relation) and Octavius Catto. Rosetta did not secure a position there, but she did get an education in the perils of being a young, single, and independent black woman.[4] Within six weeks, she was miserable. "I did not know I could be so unhappy and friends so false," she declared to her parents. Thomas Dorsey proved "quite genial," but his wife and daughters, Louisa, Sarah, and Mary, had taken an immediate dislike to Rosetta. "Mrs. [Louisa] Dorsey is tyrannical," she reported, and Louisa had enlisted daughter Sarah

Figure 7.1 Rosetta Douglass at around the time she taught school in Salem, New Jersey. National Park Service, Frederick Douglass National Historic Site, Washington, DC, Rosetta Douglass, [c. 1863], FRDO 3904.

and Sarah's future mother-in-law in a campaign to control Rosetta. Although Thomas Dorsey encouraged his young guest to walk about the city, pointing out "that white ladies walked out" while "colored ones were too lazy to dress and go," Louisa took it as her duty to ensure Rosetta's respectability more zealously than Rosetta herself was accustomed to. When Rosetta ventured to the post office alone, then called on a Dorsey in-law for lunch, Louisa accused her of being a "*streetrunner*" (a prostitute), adding to Rosetta's humiliation by upbraiding her "before a room full of folk." Confined to the house, Rosetta was forced to snub

Emily Minton, wife of a well-to-do black restaurateur and a friend of her father, just to keep peace with her hostess. She lamented that in going to Philadelphia, she had "anticipated so much pleasure in an innocent way" with "no idea of being a hermit." Instead, "nothing but unhappiness has followed."[5]

Compounding Rosetta's isolation, Louisa disapproved of anyone visiting her at the house. Rosetta protested to her father that "there are plenty of young ladies who are ready and willing to take me about." Unfortunately, "Mrs. Dorsey will not allow it and would treat them in such a way they dare not approach." As she awaited the arrival of one of those young women, she found herself "fearful of an explosion." When Catto and William Minton, Emily's son, stopped in to visit her, Rosetta noted that "the family did not like it."[6] Louisa also prevented her from finding a job. "All the time I am here I feel in bondage," she told her father, "for I must not even go out which is necessary to get or at least to try and negotiate for a school."[7] Feeling a failure, Rosetta longed to return home, "but I feel ashamed." Before she gave up, she decided first to investigate a prospect sent by "Uncle" Perry Wilmer from Salem, New Jersey, near the border of Delaware and Maryland. Wilmer was either Anna's younger brother or saw himself in that role through the fictive kinships typical of southern black communities. He recommended Rosetta for a school in Claysville, in a very poor section of Salem County. She gratefully accepted and moved in with Wilmer, his wife, Elizabeth, and their three young daughters. After passing the local teacher's exams, she secured a position at a school in the town of Salem. Despite the Wilmers' poverty, Rosetta considered her living arrangements a vast improvement over the Dorseys.[8]

She soon reconsidered. At first, she confessed only that the conditions did not suit her. The young Wilmer daughters were "rather unruly," she explained, and "after being in a noisy school all day one likes quiet at night." Following her experience in Philadelphia, she hesitated to say more because, she told her father, "you would begin to think me a great faultfinder." Nevertheless, the truth came out. "Aunt Lizzie is rather a passionate person," Rosetta observed. After announcing her intention to find lodging elsewhere, she faced Elizabeth's vacillation between "over fondness" in order to keep Rosetta and her board money and threats "to pitch me out doors and my washing after me." On two occasions, Elizabeth flew into a rage, chasing her niece through the house and, Rosetta informed her parents, "Lately it has been a great way with her to shake her fist in my face." Fortunately, September found her more peacefully situated in the home of Joseph Gibbs, a laborer, and his mother Lucy, a laundress. Despite Elizabeth's abuse, Rosetta expressed fewer thoughts of returning home once she moved to Salem, and none once she took up residence with the Gibbses.[9]

In her travails, Rosetta constantly drew a distinction between the trust that her parents had placed in her and the expectations of her hosts. When she went out at home, she told her father, "you and mother are satisfied of my capability to take care of myself," and her parents did not censure her acquaintances so long as they "were satisfied that those with whom I went were respectable." She had thought Thomas Dorsey's advice about taking exercise by walking about Philadelphia to be sound because it resembled that of her parents. He "talked the same as you do," she observed, and she was determined "to feel at home in the city." Years later, she referred to conflicts with her brothers as she was growing up, but in 1862, what she observed boarding in other families had shocked her. At the Dorseys', she reported that "the language and manners in the family was enough to disgust me," while at the Wilmers', "I have received harsh language from her [Elizabeth Wilmer] that my own mother never gives me." Her parents had been stern disciplinarians, but they had granted her a degree of trust, freedom of movement, and respect that she was not accorded in the homes of the black elite or her kin.

Just as distressing were the gossip and intrusive questions that circled around the themes of an unhappy home life and her own morality. "I am amidst slanderers," she declared. Louisa Dorsey had insisted to Rosetta that her father had said Rosetta must be "kept from the boys as if that was my particular failing." Dorsey's fixation on the subject led Rosetta to conclude, "One would think she would be glad to have me enjoy myself in connection with street running." Indeed, the older woman may have misinterpreted or misused advice from Douglass that Rosetta was innocent of the fast ways of young city men. Nevertheless, even in Salem, Rosetta endured Elizabeth Wilmer "repeatedly asking me questions about my former habits" because "she had heard I was not altogether what I should be" and that "I was driven from my home on account of my growing intimacy with men and again on account of my quarrelsome disposition toward my mother."[10] Rumors drifted in from elsewhere, too. Rosetta told her father of a minister, allegedly from Rochester, who insisted that he "knew of you [Douglass] having been obliged to send me away," and recounted tales of other whisperings that "I was sent from home on account of my ill conduct" or "that you and mother could not live with me." Elizabeth Wilmer accosted Rosetta with another story, this one coming from "some Lucy Oliver from New Bedford." Rosetta recognized that, on both occasions, she had been confused with William Wells Brown's daughter, Josephine, who had met with some trouble in 1857. Rosetta attempted to correct the mistake, but to no avail.[11]

Others insinuated that her background was less than respectable. Sarah Dorsey, in one instance, pointedly said that "she did not like too dark a face to come in their house to make much of a stay there," suggesting that Rosetta's darker skin was a detriment to their household. Some people believed that she was a con artist making a living by pretending to be Frederick Douglass's daughter. She informed her father that the minster allegedly from Rochester "told it that Fred. Douglass himself was a very nice man but the daughter of his is one who had become low." Two Quaker women interrogated Rosetta about her parentage, asking if Anna and Frederick had been married before Frederick had escaped from slavery. Rosetta took umbrage not only at the insinuation of illegitimacy and insult to her mother, but also to the intrusiveness of the question. Another Quaker woman and her companion scoffed at Rosetta having taught in Claysville, "as those in that district were very low indeed." She seemed to think Rosetta was tainted by the connection and with a "curled lip" told Rosetta, "I wonder at thee going there to teach them."[12] In sum, she told her father, "Every thing that is vile has been said of me by persons living here and strangers coming here pretending to have known me."[13]

Although Rosetta's friend Caroline Reckless, the wife of a Philadelphia merchant and friend of the abolitionist Pugh family, assured her that the gossip resulted "more from envy than anything else," part of the problem lay in the particular oddity Rosetta presented to the people she encountered.[14] From a good, well-known family, she seemed not the type who would have to work for a living, much less travel so far from home for a job. She lived among people for whom no model existed to explain the reasons a young, single, educated woman was willing to leave her comfortable home to seek independence, especially if she was the daughter of the famed Frederick Douglass. Others could only imagine dreadful scenarios that drove her away, thinking that her home must have been unhappy or that she must have fought with her parents. The theory that she chased boys had the greatest resonance in a culture anxious about black women's sexuality and independence, and that stereotyped black women as inherently lascivious.

Rosetta only stoked their imagination with her reticence about her home life in Rochester. When her father asked her if she may have brought these rumors on herself through idle talk that "spread family differences," she replied, "Father, I trust I have too great a family pride, pride for yourself to say any thing to make people acquainted with such things with which they have no business." She had, after all, lived through the gossip about her father and Griffiths. Nor did she want to praise her family too much for fear that others might assume she was making an unfavorable comparison with their own. In both the narrow world of Philadelphia's aspiring elite and the close-knit small town of Salem's black working class, Rosetta encountered the guarded values of respectability familiar to her from home, to which she believed she had adhered. Outside the immediate context of that home, however, others saw her as aberrant.[15]

Rosetta's convictions also made her a target. Ever her father's daughter, and not a little her mother's, she would not let an injustice go without comment or hide her opinions. Just as her parents hated "shams" and hypocrisy, she detested "the feeling of caste" that she witnessed in Philadelphia, much of it directed at her. In Salem, when the Quaker woman who questioned her association with the Claysville school sneered that its students were beneath her, Rosetta became "quite indignant." She told her father that "I tried to show as well as I could that much of degradation was owing to the whites." The woman and her companion, both being white, did not take her point well, and "much was said on both sides." The encounter earned her a rebuke from Perry, who told her that he "did not think it was proper to say such things to persons who were our friends." Rosetta retorted that "I should certainly say what I thought when people speak so carelessly of slavery." To which Perry ordered, "You cannot speak here." "I try and have always tried to govern my temper," Rosetta insisted to her father, "but I do not wish to be tyrannized over." Hers was a family trait.[16]

She did not go to church, either. Echoing her father, she told him that reading and experience had convinced her that "most of this religion is a cloak for sin." Her opinion was not much helped by the southern minister who issued her teaching exam in New Jersey. "We have every reason to believe [he] is a secessionist," Rosetta reported, because his son had been arrested "for giving information to the enemy [the Confederacy]." In Philadelphia, where the African Methodist Episcopal church served as a vital social political force in the black community, her absence was noted and had probably contributed to Louisa Dorsey's opinion of her. Moving to Salem, she observed that she had become "sort of a mystery" because "I am never seen going to church and I never talk of the Bible." She did, however, agree to lead a Sunday school class of older girls because it was a Sabbath School where "the children are taught to read the bible," emphasizing literacy more than religion. She wanted her father to know that this was all the product of following his lessons and example. "Most of my ideas of morality and uprightness of character I have learned from you father," she assured him. "You may think you were talking in vain," she declared, but "here is one that remembers."[17]

Rosetta downplayed her mother's influence, writing that "for smaller things also mother has given some counsel," but Anna emerged in her daughter's economizing. Rosetta earned very little, and at one point she had to beg from door to door for the portion of her salary that her students' parents were supposed to donate. Not wanting to burden the Wilmers, she voluntarily turned over her earnings to them, "except what amount it took to do my washing," and used the sums that her father sent "to buy my paper and ink and postage stamps and thread." She explained that the thread allowed her to sew and thus not burden Elizabeth with mending. She also skipped lunches to the point that she "was sometimes very faint," so as to relieve Elizabeth of the cost and trouble of preparing at least one meal. Finding that the family had a single towel used by everyone, she used the money from her father to buy three new ones. Wishing to stay up late to work, she purchased her own candles, which the Wilmers also used. Although "some Quaker lady had said it was a pity I was here on Perry as he was struggling," she assured her father that Perry and Elizabeth would agree that "I have been of some help instead of hindrance." When she relocated to the more hospitable Gibbs home, she took on needlework and added an evening school for adults to her Sunday school and regular day classes.[18]

She took some pride that before she arrived, her "school was noted as being a very bad one" but had become "very orderly and the scholars are more or less attentive" under her management, and they "appear to love me." No longer having to skip meals, she became healthy enough to worry that "I am to be large like Aunt Charlotte." She could save more of her salary once she did not have to turn the whole over to the Wilmers. Then, in the autumn, her brother Lewis moved to Salem. Lewis continued to feel the lack of opportunities for black men in the United States, more so since he had become engaged to Amelia Loguen, daughter of the Reverend Jermain Loguen, Douglass's compatriot in Syracuse. Despite his father's opposition, Lewis joined Kansas senator Samuel C. Pomeroy's expedition to establish a black colony on the Panamanian isthmus. News of the project's cancellation reached Lewis in Philadelphia, en route to Washington. While Douglass rejoiced that a "scheme for getting quit of the free colored people of the United States" had collapsed, Lewis felt "dejected and miserable." Rosetta asked him to visit her, and shortly thereafter, he reported to Amelia from Salem that "I have gone into the Restaurant business with good prospects." "I see him every day," Rosetta informed their father, "he seems to be doing well in his business." Now she had a brother to keep her company and vouch for her respectability. As Lewis pined for his fiancée, Rosetta had no harassment to report as the year ended.[19]

Douglass awaited the chime of midnight on New Year's Eve 1862, anticipating "the great day which is to determine the destiny not only of the American Republic, but that of the American Continent."[20] Then, the deed was done. Lincoln signed the Emancipation Proclamation on January 1, 1863. For all of its limitations to territory in rebellion, already freed slaves were effectively liberated in territory controlled by the Union Army and the Border States that had not seceded had begun the legislative process of ending slavery inside their borders. This revolution could not go backward. Still, the Proclamation was only a preliminary step for black men. With emancipation still tenuous, black men unable to vote on an equal footing with white men in all states, and the *Dred Scott* decision still excluding African Americans from federal citizenship, the struggle had hardly begun. "The manhood of the slave has been a test of all our laws, customs, morals, civilization, governments, and our religions," Douglass had declared at the beginning of the war. Although he often spoke in universal terms, indicting slaveholders as "rebel[s] against manhood, womanhood and brotherhood" desiring "nothing less than the complete destruction of all that dignifies and ennobles human character," his rhetoric increasingly invoked black masculinity as the force for black liberation and the path to black citizenship.[21]

Ever since his days battling the slavebreaker Edward Covey, Douglass had argued that militance, and now military service, was the means by which black men could demand respect. "The colored man only waits for honorable admission into the service," he declared at New York City's Cooper Union in February, depicting black men as the defenders of the Union.[22] Already, the Confiscation Act of 1862 allowed the military to use "men of African descent," but Congress had not yet sought to raise black troops. So, in January 1863, Massachusetts governor John A. Andrew asked for and received the US War Department's permission to enlist black men for the state's Fifty-Fourth Infantry regiment. "Men of Color to Arms!" Douglass called, invoking the names of black rebels Denmark Vesey, Nat Turner, and Shields Green. He began traveling through the North to encourage black men, who had been told for so long that this was a white man's war, to trust that they would not die in vain. There was no question that the Douglass sons would join.[23]

They seemed eager to, as well. Nineteen-year-old Charles was the first New Yorker to sign on. Lewis, the oldest Douglass son, followed. As were his brothers, Frederick Jr. too may have been eager to prove himself a man, a patriot, and his father's son. Other families saw all their sons off to war and, because men from the same town usually served in the same regiment, lost more than one. Either at the urging of his family or by his own decision, this middle son did not become a soldier. That may have been small consolation to Anna since he instead went to the Deep South to recruit soldiers from among the emancipated slaves along the Mississippi River, close to a war zone and in danger of capture, enslavement, or assassination by guerillas. Meanwhile, through the summer, Frederick Sr. pursued a commission in the army. Although his efforts may have been a means to force the military to bring black men into the officer ranks, he seemed eager to be closer to the action as well. From England, Julia Griffiths Crofts begged Douglass, "By everything dear to you, my friend, do not *take any commission* that leads you, *personally*, into the fighting ranks." Anna may have agreed, but she alone had seen and touched the scars on her husband's back. She knew the core of anger that fired his work. She had given birth to his free children, raised his family amid the public quarrels of his colleagues, and provided the stability that enabled him to fight for their cause. This war was one more sacrifice.[24]

Having all her sons and her husband leave home not only strained Anna emotionally but also isolated her because she relied on her children to read and write for her when she corresponded with her absent husband. Now that the brothers were serving the cause, Rosetta's presence at home became necessary. Perhaps she also wished to be closer to her loved ones should the worst news arrive. May found Rosetta back in Rochester. From there, she and Anna traveled to Camp Meigs, outside Boston, where Charles and Lewis trained. Charles had contracted what Lewis determined to be "a severe cold," but Lewis prepared to ship out to Port Royal, South Carolina, on May 28. His fiancée, Amelia, was not there to see him off, much to his chagrin. Rosetta and Anna, however, stood in the crowd to hear Frederick Sr. speak to the hope that African Americans would become fully incorporated "into the great national family of America," and to watch Lewis march through Boston's streets in uniform.[25]

In spite of black men risking their lives for the Union, the double battle against slavery in the South and discrimination in the North continued. The Confederacy vowed to execute the white officers of black troops and enslave any captured black soldiers. Then, in June, Lewis and Charles learned that while white soldiers received a monthly pay of $13, they and their comrades would receive only $10, and that an additional $3 would be deducted for their uniforms. None had access to the rank and much higher pay of commissioned officers. In protest, the black soldiers refused all pay until granted equal salaries. The burden fell particularly hard on their dependents back home. Anna and Rosetta were better off than the families of working-class men, but with only *Douglass' Monthly* and whatever wages the two Fredericks received for recruiting, they had probably hoped for supplements from the two brothers in arms. Amelia Loguen, too, may have wondered at the financial circumstances she would later face if Lewis was not putting aside savings to start their life together. The senior Frederick became more disillusioned as the summer progressed, wondering how he could ask black men to give their lives for a country that considered them, quite literally, less valuable.[26]

Secretary of War Edwin Stanton and President Lincoln both personally reassured Douglass that they were doing everything in their power to pressure Congress to change the policies on pay and black officers. They had also left Douglass with the impression that they would grant him a commission, which might open the door for other black promotions. Douglass so much expected this development that he ceased publication of *Douglass' Monthly* with the August 1863 issue, announcing to his readers that "I am going South to assist Adjutant General Thomas, in the organization of colored troops, who shall win for the millions in bondage the inestimable blessings of liberty and country." Through the month, he received passes and recommendations to enter Vicksburg, Mississippi, now in the hands of the Union Army. No commission arrived, despite his prodding, but by September, events at home may have altered his plans in any case.[27]

In July, the Fifty-Fourth assaulted Battery Wagner on Morris Island at the mouth of the Charleston Harbor. Lewis described the attack as "the most desperate charge of the war." The regiment suffered heavy losses, leaving him to lament that "the splendid Fifty-fourth is cut to pieces." He himself had led men up a parapet where, he told his father in a dashed-off note, "The grape and canister shell and Minie swept us down like chaff." To Amelia he wrote, "a shell would explode and clear a space of twenty feet." The barrage forced the men to fall back. In the fray, Lewis remembered, "I had my sword sheath about blown away," the blast spraying shrapnel across his groin. In light of the carnage that he witnessed, Lewis thought his injury so unimportant that he concealed the extent of his injuries from his parents and told Amelia that "I escaped unhurt from amid that perfect hail of shot and shell." By August, however, he wrote his letters from the military hospital in Beaufort, from under the watchful care of Harriet Tubman and the poet Charlotte Forten, both of whom had volunteered to nurse wounded black soldiers. Although Lewis had thus far remained immune to the diseases of the Low Country that had felled so many from the North, he confessed to Amelia, "I now fear that I am going to be sick." He promised her that his letters would remain cheerful, but what he had thought was a minor wound grew worse. September found him evacuated to New York City, where family friend Dr. James McCune Smith declared him too ill to be moved.[28]

In Syracuse, Amelia Loguen had particular concerns about the nature of Lewis's injury. According to Smith's report in October, Lewis had "spontaneous gangrene of the left half of Scrotum," with "the slough having separated leaving the part named entirely denuded." He never returned to serve and ultimately received a disability discharge due to "Scrotal Abscess gangrenous in its nature" and "a fistulous opening in Perineum." Facing a childless future in an era that expected her to become a mother, and with a fiancé whose wound might cause chronic medical problems, Amelia reconsidered her engagement. She did not commit to a wedding date; neither did she release Lewis from his promise. Instead, in early 1864, she left Syracuse to teach in Binghamton, New York. When he heard the news while awaiting his discharge, Lewis inquired, "What will become of your promise to me?" He tried to joke about rumors connecting him to a young woman in Rochester, teasing her about the many marital options available to a young veteran. Nevertheless, his concern was real. They did not marry until 1869, and they never had children.[29]

Even before he realized that Lewis's condition had become dire, Douglass told an acquaintance that "I am full of hope for the country, but deeply anxious for the safety of some who are very near me and who are now exposed to all the horrors of war." These might also have been the sentiments felt back at his home in Rochester. Although Lewis was now out of the line of fire, his health remained fragile for some time. As his brother gained strength, Charles sent word that he expected to go south to the war front. Frederick Jr. had moved his recruiting efforts north to Buffalo by the end of the year, but then he returned to Vicksburg. Frederick Sr. continued to agitate. Yet, for all the danger and frustration, the men could, at least, act. With *Douglass' Monthly* shuttered and the number of freedom seekers declining after the Emancipation Proclamation, Anna and Rosetta moved further away from the center of activism.[30]

Not all options to serve the war effort had evaporated, however. Activist women had always asserted their political and social consciousness through their own organizations. Amy Post became involved in relief for freed people both through her friend, former slave Harriet Jacobs, who went south to work among the emancipated, and through Susan B. Anthony. In May 1863, Anthony and Elizabeth Cady Stanton had formed the Woman's Loyal National League after two years of frustration that included the New York State Legislature's repeal of portions of the 1860 Women's Property Act and little interest in woman's rights or antislavery conventions. The organization would petition for a thirteenth amendment to embed the demise of slavery into the Constitution, allowing women to "make an opportunity to speak her thoughts on the war." In their founding document, they resolved that "there can never be true peace in this Republic until the civil and political rights of all citizens of African descent and all women are practically established."[31]

The Rochester Ladies' Anti-Slavery Society had geared its efforts toward contraband aid in 1862. They intended to engage a black woman to work among freedmen in Alexandria, Virginia, and could rely upon support from Julia Griffiths Crofts overseas. They briefly considered Rosetta for this position, a logical choice, but she seemed unaware of their plans from her post in Salem. Instead, the society sent the more experienced, Haverford College–educated Julia A. Wilbur. The American Missionary Association also recruited teachers for schools being established to teach the freedmen. Among them was Helen Pitts, a woman of Rosetta's age from Honeoye, New York, south of Rochester. By 1864 the association called for black teachers, and Edmonia Highgate, a Syracuse friend of the younger generation of Douglasses, volunteered. Rosetta, however, could not. Although she had never been deeply involved in organizational work and she was needed at home, by the end of 1863, her life had taken another course.[32]

Rosetta had returned to Rochester earlier in the year, and from there, she may have considered her future with some ambivalence. Rosine Ami-Droz, a Swiss governess working in England with whom she had been corresponding, might have warned Rosetta about the difficulties for single women living in alien families and holding firm to their convictions. If her father, in his admiration for Griffiths and Assing, had thought Rosetta might find inspiration in them, her own experience and what she saw of theirs cast their lives in a different light. Both had been a source of disharmony in her own home; and Griffiths had become the target of vituperative attacks, while Assing lived at the constant mercy of landlords. All of this Rosetta had experienced for herself while living with the Dorseys and Wilmers. Griffiths and Assing, at least, had the emotional support and companionship of Frederick as well as of their friends in Rochester and Hoboken. Rosetta had nothing similar in Philadelphia and Salem until Lewis arrived. She had found that, for a young, single woman, she had more freedom as her parents' dependent than she did on her own. Her hosts had policed her behavior and manipulated her with threats to tell the Douglasses that she was "saucy" and "quite unruly." She had experienced racism at school, knew of the dangers her father faced as an outspoken man of his race, and understood the importance of respectability. Yet, the enmity in those cases had come from unexpected sources. In her excursion from home, Quakers, middle-class African Americans, and extended kin, people whom she had every reason to trust, had antagonized her. In disgust, Rosetta vowed, "I never expect to visit any colored family who make such great pretentions" as those she had met in 1862. Although she had planned "to make another year more profitable to me as well as others," she may just as well have been open to other offers.[33]

Nathan Sprague presented another option. A gardener by trade, Sprague probably worked in the nursery next door to the Douglass's three acres in Rochester, and Anna may have hired him to do some of the heavy work on their property. Sometime in 1863, he caught Rosetta's eye. The young man, generally considered handsome, had grown up under slavery on the Prince Georges County, Maryland, plantation of former governor Samuel Sprigg, who was also his grandfather. He knew that he had been born on October 21, 1839, because his grandmother was the plantation midwife, and she and his mother had passed the information down to him. He may have run away around 1858, but by 1863, all of the Spragues were free. Leaving his family behind in the Washington, DC, area, Nathan migrated to Rochester, where he could easily have been one of the refugees receiving aid from the local abolitionists. Gardening and memories of rural Maryland offered common ground for conversation between Nathan and Anna, and neither would judge the other's dark skin color, inability to read, or manner of speaking. Whether or not Anna considered Nathan a good match for her daughter was another matter. He was certainly not the sort of husband that Frederick had imagined for Rosetta, and he stood in stark contrast to the spouses of the Douglass sons, all of whom came from free, educated black families.[34]

Frederick's objections, if he had any, would have revolved around class and education. Two decades earlier, in more reduced circumstances, Frederick had become distressed at the mere prospect that Harriet Adams, "altogether too refined and intelligent," might marry an "ignorant and unlearned" or "idle worthless person unable to take care of you or himself." More recently, in 1856, a white correspondent, whom Frederick suspected had written from the state prison in Auburn, had heard a rumor that the great abolitionist would pay "$15,000 to $20,000 dollars" to marry his daughter to a "whight man." The correspondent offered himself as a groom. Frederick responded that he did not have the money,

Figure 7.2 Rosetta Douglass met Nathan Sprague while he was working as a gardener in Rochester in 1863. National Park Service, Frederick Douglass National Historic Site, Washington, DC, Nathan Sprague, [n.d.], FRDO 4921.

but even if he did, "there are certain little faults of grammar and spelling as well as other little points in your letter, which compel me to regard you as a person, by education, manners, and morals, wholly unfit to associate with my daughter in any capacity whatsoever." His jesting did not hide the real expectation that the expense of educating and polishing Rosetta would not go to waste.[35]

Therefore, in 1863, Frederick likely looked on Rosetta's engagement to Nathan with trepidation. Nathan's history as a former slave and manual laborer, as well as his intention to learn to read, perhaps through Rosetta's instruction, gave the young couple the material to fashion the prospective groom as a latter-day Douglass, working to become a self-made man. They could at least point out that Douglass at twenty-three was hardly better off than Nathan, and while Anna made a good wife for a working-class man, Rosetta was much better situated than her mother had been to help her husband rise to the middle class. They could have likened their union to that of the Loguens, in which the former slave Jermain had married the wealthy Caroline Storum, who supported him as he devoted himself to aiding fugitive slaves.

As for Rosetta's decision to marry someone about whom her parents might have reservations, she had her own future to consider. She could return to a life of boarding in other people's home, low wages, supervision of other people's children, and gossip about her independence, with few emotional bonds. She had no reason to believe that a life in that direction would improve, other than that she might save a little money. If she chose matrimony, then she would head her own household, gain the respectability of marriage and motherhood, and raise her own family. She would be recognized as an adult. As had her mother before leaving Baltimore with Frederick so many years earlier, Rosetta chose the latter. More than her parents, too, she probably placed affection and attraction ahead of practical considerations, as was becoming the norm for middle-class marriages at mid-century. If either parent had objections, both bowed to her decision. On Christmas Eve 1863, Nathan Sprague and Rosetta Douglass married in the parlor of her parents' home.[36]

Unfortunately, the newlyweds were not in a position to set up their own household. Anna may have found having the couple in residence a convenience, but living with her parents did not convey to Rosetta the adulthood bestowed by marriage. In the late spring, she became pregnant. By the time of the baby arrived, later that year, the gardening season had ended and work become sparse for Nathan. Meanwhile, over the summer the government had finally relented and agreed to equal pay for black soldiers. Financial decisions, then, provided the backdrop for his next move. At their wedding, Nathan had been the only man in attendance not involved with the war effort. Lewis was on leave, having been wounded the previous July. Charles barely had enough time to get to Rochester from his post at Camp Meigs, and Frederick Jr. took time off from recruiting to attend the wedding. Rosetta and Anna may have been relieved that they would not have to worry for Nathan's life; however, the new husband and his father-in-law had different ideas. Faced with impending fatherhood, possible pressure from the Douglass men to do something in the fight against slavery, and perhaps his own desire to be a part of great events, Nathan enlisted for a year in the Massachusetts Fifty-Fourth, on September 13, 1864. He could send his salary back to his wife and new daughter Annie, born in November, while also fighting for the demise of the institution into which he had been born. "Poor Rosa!" cried Julia Griffiths Crofts from overseas. "I'm quite sorry he sh'd have to go—I tho't he tilled the ground."[37]

Nathan served the winter in Elmira, New York, before moving to Savannah, Georgia. Lewis, discharged from the army in February, found himself chafing at his idleness in Rochester and signed on with a series of sutlers who sold nonmilitary supplies to the Fifty-Fourth in South Carolina. "I feel more self reliant," he assured Amelia, "more independent than I should had I forever hung around home." Charles had proven himself an excellent clerk, but a transfer to the Fifth Cavalry brought him into the action in the South. After his discharge in September 1864, he found work with the Freedmen's Bureau in Washington, DC; and Frederick Jr. continued recruiting in Vicksburg. Their father pressed the government to seize the momentum of the war and the victories of black regiments to pass the Thirteenth Amendment to abolish slavery and to pass measures that would ensure the civil rights of all black Americans. Rosetta stayed home with her mother, taking care of the house, her new baby, and her father's correspondence. The Spragues' was not an atypical experience for families of servicemen, and it was more privileged than that of the families of many black soldiers, who increasingly came from the ranks of freedmen as the fighting wore on. Directly or indirectly, Nathan and Rosetta each saw themselves as part of the conflict, but in the context of the great questions about the nation, their difference reflected one of the core problems in the fight for universal civil rights.[38]

In October 1864, three-and-a-half years into the war, the most prominent black men of the day met in Syracuse's Wesleyan Methodist Church to outline their demands for "the immediate and unconditional abolition of slavery"; equality of "pay, labor, and promotion" for black soldiers; and the rights to remain in the United States, to receive public land, and to suffrage and representation in the coming reconstruction of the nation. On the way there, Douglass overheard a group of white men ask, "Where are the d——d niggers going?" The slurs on the street only reminded African Americans of the battles yet to be fought, and their argument for "equality" rested on the military service of black men who "vindicate[d] our manhood." Douglass's rhetoric had been consistent from the start of the war. Unchaining the "iron hand of the black man" would unleash the full force of American manpower upon the southern rebellion. Black soldiers had demonstrated loyalty to the nation on par with white Union soldiers against traitors to both the government and the ideals of the United States. This very masculine type of patriotic service had proved their right to participate in the social contract on which American freedom was founded.[39]

The men attending the 1864 convention were in no way hostile to the public roles that women had taken in service to the race. They praised the organizations aiding freedmen, as well as the new black schools and academies, both of which served girls and relied on the work of women. Douglass, as president of the convention and a member of its credentialing committee, likely had a hand in allowing statements from two women at the convention. Edmonia Highgate, physically and mentally worn down from teaching freedpeople in Virginia, "urged the Convention to trust in God and press on, and not abate one jot or tittle until the glorious day of jubilee shall come." Frances Ellen Watkins Harper, veteran of the abolition movement and a newly widowed mother, "spoke feelingly and eloquently of our hopes and prospects in this country." As before the war, neither addressed the place of woman's rights in this agenda, but men did not equate their appearance with an endorsement of woman's rights. The voices of Highgate and Harper represented a significant advancement for women in public. Indeed, Highgate wondered, if "girl as she is, she should tell the Convention what they ought to do," and in doing so was deemed by a reporter as "a strong *Lincoln* MAN." She justified herself by claiming to represent those who "*thought* about what had been proposed," and they likely included the freedpeople she had worked among and other women, all of whom had a stake in the outcome. Throughout the war, both black and white women defined the work that they were doing as patriotic service. Yet, just as that work was considered to be ancillary support, so, too, were women considered "helpmeets" to change.[40]

As excluded classes of people demanded access to power, they were forced to convince those with power that they had some self-interest in ceding it. The ascendant Republicans could see the benefit of admitting into the body politic millions of men whom they could organize, thereby ensuring that the party maintained control of the federal government. Many black men, as the conventions before the war had proven, felt that woman's rights undermined manhood and pitted wives against husbands, and they were thus reluctant to grant their brides political rights equal to their own. Meanwhile, the enfranchisement of African Americans as a class was at stake. At the time of the Syracuse meeting, the Thirteenth Amendment had not yet passed Congress, and so emancipation was not yet a fully guaranteed constitutional right. This made women's rights too risky an issue even for the most sympathetic men at the convention. Highgate's trepidation at the Syracuse convention conveyed the reluctance of many women to publicly challenge their men on this point.[41]

The American Anti-Slavery Society, which had married racial and gender equality from its founding, followed suit. Wendell Phillips had assumed leadership after Garrison had declared the antislavery movement over and resigned his presidency. Maria Weston Chapman had also relinquished her position. The organization as a whole, however, reached a consensus that freedom meant nothing without political equality and voted to work for that end. Phillips, making an observation as much as a proclamation, declared, in May 1865, that "this hour belongs to the negro," and all energies went toward black suffrage. Susan B. Anthony, Elizabeth Cady Stanton, and Lucy Stone, who had loyally defended the cause for decades, retorted that this was also "the hour for woman to make her demand."[42]

The "hour" extended to the 1866 congressional debate over the Fourteenth Amendment. While section 1 of the amendment defined citizens as "all persons born or naturalized in the United States," section 2 seemed to qualify that citizenship by the use of "men" and "male inhabitants." Stanton, an autodidact legal scholar, understood the importance of this language. "The sons of Pilgrims in Congress," she bemoaned, were doing "nothing less than trying to get the irrepressible 'male citizen' into our immortal Constitution." The language of the second section was intended to persuade southern states to enfranchise black voters, which they proved unwilling to do. Stanton, however, saw an interpretation in which black men were entitled to suffrage but women were not. Cut off from the institutional support of the American Anti-Slavery Society, she and Anthony asked the Eleventh Annual Woman's Rights Convention of May 10, 1866, "to broaden our Woman's Right platform, and make it in *name*—what it ever has been in *spirit*—a Human Rights platform."[43]

In those early revolutionary days of change so idealistic a union was not as ill-conceived as it seemed in hindsight. The federal government was at the height of its power and congressional leaders had never been as supportive of civil rights as they were for the former slaves, and the Republican Party hoped to maintain its ascendancy with black votes. Using the language of rights, protection, and consent, woman's rights activists intended to maintain the universal agenda that had existed in the 1840s antislavery movement. The new incarnation of their convention movement, the American Equal Rights Association (AERA), sought to ensure that the rights of women kept pace with those of black men and that no black civil rights legislation passed unless it included women.[44]

In principle, Douglass supported the goals of the new organization. "The cause which it aims to subserve is the cause of the whole human family," he observed, and it was "in a sense the broadest and most striking ever hit upon by any other association." At a New York Equal Rights Convention, he emphasized that "by every fact to which man can appeal as a justification of his own right to a ballot, a woman can also appeal with equal force." He also signed his name to a memorial of December 22, 1866, in which the AERA pledged to oppose any federal legislation or constitutional amendment that would make "proscriptive distinctions in right of suffrage and citizenship, on account of color or sex." The association appointed him a vice president all four years of its existence, although he did not attend its first two national conventions. Still, he consistently repeated his belief in woman's right to suffrage. "My heart and my voice go with the movement to extend suffrage to women," he affirmed in 1865, emphasizing at the 1868 convention that "I have always championed women's right to vote." A few months later, he reiterated to Ohio abolitionist Josephine Griffing that "I am quite willing at any time to hold up both hands in favor of this right," insisting that "I am in favor of woman's suffrage in order that we shall have all the virtue and vice confronted." At no point did he waver in his belief that women should stand on equal political footing as men, both black and white. Yet, for all their idealism and agitation, activists could only support or oppose legislation as it was written, and they formed their alliances accordingly.[45]

The years 1867 through 1870 deepened not only the divisions in the AERA but also those between leading woman's rights activists and Douglass. In 1866, Stanton and Anthony had insisted that only the Democrats had done anything to advance universal suffrage, citing the support of two Copperheads, a stripe of Democrat characterized by its lack of interest in ending slavery, much less in extending the rights of African Americans. Douglass warned the two women that support for their cause from such quarters was "the trick of the enemy to assail and endanger the rights of black men," and he worried that such alliances would only lead to "trouble in our family." Trouble appeared in Kansas in 1867, when the state proposed two separate referenda, one on woman suffrage and one on black male suffrage. Lucy Stone and her husband, Henry Blackwell, began campaigning for the woman's suffrage bill and were later joined by Anthony and Stanton, who had been working on similar measures in New York. Douglass had little to do with the campaign and did not visit Kansas that year, although Anthony had hoped to include him in a series of lectures. He continued to sympathize in spirit and word with woman suffrage, but, in deed, he pressed the necessity of expanding black civil rights at Republican conventions throughout the North, unable to escape the constant violence directed at his people.[46]

White hatred of African Americans was very personal, striking at the Douglass family as well as millions of others throughout the nation. In 1866, President Andrew Johnson, whose interest in Reconstruction extended little beyond humiliating the former slaveholding elite, accused a delegation composed Douglass, his son Lewis, and three other black men of fomenting a race war. Lewis had been representing his extended kin and their neighbors in Talbot County, where he taught school, and where, he reported, white property owners refused to sell land to African American buyers. When the group departed, Johnson was supposed to have turned to his secretary and used a racial epithet to refer to Douglass. Afterward, not only did the black men receive hate mail for daring to confront the president, but Frederick Jr., who lived in the capital at the time but was not at the meeting, also received threats. "You old son of a Bitch," began the note sent to him by "Ichabod." "We give you twenty four hours

from Date to leave the D.C. if you Donot You must take the consequence." Both
Frederick Jr. and Lewis fled to Colorado, where their father's old friend Henry
O. Waggoner helped them to find safer work. When Douglass later charged that
"murder runs riot in Texas," he was referring to a Ku Kux Klan attack on the
besieged black community of Millican, Texas, an incident that his brother, Perry,
with whom he had recently reunited, had escaped. Even in the North, his son-
in-law faced violent retribution for daring to enter a profession dominated by
white men. Therefore, when Douglass stood before the AERA meetings in 1866
and 1868 to insist that that black suffrage was "a question of life and death," he
was begging for compassion. The failure of Stanton, Anthony, and their cohort
to offer it suggested to him that, for all of their abolitionism, they devalued black
lives, including his and those of his family.[47]

In 1867, with these events in mind, the news Douglass received from the
west about Stanton and Anthony must have sickened him. Campaigning for
the woman suffrange referendum in Kansas, the two women found themselves
cut off from American Anti-Slavery Society funding and lacking an effective
fundraising apparatus in the AERA. Acting independently of the AERA, they
accepted financing from George Francis Train. A flamboyant and flagrantly racist Democrat, whose sincerity on the woman's rights question was questionable, Train was "the most wonderful man of the century in some respects," in
Stanton's estimation. The association horrified their allies, including Stone and
Blackwell. When both Kansas proposals failed, Anthony and Stanton blamed
lack of support from former abolitionists and the Equal Rights Association and
accepted Train's funding for a woman's rights newspaper, *The Revolution*, which
they published from 1868 until 1870. Their alliance with Train severed the suffrage cause from black civil rights and allowed the two women to vent unsavory
racial prejudices and nativism.[48]

The December 1868 congressional debates on the Fifteenth Amendment
ended any hope that black male and woman's suffrage could advance together.
Several proposals came before Congress, but, collectively, they made it clear
that women were not a consideration. The final draft, which Congress passed in
February 1869, eliminated "race, color, and previous condition of servitude" as
acceptable reasons to restrict voting rights, but not gender. Many in the AERA
opposed the amendment because it did not accomplish the complete goal, and
they rejected suggestions that they turn their energy toward the proposal of a
sixteenth amendment to secure voting rights for women. Stanton and Anthony
led the defection. The lesson that they had taken from Kansas was that the separation of the two causes would "create an antagonism between the rival parties."
Both must advance together or not at all.[49]

In objecting to the Fifteenth Amendment, Anthony insisted that she had not
"opposed the enfranchisement of the negro" and found the suggestion insulting.[50]

Her complaint about the legislation, she explained, came "not because it enfranchises black men, but because it does not enfranchise all women, black and white." Like Douglass, she understood the justice and claim of both parties to the ballot box, but she was not willing to allow one to advance before the other. "Neither has a claim to precedence upon an Equal Rights platform," she told him at the final, sparsely attended, meeting of the AERA, in May 1869. He pleaded that she understand that "when women, because they are women, are hunted down through the cities of New York and New Orleans; when they are dragged from their houses and hung upon lamp-posts; when their children are torn from their arms, and their brains dashed out upon the pavement," continuing a litany of depravations against African Americans, "then they will have an urgency to obtain the ballot equal to our own." Exasperated, Douglass finally asked if "granting to woman the right to suffrage will change anything in respect to the nature of our sexes." "Anything for a fight today," Anthony shot back, offering her own equally valid inventory of the tyrannies and dangers suffered by women. In the end, having nothing at stake in a defeat of the Fifteenth Amendment, she had nothing to lose by opposing it.[51]

The black women at the convention might have pointed out to Douglass that they were "hunted," both because they were black and because they were women, since he omitted rape from his list. Like the white women, they, too, were vulnerable under the existing law and had fewer avenues through which to redress their grievances. Sojourner Truth, at the 1866 AERA meeting, had maintained that "if colored men get their rights and no colored women get theirs, there will be a bad time about it." She and Frances Ellen Watkins Harper testified to the ways in which black men could be just as abusive as white men toward their wives and children, and the ways in which single black women were more vulnerable in the absence of a husband or father to protect them. Still, they also required power against the hatred directed against them as African Americans, including from white women. As much as she, a destitute widow, required the means to defend herself, Harper found herself making the sacrifice that "when it was a question of race, I let the lesser question of sex go." If the matter came down to opposing an imperfect amendment that provided their communities with at least some protection, they could not join Anthony. Both Harper and Truth, along with many other black women, campaigned for black male suffrage because they had plenty to lose if the measure did not pass.[52]

Black women's critique of their own community was quite different from the blanket condemnation of all black men that flowed from the pages of The Revolution as it resorted to the worst stereotypes. When Congress adopted the Fifteenth Amendment, in February 1869, Stanton predicted that the law would unleash "fearful outrages on womanhood, especially in the southern states." Anthony used the same language in proposing a resolution at an Illinois Woman Suffrage meeting, insisting that black suffrage without woman suffrage would escalate antagonism between the two. That they ignored the outrages—usually a euphemism for rape—already being committed against black women by white men suggested that, in their formulation, the danger came from black men targeting white women. That type of rhetoric could and did lead to the murder of innocent black men. While Stanton took some pains to exempt Douglass from these depictions, she could not resist stereotyping him as an intimidating black man, describing him as a fairytale villain, "dressed in a cap and great circular cape of wolfskins," when she and Anthony met him on their March 1869 tours through Ohio. "He really presented a most formidable and ferocious aspect," Stanton feigned shuddering. "I trembled in my shoes and was almost as paralyzed as Red Riding Hood in a similar encounter." She tempered the description by noting that "Douglass's hair is fast becoming white as snow, which adds greatly to the dignity and purity of his countenance."[53]

Stanton's and Anthony's dystopian prophecies about the consequences of the Fifteenth Amendment lay as much in their elitism as in racist visions of rape and anarchy. The majority of black men had no education and lived in poverty in the South, and the women appealed to class prejudices against the nonwhite working class. By promoting black male suffrage, Anthony insisted, "the Republican Party has elevated the very last of the most ignorant and degraded classes of men to the position of master over the very first and most educated and elevated classes of women." Although Stanton had, in 1866, opposed establishing an educational qualification for suffrage because "the negro at the South has not the free school, and cannot obtain it without first obtaining the ballot," she now protested "putting Sambo, Hans, Patrick, and Yung Tung above your noblest countrymen." After all, she argued, "the influence and vote of an educated woman are of more value to a government than those of an ignorant man." Receiving criticism for these remarks, the two attempted to point out the nuances of their argument, maintaining that they only used such examples to illustrate "the principle and the practice that gives them [uneducated black men and immigrants], civil and political superiority over the women by their side, not only, but over the educated and cultivated as well."[54]

The distinctions did little to persuade Douglass, who objected to "the employment of certain names, such as 'Sambo'" and its like, in *The Revolution*. When, after the Fifteenth Amendment was ratified, Stanton and Anthony continued to degrade black men in their woman suffrage rhetoric, he counseled them "that their flings at the negro and their constant parading him before their conventions as an ignorant monster possessing the ballot, while they are denied it, are of no real benefit to their cause" as they alienated black women and sympathetic black men like himself. Furthermore, every assault that they made on the Fifteenth Amendment to build the case for their own claim to voting

Figure 7.3 Frederick Douglass at the height of his career, during the Civil War. "Frederick Douglass," c. 1862. J. W. Hurn, photographer, Library of Congress, Prints and Photographs Division.

rights struck Douglass personally, whether intended to or not. He himself had grown up "ignorant," stolen his own education, and been beaten for teaching other slaves. In freedom, anti-abolitionists and abolitionists alike had used the image of an intimidating, hypersexual black man to discredit him. Anthony had already shown her proclivity to resort to such tactics by stoking rumors about his friendship with Julia Griffiths back in 1853, but Stanton had not, and her jovial wit had kept her in Douglass's good graces. Even as she likened him to the Big Bad Wolf in their 1869 encounter in Ohio, he greeted the two women with "hearty words of welcome and gracious smile." At one time, Douglass joked with Stanton that "I have about made up my mind that if you can forgive me for being a negro—I cannot do less than to forgive you for being a woman." He had shown patience with white allies who "were nobly struggling" to free themselves from racial prejudice, but his tolerance of her "forgiveness" for something that needed none must have worn thin as she constantly berated the type of man he might have become but for moments of good fortune. Stanton's tactical deployment of caricatures of black men in the interest of woman's suffrage, while black men and women lived and died in terror, could only have strained his sense of decency.[55]

The fact that they stood on the same side for woman suffrage, sometimes speaking at the same meetings, could not compensate for the knowledge that Stanton and Anthony, at worst, despised black men and, at best, considered them expendable, all the while using black women as rhetorical devices rather than partners. Although Stanton never overcame her elitism, she and Douglass over the years appeared able to discuss the issue and negotiate their way back to friendship. Along with his old friend Martha Greene in New England, Stanton remained his main point of contact with most projects related to woman's suffrage. The two also had much in common personally, with their marriages, children around the same age, sharp senses of irony, and an abiding awareness of the injustice that the world only saw the body into which they were born rather than the intelligence within. Anthony, on the other hand, not only continued to ignore problems with race in the woman's movement, she never forgave Douglass for throwing "the principle of Equality of Political Rights to women—overboard—in '69." Theirs was hardly the "lifelong friendship" that Anthony described after Douglass had died. While he supported her cause and they found one another useful political allies, they had little fondness for one another.[56]

When the AERA collapsed at the May 1869 meeting, so too did unity among woman's rights activists. Stanton, Anthony, and their allies opposed to the Fifteenth Amendment immediately formed the National Woman Suffrage Association (NWSA). Anthony thwarted debate about the amendment for the rest of the year, saying that "she was unwilling a resolution should ever again be offered in any Convention of women for or against the Fifteenth Amendment." For her part, Stanton praised an Ohio convention where "the Fifteenth Amendment laid in state," and "as sacrifice is woman's pet virtue," she criticized women who supported it for "boosting some male, black or white, over her own head." Meanwhile, Lucy Stone founded the rival American Woman Suffrage Association (AWSA). Many saw little reason to keep the two organizations separate after the Fifteenth Amendment passed, and Douglass was among those who signed a circular urging a union of the two. "Whether what ought to be, will be, in this case, is quite open to doubt," he mused in the *New National Era*, the Washington-based newspaper that he began editing in 1870, "there cannot, however be any harm in making the endeavor."[57]

Over the next decades, many of the advances in woman's suffrage took place at the local and state levels, usually in the western territories, and over particular issues. Douglass participated in many of those meetings and endorsed efforts to expand woman's suffrage at the local level, but his greatest connection with the movement lay at the national level and his support for the Sixteenth Amendment for woman suffrage at national conventions. This strategy was a logical outgrowth of lessons he had learned through abolitionism, which had been accomplished through federal action. In the divide between the two different woman suffrage organizations, Douglass for the most part remained nonpartisan. He was not particularly close to either Anthony or Stone, and had no special interest in their feuds with one another. His sympathy would more likely have gone to the AWSA, whose members had endorsed the Fifteenth Amendment and the Republicans, and who focused on suffrage as an end unto itself. The NWSA, led by two women who continued to set black men up as implicitly unworthy of the vote and who continued their association with Train, positioned itself as independent and, often, in opposition to the Republican Party and the vestiges of abolitionism. The organization also discussed suffrage as a means to other ends, sometimes drifting into issues that Douglass did not necessarily support, such as divorce.[58]

Nevertheless, of the eight woman suffrage meetings that recorded his attendance in the 1870s, one was for the AWSA, one was a Rochester convention celebrating the thirtieth anniversary of the Seneca Falls meeting, two were state conventions, and four were for the NWSA. The New National Era covered the 1873 annual convention and in 1871 and 1872 backed Theodore Tilton and Victoria Woodhull, both associated with the NWSA, as they argued for an interpretation of the Fourteenth Amendment that would allow women to vote. He, however, did not formally acknowledge Woodhull's presidential bid or that she had named him her vice-presidential running mate, and he found her views on free love distasteful. After 1880, Douglass attended meetings more regularly. He was more likely to appear at the NWSA meetings because they were held in Washington, DC, where he and his family had moved in 1872. Still, he did not neglect New England, where the AWSA was based.[59]

Then, in the late 1870s and 1880s, Anthony and Stanton began courting Douglass as they embarked upon their multivolume project, History of Woman Suffrage. They included him for his stature and because he had been a player in the beginning of their story. They also wanted his endorsement in order to gloss over their checkered history with black civil rights and to portray woman suffrage as the victim of the unfulfilled promise of republicanism that had died with Reconstruction. They finished the second volume of their history in 1882, the same year that Douglass completed his third autobiography, Life and Times of Frederick Douglass, and the same year that the Supreme Court overturned the bulk of the 1875 Civil Rights Act.[60]

Douglass was, to some degree, complicit in their construction of history. Yet, he diverged from their account on important points in Life and Times. Anthony and Stanton portrayed woman's rights as emerging in opposition to abolition by constructing a history of the movement that preceded abolition and dating its origins to women's exclusion from the 1840 World Anti-Slavery Convention. Douglass, however, connected the two movements directly. "Gratitude for this high service" of antislavery activism, he recalled, "early moved me to give favorable attention to the subject of what is called 'Woman's Rights,'" and Stanton had been "an earnest abolitionist" when she first lectured him on the matter after an antislavery meeting. *History of Woman Suffrage* received publicity in his account but only to point out an excerpt in praise of Abby Kelley Foster's early abolitionist work. Only after lauding the antislavery work of several women did he point out the "folly" and "degradation" that resulted "when one-half of the moral and intellectual power of the world is excluded from any voice or vote in civil government."[61]

The Seneca Falls convention of 1848 was conspicuously absent from Douglass's autobiographies, although it figured as the starting point for the movement in *History of Woman Suffrage*. Thus, he simultaneously declared himself a woman's rights man while erasing his role in its origin story or subsequent history. He skirted around any grievances emerging from disagreements in the 1860s or the white woman suffragists' depiction of freedmen by ignoring the entire episode, even as Stanton and Anthony continued to justify their actions. Indeed, he gave credit to their heroine, Anna Dickinson, for proposing the Fifteenth Amendment, a story that he allowed Stanton to include in *History of Woman Suffrage*. Given that Dickinson later joined NWSA and was briefly a pet of Anthony, the story could have been interpreted as either showing unity between their causes or implying that even their star sympathized with Douglass's position on the schism of 1869. In either case, he neither publicly disputed their version of events nor resorted to promulgating stereotypes about women's intelligence or place in society in the same way that they did about African Americans. He was, in these respects, a better woman's rights man than they were civil rights women.[62]

As he always had, Douglass employed, endorsed, and advanced both individual women and the causes that they supported. They, too, had been the silent army that had brought their organizational and fundraising skills to ensuring that his voice was heard in print and on stage. Their success helped propel him to the forefront of the nation's movement to end slavery, making him an influential national force in the 1860s and 1870s. Yet, his activism took him into arenas barred to women as he grounded citizenship in the exclusively male experience of military service and protected the gains of African Americans through the Republican Party. Women's support became less necessary as he moved into circles that not only barred them but also left them powerless to sustain his work.

That did not render women ancillary to his life, however. Party politics proved fickle and could not cover the myriad ways in which Douglass challenged racism. His home became ever more the representation of his and, by extension, African American success and the seat of political actions. The women who ran and inhabited his homes remained central to his work and legacy even as they lived out the contradictions in his ideology.

8

"Her True Worth," 1866–1883

After forty-four years of life together, Frederick recognized that "Mother was the post in the center of my house and held us together." By "Mother" he meant his wife, Anna. In its formality the appellation reflected both her reserve and the role that she had assumed as caretaker of everyone who became part of their household over the years. Rosetta believed that "my own dear father hardly understood her [Anna's] true worth until she was about to leave him." Frederick, in Rosetta's view, "was father, mother, brother and even sister to me." He was the exciting parent, the one engaged with the world, and the one to impress. Anna, on the other hand, was so eclipsed by her husband that even their daughter conceded that "it is difficult to say anything of mother without the mention of father, her life was so enveloped in his."[1]

Before the Civil War, Frederick's newspaper, lectures, and movement would not have survived without the constant vigilance of women, but as he moved deeper into Republican Party politics in the 1870s, women no longer had a prominent, visible role in his work. Instead, his life took on a more traditional nineteenth-century cast in which his public work could be described without any reference to women aside from his support of suffrage. Anna, as Rosetta noted, was portrayed as the cliché of the woman behind the great man and their marriage as the contemporary ideal of "separate spheres." Such women, however, did the caretaking that enabled the work of their famous husbands by, as Rosetta had said of her mother, "relieving him of all the management of the home as it increased in size and in its appointments." Moreover, Frederick and Anna might have seemed to conform to the ideal, but in the context of nineteenth-century racial prejudices and his increasing public visibility, they formed a caretaking partnership that covered a spectrum extending from their marriage to family to community to race. Their home was Anna's domain, and there she provided solace to the individual sufferers of the injustices against which her husband railed.[2]

If Rosetta later said of her mother that "so few there were who could see and know her [Anna's] true value," in her youth she might have counted herself in their number. Yet, once she married, she found that she required Anna's particular set of skills just as much as she did her father's counsel and approval. If Rosetta had thought the prospects of being a single woman and teacher bleak when she met Nathan Sprague, marriage proved no better. Nathan's status as a veteran and his connection to Frederick Douglass could not compensate for racism, his limited education, or his poor choices over the years. His difficulties in securing employment placed burdens on his wife that she could not assume with a growing family. As a result, for Rosetta, the woman's cause and civil rights were more elemental than suffrage and access to education or employment. In fact, many of the woman's rights activists faced the same problems of marriage and motherhood, causing the unmarried Susan B. Anthony to chide many of them for increasing their families. This was a problem endemic to the working class, as well. Children limited women's ability to work for wages or for a cause, and women of Rosetta's background expected their husbands to take care of the former so that, as the children grew older, they could devote their energy to a movement. Rosetta could look to the early years of her parents' marriage and cast herself in her mother's role, working as a partner to support a new family as her husband rose to prominence. She, instead, found herself relying on her parents to help her keep her family afloat.[3]

The Spragues tried repeatedly to make an independent life for themselves, but the family expanded at a faster pace than they could manage. Rosetta gave birth to their first child, Annie Rosine, in November 1864, when Nathan was away in the war. She found herself pregnant again in early 1866, but by that time Nathan could move his family to their own first home on a farm outside of Rochester. There, little Annie received a little sister, Harriet "Hattie" Bailey (sometimes spelled "Harriette"), for her second birthday. Soon, however, the Spragues could not earn enough from the farm to pay the rent. With help from the Douglasses, they purchased a home on Pearl Street in the city in 1867. Nathan secured a license to operate a hack, but facing competition from a black man infuriated Rochester's white drivers, who vandalized Nathan's vehicle. He planned to buy another, although he still owed money on the first, but ended up out of business and further in debt just as Rosetta discovered she was pregnant with their third child. To survive, they rented out the Pearl Street house and returned to her parents' home.[4]

The family grew in other ways during 1867, as emancipated, extended families joined both the Spragues and the Douglasses in Rochester. "The happy reunions now taking place all over the South, after years of separation and sorrow," Frederick reflected, "furnish a subject of the deepest pathos." Already, Louisa Keys, a young widow and Frederick's niece from Maryland, had joined the family in 1865. In 1867, Douglass received a letter from his brother, Perry Downs, whom he had not heard from since they had both lived under the supervision of Aunt Katy at Wye House plantation forty years earlier. The Anthony descendants had sold Downs and his wife away from Maryland and away from one another around 1862. After the war, Perry found his wife in the east Texas town of Millican. "I have a great desire to see you if it is possible," Downs wrote to Douglass through an amanuensis, asking his younger brother "to make arrangements to bring me to you." Douglass secured passage for Perry, his wife, and their children and grandchildren to Rochester in July, and over the summer, Frederick had a house built for them on his South Street property.[5]

While the toll that slavery had taken on Perry shocked Frederick, others, including the immediate family, did not quite know how to reconcile the incongruity of the two brothers. "I don't understand in what way those people you have at home are related to you," Charles wondered from his new post at the Freedmen's Bureau in Washington. "Is it that Mr. Downs is your half brother?" Charles's wife, Elizabeth—called "Libbie"—had been staying with the Douglasses after giving birth to their first child when the Downses first appeared, and after hearing Libbie's observations, Charles believed he "should be afraid even to have them in the same neighborhood and more especially when you are away in the winter months." Ottilie Assing, there for her annual summer visit, described them as "an incorrigible group of people" and was particularly horrified by Perry's wife, "who smokes her pipe while doing other things and who whips her children with a riding crop." Assing believed that this family of former slaves neglected their children, and she wanted to abscond with Douglass's two-year-old great-niece, whom she described more as a pet than a person. Assing abandoned the idea as soon as she thought of it, seeming more concerned about the disruption that the girl would cause back in Hoboken, where she planned to turn the child over to her landlord's wife, than about severing the girl from her own kin.[6]

The German visitor may have been accurate in observing that "Douglass does not want to sustain them in glory and absolute idleness"; still, he could not deny his brother. The class differences between the two branches of his family only highlighted the consequences of bondage and the different life Frederick would have lived had the Auld women not sent him to Baltimore and taught him to read, had Anna not helped him escape, and had Griffiths not helped his business thrive. Whatever his frustrations that his people did not always behave in the ways that he wished they would, he felt a responsibility to help them, whether they were other African Americans in general or his family in particular. Anna may have had equally complicated feelings. Although she may not have felt the survivor's guilt that her husband might have experienced, she had only narrowly escaped being born into slavery and, through turns of good fortune, had risen into the middle class and adopted many of its norms. Perry's family, especially the women, might have respected her position without judging her manner of speech, skin color, demeanor, or lack of education. At the same time, given Anna's high standards of deportment, she may have been just as shocked as Assing at some of her guests' behavior. Regardless, she incorporated them within the elastic bounds of their household.[7]

When the Downses settled in their house on the Douglass's property, Nathan's older brother, Lewis Sprague, had already arrived from Maryland with his wife, Emma, and their six children. A younger sister, sixteen-year-old Louisa, followed shortly thereafter, and other Spragues arrived over the next few years. Lewis Sprague's family found a farm to rent in nearby Henrietta, and Louisa moved in with them. But life in Lewis's household made Louisa unhappy. On more than one occasion, she sought refuge at the Douglass house with Nathan and Rosetta, preferring life with them because, according to Rosetta, "Nathan never speaks harshly to her," and she felt that "she was never treated as kind in her life" as by him. Louisa also worried that Lewis Sprague might return his family to Maryland, and she had no desire to go with them. Twice, in February 1868, Louisa trudged through the snow from Henrietta, arriving sick and upset on the Douglasses' doorstep. Nathan and Emma got into a row over Louisa's treatment in Lewis's household, and Louisa begged to stay with the Spragues. They agreed, an arrangement to which Anna must also have acquiesced, and Rosetta assured her father that "it will cost quite a little to take care of her." Louisa moved in with the Douglasses and Spragues, and Nathan recommended that she attend school, all of which satisfied Louisa. Just after taking her in, however, Nathan struck out for Omaha, Nebraska, where he again attempted to operate a hack and then a boarding house. Rosetta remained behind. Louisa and Anna managed the house and children together, and Rosetta helped her father maintain his correspondence.[8]

Anna, Rosetta, and Louisa formed a triumvirate of women sustaining one another in a stress-filled household, even when they quarreled, especially when ill health and childbirth took their toll on each of the older two women. Anna's neuralgia from the previous decade had subsided, but the weather began to affect her health as rheumatoid arthritis set in. She had also suffered an episode in April 1867 that indicated deeper health issues. Charles identified her condition as "bilious," a term usually used in reference to stomach ailments, but Rosetta described something neurological, possibly a stroke. She told her father that Anna "had complained of dizziness in the head" and, a few weeks later, "while at the sink she [Anna] fell across it." Afterward, Anna "seemed stupid" and, following a vomiting spell, "complained mostly of her head." She remained in bed, unable to work for some time and in need of nursing. Rosetta stepped in to take care of Anna while also taking care of the demands of the household. At the same time, with her own small daughters tumbling about, she found the company of Anna, despite her illness, beneficial. As a new mother, in 1865, Rosetta had been grateful that "Mother takes charge of little Annie," so that she could have a moment to herself to simply visit the post office among other things. Anna had also "helped me to get somewhat put to rights," the following year, when Rosetta was trying to set up her own household on Pearl Street, "with Annie crying for bread on one hand and Hattie fretting to be taken." Things had changed by 1868, when Rosetta, again living with her parents, wrote, "Mother seems delighted to have me near, and sits with me every day," and Anna was "certainly very thankful for the change" of having Rosetta back in the house. When Louisa joined them, she simply wanted a home and a family, and she was the physically strongest and least encumbered of the three. Together, they shared the work of running the South Street house.[9]

Back at her own home in Hoboken, reading Frederick's descriptions of his household, Ottilie Assing was left with the impression of "screaming children, people who are constantly at the verge of armed peace with one another and who do not love another human being apart from themselves," but Louisa, Anna, and Rosetta would have had different interpretations. If they had "armed peace," that was simply a natural outgrowth of multiple generations and blended families living under one roof. For Anna and Louisa, who both had grown up among extended kin networks, this pattern was no different from the patterns of community, familial conflict, and support common to working-class, immigrant, and enslaved families, and that was typical of many African American women's experiences. Rosetta's upbringing, however, was slightly different and she might have had some ambivalence about her position. She could accept the communalism, but she had grown up with influences emphasizing the individualist self-reliance of the urban middle class. It was one thing to draw on the support of the women around her, but quite another to be married with children and still occupy a child's position in her parents' home. Whatever benefits she received in living with her parents could have been offset by the shame that she shared with her husband at his failures, their dependence on Frederick and Anna, and the conflicts they caused among the men in her family.[10]

This conflict became evident when Nathan's ventures in Nebraska met with little success. He returned before the end of the year, arriving in time for the birth of his third daughter, Alice Louise, on October 14, 1868. He found employment as a gardener, but his wages did not allow him to support his family independently of the Douglasses. His standing in the rest of the family deteriorated, and Rosetta found herself negotiating among her husband, her father, and her brother Charles. The tension came to a head during a dispute between Nathan and Charles over borrowed money, but class prejudices tinged every insult. Nathan had taken loans from Charles and Frederick Jr., and Charles had later borrowed from Nathan. They all borrowed from Frederick Sr., and all had difficulty with repayment. Relatively privileged, Charles became particularly resentful of working-class Nathan because, he explained to his father, the former slave had often "boasted that he could make a living" because he had no fear of hard work and "acted as though he could get along and we could not." Charles was also certain that Nathan had poisoned Frederick against his own sons and had recruited Rosetta to prevent Charles from appealing to Anna in their quarrel. When, in 1869, a frustrated Douglass complained to Rosetta that his family had become "all mouths and no hands," Nathan took umbrage and made arrangements to move his family back to the Pearl Street house.[11]

That decision did nothing to resolve the argument. Charles deemed Nathan ungrateful, and Douglass was hurt. Rosetta begged her father to understand her husband's pride, explaining that Nathan "took exception" when it seemed that Frederick "included him with the rest as being a burden." The accusation, Rosetta insisted, was all the more painful because Nathan "has been very sensitive all winter because he has laid idle so long" and knew that he was disappointing his father-in-law.[12] She had turned to her father to buy her a sewing machine, so that she could earn an income herself, but with three children, she lamented that "I have not been able to use it more advantageously." At one point, Rosetta found herself "compelled to keep Louisa from school" to work. "If she learns to read and write," a harried Rosetta declared, "then she can do so at home." Exhausted and feeling hopeless, not only did Rosetta ignore Louisa's own wishes, but she had inverted her own educational experience and gone against the Douglasses' emphasis on formal schooling.[13]

In her embarrassment over her predicament, years of resentment against her brothers and the family dynamic bubbled to the surface. "My position at home has been any thing but pleasant," she snapped at her father, accusing him of a lack of sympathy. "I never dared to show much zeal about anything where you were concerned as I could never bare ridicule," she explained, pointing out that "jealousy is one of the leading traits in our family." Should he doubt her loyalty, she reminded him that taking his side could "very readily bring a storm around my ears." In the high emotion of her missive to Douglass, Rosetta conflated her past familial position of attempting to please two very different parents with her current place between her brother and her husband and her father and her husband, with all sides demanding fidelity and none showing her any compassion. "You say to me 'Husbands first and fathers second,'" she finally pointed out to Frederick, but, "where I am compelled to act other than what you think is for my benefit I feel troubled" because "your words whether of censure or praise remain with me always and affect me accordingly." She relied on his approval, but in this case, her father's advice to follow her husband was at odds with his wishes that she remain in his house.[14]

Ultimately, Rosetta determined to be the proper wife and to go "where I can assist Nathan get *himself* out of the entanglement he finds himself in." After all, she, too, hated being in a "position where it looks as if he depended so much to your kindness." She also hinted that she received some of the brunt of her husband's shame when she told her father that Nathan "has never been seriously offended with me" except when "he has been conscious of the feeling of the family toward him." Although she told her father, "I do not consider his harshness toward me just," she agreed to "bury it in the past" as he advised because "our happiness mainly depends on me." She explicitly meant the happiness of herself and Nathan, but the desire to please her father haunted her, as well. This cycle repeated itself over the next two decades as Nathan disappointed the Douglasses, redeemed himself, and then disappointed them again, leaving Rosetta torn between her loyalties. Meanwhile, the Spragues did not stay long in their Pearl Street. Rosetta gave birth to another daughter, Estelle—called "Stella"—in August 1870, by which time, they were back with the Douglasses.[15]

They were there when, just after midnight on June 2, 1872, Rosetta awoke to the smell of smoke. A fire had begun in the barn and jumped the space to Anna's kitchen. By the time that Anna, Nathan, Louisa, and a heavily pregnant Rosetta herded Annie, Hattie, Alice, and Stella outside, flames engulfed the house. Baby Stella nearly suffocated before they reached fresh air. Neighbors sounded the alarm and hurried to help the family salvage what they could. They concentrated on Frederick's library, rescuing a few pieces of furniture, his books, and some of his personal documents, but copies of the entire run of all of his newspapers burned. Frederick, away from home when tragedy struck, dashed to Rochester as quickly as he could, arriving after midnight a few days later. He later recounted that two hotels had turned him away, which only heightened his suspicions that an arsonist had targeted his home.[16]

Although an insurance policy covered the nearly thousand dollars of the damages, Ottilie Assing pointed out that "the thing that cannot be replaced is the now destroyed beautiful place to which so many memories are tied, a 'historic' site." Frederick and Anna felt the loss more intensely. Their home represented the accomplishments and work of their lifetime together and contained all the memories and mementoes of their family's life. In particular, the destruction of the copies of the newspapers pained Frederick. "If I have at any time said or written that which is worth remembering or repeating," he believed, "I must have said such things between the years 1848 and 1860, and my paper was a chronicle of most of what I said during that time." A significant chunk of the record of his intellectual life had been lost. For Anna, if the house had been her creation and the apotheosis of her own sacrifices and work, as well as her life among her own family, its destruction left her with a parallel bereavement.[17]

At the time of the fire, Washington had become the gravitational center of Frederick's work life and the home to all of his sons. There, he found that the postwar world of activism functioned much differently than it had during the abolition movement. The diffuse, grass-roots organization of antislavery women who had supported the *North Star, Frederick Douglass' Paper,* and *Douglass' Monthly* gave way to activities that would soon be known as "lobbying," pressuring those in the seat of power to pass and enforce legislation. While Douglass continued to lecture, he found himself drawn to the nation's capital more frequently to address lawmakers and, in 1870, he decided to return to newspaper publishing by investing in the city's *New National Era.* The *Era* was originally the joint venture of Lewis Douglass, self-educated former slave and Presbyterian minister J. Sella Martin, and black activist George T. Downing. Only Lewis had prior newspaper experience. They brought in Frederick, who continued to emphasize the importance of black enterprises and the necessity for black journalists to inform and express the views of African Americans. He initially signed on as an investor and corresponding editor at the beginning of 1870, but in September he became half-owner and editor-in-chief; Lewis and Frederick Jr. took over as printers.[18]

The paper primarily covered African American politics but included other stories of interest to black readers and those interested in the transatlantic movement for greater democracy. Although Amy Post took the Douglasses to task for not taking stronger stands on woman suffrage, Frederick Jr. responded that she was correct, but that "those who are acquainted with its Editor are satisfied that he leans on the right side of the question of female suffrage." Frederick Jr. himself supported the issue, and his wife Virginia, along with Rosetta, and twelve other black women signed a petition to Congress requesting that it "adopt measures for so amending the Constitution as to prohibit the several States from Disfranchising United States Citizens on account of Sex." The *New National Era* ran periodic notices on the progression of the suffrage movement because it considered all democratic movements to be of interest to its readers. Douglass also accepted article contributions on both domestic and international politics from journalists, including Ottilie Assing, who had little work after the *Morgenblatt* closed its doors in 1865, and Mary Ann Shadd Cary, an African American editor in her own right.[19]

The paper proved to be a financial disaster. As before the war, the newspaper business was risky, and the *New National Era* faced far more competition from both black and white papers that focused on Washington politics than *Frederick Douglass' Paper* ever had. The *Era* also lacked the fundraising and management acumen of a Julia Griffiths Crofts. Although Assing told her sister that she had a strong hand in editing the paper, her skill was writing, not business. British philanthropy had turned its attentions elsewhere by the 1870s, so the networks Crofts had cultivated had dissolved, as had the Rochester Ladies' Anti-Slavery Society and the Western New York Anti-Slavery Society. In 1872, shortly after Amy Post had pointed out the lesser coverage woman suffrage received in the *New*

National Era's pages, she lost her beloved husband, Isaac. Post was entering her seventies, and now most of her energy went to advancing woman suffrage and to her work in the National Liberal League. Later that year, she was among the fifty Rochester women who registered to vote, an act that resulted in Susan B. Anthony's arrest. In 1873, Post again attempted to register for the state elections. In Washington, black women had begun to emerge as a powerful force in churches and in benevolent associations, but while they might contribute articles or the occasional donation, they did not support any particular paper in the way that abolitionist societies had supported the *Liberator* or Douglass's paper. No key philanthropist like Gerrit Smith emerged. Indeed, Douglass himself served as the primary backer for the *Era*. During the economic depression of 1873, Douglass withdrew from the paper, and the entire venture collapsed a year later.[20]

By the time the fire destroyed the Douglasses' Rochester house, Frederick had already purchased a home in Washington, on A Street NE, near the Capitol, to use as a base when Congress was in session. After the fire, Anna returned to Washington with him to take charge of the house. The Spragues remained in Rochester and moved back into the Pearl Street home. In the end, despite the loss of the home, the change may have suited Anna. "There are forty thousand colored people in Washington," Frederick informed a former abolitionist colleague who had urged him to return north, "my wife is in her element there." The relocation to the capital was also an improvement for Assing, although she grumbled that the fire in Rochester had interfered with her summer plans. With Frederick editing the *New National Era* and the 1872 presidential election heating up, "you can imagine what kind of pleasure it is for me," she boasted to her sister, Ludmilla, "not only to be introduced to all the depths of political conditions, but also to have my hands in it as a journalist." She descended on the Douglass household in August and stayed until the day after the election on November 5, her longest visit yet.[21]

Frederick took to the campaign trail in support of Republican candidates for most of that autumn, leaving Assing to write from Douglass's study during the day or in the evenings if she worked at the offices of the *Era*. "Armed peace" may have been an apt description here, as well. Assing already resented Anna, whom she blamed for the extent of the losses in the Rochester house if not for the fire itself. She was certain that "the stupid old hag lost her head, as often happens with uneducated people," and that Anna was less concerned with saving bonds than "her wig and a few dozen silver spoons." Her explosion indicated how little she knew of the woman who had hosted her for so many summers. Anna had always taken care of the household finances, including the bonds, and the spoons were likely those that she had purchased in the first years of her marriage. More likely, Anna had, above all, rushed to save her granddaughters. Assing had once dubbed

Figure 8.1 Ottilie Assing in the 1870s, when she became the source of tension in the Douglass household. National Park Service, Frederick Douglass National Historic Site, Washington, DC, Ottilie Assing, [c. 1871], FRDO 4804.

Anna "Border State," a reference to the slaveholding states that had remained in the Union and thereby impeded the federal government's advance on abolition. In the German woman's estimation, like those states, Anna prevented Frederick from advancing because she was "ignorant and uneducated." At one point, she dismissed Anna as "a veritable beast which itself neither has love to give nor knows how to appreciate it." Anna was unfathomable as a person to Assing, who, without any sense of irony, regarded the black woman as an unintelligent servant requiring "feeding" with gifts, a boarding house matron or, when she herself contracted a cold and ear infection later in the autumn, a nurse.[22]

That autumn, however, Anna did not have to endure Assing's visit alone. In October 1872, Louisa Sprague, who had stayed with Rosetta's family after the fire, moved down from Rochester, likely sensing that her brother's family regarded her as a servant. In many households, the unmarried women in the family were expected to contribute. However, Louisa's desire to go to school and her choice to be where she was treated kindly indicated that she saw a difference between her status as a family member and her treatment at the hands of Emma

Sprague or even Rosetta when she was overtaxed. Anna, on the other hand, had embraced Louisa as another daughter, one more like herself than Rosetta. Louisa adored Anna and Frederick, whom she began to call "mother" and "father," and for a brief period she experimented with the last name "Douglass." Under Anna's direction, she learned to bake "Maryland" beaten biscuits and became so integral to the operation of the Douglass household that, by 1874, Frederick found himself helpless when he had to spend much longer than a week at home without either Anna or Louisa. He considered them equals in the task of housekeeping. Over the years, as Anna's rheumatism worsened and her mobility declined, the younger woman took over more of the physical labor. Louisa also learned to read and write, although never very well, apologizing for her grammar and spelling mistakes in letters to Frederick. "Do not Laughte at this," she admonished him in one postscript. Still, her limitations in this regard worked in her favor. At one point, Frederick preferred that she transcribe Anna's letters because "It will seem more like coming from her [Anna] if Lew [Louisa] writes than if I should."[23]

When Assing arrived in 1872, Louisa and Anna let her know that she was an interloper, whatever Frederick might wish. Anna and Louisa's teamwork loomed over the summer of 1873 as well and gradually incorporated other family members. "Mother and Louisa are pursuing the even tenor of their ways," Frederick informed Rosetta, "for Miss Assing is still with her friends in Boston and we three are alone." That winter, he began to enlarge the A Street property, adding an adjoining house, and Assing bragged to her sister that Frederick "says that I should move in with him for good." Although she considered "how happy it would make me to be with him all the time," she thought twice about the reality, wondering "about whether it is advisable to constantly live in the immediate vicinity of his lovely wife." She arrived on July 2, 1874, and adored the new suite for her accommodation, but found, to her dismay, that Lewis had been living with his parents for the previous year and was still in residence in the house. When he secured a job at the post office, she groaned that he "immediately went and got his terrible wife from Syracuse, with whom he is planning on spending the winter at Douglass' house." She had hoped to stay longer than four months, but "there is now such a lovely group of people, without any 'redeeming features'" that she departed at the end of October.[24]

On her next visit, in 1875, Frederick observed that "Miss Assing is fighting her way here as usual." Even a simple game of croquet became a reminder that she was not part of the family. "Everbody seems to hit the blue ball," Frederick told Rosetta, as he watched other players knock Assing's piece out of bounds again and again. "As usual," he sighed, "I fight on the side of my old friend," only to be met with Lewis's indignation. Yet, the Douglass home was no longer her "green magic island" of the Rochester summers when Frederick was "surprisingly free of bothersome visitors." The Washington house teemed with activity every day. Lewis and Amelia were still living with the Douglasses, and Rosetta's daughter Stella had joined her grandparents. African American Senator Blanche K. Bruce and the Barrier sisters, two African American teachers from Brockport, New York, boarded with the family and provided the sort of constant intellectual and political companionship that Frederick craved. Assing had no practical function at the house, and the defunct New National Era no longer offered her an outlet for her journalism, as it had during her first summer in Washington. She cut her visit short, staying only about a month, and decided to take a long-planned trip to Europe that lasted through the next two years.[25]

When Assing returned, in 1878, she resumed summer vacations with Frederick, but complained that the household continued to incorporate his extended family. She expressed little sympathy for the deaths and illnesses that had placed them there, telling Frederick that they were all "hangers-on and parasites who abuse your kindness either on the plea of relationship or on that of being allies in opinions." She betrayed no sense of irony that some of them might have put a woman who took up residence for months at a time, paying no room or board or contributing to the operation of the household, in the same category. Her last visit, in 1880, lasted little over a month, although she was there when President Rutherford Hayes stopped in for an unannounced and unpublicized call. The next year, instead of going to Washington, she returned to Europe and, again, Frederick urged her to go.[26]

Assing's long holidays with the Douglasses were not unusual for their length. Hostesses in the nineteenth century could expect houseguests for a duration that would strain later generations' notions about the limits of hospitality. Throughout her life in America, Assing escaped the muggy Hoboken summers by spending weeks on end with the Koehler family in Boston and friends in Stamford, Connecticut, among others. Yet, her admitted inability to "find time for independent work" when she was with Douglass, her distaste for any of his associates who were outside of her circle of friends, her aversion to his family and their hostility toward her, make her long summer stays seem peculiar. Indeed, they perplexed Anna, who had accused Assing of "bewitching" Frederick.

Part of the explanation was their friendship, which survived after she had failed to expand his audience. He continued to correspond with her, invite her to stay in his home for weeks on end, and share ideas with her. She was, as he said, "my old friend" for whom he felt loyalty, gratitude, and affection. Another part of the explanation lay in the way he structured his life. The design of the house on A Street suggested that two separate lives occurred within the same space. His granddaughter Fredericka remembered the house as being "really two connecting houses" in which "communicating doors were cut through the halls both up and down stairs." She also chuckled that the playroom for the grandchildren was set up "at one extreme side of the house, up stairs and far away from grandpa's study." Later, when the Douglasses moved to Anacostia in 1878, his office was behind the formal parlor, which was separated from the family parlor by a hall. Anna's kitchen was behind the family parlor and the dining room. When the study did not offer enough solitude, Frederick moved out to a small outbuilding called the "growlery," after a similar space in Charles Dickens' *Bleak House.* Fredericka remembered a temporal division, as well. "He had *two* distinct periods that he daily observed—his Work-time and his Playtime," and she was particularly aware of the distinction because "he was visibly annoyed by any infringement upon either." Anna and Rosetta enforced this division, keeping children quiet during "work time" and visitors for work away during "playtime." Assing was part of that "work-time" and work space, but she stayed through "playtime."[27]

Figure 8.2 Frederick, Anna, and Rosetta's family outside of the Douglasses' A Street home in Washington, DC. Because they lived only a block away from the Capitol, Anna stayed busy protecting her husband's "work-time" from visitors of all classes and tending to the needs of extended family and long-term guests who occupied the house. National Park Service, Frederick Douglass National Historic Site, Washington, DC, Capitol Hill home, [c. 1871–77], FRDO 11001.

Still, although Douglass clearly enjoyed Assing's companionship, their friendship became unequal as his fame continued to grow. Whereas he had once looked to her to expand his audience and his knowledge about the world, she had become dependent on him for work as a journalist and her sense of self. "Your company for me has such a charm and affords me a gratification the like of which I never feel elsewhere," she effused to Frederick. "Aside from other attractions it is such comfort to be allowed to communicate anything and everything to each other, to confide unconditionally without the least reserve or distrust." He, on the other hand, silenced such outpourings as "incendiary," inappropriate to the platonic nature of their friendship and a sign of disrespect to his marriage, although she protested that she had only "honest intentions and promises to the contrary." She boasted of corresponding with a wide array of people, many quite important, but in reality she had only a small group of close friends, most of them German expatriates and none approaching the fame of Frederick. He, as she herself noted, had far more friends and associates, many of great stature, who filled his life and his house regularly and who rearranged their lives around his. She was only one of them, closer to him than most and certainly dear, but not as close or as dear as she liked to think, and unwilling to acknowledge or unaware of the intimacies that he shared with other people. As a result, he figured much larger in her life, or in the life that she portrayed to her other correspondents, than she in his.[28]

"If you are in as close of a relationship with *one* man as I am with Douglass," she intimated in a letter to her sister, Ludmilla, "you get to know the whole world, men and women, from perspectives that would otherwise be hidden." She possibly intended her sister to infer a sexual liaison from this passage in order to elicit intimate details about Ludmilla's collapsing marriage. The two had an often acrimonious rivalry in which Ludmilla had bested Ottilie not only by surpassing her professionally but also by getting married. Ottilie followed the alleged disclosure with a direct request for more explicit information, "Let me know, I beg you!" She sought the evidence to satisfy her schadenfreude over her sister's misfortune. In truth, she more likely described what she believed to be her special insight into the life of a famous man as his confidante and devotee, more intimate than all others and closer than a wife. Moreover, she possessed an exceptional knowledge because Frederick, like Ludmilla's errant husband, was "a man who has seen so much of the world and has been loved by so many women."[29] Still, however much he may have appreciated her friendship and the ideas to which she had introduced him, he did not seem to share her perception of their relationship. Her letters to and about him brimmed with advice, directions, and opinions, but did not indicate that he took the same depth of interest in the details of her life. More often, he cautioned her to keep some distance. "I know too well how lonely and dependent he would feel for the entire long summer despite all visitors that he constantly has to endure," she insisted as she contemplated a trip to Europe in 1868, but, by her own admission, "he himself does not try to hold me back, and even advises me to take the trip." He did the same in 1881, knowing both times that she would be gone for years.[30]

As long as the Douglasses lived in Rochester on a large property outside of the city with plenty of space to roam and with her visiting during summer and early autumn months of little activity, she could believe that she was essential to his life. She could do the same when he passed through the German community in Hoboken. His move to Washington, where he fretted that "the demands upon my time and attention by my Books and papers and by visitors are incessant," challenged her perception. He was not really, as one of her acquaintances later put it, "the handi-work of her spirit," nor was she a central figure in his life. Her own experience of family had been of sorrow, abuse, alienation, rivalry, and limitation, so she had cut herself off from entanglements that were not voluntary and satisfying, and she counseled others to do the same. She could not understand Douglass's complicated, enmeshed responsibilities to his family, and she resented their competition for his undivided attention. Any affection that he felt for her was probably blunted by her refusal to accept that his family was of primary importance to his sense of self, regardless of the ways that they frustrated him. She was, ultimately, an outsider.[31]

Rosetta, on the other hand, was very much an insider, who admitted that "I should feel lonely indeed if I had no family." Her life continued to cleave to that of her parents, even while living in separate cities. Louisa had stayed in Rochester through the birth of Rosetta's fifth daughter in August 1872. Possibly despairing of ever having a boy to name after his famous and beloved grandfather, the Spragues named the girl Fredericka Douglass. Although Rosetta hired a young woman to replace her sister-in-law, taking care of five children ranging from infancy to age eight proved a strain, particularly in hard times. After an illness in the winter, she took six-year-old Hattie to stay with the Douglasses in Washington. There, the little girl also had the attentions of her childless Aunt Amelia and Uncle Lewis who, Frederick was happy to say, "bought her some nice little Story Books." Frederick was delighted with her and took her out riding in his carriage. Meanwhile, he used Rosetta's house as a base when he traveled through Western New York or, when passing through the area, would "slip over to Rochester to see Rosetta and the children." Fredericka, only a baby at the time, first remembered her grandfather as "a very tall man" who appeared at their door one day. Her "mother uttered a little cry and ran into his arms," then the "strange man" picked up his grandchild, "way up high," and hugged her "very close to a very stiff, white shirt bosom." Her sisters gathered around, and then they all went outside for a game of croquet, the family's favorite.[32]

Rosetta's memories of those years were less rosy. In April 1874, as Rosetta was nearing confinement with her sixth pregnancy, seven-year-old Alice became ill. Anna and Louisa rushed to Rochester from Washington to help Rosetta, and her son Herbert Douglass was born on May 17. His grandfather predicted, "If I shall like him as well as I like your girls—he will be very well liked." Alice, however, did not improve. By June 2, they were expecting the worst. Frederick wished that he could be at his daughter's side, but he did not want to leave Amelia and Lewis alone while they all feared a nightrider attack on the Washington house. "The pain of death is with the living not with the dead," he reminded Rosetta, and he hoped "that you are thoroughly nerved for the event, that you are wholly emancipated from the superstitious terrors with which priest craft has surrounded the great and universal fact of death." He counseled her to accept that the little girl "could never be strong and healthy if she did live" and that "her passing away will be a happy release from a life of misery." In the end, "We shall all miss our dear little Alice," who died on June 8. For Frederick, Anna, and Rosetta grief over the loss of Alice mingled with remembered grief for Annie, as they once again found themselves preparing a small child's body for burial. When Anna and Louisa returned to Washington in August, they brought four-year-old Estelle with them. "She seems quite contented and happy," Frederick reported to her mother, as the little girl joined him in his new study to watch the outside world from his window.[33]

Then, four months later, while helping investigators in a case of mail fraud, Nathan was arrested for stealing mail. He pled guilty and served a year in jail. Creditors began badgering Rosetta to pay Nathan's debts, especially after they learned that she was planning to leave the city and join her parents in Washington. As painful as it was to have to stand by while constables carted off their furniture, carpets, and chronometers, the threat to her piano hurt the most. "My piano is my personal property and it can be seized to settle debts contracted by Nathan," she cried, echoing the indignation of woman's rights activists as they petitioned for married women's property rights. The rights to their own property that New York wives had gained in 1848 and 1860 had been rolled back in 1862, and Rosetta deemed it "a poor law that does not work both ways," allowing her property to be seized and auctioned to pay Nathan's debts without allowing her to sell his property to pay the same. When all was settled, she once more rented out the house on Pearl Street, packed up the belongs she had left, and took her children to her parents' home in Washington. Whatever shame she felt, she at least did not have to face her Rochester neighbors. Whereas some woman's rights activists, such as Elizabeth Cady Stanton, used just such catastrophes as a good reason to liberalize divorce law and ensure that married women had financial independence, at no point did the Spragues consider separating or dissolving the marriage. Instead, after Nathan's release from prison at the end of 1876, they immediately conceived their last child, Rosabelle Mary, who was born in September 1877. By that time, Rosetta was thirty-eight years old and had given birth, on average, every two years since she was twenty-five. She had also lived with her parents for the majority of her married life.[34]

In 1878, the Douglasses had saved enough to purchase a new home across the Anacostia River in a new neighborhood called Union Town, far from the commotion of the city, but close enough to drive or walk there when necessary. In family lore, as told by their granddaughter, Fredericka, "grandpa bought Cedar Hill as a surprise to grandma." One of the developers of the community, John Van Hook, had refused to sell property to African Americans or Irishmen, so Frederick's choice to buy there carried a note of defiance. As a reporter quipped, "The ex-slave Douglass now owns Van Hook's house and Van Hook doesn't own anything." The two-story house sat atop a hill, surrounded by trees. Anyone resting on the veranda or peering out the windows could overlook the capital and the countryside of Maryland. The poetry of the view was not lost on one journalist,

Figure 8.3 In 1877, Frederick and Anna purchased a large home and several acres in a previously segregated neighborhood, Union Town, near the Anacostia River. The porch offered a view of both the nation's capital and the Maryland countryside. The home represented Frederick's fame and the couple's rise from poverty to prominence over the previous four decades. Photo by Leigh Fought.

who noted, "From his door he can see the dome of the Capitol of a free country; he can see Arlington Heights where sleep the brave who made it free; and slavery and the fields of Tuckahoe, dark with the memory of blood and toil and tears, are behind him." The sixteen rooms, later expanded to twenty-one, were, according to one observer, "very handsomely furnished" and had "the appearance of being the home of a cultured, refined gentleman." While Frederick received credit for the décor, and certainly influenced some of the choices, Anna probably had the stronger hand.[35]

More importantly, Douglass had accepted some measure of legal equity in regard to marital property. This had been a concern of his two decades earlier, at the 1853 Rochester Woman's Rights Convention. The women had called for an expansion of the 1848 New York Married Women's Property act to include joint ownership of property acquired by a couple during the marriage. Douglass wondered, in the event of a disagreement over that property, "how shall the matter be settled between them?" He elaborated by insisting that "law is not a necessity of human nature; if love ruled, statutes would be obsolete; genuine marriages and harmonious co-operations would prevent any such necessity." By 1869, however, Anna's name began appearing with her husband's on deeds and financial transactions involving Rosetta. When Frederick purchased Cedar Hill, Anna also made her mark on the deed. Legally, the home was hers in partnership with her husband, and as a representation of their rise from slavery and poverty to economic security and social status. Whereas at one time she could not even hope to be mistress of her own home, she was now an owner. As usual, they had their own spheres in the house, with Anna's kitchen, dining room, and family parlor on one side of the central hall, and Frederick's office on the other.[36]

The arrangement within the house reflected other ways in which the two Douglasses took care of their extended family. As he became embedded in Republican Party politics, Frederick realized the ways that the much reviled patronage system could work to many African Americans' benefit. His early positions facilitated his sons' entrance into civil service. Lewis finished a term on the territorial legislature of Washington, Charles received a diplomatic appointment to Santo Domingo, and Frederick Jr. became a bailiff in the District courts, all through their father's connections. Then, in 1881, President James A. Garfield appointed Frederick Sr. as Recorder of Deeds of the District of Columbia. "The office is one that imposes no social duties whatever," Douglass explained, "and therefore neither fettered my pen nor silenced my voice in the cause of my people." Although seemingly a demotion from the post as US Marshal to the least exciting position of his career, in a booming real estate market the Recorder's office proved both lucrative and a means to offer far more people employment. As he pointed out, not only did the post become much coveted by black office seekers after his tenure, but he believed he had "opened the gate and led the way upward for the people with whom I am identified." All three of his sons held management positions, and his fourteen-year-old grandson Charlie, Charles's oldest son, worked there as a messenger. The majority of the jobs, however, were for copyists and clerks. Throughout the Civil War and after, the number of these positions in the federal government expanded and they were considered acceptable employment for women. Douglass took full advantage of the situation, and Rosetta was among the first women he hired, providing her with a steady income for her family.[37]

Douglass believed that the handful of black men with access to privileged positions such as government appointments had a responsibility to bring along as many African Americans as possible, despite accusations of nepotism and presumptions of incompetence. His ethic of self-help focused on the individual, but it was not selfish. Individuals should strive to improve themselves, but should also use any success they achieved to help their families and communities. His sympathy sometimes faltered in his presumption that most people were as extraordinary as himself and when ne'er-do-wells expected him to offer what they presumed was his limitless charity. His forgiveness of Nathan's failings, for instance, ranged from anger at the racism that the younger man faced, to annoyance at Nathan's own shortcomings, to concern for the welfare of Rosetta and her children. Frustration also tinged his relationship with his sons, who, in living beyond their means to keep up appearances, did not realize that the standard of living that they had enjoyed under their parents' roof had resulted from decades of the Douglasses' toil. Nevertheless, as their father, creditor, and a fellow black man, he saw himself obligated to help them, just as he helped other African Americans make their way in Washington, by providing them with jobs, shelter, and other forms of patronage, and just as he helped all African Americans by lobbying for civil rights legislation, speaking out against injustice, and supporting educational institutions. It was all of a piece. At the same time, Anna performed the unpaid and often unseen labor of women that enabled others to devote more time and energy to that type of public work. Family formed a significant component in this spectrum of black life in America, and Anna's care for their extended, blended, and elastic household was the domestic version of Frederick's politics.[38]

Even away from Capitol Hill, the Douglasses' numbers expanded, and the distance may have allowed some privacy for the troubles that drove family in need to their house. Charles's wife, Libbie, who had suffered from tuberculosis for over a year and through her last pregnancy, died on September 21, 1878, and her husband took her body to her family home on Long Island. He stayed there for some time, leaving the youngest two children, Mary Louise—called "Mattie"— barely four, and Edward Arthur, not yet a year old and sickly, to live with their grandparents. The little boy, unfortunately, did not thrive and died in March. He was the sixth grandchild that Anna and Frederick had lost by that time, having seen the deaths of not only Alice Sprague, but also three of Frederick Jr.'s children and another of Charles's. Rosetta's daughter Hattie, now twelve, moved into Cedar Hill, followed by her older sister, sixteen-year-old Annie, and their cousin, Charles's seven-year-old daughter, Julia Ada, in 1879. The family, by then, had already grown wider.[39]

In November 1878, Frederick brought more family to Cedar Hill. He had returned to visit Talbot County for the first time in forty years. A version of this journey appeared in his 1881 memoir *Life and Times of Frederick Douglass*, and at the time of his visit, the press covered his speech "Self-Made Men" at the Asbury Church and his visit to Thomas Auld's deathbed. The message of both his autobiography and the newspaper coverage stressed reconciliation and racial uplift. Neither reported on Douglass's visit to the family whom he had left behind in slavery, who could clarify details of his childhood, and who might make the official message more complicated. After this visit, the passage about his paternity appearing in *Life and Times* was shortened from the longer speculations of his earlier autobiographies to a blunt dismissal that "of my father I know nothing."[40]

During this visit to Talbot County, Douglass may also have learned the fate of his older sister, Sarah, as well as that of his younger sisters, Arianna and Harriet, his aunt Hester, and others who appeared in his earlier writings. His sister Eliza had died around 1875, but he had been reunited with her at some point after the war, and she had met Lewis when he taught in St. Michaels. She had seven adult children, one named after her famous brother, and they had children themselves. He also found Perry, who with most of the Downs family had returned to Maryland sometime before 1870. The intervening years had worn the older brother down further, leaving him "old and decrepit" in the words of one reporter and suffering from tuberculosis. Douglass brought Downs back to Cedar Hill along with their sister Kitty Barret and her son and daughter-in-law, Henry and Martha Wilson. Once more, he installed them all in a house on his property. When, two years later, Eliza's orphaned grandson, Charlie Mitchell, contacted Frederick, he invited the ten-year-old boy to move in and receive a better education than rural Maryland could offer a black child. Assing predicted that "the boy may bring him some joy." Barret and her family stayed on a few more years, then she moved to her own house in the city. Downs's condition, however, only worsened. He died on August 18, 1880, at his brother's home.[41]

Assing considered all of these relatives to be a drain on Douglass, but a journalist visiting Cedar Hill in 1881 described Frederick as "a patriarch indeed," surrounded by Anna, Kitty, Henry, Rosetta, Annie, Mattie, Louisa, and Charlie. Just as he continued issuing the German woman invitations, he drew his family close and offered them refuge, considering both actions to be his prerogative as the head of the family. He enlarged his houses to accommodate all, doubling the size of the dwelling and including a children's playroom in his house on A Street, and adding cottages on both the Rochester property and Cedar Hill to permit more. Anna had grown increasingly disabled over the years, making her job as mistress more difficult. As that journalist noted, she had become "infirm from rheumatism," and her grandchildren were told to "be quiet in her presence" because she was so "feeble." Her housekeeping had most likely become entirely supervisory by this point, with Louisa and the granddaughters carrying out her orders in the home, and the various young men whom she fostered taking care of the garden and livestock. That was the privilege of her position.[42]

Anna's grandchildren had memories of their grandfather allowing them to braid his hair, "scramble atop of his broad back" to play horse, slide down the banisters, or join him in calisthenics. She was less jocular. Rosetta recalled her as "firm in her opposition to alcoholic drinks," disapproving of "gaieties" that were "frivolous in the extreme," and "a strict disciplinarian." Yet, she also took over the care of Rosetta's infant daughter Annie, taught Estelle and Fredericka about charity, allowed a "pleased and happy" Mattie to cling to her skirts, and proudly let Rosetta know that Estelle had grown "fat and plump" and "much improved in every way" under her care. Fredericka remembered Anna as "always kind and sweet, and saw to it that we had the loveliest cookies, delicious apple sauce, cottage cheese, milk and cheese." William Oliver, a young apprentice taken in by the Douglasses in Rochester, remembered her as "a motherly woman" who enjoyed "making home pleasant." One young woman, Julia D. Lucas, thought of her as "ever a true friend and mother." Nearly twenty years after having last seen Anna mother the Douglass children, Julia Griffiths Crofts suspected that, as a grandmother, she was "very fond of the little ones." Even her husband took to referring to her as "mother." The people she cared for were all the personal element of her husband's politics, and she carried out his interpretation of family as resistance. In this she was his partner.[43]

Anna's health finally got the best of her in 1882. She had a respite from Assing in 1881, and 1882 looked to be free of intrusion, as well. Frederick had scaled back his speaking engagements over the years, so he was at home on the morning of July 7, 1882, when, sometime between seven and eight o'clock, probably while overseeing preparations for the day, Anna suffered a stroke. Rosetta remembered that "altho' perfectly helpless," paralyzed, and "a great sufferer," Anna "insisted from her sick bed to direct home affairs." The youngest children had been sent to their respective homes because, Fredericka remembered, "grandma was too ill for noise." Louisa, Rosetta, and the older granddaughters stayed at Cedar Hill to nurse the dying matriarch. Frederick had suspended all invitations to speak and stayed by her bedside. "Ah! Rosa," she remembered him sighing as he pulled her close, "if she could have only lived a few years longer." Rosetta, watching him, realized that "he seemed to feel that she was a protection to him in many ways" throughout their life. Anna held out for four weeks, unconscious for the last ten days. Early in the morning of August 4, 1882, she passed away.[44]

Over the next two days, the women would have prepared her for burial, washing her, dressing her, setting her hair, and arranging her body in the front parlor. To them also fell the task of notifying friends, family, and the press, and arranging for all other details of a funeral, including a floral arrangement spelling out "Mother." Annie, now a "little woman" of eighteen, took over at the Sprague house, scrubbing her little sisters and brother and herding them to her grandfather's house for the ceremonies. There they scampered down the hillside in search of Frederick. Finding him weeping, they cuddled up to his side, "still as mice," Fredericka remembered, "wiping our tears away because grandpa wiped his." "Mother was dead!" he cried, moaning over and over, "Your grandma has gone away—you have no grandma now!" Fredericka concluded that "he did not want us to forget grandma."[45]

Figure 8.4 Anna Douglass in one of the two known images of her, taken during the Civil War. After forty-four years of an eventful marriage to Anna Douglass, Frederick believed her to be the "post in the center of my house." National Park Service, Frederick Douglass National Historic Site, Washington, DC, Anna Douglass, [c. 1863], FRDO.

The funeral was a huge affair. One newspaper estimated that three thousand people, both black and white, crowded outside of the Douglass house. The ceremony of invited guests, among whom were senators and congressmen, took place in the Douglass front parlor. Blanche K. Bruce served as a pallbearer, while Bishop T. M. D. Ward gave a eulogy that invoked such notable figures as "Lundy, Torry, Nat Turner, Denmark Vesey, Allen, Lovejoy, Garrison, John Brown, Ward, Stephens, Giddings, Beman, Shaw, Sumner, Lincoln, Gerritt Smith, Garnet, Garfield." Yet, all the pomp appeared designed to honor Frederick, referring to his accomplishments and repeating his autobiography. Few seemed to know much about her, which was probably how this very private woman would have liked it, and she might have been discomfited by the scale of the affair. According to one report, "nearly an hundred carriages" and "a great number on foot" followed her mahogany casket to Graceland Cemetery across the Anacostia River. Although the Douglasses still held the deed to the Mount Hope lot in Rochester, the family choose to keep her remains in Washington, where they all now lived.[46]

Frederick and Anna had bickered over the years. If he had hoped she would embrace more of his interests, she probably wished he would have respected her control over the household more often. If he had expected she would become an activist, she probably insisted he tour less. They clashed over particular houseguests, she asserting dominance in the home and he asserting dominance over it. Hints of the domestic dramas that played out over the years slipped into the family's correspondence. Yet, these conflicts were no more the whole story of the Douglass marriage than were the nostalgic paeans to nobility and bliss that appeared in the commemorations. Forty-four years of life near the center of the most important events of the nineteenth century could not be reduced to a set of adjectives, and even Frederick did not try. The year before Anna died, Frederick had finished his third autobiography. He had omitted his wife's name and the transcript of their marriage certificate because no longer had to establish the legality of their union. The story of their wedding and her intention "to share the burdens of life with me" remained, as well as his use of plural pronouns in describing the beginning of their journey together. Her reduced role was not intended as an insult, as his was meant to be a tale of a public life and wives did not appear in biographies of great men except in formulaic, respectful acknowledgments. The fact of their marriage was enough for his audience to know.[47]

In the end, romantic love and happiness were beside the point and belonged to a later generation of marital expectations. Anna and Frederick had accomplished what they had set out to do in September 1838. They married in freedom. They raised a family. They kept it together. Their children and grandchildren had better opportunities than they themselves ever could have imagined. They owned a home. His work, and hers by extension, helped to end slavery. They coped with daily life, mundane and enervating. Anna and Frederick knew one another longer and better than anyone else. His grief at her passing suggested something beyond love, a loss of part of himself. "The main pillar of my house has fallen," he grieved. "Life cannot hold much for me, now that she has gone."[48]

The year after Anna's death did nothing to comfort Frederick, and he seemed to feel himself at the end of his own life. He concluded *Life and Times* anticipating no "great changes in my fortunes or achievements in the future." The militant young men of the civil rights movement insinuated that he was an irrelevant tool of the Republican Party, an office seeker rather than an agitator. Cedar Hill, with its reminders of Anna and with visitors who still dropped in, and Washington, DC, with its intrigue and disappointment, offered no respite. In the summer of 1883, he retreated to the Poland Spring resort in Maine for solitude. Louisa kept watch over Cedar Hill with a rotation of Sprague daughters, each spending several days at a time and all sending Frederick letters hoping to cheer him. Lewis and Charles looked in periodically, and Rosetta wrote so often to her father from his study that she was certain, "You will begin to think I am living here." She did not want her father to marry again, "at his age," and may have seen herself as stepping into her mother's role as mistress of Cedar Hill. Already she worked for him as a copyist in the Recorder of Deeds office and could have envisioned herself reenacting the antebellum Rochester days, when she had followed him from home to office and back.[49]

Poland Spring, however, rejuvenated Frederick. When Anna had died, Frederick's old friend, Henry O. Waggoner, recognized that the loss of Anna, "with whom you have lived so long," was "especially sad to you, because she was the choice of your youth." He was now ready for the "choice of his old age."[50]

9

Helen Pitts, Mrs. Frederick Douglass, 1837–1890

Frederick Douglass and Helen Pitts had worked through the day normally enough, he the Recorder of Deeds and she a clerk in his office, copying documents. Her fellow clerks, including Lewis Douglass and Rosetta Sprague, noticed nothing amiss. They closed the office that afternooon, and everyone went home as usual; but Frederick and Helen had evening plans that they had kept to themselves. Changing into a black suit at home, Frederick returned to the city, stopping by Helen's lodgings on E Street NE. She alighted from the building wearing a garnet-colored velvet dress. Then, they proceeded to Francis Grimké's parsonage, as Frederick had arranged a few days earlier. There, they met Senator Blanche K. Bruce and his wife Josephine, as well as Grimké's wife, Charlotte Forten Grimké, and their houseguests, Josie Martin and her mother, the widow of J. Sella Martin. At six o'clock, Francis Grimké pronounced Frederick and Helen husband and wife. Congratulations passed all around, and then the newly married couple returned to E Street, where Helen gathered her belongings, and rode to her new home at Cedar Hill. Hours later, reporters appeared at Grimké's door, demanding confirmation and explanation of the marriage of one of the most important black men in the nation to a white woman. Frederick later proclaimed that he and Helen had "set the world ablaze with indignation."[1]

Much ink was spilled over the rights and wrongs of the great Frederick Douglass having married a white woman. Yet few have paid attention to the woman herself, except to insult her husband, as when the *Harrisburg State Journal* quipped that "the Miss that Fred Douglass fell in love with" was "Misgeneration [*sic*]." Her age—forty-six—was sometimes lowered by over a decade, while his—sixty-six— was advanced nearly as much to portray him as doddering or lecherous.[2] Critics deemed her "common" or "low," of a lesser class socially than Douglass. The *Washington Grit* referred to her as "second rate," and the Honorable A. W. Harris of Virginia went "just a step too far in his speech in the Virginia Legislature in passing his opinion upon the character of

Mrs. Frederick Douglass."[3] Even her husband's biographers spent more time on the fact of her whiteness and her fitness as a partner for Douglass in contrast to Anna than the reasons that she might risk so socially transgressive a relationship as an interracial marriage after decades of being single.[4] Moreover, if Frederick had his pick of refined, educated, respectable women, both black and white, then Helen must have distinguished herself beyond superficial common interests. The abolitionism of her childhood might explain her willingness to cross the racial divide in the most intimate of human relationships. But even the most radical of antislavery activists supported miscegenation more in theory than in practice, and members of her family ostracized her after her marriage. Instead, abolitionism was only the starting point of her ideology, conditioning her to make decisions that placed her in the vanguard of interracial relations and shaping the way that she understood her role as Mrs. Douglass into her widowhood.

Helen and Frederick descended from two vastly different parts of the American story. Frederick's family history told a distinctly African American narrative of enslavement, purloined freedom, and disfranchisement, regardless of black participation in the creation of the nation or their European ancestry. His ancestors had been forced to the scruffy settlements on the Chesapeake Bay, used for the benefit of European planters, and, when freed, told that their presence blighted the nation. As he observed in his 1852 speech, his ancestry was not celebrated on the Fourth of July. Helen's was. Her family tree included John and Priscilla Alden, celebrated as immigrants on the *Mayflower*. Her great-grandfather, Peter Pitts, had earned the title "Captain" during the American Revolution and received land bounties in Western New York in payment for his service. Drawing a lot that granted him a tract at the northern end of Honeoye Lake, he and his sons moved their families west in 1789. Like their Pilgrim ancestors, they settled on land that had already been partially cleared by the Native people who were slaughtered during the war and they named the settlement Pittsville for themselves. From the *Mayflower* to these pioneers, Helen's family was the sort enshrined in Anglo-American mythology. By the end of her life, Helen worked to combine these narratives into one racially integrated American story and to ensure that story survived for later generations.[5]

For all their ancestral glory, Helen's parents, Jane Wells and Gideon Pitts, lived a relatively modest, rural life. Helen, their first child, was born on October 14, 1837, eleven months before her future husband escaped from slavery, and twenty months before the birth of his daughter, Rosetta. Helen's little sister, Jane, called "Jennie," followed in 1840, with two others, Lorinda and Eva, arriving in 1843 and 1849, respectively. A brother had been born after Lorinda, but had died within the year. Another, Gideon III, came later, in 1852. Like most other families in their village, the Pittses were farmers, and while they were not the wealthiest family in the village, they were among the well-to-do and had the prestige of being descended from the town founders. Gideon and his brothers George and James, however, distinguished themselves by founding the Richmond Union Church.[6]

The Union Church was the strongest statement of antislavery sentiment in Honeoye. Members of the Presbyterian and Methodist churches had asked their congregations to condemn slavery and, finding their fellow worshippers reluctant to do so, left their respective churches to form their own. They approached William Goodell to lead them, although he was neither trained nor ordained as a minister. He had, however, been among the founding members of the American Anti-Slavery Society and the editor of several temperance and abolitionist newspapers. His lectures and editorials on the necessity of individuals "coming out" or leaving churches that refused to condemn slavery had made him appealing to the Union Church members. He accepted their invitation, bringing his newspaper operation with him.[7]

Over the next ten years in Honeoye, Goodell became more invested in political action against slavery, promoting the Liberty Party and then the more radical Liberty League, naming his paper the *Liberty Leaguer* in 1849. His embrace of political action also brought him into the company of Frederick Douglass as the black abolitionist gravitated toward that branch of the movement. Local tradition remembers Goodell inviting Douglass to Honeoye, usually described as a center of abolitionism and a stop on the Underground Railroad. There, Douglass met the Pittses, including his future wife, and he returned "frequently" through the 1850s.[8] This is all plausible, given that Douglass had toured Western New York in 1842, 1843, 1845, and 1847, before moving to Rochester. Yet, from the announcements in the *Liberator*, his schedules for those tours had him speaking almost every day and provided him little time for a detour to Honeoye. Not until April 1852 did he venture to Helen's home village.[9]

That first visit was not part of a tour, sandwiched as it was between engagements in Rochester, and therefore probably had come at the invitation of someone in town. Goodell and members of the Union Church congregation, such as the Pittses, held fast to their beliefs, making Goodell, the Pittses, or another congregation member the likely hosts. Whether or not Douglass lodged with the Pittses for the several days he visited, in a town with fewer than two thousand residents and only one black family, he must have made some impression on Helen. He, after all, was the living embodiment and apotheosis of the ideals that had permeated her life since she was at least six years old. At age fourteen she may have been wondering about ways in which she might better live those ideals herself. She alone among her family returned to the question of racial equality throughout her life, and her younger sister Jennie—twelve at the time of Douglass's visit—supported her through decisions that frightened the rest of her family. Their much younger siblings might not have been quite so impressed, and they found Helen's later choices perplexing if not distasteful.[10]

As Helen grew up, too, the Pitts family appeared to emphasize education beyond the normal expectations for daughters. All their children attended college, and the youngest, Eva, earned a master's degree in literature in 1875 as part of the second class of women to graduate from Cornell. Yet, Eva's older sisters had already set the precedent for higher education fifteen years earlier. Helen and Jennie both attended the Genesee Seminary in nearby Lima, New York, which prepared them either for a career in teaching or for college. The course of study lasted three years and included lessons in English, Latin, Greek, German, French, math, geography, and various sciences and philosophies, as well as the practical skills of penmanship, bookkeeping, drawing, and elocution. Jennie, at least, appeared to have ambitions to go to college. In 1856, she enrolled at Mount Holyoke Seminary, in Massachusetts, one of the earliest educational institutions for women. Helen followed a year later.[11]

Helen and Jennie attended Genesee and Mount Holyoke during the same years that Rosetta was enrolled at Oberlin, but with drastically different experiences. The Pitts sisters boarded at both schools, thus they had each other's companionship, whereas Rosetta was alone. Furthermore, Rosetta belonged to a minority within two other minority segments of the student population, but Helen and Jennie studied among an equal number of women as men at Genesee, and among only women at Mount Holyoke. In both cases, they belonged to the majority race and class represented by the student population. Pursuing degrees at Mount Holyoke also suggested that both saw their education as something other than a means to an end. They could have entered the teacher's department at Genesee or moved up to the Genesee College, as their sister Lorinda did a few years later. Although the extra years of schooling and connections they made in New England could have led to employment at better schools or in better families than they might find at Genesee, going beyond the basics of teacher training indicated that Helen and Jennie liked the pursuit of knowledge for its own sake.[12]

Just as importantly, they may have been attracted by Mount Holyoke's commitment to producing missionaries as well as teachers, an exciting and meaningful prospect for young, evangelical American women like themselves. The school stressed individual moral perfectionism and selfless Christian service to others, a message that the Pitts sisters had received throughout their childhood. While the school itself did not promote antislavery, in 1854 and 1856, the students staged Fourth of July protests in which they dressed in mourning to denote the demise of freedom in the United States. During Reconstruction, Mount Holyoke alumnae, Helen among them, were surpassed only by Oberlin graduates in providing the largest percentage of teachers to freedmen's schools in the South. Although the Pitts sisters did not appear to participate in any formal reform organization or stage any demonstrations at college, their education at Mount Holyoke and their background at Goodell's church in Honeoye placed them in sympathy with the sort of women who backed Frederick Douglass throughout New York and overseas.[13]

The Pitts sisters graduated in 1859 and appeared to have rejoined the Honeoye household routine for the next four years.[14] When the Civil War broke out Helen was every bit as patriotic and determined to contribute to the war effort as the young men in her town, and she intended to put her education and convictions into action. Seeing the war as one against slavery and racism, in March 1863 she applied to become a teacher with the American Missionary Association, the largest organization addressing the condition of the freed slaves before the creation of the Freedmen's Bureau. Although she specifically requested a "*healthy location,*" few of those were to be had. Three weeks later, she was heading to Norfolk, Virginia, where slaves from the surrounding countryside had flooded federal lines since the Union forces had seized the area in 1862.[15]

Figure 9.1 Helen Pitts in her youth, around the time that she attended Mount Holyoke Female Seminary, which trained young women to become teachers and missionaries. National Park Service, Frederick Douglass National Historic Site, Washington, DC, Helen Pitts, [n.d.], FRDO.

With little more than the rags on their backs, men, women, and children arrived seeking freedom as contraband of the war. Few organizations, including the federal government, were prepared to meet their needs. Abolitionist societies, such as the Rochester Ladies' Society, stepped in, but the American Missionary Association was the largest. While many of the freedpeople had little use for the association's religious ministering, they hungered for the education that the missionaries provided, and the association concentrated their efforts on meeting that demand. As one northern white minister noted, "the work of teaching will be *the work* among this people for some time." Pitts's supervisor, George N. Greene, begged that she be allowed through the lines, despite an order barring "ladies'" travel to Norfolk, because he anticipated at least two hundred students for the first day of classes.[16]

When Pitts left Honeoye in April 1863, she joined a vanguard of association teachers headed for the center of emancipation and the heart of the movement to turn former slaves into citizens.[17] She had spent her life in the peaceful northern countryside of rolling hills and moderate summer temperatures, living among her family and people much like herself. Now, she entered a sea-level southern city at the beginning of a hot and humid summer, in a war zone, where large groups of people from all classes swelled the population and taxed the city's infrastructure, and where she encountered few familiar faces and more than enough hostile ones, not to mention a workload that would occupy her every waking hour. She had no frame of reference for what she faced.[18]

Almost a year before Helen's arrival in Norfolk, the thrust of the fighting had moved up the James River, but the local whites had favored secession and were not pleased to have Union soldiers, abolitionists, and growing numbers of freedpeople in their midst. Guerilla fighters threatened the countryside, cutting off supply lines and preventing the rapid organization of schools outside the city throughout the year.[19] In January, before Pitts arrived, they had burned several buildings and regularly harassed African Americans.[20] "*Secesh* shows its cloven foot in many ways," reported William Coan, the head teacher, in May, "our scholars are stopped on the streets, bricks flying at and against them—*books* occasionally taken from them &c."[21] Even Pitts, who expressed determined optimism in the face of every challenge, noted "the bitter hostility" that was "too freely expressed by some."[22]

Camaraderie among the missionaries became a necessity. Pitts joined the "family" who occupied the ex-mayor's house, who soon appointed her temporary housekeeper. Twelve ministers, teachers, and servants lived there in close quarters, often joined by visitors, and their numbers swelled as the year progressed. Men and women shared accommodations, although by December mainly women occupied the house. Black teachers were in demand, so blacks and whites were expected to share the same space, as well. James Edward, a black monitor, roomed among the white teachers later in the year, and Blanche Harris, the first black teacher from the North, moved in not long afterward. As a result, no one could demand special treatment and, after one finicky lady made too many demands for her personal comfort, Greene requested that no one be sent who was too set in their ways. "We do not wish any old Maiden ladies or those of confirmed old maid's habits," he stipulated, because "so many of us must necessarily be together."[23]

Working conditions demanded the same flexibility, as well as stamina and creativity. Pitts, like the other teachers, supervised classes from Monday through Saturday for two hours every morning and two hours every evening. On Sundays, they held Sabbath schools in both mornings and evenings. The size of the classes every day overwhelmed both the teachers and the two church buildings in which they taught. When the first two schools opened on May 4, 1863, the numbers surpassed Greene's estimations as 350 students showed up in the morning and another 300 that evening. The next day, the numbers jumped to over 550 and 500. When Charles Reed, an old acquaintance of Helen's from Honeoye now stationed in Portsmouth, dropped by for a visit on the third day, he estimated "300 scholars present of all ages from old men to four years old." Over a thousand people from a black population of six to eight thousand hoped to learn to read, write, and do arithmetic every day, and attendance continued to climb, even when individual students could not appear regularly. No wonder Reed observed that Pitts "has got a great undertaking before her."[24] Greene searched for more buildings and asked for more teachers, but resources were stretched so thin that he enacted a policy in which no "day scholars are allowed in evening."[25] Sabbath Schools on Sundays proved equally popular, even as the freedpeople preferred their own ministers for worship.[26]

Pitts was one of the four teachers to oversee these classrooms, assigned to the "higher department" of students who already had some sort of education or who progressed quickly. With classes so large and the pedagogy calling for repetition and recitation, the teachers required assistants to help control, discipline, and drill their charges. The most advanced pupils filled these positions, although Greene noted that "their *little* learning was *exceedingly superficial.*" Pitts realized that many of her pupils showed much promise as monitors and "many would make without doubt very effective teachers" but for a lack of experience and instruction. To that end, she proposed a separate class in the afternoons to train them.[27] Discoving that even they had little basic knowledge of the world beyond their own neighborhoods, she included a globe in the list of books, slates, pencils, and lantern oil requested from donors.

Daily contact made the teachers ever more aware of the problems facing the freedpeople.[28] New arrivals to the city lived crammed together in any available building, and one group of refugees had nowhere to stay but the old slave pen, which only compounded illness in the already weakened population. Clothes also proved scarce. "All the clothing you can spare for this place wanted," appealed Greene. "Many have not clothes enough to get out of doors. Not a rag scarcely on as to put on."[29] Nearly a year later, teacher Blanche Harris also reported that "many would send their children to our schools, had they sufficient clothing."[30] The demand was so great that Greene decided that the mission was compromised until "we can get *clothing* and teachers."[31] Bedding, blankets, and mosquito netting were in short supply, as was adequate medicine.[32] "The sooner we can *have* the *articles* sent *for*," Greene explained in his request for donations of these items, "the sooner and more good we shall do the people."[33] Moreover, although the Union army proved willing to protect the white missionaries from "Secesh," they had less interest in protecting the black population and quite often exploited them. The black population was at first wary of the missionaries and teachers because of their association with the army. Gradually, however, as they learned that the missionaries condemned these acts, African Americans began to appeal to them as intermediaries with the military.[34]

The return of General Benjamin Butler to command at nearby Fort Monroe in November 1863 gave the missionaries in Norfolk hope that black grievances against the military might be addressed. Butler, after all, had enacted the contraband policy that had effectively freed many of their pupils, and he had done much to prevent epidemics in New Orleans by improving its sanitary conditions. As they awaited his return, association superintendent William Woodbury, with Pitts's assistance, began compiling petitions from the freedpeople protesting military abuses. Because he had so many other duties, much of the work fell on her shoulders.[35] "I find her service almost indispensible," Woodbury wrote to the Missionary Association's secretary in New York, and begged that a teacher be sent to replace Pitts in the classroom so she could focus all of her attention on collecting complaints.[36] In seconding his request, Pitts explained that she had already "taken the names of one hundred and seventy men cheated out of their pay *in our department*" alone. Each person "must be patiently listened to, their statements written down, their cases looked after, their claims investigated and a thousand and one little matters attended to." The task, she insisted, was "not only necessary but something for which the whole public is suffering" and thus she could do "the greatest good to the greatest number."[37] The work brought her deeper into the problems faced by African Americans, even in freedom, and the difficulties of forcing apathetic, powerful, white men to respond. The Missionary Association, at least, appeared to have answered their request for more teachers, and William Henry Morris and Blanche Harris, both African American, arrived shortly thereafter.[38]

By this time, the system had become more complex. The original two schools in the churches continued, with classes in morning and evenings, as did the class for training monitors. Smaller schools had been established in the countryside and, in the city, students could advance out of the large classes and into smaller ones of fifty pupils held in public school buildings. Pitts taught one of those classes as well as a Sabbath school of 400 students. She also proposed yet another class for students who had surpassed the classes in both large and small schools, and she and some of her fellow teachers began hour-long lessons with black soldiers in the city. After she began investigating complaints against the army as her main work, she was called back to a large church classroom as substitute for William Coan when he took a leave in December. She remained there into the new year.[39]

Despite the grueling schedule, Pitts consistently found purpose in the work. She boasted of "two or three of my special prides who I am sure with the right influence will someday make their mark."[40] Of her lessons with the soldiers, she declared, "It is a most impressive hour and I trust a prophetic one." When her parents repeatedly demanded that she return north in August, if only for a visit, she put them off until she conceded that "I do not feel it right to disregard their wishes."[41] Even then, she delayed her departure, and when she did arrive in Honeoye, she used the time to collect donations for Norfolk.[42] If her parents had called her home out of worry, her mother soon saw that "her whole heart & soul are in the work."[43] Her colleagues noted her dedication, as well. Just after she had arrived in May 1863, Coan praised her as "all and more ever I think than any of us predicted." Greene asked for more teachers "like Miss Pitts."[44]

Enthusiasm and dedication could not overcome the limits of the human body, however. Not only did many northern teachers and soldiers acclimate to the southern heat and humidity with difficulty, but the transient population of merchants, soldiers, and refugees brought in germs from elsewhere, while the growing population overtaxed the city's infrastructure and led to an accumulation of human filth. Disease ran rampant, as malaria, dysentery, typhoid, and yellow fever, as well as exhaustion, felled people regardless of race. In July 1863, smallpox broke out in Portsmouth, across the Elizabeth River, and a yellow fever epidemic threatened Norfolk the following spring.[45] Within a month of her arrival, Pitts contracted "dumb ague," the common term for malaria without chills, which the doctor first feared was "heart disease."[46] Citing "the fatigue of a crowded school, and the confinement of the city" as reasons for her illness, she suggested that the association take more initiative to address the missionaries' complaints about the "sanitary influence" of the city.[47] In February 1864, Pitts either contracted another sickness or experienced a relapse of malaria so worrying to her supervisors that they notified her parents. She herself assured her mother that she was recovering, and by early March she returned to her classroom.[48] Nevertheless, at the end of the month, she could no longer continue her work. To the dismay of her colleagues, her father had to travel to Norfolk to retrieve her, by which time she felt she "had hardly strength to reach home."[49] She was not the sole casualty. Disease sent Blanche Harris home in April, and replacements Sarah Stanley and Edmonia Highgate succumbed to the climate, conditions, and stress within a year.[50]

Despite Pitts's constant reassurances that she was on the mend and would soon return to her post, she did not recover for a long time. Horrified by reports of "the great sufferings" continuing in Norfolk and "the dreadful atrocities of Paducah and Ft. Pillow," in which Confederates had slaughtered black men, she informed the association that she "began to recruit" immediately upon her arrival home, "even before thoroughly rested."[51] A month later, she swore, "I have had scarcely an ill day since my return" and that her doctor believed that "there was no organic d[is]ease, only functional derangement." She fully expected to resume her work in "a few months."[52] Still too weak in September, however, she could not reply to George Whipple's inquiries about her health and, in December, finally admitted that "it is now uncertain when I shall be strong enough" to return.[53] She was, in fact, much worse than she let on. Jennie had left her teaching post in Iowa to nurse Helen and reported, as late as 1866, that, although Helen "never complains" and was "in some respects better than she was a year ago," she only "sits up about an h[ou]r a day."[54] Like a soldier, Helen's work in Norfolk had disabled her, but she had also put into practice her ideals and learned through close observation the extent of deprivation and racism that afflicted African Americans despite the end of slavery. They were no longer abstractions to her.

By the time she had fully recovered, the war had ended and Reconstruction begun, but Helen did not continue the work that had been so important to her. As she watched her sister Lorinda's family grow and Eva and Gideon III leave for Cornell, Helen and Jennie seemed not to wander far from home for nearly a decade.[55] Still, her strength grew and, by 1876, Helen had become involved enough in temperance to lead a discussion on "the danger of moderate drinking" at a September meeting of the Woman's County Temperance Union for Ontario County. The organization subsequently appointed her to be their alternate delegate at the national meeting in Newark, New Jersey, that October.[56] The new year found her in Washington, living in the Union Town home of her uncle, Hiram Pitts, who had been a clerk in the treasury department since the end of the war.[57]

As with many young, educated women in those postwar decades, the prospects of a job in the expanding government bureaucracy had attracted Helen to the capital. Hiram could serve as a crucial connection in an era of patronage. Another potential source of patronage, the US Marshall for the District of Columbia, moved into the house next door a year after Helen's had arrived. By summer 1878, when Martha Greene, her daughter Minnie, and Ottilie Assing all visited the Douglasses' Cedar Hill, the Pittses and Douglasses had become neighborly. Assing loathed Helen's aunt, Frances Pitts, whom she described as "crafty," "plotting," "unscrupulous," and insincere, and extended her distaste to the whole "Pitts set and those connected with them."[58] Greene, on the other hand, was initially polite to Helen, later inviting her and her sister Eva to visit the Greene family in Fall River.[59]

Shortly after arriving in the city, the Moral Education Society attracted Helen's attention, and she was elected its corresponding secretary in Febrary 1877. Although the group was later characterized as radically feminist, the politics of the Moral Education Society, its president Dr. Caroline Winslow, and its journal *The Alpha* were much more complex. Members took the view that women were the moral guardians of the nation. As such, they promoted strengthening the influence of women as citizens through education, suffrage, entrance into the professions and business, and protective legislation. Belva Lockwood, the first woman attorney admitted to the DC bar, advertised in *The Alpha's* pages, and Clara Barton of Red Cross fame, suffrage leader Matilda Joslyn Gage, former Sanitary Commission officer and woman's rights activist Mary Livermore, and abolitionist Parker Pillsbury all lauded the work of the organization.[60] The society and *The Alpha* lay firmly in the woman's rights camp, and Winslow had been among a group of women who had attempted to register and vote in 1871. They also believed that the moral health of the nation lay in the physical health of women and children, and their most controversial stand was on the issue of sex education. Members applauded the portion of the Comstock laws aimed at pornography, but they also insisted that the good health of women and children could only be protected by throroughly educating women about their bodily functions. That included a complete understanding of reproduction. They in no way endorsed promiscuity or free love. Instead, they insisted that "marriage is with us a religion," calling for mutually respectful companionate unions. Indeed, except for childbearing, they advocated celibacy as the best means for women to control their own destiny, even within marriage.[61]

Nevertheless, such frank talk about sex offended many. One correspondent denounced *The Alpha* as a "disgusting sheet" and asked that it "be suppressed by Anthony Comstock." Winslow replied by letting readers know that she sent Comstock the journal from time to time, without receiving any threats. Frederick Douglass apparently never read *The Alpha*, but Ottilie Assing did, if only "for the sake of having a right to denounce it," she insisted. "No pure-minded woman can advocate those monstrous doctrines," she pronounced. Despite her atheism, Assing was more offended by the content of the paper than its moral rhetoric. In her estimation, only someone "incurably and irredeemably stupid as to be considered altogether irresponsible" could possibly "allow her imagination to run always in that same channel, read all that obscene stuff hidden under religious cant."[62]

Yet, that "religious cant" was their main weapon, and the "obscene stuff" of reproduction was the defining feature of most women's life. The women of the association claimed moral guardianship of the domestic sphere, but used it to gain entrance into an unreceptive public sphere. They may not have seen themselves as demanding equality with men, but they expected to have direct influence in all areas of life that affected them, from healthcare to business to the law. A similar ideology had permeated the antislavery movement, Pitts's education at Mount Holyoke, and the American Missionary Association. For Helen, apparently uninterested in marriage at the age of forty, the concept of autonomy through celibacy gave her a way to understand her personal choices as empowering because they liberated her from a life of constant childbearing. As a moral reformer focused specifically on women, she could retain the femininity and respectability that women were expected to foster through marriage and motherhood.

Pitts's active association with the society, however, lasted perhaps a year. She did not appear in the list of officers after 1877, nor did she contribute any columns or articles using her own name or initials. Caroline Winslow complained that the production of the paper lay entirely in her hands, and no other evidence indicated that Pitts participated in its publication.[63] She did remain in contact with at least one of the society's members. Her aunt Frances Pitts had become involved with the organization by 1878 and served as its recording secretary from 1882 through 1884, which led to some of the later confusion over the length of Helen's tenure. A newspaper reporting on Helen's wedding in 1884 referred to her as "an associate of Mrs. Winslow in the publication of the *Alpha*." When another associate asked Winslow's opinion on Helen's marriage, Winslow counseled against it and implied that the two were still in communication.[64] Also, in 1884, the Boston branch of the association referred to Helen as "a long time worker in the cause" but may have inflated the connection because they supported the marriage. Overall, Pitts seemed to keep abreast of the organization's progress but did not play a visible role after her tenure as secretary.[65]

Pitts's drift away from the organization probably came as a result of her employment prospects. Her search for a government position appeared fruitless by 1879, when she spent a short time teaching in Huntington, Indiana, substituting for her sister Eva.[66] The next year, she accepted an appointment in a boarding school in Darien, Connecticut.[67] Yet Pitts had either little luck or little interest in teaching students who were less enthusiastic than her Norfolk pupils, and these schools probably lacked the sense of excitement and purpose that had characterized her days with the American Missionary Association. In September 1881, she returned to Washington and never taught again. This time, patronage worked in her favor. Douglass, now the new Recorder of Deeds in the District of Columbia, had the power to hire his own staff. Along with his sons; Rosetta; and, later, Rosetta's oldest daughter, Annie, he brought Helen on as a copyist.[68] While the pay was not grand, she no longer had to room with her uncle's family and found her own lodgings closer to the office. A year later, she moved to Cedar Hill.

Judging from the universal shock in response to their wedding on January 24, 1884, no one had noticed anything between Frederick and Helen before then.[69] She had visited the Douglass home, knew the Douglass family, was acquainted with Anna, and worked with the Douglass children. Her visits to the Cedar Hill before Anna's death probably did not differ in any way from the visits of other acquaintances who admired Douglass, shared his interests, and, by extension, showed concern for the well-being of his family. Unlike Julia Griffiths and Ottilie Assing, Helen stayed no longer than an afternoon or evening when she visited him. If Frederick and Helen attended literary society meetings, church, plays, or any other gathering, then they did so in a way that attracted no notice either before or after Anna's death. Only Frances Pitts seemed to suspect something, and Frederick confronted her about the "hints, innuendos or implications" and "rumors and mean suspicions" that she harbored. He suggested that she meet him either "with or without Miss Helen" to address "anything you may think it well to say to either or both of us."[70] Otherwise, no one recalled any signs of a courtship. Indeed, when Frederick approached Francis Grimké to perform the wedding ceremony, Grimké was of the impression that the bride would be "one of two prominent women of the race" with whom Frederick had been connected. He was surprised to discover that his friend's intended was the white woman whom Grimké had met in passing only moments earlier.[71]

As Grimké indicated, rumors about Frederick's intention to remarry began within a year of Anna's death. In fact, when Rosetta Sprague first heard about her father's wedding, she dismissed it as yet another fabrication, laughing because "that has been the tale for a long time."[72] Women, after all, had long been attracted to her father and many could not imagine him enduring a lengthy widowhood. Within months of Anna's death, Elizabeth Thompson, a widowed philanthropist and long-time correspondent of Frederick's, intimated that she "should not be surprised to some day find a little young bird of a lighter plumage than the other caged there" at Cedar Hill, and her reference to color suggested that she, too, may have suspected Douglass of harboring fondness for a white or lighter-skinned woman. Her effusive letters in the 1870s implied that she might have considered herself a possible candidate in another period of life, but now, she suggested he find a younger woman.[73] Mary Ann Pierson, a daughter in the family that had housed Charles after the John Brown raid, begged Douglass to destroy letters she had written to him in 1881, if "looked over by a curious person they could & probably would be misconstrued and misinterpreted both for your sake and mine its best to burn them up."[74] Not long after Anna's death, Martha Greene had indicated that she was available, although she backtracked quickly when Douglass politely demurred. Still, with her own fortunes declining, and living on the hospitality of her son-in-law, she would hardly have rejected an offer from her cherished friend.[75] Ottilie Assing had of course for decades let him know that she considered herself a more suitable partner than anyone else. Frances Grimké's wife, Charlotte Forten Grimké, could have introduced Douglass to a host of genteel black ladies from her husband's church, or he could have met the same sort of woman at meetings of the literary society to which he belonged. Indeed, as Francis Grimké indicated, Frederick already had the attentions of at least two, while a newspaper in Georgia repeated a rumor that the great man "has for some time paid addresses to one of the most worthy and accomplished colored ladies of Washington,"[76] and a paper in Washington speculated that he "was soon to marry a very handsome woman, almost white, and many, many years his junior."[77]

Despite the rumors and attentions of available women, Douglass himself never intimated that he at all wanted a wife, and he certainly had no practical need for one. He was not a young man hoping to establish a family, as he had been when he and Anna married. Older men tended to remarry in order to have someone to take care of the children and household, as his son Charles had.[78] Frederick's own children, however, were grown with their own families. Louisa oversaw the operation of Cedar Hill, and he could afford to hire servants. He was self-supporting, so he had no need for someone who could contribute to the household income, and had managed thus far without a political wife to accompany him to social gatherings. In other words, if Douglass wished to marry, he had the luxury of choosing a wife purely for affection and desire. Companionship, white or black, with or without controversy, could be had. When his mourning for Anna had subsided, he chose Helen Pitts.

Helen chose him, too. At forty-six, she was more than twice the usual age for a bride and, like her sisters Eva and Jennie, appeared to have consciously avoided matrimony. Helen's participation in the Moral Education Society indicated a respect for the institution but also suggested a desire for some sort of self-determination that freed her from childbearing. For her, that freedom meant that she must sacrifice marriage, with its expectation of motherhood shortly thereafter. Futhermore, marriage meant dedicating oneself to husband and family first, but many of Helen's influences and decisions indicated that she found more satisfaction in serving an ideal. Marriage to Frederick reconciled both urges, allowing her intimacy and providing her with her own household while also connecting her to a movement for racial equality, something that marriage to a Honeoye farmer or another government bureaucrat would not. Like Julia Griffiths, who had understood her work for Frederick as directly abolitionist, like the children's interpretation of Anna's housewivery as inherently antislavery, Helen considered her marriage to one of the leading black civil rights activists a contribution to that cause. Given her family's abolitionist background, she had no reason to think that her decision was anything other than in accordance with the very ideals they had taught her.

Forty years earlier, when Frederick and Anna had agreed to marry, Maryland law would not recognize their union, although they would have been universally accepted as husband and wife until Thomas Auld decided otherwise. In 1884, the District of Columbia recognized Frederick and Helen's marriage, but neither spouse was naïve enough to believe that they would be popularly accepted as anything but race traitors. Grimké, who fielded the first questions from reporters, observed that "the colored people, generally, did not approve of his marriage to a white woman."[79] Disgust more aptly described the reaction in the black press. One Washington newspaper proclaimed the Frederick had made "the mistake of his life," one that was nothing less than "a national calamity."[80] Another followed suit, calling the marriage "the fatal error of his life" and "a foolish and unwise step."[81] A correspondent in Springfield, Ohio, wondered if Frederick were "possessed of weakness or succumbing to the influences of a second childhood."[82] Many agreed with the reporter from Raleigh, North Carolina, who wrote, "he does not represent the intelligent and more self-respecting colored men of the South."[83]

Few on either side of the debate denied his right to choose a white wife. Instead, the problem for Douglass's critics lay in the result of that choice. Most believed that Frederick had a responsibility to marry a black woman. His choice

Figure 9.2 This advertisement for a skin lightening cream lampooned Douglass's marriage to Helen Pitts and is only one small example of the vitriol aimed at the newlywed couple. "Sulphur Bitters ad." Courtesy of Donna Albino, Mount Holyoke alumna.

of a white woman was seen as an explicit rejection of black women and, by extension, all African Americans. "Africanus," a columnist writing for the *Cleveland Gazette*, believed that Douglass was attempting to "bleach out the race." The *American Baptist* proclaimed that "he had little sympathy with his race," a North Carolina paper that he had "branded" African Americans as "inferior," the *Leader* that he had "deserted" them, and the *Washington Critic* that "he acknowledges the superiority of the Caucasian by marrying one." "He may be deply concerned about the Negro in words," insisted the *Virginia Baptist Companion*, "but in actions does not wish to be identified with the dear people." Others looked to the future of his family. "If he had married a colored woman," speculated the *People's Defence*, "his fortune might have remained in the race." A Pittsburgh commenter concluded, "Good bye black blood in that family."[84] Even his black allies, those who supported his marriage and genuinely liked Helen, felt disappointment that, in the words of Ida B. Wells, Frederick had not "chosen one of the beautiful, charming colored women of my race for his second wife."[85] Most deferred to his right to make a private choice without registering their opinion of that choice.

To Frederick and Helen, critics missed the point. For all Frederick's rhetorical demurral that that his interracial marriage should be of no consequence, both he and Helen understood the symbolic importance of their union. In 1838, Anna and Frederick's marriage, coupled with his self-emancipation, asserted their will against the conditions imposed on black families in the South. Now, in 1884, Helen and Frederick's marriage asserted their will against racial segregation at the most basic level, the one at which white supremacy was most strongly enforced, and the one in which biological arguments for racial difference were propagated. Frederick's own existence was proof that such transgressions took place. As he joked, "Some folks have tried to read me out of the race because I have done in one direction what my father did in another."[86] Yet, those liaisons were often either clandestine or lacked consent. They also usually took place between a white man and black woman; whereas black men were viciously punished for the mere rumor of a liaison with a white woman. In this hierarchy of sex, white men considered the sexuality of both black and white women as their possession and saw black male sexuality as something to contain. That attitude emerged most explicitly in a letter written to the *Washington Sunday Gazette*, whose author insisted that the marriage had come about merely "by reason of Douglass' cultivation of much of the Southern niggerism, which inclines them to win and belittle any white woman who condescends or tolerates the advance or amours of an impudent Negro."[87] Yet, in this marriage, Helen herself had denied white male control over her affection and body by asserting her own sexual and marital choice, taking a black man for a husband. Their union was mutually consensual, legally

sanctioned, and a matter of public record, which made it threatening to the social order of white male supremacy.

Still, though Frederick called for interracial mixing as a means of eliminating
race and therefore racism, his marriage to Helen was not likely to produce children. Although some newspapers had reported her as much younger, Helen was
forty-six on her wedding day and either past or at the end of her childbearing
years. She expressed no desire to become a mother, and, while she supported
at least one young woman who was pursuing a professional career, she did not
foster young girls or boys, as Anna had. Frederick could have chosen a wife who
had a better chance of having babies, but his choice of a woman not likely to do
so conveniently avoided future questions about inheritance. With Helen and no
additional children, he had only to provide for his surviving heirs and a widow,
as he would have done had Anna outlived him. At the same time, Helen was
young enough that she would not likely die before he did and could, therefore,
guide the commemoration and public image of him after his death. His stipu-
lation in his will, drawn up in in the summer after their wedding, that she have
sole posession of Cedar Hill, his papers, and his books suggested that this was,
perhaps, a consideration.

Although their union presented no material challenges to their families,
not all members on either side took the news gracefully. Having been raised
in a household that condemned racial prejudice and embraced her husband
as a hero, Helen was surely disappointed in her family's reaction. The marriage exacerbated tensions between Frederick and Hiram, who argued over
debts and property boundaries in the following years, but only in memos.
Two years later, according to one newspaper account, Hiram and his family
still "have not forgiven her [Helen], and hold no intercourse with her in
any way."[88] Helen's mother, Jane, would not speak to her daughter for over a
year, either of her own choice or in obedience to her husband. She eventually visited Cedar Hill, in spring 1885, reconciling with Helen and restoring
Frederick in her affection.[89] Helen's father, Gideon, shunned his daughter's
new home, visiting the capital only when she and Frederick were out of town,
and cut Helen entirely out of his will.[90] Her sister Eva left Frederick with the
impression that "she hates me";[91] and as far as her other sister, Lorinda Short,
was concerned, Helen's marriage became "a dark scandal" that she only whispered to her grandaughter "in the privacy of her room."[92] The hostility was so
great that, when Helen abbreviated her and Fredcrick's 1887 tour of Europe
to rush to the side of her ill mother, her husband worried about the family's
reception and wished "your welcome civil if not cordial." He tried to comfort
his wife with humor, advising her to rely on "your own dignity" and have "no
concern about the hate and malice" of her sister's family because "we move in
very different grooves." He also thanked her sister Jennie for being "as good

as she is brave." Jennie alone, always the sister closest to Helen, stood by her side throughout. Her inclusion in a portrait with the couple (see Figure 9.3), in which all appear to enjoy themselves, indicated her place in their lives.[93]

Some members of Frederick's family also objected. His sons and their wives accepted that their father had chosen Helen for his wife. "Father had a right to marry whom he pleased," Lewis told a reporter, "and that is the way we regard it." During their father's life, they and their families remained on polite, if not intimate, terms with his second wife. Frederick's sons, however, had not relied as heavily on their parents for support as the Spragues, who had depended on Frederick and Anna through their very frequent financial, legal, and emotional difficulties. The Spragues broke from the official family position both on Frederick's marriage and in airing their grievance in public. "I would have

Figure 9.3 Of Helen's family, only her sister Jennie Pitts, standing between the seated Frederick and Helen, supported her choice. This joint portrait demonstrates the Douglass couple's gratitude to her. National Park Service, Frederick Douglass National Historic Site, Washington, DC, Frederick Douglass, Jennie Pitts, and Helen Douglass, [c. 1885], FRDO 3912.

prefered, at his age," Rosetta confessed to a reporter, that "he should not have married again." Although she had dismissed early news of her father's marriage, her daughter Annie and Louisa, who lived at Cedar Hill, had confirmed it. As soon as Rosetta received word that there would be a new mistress of Cedar Hill, she went to retrieve Annie. Frederick hoped his granddaughter would stay, but when asked if she could respect Helen as she had Anna, Annie replied, "I cannot do that." "Then you had better go," concluded Frederick, which Rosetta took as having her daughter "turned out of the house." She extended this interpretation to Louisa's situation, as well, when Louisa shared Annie's reaction.[94]

Louisa faced a complicated proposition when Frederick brought Helen home. She remembered being a slave, during which time she had experienced an unspecified trauma about which she had told only Anna. In freedom, she had refused to live in her brothers' houses when she felt they treated her like a servant.[95] Anna and Frederick, on the other hand, had welcomed her as a daugher, and she had been running Cedar Hill on her own for the two years between Anna's stroke and Helen's arrival. This new arrangement placed Louisa under Helen's supervision, and Louisa evidently understood this as a return to servility, made worse because her mistress was a white woman. Powerless to change the situation, she sought refuge with the Spragues.

Nathan regarded this change as an actionable insult and approached attorney and former judge Thomas J. Mackey for legal advice on his sister's behalf. A South Carolinian, alumnus of the Citadel, and former Confederate, Mackey had a checkered past in relation to race. He had belonged to the Democratic Party until 1876, when he switched to the Republicans and thereby received a judgeship. Hardly a radical, he believed that African American civil rights had gone far enough and later returned to the Democrats' fold.[96] When he was approached to take on a suit against one of the leading black men of the day, he welcomed the case. On Mackey's advice, Nathan presented Douglass with a bill for services that Louisa had rendered since October 21, 1872, when she had moved into Douglass's Capitol Hill house. Frederick and Helen were departing for abolitionist Wendell Phillips's funeral in Boston when Nathan appeared at Cedar Hill. Impatient to leave and annoyed at facing yet another demand for money from his son-in-law, he told Nathan to draw up an invoice, promising to attend to it after the funeral. While he was in Boston, however, the *Philadelphia Press* ran a story detailing Louisa's plans to sue him if he did not pay the as yet unspecified amount.[97]

When Frederick returned to Washington, a messenger appeared at his door with the invoice. Louisa and Nathan asked for a total of $2,640, for which they were willing to subtract $675 for the sums that she received over the years for clothing. To give Louisa's claim legal grounds, a story also began circulating that, in 1872, Louisa had actually entered into a contract with the Douglasses for a salary of $25 per month, but that she never received pay beyond "an average about $40 a year, on which to dress herself." Even then, ran one version, "this paltry sum was wrung with great difficulty." The Spragues and the press played on Douglass's history of demanding just payment for labor, attempting to underscore his hypocrisy by reporting that his annual income exceeded $200,000. This gave ammunition to civil service reformers who charged public servants like Douglass with using their offices for financial gain. "You were not raised in a parlor yourself," Nathan charged Frederick, "your experience and the doctrines you preach should have taught you not to deny to any one a fair day's wages for a fair day's work, even though the work was done in *your* kitchen." To ensure that this was not seen as an act of vengence against Helen, the Spragues distanced Louisa's complaint from Frederick's marriage by claiming that she had planned to take action long before the wedding.[98]

Frederick dismissed the accusations because such a "contract has no existence, and never had." He had no objection to compensating Louisa so long as the price was "reasonable," but he deemed their bill "larger than I should have paid her had I offered to hire her, or had she offered to hire herself." He, Lewis, and Charles suspected other motives behind the gambit. Combined with intimations that Mackay "intends to show Douglass up as very different to what he appears to be to the public" by exposing "a number of breezy peculiarities about the local and domestic life of the colored Moses," Douglass believed that the charges against him were "an attempt to take a mean and cowardly advantage of the supposed unpopularity of my recent marrage to malign and blackmail me, to extort money." He did not blame Louisa, but instead pointed to "those who are managing the business in her name."[99] If he included his daughter in that category, it was the closest he ever came to criticizing one of his children in public.

Charles and Lewis, however, had always accused Nathan of preying too much on their father's generosity and were more specific in their statements. Lewis did not believe that Louisa had taken part in the initial proceedings of the claim, nor did he think Mackey was its source. "There is someone else behind who wants to injure father for his own purpose," he told a reporter, implying that the insinuations being made about Frederick's home life pointed to Nathan as the culprit.[100] Charles tabulated Nathan's history to his father privately, pointing out that, "He came to you without a shilling, was given a home, married into your family, started in business, put into office, betrayed his trust by stealing, served a light sentence through your kind influence, taken back to the family and encouraged to do better." Now, Charles fumed, Nathan was "the first and only one to drag you before a court, and through a malicious conspiracy."[101]

Nathan agreed that money was central to the claim, but denied any vengeance. "It was not a personal matter at all," he insisted, only "a matter of dollars and cents."[102] Although the Spragues had fared better since moving to Washington, they continued to struggle. Nathan had entered the feed business and worked as a drover, a baker, and a milkman, with moral and financial support from his father-in-law. Yet, the capital was an expensive city to live in, and having outstanding debts in Rochester, Nathan could not earn enough to support his family, and Rosetta worked constantly to make ends meet.[103] Now that Annie and Louisa had returned from Cedar Hill, and with four children not yet old enough to contribute to the household income, the Spragues had two more mouths to feed. They probably also believed that they could no longer rely upon the Douglass household as a refuge or appeal to their father's wife for sympathy as they had when Anna was alive. Financial recompense was no small matter, but notes of resentment permeated Nathan's statements. He and Rosetta had spent much energy attempting to live up to Frederick's standards, often feeling the sting of failure. Nathan in particular seemed intent on venting his frustration and shame by humiliating his father-in-law in public. "According to your well known habit," he accused Frederick, "you place yourself on a lofty pedestal and flaunt your assumed dignity before the public." Having essentially called one of the most important black men of the century "uppity," Nathan then intended to tear down his father-in-law by exposing Frederick's private life to public scrutiny.[104]

Nathan began by violating the Douglass practice of protecting the household from intrusion by alerting the press to the problem. Then, through his attorney, he threatened to expose damning material about Douglass's home life as the suit proceeded. He knew to take the disagreement into the political realm by framing his sister's demand for compensation as a violation of a labor contract, not quite saying that Louisa was Frederick's slave, but certainly accusing Frederick of exploiting a black woman's labor. Despite his denial that there was any connection between Frederick's marriage and Louisa's claim for wages, he described both as betrayals of racial solidarity in general and black women in particular. "In common with many of your friends," he informed Frederick, "I have viewed your marriage more in sorrow than in anger." In this threatened lawsuit, Nathan portrayed himself in a role much like that of a younger Frederick. He, the former slave, defended two black women from ill treatment, demanding recognition and compensation for their labor and suffering. Frederick, on the other hand, he portrayed as betraying his origins, which were so much like Nathan's own, by marrying a white woman and by refusing to pay a black woman back wages.[105]

As for Rosetta, she tried at first to keep this particular family dispute from spilling into the political arena in which her father's marriage was debated. Failing that, she intended to separate Louisa's complaint from any suggestion that the family objected to Frederick's marriage to a white woman. Louisa, Rosetta insisted to a reporter, "did not dislike her [Helen] because she was white or because she married

Mr. Douglass," but rather had "disliked her long before" the wedding.[106] The matter was one of personality, nothing more. Although she usually acted as diplomat between her husband and her father, here she sided with Nathan, and her actions in ensuing decades indicated that she never accepted that Helen had any rights as her father's second wife. Because Rosetta had mediated many of the differences between her parents, she understood the complexities of race and class among her mother, father, and his white female friends. Her mother had been dead for approximately a year and a half and she had not wanted her father to remarry at all. She even may have seen herself as stepping into a caretaking role in his old age, the devoted daughter of the Great Man, serving as hostess of Cedar Hill and preserving his legacy after his death. Therefore, she likely perceived her father's marriage to Helen as a repudiation not merely of black women but of her mother in particular and herself by extension. The Spragues, then, took Douglass's remarriage as a personal insult. With no other means or right of protest, a lawsuit was a way to strike back if only through the publicity.

Louisa had the most at stake in the case. Regardless of the accumulating pain and betrayal within the family, she occupied the precarious position faced by single women who were dependent on extended family members. Providing unpaid labor that would otherwise have come from hired servants, these women had little long-term security or negotiating power in the arrangement. For over a decade, Louisa had worked for Frederick and Anna, proving as capable and almost as valuable to the household as Anna herself. Yet, while they clothed, fed, sheltered, and otherwise cared for her as a daughter, she had no authority in the household and no form of property or savings to fall back upon. "It is true that I never asked him for money and that I often refused it," Louisa conceded, "but then I understood that I had a home there and would always be cared for." When conditions changed, she had to accept the new arrangement or find somewhere else to go, without income, shelter, or references. "Twelve years out of a woman's life is a great deal," her brother pointed out. "If she had not given this service to him [Douglass] she might have been at work at something else, and providing for her old age." This lawsuit might ensure that those years had not been for nothing. Nevertheless, much of the vitriol seemed to come from her brother. Even after both Louisa and Frederick indicated that they would prefer independent mediation, Nathan had his attorney file a suit. Ultimately, Louisa and Frederick prevailed. They came to a private agreement that he would pay her $645 if she would drop the case.[107] Given Rosetta's place in the family, she probably brokered the deal. Louisa then found a job with a confectioner, where she worked for the next seven years. She never returned to Cedar Hill, and she and Frederick avoided one another thereafter.[108]

As the fracas unfolded, Martha Greene insisted that her old friend could have avoided the whole affair had he proceeded with the marriage more publicly.

Perhaps expressing her own opinion of the marriage, she believed that the outcry resulted not so much from whom he married as from "the *way you did it*." She was certain that "had your courtship been open, and above-board, your marriage announced, and consummated in presence of your children and friends, yourselves conducting the whole affair, with the dignity and propriety which have ever before marked all your public proceedings," then there might have been merely "a ripple of displeasure" that would have soon dissipated.[109] Her growing mistrust of Helen clouded her opinion, and this line of argument was the only one that she could make without seeming hypocritical. Frederick and Helen, however, were not so unworldly as to believe that the manner in which they had proceeded would have made any difference in the reception. Had they followed Greene's advice, then they would have faced protests before the wedding as well as afterward, in public and at home. By marrying without warning, they kept the ceremony a happy affair and presented their marriage to the world as a fait acccompli, something to which people could object but not attempt to prevent. They thereby controlled the timing of the outrage and made a statement about their right to marry. Rather than implicitly ask for permission by announcing their intentions beforehand, as a *Washington Post* reporter later wrote, they "married without asking any one but themselves if it were best or suitable."[110]

Meanwhile, the *Washington Grit* was of the opinion that "Barnum could make a mint of money out of this couple if they would consent to go on exhibition."[111] The *Grit* intended to insult, but Frederick and Helen knew that they were on exhibition with or without the showman's help and did not shy from the attention. In May, they arrived together at the House of Representatives after a heated debate had begun on the floor. "Scores of opera glasses were leveled at them" as they took their seats in the Ladies' Gallery, reported a Washington DC paper, noting that "Mrs. Douglass bore herself with much grace and dignity, and was subject to many admiring remarks."[112] In 1885, they were rumored to have sat in a pew in front of President Cleveland during a Sunday service at Washington's First Presbyterian Church. Another paper reported that they had been denied the rental of a pew not "because of his [Frederick's] race but because of the race of his wife."[113]

In February 1886, just after Frederick had tendered his resignation from the Recorder of Deeds Office, he and Helen attended a White House reception with Helen's sister Jennie and one of Rosetta's daughters, probably Annie, now an employee in Frederick's office and on better terms with the Douglasses. In the receiving line, Frederick found himself in the position of explaining to President Cleveland that the "young mulatto girl" on his arm was not his wife, as announced, but his granddaughter. The "demure-looking white lady" with them was his wife. "It is safe to say," the press reported, "that Fred. Douglass and his white wife attracted more general attention and comment than any other couple present."[114] Frederick and "the ladies of his family" were invited back to the White House in March.[115] Accusations later abounded that the Douglasses had dined at the Executive Mansion and attended Cleveland's wedding, Frederick denied the rumors, explaining that the president had only "repeatedly and over his own signature invited us to attend his receptions."[116]

The National Woman Suffrage Association convention also met in March, and "Frederick Douglass and his new wife have been conspicuous attendants each day," sitting in the front row, according to one report.[117] On the surface, this would not have been unusual since both professed to be suffragists, and Douglass had attended NWSA conventions before. Behind the scenes, however, Susan B. Anthony had a fit. Elizabeth Cady Stanton, still lecturing Frederick on woman's rights after forty-two years, had parodied the most virulent of the reactions to the Douglass marriage in a letter addressed to him. "To think," she huffed in jest, "that you should unite your future destiny with 'a woman.'" After all, she pointed out, "did you forget that according to some authorities, a woman is not even 'a person' much less 'a citizen'?"[118] She intended to have the letter published in Washington and New York, but Anthony all but ordered her to remain silent. "The question of the amalgamation of the different races is a scientific one," which she separated from the *"perfect equality of Rights—civil and political—for all women."* Frederick had "shocked the general feeling—the general sense of propriety" and therefore endangered the woman suffrage movement, Anthony argued, declaring that "He has by this act compromised every movement in which he shall be brought to the front!" With pen, paper, and many underlined words, she ranted for two days, including Helen in her barbs by suggesting that she was not a suffragist because she was not on the NWSA rolls and that she was not Frederick's *"peer in intellect, position, & wealth."* In the end, she could do nothing but announce, "I shall *not* invite him," and threaten Stanton that, "if you do—you will outrage the best feelings of the best friends here."[119] Heart problems kept Stanton from attending the meeting, and while she capitulated to Anthony, she sent her letter to the Douglasses privately.[120] Helen and Frederick, however, defied Anthony's wishes, putting her in the position of either accepting their presence or tossing them out of the convention and thereby calling attention to an issue that she intended to avoid.

Such stories led scandal-mongers to repeat rumors that the Douglasses had been shut out of polite society, but the couple continued to receive invitations to weddings, funerals, and other social and official gatherings.[121] In a change from Anna's tenure as mistress, Helen began holding parties and "open houses" at Cedar Hill, during which vistors dropped by.[122] Clusters of signatures in their autograph book suggest that they held dinner parties, luncheons, or teas on those days.[123] From 1884 to 1886, they hosted literary society gatherings that could number up to one hundred participants. Guests included family members, such as Lewis, Amelia, Charles, Laura Douglass, and Frederick Jr.'s brother-in-law E. M. Hewlett, as well as reporters, Howard University professors, and other members of Washington's black elite, including James M. Gregory, who later wrote *Frederick Douglass the Orator*.[124] At an 1886 party, Annie Sprague, "the talented pupil of Prof. Bischoff," played the piano, and Charles's son "little 'Joe Douglass,'" aged sixteen, thrilled his grandfather by demonstrating his emerging talent on the violin.[125] They also held a Fourth of July celebration in 1885, and a bon voyage party before embarking on a tour of Europe in September 1886. When they returned, the Washington papers noted that they continued to be "hospitable and entertain many visitors," including on the Fourth.[126] They scaled back their entertaining, however, after Helen's disabled mother moved to Cedar Hill in 1888. She lived there until her death in 1892. Then, in 1894, Jennie became seriously ill. Caregiving and mourning took up much of Helen's energy, although she and Frederick neither ceased to socialize nor turned away visitors.

In opening her home so frequently to so many guests and in mingling with those guests as hostess, Helen differed from Anna. Anna had probably had a greater sense of ownership over the house. Cedar Hill was, after all, the product of the previous decades of her life with Frederick and a space that she defined as her domain. Helen, on the other hand, more likely saw the house as part of her husband's legacy, and herself in the role of caretaker. Literary gatherings alone presented the couple as engaged not only with the ideas represented in books but also with an integrated world of intellectuals. A Fourth of July celebration, held two years after the Supreme Court had ruled that African Americans were not entitled to equal protection under the US Constitution, indicated their defiant patriotism. These events, which were covered by newspapers, demonstrated that they had not been rejected by black society and that the races could socialize peacefully as intellectual and social equals. They defied the critics who had prophesized a doomed marriage.

Most importantly, when Helen and Frederick opened parts of their house to the public, it became a theater for their marriage, from which they projected the image of an affectionate couple, less reserved with one another than Frederick had been with Anna. The *New York Globe* noted that, at their 1884 literary society celebration, their "chief anxiety seeemed to be to render each guest as happy as themselves."[127] Henry O. Wagoner, now a widower, told his age-old friend that a recent, published account of the Douglass couple had moved him as "a truthful description of the purely mutual affection existing between you and your womanly wife," and reminded him of his own marriage to a woman whose "very bones in the grave are sacred to me."[128] A paper in Bennington, Vermont, reported that Frederick "is very happy with his new white wife, and she seems happy with him," and could not help making the comparison that "she is much more congenial to Douglass than his first wife."[129] Yet, for Frederick and Anna, their reserve in public was consistent with an image of mid-nineteenth-century respectability that shunned public displays of affection. The obvious warmth between Frederick and Helen not only conformed to the expectations in a late-nineteenth-century marriage, but also demonstrated that interracial affection was both possible and desirable, not violent and exploitative.[130]

They did not limit their public appearances to Washington. Hardly a month after their wedding, they attended Wendell Phillips's funeral together in Boston;[131] they visited Rochester the following April.[132] Through the late summer and autumn, when Frederick campaigned for the Republican Party in the Midwest, the press did not fail to note Helen as his intrepid companion in Chicago and Battle Creek, as well as on stops throughout Ohio and Indiana. They also took detours to Providence, Syracuse, and Rochester.[133] In January 1885, they visited Vermont and, in August, they spent a week in Nantucket.[134] Although Helen did not accompany Frederick on every engagement, they traveled together often enough that, while on a five-week trip to Boston in 1890, he told reporters that "this is the first trip of any length since his marriage, upon which Mrs. Douglass has not accompanied him." By that time, he and Rosetta had reconciled. She accompanied him and visited scenes from his days as a newlywed to Anna.[135]

Helen and Frederick could not have avoided publicity each time they stepped outside of Cedar Hill or held a gathering at their home that included prominent members of Washington's black bourgeoisie and the press. Yet, their appearances in the capital contained an element of calculation in that it took place against an overtly political backdrop. Their visit to the House of Representatives was reported as "their first appearance in public since their union." While they would have garnered attention at any public event, this one placed a black man with his white wife among other white women in the nation's Capitol, located in a district situated between two formerly slaveholding southern states. Helen joined Frederick on the campaign trail, although no one at the time expected political wives to do so. They risked potentially violent acts of retribution and being refused service at hotels, much like the treatment Frederick had received forty years earlier. Likewise, because the Republican Party continued to pretend to be committed to black civil rights, in the face of criticism from black activists, they needed Frederick to maintain their façade. They could hardly shun him in the midst of a decisive campaign just because he had brought along his white wife. Thus, he and Helen forced the Republicans to condone interracial marriage by accepting them together at campaign events. Whether they were welcomed or rejected, they could rely on the press to cover the reactions wherever they went.

When the Republicans lost the presidency, the Douglasses placed the new Democratic president in the same position during that first reception at the White House in 1886. Not only did they accept the invitation, but they entered late, and Frederick specifically requested to meet the president. Then, they approached President Cleveland in such a manner as to cause confusion about the black woman on Frederick's arm in order to draw greater attention to his introduction of his white wife. At the same time, they embarassed those who assumed, based only on skin color, that Frederick would be married to the twenty-year-old Annie rather than the nearly fifty-year-old Helen. The *New York Freeman* understood the importance of that move, editorializing that any African American concerned with "the elevation of his race" could not fail to look on the event "without experiencing a feeling of pride; without having hopeful feelings." The paper added that "the President in his act has reported the effort to reflect on Mr. Douglass because he exercised his right to select a white lady to be his legal companion as wife."[136] By 1888, the factions among the Democrats and the Republicans challenging Cleveland used the president's apparent acceptance of the Douglasses as evidence of his favorable position on racial integration, for better or worse.[137] Indeed, Cleveland's congeniality toward them haunted him well after both Frederick and Helen had passed away as critics used his cordiality to discredit him.[138] Unlike the many black men who were tortured to death on the mere accusation of interracial liaisons, Frederick had the political clout to dare men in power to squander their moral capital by condemning his interracial marriage. When they traveled to Europe in 1886 and again when Frederick served as the American consul in Haiti, they expanded this message to the international stage.

Frederick "had long desired to make a brief tour through several countries in Europe," a sentiment shared by Helen, and the Grand Tour of the continent had been a mark of culture among Americans for nearly a century. He also planned "to meet once more the friends" in England, Scotland, and Ireland from his antislavery days, a prospect appealing to Helen, as well.[139] They departed for Liverpool in September; and while tours of Europe typically lasted approximately three months, the Douglasses did not return to America until the following summer.[140]

The first part of their jouney covered the route between Liverpool and Paris, by way of Julia Griffiths Croft's home in St. Neots. After two months in Paris with Crofts—who, Frederick was relieved to find, "speaks French like a native"— Theodore Tilton, and Theodore Stanton serving as guides, they then turned southward for Rome. Along the way they stopped in Dijon, Lyon, Avignon, Arles, Marseille, Nice, Genoa, and Pisa, and arrived at their destination on January 19, 1887, in the middle of the night. Two weeks later, Naples drew them further south, from whence they proceeded to Amalfi, Salerno, and Pestum. There, on February 11, they suddenly decided to depart from the usual American itinerary and venture across the Mediterranean to Egypt. Frederick confessed that the change of plans "will probably keep me awake to night" as he pondered seeing "the land of Joseph and his brethren, and from which Moses led the Children of Abraham out of the house of Bondage."[141]

They set out the next day aboard the Australia-bound British steamship *Ormuz* for the four-day voyage to Port Said, passing through the straits of Messina and sighting Stromboli, Mt. Etna, and Crete. Frederick pronounced Said "the queerest of queer places," but the quiet of the journey down the "weird, silent and dreamy Suez Canal" unnerved him. He pondered the "vast, profound, unbroken sameness and solitude" as the ship glided between expanses of desert, amazed at "such a deep sense of unearthly silence." A day later, they disembarked at Ismailia, then took the train to Cairo, passing a camel caravan as they sped westward through Goshen. During the next two weeks in Cairo, they both climbed to the top of the pyramid Cheops at Giza, which proved the most exhausting event of the entire tour.[142] Frederick described the process as involving "two Arabs pulling me in front and Arabs pushing me behind," as he "took my seventy years and my 230 pounds" up the 451 feet of sometimes three-feet-high blocks.[143] Helen, a mere fifty-one years and more diminutive but encumbered by a traveling dress, ascended in the same manner. She pronounced it a "dreadful climb," and Frederick declared that he was "completely played out" and "did not recover from the terrible strain in less than two weeks." Nevertheless, recalling how he felt as they stood gazing out over the desert, he later admitted, "I am very glad to have had that experience once," and Helen believed she "had never breathed such air."[144] After recovering from the escapade, they boarded a river craft for a journey down the Nile to spend four days in Alexandria. Their next destination was Athens, where they spent a week before returning to Naples on March 28.[145]

In Naples, they learned that Helen's mother, Jane Pitts, lay near death back in Honeoye. Helen dispatched a telegram to Jennie asking, "Shall I come?" Jennie's reply arrived two days later with the news that their mother would survive and that Helen was not required.[146] The Douglasses continued their travels, arriving in Rome in time for Easter.[147] After a month there, they hurried through Florence, Venice, Milan, and Lucerne, returning to Paris on the twenty-fifth and arriving in London at the end of May. Helen continued to worry about her mother and left for New York a week later, but Frederick stayed on in England for another two months, rushing about to visit old friends or their children and grandchildren. All expressed disappointment at not having met another Mrs. Douglass.[148] Torn between the melancholy desire to visit people whom he might never see again and his "want" of Helen's companionship, he finally departed from England for the last time, on August 3, 1887.[149] Helen, who missed her husband after enduring months of hostility from her sister Lorinda's family and coldness from her father, welcomed her husband at Cedar Hill eight days later.[150]

Frederick later explained that "Man is by nature a migratory animal" as far back as Adam and "Mrs. Adam," who "both seemed to have had a very strong desire for knowledge, and something of a roving disposition" and curiosity about the world.[151] The Douglasses, like so many others on the Grand Tour, had searched for the culture about which they had read and the authentic and transcendent experience that it should inspire. With either the Murray's or the Baedeker's travel guide in hand, they were, in Frederick's words, "busy, very busy I may say day and night," cramming as much sight-seeing as possible into every day, no small feat.[152] By all indications, they threw themselves into European culture and fashion. They had their picture taken in Rome. African American artist Edmonia Lewis sculpted a bust of Frederick. Helen purchased a French dress and ordered cameos brooches depicting her husband's profile.[153] Even Frederick's request to see his own book in the Paris Library, which the librarians produced to his surprise, typified the desire of Americans to make their mark upon the Old World in one way or another. Like American tourists just after the Civil War, they, too, were sensitive to militarism; but while those earlier travelers looked to their experience in Europe as a peaceful balm, the Douglasses noted with distress a pervasive arms build-up throughout their journey.[154]

They also experienced the odd mix of admiration for Europe's sophistication and disdain for the features they considered "superstitious," such as the Roman Catholic Church and Sufi whirling dervishes, or the vestiges of despotism represented by the Crown jewels housed in the Tower of London, sites of the French Revolution, or the inaccessibility of England's Parliament and the French legislature. Both included on this list the status of women in Egypt. "The most painful feature met with in the streets are the hooded and veiled women," Frederick insisted, lamenting that they were captive "to the pride and lusts of the men who *own* them as slaves are owned."[155] Helen exclaimed that a woman in Egypt was "a plaything and a beast of burden and that is all!" She was incensed that "divorced by the husband at his merest whim, she never knows when she is to be driven from her home and children. It is all dreadful!"[156]

Yet, they could hardly have seen themselves as typical. Certainly, they had particular interests from their own encounters with art and literature at home. Frederick had wanted to see Genoa because Wendell Phillips had described it so vividly in one of the first antislavery speeches that Frederick heard him give, in 1842. They both made a pilgrimage to the Château d'If, portrayed in Frederick's favorite novel, Alexandre Dumas's *Count of Monte Cristo*, Frederick helping the wizened hired boatman row them out to the island prison. Helen could hardly wait to tell her sister that she had seen the room in the Capitoline Museum that Nathaniel Hawthorne had described in *The Marble Faun*. In Venice, with Helen at his side, Frederick noted that they have visited "the house where Desdemoni resided when wooed by Othello," a place that held particular romantic attraction for the man called "the Modern Othello" and the woman framed as Desdemona upon their marriage. While Shakespeare's story ended in a tragedy of manipulation, jealousy, and murder, the Douglasses chose to focus on the early romance of the Moor and his Venetian love. A print of the same scene of courtship adorned the walls of Cedar Hill.[157]

Because they were an American black man and a American white woman traveling together, their journey carried a different meaning and included a different quest than it did for the white Americans of contemporary travel literature. Few African Americans had the means to follow in their footsteps, and those who did traveled within the network of reformers, as Frederick had on his previous two visits. This tour, designed to demonstrate and refine their status as cultured people, also provided them with the opportunity to find other African Americans engaged in the same pursuit and to search for and observe black communities that had developed in the absence of chattel slavery. They could compare the Old World and the New in regard to race in ways that other travelers could not.

In Paris they saw students from the African diaspora of the French colonies studying at the universities and met one of these students, "M. Janvier," at the home of dissident priest Père Hyacinthe. Hyacinthe assured the Douglasses that Janvier "surpassed all his fellow-students and carried off all the prizes." Later Frederick was careful to point out that Janvier's skin was "perfectly black" and "shows no traces of Caucasian blood" to deflect speculation that Janvier's refinement was a product of European ancestry, something with which Frederick himself was all too familiar. Frederick appreciated, too, finding "the bushy head and African features" of Alexandre Dumas's bust in the Théâtre Paris. As they traveled south, they observed the cultural and genectic diffusion of Europeans and North Africans that complicated racial dichotomies. Frederick told his later audiences that they could see "an increase of black hair, black eyes, full lips and dark complexions," as well as the styles of clothing and jewelry and "the habit of carrying the burdens on the head." The latter, he explained, was supposed to be "a mark of the inferiority peculiar to the negro," but seeing the practice in southern Europe and "copied by some of the best types of the Caucasian" either proved otherwise or served "as proof of a common brotherhood" and that "the wisdom of African and the social dispositions of Africa" could be copied without degradation. Their discussions of these observations had resulted in the decision to go to Egypt, an uncommon detour for Americans, where Frederick hoped to determine whether "the people who built the Pyramids were of the white race" or if "they were veritable negroes." Although he saw evidences of sub-Saharan African people, he came to the conclusion that the ancient Egyptians "were neither Caucasian nor negro, neither black nor white."[158]

Rome, however, proved to be the center of African American expatriatism. There, the Douglasses stayed at the hotel Palazza Moroni, run by Maricha Remond and Caroline Remond Putnam, sisters of Frederick's earliest black abolitionist companion, Charles Lenox Remond. The two had followed their father into the hairdressing business back in their hometown of Salem, making their fortune with their Ladies Hair Work Salon, a wig factory, and from the sales of a hair-loss tonic. A third sister, Sarah, was visiting from Florence. Frederick had last seen Sarah in England in 1860, when they were both denied passports to France under the *Dred Scott* decision. Sarah, now a doctor and married to a Sardinian, was not ostracized for either her race or for marrying outside of her race, and she was among the most highly educated women of her time. Caroline's son Edmund Quincy Putnam, whom the Douglasses also met, was married to a white English woman and experienced no criticism either.[159]

In this circle they found Edmonia Lewis, a sculptor of African American and Chippewa ancestry. She had lived in Italy since 1865, so long, Frederick noted, that "constantly speaking Italian has some what impared her English."[160] Like Frederick, Lewis struggled with many of the same themes about the place of African Americans in Western culture as she attempted to apply classic sculptural techniques to black and Native American subjects. She had also encountered among Boston abolitionists the same patronization and amazement at African American talent that Frederick had. Helen and Lewis, who were near in age, got along famously.[161] Lewis loaned Helen books, and the two spent long days perusing the Vatican sculpture gallery and Capitoline Museum. "We go together as you and I do," Helen wrote to her sister Jennie of her outings with Lewis, "looking slowly at what we want to see, and passing by what we do not want to see—and generally wanting to see the same things."[162]

Meanwhile, every notice of their movements that appeared in American papers served as a reminder to white Americans and an inspiration to African Americans that a black man could not only become successful and cultured enough to travel Europe, but that racial segregation and violence was also not an immutable fact of human existence. Early in the Douglasses' tour, the *San Francisco Daily Evening Bulletin* noted that "Frederick Douglass and his white wife are a great success socially in London."[163] Theodore Stanton, son of Elizabeth Cady and Henry B. Stanton and a resident of France, reported the same thing from Paris, where the Douglasses had received "much attention from Americans and Frenchmen," all good.[164] The *Kansas City Times* informed readers that Frederick and "his white wife" had "made an eleven months' tour of Europe and Egypt without the slightest unfavorable comment or unfriendly treatment," adding that "At home he knew very well that he would be treated socially no better than one of his own servants."[165] Henry O. Wagoner, probably with permission, had published a letter in which Frederick specifically stated, "I am accompanied by

Mrs. Douglass" and that "we passed along with out resistance, aversion or insult." He added, "the absence of colorphobia is as notable as its presence in the land of the free."[166] In his speeches on his trip and in sections in the 1892 edition of *Life and Times*, he used the pronoun "we" to include Helen in the telling without violating decorum. Implied in all of these comments and occasionally explicitly stated was that Frederick had been welcomed regardless of his race or that of his wife, and reports mentioning Helen's race only underscored their criticism of American racism.

Europe, however, was a continent where configurations of race did not fall into the black and white dichotomy that had emerged from justifications of slavery in the United States. Haiti, with its own history intimately tied to slavery, provided a different context for the Douglass marriage when Helen accompanied Frederick there two years after their return from Europe when he received an appointment as Minister Resident and Consul General to Haiti, only the second to serve in that black republic. Unlike the sojourn across the Atlantic, it was an official trip in service of the United States' imperial interests rather than the couple's self-conscious attempt to expand their knowledge of the world and themselves as cultured people. Whether Douglass expected to go alone or not, Helen insisted on accompanying him and remaining at his side, despite suffering a bout of rheumatic fever. She likely proved an asset because, as he noted, she could take dictation when his hand tired of writing and she had a better command of French, a language he had despaired learning.[167] "She says 'she *fights with*' Frederick," he told Rosetta, "and will stay here as long as I stay—That is the true woman of her."[168] Helen had good reason to believe they were engaged in a struggle together in Haiti. The racist underpinnings of American imperialism, the limited negotiating power granted to Douglass, the restrictions on his use of the press to defend himself, his isolation from advisers, his lack of French, the jealousies among the black elite in the United States over his obtaining the position, the island's climate, and his own frustration at the Haitians' different lifestyle and habits plagued Frederick incessantly. In criticizing him, some could not refrain from implicating his wife.

One friend with a low opinion of any job in Haiti believed that Frederick had received it because of many "who would like to have Mrs. Douglass punished for her treachery to the Anglo-Saxon race and both of you buried among the 'niggers' of the Island."[169] Another friend, Jane Marsh Parker, who had accompanied them to Haiti, started a rumor that the Douglasses had gone to the black republic "because we were ignored by the white and colored people of the United States."[170] She likely intended to emulate Frederick and Helen by contrasting foreign and American racial attitudes, wanting to generate sympathy among the Haitians, but her words did not please Frederick because they potentially gave ammunition to the stories that his appointment was a calculated offense to the Haitians. "A Miscegenation Administration" ran one American headline above an article that predicted that Frederick's term would be short. Frederick, the author estimated, had "an objectionable social reputation" because of his marriage to a white wife. Sending a black man with a bad reputation and a white wife to a black nation was, the author argued, "a bad piece of diplomacy."[171] A few months later, "a commercial traveler" returning from Haiti reported that Frederick was "badly handicapped by his wife." He insisted that "the leaders of society there, the ladies and gentlemen of pure black blood, won't look at her." In particular "the black ladies are especially antagonistic and manifest their displeasure at her presence," snubbing Helen into seclusion, "which she is compelled to submit to because she is white." These same "leaders of society," according to the traveler, "have a slight opinion of Douglass for having married outside of his color" and, as a consequence, "this diminishes his influence."[172]

Frederick himself noted that "there is much of race prejudice here" in the black republic. He observed that "the blacks hate the mulattos and the Mulattos look down upon the blacks," yet "many of the whites have colored wives and black men have white wives," and "in the face of all mixture fools indulge in prejudice and turn up their noses."[173] Still, he did not mention any insults directed specifically at himself or Helen, nor did Helen note any expressions of discrimination. Black Congressman John Mercer Langston also denied that the Douglasses faced any ostracism because of their marriage. "Not a few of the most noted people of the Island are blacks who have white wives, and this was the case of the late President Salomon," he insisted, when asked about the matter, instead pointing to American designs on Haiti as the possible reason "that the Haytians fear Douglass."[174]

Once again, the Douglasses used their position to challenge antimiscegenation sentiments. Haitian president Florvil Hippolyte could not refuse to receive Douglass for so minor an objection as Helen's color and therefore was forced to accept them as a married couple. At the same time, the Republican administration needed the moral capital Douglass brought to his position as their black representative to a black nation. The Douglasses were probably more concerned about the ways that American audiences perceived Frederick's appointment to an international position with Helen at his side, and the author of "Miscegenation Administration" deduced that many in the United States understood his appointment as presidential "approval of intermarriage between blacks and whites."[175] American newspapers found better fodder in rumors that the black republic rejected Frederick because he was black. Knowing the low esteem in which Americans held black men, ran the reports, the Haitians took his appointment as an insult.[176] "It is not so," Frederick insisted, "and the whole free history of Haiti proves it not to be so."[177]

By the time these stories were published in the paper, in December 1890, however, Frederick had begun to sense the futility of his mission in Haiti and his impotence in the face of America's imperialist designs. He and Helen had returned to the United States for a vacation in late 1890. In the new year, they resumed their position, and Frederick learned that he was to help US Admiral Bancroft Gherardi persuade the Haitian government to agree to the establishment of an American naval base in Môle-St. Nicolas. Both Frederick and the Haitians believed that the base would serve to intimidate the Haitians into subservience. Gherardi ultimately usurped Frederick, and negotiations with President Hyppolite deteriorated; Frederick received much of the blame and the terms of his appointment forbid him to defend himself in the press.[178] Meanwhile, Helen suffered a near-fatal attack of rheumatic fever in the spring, and news of illness and death filled the letters she received from home. When Frederick's three-month leave of absence back in the United States became permanent, they could pretend that his public life had ended.[179]

Now fifty-four, Helen had made a long journey from her origins in rural Western New York. For much of her life, she had seemed to be searching for a way not merely to support an ideal but to live it, and that ideal included racial justice and individual self-determination. The church of her childhood, in which her father and uncles were leaders, had steeped her in an ethos of defiance of institutional authority in service to a higher moral authority. Yet, the abolitionism of her youth had essentially been theoretical, since she had little contact with actual slaves or African Americans. The educational opportunities that she pursued drew her toward missionary work as a means of using her privilege to help those she considered less fortunate. She alone among her sisters followed her conviction into war in order to bring education to former slaves, the significance of which was not lost on the man who had purloined his own literacy and faced punishment for spreading it to his fellow slaves. While paternalism born of class and race prejudices had tinged her sympathy for African Americans, her sentiments allowed her to break through the ingrained racism that would have made romantic love for a black man taboo and exclude him as a prospective life partner.

Neither Helen nor Frederick were libertines, nor was their union one of necessity, which made their marriage all the more challenging to critics. For Frederick, this marriage, like his first, emerged from the desire to choose his companion and to have that choice legally and socially recognized. In doing so, he had defied slavery with his marriage to Anna and the prohibitions against interracial marriage with his wedding to Helen. Yet, this expression of lived activism worked mainly because Helen and, especially, Frederick had the privileges of class, position, and fame. Their acceptance on tours in the cradle of Western civilization, in Egypt, and in a black nation came as the result of those privileges, and those privileges kept them safe in spite of their critics. As the outcry following their wedding indicated, the Douglasses' message was dangerous. White fear of miscegenation came from a desire for white purity on which rested concepts of racial superiority, while African Americans saw in this type of integration internalized racism that devalued their experience. As the last decade of the nineteenth century and last years of Frederick's life saw the potential for racial justice crushed, a new generation of Douglass women and activists navigated these tensions between integration and racial pride.

10

Legacies, 1891–1895

Mortality had followed the Douglasses to Haiti, and it continued to haunt them at home as funeral notices piled up from both the Douglass and Pitts families and friends. Confessions such as "I am now an old man,"[1] "I am no longer strong,"[2] "I am getting a little stiffened by time,"[3] and "My dear old eyes refuse to see what and how I am doing"[4] peppered Frederick's correspondence, as he concluded that "I have already lived beyond the allotted space."[5] Back at Cedar Hill, Frederick revised and expanded his third memoir, *Life and Times*, and Helen typed the drafts, but the gains in the struggle told in its pages eroded each year. No black civil rights movement on the scale of abolition had yet risen in opposition. The old antislavery leaders passed away one by one, leaving Frederick with the feeling that "the great men of our country are rapidly sinking down below the horizon"[6] and wondering if "my turn may come next."[7] Meanwhile a new generation of black activists, struggling to overcome class and regional differences, debated new strategies and tactics, including the wisdom of interracial alliances. Frederick still occupied the position of Old Man Eloquent and the Sage of Anacostia, but he had reached a time of life in which men wonder if their life's work will carry forward through their family, their successors, and their writing. For all of his life, women had cared for Frederick, fed him, taught him, and ensured his survival in many ways. To the end and after, they would do the same, shaping the importance and meaning of his work, and ensuring his legacy.

Many of Douglass's old comrades, both friends and foes, passed away, leaving little record of his role in the movement. Gerrit Smith had died in 1874, followed five years later by William Lloyd Garrison. Garrison's sons had collected their father's papers and published his autobiography in several volumes between 1885 and 1889. By 1890, all of the Weston sisters, including Maria Weston Chapman, had passed on. They, too, had collected and edited the correspondence and papers relating to the American Antislavery Society, with a view to preserving its history, and they retained much of Chapman's assessment of Douglass as a traitor.[8] Susan F. Porter and Samuel D. Porter, Frederick's old allies in Rochester, had died in 1881, by which time most of their circle had also gone.[9] Abby Kelley Foster, the woman who had so impressed Douglass on his first speaking tours, despite her suspicion of him, and who later found herself on his side during the debates over the Fifteenth Amendment, had passed away in 1887. A letter from Isabel Jennings in 1888 informed him that much of her family no longer walked among the living and that he "would scarcely see on old friend" from those early days in Cork.[10] Early February 1889 brought news of the death of Frederick's dear old friend Amy Post.[11] Julia Griffiths Crofts lived, but her eyesight failed. With no heirs of her own, she had no one to preserve the records of her collaboration with Douglass.

Ottilie Assing, too, had gone. On August 22, 1884, her lifeless body was discovered, without identification, in the Bois de Boulogne in Paris. Sometime around her arrival in the city earlier that month, Assing had learned that she had breast cancer. The only treatment for the condition was the removal of her breast and, in rare cases, the extraction of the lymph nodes. Yet, even with radical surgery, patients like Assing faced a long, lingering, and painful death, and she had no family or friends close enough to nurse her. Although two years earlier she had counseled a "slightly depressive young woman" against suicide, Assing had confided to Douglass that "if at any time she found that she was inflicted by an incurable disease she would terminate her life." Faced with that very prospect, she poisoned herself with cyanide in a place where she could be sure that she would be found, but not until she was already dead. The police took her body to the city morgue, where her remains were put on display with other unknown victims of the night in the hopes that someone could identify and claim her corpse. Parisians, with a Victorian sense of the macabre, regularly visited the morgue for a lark, and among them was an old acquaintance of Assing, Rinaldo Kuntzel. Two weeks after her death, and just as the medical school was about to claim her body, Kuntzel passed through the viewing room with friends and recognized the cadaver on display. He arranged for Assing's burial in "the cemetery de la morgue á Ivry" and notified her friends and attorney of her passing. She had remembered her closest friends in her will, including Douglass. Although he had assumed that Assing had little money, she left $13,000 in trust for Douglass's lifetime, as well as her photo albums and other small items. A harsh critic and thorn in the side of his family, she was his friend, nonetheless, and one whom he valued. When he heard the news of her suicide, he confessed to Martha Greene that "I have been made inexpressibly sad" because "in her death I have lost a precious friend." Only a few lines later he repeated, "You will easily believe that this is a distressing stroke to me for I ever held her as one of my most precious friends." All of her papers, including those that Douglass had sent to her, were consigned to the flames according to her wishes.[12]

The death of two other friends at the same time, as well as the many funerals for family and friends that he had attended in the preceding years, compounded the grief Douglass felt over Assing. Indeed, the survival of future generations of

Douglasses appeared to be in danger, particularly if men were supposed to be the progenitors of families. By the time he had married Helen in 1884, Frederick had already buried his daughter Annie, in 1860; his older sister Eliza Mitchell, sometime in the 1870s; his brother Perry, in 1880; and five grandchildren since 1872, not to mention Anna in 1883. After their marriage, Frederick and Helen attended a funeral in one or both of their families at least once every year until 1895.[13] They began with that of Kitty Barret, Frederick's younger sister, who died in Washington on February 29, 1884, leaving him the last known survivor among Harriet Bailey's children.[14] By 1891, Frederick confessed, "It seems I can never return to Washington but to find some chair vacant and some dear face gone."[15] He found himself "almost afraid to open a letter from home lest I should find sickness death or disaster staring me in the face"[16] Still, the death notices arrived.

The families of Frederick Jr. and Charles suffered particularly. Charles had lost his year-old daughter Annie in 1872, and his first wife Mary in 1878. Frederick Jr. had lost three children, all in infancy, by 1877. In 1886, his oldest son, Frederick Aaron, died at age sixteen. Twenty-year-old Charles Frederick, Charles's son and a budding photographer, succumbed to typhoid fever on November 3, 1887, followed the next day by his sister, fourteen-year-old Julia Ada, and a week later by their cousin, four-year-old Gertrude, daughter of Frederick Jr. While the Douglasses were in Haiti in 1889, Frederick Jr.'s wife, Virginia, died of a hemorrhage, devastating her husband. "I believe they truly loved each other," the elder Frederick observed, "and where love is there is happiness within however the wind may blow without."[17] By then, of Frederick Jr.'s seven children, only two sons survived.[18] The death of fifteen-year-old Mattie in 1890 left Charles with only two children, as well, but Joseph Henry and Haley George both survived their father. When Frederick Jr. died in 1892,[19] Fredericka Douglass Sprague, Rosetta's daughter, remained the only namesake of Frederick Sr. to survive into the next century.[20]

With the exception of little Alice's death at age six in 1875, Rosetta's family proved more robust. "La grippe" (influenza) had incapacitated the whole household in 1890, but everyone had recovered.[21] Then, in 1891, while Frederick and Helen were still in Haiti, tragedy struck. Both Rosetta's twenty-five-year-old daughter, Hattie, and thirty-eight-year-old sister-in-law, Louisa, became mortally ill. Frederick first heard of Hattie's sickness in February, and his concern for her disturbed his sleep. "I dreamed of her two nights ago," he worried to Rosetta, "I saw her pail and weak as she describes herself."[22] Then, he received news of Louisa's poor condition. "I am trying to hope for the best for both, but cannot but have serious fears," he wrote to Rosetta of her two patients, lamenting that "Hattie was never strong and the trouble with which Lou suffers has an old foundation of which I heard years ago."[23] Worry about the three women made him "anxious," and "gloomy," and he admitted to Rosetta that "my own health is poor and my spirit depressed." Hattie's recovery came as a relief.[24]

The ordeal worsened with the near fatal illness of Helen in January 1891, hardly a month after they had returned to Haiti from their vacation in the United States. "She is usually so well that it is all the more serious when she is taken down," fretted her husband, alert to the dangers of a climate in which "people are here to day and are gone tomorrow." The doctor diagnosed "articulate rheumatism" (rheumatic fever), a general inflammation that would have caused her body to twitch and her joints to swell, damaging her nervous system and heart.[25] As weeks passed and Frederick also received word of the conditions of Hattie and Louisa, he worried that "My dear Helen is still confined to her bed with Rheumatic fever, and she does not seem to mend" despite being "on the Doctor's hands" and "well cared for by friends who are willing and glad to nurse her for both my sake and hers." Yet, Helen suffered so greatly that he confessed, "at one point I feared the worst for her."[26] By April, she had finally recovered.

Louisa, with cancer, would not get better. Her impending death distressed Frederick. "She lived with me a long time and was devoted to my welfare," he reminisced to Lewis. "I cared much for her." He had forgiven her for her suit against him because "I know how it all came about and do not now feel any resentment." He very much hoped to see her again, "alive if I cannot see her well and strong." Barring that, he all but begged for a letter from the still young woman, declaring to Rosetta that "my heart aches to hear from Aunt Louisa." He confessed that "I have thought about her and dreamed about her very much since I learned she was ailing," and that "I wish I could be near her and give her such comfort as I know she would gladly give me if I were on a bed of sickness and within her reach." When the cancer took her at the end of March, he mourned to Rosetta that "she held a place in my heart only second to yourself and the grandchildren" and that he had lost "my precious friend." As Louisa had requested, the Spragues buried her with her niece Alice in the family lot in Rochester's Mount Hope Cemetery.[27]

Rosetta's daughters, however, thrived. Annie, Harriet, Estelle, Fredericka, and Rosabelle, along with their brother Herbert, lived into adulthood. The five sisters relieved one another from the type of domestic stress that Rosetta had felt as the oldest and ultimately only girl, and they also had more examples to follow in the black women whom they encountered through their grandfather. From childhood, Sprague daughters had constantly visited or lived in Frederick's home. Harriet had stayed there in 1873, then Estelle in 1875. The next year, Rosetta moved her entire family to the Douglass house while Nathan was in jail.[28] Later, Annie and Harriet stayed with the Douglasses often enough at Cedar Hill to be counted as part of both their parents' and their grandparents' households in the 1880 census, and Annie remained in the house after her grandmother's death in 1882 and returned in 1893 after a fight with her father.[29] Estelle also spent two summers there around that time, and Fredericka, too, took up residence in 1894.[30] These extended visits had provided relief for both households, where a child might be a burden in one but a boon in the other, especially if either Anna or Louisa felt poorly. As their grandfather noted about Estelle's first stay, a little girl might find it "pleasant to be the only child about the house" after living in one that had a toddler, a baby, and two much older sisters.[31] An older child might escape conflict with her parents.

Living with their grandfather brought the young Sprague women into contact with the elite of Washington reform and social circles. Estelle, for instance, lived with her grandparents at a time when the household included newly elected Senator Blanche K. Bruce and Fannie and Ella D. Barrier. While living there, Bruce began courting Josephine Wilson, who became a leader in Washington's black social circles.[32] Both Barriers had graduated from the Brockport Normal and Training School in New York, and Ella taught black children in Washington's schools. She and Fannie were at the beginning of long activist careers with a strong focus on education.[33] Estelle's younger sister, Fredericka, remembered her awe that Estelle "knew *everything*" after living in this *milieu*. She credited the Barriers' influence with providing the "various forms of guidance and instructions" that helped her older sister develop "into a very wide awake, independent and wise young miss."[34] All of the sisters attended gatherings at Cedar Hill that included professors, ministers, and other leaders and their wives, and Annie was living there when Ida B. Wells visited in the 1890s.

They had similar examples in their own extended family, too. Their aunt Amelia, Lewis's wife, was the daughter of the self-emancipated and self-educated Reverend Jermain Loguen and the well-educated and well-off Caroline Storum, who made their home the center of abolitionism in Syracuse.[35] She had also taught for some years before her marriage, and Estelle had stayed with Amelia and Lewis in Syracuse when creditors harassed Rosetta during Nathan's imprisonment, in 1876.[36] That year, Amelia's sister Sarah, also known as "Aunt Tinnie," became the first black woman to receive a medical degree from Syracuse University. She later practiced in Santo Domingo, continuing after her marriage and the birth of her daughter.[37] Frederick Jr.'s wife, Virginia Hewlett, was the daughter of the only black instructor at Harvard, Aaron Molineaux Hewlett, and the sister of attorney E. M. Hewlett and Shakespearean actor Paul Molyneaux Hewlett. Also well-educated and a teacher, she continued her involvement in the Washington education system as her own family grew to seven children. Mary Elizabeth Murphy, Charles's first wife, did the same. His second wife, Laura Antoinette Haley, was of the same mettle, although they limited their childbearing to one son.

At their grandparents' house, too, Rosetta's daughters could observe their grandmother. Anna ran a busy but financially secure household, and the little girls understood that the home was her domain. At the same time, she brought them to at least one camp meeting and taught them about generosity and charity.[38] Fredericka remembered that the indigent former slaves in Washington who begged door-to-door with baskets "seldom left [her grandparents'] door as empty as when they were presented." When Anna had nothing to spare for a poor woman one day, Estelle offered up her own slice of jellied bread. "Grandma stooped and kissed her," Fredericka remembered, and rewarded Estelle for her kindness. Such encounters, too, led Fredericka to realize "the narrow margin in years that existed between the fate of these exslave women and me."[39] Louisa, who was Anna's companion at that time, however, became a cautionary tale of the precarious position a young woman might hold even in her own family if she had not the background that might offer an opportunity to propel herself out of domestic service.

Then, of course, they had their own mother. Neither Rosetta nor her daughters attached any stigma to doing work outside the home, although Anna and Frederick had hoped that their daughter might have a future similar to those of her contemporaries, the Barriers, Sarah Remond, Charlotte Forten Grimké, or the Loguens, as a teacher, reformer, or pioneering professional. Rosetta had grown up with the expectation that the educational advantages she had received would enable her to contribute to her own household, either as daughter or wife, as much as to improving the conditions of less fortunate African Americans. Most of her effort, however, went into the former. Her daughters watched her take in sewing, run a grocery store, and, finally, settle into a copyist position in the Recorder of Deeds office from 1881 to 1886, providing the most consistent financial support for their family as she raised six children.[40] As one family friend worried in 1885, "What will become of them when Rose leaves her present position[?]"[41] Only in the 1890s, when the baby Rosabelle was entering her teen years, could Rosetta turn her attention to other activities. She joined a reading club that met at the Grimkés' home, served as secretary of the Women's Union Christian Association when it was setting up a "home for friendless colored girls" near her home in the Meriden Hill section of Washington, and wrote the editorial, "Colored Women, Arouse," for the *Washington Post* in 1891.[42]

For the Douglasses, Rosetta's employment outside the home was not a failure of her femininity or as a woman, but the failure of Nathan in his masculine role as head of the family. After being released from prison in New York, Nathan joined the family in Washington, where he went through a succession of jobs between 1877 and 1886. He moved from the feed business to droving to delivering milk, at one point seeking work outside the city.[43] Meanwhile, he relied on Frederick's support, even as he antagonized the Douglass family. Not only did Nathan help his sister file her suit against his father-in-law, but he demanded the return of furniture that he had sold to Douglass some years earlier. He also caused enough people to suspect him of unscrupulous business dealing that they appealed to Frederick to intervene, and he threatened to blackmail Frederick with unspecified allegations involving his family life.[44] By the 1880s, Nathan had earned a reputation as "shiftless" and a "poor miserable good-for-nothing" among the Douglasses' friends and associates.[45] Only after he entered the real estate business in 1886 did he appear to find solvency. "I hope in truth he is as successful as he thinks he is," prayed old Douglass friend Elizabeth Pierson after Nathan paid her a visit.[46] In this endeavor, he did prove successful enough to earn the short-lived respect of both his brother-in-law and father-in-law, Fredericks Jr. and Sr. The younger Frederick, now an editor of the Washington *Leader*, echoed the *Washington Bee* in singing Nathan's praises as "one of the most enterprising real estate men that we have" by adding that "it will pay to consult Mr. Sprague before buying or selling property."[47]

Nathan also experienced a brief period of admiration from the elder Douglass when, in February 1891, he purchased an interest in *The Pilot*.[48] Knowing from experience that "the money part of the enterprise is the one that is to ensure success," Frederick expressed trepidation about his son-in-law's foray into journalism. Nevertheless, he praised the younger man's "industry mutual activity & pluck" and complimented the first two issues that were published under Nathan's management as making "a fine appearance."[49] "I do not see why the Pilot with your business talents and the literary ability of Mr [Charles] Morris [the editor] should not succeed," he predicted, and the old newspaperman in him could not help but offer a list of advice to ensuring that end. "Make friends wherever you can," he urged, much like a character in his beloved Shakespeare, "Never make an enemy if you can possibly help it," and "Praise every good deed whether done by friend or enemy." Of course he had to admit, "I have not always been able to follow my own advice—but I am now old enough and wise enough to wish I had."[50]

With limited access to English-language newspapers in Haiti, Frederick did not hear about the shadier aspects of his son-in-law's purchase of the paper or his questionable journalistic practices.[51] The criticism grew worse after Nathan fired his editor, Charles Morris, an experienced writer, friend of Ida B. Wells, and fiancé of the oldest Sprague daughter.[52] Following Morris's departure, one paper charged, *The Pilot* had "been gradually lowering its moral and intellectual standard until it has reached a point beyond the limit of decent journalism."[53] Some in Washington press circles suspected that Charles Douglass, now working in the pension office, had replaced Morris as editor, and that he and Nathan were using *The Pilot* to defend Frederick against attacks about his performance in Haiti.[54] Rather than flatter Frederick, however, Nathan only embarrassed him. The former newspaperman had counseled the neophyte to "say as little about me in it [*The Pilot*] as possible" because "it would not do for it to get the reputation of being a Douglass paper."[55] Now, the competition asked, "Wonder what Hon. 'Fed' Douglass thinks of son-in-law Sprague, editor of the Pilot?"[56] and suspected that the elder statesman might "well exclaim 'save me from my friends!'" due to "the unhealthy zeal displayed by the editor of *The Pilot*, whoever he is, son or son-in-law, in rushing to his defense at every imaginary rejection," with results "more painful than ludicrous to his thousands of real friends."[57] By 1892, Nathan's editorial attacks led W. Calvin Chase, editor of the *Washington Bee*, to charge him with libel.[58] The paper had folded by 1894. Although his real estate business continued, Nathan was charged with various offenses, including plagiarism,[59] assault,[60] embezzlement,[61] and three instances of fraud.[62] Whatever good will he had earned with his wife's family, he lost.

Like their mother, the Sprague daughters would have seen their father's problems from a different perspective than that of their grandfather or uncles. For instance, when Frederick first brought home Helen as his wife, Annie was living at Cedar Hill and refused to accept the new Mrs. Douglass as mistress. Her sister, Estelle, later had to answer to her grandfather for rumors that she had spoken badly of Helen. Estelle denied the charges, which may have been mere gossip, but that her grandfather granted them enough credence to approach her suggested that he sensed some tension. If they did not accept Helen, they did adore their Aunt Louisa, who had been a part of their family all of their lives. Thus, when their father urged their Aunt Louisa to file a suit for back wages, the Sprague daughters may have had more sympathy for the woman who had helped to raise them, who had fewer advantages than they had, and who illustrated one of their possible futures. Their father, in their eyes, would have played the role of protective brother. Likewise, when the Spragues nursed Virginia Douglass, Frederick Jr.'s wife, during her dying days and took in both their young nephews, the daughters saw their father overcoming long-held animosity toward their uncle, possibly believing, as Nathan did, that he had "not allowed personal feeling to interfere where I could do any good to them."[63] In *The Pilot* venture, he had followed in their grandfather's footsteps, contributing to the discussions about race and defending Frederick at a time when the older man could not speak out in the press. Like their grandfather, their father used the paper as a means of training their less-than-scholarly brother in a trade.[64] The criticism leveled at Nathan harped on his criminal history and his lack of education, which the Spragues may have interpreted as class bias, coming as it did from middle-class African Americans and directed at a former slave.

From the perspective of the Sprague household, Nathan was not the opportunistic and ungrateful son-in-law of Frederick and his sons' accounts, but a man born with few advantages who struggled to find work and, in his words, to "do my duty to my family" both immediate and extended.[65] His daughters could see that their uncles and mother experienced similar difficulties. Lewis and Frederick Jr. had faced racial exclusion in the Washington printers' union, struggled to survive in the competitive market of black newspapers, and found government jobs primarily through the connections of the Grand Army of the Republic and their father. Their mother, uncles, and eventually Annie all got jobs in the Recorder of Deeds office through their grandfather's patronage, and all were removed from their jobs by his successor while Frederick was touring Europe with Helen. For all their advantages and connections, employment was still precarious for middle-class African Americans. Frederick could use his influence to find positions for his friends and family, but he could only do so successfully if those receiving the patronage had the skills to do the job. The Sprague daughters could see that the decisive factor separating their uncles and mother from their father and Aunt Louisa was education.

To become educated not only ensured their own future security, but also justified the struggles of their mother and grandfather to provide them with access to schools and served as a political act in defiance of assumptions about black intellectual inferiority and continuing efforts to suppress black education. Thus, both Rosetta and Frederick emphasized the education of her children, keeping one another updated on the progress of the younger generation. Frederick praised nine-year-old Harriet for her "admirable good sense" and reported to Rosetta that the little girl "reads well and remembers well and has some marks of being a scholar."[66] Harriet's brother, Herbert, proved less pleasing when, at the age of fifteen, he showed little aptitude for school. "Not everybody can be a scholar, and not every scholar is a success in life," Frederick counseled Rosetta after a dismal report. "Have patience with him."[67] Rosabelle, on the other hand, "much pleased" her grandfather with her success, as did Fredericka. By age fourteen, Fredericka was keeping her grandfather posted on her scholastic progress.[68] As the young woman looked toward a career in education, Rosetta let her father know that his namesake "has been kept busy with her books preparing for her examination" to the neglect of her violin.[69] Frederick, a violinist himself, replied that "I am sorry to know that she does not practice."[70] Nevertheless, he understood the necessity of focusing on her lessons, telling Fredericka, "A colored young lady will have enough to contend with, in the battle of life without having her hands tied as mine have been by a want of education."[71] Beyond their own security, however, pursuing education, either as student or as teacher, was a defiant political act. "The South as little wants the Negro educated as it wants them to vote," their grandfather observed as Mississippi proposed the first literacy laws, "and it would see in every effort to educate the negro an effort to give them supremacy."[72]

The advantages that the Sprague daughters acquired as well as the examples of domesticity and domestic work, professional life, marriage, the necessities of providing for a family and having a husband who could do so, and emphasis placed on education, both as students and as teachers, all shaped their choices in their own lives. Annie, the oldest, made her way first, joining her mother in the Recorder of Deeds office as a copyist. Her tenure began after her twentieth birthday, at the end of 1884, a year that began with her departure from

Cedar Hill and Helen's departure from the office, and coincided with a lull in her father's employment.[73] Whatever disagreement she and her grandfather had over his new wife paled in comparison to the responsibility that Frederick felt to help his granddaughter earn a living.[74] She may have been the single "very smart and industrious clerk" working in her father's real estate office in 1888 or she may have been retained by the Recorder's office.[75] She also appeared in society, joining her grandfather at White House receptions, appearing among the list of guests at parties of the black Washingtonian elite, sometimes playing the piano and organizing a fundraising gathering for a rising violinist at one point.[76]

Around the late 1880s, a young journalist entered her grandfather's circles. Charles Morris had "the walk of a peacock," a singing voice good enough for concerts, and a speaking style that placed him among "the first class Afro-American orator[s]" of his generation.[77] He was quick enough to spar with Ida B. Wells, who entertained him as a long-distance suitor in the mid-1880s. Wells, however, not only had other prospects, but realized that marriage would interfere with her career as a journalist. Their romance had become friendship and collaboration by the time rumors emerged in 1888 about his connection to the oldest granddaughter of Frederick Douglass. When their engagement continued into 1891, the old man became perturbed. "If Morris and Annie are going to make a match, I hope they will not delay the matter," he wrote to Rosetta. "These long delays bring trouble." He admitted that it was "none of my business I know." Nevertheless, he registered his concern because "I have known young men to keep company with a lady and then keep all others at a distance and when the lady was no longer young leave her."[78] When Rosetta questioned his concern, he reiterated his point. Morris "should declare his purposes of keeping company with her or leave her course in clear in the world," he insisted, adding, "Nathan should tell him so." Annie, at twenty-seven years old, was "no longer a child to be trifled with." Reminding Rosetta that "the life of a young woman is a solemn concern" and that "if after keeping her company two or three years she is not married but all at once dropt— people draw conclusions unfavorable to her." He urged his daughter and Nathan to intervene. Both being fathers of daughters, he insisted that Nathan, for once, "will see the matter in the same light as I see it in."[79]

The extended romance probably had more to do with Morris's employment prospects than his "trifling" nature. While better situated than Annie's father had been at a similar point in life, Morris had ambitions as a journalist and politician that did not bode well for a secure future. An 1899 rumor held that Douglass was campaigning for Morris to be appointed minister to Liberia. Another, in 1890, reported that Morris had plans to study law at Harvard.[80] Instead, in March 1891, he went to work for Annie's father as editor of *The Pilot*, where the two men clashed almost immediately. Morris charged "one of my truest friends" and prospective father-in-law with "having disposed of all my savings of the last

three years," "having taken my interest in the Pilot which according to a written contract is exactly equal to his," "having broken open my private mail," and
"assaulting me like a ruffian on the street and threatening my life," as well as slan-
dering him in the pages of the paper and forcing him out of the partnership.[81]

Annie, like her mother, found herself caught between a father and the man
she loved. Echoing his insistence to Rosetta decades earlier when he had counseled, "Husbands first and fathers second,"[82] Frederick believed that "if she
[Annie] cares for him [Morris] she will side with him against every body else
in the world."[83] Annie did, but the animosity was between herself, Rosetta, and
Morris on one side and her Nathan on the other.[84] Frederick sided with the
women of his family, and he and Helen gave Annie shelter at Cedar Hill. Morris,
meanwhile secured a job with the Treasury Department, considered a position
in Haiti with Douglass, then toured with a singing troupe before heading to Ann
Arbor to study law.[85] As those plans took shape, the young couple finally married
on April 6, 1893. As much as Annie hoped that her father and grandfather could
call a truce long enough to wish her well together, she worried that a scene might
erupt if they both showed up at the wedding or to see her off at the train station.
Only Frederick did, and she was grateful that "I left very quietly with nothing to
mar the peace and quiet of the occasion." Her "kindest regards to Mrs. Douglass"
indicated that she had overcome her earlier animosity toward Helen.[86]

The bride became pregnant almost immediately, just as her grandmother
had after marrying, and just as immediately the pregnancy proved difficult. In
Harpers Ferry, en route to the World's Exposition in Chicago, where her husband was working for her grandfather at the Haitian Pavilion, the situation
became dire.[87] The couple agreed Annie would stay in West Virginia until she became strong enough to rejoin Charles in either Chicago or Ann Arbor. Rosetta
visited her in July and, consulting with Annie's doctor, learned that the expectant
mother was suffering from complications that "would have to be very carefully
attended to to enable her to pass through the ordeal of child bearing safely."[88] In
November, only weeks before her twenty-ninth birthday, and despite her doctor's orders, Annie felt well enough to join her husband. Rosetta believed that
the journey caused her to go into premature labor. Neither Annie nor the baby
survived. Rosetta, having lost both her first child and first grandchild, turned to
her father for comfort. "I am utterly dazed and crushed," she mourned.[89]

Rosetta also mourned that all her children except sixteen-year-old Rosabelle
were leaving her alone in Washington, although they were all doing exactly what
had been expected of them. Annie and Charles appeared to have been planning a
life as a political couple, in which he would seek office and work for the improvement of African Americans through the law and she would manage their social life,
household, and children. Her sisters did not pursue life in society, if their absence
from those columns in the Washington newspapers is a measure. Like Annie and

Rosetta, Fredericka worked as a clerk in the Recorder of Deeds office in 1894 and 1895, but all of the young Sprague women became teachers at some point.[90]

Harriet and Estelle turned south. Hattie went first, and her grandfather pronounced her "a noble woman" with "real, not make believe talent."[91] His pride did not prevent him from being "especially anxious" for news about her progress "because she is trying the world for herself and is in some sense alone."[92] By 1891, she found her way to Jacksonville to teach at the newly opened Florida Baptist Academy, a school operated by the Baptist Home Mission.[93] Estelle shortly followed a similar route, taking a position at the Gloucester Agricultural and Industrial School in Cappahosic, Virginia, founded in 1888 by graduates of the Hampton Institute. Her grandfather's support of Estelle's work, as well as the founders' willingness to take advantage of the connection to Douglass, showed in his donations to the school, particularly after they named their second building after him. Both the Florida Baptist Academy and the Gloucester School continued the types of educational programs begun during Reconstruction by such organizations as the American Missionary Association, for which Helen Douglass had worked in the Civil War. Indeed, Hampton Institute itself was founded by the AMA, which provided funding for the Gloucester School beginning in 1891.[94] Both the Virginia and Florida schools provided educational and vocational curricula modeled on that promoted by Booker T. Washington, a Hampton alumnus who was fast joining Frederick Douglass as one of the most influential African American leaders of the time.

About 1898, Estelle married David D. Weaver, a fellow instructor and brother of one of the Gloucester School's founders. If the couple had not taken to farming, their eight children would probably have kept Estelle from the classroom until David's death, sometime between 1910 and 1916. Harriet, on the other hand, never married. By 1916, she admitted that "I would stop teaching if I could secure something else to do" because of the toll the profession had taken on her health, which her grandfather had once pronounced "never strong."[95] She searched for clerical work, but ended up at the Conroe Normal School in Texas, where she also found a position for Estelle so that she could support her family.[96] Estelle later taught at Paul Quinn College in Waco in 1920, presumably leaving her youngest children with her husband's family.[97] When Harriet died in 1940, her obituary listed her as having "devoted much of her life to teaching in Jacksonville, Fla.; Concord, Del.; Princess Ann, Md.; Conroe, Texas; and Lincoln Institute, Jefferson City, Mo." and as having served "for three years as secretary to the principal of Tuskegee Institute, Tuskegee, Ala."[98]

Fredericka also took a job in a school in Culpeper County, Virginia, in early 1893. She taught a younger set of pupils than her sisters did. Reminiscent of her mother's time in Salem, she described a poor rural district where she walked "a mile each way" to her schoolhouse, being "compelled somedays to ride 24 miles in an open wagon through snow and wind." Nevertheless, she enjoyed the work and had antic- ipated little comfort because "pa fore warned me against all high expectations."[99] Fredericka stayed in Virginia until spring 1894, when she returned to Washington to find work as a copyist in the Recorder of Deeds office, living with her grandfa- ther to help him through the illnesses of Jennie Pitts and Helen.[100] By the end of the decade, her youngest sister, Rosabelle, had taken a position in the segregated Washington schools, in the same division as Ella Barrier and where Fredericka, who was asked to resign her position in the Recorder's office in June 1897, was also sup- posed to have taught.[101]

Fredericka, Harriet, and Rosabelle remained in Washington until the deaths of their parents. Then, around 1910, Fredericka found a position in Kansas City, Missouri, where she met and married a widower, Dr. John Edward Perry, in 1912. By 1920, Harriet and Rosabelle, along with Rosabelle's husband, Dr. Thomas Jones, and son, Thomas Perry Jones, joined Fredericka in Kansas City.[102] The Perrys never had children, but Fredericka occasionally substitute taught and be- came one of the black clubwomen who provided community support and ac- tivist networks that sustained a long African American civil rights movement in an era of institutionalized Jim Crow. These included an auxiliary support- ing the Wheatley Provident Hospital, where her husband practiced, the Civic Protection Organization, which provided legal assistance to African Americans filing civil rights suits; the Missouri Association for Colored Girls; the National Association of Colored Women; and commemorative activities for John Brown, some of which she founded.[103] The Sprague daughters, then, carried forward the Douglass family legacy of education and public service.

Rosetta's daughters followed paths that their mother had hoped to take before she married their father, one supported by their grandfather. They also drew from the black clubwomen around them, including the Barriers, Anna Julia Cooper, and Mary Church Terrell, who, in turn, looked back to antebellum ladies' church auxillaries, charitable Dorcas societies, and antislavery societies. As teachers and in their association work, they embraced and cared for African Americans in a nation that would not. They followed a typical path for conscientious black women as leaders in their communities, but they were not the leaders *of* their communities, roles usually reserved for men. The Douglass sons became activ- ists in their own right, though they did not approach the level of their father, nor did the Douglass grandsons. Still, they maintained a presence in the newspapers, as Frederick Jr. was an editor of the Washington *Leader*, and through editorials. They also continued to highlight their service during the Civil War. Rosetta's son Herbert lived a respectable life as a house painter, husband, and father of a large family in New Rochelle, New York. Charles's oldest surviving son, Joseph, became a concert violinist of some note and a music teacher, while his youngest, Haley George, attended Harvard and became a teacher in Washington. They all felt the responsibility of the opportunities that Frederick and Anna's lives had afforded them, but none appeared to aspire to take Douglass's place, in the way so many other young men did, either by allying themselves with him or attacking him. Instead, his heir apparent in civil rights appeared to be a young woman imbued with every bit of the same fiery passion, intelligence, and independence as Douglass himself had exhibited at her age. In this woman, Ida B. Wells, he found not so much a daughter-activist in the civil rights movement, but a female version of his younger self. He had likely heard of her long before their first meeting, in June 1893. The former schoolteacher from Mississippi had made a name for herself as a writer for various black newspapers throughout the country and then as editor of her own paper, the *Free Press*, in Memphis, Tennessee, which was destroyed by a white mob in May 1893.

The attack had followed Wells's investigation of the intimidation and lynching of two successful leaders of the black Memphis community. That black men were still being illegally executed was not unknown to Wells, or to most African Americans, in 1892. Since emancipation, white mobs had been murdering African Americans as part of terrorism targeted at black community organizers.[104] In the 1880s, however, white propaganda had begun citing the rape of white women by black men as the cause for lynching, and the lurid sensationalism of such stories made them linger in the popular imagination until they were accepted as conventional wisdom. The victims usually came from the rural working class and were presumed to be guilty, which garnered them little sympathy from the black urban elite who led civil rights campaigns.[105] Thus, "to the better class of Afro-Americans," Wells explained, "the crime of rape is so revolting they have too often taken the white man's word and given lynch law neither the investigation nor condemnation it deserved."[106] Even Douglass, who had more than a little experience with the obscenities leveled at black men seen in the company of white women, confessed to Wells that he "had begun to believe it true that there was increasing lasciviousness on the part of the Negroes."[107] Despite the injustice of lynching, respectable race leaders did not want to expend political and moral capital on men they otherwise deemed lowlifes and criminals. Wells admitted that she, too, "accepted the idea meant to be conveyed" in the southern press: "that although lynching was irregular and contrary to law and order," the crime was so terrible that ultimately "the brute deserved death anyhow and the mob was justified in taking his life."[108]

The murder of three successful and upstanding leaders of the black community, in a place that had not experienced racial violence on such a scale in a quarter of a century, and with nary a mention of a violated white woman, "opened my [Wells's] eyes to what lynching really was."[109] She began to question the conventional wisdom, and her investigation led her to publish an editorial in the *Free Press* that aimed at the heart of the myths surrounding victims

Figure 10.1 Ida B. Wells at the time she worked with Frederick Douglass. "Ida B. Wells-Barnett," Mary Garrity, c. 1893, Albumen silver print. National Portrait Gallery, Smithsonian Institution.

of lynching. "Nobody in this section of the country believes the old thread-bare lie that Negro men rape white women," she declared. If white men kept falling back on that excuse, she insisted, they would stretch credulity to the breaking point and "a conclusion will then be reached which will be very damaging to the moral reputation of their women." The white press in Memphis, reporting as if a man had written the words, threatened to "brand" the author of the editorial "in the forehead with a hot iron and perform upon him a surgical operation with a pair of tailor shears."[110] Then a frenzied mob destroyed the offices of her paper. Fortunately, friends had warned her business partner of the riot beforehand, and he escaped unharmed in body but mentally traumatized. Wells was in New York to interview T. Thomas Fortune of the *New York Age* at the time of the attack.[111]

Douglass read Wells's account of the violence on June 25, 1893, and hurried to see her in Manhattan. She recalled that he had come "to tell me what a revelation of existing conditions this article had been to him." When she compiled her research into a longer analysis, published in October as the book *Southern Horrors*, she asked him, "if you will be so kind as to put in writing the encomiums you were pleased to lavish on my article" and she "would feel highly honored if you would send me a letter with your opinion of it, which I could use as an introduction."[112] He granted her request, telling her "there has been no word equal to it [*Southern Horrors*] in convincing power." Pointing out that "you give us what you know and testify from actual knowledge," he praised her for having "dealt with the facts with cool, painstaking fidelity, and left those naked and uncontradicted facts to speak for themselves."[113] With little existing protest or organization in opposition to lynching, he insisted she pursue her exposé and "devote" herself to building a movement.[114] The clear travesty of justice, the brutality, and the photographs of lynched bodies all recalled antislavery arguments and the role of ex-slaves like Douglass himself in the antislavery movement. As with antislavery, antilynching proponents would have to use those elements to shift the popular narrative away from alleged rape to actual murder.

Later that year, Wells spoke to what she deemed a "very poorly attended" gathering at the Metropolitan African Methodist Episcopal Church. She recalled that Douglass afterward "apologized for Washington's seeming indifference to the important message I brought" and insisted she schedule another speech for February, "when he would undertake to have a larger meeting for me."[115] In a reversal of roles from the abolitionist days, he used his connections to ensure that she would be heard and contacted the networks of black clubwomen who could guarantee a full house. Already, Wells had galvanized audiences of women, much as a younger Douglass had, and they gladly came to her aid. Women in Brooklyn had raised the funds to finance the publication of *Southern Horrors*; and, in Washington, with Douglass as their escort, they went so far as to meet with President Benjamin Harrison to personally invite him to the event. Harrison, of course, did not attend and pled forgetfulness for not writing a letter in support.[116] Douglass and the clubwomen also worked to get her an audience with the Senate Judiciary Committee in the following months, to no avail.[117] Nevertheless, Wells marveled that "they filled Metropolitan Church with one of the biggest audiences I had ever seen."[118]

Over the next two years, the relationship between Douglass and Wells might have been characterized as one of father and daughter or master and protégé. Wells certainly turned to Douglass for help, and he both granted it and offered her guidance. His endorsement, at her request, in *Southern Horrors* and the crowd

at the Metropolitan Church testified to that. He also urged her to go abroad, although the invitation contained an unintended insult to himself. When she was
staying at Cedar Hill either at the time of her lecture or later that spring, she received a letter from Catherine Impey, a British anti-imperialist activist, founder
of the Society for the Recognition of the Universal Brotherhood of Man, and
editor of the journal *Anti-Caste*. Impey had followed Wells's reports and, on behalf of her organization, she hoped Wells would consider speaking in England.
Although she understood that Wells and Douglass were working together in the
nascent antilynching campaign and that his name would draw large audiences,
she, Wells recalled, "said that they knew Mr. Douglass was too old to come." She
showed him the letter, which must have stung. Still, remembering the liberation of his own first journey to England nearly fifty years earlier, he urged her to
accept. "You are the one to go, for you have the story to tell," she remembered
him encouraging her.[119] She did, touring England from April to June 1893 and
again the next year.

Her second visit to England met with significant difficulties that resulted in
the loss of both her funding and the endorsement of her sponsors. She discovered none of this until her arrival. Isabelle Mayo, Catherine Impey's wealthier
colleague, had ostracized Impey for an overture she had made to one of Mayo's
male friends. "I will not consent to a denunciation of poor Miss Impey," Wells
declared to Douglass, so Mayo "will therefore have no part in the work" of her
tour. Impey, "practically retired," could be of no service, and the main funder of
the tour was suffering from influenza, all of which left Wells "compelled to depend on myself somewhat." She developed a new contact, the Reverend Charles
Aked, but since Wells did not have the backing of the Society for the Brotherhood
of Man, Aked recommended that she obtain letters of introduction. "You know
about my work," she pled to Douglass, "and can better commend me to these
forces than I can speak for myself."[120]

Wells's letter perplexed Douglass. He complied with her request by sending a letter to Aked, but he focused on his own opposition to lynching. "I deem
it highly important to the cause of justice and humanity," he wrote, "that the
English people should know the truth concerning the outrages committed upon
colored people in the Southern states of our Union." He assured the minister that
"if I were a few years younger, I would willingly join Miss Wells in her work." As
for the young woman herself, he noted her gratitude that Aked had taken her in
and pointed out that she had been attacked in southern papers "as an unworthy
person," but "the motive for assaults is simply to destroy the effect of her dis-
closures."[121] From Wells herself, however, he demanded explanation. Beginning
with the formal "Miss Wells," when she preferred that he call her "Ida," he
pointed out that "I had not supposed that, being invited to England, you needed
my endorsement," and did not understand why those who had invited her had

cut her off so suddenly. "If they have promised and have failed to perform what they promised they should be exposed," he insisted, but "if you have not been invited and have gone to England on your own motion and for your own purposes, you ought to have frankly told me so."[122] His suspicion was probably also aroused because he had loaned her $25, and his general philosophy on lending was "lend your money and lose your friends."[123]

"Your letter which I received this morning has hurt me cruelly," she responded. "I have never felt so like giving up as since I received your very cool and cautious letter this morning, with its tone of distrust and its inference that I have not dealt truthfully with you." In a rush, she detailed the way her sponsors had essentially abandoned her, and she remitted the cash she had borrowed. "While my heart bleeds that you should class me with that large class who have imposed upon your confidence," she concluded, "I still love you as the greatest man our race has yet produced and because of what you have suffered & endured for the race's sake."[124] His reply indicated that he forgave her now that he understood her position more clearly. "It lightens my heart wonderfully to have you say at the close of your letter that you have stood by me in every time of trial and will for all time to come," she thanked him, and begged "your forgiveness for my hasty words." Nonetheless, Aked pronounced Douglass's recommendation inadequate. "While they did not expect 'gush' (nay they pay you the same compliment I do, in knowing you to be incapable of such a thing)," she explained, "they would have been better satisfied if you had spoken more positively regarding me and my work."[125] A few days later, she gave him more detailed instructions on writing his recommendation. Once again, he complied. Meanwhile, she had visited Ellen Richardson, who had helped secure Douglass's legal freedom in 1846 and who could vouch for Wells among the remnants of her circle of Quaker reformers. Helen Bright Clark, daughter of parliamentarian John Bright, who had welcomed Douglass on previous visits, also became one of her hosts.[126]

As if he were Wells's father, Douglass was often called upon to either defend or reprimand her, which could either buoy or sink her credibility. In late 1893, while she was working for Ferdinand Barnett's Chicago-based *Conservator*, the *American Citizen* published an editorial that urged Barnett to "put a muzzle on that animal from Memphis" and threatened to "make her wish her mother had changed her mind ten months before she was born."[127] Incensed, she turned to Douglass, "It is very hard to have to stand such insults from white and black men too." She begged him to "come to my relief and teach him a lesson he will not forget," pointing out that "this is the first request of the kind I ever made any one and I feel you will not fail me in this my hour of need."[128] Usually, however, she could take care of herself, and others turned to Douglass to "muzzle" her. In early 1893, she opposed the planning of "Colored People's Day" at the World's Columbian Exposition, a controversial example of tokenism at an event that largely ignored African Americans as anything other than caricatures. The head of the planning board for the event, which included Douglass, asked him to "say something to the press in defense of this committee," knowing that Douglass's voice would carry greater weight than either her own or Wells's.[129] Meanwhile, Josephine Ruffin, a Wells ally, had approached the editor of the *Boston Courant* and demanded that he denounce "Colored People's Day." "Miss Ida Wells has been pretty influenced by Mrs. Ruffin," he wrote to Douglass, implying that Douglass should use his influence with Wells to stop the opposition.[130] Douglass did not appear to jump to Wells's defense in the first case, but neither did he comply with the requests in the matter of "Colored People's Day," although he disagreed with Wells about it.

His refusal to restrain Wells probably stemmed not only from his respect for her as an activist, but also because they had begun to collaborate on a protest to the overall exclusion of African Americans at the World's Columbian Exposition, held in Chicago in 1893. Although the Haitian government had appointed Douglass manager of their pavilion, African Americans were woefully underrepresented in all other exhibits and held no positions of authority. In theory, some of the exhibits integrated black achievements into the appropriate categories. Pieces by Edmonia Lewis and the Kentucky art student Fannie Hicks, for instance, were accepted for the Women's Pavilion, and the Louisiana Pavilion boasted a "comprehensive exhibit of the schools for negro children." At the same time, for all the black seamen and watermen in the history of the nation, the fisheries exhibit only depicted a "darkey" with a crude, homemade pole sleeping on the banks of a trout stream, in contrast to the white "fancifully equipped angler" who fished a few feet away.[131] Former slave Nancy Green also made her debut as Aunt Jemima for the Quaker Oats Company. Dressed as the "Mammy" character she played in minstrel shows, Green demonstrated the conveniences of a pancake mix while telling nostalgic stories about the antebellum South. Worse yet, the African pavilion exhibited a group of Fon people in a cage, like animals in a zoo, and all references to Africa portrayed the continent and its people as primitive and uncivilized. To placate protesters, fair managers offered to include African Americans in a series of days featuring a particular ethnic group or nation. Called variously "Colored People's Day," "Jubilee Day," and, with both sarcasm and sincerity, "Nigger Day," the plan stirred up more controversy, especially when the managers of the Agricultural Pavilion offered to serve free watermelon. The debate divided those who saw the day as characterizing black Americans as somehow not wholly part of the United States, those who hoped to use the day to emphasize African American advancement, and those who saw the day as an opportunity to protest racial injustice in the country. Wells saw the day as an insult, but Douglass saw it as an opportunity and agreed to be part of the planning committee.

The difference of opinion between Douglass and Wells was no secret when Wells stayed at Cedar Hill in February 1893, but rather than create a rift between the two, it strengthened their respect for one another. During that visit, they began planning a pamphlet that would expose the hypocrisy of an event that, according to the Fair's guidebook, represented the United States as "mankind's choicest blessings—personal and political freedom," dedicated to "the enfranchisement of the human being" and "stewardship in matters intellectual and spiritual."[132] "Let the truth be told," Douglass demanded, "let the light be turned on ignorance and prejudice, let lawless violence and murder be exposed."[133] The idea for *The Reason Why the Colored American Is Not at the World's Columbian Exposition* was more likely Wells's because she did the lion's share of the work. but she framed the idea as a joint effort, insisting that "we had decided" that they should produce the pamphlet.[134] Douglass wrote the introduction, Ferdinand Barnett contributed a chapter on the ways that fair organizers had denied African Americans jobs and leadership positions, and I. Garland Penn offered a chapter celebrating black advancements in the thirty years since the Emancipation Proclamation. Wells wrote chapters on lynching, legal restrictions on African Americans, and the convict lease system, as well as a preface and concluding letter "to the Public." She also did the bulk of the fundraising and distribution at the fair. Douglass, meanwhile, ensured that the Haitian Pavilion provided a haven for African Americans, hired the as-yet-unknown poet Paul Laurence Dunbar as his secretary and scheduled him to give a reading on "Colored People's Day," and provided a platform for violinists William Cook and Joseph Douglass, his grandson. He himself gave a speech pointedly addressing northern whites. "The sunny south does not love you: it never will," he observed. "We do. Yet, why in heaven's name do you take to your breast the serpent that once stung and crush[ed] down the race that grasped the saber that helped make the nation one and the exposition possible."[135]

The following year, Wells returned to England and became embroiled in another controversial tangle that again required Douglass's mediation. This one involved Frances Willard, president of the Women's Christian Temperance Union, a national organization that included thousands of white southern members. In a debate reminiscent of the 1846 "Send Back the Money" campaign that saw Douglass joining other abolitionists to urge the Free Church of Scotland to reject monies raised by slaveholders, Wells believed that Willard should lead the organization in denouncing lynching, regardless of the disapproval of her southern members. Willard insisted that she did not condone lynching, but indicated that she supported restrictions at the ballot box "that would sift out alien illiterates," which included African Americans, and that she believed black men terrorized the southern countryside.[136] Wells questioned the depth of the organization's Christianity. Lady Isabella Somerset, president of the British Women's

Temperance Association and a friend of Willard, sent Douglass a clipping of an editorial in which she had written, "If Miss Ida B. Wells, the coloured woman who is in this country enlisting sympathy for her race, is not careful she will kill her cause with imprudent speeches."[137] Like others, she expected Douglass to reprimand Wells. Instead, he cabled the reply, "I endorse her mission."[138]

Himself a temperance man since his first encounter with David Ruggles in 1838, and a supporter of Willard's other cause, woman's suffrage, Douglass conceded that she was "an excellent lady" and that "it is too bad to have a noble-minded woman like Miss Willard, so abundant in influence, to go wrong."[139] Nevertheless, she had written to him in defense of lynching. "I pity the Southerner," she told him. "The colored race multiplies like the locusts of Egypt," she insisted. "The safety of woman, of childhood, of the home is menaced in a thousand localities at this moment, so much that men dare not go beyond the sight of their own roof-tree."[140] Willard asked to interview Frederick, probably to persuade him to restrain Wells. Helen, having buried her sister Jennie two weeks earlier, extended Willard an invitation to discuss the matter at Cedar Hill.[141] Douglass held firm and likely had more influence on the temperance activist than she might have hoped to have on him. The pressure from Wells, Douglass, and other quarters forced Willard to finally condemn lynching in her "Fifteenth Presidential Address" of November 16, 1894, although she held firm to her belief in other forms of disfranchisement.[142]

The sexist and patronizing calls to restrain Wells cast her in a role subordinate to Douglass. His responses and their interactions, however, suggest that neither of them saw the relationship in those terms. When he disagreed with her, he did not use her respect for him to try to influence her to change her mind. When he defended her, he did so as a fellow activist, not a protector. She was not like many of the young men who turned to him to recommend them as they began their careers, including Paul Laurence Dunbar, Charles Morris, or even his sons and son-in-law. Nor was she like him when he had first entered the abolitionist movement or launched the North Star. Wells was a grown and experienced woman. She had taken care of herself and her siblings since age sixteen. When she met Douglass, she was thirty years old and an established teacher, journalist, editor, and activist. She had fled a lynch mob and sued a railroad company for relegating her to a Jim Crow car. She did not need a father, or even a Garrison or Gerrit Smith, she needed the weight and credibility of an established, male activist to help promote her crusade.

Naturally, because of their age difference, their relationship contained a filial element. Douglass had referred to Wells as "my child" in urging her to go to England, and his recommendations for her always thanked her hosts as if he thanked someone for their kindness to one of his own children. "I cannot thank you to heartily for the aid you have rendered to Miss Ida B. Wells, in her mission to the English people," he told one English supporter; to another, he expressed gratitude "that the brave little woman found sympathy and shelter under your roof."[143] Indeed, referring to her as "the brave little woman" and "my child" was patronizing, even as he meant it to be an endearment. She, for her part, looked up to Douglass with gushing adoration and was more than honored when he found her work honorable. "I have always adored you as our greatest man and hoped that I had been fortunate to win for myself a slight measure of your regard from a personal point of view," she told him. "However I feel myself favored to have won your encomiums for my work."[144] Nevertheless, while their affection was personal, their respect was mutual and professional. Both posited themselves as engaged in a struggle as equals and allies, with Douglass as the senior member rather than her superior. As in their encounters with Willard, he threw the weight of his reputation behind her. "With Miss Wells, I plead for him [African Americans] against persecution and lawless outrage,"[145] he declared.[146] She did the same, bringing with her the strength of her research and personal experience in the South. Thus, when Senator Henry Blair of New Hampshire proposed the first federal anti-lynching bill in 1894, she suggested to Douglass "that you take necessary steps to get us,—you and me—a hearing" in Congress.[147]

The relationship benefited both of them. She drew on his more extensive influence, but not because she had none of her own. As a young black woman, already subject to attacks that used her gender to discredit her ideas, she required the powerful presence of a black man to legitimize her work, much as fugitive-slave narratives like Douglass's had needed the endorsement of white abolitionists. While Douglass had later portrayed himself as an activist "child" when his *Narrative* was published, and called on a black man to write the introduction to *My Bondage and My Freedom*, Wells did not construe herself as anything other than an adult trying to build a movement. Finding that the most influential black man of her time supported her work, she shrewdly called on his authority, and he placed himself in the role of student in providing support at that early stage. Just as importantly, Douglass proved to be very popular with white audiences who liked to remember themselves as faithful abolitionists, true or not. These audiences probably believed, like Willard, that black men raping white women excused lynching. Like Willard, too, if exposed to the facts, they might sympathize with an antilynching crusade, even if that sympathy did not extend to other civil rights. As under slavery, the people most affected by lynching lived under fear and disfranchisement, while whites, especially northern whites, became a crucial audience because they had political power.

Yet, for all his celebrity as a civil rights icon, many young activists of the time saw Douglass as a relic of the past, rapidly growing irrelevant. Young men turned to him for patronage and endorsement, but did not necessarily ask him to participate in a movement. Black colleges called on him as a graduation speaker, and commemorations of the abolition movement could rely upon his presence. Even the National Woman's Suffrage Association and National American Woman's Suffrage Association seemed to desire his endorsement as a way to elide their attacks on black men in the 1870s. Douglass's most popular and frequently delivered speech at that point was "Self-Made Men," a practical but hardly militant call for self-help. Although he was still a fixture in denouncing racism from all angles, he had become less an activist than an office-holder, speech-maker, and symbol of a fading past. Wells approached him for his patronage, but she also seemed to expect involvement, offering him a role in opposing Jim Crow that would bring to bear his experience and influential reach on both sides of the ocean and connect his abolitionist past to her antilynching present. Focused, multilayered, unified, and incorporating class and gender analyses that had eluded Douglass for the previous thirty years, she offered him an intellectually exciting and important role in current racial politics. In that respect, Douglass followed Wells as much as she followed him.

Their conversation on lynching became the apotheosis of this symbiotic relationship. After Wells published *Southern Horrors* in 1892, Douglass made his own contribution in January 1894 with "Lessons of the Hour," published as "Lynching Black People Because They Are Black" in the April 1894 issue of *The Christian Educator*. This was his first major speech that specifically addressed lynching and the last major speech of his career. Wells followed later that year with *Red Record*. Douglass the Orator tended toward a rhetorical approach, puncturing the logic that imagined hordes of black men ravaging white feminine virtue across the South. Wells employed the tactics of a journalist, ferreting out data and demanding further investigation. In these essays, they both agreed that lynching was a failure of the legal system in which the federal government, by its inaction, stood as culpable as the state and local governments. The reasons for this failure came from the nature of the accusation of rape and the low value placed on the lives of African Americans by both the mob and people in authority, but rape had very little to do with the real purpose of lynching. Indeed, rape was not as prevalent as the press would have the public believe, nor were actual rapes as numerous as the accusations. Lynching terrorized African Americans into subservience, and disfranchisement and disempowerment were the hidden motives behind the accusations of a crime that disgusted most Americans, both black and white, and played upon white stereotypes of black men with white women.

Both Douglass and Wells agreed that rape was a heinous crime. Douglass learned more than he cared to know about the subject at an early age, hearing the "whispers" about his father and witnessing the brutalization of Aunt Hester. Wells had heard similar stories from her mother and, like other black women, she understood the continuing danger of sexual violence. Yet, they were both well aware that in denouncing lynching, they opened themselves up to accusations that they were defending the crime instead of demanding due process for the accused. As Douglass pointed out, rape "is a crime that places him [the alleged rapist] outside of the pale of the law, and settles upon his shoulders a mantle of wrath and fire that blisters and burns into his very soul," making him "an object of suspicion and avoidance."[148] Wells echoed these sentiments, observing that "humanity abhors the assailant of woman hood, and this charge upon the Negro at once placed him beyond the pale of human sympathy."[149] Therein lay the power of the accusation. In raising a specter of brutish black male sexuality, Douglass reasoned, "it throws over every colored man a mantle of odium and sets upon him a mark for popular hate more distressing than the mark set upon the first murderer."[150] These assumptions cloaked any crime against a black man and, as Wells demonstrated, lynch mobs attacked black men merely for being successful rather than subservient.

The means of undermining the widespread acceptance of mob violence thus lay in exposing the lie of the black rapist. In *Southern Horrors,* Wells marshaled the data, citing a *Chicago Tribune* report demonstrating that allegations of rape accounted for only "*one-third* of the 728" lynchings in 1892. Her pamphlet, however, began with an explanation that the attack on the Memphis office had occurred after she had suggested that white women could be sexually attracted to black men. To make the case, she presented several examples of white women who had either seduced, conducted extramarital affairs with, or fallen in love with black men. In looking at the evidence, she concluded that "there are white women in the South who love the Afro-American's company even as there are white men notorious for their preference for Afro-American women."[151] Douglass did not have to incorporate this argument into "Lessons of the Hour." That he had married one of those women was a matter of public comment, as was his mixed parentage. As with all of his interracial interactions with white women, his actions carried far more weight than his words. His line of argument, too, had more to do with black masculinity than the sexual and romantic preferences of women.

He, instead, picked up on Wells's remark that "there is little difference between the Ante-bellum South and the New South."[152] Recalling the scope of his life, he began by placing the new wave of lynchings into historical context. Lest his audience forget that the Confederacy had begun the "late war," he reminded them that, for four years, "the slave-masters of the South were absent from their homes in the field of rebellion, with bullets in their pockets, treason in their hearts, broad blades in their bloodstained hands, seeking the life of the Nation, with vile purpose of perpetuating the enslavement of the Negro." As white southerners took up arms against the US government, back home, "their wives, their daughters, their sisters, and their mothers were left in the absolute custody of these same negroes." Despite having ample and extended opportunity to resort to any sort of depravation toward these helpless females, slave men were never "accused of assault, insult, or an attempt to commit an assault upon any white woman in the whole south."[153] That state of affairs continued during Reconstruction when "there never was a charge then made against a Negro involving an assault on any white woman or upon any little white child."[154] Instead, the defeated former rebels began to wage war against the freedmen who had committed no crimes.

Nonetheless, during the antebellum and Reconstruction eras, whites often used violence to control African Americans. Then, "the justification for the murder of Negroes was said to be Negro conspiracies, insurrections, schemes to murder all the white people, to burn the town, and commit violence generally."[155] With the Confederacy, however, only white southerners had resorted to uprisings against the government. Still, the outlaw violence against African Americans continued, first "to check the domination and supremacy of the Negro, and to secure the absolute rule of the Anglo-Saxon race," and then as retaliation for the "assault upon defenseless women." Expounding upon Wells's connection between lynching and "the lesson of subordination," by which, Wells argued, white mobs "Kill the leaders" in order to "cow the Negro who dares to shoot that white man, even in self-defense," Douglass drew a more direct line between terrorism and political disfranchisement. The rape charges appeared, he asserted, "simultaneously with well-known efforts now being industriously made to degrade the Negro by legislative enactments, and by repealing all laws for the protection of the ballot, and by drawing the color-line in all railroad cars and stations and in all other public places in the South." If that were not clear enough, he added, "I see in it a means of paving the way for our entire disfranchisement."[156]

Wells incorporated Douglass's periodization into Red Record, adding data to bolster his argument. She also refined his point by suggesting that, under slavery, southern whites had forced African Americans into subservience and had an investment in the lives of their human property. Emancipation had eliminated the investment but not the desire to control. Douglass had made a similar argument in his autobiographies when he explained that the masters who fed him well did so because a well-fed slave made a better worker. After emancipation, however, "a new system of intimidation came into vogue," Wells argued. "The Negro was not only whipped and scourged; he was killed."[157]

Wells and Douglass thus pushed one another to develop their overall arguments. The major difference between the two lay in their interpretations of the role gender played in the crime. Douglass emphasized the male victim of the crime and the implications for black masculinity, without addressing black victims of rape or the role of white women in the lynching. Charges of rape "blast and ruin the Negro's character as a man and a citizen" and counteracted the Negro's advancement by leading "men and women to regard us with averted eyes, increasing hate, and dark suspicion."[158] His rationale flowed from his opposition to slavery, the service of black men during the Civil War, and advocacy for black male suffrage. Black men led and protected the black community. Therefore an attack on one assaulted the whole. Violence against women under slavery, such as Aaron Anthony's beating of Aunt Hester, the unspoken rapes of his mother, and the separation of mothers from husbands and children through sales, violated not just the woman in question but African Americans' right to form and protect their own families. As such, they infringed on the paternal right over that family. The right for black men to bear arms in the Civil War extended from a demand for manhood and citizenship, interchangeable concepts by that time, in which the black soldier defended his nation and family. Male suffrage was based in part on a patriarch's representation of the people within his household. Removing the right to vote, the right to defend their communities, and the right to protect their families effectively emasculated black men. Casting black men as sexual brutes served as a more effective means of doing the same, a point too finely made on those victims castrated by mobs.

Although Wells did not disagree with Douglass, she made a more complicated argument that incorporated both black and white women. She approached the question of lynching with a triple consciousness, aware of the proscribed behavior for African Americans, the proscribed behavior for women, and her own experience as both. She saw the predicament of white women in interracial love affairs clearly, believing "there are many white women in the South who would marry colored men if such an act would not place them at once beyond the pale of society and within the clutches of the law." Moreover, by southern logic, "the woman was a willing partner in the victim's guilt, and being of the 'superior race' must naturally have been more guilty." Southern antimiscegenation laws kept white women's sexuality as tightly controlled as black men's in order to ensure the purity of the white race. White women, however, had greater power through the privilege of their race, which made them culpable in the lynching of their paramours and white male domination through false accusations.[159]

In addressing the rape of black women by white men, Wells made a subtler argument than Douglass had. "The utterances of the leading white men show that with them it is not the crime but the *class*" that is offensive, she declared, pointing out that those defending mob violence did so for "lynchers of *white* women only" and citing South Carolina governor Benjamin "Pitchfork" Tillman's promise that "he would lead a mob to lynch a *negro* who raped a *white* woman." Then she provided a series of examples in which the white rapists of black women escaped accusation, conviction, and lynching. In the case of the rape of an eight-year-old girl, Wells seethed that "the outrage upon helpless childhood needed no avenging: she was black."[160]

In Wells's formulation, lynching was violence committed against the black community because it was an injustice against the lives and rights of both men and women in the community. On the one hand, lynching was the murder of a man committed as a means of intimidating the entire black community and as punishment for violating a code of white superiority. Whether or not the man was in fact guilty of any crime, his right to due process was violated, and his killers not only escaped prosecution but received accolades. Yet, rape also trampled the rights of black women in the violence done to their bodies and in the legal failure to see the rape of black women as a crime. A black woman's bodily integrity and virtue were not considered equal to that of a white woman, and her rights as a victim were ignored. In this respect, Wells implicitly argued that black women were citizens equal to black men and entitled to the same demands for legal action that their husband, fathers, and brothers made. Whereas Douglass made the argument that rape and lynching violated the male prerogative to protect and defend women, Wells argued that women were entitled to that same prerogative in protecting themselves. Sojourner Truth and Francis Watkins Harper had tried to impress this point upon Douglass during the AERA's debates about the 15th Amendment.

Douglass and Wells both used lynching as the issue around which to build a black civil rights movement. Unlike his relationships with antislavery women like Julia Griffiths, who served a different function in the movement than did Douglass, or Ottilie Assing, who introduced Douglass to an intellectual world outside activism, he and Wells worked in a similar arena, giving speeches and writing editorials. They pushed one another and had their collaborations continued, it may have forced Douglass to develop an integrated analysis of black and woman's rights. As events unfolded, by the end of 1895, Wells had married, and was soon starting a family. Like other women activists, she learned the difficulties of combining a public and a private life. A few years earlier, Douglass had said of Fannie Barrier Williams that he was glad that "marrying has not destroyed her ambition," and perhaps he would have been delighted to see Wells continue the cause with a child on her lap.[161]

The Sage of Anacostia, however, was not there to see Wells marry Ferdinand Barnett, the business partner of Fannie Williams's husband. On January 26, 1895, Douglass attended the Women's Council Convention being held in Washington. Late that afternoon he returned to Cedar Hill for dinner. Helen had not attended the convention, but wanted to know all about the proceedings. Frederick complied, and storyteller that he was, his account continued through the meal and into the hallway as they awaited the carriage to take him back to the evening sessions. According to the *New York Times*, "He grew very enthusiastic in his explanation of one of the events of the day, when he fell upon his knees, with hands clasped." Knowing his penchant for the dramatic, Helen assumed for an instant that he was re-enacting part of the meeting. A moment later, she knew that her husband was dying. Neighbors responded to her cries for help, but to no avail. Frederick died in his front hall with Helen at his side, twenty-seven days after their eleventh anniversary. Impressive funerals followed in both Washington and Rochester, and then she buried his body in the Douglass plot at Mount Hope Cemetery and returned to Cedar Hill alone.[162]

Epilogue

Afterlife, 1895–1903

As Helen Douglass headed home after burying her husband, she had a mission: to ensure that Frederick Douglass and his work would be remembered. Her plan lay on the cutting edge of a movement to preserve the homes of famous Americans and matched the efforts of white abolitionists to preserve an antislavery history and records in an age of Jim Crow. To succeed she would need the support of the leading African Americans in Washington; instead, she found herself pitted against her stepchildren in legal battles over the control of Cedar Hill and her husband's papers. As a result, in attempting to preserve Frederick's history and commemorate his life, the image of her, the white wife of his last eleven years, clashed with the image of Anna, the enigmatic black wife of the previous forty-four.

Newspapers across the country recounted his life and praised his accomplishments, as Helen and Frederick's children prepared for his funeral. Anna's remains still lay buried at Graceland Cemetery in Washington, but the family decided to have Frederick buried in Mount Hope Cemetery next to little Annie. No stone marked either grave, and two years passed before Helen could attend to the matter. Meanwhile, friction within the family preoccupied her. At Frederick's funeral in Washington, Helen reportedly sat alone in a pew, separate from the Douglass children and grandchildren and with none of her own family at her side.[1] Within weeks the *New York Times* repeated rumors from Rochester that "The children by [Douglass's] first wife claim that their white stepmother unduly influenced their father and got his property."[2] Helen, Charles, and Lewis moved quickly to quash the rumors as a "tissue of falsehood" and "utterly false."[3] Nevertheless, within days of the denial, Rosetta challenged her father's will.[4]

Written seven months after his marriage to Helen, the will left her $10,000, all of his bonds, and Cedar Hill, which included the house, its contents, and the surrounding acreage. Douglass stipulated that "all my writings, books, papers" should go to Helen, excepting only "a certain portrait of myself," which he bequeathed to Rosetta. He left the remainder of property in Rochester, Washington, and Maryland to be divided equally among his children, estimating that the value would provide each with $15,000.[5] Frederick Jr.'s two surviving children, Charles Paul and Robert Smalls, became heirs, but Charles Paul died on April 4, three months after his grandfather. Robert Smalls lived until 1907, but his name did not appear in the suits filed after 1895.[6] Thus, a larger portion remained for Rosetta, Charles, and Lewis. Neither Lewis nor Charles openly objected to the terms of the will, probably understanding that their father saw it as his duty to provide for his aging widow, who would have few opportunities to support herself. Nathan and Rosetta, who had never quite accepted Helen's legitimacy, seemed to believe that he had a duty to provide for his adult children at least as equally as his widow.

In March, the press reported that Rosetta and Nathan had accused Helen and Lewis of "unlawfully retaining possession of her father's property." They targeted Helen specifically as committing fraud because the will had been drafted in Helen's handwriting and because its failure to name an administrator meant that the role fell to Helen by default. Nathan insisted to one reporter that Helen "is to get everything in sight if there is not a proper intervention."[7] Worried about the validity of the will because it had two rather than the requisite three signatures, Helen had already consulted her lawyer. He advised her to file the will, warning her that DC law would invalidate the portions relating to real estate in the District but assuring her that she could still claim her dower-rights of one-third of the value of the property. She seemed most concerned about her right to the papers, and he promised her that her claims to those were "entirely safe." Following her attorney's instructions, Helen approached Lewis and Charles with the document. Helen and Lewis together filed the will and the necessary letters to request administrative authority over the estate on the day after the Spragues threatened their suit.[8]

Just as Helen's counsel had predicted, the court named Helen and Lewis as the administrators of the estate, but invalidated the will in regard to only the real estate. She was entitled to all other bequests in the will, as was Rosetta to the portrait. The property in the District of Columbia, which included at least two other houses and all of Cedar Hill, was now up for division. By law, one-third of their value or, on the leased properties, one-third of the rent, went to Helen, and the remaining two-thirds would be divided equally among the other heirs. Rosetta, however, continued to believe that Helen and Lewis conspired to defraud her out of her portion and demonstrated a detailed familiarity with the items that she believed the two had excluded from inventories and evaluations. She demanded to be named a third administrator and that the property be divided equally among the heirs and widow, which would apportion more to the children and less to Helen than the existing arrangement.[9]

Although fifty-seven years old, Helen did have to worry about her own security and would for the remainder of her life. The key issue for her was not the
wealth of the estate but the parts of it that she would control to preserve her husband's legacy. Most public figures had widows or daughters who curated their
papers and artifacts, donated them to libraries, permitted biographers access
to them, or otherwise guarded, shaped, and ensured the preservation of the
Great Man's memory. Failure to do so could be disastrous. Thomas Jefferson had
Martha Randolph and her daughters to ensure that posterity remembered him
as the unblemished Sage of Monticello. The legacy of Aaron Burr, on the other
hand, a widower with no surviving children, fell to his enemies. Already John
Brown and William Lloyd Garrison had their chroniclers in John and Franklin
Sanborn and the Garrison sons, who published long volumes combining narra-
tive, reminiscence, and correspondence usually unavailable to researchers, and
Garrison's papers along with those of the Weston sisters and Samuel May were
collected, preserved, and later donated to the Boston Public Library.[10]

Few African Americans had the same sort of archives. As a result, abolition was being remembered as a white movement if it was remembered at all.
Antislavery and emancipation were being purged from commemorations of
the Civil War, while lynching, sharecropping, and Jim Crow eroded the rights
for African Americans won during Reconstruction. The culmination of nearly
a century of civil rights activism was being erased. Helen hoped to ensure that
it was not just remembered but also that it would serve as a cultural bulwark
against the degradations being imposed upon African Americans in her time.
Helen's concern about her control of Douglass's papers, as well as his specifi-
cation that she receive them after his death, suggested that both Douglasses
expected Helen to guarantee that Frederick in particular and black participation in general remained part of the history of antislavery and the nation. To
that end, she made plans for a reprint of the last edition of *Life and Times of
Frederick Douglass* and collected speeches and reminiscences for a memorial
volume.[11]

She had still grander plans. On March 4, 1895, the *Washington Post* reported
that T. J. Edmundson, president of the Mount Olive Sunday School Lyceum
in Washington, "urged the colored people to purchase the Douglass home on
Anacostia Heights, transform it into a national museum and the ground into a
park, and erect a monument." Either inspired by or independent of the lyceum,
Helen developed a similar idea. On March 10, 1894, she drew up her own will,
stipulating that "should I die possessed of Cedar Hill," then the property should
go to the US government for a monument to Douglass and antislavery. The
contents she left to Lewis for his lifetime, after which she directed that all of
the books, "except a few volumes kept by the children of Frederick Douglass
as heirlooms," would be maintained as the "Frederick Douglass Library" and

donated "to some most suitable and worthy colored institution." Cedar Hill was crucial to those plans and, as they evolved, she had only one example to follow.[12]

Just up the Potomac River stood Mount Vernon, the home of George Washington, and Frederick and Helen had been among the many tourists who flocked to see the mansion and its grounds. In 1858, the Mount Vernon Ladies' Association had purchased the property in order to foster a sense of national unity during a growing sectional crisis by creating a shrine where the public could learn about the nation's founding. Even in the 1890s, such sites were scarce. Monticello rotted atop a mountain, and descendants still occupied the Adams home. The idea of turning a house into a museum was unusual; and to do so for a black man's home in an effort to preserve an aspect of African American history was unimaginable, even to Frederick's children. Nevertheless, Helen planned to make Cedar Hill the antislavery version of Mount Vernon. Where Mount Vernon used the life and story of George Washington as the means of discussing the origins of the American republic and the virtues of American ideals, Cedar Hill would use the life and story of Frederick Douglass as the means of discussing the antislavery movement and the realization of those ideals that the American Revolution did not accomplish.[13]

Helen faced two problems, the first of which was securing full ownership of the property. According to Francis Grimké, while the terms of the will were being sorted out, Helen had approached Rosetta, Charles, and Lewis, asking them "to set Cedar Hill apart as a perpetual memorial to their father, and to appoint a board of trustees to whom the property should be deeded to be held as such."[14] Charles later said that he thought the idea wasteful and that any money raised for the purpose of a memorial "would be of far more service to the colored people, if it were given to some such institution as Tuskegee, for an industrial building of some kind, dedicated to the memory of Frederick Douglass."[15] Grimké, however, recalled that the children preferred that the property be "left as part of the estate and sold, divided among the heirs."[16] Since Helen controlled only a one-third interest in the property, she took out a $15,000 mortgage to buy the children's shares of the property. Because selling Cedar Hill had been their wish in the first place and because they had little sentimental attachment to the house, they had all sold their interests to her by 1896.[17]

Helen could proceed with the memorial, but the mortgage only added to her second problem. The debt and the upkeep for such a large house and its grounds, which included fruit trees, gardens, and livestock, shaped many of the subsequent actions that seemed so mercenary to the children. First, she successfully sued to ensure that she received the full amount of her claim to the property owned by her husband in Baltimore, Washington, and Rochester, which included not only her own dower-right but also shares that Rosetta had sold her. Then, she unsuccessfully sued for the $10,000 value of bonds stipulated in Frederick's will.[18] The proceeds of the 1895 reprint of *Life and Times of Frederick Douglass* and a memorial volume featuring images of Cedar Hill also went toward preserving the home.[19] Finally, she took to the lecture circuit, although this had a purpose beyond the $100 fee she charged. She focused on lynching and the convict lease system, two methods of violent disfranchisement and exploitation of black men, as well as on the conditions of poverty and police brutality toward African Americans in cities.[20] Martha Greene mocked her efforts, writing to Rosetta that "way down in Georgia the poor convicts demand her sympathy!!"[21] Yet, Helen had always been sincere and probably saw herself as continuing the work that her husband would have performed, had he lived. The fees allowed her to continue the preservation of his papers and home.

Realizing that her plans for a museum called for the same sort of institutional support that Julia Griffiths had mustered for the *North Star*, nearly half a century earlier, Helen began to court key African American activists who might be interested in preserving Cedar Hill and who could ensure that her vision survived her death. In mid-July 1896, the National League of Colored Women and the National Federation of Afro-American Women held their annual meetings in Washington, ultimately deciding to merge the organizations into the National Association of Colored Women (NACW). The *Indianapolis Freeman* had declared that the League "was composed of some of the brainiest women of the race," who included president Helen A. Cook, Charlotte Forten Grimké, wife of Francis Grimké, and Marion P. Shadd, a leader in Washington schools and cousin to newspaperwoman Mary Ann Shadd Cary.[22] Delegates to the Federation conference included Ida B. Wells-Barnett, Frances Ellen Watkins Harper, the wives of Blanche K. Bruce and Booker T. Washington, Harriet Tubman, now in her seventies, and president Mary Church Terrell.[23] Helen addressed the League's convention, decrying the poverty that led to "a steady stream from the workhouse and almshouse" and racial discrimination in the police courts, then she seized the opportunity to invite members of both organizations on a pilgrimage to Cedar Hill.[24] Many of these women and their husbands emphasized education as a key component in improving conditions for African Americans and intended to shape Cedar Hill's future as, in the words of Francis Grimké, "a great educational force, a center from which could radiate influences that would keep the race steadily pressing on."[25] They began assembling support for a preservation organization and a bill for its incorporation, which would secure tax-exempt status. Wells-Barnett also gave her endorsement, crediting Helen with "the bequeathing of the Douglass Home to the Negro race."[26]

The next year, to stimulate popular support, Helen invited a *Washington Post* reporter to tour the house. As she gave evasive answers to personal questions about the color of her wedding dress and "how you happened to fancy Mr.

Douglass," he followed her about the house noting the art, books, and mementoes of the antislavery movement on display. Just before he departed, she mentioned her plan to turn Cedar Hill into a "memorial hall of the earliest efforts in the cause of freedom." The reporter agreed that the idea was good. "It is, however, too soon for these ideas of mine to be known," she demurred, as "It might hurt the object?" The reporter declared that Helen "may be the one by which this mission to [Douglass's] people is to be carried out."[27]

Meanwhile, the Grimkés and Terrells proved instrumental to the creation of the Frederick Douglass Memorial and Historical Association (FDMHA), modeled on the Mount Vernon Ladies' Association. They intended "to preserve to posterity the memory of the life and character of the late Frederick Douglass," and "to collect, collate, and preserve a historical record of the inception, progress, and culmination of the anti-slavery movement of the United States," which would include "all such suitable exhibits of records or things illustrative or commemorative of the antislavery movement and history," which would be brought to Cedar Hill. They planned also to erect "a monument to the memory of the late Frederick Douglass" on the site according to Helen's specifications. Knowing her husband's disgust at the subservient figure in the memorial to Abraham Lincoln as Emancipator, she stipulated that the purpose of the monument to her husband would "not be to represent a slave or broken chains"; rather it was to be "be an inspiration for the colored people who come here to pay their loving tribute to his memory." A year later, in August 1898, Senator Jacob Gallinger of New Hampshire proposed a bill "to incorporate the Frederick Douglass Memorial and Historical Association."[28] The *Cleveland Gazette*, a black newspaper, declared the move "a splendid idea."[29]

As soon as newspapers reported the House proposal, a reporter from the *Colored American* approached Charles Douglass for comment. "I trust to the good sense and loyalty of the colored people of their country to set their mark of disapproval upon this scheme," Charles responded, noting that he and his siblings had not been consulted about the plan and that they would have opposed it had they been asked. Because the bill specifically exempted the property from "all taxes or charges and assessments whatever" and because the Memorial Association would fundraise, Charles believed that Helen had manipulated her supporters in order to pay off "money expended in the purchase of Cedar Hill, and to guarantee her a life of residence there and maintenance." He pointed out that "my father left her with ample means of support," so her plans for Cedar Hill could only be for profit, "sentiment and personal aggrandizement." He also believed the project ill-conceived because "Cedar Hill is situated in a community not at all friendly to the colored race," and Washington was not the site of "the greater portion of my father's work in the anti-slavery cause." He thought Rochester a more suitable location. There, he pointed out, "they are about to erect a bronze statue of my father in one of the public parks" and the University of Rochester displayed a bust of Frederick, which he considered sufficient.[30]

Yet, for all of his opposition to the project, Charles insisted, "I have no interest in Cedar Hill." He could have done little to stop the project if he had. He proclaimed that "I would not have a word to say upon this matter," except for one part that he considered personally objectionable, "the provision in this bill to desecrate the graves of my father and mother."[31] According to section nine of the bill, "the remains of the late Frederick Douglass may be interred" on the grounds of Cedar Hill.[32] Helen had sole right to determine who else could be buried on the site, and she planned to have her own remains placed next to her husband's. This, Charles insisted, went against the wishes of his father, who had purchased the lot at Mount Hope Cemetery in Rochester as the final resting place for himself and Anna, "whose remains lie beside those of my father." Moving Frederick away from Anna was, Charles believed, "conceived in a spirit of unfriendliness to the family," an insult "aimed at every other member of my father's family, as well as to the memory of my mother" and "to the race at large." He gave a second interview to the *Washington Post* reiterating his opposition, asking the interviewer to "think of taking the body of my father from the side of the wife of his youth and his manhood."[33]

That her plans would disturb Anna's grave came as a surprise to Helen. Until early August, when the bill for the Frederick Douglass Memorial and Historical Association was already before the House, Helen had believed that Anna lay in Graceland Cemetery in Washington, DC, where she had been buried in 1882. Anna's body had not figured in Helen's plans because Helen had no authority over Anna's grave. Then, on August 4, 1898, David Z. Morris, the superintendent of Mount Hope Cemetery, asked for Helen's advice on a new monument being placed on the Douglass lot. Because Helen had already placed a large marker on her husband's grave, Morris explained "the two would of necessity come quite close together, and as that already there is of considerably larger bulk it would give the appearance of two monuments set corner to corner." The new monument, "of the sarcophagus style," stood in sharp contrast to the plain slab already on the lot and was being erected by Lewis and Charles for their families, with their mother and sister Annie's names to be inscribed on its side. Helen inquired as to the reason that Anna would have a marker in a place where she was not buried. "The first wife of Mr. Douglass was moved here during last Spring and interred on the lot between Mr. Douglass and the child's grave," Morris informed her. "I believe by the order of the sons."[34]

He was correct. On March 19, 1898, Charles and Lewis had their mother reinterred next to their father and younger sister.[35] They had no reason to notify their father's second wife of the change; and while they wanted their parents buried together, they possibly also hoped to forestall Helen having herself buried by his side or to ensure that she was not remembered as the only Mrs. Douglass. Helen, in fact, was worried that she could not be interred next to her husband, should her other plans fall through, but Morris reassured her that she had the right to be buried by Frederick's side. Meanwhile, the provision about moving Frederick's body did not appear in the bill presented to the Senate, which passed in 1900. Helen, however, kept it in the final version of her will, dated September 28, 1900, three months after the incorporation of the Frederick Douglass Memorial and Historical Association. She made no mention of Anna's remains or her own.[36]

Francis Grimké later criticized the Douglass children for "doing everything they could to defeat the project" and said that, into the early twentieth century, fundraising "was hindered through the influence of some member of the family."[37] Lewis later insisted that they were, in fact, interested in the project, but "no offer on our part has been listened to." They also found the fundraising tactic of "falsely alleging poverty" distasteful and contrary to "our father's ideals" of thrift and avoiding debt.[38] Helen and the FDMHA perhaps made a misstep in not courting the Douglass family more aggressively, but Charles and Lewis had made clear that they did not like the idea of this memorial, and they intended to thwart donations with their public statements.

Rosetta and Nathan, however, remained surprisingly silent on the subject. Unlike her brothers, Rosetta and her family had a connection to Cedar Hill. Her daughters had lived there, her sister-in-law had helped manage it, and she had visited frequently enough in the summer of 1883 to tease her father that he would think that she had moved in. To her, preserving Cedar Hill as a memorial to their father may not have seemed as inappropriate as her brothers deemed it. At the same time, she had no love for Helen. She had attended the National Federation of Afro-American Women meeting in 1896, but did not appear on the guest list for the sojourn to Cedar Hill. Had she gone, she would have seen another woman acting as hostess, a role that she herself had perhaps hoped to fill and a painful reminder of the loss of her mother. She may have felt a sense that even the memory of her father was slipping out of the control of the family and that the family was being forgotten in his history.

The important issue in regard to Cedar Hill was not simply the preservation of Douglass's history but rather the interpretation of that history. Lewis, Rosetta, and Charles had collected and saved mementoes and documents of their family's life, some of which made their way into private and public collections throughout the twentieth and twenty-first centuries. The three children seemed to agree that the real problem was that Helen did not tell the story that they wanted told about their father. Helen and the FDMHA hoped to convey a message of hope, a message with which the Douglass children could agree. Yet, Helen and her supporters focused on a story of integration and achievement. In the spirit of contemporary biographies, Helen portrayed her departed husband as a Great Man, an individual guiding the nation in fulfilling its promise of equality for all. Cedar Hill asked visitors to stand on its porch, look across the river to the Washington Monument and the Capitol or across the horizon to Maryland, and to ponder the progress of Frederick from slavery to these heights. Inside, they could look over artifacts of the antislavery movement and Frederick's subsequent career to learn about the struggle for African American rights.[39]

Although the FDMHA membership was almost entirely black, the story at Cedar Hill would also stress the importance of integration and "racial uplift" during a period in which the Supreme Court had blessed segregation with the 1896 *Plessy v. Ferguson* decision and white audiences had interpreted Booker T. Washington's speech at the 1896 Atlanta Exposition as sanctioning racial separation. Helen took the message for racial integration even further when she applied for admission to the newly formed Mayflower Society. In doing so, she attempted to use her marriage to connect her husband, and all African Americans by extension, to the grand sweep of American history. The president of the local chapter, however, refused to consider her application for that very same reason. "Trampling upon Constitutional rights is becoming altogether too frequent in our land," she scolded them. "If the descendants of the Mayflower give themselves up to it, to whom may we look for fair dealing?"[40] Even as Charles charged Helen with egotism in planning the memorial project, she carefully included herself only as a symbol. She made no provision for a headstone for herself at Mount Hope, nor did she bequeath any of her own papers or objects to the association, except for the cameos that depicted her husband and two dresses, one bought on their trip to Europe and the other her wedding dress.[41] Both served to remind audiences that Frederick had transgressed that racial line against intermarriage without approbation in Europe but at the risk of lynching in the Land of the Free.

The story that the Douglass children wanted told emerged over the years in their often explicit contrast of Helen with their mother, rhetorically setting Frederick's two wives against one another. When the bill for the Historical Association first went before the House, Charles pointed to a passage that praised Helen's "devotion and sacrifices." "What sacrifices has she made?" he exclaimed. "My father left her with ample means for her maintenance, none of which has been sacrificed that I know of."[42] In later years, Lewis objected to Archibald Grimké's similar characterization of Helen as having "denied to herself sufficient food and proper clothing" in order to preserve Cedar Hill. Grimké, in Lewis's estimation, had cast Frederick as a villain who "left his wife penniless and suffering for the necessaries of life" when, in fact, "he left her well off."[43] Charles also reminded his audience that fundraising by the Historical Association went "for the purpose of clearing an incumbrance placed upon it by the donor," while his father had always attempted "to keep out of debt by never getting into debt."

Helen, in other words, had not participated in a family ethos of frugality and had squandered their father's fortune. Their mother, on the other hand, had helped their father amass that fortune. "If any sacrifice was made," declared Charles, "it was made by my mother who toiled side by side with my father."[44] Anna "labored and saved," and "went without the luxuries that came and went into the hands of another Mrs. Douglass," Lewis affirmed.[45] The Douglasses, as a family, "worked on only encouraged by the thought that they were working for the cause," while "it is a mockery to speak of [Helen] doing any thing for the good of the cause for which we had labored and worked unceasingly."[46]

Rosetta did not attack Helen in public, and instead drew attention to the role that her mother played in her father's life. Black women had deployed this tactic in the wake of Frederick's second marriage and continued to do so after his death in an effort to ensure that tales of civil rights history did not forget the work of Anna, who represented African American women. At the end of the black clubwomen's tour of Cedar Hill in 1896, Lottie Wilson Jackson thanked Helen, but made a point of saying, "Goodbye, Mrs. Douglass, I want to thank you for permitting us to see Annie Murray Douglass's home."[47] The next day, at the end of the convention's proceedings, she delivered a paper about Anna in which she "declared that much of Mr. Douglass' success in life was owing to the advice and care of his wife" and concluded that "what Elizabeth Barrett was to Browning, Anna Murray was to Douglass," for which Rosetta was grateful.[48]

Four years later, Rosetta followed Jackson's example with "My Mother As I Recall Her," a speech to the Anna Murray Douglass chapter of the Women's Christian Temperance Union. In this memoir, Rosetta portrayed Anna as her father's "helpmeet," a word that he himself had used to describe his first wife. Like Frederick, Anna worked hard, taking in piecework from Lynn shoe factories and laundry in New Bedford; like him, she saved their pennies; like him, she imbued her children with a sense of social responsibility. Understanding that she was crafting a foremother for a room full of educated and socially conscious women, Rosetta emphasized the parts of Anna's life that would appeal to her audience. She insisted that her mother could read "a little" and downplayed her wage labor once her father had begun his newspaper. She also wedged Anna, never much of an overt activist, into the role of a recognizable abolitionist by noting her contributions to the Lynn Ladies' Anti-Slavery Society, and she and her brothers included their mother in the ubiquitous tales of the Underground Railroad. Anna kept them fortified during the weekly rolling of newspapers on the day that they delivered the *North Star*, Anna insisted the boys go to work in the newspaper office to learn a trade, and Anna ensured that her husband presented an impeccable appearance on stage and on tour.[49] Rosetta also connected her mother to revolution by having a brooch with an image of Toussaint Louverture painted into a portrait of Anna. The same brooch appeared in a portrait of Rosetta, as well.

Later, Fredericka Douglass returned that portrait of Anna to Cedar Hill, and the president of the FDMHA, Mary Talbert, promised to hang it in Frederick's bedroom, because she was "determined that no other woman's picture shall hang in that room except Frederick Douglass and Anna Murray Douglass, the mother of his children."[50]

The children's preferred interpretation of their father's biography shifted the emphasis from Frederick as an individual to Frederick within his family and thereby refocused the history that his life represented. In telling a family story, they alluded to the fragility of black families in the face of slavery, economic deprivation, and violence that had plagued them throughout American history. The Douglasses existed as a family unit because of the struggle of both Frederick and Anna against the odds they faced when they joined their futures together in 1838. As a black family collectively engaged in abolitionist work, the Douglasses represented a black community that was also engaged in such work. Like their father, the Douglass children had no problem with sympathetic white people or with the fact that white people also participated in this movement, but they demanded that the centrality of African Americans as active, even militant, participants in the cataclysmic changes of the nineteenth century be recognized. For this narrative to work, Anna had to figure most prominently in the role of Douglass's wife. As Charles put it, "My mother was colored; she was one of our people, she lived with our father throughout the years of his active life. What money he made, she helped to save. His home was her home; his children were her children, reared by her."[51] The very fact of Helen, their father's white second wife, and her commemoration activities at Cedar Hill in the District of Columbia, where they had not lived or worked together as a family unit, obscured and complicated that story.

Neither depiction of Douglass was wrong. His two wives represented two parts of a long life engaged in some of the most important events of the history of nineteenth-century America and race. To ignore the aspects of his life that Helen represented would mean ignoring that integration was always part of Frederick's political and social vision, and that he was a product of both the reality of racial mingling and the racism that opposed it. White women had always been part of his activism and had always played crucial roles in his survival. Recognizing that did not mean rejecting the roles that black women played. To ignore the parts of his life that Anna represented would be to ignore the future that Frederick Bailey had envisioned for himself in the shipyards of Fells Point, before he could imagine, much less become, Frederick Douglass. To ignore her, too, would mean ignoring the struggle that black families faced and the personal costs of succeeding, as well as the black women whom Frederick worked with and supported as they, including his daughter and granddaughters, formed a broad, cross-generational front against racial oppression. Both women ensured his legacy, one through their children and all that she did to enable him to have a legacy, and the other by preserving his papers and home for generations of scholars. They were also both products of the tension in his life between his desire to smash distinctions of color and thereby challenge the notion of race itself, while also cherishing his own race and the history of his own people. The configuration of Douglass family lot in Mount Hope Cemetery still depicts that tension.

On December 1, 1903, Helen died at Cedar Hill. The long-term damage caused by the rheumatic fever she had contracted in Haiti had caught up with her and her heart valve malfunctioned. According to one report, she could not leave Cedar Hill during the last year of her life and remained in bed for the final three months. During that time she adjusted her will to ensure that Cedar Hill passed to the Frederick Douglass Memorial and Historical Association, while her own personal belongings went to her family and the close friends, both black and white, who had lived with her in her final years. She also left Haley, Charles's youngest son, mementoes of his grandfather. Although newspapers reported that the children would not challenge her will, the *Washington Post* learned that Rosetta intended to "fight for the possession of the books and other former property of Mr. Douglass" and that Lewis and Charles "will join Mrs. Sprague in her contest." They had no legal grounds for the suit because those had been bequeathed to Helen by their father and had been protected from the first lawsuit after his death. Their challenge did not proceed, and Charles simply asked for and received the family Bible to leave to his own son, Joseph. Helen's remains, meanwhile, were moved to Mount Hope Cemetery in Rochester.[52]

After her death, the FDMHA struggled to meet Cedar Hill's mortgage payments and cover the costs of maintenance. The interest of the National Association of Colored Women in preserving the property continued. Under the presidency of Mary Talbert, an Oberlin College alumna, former teacher, and civil rights activist, the association formed a fundraising committee in 1916 that was able to clear the $4000 debt on the property within two years. Gradually, women from the NACW began to hold board positions in the FDMHA and brought not only a consciousness of African American history but also the desire to incorporate black women's history into the interpretation of the home by drawing Anna into its narrative. Talbert and her successors also began to court at least one Douglass descendant to participate in the project of preservation. Fredericka Douglass Sprague Perry, then a prominent clubwoman in Kansas City, donated the portrait of her grandmother to the organization and served as a trustee in 1943.[53]

Over the years, the cost of maintaining Cedar Hill became prohibitive. The association contacted the federal government and the Ford Foundation, which had preserved many homes at Greenfield Village in Dearborn, Michigan, but to no avail. In the mid-1950s, the Department of the Interior deemed Douglass of little historic importance. The trustees continued to lobby, and Cedar Hill became part of the National Park Service in 1962, on the eve of the civil rights movement. Douglass's papers were stored on the site, until their transfer to the Library of Congress between 1972 and 1974, and there were several additions to the collection thereafter from Rosetta's granddaughter Ann Weaver Teabeau, Joseph Douglass's widow, Fannie Douglass, and descendants of Ruth Adams, who had gone by the name Harriet Bailey when she lived with the Douglasses in the 1840s. When Cedar Hill finally opened to visitors in 1972, the *Washington Post* reported that 60 percent of them were African American.[54]

Lewis, Charles, and Rosetta did not participate in the FDMHA after Helen's death, and made vociferous speeches against it. Lewis died of nephritis, a kidney

Figure E.1 The Douglass family grave site in Mount Hope Cemetery, Rochester, N.Y. The Douglasses purchased the plot after the death of their ten-year-old daughter Annie in 1860. She is buried near the bench toward the back. Frederick lies beneath the slab, where he was interred in 1895. A year later, Lewis and Charles Douglass had their mother, Anna, moved from her resting place in Graceland Cemetery in Washington, DC. She lies between her husband and her daughter, on the far side of his stone slab. The sons had the tall monument erected to the memory of Anna and Annie at the same time that Helen Douglass had Frederick's marker placed. Helen was buried in the plot upon her death in 1903. In the 1970s, the Frederick Douglass Memorial and Historical Association placed the slab over what is believed to be the location of her resting place. Photo by Leigh Fought, June 2010, Mount Hope Cemetery, Rochester, N.Y.

infection, on September 19, 1908, at the age of sixty-seven. Charles lived until 1920, and his two sons outlived him. As for Rosetta, by 1903, she had more pressing problems and did not join her brother in their attacks on the FDMHA. Nathan had abandoned her in September of that year, leaving her without support. He returned two years later "a sick man," and "his mind became so deranged" over the next eight months that he had to be committed to the Government Hospital for the Insane, later known as St. Elizabeth's Hospital, in Washington. By that time, Rosetta had developed uterine cancer. She died in November 1906. Her daughters buried her in Rochester's Mount Hope Cemetery, next to her sister-in-law Louisa and her two daughters, Alice and Annie. Nathan joined her two months later. Their daughter, Fredericka, was most active in commemorations of John Brown in Kansas, but she also helped contribute to memorial events in Rochester. The other Frederick Douglass namesake in the family, Joseph's son Frederick Douglass III, later married the granddaughter of Booker T. Washington. In the early twenty-first century, their grandson organized an initiative against global trafficking, carrying on the Douglass legacy into the future.[55]

In Mount Hope Cemetery, no marker commemorated Helen's resting place until 1972. When Cedar Hill opened that year as part of the National Park System, the FDMHA commissioned a memorial stone to mark their founder's grave. The epitaph on the marble slab ensured that she would be remembered as "Widow of orator and statesman Frederick Douglass" and that "Through her vision his greatness was memorialized at Cedar Hill in Washington, D.C." because "Mrs. Douglass was the founder of the Frederick Douglass Historical and Memorial Association."[56] The wording tied her to her husband, to her crowning achievement, to Washington, DC, and to Douglass's later life. In the same space rises the monument "erected by Lewis and Charles," noting by inscription and placement the presence of Anna and Annie to Frederick's left. In the middle lies Frederick, surrounded in death, as he was in life, by women.

Appendix

FAMILY TREES

1. Family Tree (descendants of Baly, Sue, and Selah)

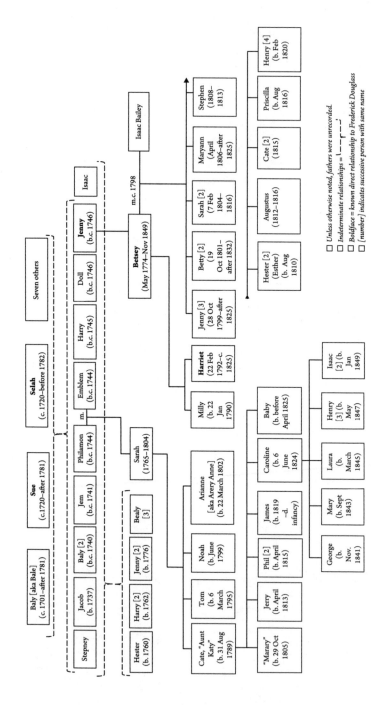

□ *Unless otherwise noted, fathers were unrecorded.*
□ *Indeterminate relationships =* ⌐⌐⌐
□ **Boldface** *= known direct relationship to Frederick Douglass*
□ *[number] indicates successive person with same name*

2. Family Tree (children and grandchildren of Betsey Bailey)

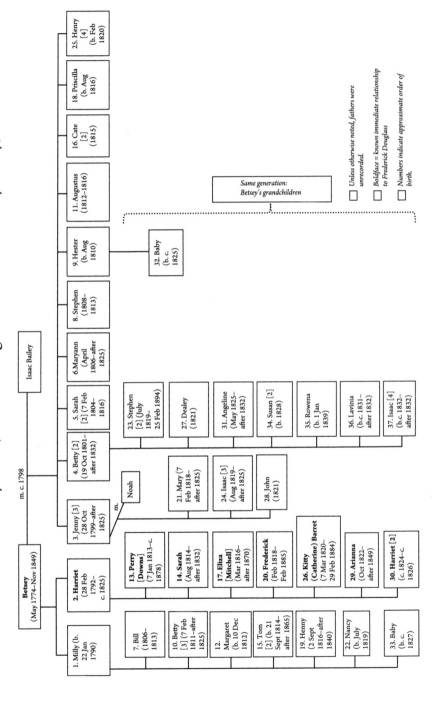

Isaac Bailey   m. c. 1798   Betsey (May 1774–Nov 1849)

1. Milly (b. 22 Jan 1790)

2. Harriet (28 Feb 1792– c. 1825)

3. Jenny [3] (28 Oct 1799–after 1825)   m. Noah

4. Betty [2] (19 Oct 1801– after 1832)

5. Sarah [2] (7 Feb 1804– 1816)

6. Maryann (April 1806–after 1825)

8. Stephen (1808– 1813)

9. Hester (b. Aug 1810)

11. Augustus (1812–1816)

16. Cate [2] (1815)

18. Priscilla (b. Aug 1816)

25. Henry [4] (b. Feb 1820)

7. Bill (1806– 1813)

13. Perry [Downs] (7 Jan 1813–c. 1878)

10. Betty [3] (7 Feb 1811–after 1825)

12. Margaret (b. 10 Dec 1812)

14. Sarah (Aug 1814– after 1832)

15. Tom [2] (b. 21 Sept 1814– after 1865)

17. Eliza [Mitchell] (Mar 1816– after 1870)

19. Henny (2 Sept 1816–after 1840)

20. Frederick (Feb 1818– Feb 1885)

21. Mary (7 Feb 1818– after 1825)

22. Nancy (b. July 1819)

23. Stephen [2] (July 1819– 25 Feb 1894)

24. Isaac [3] (Aug 1819– after 1825)

26. Kitty (Catherine) Barret (7 Mar 1820– 29 Feb 1884)

27. Dealey (1821)

28. John (1821)

29. Arianna (Oct 1822– after 1849)

30. Harriet [2] (c. 1824– 1826)

31. Angeline (May 1825– after 1832)

32. Baby (b. c. 1825)

33. Baby (b. c. 1827)

34. Susan [2] (b. 1828)

35. Rowena (b. 1 Jan 1839)

36. Lavinia (b.c. 1831– after 1832)

37. Isaac [4] (b.c. 1832– after 1832)

Same generation: Betsey's grandchildren

☐ Unless otherwise noted, fathers were unrecorded.

☐ Boldface = known immediate relationship to Frederick Douglass

☐ Numbers indicate approximate order of birth.

3. Family Tree (Harriet's children and grandchildren)

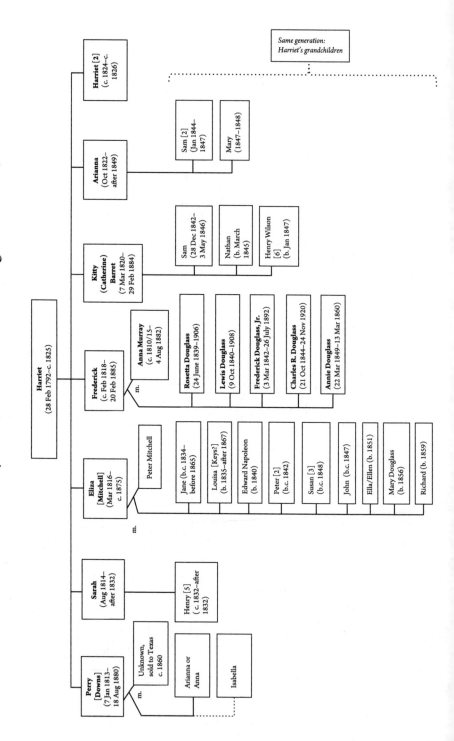

Harriet
(28 Feb 1792–c. 1825)

Harriet [2]
(c. 1824–c. 1826)

Arianna
(Oct 1822–after 1849)

Sam [2]
(Jan 1844–1847)

Mary
(1847–1848)

Kitty (Catherine) Barret
(7 Mar 1820–29 Feb 1884)

Sam
(28 Dec 1842–3 May 1846)

Nathan
(b. March 1845)

Henry Wilson [6]
(b. Jan 1847)

Frederick
(c. Feb 1818–20 Feb 1885)

m.

Anna Murray
(c. 1810/15–4 Aug 1882)

Rosetta Douglass
(24 June 1839–1906)

Lewis Douglass
(9 Oct 1840–1908)

Frederick Douglass, Jr.
(3 Mar 1842–26 July 1892)

Charles R. Douglass
(21 Oct 1844–24 Nov 1920)

Annie Douglass
(22 Mar 1849–13 Mar 1860)

Eliza [Mitchell]
(Mar 1816–c. 1875)

m.

Peter Mitchell

Jane (b.c. 1834–before 1865)

Louisa [Keys?]
(b. 1835–after 1867)

Edward Napoleon
(b. 1840)

Peter [2]
(b.c. 1842)

Susan [3]
(b.c. 1848)

John (b.c. 1847)

Ella/Ellen (b. 1851)

Mary Douglass
(b. 1856)

Richard (b. 1859)

Sarah
(Aug 1814–after 1832)

Henry [5]
(c. 1832–after 1832)

Perry [Downs]
(7 Jan 1813–18 Aug 1880)

m.

Unknown, sold to Texas
c. 1860

Arianna or Anna

Isabella

Same generation: Harriet's grandchildren

4. Family Tree (Anthonys and Aulds)

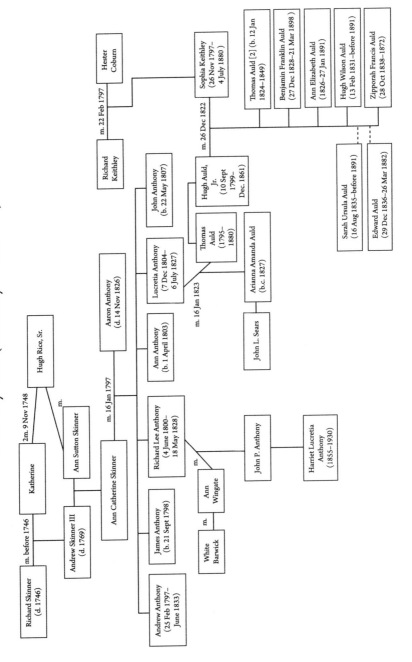

5. Family Tree (children and grandchildren of Frederick and Anna Douglass)

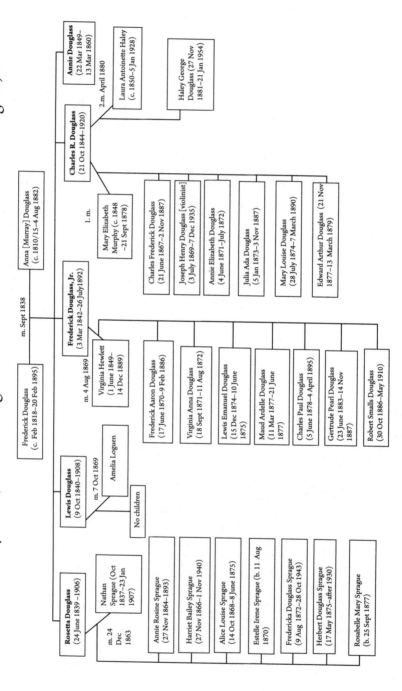

ABBREVIATIONS USED IN NOTES

People

Note: Brackets distinguish women's names before or after marriage, depending on when they wrote the document in question and how they constructed their names after marriage.

AKP	Amy Kirby Post
AK[F] or AKF	Abby Kelley [Foster] or Abby Kelley Foster
AM[D] or A[M]D	Anna Murray, Anna [Murray] Douglass
CRD	Charles Remond Douglass
ECS	Elizabeth Cady Stanton
FD	Frederick Douglass
FDjr	Frederick Douglass Jr.
GS	Gerrit Smith
HB/RCA	Harriet Bailey / Ruth Cox Adams
HP[D] or H[P]D	Helen Pitts [Douglass] or Helen [Pitts] Douglass
IBW[-B] or IBW-B	Ida B. Wells [-Barnets] or Ida B. Wells-Barnets
JG[C] or JGC	Julia Griffiths [Crofts] or Julia Griffiths Crofts
LA[G] or LAG	Ludmilla Assing [Grimalli] or Ludmilla Assing Grimalli
LHD	Lewis Henry Douglass
MJG	Matilda Joslyn Gage
MWC	Maria Weston Chapman
MWG	Martha W. Greene
OA	Ottilie Assing

RD[S] or RDS	Rosetta Douglass [Sprague] or Rosetta Douglass Sprague
RDW	Richard D. Webb
SBA	Susan B. Anthony
SHG	Sydney Howard Gay
SRK	Sylvester Rosa Koehler
WCN	William C. Nell
WLG	William Lloyd Garrison

Organizations

AAS	American Anti-Slavery Society
AMA	American Missionary Association
AERA	American Equal Rights Association
AWSA	American Woman Suffrage Association
FDMHA	Frederick Douglass Memorial and Historical Association
NAWSA	National American Woman Suffrage Association
NCWA	National Colored Women's Association
NWSA	National Woman Suffrage Association
RLAS	Rochester Ladies' Anti-Slavery Society and Sewing Circle

Repositories and Collections

AQM	American Antiquarian Society, Worcester, Mass.
AKFP	Abby Kelley Foster Papers
BPL	Boston Public Library
ASC	Anti-Slavery Society Collection
BJK	Biblioteka Jagiellonian, Krakow, Poland
VC	Varnhagen von Ense Collection
DCAWR	Archives of American Art, Washington, DC
DHU-MS	Moorland-Spingarn Research Center, Howard University
FDC	Frederick Douglass Collection
DLC	Library of Congress
FDP	Frederick Douglass Papers. Multiple repositories have collections with this name. Unless otherwise specified, all citations from the FDP collection at the Library of Congress (DLC) come from the General Correspondence series.
FDMHAR	Frederick Douglass Memorial and Historical Association Records

LDA	Amistad Research Center, Tulane University
AMAA	American Missionary Association Archives
MdAA	Hall of Records Commission, Maryland State Archives
MdHi	Maryland Historical Society
MH-H	Houghton Library, Harvard University
MiU-C	William C. Clements Library, University of Michigan, Ann Arbor
RLASP	Rochester Ladies' Anti-Slavery Society Papers
NARA	National Archives and Records Administration
NbHi	Nebraska State Historical Society, Lincoln
NRU	University of Rochester, Rush Rhees Library
IAKPFP	Post Family Papers
PFP	Porter Family Papers
NSyU	Bird Library, University of Syracuse
GSP	Gerrit Smith Papers
SRKP	Sylvester Rosa Koehler Papers
PSC-Hi	Friends Historical Society, Swarthmore College
SNN	Sophia Smith Collection, Smith College
GFP	Garrison Family Papers
ZCU	Butler Library, Columbia University
SHGP	Sydney Howard Gay Papers

Frequently cited texts

DM	*Douglass' Monthly.* Rochester, N.Y., 1856–1863.
ECS/SBAP	*Selected Papers of Elizabeth Cady Stanton and Susan B. Anthony.* 6 vols. Edited by Ann D. Gordon, *et al.* New Brunswick, N.J.: Rutgers University Press, 1997–2013.
FDP	*Frederick Douglass' Paper.* Rochester, N.Y., 1851–1860.
FDWR	*Frederick Douglass on Women's Rights.* Edited by Philip S. Foner. New York: Da Capo Press, 1992. Originally published in 1976.
L&T	*Life and Times of Frederick Douglass.* Edited by John R. McKivigan, *et al.* Frederick Douglass Papers: Series 2, Autobiographical Writings. 1892; New Haven, Conn.: Yale University Press, 2012.
LACL	*Love across Color Lines: Ottilie Assing and Frederick Douglass,* by Maria Diedrich. New York: Hill and Wang, 1999.
Lib.	*Liberator,* Boston, Mass.

MBMF   Frederick Douglass. *My Bondage and My Freedom.* 1855.
                Edited by John W. Blassingame, John R. McKivigan,
                and Peter P. Hinks. Frederick Douglass Papers: Series
                2, Autobiographical Writings. New Haven, Conn.: Yale
                University Press, 2003.

MMAIRH   *My Mother as I Recall Her.* By Rosetta Douglass Sprague.
                Washington, DC, 1900. Family Papers, FDP, DLC.

Narr.   Frederick Douglass. *Narrative of the Life of Frederick Douglass.*
                Edited by John W. Blassingame, John R. McKivigan,
                and Peter P. Hinks Frederick Douglass Papers: Series 2,
                Autobiographical Writings. 1845; New Haven, Conn.: Yale
                University Press, 2001.

NS   *North Star,* Rochester, N.Y., 1847–1851.

NYT   *New York Times*

NYTrib   *New York Tribune*

Speeches   Frederick Douglass. *Speeches, Debates, and Interviews.* 5 vols.
                Edited by John Blassingame, *et al.* Frederick Douglass
                Papers, Series 1. New Haven, Conn.: Yale University Press,
                1979–1992.

YFD   *Young Frederick Douglass,* by Dickson Preston.
                Baltimore: Johns Hopkins University Press, 1980.

NOTES

Introduction

1. FD, *Speeches*, 4:181.
2. The first generation of biographies about Douglass includes Frederick May Holland, *Frederick Douglass: The Colored Orator* (New York, 1891); James M. Gregory, *Frederick Douglass, the Orator* (Springfield, Mass., 1893); Charles Chesnutt, *Frederick Douglass* (Boston, 1899). The second generation includes Benjamin Quarles, *Frederick Douglass* (1948, 1968; New York: Atheneum, 1976), which was the first scholarly treatment of Douglass's life; Philip S. Foner, *Frederick Douglass: A Biography* (1950, 1964; New York: Citadel Press, 1969).
3. Biographies from the 1980s through the 2010s influenced by developments in African American history and, to a much lesser degree, women's history included Nathan Irvin Huggins, *Slave and Citizen: The Life of Frederick Douglass* (Boston: Little Brown, 1980); William S. McFeely, *Frederick Douglass* (New York: W. W. Norton, 1991). Although the following works are not traditional biographies covering Douglass's life from birth to death, they fall into the category of biography and reflect the trend to focus on an aspect of his life rather than the whole: Dickson J. Preston, *Young Frederick Douglass: The Maryland Years* (Baltimore: Johns Hopkins University Press, 1980) [hereafter cited as Preston, *YFD*]; Waldo Martin Jr., *The Mind of Frederick Douglass* (Chapel Hill: University of North Carolina Press, 1984); David Blight, *Frederick Douglass' Civil War: Keeping Faith in Jubilee* (Baton Rouge: Lousiana University Press, 1989); Maria Diedrich, *Love across Color Lines: Ottilie Assing and Frederick Douglass* (New York: Hill and Wang, 1999) [hereafter cited as Diedrich, *LACL*]; James Oakes, *The Radical and the Republican: Frederick Douglass, Abraham Lincoln, and the Triumph of Antislavery Politics* (New York: W. W. Norton, 2008); John Stauffer, *Giants: The Parallel Lives of Frederick Douglass and Abraham Lincoln* (New York: Twelve, 2008); Laurence Fenton, *Frederick Douglass in Ireland: The Black O'Connell* (Cork, Ireland: Collins, 2014); Tom Chaffin, *Giant's Causeway: Frederick Douglass's Irish Odyssey and the Making of an American Visionary* (Charlottesville: University of Virginia Press, 2014); Robert S. Levine, *The Lives of Frederick Douglass* (Cambridge, Mass.: Harvard University Press, 2016). As of this writing, David Blight is finishing a biography that will return to the full treatment of Douglass's life. Our correspondence has proved invaluable in working through questions that have arisen in this book.
4. Fawn Brodie's controversial biography of Thomas Jefferson was, in effect, a biography of the Sage of Monticello from the perspective of women that lay bare his misogyny. Jon Kukla and Virginia Scharff have drawn on intervening decades of research into gender to offer more nuanced versions of Jefferson; but ultimately they confirm Brodie's instincts. Annette Gordon-Reed, in researching Sally Hemings's story, found an extensive family history that also yielded a picture of Thomas Jefferson as a slave master. Cynthia Kierner gave a portrait of

him as a patriarch in her biography of his daughter, Martha Jefferson Randolph. John Matteson also made the father-daughter relationship the subject of his biography of Louisa May and Bronson Alcott. This method of biography through relationships has also led to insightful work on, among others, Dred Scott's wife, the marriages of Andrew and Rachel Jackson and Elizabeth Cady and Henry Stanton, and the women surrounding Wolfgang Amadeus Mozart, Elizabeth I, Charles Dickens, and John Brown. Fawn Brodie, *Thomas Jefferson: An Intimate History* (1974; repr. New York: Bantam Books, 1985); Jon Kukla, *Mr. Jefferson's Women* (New York: Vintage, 2008); Virginia Scharff, *The Women Jefferson Loved* (New York: Harper, 2010); Annette Gordon-Reed, *The Hemingses of Monticello: An American Family* (New York: W. W. Norton, 2008); Cynthia Kierner, *Martha Jefferson Randolph, Daughter of Monticello: Her Life and Times* (Chapel Hill: University of North Carolina Press, 2012); John Matteson, *Eden's Outcasts: The Story of Louisa May Alcott and Her Father* (New York: W. W. Norton, 2007); Lea VanderVelde, *Mrs. Dred Scott: A Life on Slavery's Frontier* (New York: Oxford University Press, 2009); Patricia Brady, *A Being So Gentle: The Frontier Love Story of Rachel and Andrew Jackson* (New York: Palgrave Macmillan, 2011); Linda Frank, *An Uncommon Union: Henry B. Stanton and the Emancipation of Elizabeth Cady Stanton* (Auburn, N.Y.: Upstate N.Y. History, 2016); Jane Glover, *Mozart's Women: His Family, His Friends, His Music* (New York: HarperCollins, 2006); Tracy Borman, *Elizabeth's Women: Friends, Rivals, and Foes Who Shaped the Virgin Queen* (New York: Bantam, 2009); Robert Garnett, *Charles Dickens in Love* (New York: Pegasus, 2012); Anne Isba, *Dickens's Women: His Life and Loves* (London: Continuum, 2011); Bonnie Laughlin-Schultz, *The Tie That Bound Us: The Women of John Brown's Family and the Legacy of Radical Abolitionism* (Ithaca, N.Y.: Cornell University Press, 2013).

5. Preston, *YFD*; McFeely, *Frederick Douglass*; Diedrich, *LACL*. See Thomas Foster, *Sex and the Founding Fathers: The American Quest for a Relatable Past* (Philadelphia: Temple University Press, 2014) for a recent discussion of the careless projection of today's sexuality onto the past. See John D'Emilio and Estelle B. Freedman, *Intimate Matters: A History of Sexuality in America*, 3rd ed. (1988; Chicago: University of Chicago Press, 2012) for the historical context of sexual behavior.

6. I began this study accepting Diedrich's understanding of a sexual affair between Assing and Douglass with few questions beyond the method of Assing's birth control. I soon found significant discrepancies between Diedrich's text and the documents that she cited, and I discovered questions that she did not ask that, once answered, disproved much of her speculation. No longer trusting Diedrich's interpretation, I realized that I would have to look at the evidence myself. The Assing letters used by Diedrich are largely housed in two repositories, the Sylvester Rosa Koehler Collection at the Archives of American Art and the Varnhagen von Ense Collection at the Jagellonian Library in Krakow, Poland. Unfortunately, Assing wrote in Kurrentschrift, a nineteenth-century German script that fell out of use by the middle of the twentieth century. This required not only a translator, but a translator who specialized in nineteenth-century documents. After procuring copies from the collection, I used a small grant from the Le Moyne College Research and Development Committee to have key letters translated by Heike Polster. I shared these with David Blight, who was generously willing to draw upon funds from the Gilder Lehrman Institute of American History to hire Katherina Schmidt to translate the entire set. Schmidt is now pursuing her own research on Assing, and her insights have both confirmed and enhanced some of my own interpretations. In order to get a stronger sense of Assing's voice and intent, I compared these two sets of translations, as well as passages appearing in Diedrich, McFeely, and an article by von Ense's biographer Terry Pickett. The fact that both Polster and Schmidt found much to admire in Assing suggests that she possessed striking qualities independent of Douglass that may not come through this narrative. McFeely, *Frederick Douglass*; Diedrich, *LACL*; T. H. Pickett, "The Friendship of Frederick Douglass with the German, Ottilie Assing," *Georgia Historical Quarterly* 72, 1 (1989): 88–105.

7. Erica Ball, *To Live an Antislavery Life: Personal Politics an the Antebellum Black Middle Class* (Athens: University of Georgia Press, 2012); Chris Dixon, *Perfecting the Family: Antislavery Marriages in Nineteenth-Century America* (Amherst: University of Massachusetts Press, 1997);

Michael Pierson, *Free Hearts, Free Homes: Gender and Antislavery American Politics* (Chapel Hill: University of North Carolina Press, 2003).
8. Cassandra Good, *Founding Friendships: Friendship between Men and Women in the Early American Republic* (New York: Oxford University Press, 2015); Martha Hodes, *White Women, Black Men: Illicit Sex in the 19th-Century South* (New Haven, Conn.: Yale University Press, 1997); Amber Moulton, *The Fight for Interracial Marriage Rights in Antebellum Massachusetts* (Cambridge, Mass.: Harvard University Press, 2015).
9. FD, *Life and Times of Frederick Douglass*, ed. John McKivigan, *et al.* (1892; New Haven, Conn.: Yale University Press, 2012), 367 [hereafter cited as FD, *L&T*].

Chapter 1

1. FD, *Narrative of the Life of Frederick Douglass*, ed. John Blassingame, *et al.* (1845; repr. New Haven, Conn.: Yale University Press, 2001), 13, 30–31 [hereafter cited as FD, *Narr.*]; FD, *My Bondage and My Freedom*, ed. John Blassingame, *et al.* (1855; New Haven, Conn.: Yale University Press, 2003), 36, 81, 87 [hereafter cited as FD, *MBMF*]; Aaron Anthony, "Negroes ages as follows," "My Black People ages," Ledger B, Dodge Collection, MdAA.
2. Although the concept of childhood changes drastically according to historical context, research on the experience of enslaved children has grown in the past two decades. Two important works that have informed this discussion of Douglass's childhood are Wilma King, *Stolen Childhood: Slave Youth in Nineteenth-Century America* (Bloomington: Indiana University Press, 1995) and Marie Jenkins Schwartz, *Born in Bondage: Growing up Enslaved in the Antebellum South* (Cambridge, Mass.: Harvard University Press, 2000); see also Rachael Pasierowka, "Up from Childhood: When African-American Enslaved Children Learned of Their Servile Status," *Slavery and Abolition* (10 April 2015): 1–23.
3. With some exceptions, few Douglass biographers have investigated his childhood beyond his own autobiographies. A notable exception was journalist and Talbot County native Dickson J. Preston. In *Young Frederick Douglass: The Maryland Years*, Preston meticulously searched local records in order to verify and expand on the information contained in the autobiographies. Preston's desire to ground Douglass's story in the records limited the scope of his inquiry to only that which Douglass discussed; but his work has immensely informed and aided later biographers. Preston, *YFD*.
4. Since Jenny and the second infant, Doll, were born a month apart, they were not sisters. Sue and Selah were probably their mothers, but there is no indication of which child belonged to which mother or of the relationship of any of the other children to any of the adults. All information about this group or their relationships with one another begins and ends with mere notation in an inventory conducted in June 1746, when Jenny was six months old. Preston, *YFD*, 3–10.
5. These cousins or siblings included two Hesters, a junior Jenny, Phil, Harry, and Bealy. The family recycled many of the names from earlier generations. Up to and including Douglass's generation, the family tree included two Hesters, two Phils, two Cates and one Kitty, three versions of Bailey (not counting Isaac Bailey, Betsey's free husband), three Susans, three Jennys and one Jane, four versions of Elizabeth (Betty, Betsey, Eliza), four Isaacs (again not counting Isaac Bailey), and no less than nine variations of Henry, including Harry, Henrietta, and Harriet. See Appendix: Family Trees. Preston, *YFD*, 3–10, 205–7.
6. FD, *MBMF*, 22.
7. The pattern of work and childcare has been noted by the historians of slave life and matches that of both Betsey's life in the 1820s and the slave management of Aaron Anthony. Douglass's perception of Betsey's age as very old came both from his own perspective as a six-year-old and from the short life expectancy of most slaves, which was approximately forty years, a time at which many slave women also entered menopause. Aaron Anthony, Return Books, 1821–25, Lloyd Papers, Maryland Historical Society; Barbara Jeanne Fields, *Slavery and Freedom on the Middle Ground: Maryland during the Nineteenth Century* (New Haven, Conn.: Yale University Press, 1985), 5; Deborah Gray White, *Ar'n't I a Woman? Female Slaves in the Plantation South* (1985; rev. ed., New York, 1995), 114–16, 126–18; FD, *MBMF*, 22–23; FD, *L&T*, 23–24.

8. Aaron Anthony, Ledger C, Dodge Collection, MdAA; FD, *MBMF*, 22. On slave mid-wives and healers, see Sharla Fett, *Working Cures: Healing, Health, and Power on Southern Slave Plantations* (Chapel Hill: University of North Carolina Press, 2002); Sharla Fett, "Consciousness and Calling: African American Midwives at Work in the Antebellum South," in Edward E. Baptist and Stephanie M. H. Camp, eds., *New Studies in the History of American Slavery* (Athens: University of Georgia Press, 2009), 65–86; Marie Jenkins Schwartz, *Birthing a Slave: Motherhood and Medicine in the Antebellum South* (Cambridge, Mass.: Harvard University Press, 2006); and White, *Ar'n't I a Woman*, 111, 114–15, 129. For slave geographic mobility, see Stephanie M.H. Camp, *Closer to Freedom: Enslaved Women and Everyday Resistance in the Plantation South* (Chapel Hill: University of North Carolina Press, 2004).

9. While Betsey may have learned midwifery from her predecessors, no evidence suggests to whom or if she passed on her own skills. The Anthony account books do not indicate if the births she oversaw were for slaves or white women. Aaron Anthony, Ledgers A and B, Dodge Collection, MdAA; FD, *MBMF*, 22.

10. Historian Dickson J. Preston was the first to point out that Isaac may not have been Douglass's biological grandfather, noting that Bailey did not show up in any records connecting him to Betsey, her children, or the Skinners and Rices until 1797. He also pointed out that the names Isaac and Bailey appear in Betsey's extended family, although he rules out any of those men as the father of her children based on their age and possible consanguinity. Aaron Anthony, "Negroes ages as follows," "My Black People ages," Ledger B, Dodge Collection, MdAA; Preston, *YFD*, 18–19, 205–6.

11. Aaron Anthony, Ledgers A and B, Dodge Collection, MdAA; 1810 U.S. Census, Maryland, Talbot County, 342; Preston, *YFD*, 26; 1800 U.S. Census, Maryland, Talbot County, 90.

12. Betsey's children: Milly (b. January 1790), Harriet (28 February 1792–c. 1825), Jenny (28 October 1799–after 1825), Betty (19 October 1801–after 1832), Sarah (7 February 1804–1816), Maryann (April 1806–after 1825), Stephen (1808–1816), Hester/Esther (August 1810–after 1827), Augustus (1812–1816), Cate (b. 1815), Priscilla (b. August 1816), and Henry (b. February 1820). Jenny ran away and Mary Ann was sold in 1825. Betty was sold in 1832. Sarah, Augustus, and Stephen, and perhaps the infant Cate appear to have died from a related illness since all were of an age to be living in their mother's cabin. The spacings used to calculate this average are 12 months between Jenny and Betty, 28 months between Betty and Sarah, 26 months between Sarah and Maryann, 18 months between Maryann and Stephen, 24 months between Stephen and Hester, 36 between Hester and Augustus, 24 between Augustus and Cate, 20 between Cate and Priscilla, and 42 between Priscilla and Henry. The longest gap was the 42 months between Priscilla and Henry, who each arrived about the time Betsey would have entered menopause, the shortest was 12 months between Jenny and Betty, and the median was the 24 months between both Stephen and Hester and Hester and Augustus. Years with uncertain months were counted as a full 12 months. The last name Bailey attached to Betsey and some of her direct descendants. Dickson J. Preston notes that varia-tions on the name Bailey appear among their kin, and William McFeely ponders a possible African source. On Betsey's side of Frederick's extended family, however, the name attached to a different branch extending from the original slaves on the Skinner plantation. More likely, because the last name of his grandmother's husband was Bailey and because Douglass had adopted the American norm of passing father's names to children, the name came from Isaac. Furthermore, by adopting his grandfather's last name, Douglass granted both his mother and grandmother legitimacy in practice, if not in law, since he could not grant the same for him-self. That may also account for his careful inclusion of Isaac Bailey, always connected with Betsey, in *MBMF*, despite knowing almost nothing about Isaac's daily life but many details of Betsey's. Aaron Anthony, "Negros ages as follows," "My Black People ages," Ledger B. Dodge Collection, MdAA; Preston, *YFD*, 3–10, 205–6; McFeely, *Frederick Douglass*, 5.

13. FD, *Narr.*, 13; FD, *MBMF*, 24; FD, *L&T*, 23–25.

14. FD, *MBMF*, 24; FD, *L&T*, 24; Aaron Anthony, Ledgers A, B, C, Nimrod Barwick Daybook, Dodge Collection, MdAA.

15. FD, *MBMF*, 23; "Negros ages as follows," "My Black People ages," Aaron Anthony, Ledger B, Dodge Collection, MdAA; Preston, *YFD*, 205–6.

16. FD, *MBMF*, 23, 24; FD, *L&T*, 24.

17. FD, *Narr.*, 13; Aaron Anthony, Return Books, 1821–25, Lloyd Papers, Maryland Historical Society.

18. Thomas Auld's younger sister, born in 1789, was named Arian and his daughter, born in 1726 or 1727, was named Arianna Amanda, suggesting a connection between Harriet and Thomas and Lucretia Auld. FD, *MBMF*, 28, 30; Emerson B. Roberts, "A Visitation of Western Talbot: Auld of Dover Point," *Maryland Genealogies*, 2 vols. (1980; Baltimore: Genealogical Publishing Co., 1997), 1:24–27.

19. Of Betsey's other children, Sarah, Stephen, and Augustus had died in 1816, and Cate died the same year she was born, 1815. "Negros ages as follows," "My Black People ages," Aaron Anthony, Ledger B, Dodge Collection, MdAA; 1820 U.S. Census, Maryland, Talbot County, District 4, 49; Preston, *YFD*, 205–6.

20. In 1825, Anthony sold Betsey's daughter Maryann and grandchildren Betty, Mary, and Isaac. The latter two children may have been included as retaliation for the escape of their parents, Jenny and Noah, weeks earlier; and the impending sale may have motivated the flight. In 1827, the death of Aaron Anthony led to the division of the Baileys among Anthony's three children, Lucretia, Richard, and Andrew. The death of Andrew in 1828 and Richard in 1832 led to further division; and in the 1832 division, Betsey's daughter Betty; her grandchildren by Betty, Angeline, Lavinia, and Isaac (the third of that name); her granddaughter by Harriet, Sarah; and her only great-grandchild, Sarah's son, Henry (also the third of that name) were all sold. Thus, between 1825 and 1832, a period of a decade, the Bailey family had experienced five divisions. "Talbot Co. Distributions," Dodge Collection, MdAA; Preston, *YFD*, 64–65, 90–91, 206–7.

21. Masters willingly hired out pregnant women in order to defray the cost of clothing and feeding mother and child. While some studies indicate that pregnancy or infants limited the ease of their hire, others have pointed out that employers continued to solicit their use, although sometimes the master paid the employer to hire the slave. In all cases, hiring, especially for long periods of time, affected families in ways similar to sales. Aaron Anthony, Ledger B, "Negros ages as follows," "My Black People ages," Dodge Collection, MdAA; FD, *MBMF*, 32; Preston, *YFD*, 21; Jonathan D. Martin, *Divided Mastery: Slave Hiring in the American South* (Cambridge, Mass.: Harvard University Press, 2009), 58; Schwartz, *Born in Bondage*, 158–59, 170–71; John J. Zaborney, *Slaves for Hire: Renting Enslaved Laborers in Antebellum Virginia* (Baton Rouge: Louisiana State University Press, 2012), 29, 34–36.

22. Aaron Anthony, Ledgers A, B, C, Dodge Collection, MdAA; Zaborney, *Slaves for Hire*, 4.

23. FD, *L&T*, 12; FD, *MBMF*, 34.

24. If this scenario in any way resembled the actual events, then Jenny too may have learned to read. If Jenny could read, her ability to do so could have played a role in her own escape from slavery, just as Frederick's had when he forged passes during his first attempt. FD, *Narr.*, 35, 62; Aaron Anthony, Ledgers A, B, C, Dodge Collection, MdAA; Donald G. Mathews, "The Methodist Mission to the Slaves, 1829-44," *Journal of American History* 51, 4 (March 1965): 615–31.

25. The average age for slave women to begin families was age 20.6 years, while the average age for menarche was 15. Betsey began having children at fifteen, Milly at sixteen, Jenny at nineteen, Betty at eighteen, and Hester at sixteen. Aaron Anthony, "Negroes ages as follows," "My Black People ages," Ledger B, Dodge Collection, MdAA; James Trussell and Richard Steckel, "The Age of Slaves at Menarche and Their First Birth," *Journal of Interdisciplinary History* 8, 3 (Winter 1978): 477–505; Schwartz, *Born in Bondage*, 188–89.

26. FD, *Narr.*, 13; FD, *MBMF*, 31, 34; FD, *L&T*, 24.

27. Dickson J Preston pushed aside speculation on the identity of Douglass's father as unknowable, instead finding more importance in Anthony as a father figure. William McFeely considered alternate candidates for Douglass's father and put forth Thomas Auld, but that hypothesis falls apart when he argues that Auld would have met Harriet Bailey and her mother at Wye House. Neither was ever recorded as living there; and, even if Auld had met the two women while they had business at Wye House, his own work as a schooner captain took him along the Chesapeake, and he had little reason to visit the opposite side of the county consistently enough to have fathered seven children at regular intervals. Furthermore, he did not appear at

the Anthony House until he began boarding there in 1823, well after Douglass's birth. Aaron Anthony, Ledger Book B, Dodge Collection, MdAA; Preston, *YFD*, 23; McFeely, *Frederick Douglass*, 8, 13–14, 21.

28. In later years, when Frederick and his son Lewis returned separately to Talbot County and interviewed both black and white residents who remembered the period from his childhood, Douglass did not publicly attempt to verify the identity of his father, nor did he reveal any conversations with his siblings about their paternity, although they did give him information about the extended members of their family. LHD to FD, Ferry Neck [Md.], 9 June 1865, FDC, DHU-MS; *New York Times*, 20 June 1877; FD, *MBMF*, 36.

29. FD, *MBMF*, 52; FD, *Narr.*, 15–16; FD, *L&T*, 24; Harriet A. Jacobs, *Incidents in the Life of a Slave Girl, Written by Herself*, ed. Jean Fagan Yellin (1861; Cambridge, Mass.: Harvard University Press, 2000), 27; Thelma Jennings, "'Us Colored Women Had to Go through a Plenty:' Sexual Exploitation of African-American Slave Women," *Journal of Women's History* 1, 3 (Winter 1990), 45–74; Margaret Washington, "'From Motives of Delicacy:' Sexuality and Morality in the Narratives of Sojourner Truth and Harriet Jacobs," *Journal of African American History* 92, 1 (Winter 2007): 57–73.

30. During that same period, 1824–1826, Jenny and her husband, Noah, ran away, and their children were sold south, along with their aunt Maryann. "Account of Sales and Inventories," Dodge Collection, MdAA; Preston, *YFD*, 206–7.

31. Jacobs, *Incidents*, 54–62, 77, 91; Drew Gilpin Faust, *Design for Mastery: James Henry Hammond and the Old South* (Baton Rouge: Louisiana State University Press, 1982), 87; Gordon-Reed, *Hemingses of Monticello*, 31, 352.

32. FD, *MBMF*, 35. The relationship of women to slaveholding and management has been the focus of study for decades. Discussion of this subject in this chapter has been informed by Anne Firor Scott, *The Southern Lady: From Pedestal to Politics, 1830-1930* (1970; Charlottesville: University Press of Virginia, 1995); Catherine Clinton, *The Plantation Mistress: Woman's World in the Old South* (New York: Pantheon, 1982); Elizabeth Fox-Genovese, *Within the Plantation Household: Black and White Women of the Old South* (Chapel Hill: University of North Carolina Press, 1988); Kirsten E. Wood, *Masterful Women: Slaveholding Widows from the American Revolution through the Civil War* (Chapel Hill: University of North Carolina Press, 2004); Anya Jabour, *Scarlett's Sisters: Young Women in the Old South* (Chapel Hill: University of North Carolina Press, 2007); Thavolia Glymph, *Out of the House of Bondage: The Transformation of the Plantation Household* (New York: Cambridge University Press, 2008).

33. Preston, *YFD*, 29.

34. Aaron Anthony, "Negroes ages as follows," "My Black People ages," Ledger B, Dodge Collection, MdAA.

35. 1810 U.S. Census, Maryland, Caroline County, 194, 195, 214; Aaron Anthony, Ledger B, Nimrod Barwick Daybook, 1815–16, Harriet Anthony's annotations in *MBMF*, 178, Dodge Collections, MdAA; Perry Downs to FD, Millican, Tex., 21 February 1867, FDC, DHU-MS.

36. Marie Jenkins Schwartz concluded, "Few slave mothers abandoned their children, no matter what the circumstances of their birth." Jeff Forret, however, has found evidence that "In scattered infanticide cases, Virginia bondwomen clearly indicated that white paternity was a source of shame." Nonetheless, historians have yet to plumb the depths of mothers' emotional reactions to their children from rape. The late-night visit incident appeared only in *My Bondage and My Freedom*. In an effort to elaborate on that already dramatic scene, biographers have embellished it by adding that Harriet brought the cake with her, that she brought the cake expressly for Douglass, that the cake was for his birthday, and that she baked the cake right there at that moment. Douglass, however, never stated that his mother brought or made the cake. Given that the scene occurred in the kitchen, she more likely took a cake already baked by Katy. FD, *MBMF*, 32, 34; Schwartz, *Born in Bondage*, 45–46; White, *Ar'n't I a Woman?*, 87–89; McFeely, *Frederick Douglass*, 19; Preston, *YFD*, 63; Foner, *Frederick Douglass: A Biography*, 15; Jeff Forret, *Slave Against Slave: Plantation Violence in the Old South* (Baton Rouge: Louisana State University Press, 2015), 377.

37. FD, *MBMF*, 32.

38. Biographer William McFeely speculated that Frederick had concluded that "his mother had not appreciated him as she should have." FD, *Narr.*, 13; *Easton Gazette*, 1 November 1825; McFeely, *Frederick Douglass*, 7.

39. The baby, Harriet, appeared in the December 1826 inventory of Anthony's slaves. She did not appear in the division of slaves, dated October 1827. In 1826, she was listed as being a year old and with a value of $10, half that of another child her age, suggesting that she was sickly and died in the ensuing months. Decades later, a woman about her age, called Harriet Bailey, lived with Douglass's family in Lynn. McFeely assumed that the Lynn Harriet was Douglass's sister, but later research proved that she was actually the fugitive slave Ruth Cox, living under that assumed name. FD, *Narr.*, 14; "Account of Sales and Inventories," Dodge Collection, MdAA; Letters from FD to Harriet Bailey / Ruth Cox Adams in Addition II, FDP, DLC; FD, *Correspondence*, Frederick Douglass Papers, Series Three, ed. John R. McKivigan (New Haven, Conn.: Yale University Press, 2009), 1:157–58n3; Leigh Fought, "Lost 'Sister,' Lost Connections: The Private and Public Dissonance between Frederick Douglass and Harriet Adams" (unpublished paper).

40. FD, *MBMF*, 42–44, 74–75.

41. Based on the ages of the Anthony slave children and on the cycles of their childhood, the other children were probably his siblings Perry, Eliza, and Sarah; his first cousins Tom, Henny, Nancy, and Mary; his aunt Priscilla; and Katy's three sons. His uncle Henry, cousins Nancy and Isaac, and sister Kitty may have also joined them during his time in Katy's kitchen, as the older ones departed. Aaron Anthony's great-granddaughter suggested that Katy should receive no blame for the poor rations even as she insisted that the rations were not meager. "Negros ages as follows," "My Black People ages," and Harriet Anthony's annotations in *MBMF*, Dodge Collections, MdAA; FD, *MBMF*, 42–43, 44, 74–75.

42. Harriet Anthony's annotations in *MBMF*, 75, Dodge Collections, MdAA; FD, *MBMF*, 42–44. The South and slavery have proven to be ripe ground for the study of violence, mostly focusing on its role in the preservation of white honor and mastery of slaves. Jeff Forret, however, has begun to explore the phenomena that Douglass describes of violence against the slave community begetting violence within the slave community. Forret, *Slave Against Slave*.

43. FD, *MBMF*, 75–76.

44. Sophia Auld was married to Hugh Auld, the brother of Thomas Auld, Lucretia's husband. Aaron Anthony, Ledger B, Dodge Collections, MdAA; Dodd, Jordan, comp. *Maryland Marriages, 1655-1850* [database online] (Provo, UT: Ancestry.com Operations, 2004); Clinton, *Plantation Mistress*, 16–36; Jabour, *Scarlett's Sisters*, 96–99.

45. FD, *MBMF*, 63, 79, 83.

46. In the autobiographies, Douglass was clear that he had been in Talbot County for approximately a month. The documents listing the value and division, however, carry dates ten months apart. Biographers have assumed that he remained in Talbot County during that time, an assumption that Douglass made more perplexing by implying, on the one hand, that he saw Lucretia during this time while also relating that he did not hear of her death, which occurred 6 July 1827, until later. More likely, he arrived for the valuation at the end of 1826. Division did not require his presence unless he fell to a new master who assigned him somewhere other than the Auld house in Baltimore; or, the division could have taken place as he led readers to infer, and the document was not drawn up until months later. Douglass himself was valued at $110; Betsey, at age 53, was valued at $20. FD, *MBMF*, 99–100; Aaron Anthony, Return Books, 1821-25, Lloyd Papers, MdHi; Harriet Anthony's annotations in *MBMF*, 173; "Account of Sales and Inventories for 1827," 19 December 1826, "Talbot County Distributions," 27 September 1827, Dodge Collection, MdAA; Lucretia P. Anthony headstone, Mount Olivet Cemetery, St. Michaels, Talbot Co., Maryland.

47. Perry, although on the valuation list, did not appear on the distribution list. In 1867, he sent a letter to Douglass indicating that he had belonged to John Planner Anthony, Andrew's son. John inherited his father's estate on Andrew's death in 1828. Katy, her children, and the members of the family who shared her direct parentage went to Richard Anthony, along with Betsey's children Priscilla and Henry. Richard Anthony died in 1829, leaving his portion of the family up for division and sale. In 1832, Andrew Anthony sold Betsy's daughter Betty, Betty's children Angelina, Lavinia, and Isaac, and Douglass's sister Sarah and her baby Henry.

When Andrew died in 1835, his son, John Planner Anthony, inherited and retained those slaves. Thus, in a single decade, the Bailey family and its kin were sold, divided, or moved five separate times, not to mention hired out and separated from children. Frederick's removal to Baltimore, for all of its benefit, constituted part of these partitions.

48. FD, *Narr.*, 31; FD, *MBMF*, 75, 81–83.
49. FD, *Narr.*, 31.
50. FD, *MBMF*, 83.
51. FD, *MBMF*, 88.
52. FD, *Narr.*, 31; 1820 U.S. Census, Maryland, Talbot Co., St. Michaels, 365; William Herbert Auld, Application, Sons of the American Revolution, 14 September 1951.
53. FD, "The Meaning of July Fourth for the Negro," Rochester, N.Y., 5 July 1852, in *Life and Writings of Frederick Douglass*, ed. Philip S. Foner (1950; New York: International Publishers, 1975), 2:194; 1820 U.S. Census, Maryland, Talbot Co., St. Michaels, 365; 1830 U.S. Census, Maryland, Talbot Co., District 2, 12, 34; 1840 U.S. Census, Maryland, Talbot Co., District 2, 28; FD, *MBMF*, 118; Stephen Deyle, *Carry Me Back: The Domestic Slave Trade in American Life* (New York: Oxford University Press, 2005), 99–100, 315n11.
54. FD, *MBMF*, 82, 88; Matthews, "The Methodist Mission to the Slaves," 615–31.
55. In addition to young Thomas, born 12 January 1824, the children of Sophia and Hugh Auld included Ann Elizabeth, born 16 November 1826; Benjamin Franklin, born 27 December 1828; Hugh Wilson, born 13 February 1831; Sarah Ursula, born 16 August 1835 and died 28 April 1837; and Zipporah Frances, born 28 October 1838. FD, *MBMF*, 88; 1860 U.S. Census, Maryland, Baltimore City, 2nd Ward, 445; 1879 U.S. Census, Baltimore City, 1st Ward, 55; 1880 U.S. Census, Maryland, Baltimore Co., Baltimore, 18; Benjamin F. Auld to FD, Baltimore, MD, 11 September 1891, General Correspondence, FDP, DLC.
56. Douglass wrote that the dispute between the Auld brothers occurred "not long after" Thomas had married Rowena. Rowena and Thomas, however, had been married five years before Frederick returned to Talbot County in his teens. FD, *MBMF*, 104; "Account of Sales and Inventories," Dodge Collection, MdAA.
57. Henny lived in Baltimore with Thomas Auld's sister Sarah Cline, Cline's husband Jacob, and their two children, George and Hugh. The U.S. Census suggests various fates for Henny. Citing the appearance of a Henny Baley in the 1840 U.S. Census for St. Michaels, Dickson Preston believed that Auld had emancipated her, although that Henny Baley was listed as between thirty-six and fifty-four years old, whereas Frederick's sister Henny was twenty-four. Meanwhile, the Clines had with them a slave woman who was between ten and twenty-three. In 1860, James Mitchell, the brother-in-law of Douglass's sister Eliza, was married to a woman named Henny. At age thirty-nine, Henny Mitchell was five years younger than Douglass's cousin. FD, *MBMF*, 115; FD, *L&T*, 79; 1840 U.S. Census, Maryland, Talbot County, District 2, 28; 1840 Census, Maryland, Baltimore City, 8th Ward, 47; 1850 U.S. Census, Maryland, Baltimore, City, 15th Ward, 17; 1860 U.S. Census, Maryland, Talbot County, Bay Hundred District, 236.
58. Recent work on slave disability from historians of slave healthcare, particularly Dea Boster, notes that infirm slaves used their conditions as tools of negotiation. Stephanie Camp cites the case of a Mississippi slave, California, whose situation resembled that of Henny. California was turned out to fend for herself and not only succeeded in living independently but also took an interest in antislavery literature. Although Frederick remained a slave, he himself had the experience of living free from immediate supervision by the Aulds in 1838. Dea Boster, *African American Slavery and Disability: Bodies, Property, and Power in the Antebellum South, 1800-1860* (New York: Routledge, 2013), 100–115; Camp, *Closer to Freedom*, 96–99; Fett, *Working Cures*, 23–26, 132–33.
59. FD, *MBMF*, 89, 93–94, 96, 105, 114.
60. Rowena Hambleton married Thomas Auld in 1828, and a previous child had died in infancy. Rowena died before 1840. Thomas Auld eventually outlived four wives, Lucretia Anthony, Rowena Hambleton, Elizabeth Ball, and Sarah Ellen Baker. "Local Matters, Funeral of an Old Marylander," *Baltimore Sun*, 12 February 1880; 1870 U.S. Census, Maryland, Talbot County, District 2, 54, 55; 1880 U.S. Census, Maryland, Talbot County, District 2, 30.
61. FD, *MBMF*, 107, 108; 1840 U.S. Census, Maryland, Talbot Co., District 2, 28.

62. Preston portrayed Eliza as having taught her brother that "it was better to play dumb than to be defiant." He quoted Eliza, but provided no source for the quotation. FD, *MBMF*, 114; Preston, *YFD*, 108. Douglass's descriptions of the Sabbath school vary among his three auto-biographies. In the *Narrative*, he tells of teaching a single school "at the house of a free colored man" while he worked at the farm of William Freeland in 1836. In subsequent versions, this takes place earlier, before Auld sent him to Covey's farm in 1834, but he also teaches a second school that met "under the trees or elsewhere" and "in the woods behind the barn" while at Freeland's. Once Frederick was sent to Covey's farm, he seems not to have seen his sister again until after the Civil War, but she was a free woman by the time of his return to Baltimore in 1836. Eliza, Peter, and James, however, never learned to read well enough to call themselves literate. In the U.S. Census between 1850 and 1880, the adult Mitchells all identified as unable to read or write. FD, *Narr.*, 59, *MBMF*, 114, 150-51; *L&T*, 87,118-19; 1850 U.S. Census, Maryland, Talbot County, St. Michaels District, 99; 1860 U.S. Census, Maryland, Talbot County, Bay Hundred District, 235, 236; 1870 U.S. Census, Maryland, Talbot County, District 2, 54, 55; 1880 U.S. Census, Maryland, Talbot County, District 2, 30.

63. FD, *MBMF*, 97, 114, 118, 150–51, 159, 178, 182; FD, *L&T*, 154.

64. FD, *MBMF*, 15, 35, 48, 51–52, 54–56, 59, 85–86, 115, 124–25, 147.

65. FD, *MBMF*, 35, 15, 48, 50–51, 54–56, 116, 140; Carol Lasser, "Voyeuristic Abolitionism: Sex, Gender, and Transformation of Antislavery Rhetoric," *Journal of the Early Republic* 28, 1 (Spring 2008): 83–114.

66. Rosetta Douglass Sprague, *My Mother As I Recall Her* (Washington, DC, 1900) 8; Family Papers, FDP, DLC [hereafter cited as RDS, *MMAIRH*].

67. See Fox-Genovese, *Within the Plantation Household*, 308–16; Glymph, *Out of the House of Bondage*.

Chapter 2

1. RDS, *MMAIRH*, 6, 8, 20. Absence of documentation between Anna and Frederick respects nineteenth-century norms of confining women to the private sphere, as well as the common practice by public figures of destroying the records of their private lives, something helped along by a fire that consumed the Douglasses' Rochester home and much of its contents in 1872. In 1900, their daughter Rosetta Douglass Sprague retold and interpreted Anna's story to the Anna Murray Douglass chapter of the Women's Christian Temperance Union, later publishing her speech as *My Mother as I Recall Her*. Most of Frederick's biographers have taken Rosetta's account at face value, forgetting that she wrote her recollections nearly twenty years after Anna's death, basing them on memories of events that had taken place over a half-century earlier, and that it must be read with a view toward her audience, agenda, and own prejudices. Nevertheless, it is the most significant source on Anna Douglass, providing insights into the Douglass household and verifiable clues about her life.

Frederick's biographers, being professional intellectuals themselves, have a difficult time understanding Anna's illiteracy, which they often confuse with lack of intelligence. This bias colors the depictions of her as an unsuitable mate for Frederick. The earliest of these works say very little about Anna beyond noting that she was Frederick's wife. The first modern academic Douglass biographer, Benjamin Quarles, praised Anna's housekeeping skills but described her as "stodgy." He wrote that Douglass "found little mental stimulation in her company" because "she was content to remain put in the low grounds," that "she was totally indifferent to the world of ideas," and that she was socially inept, particularly around white people. Arna Bontemps portrayed her as faithful and long-suffering but consistently referred to her as ugly, unimaginative, and harsh-featured. Dickson J. Preston concluded that Anna "was the practical one of the pair, a few years older than Frederick and much better adjusted to the hard realities of nineteenth century black life," an odd assessment given all that Frederick told of his life as a slave. Nathan Irvin Huggins vaunted Anna as a good housewife but believed that she was "unable to serve his mind and ego" or to "contribute to his intellectual and professional growth." Waldo E. Martin Jr. cited Anna as the prime motivation for Frederick's escape, described the Douglass family life as "close-knit," "traditional," and "warm and loving," and believed Anna was influential in Frederick's woman's rights activism. William McFeely conducted more investigation than others into the information provided by Rosetta Sprague and noted the absence of women in Douglass's autobiographies at places one might expect their appearance. Nevertheless, he also drifted into dubious interpretations about the way Douglass included Anna in those autobiographies and the reasons for their marriage, going so far as to dismiss evidence to bolster his hypothesis. He tended to allow only emotional motivations for all women, and occasionally misread the record. In one particularly unfortunate passage, he insisted that Anna's use of the word "bewitched" meant that Anna literally believed in witchcraft, surmising that "Anna Douglass was trying to hold fast to the man who had led her into a world she could compete in only with her own primal tenacity," and that she "reached into an African past for survival." While he attempts to sympathize with Anna, he tends to place the blame for any unhappiness in the Douglass family squarely upon her "resentful" shoulders. Maria Dietrich, although not strictly a Douglass biographer, focused on Douglass's private life through his alleged affair with Ottilia Assing. She also attempted to sympathize with Anna but implicitly blamed her for the problems in the Douglass family. Diedrich's own authoritative voice sometimes became indistinguishable from Assing's, and her fictional chapter introductions blurred the lines between imagination and scholarship. As a result, she went the furthest in suggesting that Frederick thought that Anna was beneath him, and that he expressed his hatred for her by carrying on a sexual affair in the same house. Quarles, *Frederick Douglass*, 99, 112; Arna Bontemps, *Free at Last: The Life of Frederick Douglass* (New York: Dodd Mead, 1971), 14, 145, 197; Preston, *YFD*, 149, 154; Huggins, *Slave and Citizen*, 12–13, 154; Martin, *Mind of Frederick Douglass*, 15, 137; McFeely, *Frederick Douglass*, 65, 68, 70, 77, 154–55, 218–19, 288, 297; Diedrich, *LACL*, 134–35, 150, 171, 175–87, 194, 226, 273, 306, 366.

2. The 1840 census listed Anna in the age category twenty-four to thirty-six, the same range as her husband, although he was actually twenty-two. If this is accurate, then Anna was born between 1804 and 1816. In 1850, the census placed her age at thirty-five, making her two years older than her husband and born in 1815. Both the New York State census of 1855 and the federal census of 1860 reported that Anna and Frederick were the same age, thirty-eight in 1855 and forty-three in 1860, making 1817 their birth years. The 1870 census had Anna aging fifteen years during the intervening ten, moving her birth back to 1812. The 1880 census, the last before her death, reported her as fifty-five years old, five years younger than her husband and three years younger than she was supposed to have been a decade earlier. According to that census, Anna was born in 1825 and Frederick in 1820. Her death certificate gave her age as sixty-nine in August 1882, which meant she had been born in 1813. The 1827 Baltimore city directory listed a woman named Ann Murray as living on Mercer Street. If this was Anna, and if she did, as her daughter wrote, live "with her parents until she was seventeen," then would have been born about 1810. RDS, *MMAIRH*, 6; FD, *Narr.*, 13; 1840 U.S. Census, Massachusetts, Bristol County, New Bedford, 411; 1850 U.S. Census, New York, Monroe County, Rochester, 7th Ward, 318; 1860 U.S. Census, New York, Monroe County, Rochester, 12th Ward, 124; 1870 U.S. Census, New York, Monroe County, Rochester, 12th Ward, 15; 1880 U.S. Census, District of Columbia, Washington, 7th Enumeration District, 143; "Certificate of Death" for Anna Murray, copy courtesy of John Muller, Washington, DC; *Matchett's Baltimore Directory for 1827* (Baltimore, 1827), 189. One of the younger Murray siblings was probably Charlotte Murray, called "Aunt Lottie" by the Douglass children, who lived with the Douglasses in Rochester in 1850 and was approximately five years younger than Anna. Another was Perry Wilmer, with whom Rosetta boarded in New Jersey in 1862. 1850 U.S. Census, New York, Monroe County, Rochester, Ward 7; A[M]D to HB/RCA, Rochester, 11 March 1851, Addition II, RD[S] to FD, Salem, NJ, 31 August 1862, 24 September 1862, FDP, DLC.

3. Had she been born in 1804, Anna would have been fourteen years older than her husband, well into her thirties at the time of their marriage, and forty-five at the birth of her last child in 1849. A pairing of that age difference and childbearing that late in life would not have been outside of the realm of possibility, but no free black Murrays appeared in the 1810 federal census for Caroline County. That does not rule out the possibility that she had been born earlier. The 1810 census only listed heads of households; if the Murrays lived in someone else's home, then they would have appeared only as marks in the appropriate columns. One free black head of household named Murray appears in the 1810 census for Caroline County: George Murray. And three free black heads of household appear in the 1820 census: Amey Murray,

Dinah Murray and John Murray. No Mary, Bambarra, or any iteration of those names appears in either year. The census of free blacks for Caroline County taken by the Maryland Colonization Society in 1832 disappeared from its papers in the Maryland Historical Society sometime in the mid-twentieth century. A similar list exists for Talbot County in the Maryland State Archives, but it does not include any Murrays that fit the description of anyone in Anna's family. 1810 U.S. Census, Maryland, Caroline County, 195; 1820 U.S. Census, Maryland, Caroline County, 72, 95, 115; "A List of Free Negroes residing in Talbot County Md as returned by the Sheriff in 1832," Talbot County, Court Records, Census of Negroes 1832, MSA Collection Number C1841-1, Hall of Records, Maryland State Archives.

4. According to Rosetta's account, Anna arrived in Baltimore in 1829, went to work for the Montell family for two years, then worked for the Wells family for seven. The Montell family, however, did not arrive in the United States until mid-1832, whereas the Wells family appeared in the census as early as 1830. Thus, Anna either worked for both families for shorter periods of time, or for the Wellses first and then the Montells. RDS, *MMAIRH*, 6; Michael H. Tepper, ed., *Passenger Arrivals at the Port of Baltimore, 1820-1834* (Baltimore: Genealogical Publishing Co., 1982), 465-66; *Matchett's Baltimore Director* (Baltimore, 1833), 133, 190-91; 1830 U.S. Census, Maryland, Baltimore Co., Baltimore, Ward 2, 75-76.

5. Slave importation to the Eastern Shore had declined significantly by the late eighteenth century, when Bambarra Murray would have been born, and most of the slaves imported to Maryland came from the Caribbean. The genealogy compiled by one of Rosetta's daughters contains no more about Anna's ancestry than Rosetta told. Genealogical Notes, Addition I, FDP, DLC.

6. FD, *Narr.*, 26-27. According to Frederick's autobiographies, Giles Hicks owned one of Anna's cousins who was beaten to death by her mistress; but if Mary's former master owned Anna's seven older siblings, then it was was probably not Hicks because Hicks did not own enough slaves in the proper categories to resemble the Murray family. He had two slaves in 1810 and six slaves and one free black man working for him in 1820. Of course, this does not rule out the possibility that some of the older Murray children died or were emancipated. 1810 U.S. Census, Maryland, Caroline County, 188; 1820 U.S. Census, Maryland, Caroline County, 107, 420. The possibility that Bambarra became free and then purchased his wife's liberty had precedent in the case of Venture Smith, who purchased his own freedom, then set about earning wages to free each of his family members. He was able to raise the sum for his wife only shortly before she gave birth. Venture Smith, *Narrative of the Life and Adventures of Venture Smith* (New London, Ct., 1798), 25-27.

7. Seth Rockman, *Scraping By: Wage Labor, Slavery, and Survival in Early Baltimore* (Baltimore: Johns Hopkins University Press, 2009), 100-106, 114-17. See also Richard C. Wade, *Slavery in the Cities: the South, 1820-1860* (New York: Oxford University Press, 1964); Fields, *Slavery and Freedom*; James Oliver Horton, *Free People of Color: Inside the African American Community* (Washington, DC: Smithsonian Institution Press, 2000); Christopher Phillips, *Freedom's Port: The African American Community of Baltimore, 1790-1860* (Urbana: University of Illinois Press, 1997); Camilla Townsend, *Tales of Two Cities: Race and Economic Culture in Early Republican North and South America: Guayaquil, Ecuador, and Baltimore, Maryland* (Austin: University of Texas Press, 2000); Wilma King, *The Essence of Liberty: Free Black Women in the Slave Era* (Columbia: University of Missouri Press, 2006).

8. FD, *Narr.*, 29; RDS, *MMAIRH*, 9; "Return of Twenty-three Slaves the Property of Frances M. Montell of the Island of New Providence, Merchant," 1 January 1831, "Schedule of one Slaver the property of the said Francis M. Montell," 1 January 1831, "Return of One Slave the Property of the Estate of Francis M. Montell late of New Providence, deceased," 31 December 1834, "Schedule of Twenty four slaves the property of the said Francis M. Montell," 31 December 1834, *Slave Registers of former British Colonial Dependences, 1812-1834*, Office of Registry of Colonial Slaves and Slave Compensation Commission: Records (National Archives Microfilm Publication 71); Tepper, *Passenger Arrivals at the Port of Baltimore*, 465-66; Matchetts' *Baltimore Directory, for 1824* (Baltimore, 1824), 319; *Matchett's Baltimore Directory for 1827* (Baltimore, 1827), *Matchett's Baltimore Directory* (Baltimore, 1829), 333; *Matchett's Baltimore Director* (Baltimore, 1831), 387; *Matchett's Baltimore Director* (Baltimore, 1833), 133, 190-91; *Matchett's Baltimore Director* (Baltimore, 1835), 183, 366; *Matchett's Baltimore Director* (Baltimore, 1837), 233, 324; *Matchett's Baltimore Director, for 1840-1*

(Baltimore, [c.1840]), 260, 366; 1840 U.S. Census, Maryland, Baltimore County, Baltimore, Ward 2, 84; Rockman, *Scraping By*, 114–15; Phillips, *Freedom's Port*, 235.

9. 1840 U.S. Census, Maryland, Baltimore, Ward 5, 223; Jane Marsh Parker, "Reminiscences of Frederick Douglass," in *Cradle of Freedom: History of the Negro in Rochester, Western New York and Canada*, by Howard W. Coles (Rochester: Oxford University Press, 1941), 156–62; "Frederick Douglass: Something about His Home Life," 20 April 1887, *Augusta Journal*; JG[C] to FD, Hanley, England, 19 May 1865, FDP, DLC; CRD, "Some Incidents of the Home Life of Frederick Douglass," 13 February 1917, FDP, Walter O. Evans Collection (private); Robert Roberts, *The House Servant's Directory*, ed. Graham Russell Hodges (1827; Amonk, N.Y.: M. E. Sharpe, 1998), xxxiv–xxxvii; Rockman, *Scraping By*, 123–24; Ruth Schwartz Cowan, *More Work for Mother: The Ironies of Household Technology from the Open Hearth to the Microwave* (1983; London, 1989), 26–39, 42–45; Jack Larkin, *The Reshaping of Everyday Life, 1790-1840* (New York: Harper & Row, 1988), 24–32. Maryland biscuits originate on the Eastern Shore. Their preparation involves lengthy pounding of the dough to facilitate rising. Anna later taught this technique to Louisa Sprague, Rosetta's sister-in-law and Anna's companion in her later years. Louisa Sprague to FD, Washington, DC, 15 July 1883, FDP, DLC.

10. Roberts, *House Servant's Directory*, xxxiv–xxxvii; Suellen Hoy, *Chasing Dirt: The American Pursuit of Cleanliness* (New York: Oxford University Press, 1995), 15–19; C. W. Harper, "Black Aristocrats: Domestic Servants on the Antebellum Plantation," *Phylon* 46, 2 (1985): 123–35; James Oliver Horton, "Freedom's Yoke: Gender Conventions among Antebellum Free Blacks," *Feminist Studies* 12, 1 (Spring 1986): 51–76; Rockman, *Scraping By*, 123–24.

11. RDS, *MMAIRH*, 20. On "masks," see Bertram Wyatt-Brown, "The Mask of Obedience: Male Slave Psychology in the Old South," *American Historical Review* 93, 5 (December 1988): 1228–52, as well as Paul Laurence Dunbar's poem "We Wear the Mask," and W. E. B. Du Bois on "double consciousness," in *The Souls of Black Folk* (Chicago: A.C. McClurg & Co., 1903), 3.

12. Ball, *To Live an Antislavery Life*, 8–9; Cowan, *More Work for Mother*, 40–68; Larkin, *Reshaping of Everyday Life*, 171–80.

13. RDS, *MMAIRH*, 9. When the Douglasses's Rochester house burned down in 1872, the German journalist Ottilia Assing lamented that Anna "probably thought more of her wig and some dozen silver spoons" than of the bonds also lost in the fire. Assing's biographer focused on Assing's perception of Anna as stupid and childish, but the spoons were possibly those Anna had purchased in Baltimore. Diedrich, *Love across Color Lines*, 306.

14. Phillips, *Freedom's Port*, 110–11.

15. RDS, *MMAIRH*, 8. The proximity of Anna to the East Baltimore Mental Improvement Society both in Baltimore and in Frederick's and Rosetta's memoirs led scholars to conflate the Douglasses' meeting with Frederick's participation in the society. Benjamin Quarles asserted, "Through this society he met Anna Murray, and fuel was added to his burning desire to change his status." Philip Foner followed suit, writing that Douglass "took a prominent part in debates and here, too, he met Anna Murray, who afterward became his wife." Dickson J. Preston, usually meticulous in his details, embellished the earlier version by writing, "the East Baltimore Mental Improvement Society also had social gatherings, and at one of these Frederick met a girl named Anna Murray, like him a native of the Eastern Shore." Waldo E. Martin Jr. repeated this version, insisting, "He had met her at a social gathering of the East Baltimore Mental Improvement Society, a secret debating club of free blacks," as did Maria Diedrich. John Stauffer retold the tale, writing, "Frederick and Anna had met at a debating club called the Baltimore Mental Improvement Society"; then he added, "Essentially a men's club, it also hosted respectable parties where black men and women could meet and court." The literary scholar Elizabeth Ann McHenry based part of her argument that Murray was interested in literature on Anna being "an active member of a Baltimore literary society when she and Frederick met." Foner, *Frederick Douglass: A Biography*, 21; Stauffer, *Giants*, 72; Elizabeth Ann McHenry, "Rereading Literary Legacy: New Considerations of the 19th Century African-American Reader and Writer," *Callaloo* 22, 2 (Spring 1999): 481; Quarles,

Frederick Douglass, 8; Preston, *YFD,* 149; Martin, *Mind of Frederick Douglass,* 15; Diedrich, *LACL,* 5.

16. "The Condition of the Colored Population of the City of Baltimore," *Baltimore Literary and Religious Magazine* 4 (April 1838): 4; William E. Lloyd to FD, Baltimore, Md., 13 June 1870, FDP, DLC; Douglass, *MBMF,* 182; *Matchett's Baltimore Director* (1833), 132; *Matchett's Baltimore Director* (1835), 133; *Matchett's Baltimore Director* (1837), 103, 180, 231; *Matchett's Baltimore Directory* (1840), 113, 212, 258; RDS, *MMAIRH,* 8; Dorothy B. Porter, "The Organized Educational Activities of Negro Literary Societies, 1828-1846," *Journal of Negro Education* 5, 4 (October 1936): 558, 573; Phillips, *Freedom's Port,* 172.

17. William E. Lloyd to FD, Baltimore, Md., 13 June 1870, FDP, DLC; *New York Globe,* 12 August 1882.

18. Douglass had not yet published his first autobiography when this incident occurred, so the details of his life in Baltimore were not yet widely known. FD, *MBMF,* 186–87; FD, *Narr.,* 72–73; Extract from letter of Anne Warren Weston, Boston, 6 March 1843, ASC, BPL. Historian William McFeely was the first to begin piecing together another scenario of the Douglasses' meeting based on additional documentation. McFeely, *Frederick Douglass,* 65–67.

19. McFeely, *Frederick Douglass,* 65; *Matchett's Baltimore Directory, for 1824,* 319; *Matchett's Baltimore Director* (1833), 190–91; *Matchett's Baltimore Director* (1835), [270]; *Matchett's Baltimore Director* (1837), 228, 324; Jordon Dodd, Liahona Research, comp. *Maryland Marriages, 1655-1850* [database online] (Provo, UT, 2004), retrieved from www.ancestry.com by author on 2 April 2011. Elizabeth Wells the teacher lived on "Caroline n of Balt st" in 1838. A seamstress named Elizabeth Wells also lived on Caroline Street in the years 1829 and 1831. Elizabeth Wells the teacher does not appear in the city directories for these years, and Elizabeth Wells the seamstress does not appear in the years that include Elizabeth Wells the teacher. Elizabeth Wells the teacher appears as a different entry from Peter Wells in the 1840 census, and neither Elizabeth appears in the 1850 census for Baltimore. *Matchett's Baltimore Director* (1829), 332; *Matchett's Baltimore Director* (1831), 387; 1830 U.S. Census, Maryland, Baltimore, Ward 2, 75; 1840 U.S. Census, Maryland, Baltimore, Ward 2, 84, Ward 3, 145; 1850 U.S. Census, Maryland, Baltimore, Ward 3, 371.

20. RDS, *MMAIRH,* 8; FD, *MBMF,* 182; Ball, *To Live an Antislavery Life,* 2–3, 8, 139n7; Phillips, *Freedom's Port,* 122.

21. RDS, *MMAIRH,* 20. Benjamin Quarles wrote, "Escape and freedom would enable him to marry as a man!" Philip Foner followed suit. "The meeting with Anna Murray intensified Douglass' desire for freedom," he asserted. "It was no longer a desire for himself alone. Freedom, now, would enable him to marry the woman he loved, not as a chattel but as a man," and he further insisted that "Anna shared his feelings." Maria Diedrich echoed Foner, writing, "The two fell in love, but Frederick, who had been determined to escape from slavery since his early childhood, decided that he would marry only as a free man." Nathan Irvin Huggins stated, "Anna Murray became one of his closest friends" and "Frederick and Anna grew very close and planned to marry." Waldo Martin, too, assumed that Frederick and Anna had "fallen in love" and characterized their marriage as "warm and loving." William McFeely in his version offered the most titillating twist, speculating that "Anna may have been pregnant with Rosetta, their first child." John Stauffer pondered Frederick's feeling for Anna and concluded that Anna was the better catch of the two without explaining her motivations for marrying Frederick. Quarles, *Frederick Douglass,* 8; Foner, *Frederick Douglass: A Biography,* 21–22; Diedrich, *LACL,* 175; Huggins, *Slave and Citizen,* 12–13; Martin, *Mind of Frederick Douglass,* 15; McFeely, *Frederick Douglass,* 70; Stauffer, *Giants,* 73.

The evidence for Anna's punning skills came from Rosetta, who described an incident in which "several young women called upon her and commenting on her spacious parlors and the approaching holiday season, thought it a favorable opportunity to suggest the keeping of an open house. Mother replied: 'I have been keeping open house for several weeks. I have it closed now and I expect to keep it closed.' One of the young women, thinking mother's understanding was at fault, endeavored to explain. They were assured, however, that they were fully understood. Father, who was present, laughingly pointed to the new bay window, which had been completed only a few days previous to their call." For other clues to Anna's personality, see RDS, *MMAIRH,* 20; Marsh, "Reminiscences," in Coles, *Cradle of Freedom,* 157–58; Sarah

Thayer to AKP, Grand Blanc [Mich.], 15 April 1855, IAKPFP, NRU; FD to Lydia Dennett, Rochester, 1857, John Greenleaf Whittier Collection, Harvard University.

22. See Stephanie Coontz, *Marriage, a History: From Obedience to Intimacy, or How Love Conquered Marriage* (New York: Viking, 2005); Carl Degler, *At Odds: Women and the Family in America from the Revolution to the Present* (New York: Oxford University Press, 1980); Steven Mintz and Susan Kellogg, *Domestic Revolutions: A Social History of American Family Life* (New York: Free Press, 1988); Steven Mintz, *Huck's Raft: A History of American Childhood* (Cambridge, MA: Belknap Press of Harvard University Press, 2004), 2–3, 75, 87–88; Lawrence Stone, *The Family, Sex, and Marriage in England, 1500-1800* (1977; New York: Harper Colophon Books, 1979).

23. Rockman, *Scraping By*, 160–73, 185–86; Townsend, *Tale of Two Cities*, 225. In 1830, 12% of the slave population in Maryland and 14% of the slaves from Talbot County had been sold in the interstate trade or migrated with their masters. Fields, *Slavery and Freedom*, 24.

24. RDS, *MMAIRH*, 9–10; FD, *Narr.*, 73. For the meaning of family stories, see Elizabeth Stone, *Black Sheep and Kissing Cousins: How Our Family Stories Shape Us* (1988; New Brunswick, NJ: Transaction Publishers, 2009).

25. FD, *Narr*, 76; Graham Russell Gao Hodges, *David Ruggles: A Radical Black Abolitionist and the Underground Railroad in New York City* (Chapel Hill: University of North Carolina Press, 2010), 135. Their preparations resemble those of the Crafts, a couple who escaped from slavery in Georgia disguised as a young, white gentleman and his slave. Their lack of privacy and fear of being caught with the disguise heightened in the three days of planning. As had happened to Frederick when he spied a familiar face from Baltimore during his own escape, acquaintances of their master nearly recognized them on their journey. William Craft, *Running a Thousand Miles to Freedom* (London, 1860), 29–44.

26. FD, *Narr.*, 76; FD, *MBMF*, 196; FD, *L&T*, 159; RDS, *MMAIRH*, 9; Ball, *To Live an Antislavery Life*, 88–89.

27. In the subsequent autobiographies, *My Bondage and My Freedom* (1855) and *Life and Times of Frederick Douglass* (1882 and 1893), Douglass shortened this section. He did not mention Anna by name in the final version but did consistently use the pronoun "we" in relating events of their early years in New Bedford. By that time, he no longer felt compelled to establish the validity of his marriage, as he had in 1845, focusing instead on his success as an abolitionist and statesman. While critics might consider Anna's abbreviated mention a slight, Frederick was both following the decorum of the day, in which respectable ladies shunned publicity, and protecting his wife from the type of public celebrity that she shunned. FD, *Narr.*, 76–77; FD, *MBMF*, 196; FD, *L&T*, 159–60.

28. See Kathryn Grover, *The Fugitive's Gibraltar: Escaping Slaves and Abolitionism in New Bedford, Massachusetts* (Amherst: University of Massachusetts Press, 2001); Hodges, *David Ruggles*, 135.

29. FD, *MBMF*, 133, 180, 201.

30. Lee V. Chambers, *The Weston Sisters: An American Abolitionist Family* (Chapel Hill: University of North Carolina Press, 2014), 109–12; Peter Hinks, *To Awaken My Afflicted Brethren* (University Park: Pennsylvania State University Press, 1997), 94, 96; Grover, *Fugitive's Gibraltar*, 118–56.

31. FD, *MBMF*, 190; RDS, *MMAIRH*, 8.

32. RDS, *MMAIRH*, 10; FD, *MBMF*, 201; *NS*, 8 September 1848; FD, *L&T*, 164; FD to Frederick May Holland, Anacostia, DC, 3 August 1889, FDP, DLC; King, *Essence of Liberty*, 67–69. William McFeely speculated that Anna was already pregnant when she and Frederick married. He based his assumption on the taunts that Rosetta endured in the 1860s, when she was mistaken for the wayward daughter of William Wells Brown. McFeely dismissed the improbability that Anna would have realized that she was pregnant immediately after conception by suggesting that the Douglasses fabricated their daughter's birth date. Rosetta, however, would not have been the first child ever conceived shortly after her parents' wedding. McFeely, *Frederick Douglass*, 70.

33. FD, *MBMF*, 204; *NS*, 8 September 1848; FD, *L&T*, 163.

34. FD, *MBMF*, 203; Grover, *Fugitive's Gibraltar*, 148–49. Massachusetts was the single state to allow all adult men to vote.

35. Richard S. Newman, *Freedom's Prophet: Bishop Richard Allen, the AME Church, and the Black Founding Fathers* (New York: New York University Press, 2008), 73-76; Ball, *To Live an Antislavery Life*, 100-108.

36. FD, *MBMF*, 203-4; FD *Narr.*, 80; FD, *L&T*, 167-69; Grover, *Fugitive's Gibraltar*, 148-49.

37. The timeline in the Frederick Douglass Papers correspondence series dates the Douglasses' move to Lynn in fall 1841. Douglass himself, however, wrote that he spent three years in New Bedford, which places the move in late 1842. Rosetta reported that she and her two oldest brothers were all born in New Bedford, which meant that they moved after 3 March 1842, Frederick Jr.'s birthday. The *Liberator* also cited Douglass as living in New Bedford on 2 September 1842, posting a notice on 18 November that Douglass's address had changed to Lynn. FD, *Correspondence*, I:xlvii; FD, *MBMF*, 201; RDS, *MMAIRH*, 10; *Lib.*, 2 September, 18 November 1842. For a history of Lynn, see Paul G. Faler, *Mechanics and Manufacturers in the Early Industrial Revolution: Lynn, Massachusetts, 1780-1860* (Albany: State University of New York Press, 1981); Mary H. Blewett, *Men, Women, and Work: Class, Gender, and Protest in the New England Shoe Industry, 1780-1910* (Urbana: University of Illinois Press, 1988); Friederick Lenger, "Class, Culture and Class Consciousness in Ante-bellum Lynn: A Critique of Alan Dawley and Paul Faler," *Social History* 6, 3 (October 1981): 317-32.

38. FD, *MBMF*, 209-25; FD, *L&T*, 171-80; FD, *Correspondence*, 1:xlvii-xlix.

39. Rosetta also exaggerated when she included Anna in the Boston societies, but no evidence in the extensive records of the Boston abolitionists indicates that Anna had participated in any of their meetings. Rosetta's account flattered the white abolitionists and conformed to the expectations of her audience in 1900. She crafted her mother's biography to preserve the memory of her mother as a worthy companion to her father, appealing to a group of bourgeois black women whose understanding of community and racial uplift had prepared them to hear about a wife who, as they did, had supported her husband by embodying the virtues of domesticity and involving herself in activism through formal organizations. RDS, *MMAIRH*, 13.

40. Jean H. Baker, *Sisters: The Lives of America's Suffragists* (New York: Hill and Wang, 2005), 110; Dixon, *Perfecting the Family*, 105-15, 117-19; Carol Faulkner, *Lucretia Mott's Heresy: Abolition and Women's Rights in Nineteenth-Century America* (Philadelphia: University of Pennsylvania Press, 2011), 52; Lori D. Ginzberg, *Elizabeth Cady Stanton: An American Life* (New York: Hill and Wang, 2009), 92-93, 105; Gerda Lerner, *The Grimké Sisters from South Carolina: Pioneers for Woman's Rights and Abolition* (1967; New York: Schoken Books, 1973), 288-93; Dorothy Sterling, *Ahead of Her Time: Abby Kelley and the Politics of Antislavery* (New York: W. W. Norton, 1991), 221, 232-33, 246. In 1841, the members of the Lynn Anti-Slavery Society included William Bassett, Christopher Robinson, Aroline A. Chase, William D. Thompson, Jonathan Buffum, Benjamin Purinton, Miriam B. Johnson, Joseph Barry, Stephen N. Breed, William B. Oliver, James P. Boyce, James P. Oliver, James N. Buffum, Charles A. Cross, Eliza Boyce, Mercy T. Buffum, Joseph Breed III, Sampson Cummings, and David Johnson. The Lynn Ladies' Anti-Slavery Society included Deborah S. Henshaw, Charlotte Purinton, Miriam B. Johnson, Abby A. Bennett, Eliza Boyce, Abby L. Breed, Hannah Buffum, Beulah Brown, Abigail Johnson, Hannah Alley, Julia A. Boyce, Ruth O. Buffum, Lydia Hallowell, Aurora Porter, and Aroline A. Chase. Benjamin F. Roberts, *The Lynn Directory and Register for 1841* (Lynn, 1841), 130-14; 1850 U.S. Census, Massachusetts, Essex County, Lynn. While Anna may have known about some form of birth control or entered menopause, that there were no more children until 1850 was probably due to Frederick's absences.

41. Debra Gold Hansen, *Strained Sisterhood: Gender and Class in the Boston Female Anti-Slavery Society* (Amherst: University of Massachusetts Press, 1997), 116; Carol Lasser, "Gender, Ideology, and Class in the Early Republic," *Journal of the Early Republic* 10, 3 (Autumn 1990): 331-37.

42. FD, *MBMF*, 229-30; Abraham Brooke to MWC, Oakland, Oh., 5 October 1843; AK[F] to MWC, Canterbury, N.H., 4 October 1844; James N. Buffum to MWC, Perth, Scotland, 26 June 1846; Isabel Jennings to MWC, Cork, Ireland, 2 August 1847, ASC, BPL.

43. Isabel Jennings to MWC, Cork, Ireland, 2 August 1847, ASC, BPL; J. B. Estlin to Samuel May, Bristol, England, 12 January 1847, ASC, BPL.

44. Leslie M. Harris, *In the Shadow of Slavery: African American in New York City, 1624-1863* (Chicago: University of Chicago Press, 2003), 186–87; Gary B. Nash, *Forging Freedom: The Formation of Philadelphia's Black Community, 1720-1840* (Cambridge, MA: Harvard University Press, 1988), 209, 269–71; Ball, *To Live an Antislavery Life*, 57–58; Grover, *Fugitive's Gibraltar*, 180–81, 230–31; King, *Essence of Liberty*, 89–115; Phillips, *Freedom's Port*, 163–69.

45. RDS, *MMAIRH*, 21.

46. Josiah Henson, *The Life of Josiah Henson* (Boston, 1849), 63–64; Marsh, "Reminiscences," in Coles, *Cradle of Freedom*, 158; "The Condition of the Colored Population of the City of Baltimore," *Baltimore Literary and Religious Magazine* 4 (April 1838): 4. Intelligent, able to solve mathematical problems, capable of recognizing shapes of certain words such as her husband's name, and avoiding situations that might expose her to shame, Anna resembled students diagnosed with reading or learning disabilities in the late twentieth and early twenty-first centuries. As with many of those students, her environment conspired against her ability or desire to address the situation. Carleton Mabee suggested a similar explanation while exploring reasons that Sojourner Truth did not learn to read. Margaret Washington took issue with that interpretation, pointing out that "Sojourner's lack of education seems more of a problem for modern historians than it was for her contemporaries." Including Anna Douglass in her explanation, Washington placed greater emphasis on the material barriers that would prevent a grown working woman from embarking on an education that seemed inessential to her vocation. See P. F. Aaron, R. Malateesha Joshi, Regina Gooden, Kwesi E. Bentum, "Diagnosis and Treatment of Reading Disabilities Based on the Component Model of Reading: An Alternative to the Discrepancy Model of LD," *Journal of Learning Disabilities* 41, 1 (February 2008): 67–84; Carleton Mabee, "Sojourner Truth, Bold Prophet: Why Did She Never Learn to Read?," *New York History* 69, 1 (1888): 55–77; Margaret Washington, *Sojourner Truth's America* (Urbana: University of Illinois Press, 2009), 133, 216, 409–10n13.

47. RDS, *MMAIRH*, 21; FD to HB/RCA, England, 16 May 1846, A[M]D to HB/RCA, Rochester, 11 March 1851, Addition II, FDP, DLC. Other examples of communication between Frederick and Anna through an amanuensis, particularly in the 1860s, can be found throughout the Frederick Douglass Papers in the Library of Congress in the letters between him and other members of the family.

48. RDS, *MMAIRH*, 13, 18; CRD, "Some Incidents," Evans Collection; Beth Maclay Doriani, "Black Womanhood in Nineteenth Century America: Subversion and Self-Construction in Two Women's Autobiographies," *American Quarterly* 43, 2 (June 1991): 199–222; Kate Clifford Larson, *Bound for the Promised Land: Harriet Tubman, Portrait of an American Hero* (New York: Ballantine, 2004), xix; Nell Irvin Painter, *Sojourner Truth: A Life, a Symbol* (New York: W. W. Norton, 1996), 230, 252; Ball, *To Live an Antislavery Life*, 8, 88–93; King, *Essence of Liberty*, 33–42; Washington, *Sojourner Truth's America*, 133, 277, 409–10n13. For writers sensitive to Anna's sense of self, illiteracy, and position, see McHenry, "Rereading Literacy Legacy," 477–82; Shirley J. Yee, *Black Women Abolitionists: A Study in Activism, 1828-1860* (Knoxville: University of Tennessee Press, 1992).

49. RDS, *MMAIRH*, 13, 18; Painter, *Sojourner Truth*, 98; Unnamed source quoting Anthony, in Holland, *Frederick Douglass*, 225.

50. FD to Lydia Dennett, Rochester, 17 April 1857, FD to HB/RCA, England, 16 May 1846, Addition II, FDP, DLC. Frederick did allow a revealing moment to surface on his marriage to the highly educated Helen Pitts after Anna had died. "How good it is to have a wife who can read and write," he confessed to Elizabeth Cady Stanton, "and who can as Margaret Fuller says cover one in all his range." FD to ECS, Washington, DC, 20 May 1884, ECSP, DLC. Anna's lack of interest in literature would not have differentiated her from many people then and now.

51. FD to AKP, Albany, N.Y., 30 January 1848, IAKPFP, NRU; FD to Anna Richardson, Lynn, Mass., 29 April 1847, in FD, *Correspondence*, I:209. Although the Motts were scattered throughout the northeast, this Abigail Mott may have attended the Society of Friends abolitionist school Nine Partners with abolitionist and woman's rights activist Lucretia Mott and complied *Biographical Sketches and Interesting Anecdotes of Persons of Color* (New York, 1837) and, with James Mott, *Observations on the Importance of Female Education and Maternal*

Instruction with Their Beneficial Influence on Society (New York, 1825). Faulkner, *Lucretia Mott's Heresy*, 30–31; Grover, *Fugitive's Gibraltar*, 180–81, 230–31; *NS*, 5 January 1849; Michael Sokolow, "'New Guinea at One End, and a View of the Alms-House at the Other': The Decline of Black Salem, 1850-1920," *New England Quarterly* 71, 2 (June 1998): 204–28; Donale M. Jacobs, "The Nineteenth Century Struggle over Segregated Education in the Boston Schools," *Journal of Negro Education* 39, 1 (Winter 1970): 76–85; Dorothy Porter, "Sarah Parker Remond, Abolitionist and Physician," *Journal of Negro History* 20, 3 (July 1935): 287–93.

52. Ball, *To Live an Antislavery Life*, 85–97, 106–8; RDS, *MMIRH*, 12; Abigail Mott to AK[F], Albany, N.Y., 18 August 1842, AKFP, AQM; Marsh, "Reminiscences," in Coles, *Cradle of Freedom*, 158–59; *Lib.*, 7 June 1847. In the introduction to an essay Rosetta contributed to *Twentieth Century Negro Literature* in 1902, Daniel Wallace Culp wrote, "Miss Abigail gave her [Rosetta] instruction in reading and writing and Miss Lydia taught her to sew." Daniel Wallace Culp, ed., *Twentieth Century Negro Literature* (Toronto, Canada: J. L. Nichols & Co. 1902), 167.

53. *NS*, 25 February 1848.

54. FD to HB/RCA, Belfast, Ireland, 1 July 1846, Addition II, FDP, DLC; A[M]D to HB/RCA, Rochester,11 March 1851, Addition II, FDP, DLC; Alice V. Coffee, "Lest We Forget" (unpublished family history), Alyce McWilliams Hall Collection, Nebraska State Historical Society; Norfolk [Nebraska] *Weekly News*, 7 March 1894; FD, *Correspondence*, 1:126–27n1; Leigh Fought, "Frederick Douglass's Lost 'Sister': Harriet Bailey / Ruth Cox Adams," unpublished paper, 2010.

55. FD to HB/RCA, England, 16 May 1846, Addition II, FDP, DLC.

56. FD to HB/RCA, England, 16 May 1846, FD to HB/RCA, Leamington, England, 31 January 1847, A[M]D to HB/RCA, Rochester, 11 March 1851, FD to HB/RCA, [n.p.], 16 May, [c. 17 July] 1846, RD[S] to HB/RCA, Rochester, 20 April 1860, Addition II, FDP, DLC.

57. RDS, *MMAIRH*, 20; 1850 U.S. Census, New York, Monroe County, Rochester, Ward 7; A[M]D to HB/RCA, Rochester, 11 March 1851, Addition II, FDP, DLC.

58. FD to Anna Richardson, Lynn, Mass., 29 April 1847, in FD, *Correspondence*, 1:208–9; FD to WLG, London, England, 23 May 1846, *Lib.*, 26 June 1846; FD to HB/RCA, England, 16 May 1846, Addition II, FDP, DLC; FD to Isabel Jennings, Glasgow, Scotland., 22 September 1846; FD to HB/RCA, England, 16 May 1846, Addition II, FDP, DLC.

59. FD to Anna Richardson, Lynn, Mass., 29 April 1847, in FD, *Correspondence*, 1:208–9.

60. RDS, *MMAIRH*, 14.

Chapter 3

1. *New Bedford Register*, 7 July 1841; FD, *MBMF*, 205; FD, *Speeches*, 1:vii, xlvi, lxxxvii–iii, 3; Grover, *Fugitive's Gibraltar*, 169; FD, *Speeches*, 1:3. W. E. B. Du Bois wrote of this double world or double-consciousness of African Americans as a "veil." W. E. B. Du Bois, *Souls of Black Folk*, 1–4.

2. Early scholarly biographers, including Benjamin Quarles, Philip Foner, and Nathan Huggins, tended to mention particular women by name, usually if they had been speakers, but otherwise took women's supporting work for granted. As the field of women's history began to challenge those assumptions and point out the value of women's work in the abolition movement, discussions of women began to filter into Douglass biographies. Waldo E. Martin Jr., for instance, believed that Douglass's advocacy of woman's rights was a direct result of their supporting abolition. William McFeely incorporated women's work and more individual women into his biography of Douglass. Unfortunately, he credited particular women with only emotional motivation, and he demeaned the fairs by referring to the sale items as "monstrosities" while ignoring the larger implications of their fundraising. The work of women abolitionists is notably absent in John Stauffer's work on Douglass. Fortunately, work on women in the abolitionist movement, their organizing, fundraising, speaking, and points of view about antislavery, proliferated in the 1990s and 2000s, identifying the players and providing the backdrop and concrete evidence for their roles in regard to one another. Quarles,

Frederick Douglass; P. Foner, *Frederick Douglass: A Biography*; Huggins, *Slave and Citizen*; Martin, *Mind of Frederick Douglass*; McFeely, *Frederick Douglass*; Stauffer, *Giants*.

3. *Lib.*, 4 November 1844.

4. *Lib.*, 8 December 1843. On integrated women's antislavery organizations, see Julie Roy Jeffrey, *The Great Silent Army of Abolitionists: Ordinary Women in the Antislavery Movement* (Chapel Hill: University of North Carolina Press, 1998); Yee, *Black Women Abolitionists*; Amy Swerdlow, "Abolition's Conservative Sisters: The Ladies' New York City Anti-Slavery Societies, 1834-1840," Jean Soderlund, "Priorities and Power: The Philadelphia Female Anti-Slavery Society," Carolyn Williams, "The Female Antislavery Movement: Fighting against Racial Prejudice and Promoting Women's Right in Antebellum America," in *The Abolitionist Sisterhood: Women's Political Culture in Antebellum America*, ed. Jean Fagan Yellin and John C. Van Horne (Ithaca, N.Y.: Cornell University Press, 1994). On the incident at Pennsylvania Hall, see *A History Pennsylvania Hall, which was Destroyed by a Mob* (Philadelphia, 1838) and Beverly Tomek, *Pennsylvania Hall: A Legal Lynching in the Shadow of the Liberty Bell* (New York: Oxford University Press, 2013). The story about Remond appears in Lillie Buffum Chace Wyman and Arthur Crawford Wyman, *Elizabeth Buffum Chace, 1806-1899: Her Life and Its Environment* (Boston, 1914), 1:139–40.

5. The trope of separate spheres, once a defining feature of women's history, has undergone multiple reinterpretations as historians investigate the ways in which women themselves understood and interacted with the ideologies of their time. For defining research on this subject, see Nancy Cott, *The Bonds of Womanhood: "Woman's Sphere" in New England, 1780–1835* (New Haven, Conn.: Yale University Press, 1977); Lori D. Ginzberg, *Women and the Work of Benevolence: Morality, Politics, and Class in the Nineteenth-Century United States* (New Haven, Conn.: Yale University Press, 1990) and *Untidy Origins: A Story of Woman's Right in Antebellum New York* (Chapel Hill: University of North Carolina Press, 2005); Nancy Isenberg, *Sex and Citizenship in Antebellum America* (Chapel Hill: University of North Carolina Press, 1998); Mary Kelley, *Learning to Stand and Speak: Women, Education, and Public Life in America's Republic* (Chapel Hill: University of North Carolina Press, 2006); Mary Ryan, *Civic Wars: Democracy and Public Life in the American City during the Nineteenth Century* (Berkeley: University of California Press, 1997); Mary Ryan, *Women in Public: Between Banners and Ballots, 1825-1880* (Baltimore: Johns Hopkins University Press, 1990); Mary Ryan, *Cradle of the Middle Class: The Family in Oneida County, New York, 1790-1865* (Cambridge: Cambridge University Press, 1983); Elizabeth Varon, *We Mean to Be Counted: White Women and Politics in Antebellum Virginia* (Chapel Hill: University of North Carolina Press, 1998); Linda Kerber, "Separate Spheres, Female Worlds, Woman's Place: The Rhetoric of Women's History," *Journal of American History* 75 (June 1988): 9–39; Carol Lasser, "Beyond Separate Spheres: The Power of Public Opinion," *Journal of the Early Republic* 21, 1 (Spring 2001): 115–23, among many others.

6. Grover, *Fugitive's Gibraltar*, 138, 139; Horton, *Free People of Color*, 101–2, 115–17; King, *Essence of Liberty*, 41, 86–87, 179; Phillips, *Freedom's Port*, 171–5; Yee, *Black Women Abolitionists*, 60–86; D. Porter, "Organized Educational Activities," 555–76.

7. Hansen, *Strained Sisterhood*, 19–28; Williams, "Female Antislavery Movement," in Yellen and Van Horne, *Abolitionist Sisterhood*, 160–77; Abraham Brook to MWC, Oakland, Ohio, 5 October 1843, ASC, BPL.

8. FD, *L&T*, 370; FD, *MBMF*, 204. Douglass, for instance, attended the December 1842 meeting of the Essex County Society, called to order by vice president Eliza J. Kenny. Mary Kenney and Susannah Dodge addressed the gathering, and then Maria French, of Salem, testified that the minister of her Congregational church had ordered her forcibly removed when she raised the issue of slavery. Douglass encountered both Kenneys again in 1844, when they were the secretaries of societies in Boston and Essex County. In November 1842, he sat on the business committee of the Rhode Island Anti-Slavery Society with Martha Brown, and the following June he served on another in Bristol County with Sarah Borden and Mary T. Congdon. At a Nantucket meeting, he joined a committee beside Charlotte Austin Joy and Eliza Barney, on which Anna Gardner acted as secretary. Barney, Phebe W. Gardner, and Harriet Pierce participated in a group that confronted the town's clergy over their churches' complicity in slavery. Lucinda Wilmarth was secretary for the Rhode

Island Society when it employed Douglass, Catherine Swann served as corresponding secretary in Worcester when Douglass spoke to that organization, and he attended a meeting of Norfolk County Society that included Eliza Taft and Catherine Spear among its managers. In 1843, when Douglass met members of the newly formed Western New York Anti-Slavery Society, its vice presidents included Margaret Pryor, Hannah Hutchinson, Sarah Hallowell, and Esther Hathaway, while Sarah Burgess, Sarah Fish, Abigail Bush, and Phebe Hathaway sat on the Executive Committee. *Lib.*, 4 November 1844, 9 December 1842, 5 January 1844, 19 January 1844, 2 February 1844, 6 January 1843.

9. FD, *Speeches*, 1:8; Deborah Bingham Van Broekhoven, "'Let Your Names Be Enrolled': Method and Ideology in Women's Antislavery Petitioning," in Yellen and Van Horne, *Abolitionist Sisterhood*, 179–200.

10. Harriet Martineau, *Harriet Martineau's Autobiography*, ed. Maria Weston Chapman (Boston, 1877), 1:349. On Maria Weston Chapman, see Jane Pease and William Pease, "Chapter 3: The Boston Bluestocking: Maria Weston Chapman," *Bound with Them in Chains: A Biographical History of the Antislavery Movement* (Westport, CT: Greenwood Press 1972); Clare Taylor, *Women of the Anti-Slavery Movement: The Weston Sisters* (New York: St. Martin's Press, 1995); Catherine Clinton, "Maria Weston Chapman," in *Portraits of American Women, from Settlement to the Present*, ed. G. J. Barker-Benfield and Catherine Clinton (New York: Oxford University Press, 1998), 147–67; Chambers, *Weston Sisters*.

11. Tomek, *Pennsylvania Hall*, 115–16, 133.

12. Hanson, *Strained Sisterhood*, 26–27, 126–30, 134–39; Jeffrey, *Great Silent Army*, 108; Lee Chambers-Schiller, "'A Good Work among the People': The Political Culture of the Boston Antislavery Fair," in Yellen and Van Horne, *Abolitionist Sisterhood*, 249–74.

13. J. Jackson to AK[F], New York, 6 September 1840, AKFP, AQM; Sterling, *Ahead of Her Time*, 16–20, 33–35, 39–46, 61–66, 85–93, 102–6, 135; Keith Melder, "Abby Kelley and the Process of Liberation," in Yellen and Van Horne, *Abolitionist Sisterhood*, 231–48.

14. FD, *Speeches*, 1:lxxxvii; Sterling, *Ahead of Her Time*, 135, 142–43; Dorothy Sterling, ed., *We Are Your Sisters: Black Women in the Nineteenth Century* (New York: W. W. Norton, 1984), 153–64, 175–76; Lerner, *Grimké Sisters*, 293–94. Sterling also suggests that Douglass, as the first black man in whose company she spent so much time, had a profound impact on Kelley.

15. *Lib.*, 13 October 1843; FD, *L&T*, 172; Sterling, *Ahead of Her Time*, 13–14.

16. Abigail Mott to AK[F], Albany, N.Y., 18 August 1842, AKFP, AQM; Anne Warren Weston to Deborah Weston, Weymouth, Mass., 1 April 1842, ASC, BPL; *Lib.*, 19 May 1843; Sterling, *Ahead of Her Time*, 135–37.

17. Abigail Mott to AK[F], Albany, N.Y., 18 August 1842, Paulina Wright to AK[F], Utica, N.Y., [c. August 1843], AKFP, AQM; Douglass, *L&T*, 172; Sterling, *Ahead of Her Time*, 13–14; Phillip Lapansky, "Graphic Discord: Abolitionists and Antiabolitionist Images," in Yellen and Van Horne, *Abolitionist Sisterhood*, 224–30.

18. AK[F] to MWC, West Winfield, N.Y., [30] October 1843, ASC, BPL; Nancy A. Hewitt, *Women's Activism and Social Change: Rochester, New York, 1822-1872* (Ithaca, N.Y.: Cornell University Press, 1984), 60–61, 108, 116–17, 119–20; Stacey M. Robertson, *Hearts Beating for Liberty: Women Abolitionists in the Old Northwest* (Chapel Hill: University of North Carolina Press, 2010), 129–38.

19. MWC to RDW, Boston, Mass, 16 August 1845, ASC, BPL.

20. MWC to RDW, Boston, Mass, 29 June 1845, RDW to MWC, Dublin, 30 September 1845, 23 January 1846, ASC, BPL.

21. RDW to MWC, Dublin, Ireland, 12 October 1845, ASC, BPL.

22. MWC to RDW, Boston, Mass., 23 January 1846, RDW to MWC, Dublin, Ireland, 30 September 1846, 29 June 1845, RDW to MWC, Dublin, Ireland, 12 October 1845, 30 September 1846, 12 October 1845, MWC to RDW, Boston, Mass., 27 October 1845, ASC, BPL.

23. FD, *L&T*, 177–78; Abraham Brook to MWC, Oakland, Ohio, 5 October 1843, ASC, BPL.

24. *Lib.*, 22 September 1843.

25. Henry Highland Garnet to MWC, Troy, N.Y., 17 November 1843; *Lib.*, 3 December 1843.

26. For a comprehensive history of the Liberty Party, see Reinhard O. Johnson, *The Liberty Party, 1840-1848: Antislavery Third-Party Politics in the United States* (Baton Rouge: Louisiana State

University Press, 2009). For the ways that women abolitionists worked with the Liberty Party in the Old Northwest, see Robertson, *Hearts*, 37–99.

27. FD, *Speeches*, 1:14; FD to WLG, Lynn [Mass.], 27 October 1844, *Lib.*, 1 November 1844; Edmund Quincy to Caroline Weston, Dedham, Mass., 9 March 1844, ASC, BPL; MWC to AK[F], Boston, 4 March, 1844, AKFP, AQM; AK[F] to MWC, Canterbury, N.H., 4 October 1844, ASC, BPL.

28. Isabel Jennings to MWC, Cork, Ireland, 2 August 1847, ASC, BPL. On the British abolition movement, see R. J. M. Blackett, *Building an Antislavery Wall: Black Americans in the Atlantic Abolitionist Movement, 1830-1860* (1986; Ithaca: Cornell University Press, 1989), 79–161; Howard Temperley, *British Anti-Slavery, 1833-1870* (London: Longman, 1972), xiii–xvi, 191–220. On Douglass and antislavery in Ireland, see Fenton, *Frederick Douglass in Ireland*; Chaffin, *Giant's Causeway*; Patricia Ferreira, "Frederick Douglass in Ireland: The Dublin Edition of His *Narrative*," *New Hibernia Review* 5, 1 (Spring 2001): 53–67; Rob Goodbody, "Quakers and the Famine," *History Ireland* 6, 1 (Spring 1998): 27–32; Lee Jenkins, "Beyond the Pale: Frederick Douglass in Cork," *Irish Review* 24 (Autumn 1999): 80–95; Douglass C. Riach, "Daniel O'Connell and American Anti-Slavery," *Irish Historical Studies* 20, 77 (March 1976): 3–25.

29. FD to MWC, Kilmarnock, Scotland, 29 March 1846; James N. Buffum to MWC, Perth, Scotland, 26 June 1846; FD to MWC, Kilmarnock, Scotland, 29 March 1846, ASC, BPL; Benjamin Quarles, "Sources of Abolitionist Income," *Mississippi Valley Historical Review* 32, 1 (June 1945): 63–75.

30. FD to WLG, Dublin, Ireland, 16 September 1845, *Lib.*, 10 October 1845; FD to Richard Dowden (Richard), Limerick, Ireland, 11 November 1845, in FD, *Correspondence*, 1:65–67; FD to AKP, Darlington, England, 28 April 1846, IAKPFP, NRU. Richard Dowden (Richard) was called just that. He added the second Richard to his name in order to distinguish himself from the many other Cork men who shared the same name.

31. RDW to MWC, Dublin, Ireland, 12 October 1846; Isabel Jennings to MWC, Cork, Ireland, 15 October 1845; Isabel Jennings to Mary Estlin, Cork, Ireland, 29 November 1849; RDW to MWC, Dublin, Ireland, 16 November 1845; Isabel Jennings to MWD, Cork, Ireland, 18 November 1845; RDW to MWC, Dublin, Ireland, 30 September 1845; Isabel Jennings to MWC, Cork, Ireland, 2 August 1847, ASC, BPL.

32. James N. Buffum to MWC, Perth, Scotland, 26 June 1846, ASC, BPL; J. F. MacLear, "Thomas Smyth, Frederick Douglass, and the Belfast Antislavery Campaign," *South Carolina Historical Magazine* 80, 4 (October 1979): 286–97; Blackett, *Building an Antislavery Wall*, 87–100.

33. FD to Isabel Jennings, Edinburgh, Scotland, 30 July 1846, FDP, DLC; Thomas Smyth, *Autobiographical Notes, Letters, and Reflections*, ed. Louisa Cheves Stoney (Charleston, SC: Walker, Evans & Cogswell Company, 1914), 362–78. Douglass gave no speeches in Manchester until October, after Smyth had leveled his charges. He may have stopped in Manchester before then, but the speaking itinerary listed in the Yale edition of his speeches shows a schedule so tight that any visit probably only lasted long enough to change trains. FD, *Speeches*, 1:xcvi-ci. Smyth appeared not to have owned any slaves. His son, Augustus, later fought for South Carolina during the Civil War and married Louisa Cheves McCord, daughter of Louisa S. McCord, a proslavery and anti-woman's-rights essayist who was Douglass's polar opposite in almost every way. Leigh Fought, *Southern Womanhood and Slavery: A Biography of Louisa S. McCord, 1811-1879* (Columbia: University of Missouri Press, 2003).

34. *NYTrib*, 21 September 1846; FD to Isabel Jennings, Edinburgh, Scotland, 30 July 1846; FD to "Mary," Edinburgh, Scotland, 30 July 1846; FD to ["Eliza"], Edinburgh, Scotland, 30 July 1846, FDP, DLC. For Smyth's version of events, see Smyth, *Autobiographical Notes*, 362–78.

35. J. B. Estlin to Samuel May, Bristol, England, 12 January 1847, ASC, BPL; Mary Ireland to MWC, Belfast, Ireland, 24 January 1846; RDW to MWC, Dublin, Ireland, 24 September 1848, ASC, BPL.

36. Catherine (Buck) Clarkson to MWC, Ipswich, England, 2 August 1846; Mary Carpenter to MWC, London, England, [1 April 1847]; Isabel Jennings to MWC, Cork, Ireland, 15 October 1845, ASC, BPL.

37. Isabel Jennings to MWC, Cork, Ireland, 2 August 1847; RDW to MWC, Dublin, Ireland, 31 October 1846; Isabel Jennings to MWC, Cork, Ireland, 2 August 1847, ASC, BPL.

38. Isabel Jennings to MWC, Cork, Ireland, 30 November 1845, Mary Estlin to MWC, Bristol, England, 1 September 1846; Mary Brady to MWC, Sheffield, England, [April 1847], ASC, BPL.

39. Mary Grew to MWC, Philadelphia, Penn., 25 February 1846, ASC, BPL; FD to WLG, Perth, Scotland, 27 January 1846, *Lib.*, 27 February 1846. The Auld letter is known to exist through internal evidence in Douglass's 16 April letter to the *Lib.* FD to WLG, Glasgow, Scotland, 16 April 1846, *Lib.*, 15 May 1846.

40. FD to WLG, London, England, 23 May 1846, *Lib.*, 26 June 1846.

41. FD to HB/RCA, Belfast, Ireland, 17 July 1846, Addition II, FDP, DLC. The letter in which he seems to have offered this invitation has a crucial line missing on a well-worn crease. Ruth Cox and her family had been the slaves of John Leeds Kerr of Easton, Maryland. She probably escaped in the wake of his death in February 1844, when his slaves were to be sold.

42. FD to HB/RCA, Belfast, Ireland, 17 July 1846, Addition II, FDP, DLC.

43. FD to William White, Edinburgh, Scotland, 30 July 1846, DLC, FDP; Mary Brady to MWC, Sheffield, England, 29 October 1846, ASC, BPL.

44. FD, *MBMF*, 215; *Lib.*, 26 February 1847, 29 January 1847; Clare Taylor, ed., *British and American Abolitionists* (Edinburgh: Edinburgh University Press, 1974), 547.

45. Catherine Paton to MWC, Glasgow, Scotland, 2 November 1846; Esther Sturge to MWC, London, England, 1 March 1847; Mary Welsh to MWC, Edinburgh, Scotland, 2 January 1847; Ester Sturge to MWC, London, England, 1 March 1847, ASC, BPL.

46. *Lib.*, 29 January 1847; *Pennsylvania Freeman*, 9 September 1847; Henry C. Wright to FD, Doncaster, England, 12 December 1846; *Lib.*, 29 January 1847, 26 February 1847.

47. FD, *MBMF*, 215–17; FD to Henry C. Wright, Manchester, England, 22 December 1846, *Lib.*, 29 January 1847; FD to Henry C. Wright, Manchester, 22 December 1846, *Lib.*, 29 January 1847. He also used much of the same language in FD to John Hardinge Veitch, Coventry, England, 22 January 1847, *Durham Chronicle*, 5 February 1847.

48. Jane Carr to MWC, Carlisle, England, 14 April 1847, ASC, BPL; FD, *Speeches*, 2:xviii; FD to Charles Francis Adams, Lynn, Mass., 27 June 1847, *Lib.*, 9 July 1847; Jane Wigham to MWC, Edinburgh, Scotland, 17 November 1846, ASC, BPL; "British Testimonial of Esteem," *Report of Proceedings at the Soiree Given to Frederick Douglass* (London, 1847), 31.

49. Mary and Margaret Howitt, *Mary Howitt, an autobiography* (London, 1889), 2:33; "Extract from a letter from Miss S. Carpenter respecting Frederick Douglass," [Mary Carpenter to MWC], [London, England], [c. 30 March 1847]; JG[C] to Francis Jackson, London, England, 17 July [1847], ASC, BPL. The letter is dated 1846, but internal evidence in the document indicates that it was written in 1847. Both her own admission and her absence from all other correspondence prior to March 1847 indicate that she did not know Douglass before March 1847. Until she arrived in the United States in 1849, she was most commonly mentioned in association with the Howitts.

50. *FDP*, 15 June 1849; JG[C] to FD, Gateshead, England, 26 March 1877, FDP, DLC; FD, *Speeches*, 2:xviii; "Extract form a letter from Miss S. Carpenter respecting Frederick Douglass," [Mary Carpenter to MWC], [London, England], [c. 30 March 1847]. Douglass's story of the Griffiths sisters contradicts both the record of his locations and Julia's account. The story appeared in an article describing the prejudice they encountered in America, and for dramatic contrast he may have incorporated an experience that had occurred regularly in Britain and Ireland, if not with the Griffiths in particular.

51. RDW to Caroline Weston, Dublin, England, 22 February 1849, and John Estlin to Anne Warren Weston, Bristol, England, 29 April 1850, ASC, BPL.

52. RDW to MWC, Dublin, Ireland, 31 October 1846; Mary Carpenter to MWC, Bristol, England, 31 March 1847, 2 November 1846, ASC, BPL. Also, Mary Estlin to MWC, Bristol, England, 1 September 1846, 19 April 1847, Catherine Clarkson to MWC, Ipswich, England, 2 August 1846, Hannah White to MWC, Cork, Ireland, 30 October 1846, Sarah Hilditch to MWC, Wrexham, England, 31 October 1846, Jane Wigham to MWC, Edinburgh, Scotland, 31 October 1846, Isabel Jennings to MWC, Cork, Ireland, 2 August 1847, ASC, BPL; FD to AKP, Darlington, England, 28 April 1846, IAKPFP, NRU; Mary Brady to MWC, Sheffield, England, [c. May 1847], ASC, BPL. Also, Lucy Browne to MWC, Bridgewater, England, 15 October 1846; Mary Estlin to MWC, Bristol, England, 19 April 1847, ASC, BPL.

53. RDS, *MMAIRH*, 18; Edmund Quincy to Caroline Weston, Dedham, Mass.:, 30 July 1847, ASC, BPL.
54. *Lib.*, 11 June 1847.

Chapter 4

1. *Lib.*, 18 November 1853.
2. *Lib.*, 16 December 1853. By placing this editorial in the "Refuge of Oppression" section reserved for depictions of pro-slavery sentiment, Garrison classified Douglass with advocates of slavery.
3. Reprinted in *Lib.*, 18 November 1853.
4. *Lib.*, 16 December 1853.
5. In the words of journalism historian Frank E. Fee Jr., Julia Griffiths is someone "about whom too little is known and too much is speculated." The number of words devoted to her has grown over the decades as biographers have incorporated more women into the story of Douglass's life. Until recently, however, they have been at a loss in placing Griffiths coherently into his life and career. Douglass himself consistently praised her as one of the most important people in his career, and his earliest biographers followed suit; Frederick May Holland, for example, echoed his subject, and Charles Chesnutt left her out entirely. Douglass's first academic biographer, Benjamin Quarles, had access to Douglass's personal papers and was able to elaborate on the extent of her influence as a proofreader, fundraiser, and advocate of political abolition. Quarles also addressed the perceptions of Douglass's relationships with white women, including Griffiths, concluding that "Douglass never lost his head." Philip Foner followed Quarles's interpretation closely, adding more detail about Griffiths's time in Rochester. Waldo Martin Jr. incorporated Anna into this dynamic and addressed not simply the perceptions of impropriety in Douglass's friendships with white women but also the anxieties about "the interrelated fears of white female dissatisfaction and black male supersexuality." William McFeely, in an attempt to give more life to his subject, contended that the motive behind Griffiths's was dedication to Douglass and his paper was purely emotional. He simultaneously increased her presence in Douglass's life and decreased her importance to his work. Maria Diedrich, technically the biographer of Ottilie Assing, made many assumptions about the relationships among Frederick, Anna, and Julia that seemed intended more to support her contention that Douglass carried on a passionate, decades-long, and "semi-public" affair with Assing than to address Griffiths's work, which was significantly greater than Assing's in regard to Douglass. She also overlooked the element of protest in the public side of the friendship between Griffiths and Douglass, inconsistently arguing that the controversy surrounding that relationship led to his secrecy with Assing. All of these biographers, however, demonstrate a singular lack of curiosity about Griffiths herself, never questioning Douglass's decision to trust her with his business or her life outside of Douglass's office and house. Yet, as early as 1971, Erwin Palmer focused on the work that the two did together, characterizing their relationship as a partnership, highlighting many of Griffiths's innovations, and suggesting her role in the friendship between Douglass and Smith. In her study on the women of Rochester, Nancy Hewitt showed the extent of Griffiths's activism by separating Griffiths from Douglass and placing her in the context of antislavery and reforming women in the city. More recently, a group of articles have turned their attention to Griffiths herself. Janet Douglas, Sarah Meer, and Frank E. Fee Jr., have teased out Griffiths's personal history in England both before and after her sojourn in America. Their work breaks Griffiths out of the earlier narrative rut as Douglass's appendage, which dated back to the Garrisonians' perspective, and includes Griffiths in a transatlantic movement against slavery, a point heretofore unconsidered. Literary scholar Hugh Egan is working on a project, based on more data, to more accurately describe Griffiths's influence on Douglass's writing. Diedrich, *LACL*, xxiii–xxiv, xvi–xvii, 117, 148–50, 171, 179–86, 188, 192, 194–95, 208–10, 223, 262, 289, 306, 369, 382, 402n45, 420n111; Foner, *Frederick Douglass: A Biography*, 87–92, 132–33, 135–36, 145–46, 150, 217, 338, 342, 352, 400, 401; Hewitt, *Women's Activism*, 136, 140–41, 150, 167, 185, 189, 234–35, 243; Holland, *Frederick Douglass*, 180, 181, 216, 262; McFeely, *Frederick Douglass*, 145, 161–82, 203, 214, 218, 240, 248, 321, 326–27, 336, 386; Martin, *Mind of Frederick Douglass*, 40–46, 99,

137-38; Quarles, *Frederick Douglass*, 87-88, 91-95, 103-7, 306; Janet Douglas, "A Cherished Friendship: Julia Griffiths Crofts and Frederick Douglass," *Slavery & Abolition* 33, 2 (June 2012): 265-74; Frank E. Fee Jr., "To No One More Indebted: Frederick Douglass and Julia Griffiths, 1849-63," *Journalism History* 37, 1 (Spring 2011): 12-16; Sarah Meer, "Public and Personal Letters: Julia Griffiths and *Frederick Douglass' Paper*," *Slavery & Abolition* 33, 2 (June 2012): 251-64; E. Palmer, "Partnership", 1-19; e-mail correspondence between Leigh Fought and Hugh Egan, January 2014.

6. FD, *L&T*, 202.

7. Samuel May to John Estlin, Massachusetts, 31 October 1848, ASC, BPL.

8. FD, *MBMF*, 227.

9. MWC to SHG, [Boston], July 1845, 19 May 1846, MWC to Francis Jackson, Boston, 11 July 1845, SHGP, ZCU; WLG to Edmund Quincy, Boston, 18 July 1845, GFP, SNN.

10. AKF to Stephen Foster, Worcester, 28 September 1847, AKF to SHG, Geneva, Ohio, 6 July, 25 July, 11 August 1845, AKFP, AQM.

11. WLG to Edmund Quincy, 4 December 1847, GFP, SNN.

12. FD, *L&T*, 202-3; MWC to SHG, Boston, [July 1845], SHGP, ZCU; Robertson, *Hearts*, 144-51.

13. Samuel May to John Estlin, Boston, 31 October 1848, ASC, BPL.

14. Edmund Quincy to MWC, Dedham, Mass., 2 July 1847, 30 July, ASC, BPL.

15. *Lib.*, 4 June 1847; *Pennsylvania Freeman*, 2 September 1847.

16. *Lib.*, 9 July 1847.

17. The other three black-edited newspapers were van Rensselaer's *Ram's Horn* (1846-1848), David Ruggles's *Genius of Freedom* (1845-47), both published in New York City, and the Washington, DC, *National Era* (1847-1860). C. Peter Ripley, ed., *The Black Abolitionist Papers* (Chapel Hill: University of North Carolina Press, 1991), 4: 10-11; FD, *Correspondence*, 1:222n4.

18. FD to SHG, Pittsburgh, 13 August 1847, SHGP, ZCU.

19. *Pennsylvania Freeman*, 2 September 1847.

20. Martin R. Delany to FD, *NS*, 21 January 1848; Robert S. Levine, *Martin Delany, Frederick Douglass, and the Politics of Representative Identity* (Chapel Hill: University of North Carolina Press, 1997), 20, 31.

21. Robertson, *Hearts*, 135, 145-47, 244n35; [Salem, Ohio] *Anti-Slavery Bugle*, 17, 24 September, 1, 8, 22, 29 October, 26 November 1847, 21 January, 14 April 1848.

22. AKF to MWC, Worcester, Mass., 5 October 1847, Samuel May to John B. Estlin, Boston, 30 September 1847, ASC, BPL.

23. AKF to Stephen Foster, Worcester, Mass., 28 September 1847, AKFP, AQM.

24. Douglass's prospectus for his paper appeared in the *Anti-Slavery Bugle* from 17 September through 22 October 1847. On 3 October, the publishing committee of the *Bugle* called a meeting in the morning, and the executive committee of the Garrisonian Western Anti-Slavery Society met that afternoon. "Business of importance will claim the attention of both," ran the notice. Five days later, "A Special Notice to Subscribers" announced that control of the *Bugle* would transfer to the Western Anti-Slavery Society executive committee, "and will in the future, be the property, as well as the organ of that Society." As their first order of business, they called in all overdue subscription payments amounting to "more than one thousand dollars" in order to pay the paper's debt, which had heretofore been covered by "the generosity of one individual," Brooke, who was owed $508.75. The next month, Brooke resigned as agent for the society due to poor health. In January 1848, the *Bugle* reported that Brooke had become an agent for the *North Star*. In July 1849, Oliver Johnson took over as editor. Like the *Star*, the *Bugle* struggled with debt for the next several years. [Salem, Ohio] *Anti-Slavery Bugle*, 17, 24 September; 1, 8, 22, 29 October; 26 November 1847; 21 January; 14 April 1848; 11 May; 1, 15 June; 6 July 1849; *NS*, 3 December 1847; Robertson, *Hearts*, 135, 145-47, 244n35.

25. FD to SHG, Rochester, 8 January 1848, SHGP, ZCU.

26. AKF to MWC, Worcester, Mass., 5 October 1847, ASC, BPL.

27. MWC to John Estlin, Boston, 30 September 1847, ASC; Samuel May to John Estlin, Boston, 30 September 1847; WLG to Helen Garrison, Cleveland, 20 October 1847, ASC, BPL.

May reported that Douglass insisted that he had told Garrison of his plans, "just before he [Garrison] was taken ill at Cleveland. Mr. Garrison, however, has no recollection whatever of it." May to Estlin, Boston, 4 March 1848, ASC, BPL.

28. Amy Kirby, born in Jericho in 1802, was the second oldest of eight children of Jacob and Mary Kirby. Isaac was born in 1798 in Westbury, the son of Edmund and Catherine (née Willets) Post. The families had intricate relationships through business and marriage. Isaac had originally married Hannah Kirby, Amy's older sister, and they had two children, Mary and a boy named either Edmund or Henry who died before reaching adulthood. Amy carried on an epistolary romance with Charles Willets, who died in 1825 before they could marry. Hannah Post died two years later. Amy acted as guardian to the two children. For expediency and affection, she and Isaac married a year later and had four children in the course of their marriage: Jacob (b. 1829), Joseph W. (b. 1832), Matilda (c. 1840–1845), and Willet E. (b. 1847). They may also have had a son, Henry, in 1837, who died in infancy. Amy's younger sister, Sarah Kirby, joined the Posts in 1834, and married Jeffries Hallowell in 1838. He died in 1844, leaving the Posts with the burden of his debts. Sarah returned to the Post household until she married Isaac's business partner, Edmund P. Willis, in 1853. Mary, daughter of Hannah and Isaac, married William Hallowell in 1843. Amy herself was an important figure in Rochester reform but has received little attention. For full biographical treatments, see Nancy Hewitt, "Amy Kirby Post: 'Of whom it was said, "being dead, yet speaketh,"'" *University of Rochester Library Bulletin*, 37 (1984): 1–9; Blake McKelvey, "Civic Medals Awarded Posthumously," *Rochester History* 22, 2 (April 1960): 1–24. For her work with other activists, see Hewitt, *Women's Activism*; Painter, *Sojourner Truth*, 118–19; Sterling, *Ahead of Her Time*, 164–65; Washington, *Sojourner Truth's America*, 214–16; Jean Fagan Yellin, *Harriet Jacobs: A Life* (New York: Basic Civitas Books, 2004), 101–5. Additional biographical information can be found in the finding aids for IAKPFP, NRU; Amy Kirby Papers, MiU-C.

29. Paul E. Johnson, *A Shopkeeper's Millennium: Society and Revivals in Rochester, New York, 1815-37* (New York: Hill and Wang, 1978); Hewitt, *Women's Activism*, 21–3; Hewitt, "Amy Kirby Post," 1–9; Biographical Sketch, Finding Aid, IAKPFP, NRU; Finding Aid, Amy Kirby Papers, MiU-C.

30. Abigail Mott to AK[F], Albany, 18 August 1842, AKFP, AQM; Mary McClintock to Elizabeth Gay, Waterloo, N.Y., 9 August 1857, SHGP, ZCU; FD, *MBMF*, 229–30.

31. Correspondence in IAKPFP, NRU.

32. Mary Ann Johnson to AKP, Boston, 15 November 1842, IAKPFP, NRU; Hewitt, *Women's Activism*, 126–28.

33. AKP to MWC, Rochester, 1 May 1846, ASC, BPL.

34. Douglass lamented to Post that he was having difficulty funneling donations directly to her fair because "it is very difficult to turn off attention from one society to another," especially when British societies identified Boston as the sole repository of American abolitionism. FD to AKP, Darlington, England, 28 April 1846, IAKPFP, NRU.

35. *NS*, 3 December 1847. The day that the *Bugle* reported his plans to open shop in Cleveland, Douglass spoke in Rochester. FD, *Speeches*, 1:xix.

36. *NS*, 3 December 1847.

37. *NS*, 3 December 1847.

38. *Lib.*, 16 December 1853; Robert P. Smith, "William Cooper Nell: Crusading Black Abolitionists," *Journal of Negro History* 55, 3 (July 1970): 182–99.

39. FD to AKP, [Albany], 30 January 1848, IAKPFP, NRU.

40. AKP to Anne Warren Weston, Rochester, 14 November 1848, IAKPP, NRU. Anne Weston had taken over the management of the fair when her sister, Maria Weston Chapman, departed for an extended tour of England earlier that year. Chapman continued to solicit foreign donations for the Boston fair while overseas. Clinton, "Maria Weston Chapman," in Barker-Benfield and Clinton, *Portraits of American Women*, 157.

41. Circular for Rochester Anti-Slavery Bazaar, [c. May 1848], ASC, BPL.

42. Draft of Anne Warren Weston to AKP, Boston, 19 December 1848, ASC, BPL.

43. AKP to Anne Warren Weston, Rochester, 10 January 1850, ASC, BPL.

44. Isabel Jennings to MWC, Cork, Ireland, 1 November 1848, ASC, BPL.

45. John Estlin to SM, Bristol, England, 30 August 1848, ASC, BPL.
46. RDW to MWC, Dublin, Ireland 24 September 1848, ASC, BPL.
47. A. H. Francis to John Dick, Buffalo, 5 January 1849, NS, 12 January 1849.
48. Samuel May to Mary Carpenter, Boston, 4 March 1848, ASC, BPL.
49. Samuel May to Mary Carpenter, Boston, 4 March 1848, ASC, BPL.
50. John Estlin to Samuel May, Bristol, England, 30 August 1848, ASC, BPL.
51. Samuel May to John Estlin, Boston, 31 October 1848, ASC, BPL.
52. Samuel May to Mary Carpenter, Boston, 4 March 1848, ASC, BPL.
53. Samuel May to John Estlin, Boston, 31 October 1848, ASC, BPL.
54. Joseph Lupton of Leeds wrote Chapman that he "was sorry to find what you thought of Douglass's prospects both as to the Bazaar, & more particularly his paper." Lupton to MWC, Buxton, England, 21 September 1848, ASC, BPL.
55. Circular, "Rochester Anti-Slavery Bazaar," [May 1848], Anne Warren Weston to Caroline Weston, Boston, 12–14 November 1848, ASC, BPL.
56. RDW to MWC, Dublin, Ireland, 24 September 1848, ASC, BPL.
57. RDW to MWC, Dublin, Ireland, 14 November 1848, ASC, BPL.
58. Joseph Lupton to MWC, Buxton, England, 21 September 1848, ASC, BPL.
59. Samuel May to John Estlin, Boston, 31 October 1848, ASC, BPL.
60. Henry Mayer, *All on Fire: William Lloyd Garrison and the Abolition of Slavery* (New York: St. Martin's Press, 1998), 101.
61. NS, 11 February, 30 June 1848; Samuel May to John Estlin, Boston, 15 December 1847, ASC, BPL. As tempting as is the urge to call Dick an experienced printer, his full biography remains to be sorted. May believed him to be the son of Scottish astronomer Thomas Dick, whom Williams Wells Brown and William and Ellen Craft met in Dundee in 1851. John Dick and Eliza Griffith married in 1850 and lived in Philadelphia and Toronto before immigrating to Dunedin, New Zealand, in 1862. Both Griffiths's brother and many of the Dick family had also moved to New Zealand in the 1850s, and Julia believed that Dick's father had become a New Zealand representative. The noted Dick of New Zealand's government, however, was Thomas Dick, a Scottish-born merchant and the son of a merchant, of an age to be John's brother, who had immigrated to Dunedin in 1857. As for John's printing experience, Douglass probably would not have hired him had he been unskilled; and after he left Rochester, he worked as a printer for both the *Provincial Freeman* and the *Toronto Globe*. His son, Thomas Edwin Dick, also became a printer. William Wells Brown, *Three Years in Europe* (Edinburgh, 1852), 181–83; JG[C] to FD, Leeds, 1 September 1862, FDP, DLC; "Dick, Eliza Griffiths," "Dick, John," "Dick, Thomas Edwin," Cemeteries Database, Dunedin City Council (www.dunedin.govt.nz/faciliites/cemeteries, retrieved 24 January 2014); "Dick, Thomas," *An Encyclopaedia of New Zealand*, ed. A. H. McClintock (1966; http://www.teara.govt.nz/en/1966/dick-thomas, retrieved 24 January 2014).
62. Anne Warren Weston to Caroline Weston, Boston, 12–14 November 1848, ASC, BPL.
63. Samuel May to John Estlin, Boston, 31 October 1848, ASC, BPL.
64. FD to SHG, Rochester, 8 January 1848, SHGP, ZCU; WLG, "Preface," to FD, *Narr.*, 4–5.
65. FD to AKP, Albany, [11 April 1848], IAKPFP, NRU. Douglass wrote this letter from Albany because he mentioned seeing the Mott sisters who lived there, but the date is more likely around 7 May 1848, when he had a speaking engagement in the city. On 11 April, he was speaking in Millport, followed by Springport, Auburn, Rochester, and Syracuse. FD, *Speeches*, 2:xxi–xxii.
66. "Prospectus for an Anti-Slavery Paper," 19–20 July 1848, IAKPFP, NRU.
67. Frederick Douglass to AKP, Westbury, N.Y., 22 April [1849], IAKPFP, NRU.
68. AKF to SHG, Union Village N.Y., 1 March 1850, SHGP, ZCU.
69. FD to GS, Rochester, 1 May 1851, GSP, NSyU.
70. Isaac Post to AKP, Rochester, 7 May 1849, IAKPFP, NRU.
71. FD to AKP, Macedon, N.Y., 11 September 1849, IAKPFP, NRU.
72. FD, *Speeches*, 2:xxvi.
73. Draft of AKP to FD, Rochester, [11 September 1849], IAKPFP, NRU.
74. FD to William Hallowell, Fulton, N.Y., 16 September 1849, IAKPFP, NRU.

75. Mary and Margaret Howitt, *Mary Howitt, an Autobiography* (London, 1889), 2:33; "Extract from a letter from Miss S. Carpenter respecting Frederick Douglass," [Mary Carpenter to MWC], [London], [c. 30 March 1847]; JG[C] to Francis Jackson, London, 17 July [1847], ASC, BPL. The letter is dated 1846, but internal evidence in the document indicates that it was written in 1847. Both by her own admission and her absence from all other correspondence prior to March 1847 indicate that she did not know Douglass before March 1847. Until she arrived in the United States in 1849, she was most commonly mentioned in association with the Howitts.

76. RDW to Caroline Weston, Dublin, Ireland, 22 February 1849, ASC, BPL. Fee counted two songs as being attributed to Griffiths. A cover of the music surfaced in a 2012 auction at Swann Galleries, which indicated that Griffiths had composed the music and her brother, Thomas Powis Griffiths, wrote the lyrics. The accompanying lithograph of Douglass presented him from chest up, wearing a Roman toga with one shoulder bared. "Very Rare Portrait of Douglass," Printed & Manuscript African Americana, Lot 45, Sale 2271, 1 March 2012, Swann Galleries (http://catalogue.swanngalleries.com/asp/fullCatalogue.asp?salelot =2271++++++45+&refno=++653331&saletype=, retrieved 22 July 2014).

77. John Estlin to Samuel May, Bristol, England, 30 January 1849, ASC, BPL.

78. John Estlin to Anne Warren Weston, Bristol, England, 29 April 1850, ASC, BPL.

79. John Estlin to Samuel May, Bristol, England 30 January 1849, and Samuel May to John Estlin, Boston, 21 May 1849, 5 June 1849, ASC, BPL; FD to AKP and Isaac Post, Westbury, N.Y., 22 April [1849], FD to Isaac Post, Canada West, [15 July 1849], FD to AKP, Niagara, 17 July 1849, IAKPFP, NRU. Some of Douglass's biographers, such as Maria Diedrich and Erwin Palmer, have written that Griffiths "followed" Douglass to the United States. This mischaracterization invites an easy inference that Griffiths was unwelcome and that she entertained an unhealthy interest in Douglass, and it discounts her contributions to transatlantic discussions of emancipation. A letter written in 1850 but misdated as 1847, as well as Benjamin Quarles's dating of her arrival to 1848, has contributed to this view. Internal evidence in that letter and all other documentation indicates that the Griffiths sisters arrived in New York in May 1849, two years after Douglass had returned. Diedrich, *LACL*, 86; E. Palmer, "Partnership," 1–19; Quarles, *Frederick Douglass*, 87; Julia Griffiths to Anne Warren Weston, Rochester, 11 January [1847], ASC, BPL; Steamer *Sarah Sands*, Liverpool, England, 2 May 1849, Passenger Lists, District of New York, Port of New York.

80. RDW to Caroline Weston, Dublin, Ireland, 22 February 1849, ASC, BPL.

81. Isaac Post to AKP, Rochester, 15 May 1849, IAKPFP, NRU; Anne Warren Weston to MWC, Weymouth, Mass., 5 June 1849, ASC, BPL.

82. Anne Warren Weston to MWC, Weymouth, Mass., 5 June 1849, ASC, BPL; Jacob Kirby Post to Amy and Isaac Post, Jericho, N.Y. 28 October[1850], IAKPFP, NRU.

83. *NS*, 25 May 1849.

84. *NS*, 15 June, 20 July, 31 August 1849; Samuel May to John Estlin, Boston, 5 June 1849, ASC, BPL.

85. Samuel May to John Estlin, Boston, 5 June 1849, ASC, BPL.

86. Anne Warren Weston to MWC, Weymouth, Mass., 5 June 1849, ASC, BPL.

87. *NS*, 30 May 1850.

88. Jane Marsh Parker, "Reminiscences of Frederick Douglass," Howard W. Coles Collection, RMSCL.

89. "Stories of Douglass," Scrapbooks, Evans Collection.

90. Isaac Post to AKP, Rochester, 22 May 1849, IAKPFP, NRU.

91. Samuel May to John Estlin, Boston, 5 June 1849, ASC, BPL; Marsh, "Reminiscences," Coles Collection, RMSCL.

92. Draft of AKP to Frederick Douglass, [Rochester], 11 September 1849, IAKPFP, NRU.

93. *NS*, 15 June 1849.

94. *NS*, 25 May 1849. Fredericka Bremer, on a visit to Rochester, visited the Douglass household and commended the bravery of a governess living there. While the Douglasses had employed Phebe Thayer in that role, the timing of Bremer's visit suggests that she may have mistaken one of the Griffithses for the governess. If not, then the same sort of praise would also apply to the Griffithses, who were also white women living in a black family. Frederika Bremer, *Homes of the New World: Impressions of America*, trans. Mary Howitt (New York, 1853), 1:585–86.

95. FD to JG[C], Rochester, 28 April 1848, FDP, DLC.

96. *NS*, 21 September 1849.

97. FD, *Speeches*, 2:xxviii.

98. *NS*, 25 January 1850; *NS* ledger books, 1847–49, 1850–53, Financial Papers, FDP, DLC. Griffiths's name was seldom in the paper except as the author of her columns, so her official role did not appear on the masthead. The 1855 state census listed her as the assistant editor of the paper. 1855 New York State Census, Monroe Co., Rochester, Ward 7, 461.

99. Many seemed not to have understood Griffiths's role at the office. The first indication that Griffiths had begun acting in an official capacity appears in a letter from Griffiths to Anne Warren Weston in which Griffiths wrote, "I am requested by Mr. Douglass, to acknowledge the receipt of your letter," and then issued instructions for sending along donations from Cork for the Rochester fair. Such missives and others frustrated many of Douglass's correspondents, who viewed Griffiths as meddling rather than doing her job. JG[C] to Anne Warren Weston, Rochester, 11 January 1847 [1850], Isabel Jennings to Mary Estlin, Cork, Ireland, 24 March [1851], Parker Pillsbury to MWC, Glasgow, Scotland, 3 September, 1853, ASC, BPL.

100. Until recently, this development has piqued little curiosity. If the paper did face collapse, and if a committee of businessmen had appointed an experienced publisher such as John Dick to manage that aspect of the concern, then the appointment of a woman who had little to recommend herself but her devotion to Douglass was a spectacularly unwise decision. His biographers all noted her subsequent success but offered no explanation for the reversal of fortunes under her tenure. Neither have they explored the connection between the paper's success and the ensuing controversies that targeted this particular friendship and dragged Anna Douglass into public notice far beyond accepted parameters of decency. Indeed, even at the time, no one questioned the wisdom of Griffiths's role in the *Star*'s office.

101. Circular for Rochester Anti-Slavery Bazaar, [c. May 1848], and Circular advertising *NS* in Britain [c. May 1848], ASC, BPL. Letters in which Griffiths is noted as being in company of or communication with Mary Howitt include Anne Warren Weston to Caroline Weston, Boston, 12–14 November 1848, John Estlin to Samuel May, Bristol, England, 30 January 1849, RDW to Caroline Weston, Dublin, 22 February 1849, Anne Warren Weston to MWC, Weymouth, Mass., 5 June 1849, ASC, BPL; FD to JG[C], Rochester, 13 October 1847, in FD, *Correspondence*, 1:262.

102. *NS*, 20 July 1849. The correspondent also identified the Griffithses as having just toured "on the continent, in Austria, Germany, &c," which was not the case.

103. Isaac Post to AKP, Rochester, 15 May, 19 May 1849, IAKPFP, NRU.

104. James McCune Smith, introduction to FD, *MBMF*, 12.

105. In addition to Eliza (b. 1822), Julia's siblings included Joseph Littleton (b. 1814), Thomas (b. 1817), and Charlotte Augusta (b. 1819). The Saint Marylebone baptismal registers indicate that Charlotte and Thomas Griffiths also had a daughter, Mary Eliza, born in February 1813, early enough to allow for Joseph Littleton's birth nineteen months later. Other records indicate, with surprising consistency, that Eliza Griffiths was born around 1822. London Metropolitan Archives, Saint Marylebone, Register of Baptisms, January 1811–December 1812 P89/MRY1, Item 013, Births and Baptisms, 1813–1906, P89/MR1, Items 014, 015, 020, St. Mary Abchurch, Register of Baptisms, Guildhall, P69/MRY1/A/01, Item MS 24742; *London Gazette*, 12 May 1835; Fee, "To No One More Indebted," 15–16, 24n35; Douglas, "Cherished Friendship," 265–66, 272n3–7.

106. FD to GS, Rochester, 1 May 1851, GSP, NSyU.

107. *NS*, 1 February 1850; Mary Springstead to AKP, Cazenovia, 9 September 1850, IAKPFP, NRU.

108. Salmon P. Chase to FD, Washington, DC, 4 May 1850, in FD, *Correspondence*, 1:414–16; JG[C] to William H. Seward, Rochester, 26 March [1851], William Seward Papers, NRU.

109. Isaac Post to AKP, Rochester, 19 May 1849, IAKPFP, NRU.

110. William McFeely described the merger of the two papers as collapsing, but evidence indicates otherwise. McFeely, *Frederick Douglass*, 167–68; FD, *Correspondence*, 1: 445–67; FD

to GS, Rochester, 31 January, 1 May, 15 May, 21 May, 28 May, 29 May, 4 June, 10 June, [18 June] 1851, GSP, NSyU.

111. Samuel May to John Estlin, Boston, 21 May 1849, ASC, BPL.

112. FD, L&T, 205. The numbers are difficult to corroborate. Surviving subscription books are incomplete, as are full runs of Douglass's papers, which often listed new and delinquent subscribers. His son Charles, who worked in the paper's office during the 1850s, insisted they had 5,000 subscribers, while clerk William Oliver later insisted that the circulation had never gone over 1,500. These estimates, however, were cited in 1882, 1895, and 1917, without documentation. "Stories of Douglass," Scrapbooks; CRD, "Some Incidents," 13 February 1917, Evans Collection.

113. JG[C] to GS, Rochester, 23 July 1851, GSP, NSyU.

114. JG[C] to GS, Rochester, 13 December [1851], GSP, NSyU.

115. JG[C] to GS, Rochester, [c. 1852], GSP, NSyU.

116. FD, L&T, 205.

117. NS, 1 February 1850. This practice was also used by the Washington National Leader, when Frederick Douglass Jr. was associate editor, in 1889. National Leader, 26 January 1889.

118. Deborah Weston to Anne Warren Weston, New York, N.Y., 21 April 1850, ASC, BPL.

119. Anne Warren Weston to Mary Ann Estlin, Weymouth, Mass., 4 April 1852, ASC, BPL.

120. JG[C] to GS, Rochester, 22 February [1852], GSP, NSyU.

121. NS, 1 February 1850.

122. JG[C] to GS, Rochester, 24 September [1851], GSP, NSyU.

123. FD to GS, Rochester, 1 May 1851, GSP, NSyU. Douglass had initially purchased a steam press with the British donation, but John Dick and William C. Nell deemed it insufficient to meet the paper's needs. They hired another company to cover that part of production, whose work Douglass considered inadequate; he preferred to control all stages of the publishing process once he was able. In the same letter in which Abby Kelley Foster wrote of Douglass's plans to turn the North Star over to the Standard, she mentioned that "his press is already gone," suggesting that he also may have sold the old press to pay his debts. AKF to SHG, Union Village, [New York], 19 March 1850, SHGP, ZCU.

124. JG[C] to GS, Rochester, 23 July 1851, GSP, NSyU.

125. GS to JG[C] (copy), Peterboro, N.Y., 25 July 1851, GSP, NSyU.

126. FD to GS, Rochester, 2 September 1851, JG[C] to GS, Rochester, 31 March [1852], GSP, NSyU.

127. JG[C] to GS, Rochester, 26 August [1851], GSP, NSyU.

128. JG[C] to GS, Rochester, 22 February [1852], 3 May 1852, [c. 1852], GSP, NSyU.

129. FD to GS, Rochester, 10 July [1851], GSP, NSyU. This letter has sometimes been used to suggest that Griffiths was a constant source of embarrassment to Douglass, but this is the only one of its kind and appears early in their dealings with Smith as a primary donor, something Douglass had not had earlier. Therefore, his embarrassment may have been the result of his inexperience with this type of negotiation and his insolvency being made known before the first issue of Frederick Douglass's Paper came off the press. FD to GS, Rochester, 2 September 1851, GSP, NSyU; Fee, "To No One More Indebted," 16; E. Palmer, "Partnership," 4-5.

130. JG[C] to GS, Rochester, 10 July [1851], GSP, NSyU.

131. JG[C] to GS, Rochester, 26 August [1851], GSP, NSyU.

132. JG[C] to GS, Rochester, 24 November [1851], GSP, NSyU.

133. JG[C] to GS, Rochester, 26 August [1851], GSP, NSyU.

134. JG[C] to GS, Rochester, 13 December [1851], GSP, NSyU.

135. JG[C] to GS, Rochester, 22 February [1852], GSP, NSyU.

136. NS, 1 February 1850.

137. AKP to FD, Rochester, 2 February 1850, IAKPFP, NRU; Elizabeth McClintock to Elizabeth Gay, Waterloo, N.Y., 9 April 1850, SHGP, ZCU.

138. FD to AKP, Rochester, 4 February 1850, IAKPFP, NRU.

139. Mary Springstead to AKP, Cazenovia, N.Y., 9 September 1850, IAKPFP, NRU.

140. JG[C] to GS, Rochester, 26 August [1851], GSP, NSyU.

141. FD to GS, Rochester, 2 September 1851, GSP, NSyU.
142. JG[C] to GS, Canandaigua, N.Y., 26 October[1852], GSP, NSyU.
143. WCN to AKP, Boston, 21 November 1854, IAKPFP, NRU.
144. Nancy Hewitt painstakingly traces the evolutions and intersections of the careers of white Rochester women. Chapter 5, "Coalitions and Confrontations," particularly informed this description. Hewitt, *Women's Activism*, 139–76.
145. Robertson, *Hearts*, 37–66; R. O. Johnson, *Liberty Party, 1840-48*, 276–85.
146. *The First Report of the Rochester Ladies' Anti-Slavery Sewing Society*, 1852, RLASP, MiU-C.
147. *First Report*, 1852, RLASP, MiU-C.
148. Account Book, RLASP, MiU-C. They also sent aid to former slave Emily Edmonson during a famine among the freedpeople of Canada West. Although the primary beneficiary in the abolitionist press was Douglass, when Rebecca Bailey, the daughter of abolitionist newspaperman William S. Bailey, wrote to tell them that a mob had destroyed her father's press in Newport, Kentucky, they raised $20 in 1857 and $30 in 1859 to help the Baileys continue publication. During the Civil War, they turned their attention to freedpeople in Alexandria, Virginia. Rebecca Bailey to Anna M.C. Barnes, Newport, Ky., 21 September 1859; Rebecca Bailey to Anna M.C. Barnes, Newport, Ky., 20 February [1859]; Account Book, RLASP, MiU-C.
149. *First Report*, 1852, RLASP, MiU-C.
150. JG[C] to GS, 26 August [1851], Rochester, GSP, NSyU.
151. AKP to FD, Rochester, 2 February 1850, IAKPFP, NRU.
152. Account Book, Annual Reports from 1853–55, RLASP, MiU-C. They also increased the proceeds of the year by selling surplus or late items throughout the year. *Autographs for Freedom*, also available throughout the year, included contributions from prominent abolitionists followed by an engraving of their signature. The title was suggested by Harriet Beecher Stowe, *Autographs for Freedom*. Harriet Beecher Stowe to Susan Farley Porter, Brunswick, 20 June 1852, PFP, NRU.
153. JG[C] to Anna M. C. Barnes, Halifax, England, 5 August [1859], RLASP, MiU-C.
154. Account Book, Annual Reports, 1853-55, RLASP, MiU-C. Proceeds from the RLAS fair were $408.00 in 1852, $515.62 in 1853, $579.35 in 1854, $579.35 in 1855. Donations to *Frederick Douglass' Paper* were $233.12 in 1852, $300.00 in 1853, $275.00 in 1854, and $320.00 in 1855. Proceeds from foreign goods were $144.02 in 1852, $103.32 in 1853, $294.40 in 1854, and $365.39 in 1855.
155. WCN to AKP, Boston, 20 January 1854, IAKPFP, NRU.
156. WCN to AKP, Boston, September 1854, IAKPFP, NRU.
157. WCN to AKP, Boston, 10 September 1854, IAKPFP, NRU.
158. WCN to AKP, Boston, 21 November 1854, IAKPFP, NRU.
159. FD, *MBMF*, 228.
160. WCN to AKP, Boston, 22 June 1853, IAKPFP, NRU.
161. *Lib.*, 18 November 1853.

Chapter 5

1. *Lib.*, 2 December 1853. Maria Diedrich questioned Anna's authorship of this letter, insisting that it "amazed everyone who knew the Douglasses enough to know of Anna Murray's illiteracy." Anna Douglass, who did not use the name Murray after her marriage, dictated letters to others, as did most people who could not read or write. Diedrich, *LACL*, 183.
2. SBA to WLG, Rochester, 13 December 1853, ASC, BPL.
3. *Lib.*, 16 December 1853.
4. *Lib.*, 16 December 1853.
5. *Lib.*, 16 December 1853.
6. Milette Shamir, *Inexpressible Privacy: The Interior Life of Antebellum American Literature* (Philadelphia: University of Pennsylvania Press, 2006), 15–16, 24–26.
7. RDS, *MMAIRH*, 16, 17; LHD, Essay [n.d.], Addition II, FDP, DLC; CRD, "Some Incidents," 13 February 1917, Evans Collection; Ball, *To Live an Antislavery Life*, 2–3.

8. The four boys included Jeremiah Perkins, William [last name illegible], William Winston, and Floyd Richard. Anna also took in Rosetta's sister-in-law, Louisa Sprague. 1855 New York State Census, Monroe County, Rochester, Ward 7, 461; 1879 U.S. Census, New York, Monroe County, Rochester, Ward 12, 15; CRD to FD, February 1869, Washington, DC, FDP, DLC; RDS, *MMAIRH*, 18; CRD, "Some Incidents," Evans Collection; *Rochester Post Express*, 7 June 1884; Ball, *To Live an Antislavery Life*, 106–8; Stephanie Coontz, *The Way We Never Were: American Families and the Nostalgia Trap* (New York: Basic, 1992), 9–12; Wendy Gamber, "Tarnished Labor: The Home, the Market, and the Boardinghouse in Antebellum America," *Journal of the Early Republic* 22, 2 (Summer 2002): 177–204. Additionally, all three Douglass siblings wrote these memoirs around the turn of the nineteenth century, when they were battling with their father's second wife and the Frederick Douglass Memorial and Historical Association over commemorations of their father.

9. Jane Marsh Parker, "Reminiscences of Frederick Douglass," Howard W. Coles Collection, Rochester Museum and Science Center Library; Clifford E. Clark Jr., "Domestic Architecture as an Index to Social History: The Romantic Revival and the Cult of Domesticity in America, 1840-1870," *Material Life in America, 1600-1860*, ed. Robert Blair St. George (Boston: Northeastern University Press, 1987), 535–49; Larkin, *Reshaping of Everyday Life*, 119–20, 125–26; JG[C] to GS, Rochester, 13 December [1851], GSP, NSyU. Neither of Douglass's homes in Rochester survived to the twenty-first century. A single image purporting to be of the Alexander Street home, taken in the early twentieth century, shows a two-story brick building with a gable end front, shallow wooden porch, and a rear addition with two chimneys, sitting near the front of the lot, near the street. This home was probably the first that Douglass owned. Charles Douglass believed that his father had purchased the house in Lynn, whereas Rosetta insisted that her father had built it. The latter seems unlikely given the amount of time, skill, and cost required, none of which Frederick possessed at that time. He did own the Rochester house, which he mortgaged to Eliza Griffiths in order to stabilize the finances of his paper. No known photograph exists of the home on South Street, which burned down in 1872. "[Frederick Douglass Home on Alexander Street]," 1920-40?, image number rpf02425, Local History Division, Rochester Public Library; CRD, "Some Incidents," 13 February 1917, Evans Collection; RDS, *MMAIRH*, 10.

10. RDS, *MMAIRH*, 16; Shamir, *Inexpressible Privacy*, 15–16, 24–26.

11. A lecture tour took Frederick to Lynn around 3 February 1848. He did not return to New England until the following May or to Lynn itself until October. The February visit may have included settling business there to prepare his family to move to Rochester at that time. Through the spring, he passed through Albany, writing from the Motts's home in January and in April, but he only mentioned Rosetta during the winter visit. It appears that she did not begin school in Rochester until September. Although Lewis and perhaps Charles had reached school age, little documentation exists in regard to their education during 1848. FD, *Speeches*, 1:xxi–xxii; FD to AKP, [Albany], 30 January 1848, [11 April 1848], IAKPFP, NRU.

12. Harriet Bailey, also known as Ruth Cox, married Perry Frank Adams, a free black man who, like herself and Douglass, hailed from Talbot County, Maryland. She and Adams had three children, Matilda Ann, Perry Frank, and Ebby, and later adopted a son, Samuel Hall, after his mother died. In the 1850s, they became involved in the League of Gileadites, a vigilance committed composed of fugitive slaves and their families and endorsed by John Brown. After their daughter, Ebby, died, they immigrated to Haiti in 1861, part of a colony that included Eli Baptist and Bishop J. C. Holly. The expedition was a disaster, and Harriet, Matilda, and Perry Sr. returned to Springfield. After Perry Sr.'s death, Harriet and Matilda moved to Providence, where Matilda married William Van der Zee, and the three migrated to Nebraska in the 1880s. Alice V. Coffee, "Lest We Forget" (unpublished family history), Alyce McWilliams Hall Collection, Nebraska State Historical Society; Norfolk [Nebraska] *Weekly News*, 7 March 1894; Clifford L. Stott, comp. *Vital Records of Springfield, Massachusetts to 1850*, 4 vols. (Boston, 2003), 2:1420, 1583; "Resolutions of the Springfield Branch of the United States League of Gileadites. Adopted 15th Jan., 1851." Sanborn, *Life and Letters of John Brown*, 126–27; *Massachusetts Vital Records: Springfield, 1640–1894*, vol. 4: *Deaths, 1858–1861*, 60; Hampden County Register of Probate, Case 5198, Estate of Eliza A. Hall, 1859; Joseph

Caravalho III, *Black Families in Hampden County, Massachusetts, 1650-1855* (Boston, 1984), 25, 64; 1860 U.S. Census, Massachusetts, Hampden County, Springfield, 205.

13. 1850 U.S. Census, New York, Monroe County, Rochester, Ward 3, 258; 1855 New York State Census, Monroe County, Rochester, Ward 7, 461; A[M]D to HB/RCA, Rochester, 11 March 1851, Addition II, FDP, DLC.

14. William C. Nell described Dick among the occupants and Thayer as "installed as governess" at 4 Alexander St. In 1850, Dick married Eliza Griffiths and moved to Philadelphia, while Thayer had already joined two of her sisters in her brother-in-law's home. Although Fredericka Bremer described a governess living in the Douglass household in 1852, she seemed to mistake Julia Griffiths in that role. Whether Thayer lived in the house or not, she presented a regular, if invited, intrusion on the family's space, and she belonged to the Garrisonian faction in the city that grew increasingly alienated from Douglass after 1850. WCN to AKP, Boston, 2 June 1850, IAKPFP, NRU; 1850 U.S. Census, New York, Monroe County, Rochester, Ward 3, 258; *NS*, 10 August, 19 October 1849; Gamber, "Tarnished Labor," 177–204.

15. Parker, "Reminiscences," Coles Collection, RMSCL; Bremer, *Homes of the New World*, 1:585–86; JG[C] to GS, 23 July 1851, GSP, NSyU.

16. Bremer, *Homes of the New World*, 1:585–86; RDS, *MMAIRH*, 14.

17. *NS*, 22 September 1848; Judith Polgar Ruchkin, "The Abolition of 'Colored Schools' in Rochester, New York, 1832-1856," *New York History* 51, 4 (July 1970): 376–93; FDjr "In brief, 1842–1890" (notation in Scrapbook), Evans Collection.

18. Parker identified the instructor as "an English woman" and the period of the incident as being during "that first summer of their living on Alexander Street," in 1848. Parker may have confused some of the details by the time she wrote her memoir a half-century later. Phebe Thayer was Canadian and did not begin teaching Rosetta until the fall. She may have left the post by 1850, when the U.S. Census records her as living with her sister Abby, in the home of another sister, Dorcas, and her husband, Henry Collins. The English Griffiths sisters did not arrive until late spring 1849, before the Douglasses' second summer in Rochester. Julia became occupied with the business of the *North Star*, but Eliza Griffiths may have assumed the position of governess for a time. She, however, could not have been the white woman described by Bremer in 1851 because she had married and moved to Toronto a year earlier. RDS, *MMAIRH*, 21; Parker, "Reminiscences," Coles Collection, RMSCL; 1850 U.S. Census, New York, Monroe County, Rochester, 3rd Ward, 265; *NS*, 27 June 1850.

19. FD, *Narr.*,76; RDS, *MMAIRH*, 18; Ball, *To Live an Antislavery Life*, 93–100; Dixon, *Perfecting the Family*, 181–88.

20. Parker, "Reminiscences," Coles Collection, RMSCL; Wendy Gamber, *The Boardinghouse in Early America* (Baltimore: Johns Hopkins University Press, 2007), 40–41. Decades later, one of the Douglasses' granddaughters recalled that Anna demanded that the grandchildren remain quiet and far from Frederick's office when he was inside. Fredericka Douglass [Sprague] Perry, Recollections of her grandfather, FDC, DHU-MS.

21. WCN to AKP, Boston, 15 July 1850, IAKPFP, NRU; *FDP*, 27 June 1850; WCN to AKP, Boston, 3 July 1850, 15 July 1850, IAKPFP, NRU; Betsey Mix Cowles to AKP, Canton, 1 December 1850, IAKPFP, NRU; WCN to AKP, Boston, 15 July 1850, IAKPFP, NRU; Isabel Jennings to Mary Estlin, Cork, Ireland, 24 March [1851], ASC, BPL; George Thompson to Anne Warren Weston, Rochester, 17 March 1851, ASC, BPL.

22. FD to GS, Rochester, 21 May 1851, GSP, NSyU; JG[C] to Samuel Porter, [n.p.], [n.d.], PFP, NRU.

23. JG[C] to GS, Rochester, 24 September [1851], GSP, NSyU; FD to Samuel Porter, Rochester, [between 11 and 24 September 1851], PFP, NRU; Monique Patenaude Roach, "The Rescue of William 'Jerry' Henry: Antislavery and Racism in the Burned-over District," *New York History* 82, 2 (Spring 2001): 135–54; Sarah Hallowell Willis to AKP, Rochester, 7 October[1857], IAKPFP, NRU. In 1917, Charles Douglass declared that the Douglasses "were marked as constant violators of the Fugitive Slave laws" and "my fathers home in Rochester being the last Station on that road before reaching Canada the good of the fleeing slaves ambition." In 1901, Rosetta insisted that "father enlarged his home where a suite of rooms could be made ready for those fleeing to Canada," while "It was no unusual occurrence for mother to be called up at all hours of the night, cold or hot, as the case might be, to prepare supper for a hungry lot of

fleeing humanity." Like many Underground Railroad legends, the two shaped their accounts for the preconceived notions of a later audience and in order to include their mother in recognizable antislavery activism. Frederick more likely enlarged his smaller South Street home to make it more comfortable to family and to reflect his growing status. The RLASS account books, which recorded aid to freedom-seekers, show that most arrived by way of the actual railroad and sought out Douglass's office. Rosetta's description, however, belies the usual tales of fugitives hiding in crawl spaces, for which there is very little documentation, and supports the children's depiction of abolition as a family business by basing it in the home rather than in their father's workplace. The RLASS records also reveal that the Douglass children, working at the paper, played a part in the process and that the occasional overnight guest sometimes stayed with the family. A. Bates to Frederick Douglass or William Bloss, Syracuse, 11 February 1853; Jacob R. Gibbs to "Dear friend Morris," New York, 14 March 1854; W. E. Abbott to Maria G. Porter, Syracuse, N.Y., 9 November 1856; William J. Watkins to Mrs. Armstrong, [n.p.], [c. after 9 August 1857]; Frederick Douglass to Maria G. Porter, Rochester, 13 October 1857; Maria Webb to Anna M.C. Barnes, Dublin, Ireland, 10 October 1859; Frederick Douglass to Maria G. Porter, Rochester, 22 February [n.d.], 27 March [n.d.], 29 April [n.d.]; William Oliver to Maria G. Porter, Rochester, [n.d.]; William J. Watkins to Maria G. Porter, [n.p.], [n.d.]; Account Books, 1853-64, RLASP, MiU-C. For a dissection of the myths of the Underground Railroad, see David Blight, *Race and Reunion: The Civil War in American Memory* (Cambridge, Mass.: Belknap Press of Harvard University Press, 2001), 231–37, and Larry Gara, *The Liberty Line: the Legend of the Underground Railroad* (Lexington: University of Kentucky Press, 1961).

24. JG[C] to GS, Rochester, 24 September [1851], GSP, NSyU; FD to Samuel Porter, Rochester, [between 11 and 24 September 1851], PFP, NRU; JG[C] to GS, Rochester, 23 July 1851, GSP, NSyU. Anna also may have already begun suffering the frequent bouts of illness that afflicted her in later years. Frederick had described Anna as "seldom enjoying good health these days" when he returned from England, and he and Julia fell ill during a trip to the West just after the Griffithses had arrived in America; only Eliza escaped with good health. FD to Anna Richardson, Lynn, 29 April 1847, Newcastle-upon-Tyne *Christian*, 1 June 1847; FD to Isaac Post, Canada West, [c. 15 July 1849], FD to AKP, Niagara, 17 July 1849, IAKPFP, NRU.

25. JG[C] to GS, Rochester, 24 November 1851, GSP, NSyU.

26. JG[C] to GS, Rochester, 13 December [1851], GSP, NSyU.

27. A. James Hammerton, *Cruelty and Companionship: Conflict in Nineteenth-Century Married Life* (New York, 1992), 3, 14, 138–40; JG[C] to AKP, Rochester, 16 October 1852, IAKPFP, NRU. For the shared table, see JG[C] to GS, Rochester, 24 November 1851, GSP, NSyU. For an example of closings, in another letter that also gave a glimpse into daily work life, Frederick bid farewell to Gerrit Smith by concluding, "I write from the office or I am sure that my wife would write with Miss Griffiths (who is industriously wielding her pen at another desk) in sending love to yourself and Dear Lady." FD to GS, Rochester, 21 May 1851, GSP, NSyU.

28. SBA to WLG, Rochester, 13 December 1853, ASC, BPL; Samuel May to RDW, Boston, 9 March, 13 April 1858, ASC, BPL; *North Star*, 8 September 1848.

29. Isabel Jennings to Mary Estlin, Cork, 24 March [1851], ASC, BPL.

30. MWC to John Estlin, Paris, 9 March 1852, Anne Warren Weston to Mary Estlin, Weymouth, Mass., 4 April [1852], ASC, BPL. Rumors that issued from Estlin most likely came from Chapman. Her grapevine probably passed from the unwitting Amy Post to Nell to Garrison to the Weston sisters. The Weston sisters and Samuel May kept the Estlins informed.

31. FD to GS, Rochester, 5 February 1852, JG[C] to GS, Rochester, 9 September [1852], GSP, NSyU; Sarah L. Hallowell Willis to Mary H. Willis, Jericho, 27 December 1852, IAKPFP, NRU. Willis mentioned Australia because she had learned that one of the Griffithses' brothers had immigrated there.

32. 1850 U.S. Census, New York, Monroe County, Rochester, Ward 3, 13; *FDP*, 12 November 1852, 9 December 1853. The Weddles lived on the corner of Glasgow and Exchange streets, the same address given by Julia Griffiths as her home in 1852.

33. FD to Samuel Porter, Rochester, 12 January 1852 [1853], PFP, NRU. This letter is dated 1852 but notes that Griffiths had moved out of the Douglass home two months earlier, in

November 1851. Since Griffiths identified herself as living with the Weddles in November 1852, since Douglass could hardly conceal for a year Griffith's residence at South Street from Porter or his family, all of whom worked with Douglass and Griffiths in the same organizations, at the same events, and in the same company, and since January is a month in which people are likely to write the previous year in their dates, Douglass most likely wrote this letter a year later than the document indicates.

34. FD to Samuel Porter, Rochester, 12 January 1852 [1853], PFP, NRU; *NS*, 20 July 1849, 30 May 1850.

35. Anne Warren Weston to Mary Estlin, Weymouth, Mass., 4 April 1852, ASC, BPL.

36. 1855 New York State Census, Monroe County, Rochester, Ward 7, 461; A[M]D to HB/RCA, Rochester, 11 March 1851, Addition II, DLC; Parker, "Reminiscences," Coles Collection, RMSCL; RDS, *MMAIRH*, 18.

37. FD to Samuel Porter, Rochester, 12 January 1852 [1853], PFP, NRU. For the William Wells Brown marriage, see William Wells Brown to AKP, Buffalo, 23 June 1844, Plymouth, 16 July, 20 September 1848, Susan Doty to AKP, Macedon, N.Y., 22 November 1848, IAKPFP, NRU; *Lib.*, 12 July 1850; Sterling, *We Are Your Sisters*, 147.

38. FD to HB/RCA, London, 18 August 1846, Leamington, England, 31 January 1847, Addition II, FDP, DLC; FD, *MBMF*, 196-201; FD to Lydia Dennett, Rochester, [n.d] 1857, Houghton Library, Harvard University. Historians have used the letter to Dennett to demonstrate that the Douglass marriage was essentially contentious and unhappy, forgetting that this was a singular letter in a union of forty-four years. The letter taken at face value, while not entirely vicious, portrays both Anna and the children as disappointments whom he endures. This is not typical of any other known letter in which Douglass discussed his family, and Dennett, an abolitionist in Maine whose husband served as an agent for Douglass's paper, did not appear to have been a particularly close friend. A reader might easily wonder whether the letter was a prank of some sort or the tone would have been understood by Dennett and her circle as ironically jocular, or whether Douglass began it with that intention but real frustrations emerged in an unguarded moment.

39. *Lib.*, 18 November, 16 December 1853; SBA to WLG, Rochester, 13 December 1853, ASC, BPL; Lucy N. Colman to AKP, Boston, 27 [December], 1853, IAKPFP, NRU.

40. SBA to WLG, Rochester, 13 December 1853, ASC, BPL; *Lib.*, 18 November 1853.

41. Parker, "Reminiscences," Coles Collection, RMSCL.

42. Jane Swisshelm, "Frederick Douglass and the Garrisonians" reprinted in *Lib.*, 12 January 1854, originally published in the *Saturday Visiter [sic]*; *Lib.*, 16 December 1853; Jane Gray Swisshelm, *Half a Century* (Chicago, 1880), 106, 112; Harriet Beecher Stowe to WLG, 19 December 1853, quoted in Foner, *Frederick Douglass: A Biography*, 151. Swisshelm was pro–Liberty Party and not a Garrisonian, and had founded her paper in 1847, the same year Douglass had begun publication of his.

43. JGC to FD, Leeds, England, 27 March, 1 September, 5 December 1862, 10 December 1863, FDP, DLC. In 1876, Julia wrote of Anna, "I feel sure that if she and I were to meet again it would be as good friends." Griffiths's memories are in stark contrast to those of Ottilie Assing, who referred to Anna as a "hag" and a "monster." JGC to FD, Gateshead-on-Tyne, England, 3 October 1876, FDP, DLC; OA to LA[G], Hoboken, N.J., 11 June 1872, 29 January 1874, VC, BJK.

44. SBA to WLG, Rochester, 13 December 1853, ASC, BPL; FD, *Narr*, 80; Harriet Jacobs to AKP, 11 January[1853-54], IAKPFP, NRU; *NS*, 9 October 1849; RDS, *MMAIRH*, 13–4; Parker, "Reminiscences," Coles Collection, RMSCL; Yee, *Black Women Abolitionists*, 100–104.

45. RDS, *MMAIRH*, 16.

46. *FDP*, 3 March 1854; *Provincial Freeman*, 3 June 1854; WCN to AKP, Boston, 9 April, 20 January, 21 November 1854, IAKPFP, NRU.

47. 1855 N.Y. State Census, Kings County, Brooklyn, Ward 7, [49]; Sarah Thayer to AKP, Grand Blanc, Mich., 15 April 1855, IAKPFP, NRU.

48. Isaac Post to Joseph and Mary Post, Rochester, 19 November 1849, [photocopy], FD to AKP, Rochester, [c. March 1850]; 4 August 1852, Sarah Thayer to AKP, Grand Blanc, 15 April 1855, IAKPFP, NRU. As Douglass fled America after the Harpers Ferry raid in 1859, Post

apologized to him and Griffiths for letting the friendship falter in the previous years. AKP to FD, Rochester, 13 February 1860, IAKPFP, NRU.

49. Blackett, *Building an Antislavery Wall*, 115-17; Fee, "To No One More Indebted," 21-23; Douglas, "Cherished Friendship," 268-72; *FDP*, 15 June, 17 August 1855.

50. *FDP*, 17, 31 August 1855.

51. *FDP*, 16 November 1855; Mary Estlin to MWC, Glasgow, 3 September 1853, Parker Pillsbury to Samuel May, [England], 6 September 1855, ASC, BPL.

52. See annual reports of the Rochester Ladies' Antislavery Society, in RLASP, MiU-C. Parker Pillsbury to Samuel May, [England], 4 January 1855, ASC, BPL. Only a circular issued by Griffiths and some abolitionists in Glasgow, which accused the Garrisonians of actively thwarting the success of Douglass's paper, could prove Pillsbury's case.

53. Parker Pillsbury to Samuel May, England, 21 December 1855, 1 February 1856, RDW to Samuel May, Dublin, 15 February 1856, ASC, BPL.

54. Samuel May to RDW, Boston, 9 March, 13 April 1858, MWC to WLG, Weymouth, Mass., [1858], ASC, BPL.

55. WCN to AKP, Boston, 7 June 1857, IAKPFP, NRU; *FDP*, 8 April 1859; 1871 UK Census, Gateshead, St. Neots, [43]; 1881 UK Census, [Gateshead], St. Neots, [55]; Fee, "To No One More Indebted," 22; Douglas, "Cherished Friendship," 272.

56. OA, "An Antislavery Meeting" [1854], "Colored People in New York" [1855], in *Radical Passions: Ottilie Assing's Reports from America and Letters to Frederick Douglass*, ed. and trans., Christoph Lohman (New York: P. Lang, 1999), 36, 54. For more on Assing as a journalist, see Britta Behmer, "From German Cultural Criticism to Abolitionism. Ottilie Assing: 'Zealous to give vent to her gall,'" in *German? American? Literature? New Directions in German-American Studies*, ed. Winifried Fluck and Werner Sollors (New York: P. Lang, 2002), 144-69; Tamara Felden, "Ottilie Assing's View of America in the Context of Travel Literature by 19th-Century German Women," *German Quarterly* 65, 3/4 (Summer–Autumn, 1992): 340-48; Mischa Honeck, *We Are the Revolutionarists: German-Speaking Immigrants and American Abolitionists after 1848* (Athens: University of Georgia Press, 2011), 34-55, 119, 173, 180-1. Maria Diedrich's 1999 biography of Assing, *Love across Color Lines: Ottilie Assing and Frederick Douglass*, has encouraged more scholars to consider Assing and her work. Few, however, have questioned its premise that Assing was an enormous influence on Douglass, affected German attitudes about the United States, and engaged in a passionate sexual affair with him.

57. Of the dispatches Assing sent to the *Morgenblatt* from America, the editors published seven in 1852, five in 1853, four in 1854, six in 1855, ten in 1856, seven in 1857, fourteen in 1858, twelve in 1859, ten in 1860, eight in 1861 and 1862, five in 1863, twelve in 1864, and nine in 1865. The number of her columns increased after she met Douglass, as did the number of columns she devoted to black civil rights. Diedrich, *LACL*, 121-22, 430-37.

58. Honeck, *We Are the Revolutionists*, 1; OA, "Colored People in New York," in *Radical Passions*, 58-59; Hodges, *David Ruggles*, 126-27, 133-34; FD, *Narr.*, 76; Clipping, folder 8 of 9, FD (General), Subject Files, FDP, DLC. Maria Diedrich depicted Assing as boldly knocking on the Douglasses' door without having an introduction in person or through correspondence. Although Assing told a story that might lead a reader to infer such a meeting, she did not leave any account of their introduction. She first mentioned Douglass in the same 1855 column in which she wrote about Pennington, but only indicated that she had read his autobiography. Diedrich, *LACL*, 431.

59. OA, "Preface to the German Translation of *My Bondage and My Freedom*" [1858], in *Radical Passions*, 69; FD, *Vie de Frédéric Douglass, Esclave Américain*, trans. S.K. Parkes (Paris, 1848); Caroline Weston to Samuel May, Paris, 3 July 1850, ASC, BPL; F. B. Sanborn, ed., *Life and Letters of John Brown: Liberator of Kansas and Martyr of Virginia* (Boston, 1885), 431-32; OA, "Frederick Douglass" [1859], "A Visit to Gerrit Smith," "A Negro Colony in Canada" [1857], and "Meeting of the Anti-Slavery Societies: Frederick Douglass," [1857], in *Radical Passions*, 163-64, 18-62, 99-102, 94-95. Diedrich identifies Douglass as Assing's unnamed companion on her trip to Buxton, the black town in Canada, during autumn 1857. Douglass traveled in the company of other speakers throughout New York from May through July, Illinois and Wisconsin in August, and back to New York in September. He did not tour Canada West until

November, after her article had been published. See Diedrich, *LACL*, 150–54; FD, *Speeches*, 3:xxvi–xxix.
60. On the Young Germans and Assing's connection see Henry Walter Bran, "The Young German Movement Creates a Political Literature," *German Quarterly*, 24, 3 (May 1951): 189–94; Behmer, "From German Cultural," in Fluck and Sollers, *German? American? Literature?*, 144–69; Felden, "Assing's View of America," 340–48; Honeck, *We Are the Revolutionarists*, 13–37.
61. On political proclivities of German immigrants, see Honeck, *We Are the Revolutionarists.*
62. OA, "Preface to the German Translation of *My Bondage and My Freedom*" [1858], in *Radical Passions*, 69.
63. See Behmer, "From German Cultural Criticism," in Fluck and Sollors, *German? American? Literature?*, 144–69; Felden, "Assing's View of America," 340–48; Diedrich, *LACL*, 431; Honeck, *We Are the Revolutionarists*, 13–37.
64. OA to SRK, Washington, 2 October 1878, Vienna, Va, 24 August 1874, SRKP, AAA.
65. FD to RDS, Washington, DC, 28 August 1873, 2 August 1875, FDP, DLC; OA to LA[G], Hoboken, 11 June 1872, 29 January, 26 March, 9 November 1874, VC, BJK; OA to FD, Rome, 5 January 1877, FDP, DLC; OA, "Preface" [1858], *Radical Passions*, 69.
66. FD, *Speeches*, 3:xxvi–xxvii; OA, *Radical Passions*, 70; Diedrich, *Love across Color Lines*, 431, 203; FD to LA[G], Rochester, 14 July 1858, VC, BJK; FD, *Sclaverei und Freiheit. Autobiographie von Frederick Douglass* (Hamburg, 1860).

Chapter 6

1. *Washington Evening Star*, 25 February 1895; FD, *L&T*, 370, *MBMF*, 204; FD *Speeches*, 1:lxxxvi; Judith Wellman, *The Road to Seneca Falls: Elizabeth Cady Stanton and the First Woman's Rights Convention* (Urbana: University of Illinois Press, 2004), 161. William C. Nell could possibly have attended the Seneca Falls Convention, being Douglass's printer, a friend of the Posts, and a woman's rights advocate. His name, however, did not appear among the signatories of the "Declaration of Sentiments." He did attend the Rochester convention.
2. Isenberg, *Sex and Citizenship*, xiii–xvi; Pierson, *Free Hearts and Free Homes*, 47–49; NS, 27 December 1847.
3. FD to Elizabeth McClintock, Rochester, 14 July [1848], in FD, *Correspondence*, 1:305; NS, 14, 28 July 1848. For the story and significance of the Seneca Falls convention, see "Report of the Woman's Rights Convention," Seneca Falls (Rochester, 1848); "Women's Rights Convention, Held at Seneca Falls," [19–20 July 1848], *ECS/SBAP*, 1:75–88; ECS, SBA, and MJG, *History of Woman Suffrage* (Rochester, 1887), 1:67–87; Lori Ginzberg, *Elizabeth Cady Stanton*, 43–76. Sylvia D. Hoffert, *When Hens Crow: The Woman's Rights Movement in Antebellum America* (Bloomington: Indiana University Press, 1995); Isenberg, *Sex and Citizenship*; Sally McMillen, *Seneca Falls and the Origins of the Women's Right Movement* (New York: Oxford University Press, 2008); Lisa Tetrault, *Myth of Seneca Falls: Memory and the Women's Suffrage Movement, 1848-1898* (Chapel Hill: University of North Carolina Press, 2014); Wellman, *Road to Seneca Falls.*
4. NS Prospectus and notes [fragment], c. August 1848, Mary Robbins Post to Isaac and Amy Post, Westbury, N.Y., 12 September 1848, IAKPFP, NRU; "Report," Seneca Falls (1848), 10.
5. "Report of the International Council of Women" (Washington, DC, 1888), 1:323–4; ECS, SBA, and MJG, *History*, 1:73.
6. In her description of the incident in the 1888 Report of the International Council of Women, Stanton insisted that the suffrage resolution had passed unchallenged. She, Anthony, and Matilda Joslyn Gage, her coauthors of *History of Woman Suffrage*, however, reported it as the only one that did not pass unanimously. "Report of the International Council of Women" (Washington, DC, 1888), 1:323–4; ECS, SBA, and MJG, *History*, 1:76–87.
7. NS, 11 August 1848; ECS to AKP, Seneca Falls, 24 September 1848, *ECS/SBAP*, 1:123–26; ECS, SBA, and MJG, *History*, 1:76–87.
8. McMillan, *Seneca Falls*, 104–6; Martha Jones, *All Bound Up Together: The Woman Question in African American Public Culture, 1830-1900* (Chapel Hill: University of North Carolina Press, 2007), 8–11.

9. ECS, SBA, and MJG, *History*, 1:76–87.

10. Lucretia Mott to ECS, Philadelphia, 3 October 1848, in Beverly Wilson Palmer, ed. *Selected Letters of Lucretia Coffin Mott* (Urbana: University of Illinois Press, 2002), 172–74; *Philadelphia Public Ledger*, 10 August 1848; *New Bedford Mercury*, 11 August 1848; Washington, DC, *Daily National Intelligencer*, 16 August 1848; ECS, SBA, and MJG *History*, 1:77–78. "Proceedings of the Colored National Convention," Cleveland (1848), 12; *NS*, 29 September 1848. Although referred to as "Mrs. Sanford" in the proceedings of both conventions, *The History of Woman Suffrage* identified her as Rebecca M. M. Sanford of Ann Arbor, Michigan, later a postal clerk in Livingston, N.Y. ECS, SBA, and MJG, *History*, 1: 77–8; Lucretia Mott to ECS, Philadelphia, 3 October 1848, in Beverly Wilson Palmer, ed. *Selected Letters of Lucretia Coffin Mott* (Urbana: University of Illinois Press, 2002), 172–74.

11. Ruchkin, "Abolition of 'Colored Schools,'" 376–93; *NS*, 17 August, 1849, 22 September 1848.

12. *NS*, 22 September 1848.

13. *NS*, 22 September 1848; Anne Warren Weston to AKP, Boston, 19 December 1848, ASC, BPL.

14. *NS*, 17 September 1849, italics in original; Ruchkin, "Abolition of 'Colored Schools,'" 388.

15. RDS to FD, Rochester, 17 September 1876, FDP, DLC; Daniel Alexander Payne, *Recollections of Seventy Years* (Nashville, 1888), 143. Music had an important place in the Douglass family. Frederick apparently had learned to play the violin while still in slavery, and used music to stave off hunger and loneliness in Maryland, Massachusetts, and England. Charles learned to play as well, and his son Joseph Henry Douglass became a concert violinist in the late nineteenth century. John Stauffer claimed not only that Anna also was a violinist and could read music so well that she could "enchant a room," but that she taught Frederick to play and that "soon they were playing duets." No evidence exists to support this. FD, *MBMF*, 76; FD to HB/RCA, [n.p.], 16 May 1846, Addition II, FDP, DLC; CRD to FD, Washington, 26 February 1869, FDP, DLC; "Frederick Douglass' Grandson," Clippings, Addition II, FDP, DLC; Stauffer, *Giants*, 71.

16. FD to Lydia Dennett, Rochester 17 April 1858, Whittier Collection, MH-H; FD, *L&T*, 221–22; JG[C] to GS, Rochester, 26 August [1851], GSP, NSyU.; FDjr, "In brief, 1842–1890," (notation in Scrapbook), CRD, "Some Incidents," FDP, Evans Collection.

17. Unfortunately, the industrial school plan headed by Douglass relied upon a bequest promised by Harriet Beecher Stowe, donated from the proceeds of her English tour promoting *Uncle Tom's Cabin*. She insisted that she had not promised to fund a school and therefore the plan collapsed. "Proceedings of the Colored National Convention," Rochester (1853), 30–39; *FDP*, 28 May 1858, *FDP*, 12 January 1855, 1 January, 12 December 1857, 25 March, 22 April 1859; Joan Hedrick, *Harriet Beecher Stowe: A Life* (New York: Oxford University Press, 1994), 247–48.

18. *FDP*, 25 November 1853; FD, *Speeches*, 3:213–14; SBA, ECS, and MJG, *History* 1:668, 585; *FDP*, 6 January 1854.

19. *Lib.*, 18 November 1853.

20. RDS to FD, Salem, N.J., 9 October 1862, FDP, DLC. Biographers' sharp focus on Douglass himself left little room to develop nuanced understandings of seemingly minor characters like Rosetta, as was the case with most of the women in Douglass's life. The two most complete treatments of Rosetta appear in William McFeely's *Frederick Douglass* and Maria Diedrich's *Love across Color Lines*. McFeely understood that Rosetta "bore the brunt of the disparity between her parents," but he took the rumors about her in Philadelphia and Salem at face value. He insisted that she was conceived out of wedlock, characterized the young woman as quarrelsome, asserted that "she and her mother argued rancorously," and claimed that she "almost defiantly, married Nathan Sprague." No evidence exists to merit these interpretations. Diedrich's agenda of injecting Ottilie Assing into every facet of Douglass's life in order to overemphasize Assing's importance resulted in many unsupportable assertions about his family. In fictional chapter introductions as well as her text, she invented a friendship between the two women in which Rosetta was Assing's protégé. She determined that Rosetta was "a shy, sensitive teenager, eager to please" and therefore Assing's "favorite among the Douglass children." According to Diedrich, Rosetta's "relationship to her mother was warped" because Anna was "harsher in her dealings with Rosetta than the young girl could bear" to the point

that "Rosetta could not really forgive her mother for her lack of warmth" and that their relationship "would always remain precarious." Meanwhile, Assing "brought sunshine" to the
Douglass house, and Rosetta and Assing "wrote to each other regularly for many years."
Rosetta "had learned to cherish [Ottilie] as their second mother," and her later animosity
toward Helen Pitts stemmed from her anger that she became the second Mrs. Douglass rather
than Assing. This entire characterization rests on only three sources, two of which are letters
from Rosetta that make passing mentions of Assing and one that reports rumors that Rosetta
denied. McFeely, *Frederick Douglass*, 218–23; Diedrich, *LACL*, 170–71, 194–96, 274.

21. FD to Lydia Dennett, Rochester, 17 April 1858, Whittier Collection, MH-H; FD, *L&T*, 221–
22; JG[C] to GS, Rochester, 26 August [1851], GSP, NSyU. McFeely mistakenly believed
that Rosetta had attended Salem Normal School, citing a letter that she wrote from Salem,
New Jersey, in which she mentioned taking exams. Salem Normal School, however, was
located in Massachusetts. Salem, New Jersey, had no such institution, and the exams were
more likely those to qualify her to teach in New Jersey. McFeely, *Frederick Douglass*, 220–
21. Maria Diedrich and Britta Behmer insist that Assing was responsible for the Douglass
children's education to the point of paying their tuition. No evidence exists to support even
her passing interest in their intellectual development, much less having the desire or ability
to pay for their schooling. Assing herself struggled to make ends meet, working as a music
teacher in 1860. Furthermore, by the time Assing appeared in the Douglasses' lives, Rosetta
had already returned from Oberlin. Diedrich, *LACL*, 434; Behmer, " 'Zealous to Give Vent to
Her Gall,' " in Fluck and Sollors, *German? American? Literature?*, 166; 1860 U.S. Census, New
Jersey, Hudson, Hoboken, Ward 1, 5.

22. Two of her contemporaries, although not classmates, were artist Edmonia Lewis and *Amistad*
survivor Sarah Magru Kinson. Later black alumnae included Anna Julia Cooper and Mary
Church Terrell. Roland M. Bauman, ed., *Constructing Black History at Oberlin College: A
Documentary History* (Athens: Ohio University Press, 2010), 26–44; Ellen N. Lawson
and Marlene Merrill, "The Antebellum 'Talented Thousandth': Black College Students at
Oberlin Before the Civil War," *Journal of Negro Education* 52, 2 (Spring 1983), 142–55; Ellen
Henle and Marlene Merrill, "Antebellum Black Coeds at Oberlin College," *Women's Studies
Newsletter* 7, 2 (Spring 1979): 8–11; Ronald W. Hogeland, "Coeducation of the Sexes at
Oberlin College: A Study of Social Ideas in Mid-Nineteenth-Century America," *Journal of
Social History* 6, 2 (Winter 1972/73): 160–76; J. Brent Morris, *Oberlin: Hotbed of Abolitionism*
(Chapel Hill: University of North Carolina Press, 2014), 72–80. McFeely placed Rosetta in
"Oberlin College's 'Young Ladies' Preparatory Department," in which she learned Latin.
College Archive records indicate otherwise. McFeely, *Frederick Douglass*, 220.

23. Genealogical Notes, Addition I, FDP, DLC; James M. Gregory, *Frederick Douglass, the Orator*
(Springfield, Mass., 1893), 201–2; CRD, "Some Incidents," Evans Collection; "Frederick
Douglass's Daughter. Death of Rosetta Douglass Sprague at Her Home in Washington," FDP,
DHU-MS.

24. FD to Lydia Dennett, Rochester, 17 April 1857, Whittier Collection, MH-H; 1855 N.Y.
State Census, Monroe Co., Rochester, Ward 7, 461; RD[S] to FD, Annie Douglass to FD,
Rochester, 6 December 1859, Addition I, FDP, DLC. William's last name is illegible in the
1855 N.Y. State census, in which his birthplace was listed as South Carolina.

25. FD to Hannah Fuller, Rochester, 24 May 1857, Frederick Douglass Letters, New York State
Library; A. Bates to FD, Syracuse, 11 February 1853, Jacob R. Gibbs to "Dear Friend Morris,"
New York, 14 March 1854; W. E. Abbot to Maria Porter, Syracuse, 9 November 1856;
William J. Watkins to Mrs. Armstrong, Rochester, [c. after 9 August 1857], FD to Maria
Porter, Rochester, 13 October 1857; Account Books, Annual Reports, 1852–61, RLASP,
MiU-C. Contrary to legend, fugitives in New York rarely slept in barns or outbuildings,
escaped in false-bottomed wagons or through hidden tunnels, or stayed often or long enough
to require whole wings to be added to houses for accommodation. See Gara, *Liberty Line*;
David W. Blight, ed., *Passages to Freedom: The Underground Railroad in History and Memory*
(New York, 2004); Blight, *Race and Reunion*, 231–37; FD to Hannah Fuller, Rochester, 5
October 1853, Frederick Douglass Letters, New York State Library. References to "Mrs.
Douglass and daughter" in John Brown's notebooks could mean either or both Rosetta and
Annie. Rosetta also reported on Annie's school progress to her father in 1859. As the only

educated woman in the house, common practice would suggest that she oversee the educational progress of younger children. John Brown, Memorandum Book, BPL; RD[S] to FD, 6 December 1859, FDP, DLC. The 7 October 1858 meeting to protest the use of the death penalty was arranged by Anthony. Douglass, his cool relationship with her notwithstanding, was chair. A mob ended the meeting. FD, *Speeches*, 3:242; Ida Husted Harper, *Life and Work of Susan B. Anthony* (Indianapolis, 1899), 1:164–66. Rosetta and Frederick shared an interest in Haiti. Decades later, while serving as diplomat to the black republic, Frederick reminisced about their "old time thoughts of a visit." At the end of the century, too, Rosetta had a brooch with an image of Toussaint Louverture painted onto portraits of herself and her mother, and she named her home in Takoma Park, DC, Louverture Terrace. RDS to SBA, Takoma Park, DC, 27 January 1896, FDC, DHU-MS; Gregory, *Frederick Douglass*, 200; A[M]D, Portrait in collection of Frederick Douglass National Park, Anacostia, DC, National Parks Service. For more on Douglass's opinions about Haitian emigration, see Blight, *Frederick Douglass' Civil War*, 132–34.

26. "Proceedings of the Colored National Convention," Rochester (1853); SBA, ECS, and MJG, *History*, 1:577–91; FDP, 25 November 1853; Faye Dudden, *Fighting Chance: The Struggle over Woman Suffrage and Black Suffrage in Reconstruction America* (New York: Oxford University Press, 2011), 41.

27. SBA, ECS, and MJG, *History*, 1:580–3; "Proceedings of the Colored National Convention," Rochester (1853), 8–15.

28. "Proceedings of the Colored National Convention," Rochester (1853), 8–15. For the ideology and history of the antebellum woman's rights movement, see Lori Ginzberg, *Untidy Origins: A Story of Woman's Rights in Antebellum New York* (Chapel Hill: University of North Carolina Press, 2005); Hoffert, *When Hens Crow*; Isenberg, *Sex and Citizenship*; Natasha Kirsten Kraus, *A New Type of Womanhood: Discursive Politics and Social Change in Antebellum America* (Durham, NC: Duke University Press, 2008); McMillen, *Seneca Falls*; Ryan, *Women in Public*; Rosemarie Zagarri, *Revolutionary Backlash: Women and Politics in the Early American Republic* (Philadelphia: University of Pennsylvania Press, 2008), among many others.

29. SBA, ECS, and MJG, *History*, 1:581; "Proceedings of the Colored National Convention," Rochester (1853), 8–15.

30. Julie Roy Jeffrey, "Permeable Boundaries: Abolitionist Women and Separate Spheres," *Journal of the Early Republic* 21, 1 (Spring 2001): 79–93; Lasser, "Beyond Separate Spheres," 115–23; Isenberg, *Sex and Citizenship*, xviii; Foner, Philip S. and George E. Walker, eds. *Proceedings of the Black State Conventions, 1840-65* (Philadelphia: Temple University Press, 1979) 2:62.

31. "Report of the Proceedings of the Colored National Convention," Cleveland, (1848), 1; FD to GS, Rochester, 21 January 1851, GSP, NySU; FDP, 3 February 1854; Philip S. Foner and George E. Walker, "Colored Men's State Convention of New York, Troy, September 4, 1855," in *Proceedings of the Black State Conventions*, 1:88–97; Jones, *All Bound Up Together*, 103–4; "Proceedings of the Colored National Convention," Philadelphia (Salem, NJ, 1855), 6–7, 10; FDP, 21 September 1855; Jane Rhodes, *Mary Ann Shadd Cary: The Black Press and Protest in the Nineteenth Century* (Bloomington: Indiana University Press, 1998), 108–10; FDP, 21 September 1855.

32. *L&WFD*, 2:349–50; NS, 28 July 1848.

33. *FDP*, 17 March 1854.

34. *NS*, 10 December 1850; Yee, *Black Women Abolitionists*, 139–40.

35. *FDP*, 10, 17 February 1854; *DM*, October 1859.

36. Dudden, *Fighting Chance*, 42–44; FDP, 3 March 1854; SBA to Lucy Read Anthony, Cananjoharie, 29–30 October 1848, SBA/ECS, 1:131; FDP, 25 November 1853; SBA to WLG, Rochester, 13 December 1853, ASC, BPL; SBA to Lucy Stone, Rochester, 13 December 1853, ECS/SBAP, 1: 232–5. This is, of course, an entirely different view of their relationship than Anthony established in her biography, written with Ida Husted Harper, in which she depicts an immediate and enduring friendship between the two and amiable Sunday dinners with the whole Douglass family. Harper, *Life and Work*, 1:59–60, 270.

37. Lucretia Mott to Martha Coffin Wright, Roadside, Penn., 12 March 1860, in Palmer, *Selected Letters*, 297; See proceedings of all National Woman's Rights Conventions. Whether or not five conventions in twelve years might be considered "frequent", most historians writing on

Douglass and woman's rights tend to leave readers with the impression that he was deeply engaged in the movement at this time without quantifying his engagement with the only formal organization of woman's rights activists at the time.

38. Douglass attended the 11 May protest of segregation on the Sixth Avenue railroad, held at the Shiloh Presbyterian Church of Henry Highland Garnet and the 13 May meeting of the American Abolition Society, a politically focused organization founded in 1855 by William Goodell. Douglass attended the second day of the woman's rights meeting. He had begun his career making extemporaneous speeches, in the Quaker tradition, but by this time he tended to prepare his lectures, which he published as pamphlets. Susan B. Anthony and Ida Husted Harper listed Douglass among the speakers at the convention, obscuring his marginal role. Maria Diedrich placed Assing in the audience for all Douglass's engagements that May. Although Diedrich provides no source, Assing's Morgenblatt article suggests that she attended the meetings of the American Anti-Slavery Society, the Women's Convention, and the Shiloh Presbyterian Church. Assing reported that George Curtis spoke at the women's meeting, although he did not appear in other accounts. While she gushed over Douglass as the "magnet exerting such a powerful force" at the Shiloh Church, she or her editor omitted Douglass's appearance as well as a controversial call for "Free Love" made by Stephen Pearl Andrews at the women's convention. She also did not cover the American Abolition Society meeting. Diedrich insists that during this week, "there were also spaces which Douglass could and did claim for himself, time he could set aside to be with Ottilie Assing," yet offers no evidence. Instead, she explains that segregation of rooming accommodations allowed Douglass to slip off each evening to be "a private man, even a lover" with Assing, away from the "philistine attitude" of white abolitionists who would not offer their own hospitality. This supposition ignores the black boarding houses and Douglass's black friends, such as Charles L. Reason and James McCune Smith, in New York City, as well as the white abolitionists, who tended to praise themselves for offering shelter to African Americans. While Assing's effusions about Douglass could have constituted "a public declaration of love," which is Diedrich's interpretation, this would not differentiate Assing from the many people captivated by Douglass's charisma and does not in any way imply that he reciprocated. FD, *Speeches*, 3:208–12; *NYT*, 14 May 1858; M. Leon Perkal, "American Abolition Society: A Viable Alternative to the Republican Party?," *Journal of Negro History*, 65, 1 (Winter 1980): 57–71; *NYT* and *NYTrib*, 15 May 1858; FD, *Speeches*, 3:213–4; OA, "Kansas-Anniversaries," in *Radical Passions*, 123–26; Harper, *Life and Work*, 1:163; Diedrich, *LACL*, 159–60; *NYT* and *NYTrib*, 15 May 1858; Speeches, 3:213–4; SBA, ECS, and MJG, *History*, 1:672.

39. *NYTrib*, 13 May 1859; *NYT*, 14 May 1859. In other speeches on the history of abolitionism, Douglass continued this challenge of the Garrisonian interpretation that suggested the movement began with Garrison and the *Liberator*. Ottilie Assing, incidentally, did not cover Douglass's 1859 appearance at the Shiloh Church or any other anniversary meeting except that of the American Tract Society.

40. R. O. Johnson, *Liberty Party*, 1840–48, 276–85; Laughlin-Schultz, *Tie That Bound Us*, 19–20; Isenberg, *Sex and Citizenship*, 18–21; Pierson, *Free Hearts*, 34–37, 57, 141–50.

41. FD, *L&T*, 212–13, 370; FD, *MBMF*, 204. Historians have noted Douglass's fascination with the gender egalitarianism of Brown's family because he noted that both men and women equally participated in attending the traditionally female chores of setting and clearing the table. Bonnie Laughlin-Schultz, however, has pointed out that Brown was hardly radical in his gender politics and that he was "comfortable with and even empowered by the enactment of patriarchy." Laughlin-Schultz, *Tie That Bound Us*, 19–20.

42. David S. Reynolds, *John Brown Abolitionist: The Man Who Killed Slavery, Sparked the Civil War, and Seeded Civil Rights* (New York: Alfred A. Knopf, 2005), 104, 121–25; FD, *L&T*, 236–40; Wilbur H. Siebert, *The Underground Railroad from Slavery to Freedom* (New York, 1898), 438; Alice V. Coffee, "Lest We Forget," Adams-Douglass-McWilliams-Vanderzee Family Paper, Nebraska State Historical Society; John Brown, Memorandum Book, BPL. Although Harriet Adams lived in Springfield at the time Douglass visited Brown and knew Brown herself, she and Douglass seem to have been alienated at the time after his overreaction to her failure to ask his permission to marry. FD to HB/RCA, Leamington, 31 January 1847, Addition II, FDP, DLC; A[M]D to HB/RCA, Rochester, 11 March 1851, Addition II, FDP, DLC.

43. John Brown, Memorandum Book, BPL; FD, *L&T*, 248; Lucy N. Colman, *Reminiscences* (Buffalo, 1891), 57; CRD, "Some Incidents," and FDjr, "In brief, 1842–1890" (notation in Scrapbook), Evans Collection; Laughlin-Schultz, *Tie That Bound Us*, 3–4, 48–63.

44. CRD, "Some Incidents," Evans Collection; 1860 U.S. Census, New York, Niagara County, Lockport, 230.

45. FD, L&T, 236–40; CRD, "Some Incidents," Evans Collection. Clara Marks, a New Yorker and single mother, took in boarders at her home in New Jersey. According to Diedrich, her house was supposed to be the site of clandestine liaisons between Douglass and Assing. Given the bawdy reputation of boarding houses, respectable women such as Marks tended not to advertise them as such, and took care to preserve their reputations as running legitimate businesses. As such, she would have been unlikely to permit an illicit affair, particularly an interracial affair, to occur under her roof, with servants and other boarders around who could gossip and a teenage daughter to protect. The same could be said of Assing's other landlords and their families, who all came from the middle class. Furthermore, in 1878, Assing noted that Douglass stayed in a separate room when he visited her lodging without indicating the arrangement as an exception. 1860 U.S. Census, New York, Hudson, Hoboken, Ward 1, 5; Gamber, *Boardinghouse in Early America*, 102–9; OA to FD, Boston, 21 August 1878, FDP, DLC. Maria Diedrich also speculated that Assing and Douglass spent the trip to Patterson in one another's arms and planned for Assing to join him after he arrived in England. The first claim is pure imagination, especially with Johnson along. The second is based on the suspicions of one of Assing's European friends that Douglass's visit to England might prompt Assing to visit the continent. Diedrich also interpreted his inclusion of Assing in the episode in his autobiography as proof of his love for her and of their erotic relationship, when it was just as likely a tribute to her role, much as he spoke of many other women throughout his memoir. Diedrich, *LACL*, 218.

46. FD, *L&T*, 236–40; FD to Maria Porter, Rochester, 26 September 1858, RLASP, MiU-C; William Still to AKP, Philadelphia, 21 October 1859, FD to AKP, Clifton, Canada West, 27 [October] 1859, AKP to FD, Rochester, 13 February 1860, IAPFP, NRU; *DM*, December 1859.

47. AKP to FD, Rochester, 13 February 1860, IAPFP, NRU; *FDP*, 17 February 1830.

48. FD to Maria Porter, Halifax, 11 January 1860, RLASP, MiU-C; Honeck, *We Are the Revolutionists*, 72–73, 94–95; Annie Douglass to FD, RD[S] to FD, Rochester, 6 December 1859, FDP, DLC; Blake McKelvey, "The Germans of Rochester: Their Traditions and Contributions," *Rochester History* 20, 1 (January 1958): 7, 16–17, 19. Maria Diedrich builds an entire friendship between Assing and Rosetta around Rosetta's mention that "I have just written a letter to Miss Assing in reply to one I received from her dated November 26th." This is the most evidence that Rosetta wrote to the German woman. Diedrich also insists that Annie's proficiency in German and intent to write a German letter to Frederick meant that she was "eager to fall under Assing's spell," that the two "worked at German lessons together," and that Frederick was fluent in the language by this time. Not only is there no evidence to support these claims, but Annie learned German during a period in which she had no contact with Assing. The document "German Lessons" in the Douglass Papers at the Library of Congress, which serves as Diedrich's evidence of Frederick's linguistic mastery, has neither an identified author nor a date. Helen Pitts Douglass's name in German lesson books in the Cedar Hill library suggests that the notes could have been hers. Furthermore, a German instructor at Howard University lived with Helen after Frederick's death. The notebook containing German lessons in the Douglass Collection at the Moorland-Spingarn Research Center has been assigned a date that is after Assing's death. Diedrich, *LACL*, 194, 223, 226; RD[S] to FD, Rochester, 6 December 1859, Addition I, FDP, DLC; "German Lessons," [n.d.], Subject File, FDP, DLC; RDS [and Fredericka Sprague], Notebook, 1886, FDC, DHU-MS; William L. Petrie and Douglass E. Stover, eds., *Bibliography of the Frederick Douglass Library at Cedar Hill* (Washington, DC: National Parks Service, 1994), 61.

49. RD[S] to FD, Salem, N.J., 9 October 1862, Rochester, 6 December 1859, FDP, DLC; FD, *L&T*, 250; Annie Douglass to FD, 6 December 1859, FDP, DLC; CRD, "Some Incidents," Evans Collection.

50. Annie Douglass Interment Record, Mount Hope Cemetery; CRD, "Some Incidents," Evans Collection; *Rochester Daily Democrat*, 16 March 1860; *DM*, April 1860; Sally Holley and

anonymous source quoted in Holland, *Frederick Douglass*, 225, 229. Edwards was a descendant of the First Great Awakening minister of the same name and himself influenced by Charles Finney, the leading minister of the Second Great Awakening in New York. His congregation contained many Evangelical reforming women involved in children's aid and education, which made support for Anna and Rosetta in preparing for Annie's funeral a natural concern of theirs. Charles D. Broadbent, "A Brief Pilgrimage: Plymouth Church of Rochester," *Rochester History* 40, 4 (October 1978): 3; Nancy Hewitt, *Women's Activism*, 179–80.

51. *Rochester Daily Democrat*, 16 March 1860; Mt. Hope deed, 5 July 1850, Legal File, FDP, DLC; RD[S] to HB/RCA, Rochester, 20 April 1860, Addition II, FDP, DLC. Maria Diedrich speculated that Anna was angry at Frederick for being away when Annie died and because of "an undercurrent of suspicion that he blamed her, his illiterate wife, for the child's death." No evidence exists to suggest that either had any thought along those lines or that Anna's illiteracy made her incompetent in caring for their children's health. Anna's care of Frederick through his own sicknesses, as noted by another of Anna's patients, Julia Griffiths, as well as Assing's later observation of Anna's nursing skill suggest quite the opposite. Frederick May Holland interviewed a woman who knew the Douglasses at this time who told him Anna was "ever attentive to warding of attacks of colds and rheumatism." Diedrich, *LACL* , 226; JG[C] to GS, Rochester, [n.d.], GSP, NSyU; OA to FD, Hoboken, 10 December 1878, FDP, DLC; Holland, *Frederick Douglass*, 226.

52. FD, *Speeches*, 3:xxxi–xxxii; FD, *L&T*, 253; RD[S] to HB/RCA, Rochester, 20 April 1860, Addition II, FDP, DLC; FD to John T. Hull, Washington, April 1886, in *Centennial Celebration: An Account of the Municipal Celebration of the One Hundredth Anniversary of the Incorporation of the Town of Portland* (Portland, Me., 1886), [n.p.]; FD to Lydia Dennett, Rochester, 17 April 1857; John Greenleaf Whittier Collection, MH-H; 1860 U.S. Census, Maine, Cumberland, Bridgeton, 33; Mount Hope Cemetery Deed, 5 July 1860, Deeds, FDP, DLC. The Friends of Mt. Hope Cemetery records indicate that Annie was reinterred in the family lot, but only give the date of her death. Shortly after the funeral of Jane Porter in November 1860, her sister Maria visited the cemetery with Sally Holley and identified "a small, newly-made mound" as Annie Douglass's in the Porter lot, suggesting that Annie's body lay undisturbed at least until the end of the year, and many cities had sanitary laws that forbid exhumation for a year after burial. Annie Douglass Interment Record, Mt. Hope Cemetery; Holly quoted in Holland, *Frederick Douglass*, 229.

53. RD[S] to HB/RCA, Rochester, 20 April 1850, Addition I; RD[S] to FD, Rochester, 2 February 1859 [filed in 1858], FDP, DLC. Rosetta seems to mention a second "little girl" in this letter, perhaps Adams's youngest daughter, Ebby. Ebby, however, had died in 1858 of "inflammation of the bowels." Neither Ebby nor another younger girl lived with the Adams by 1860 and Massachusetts Vital Records indicate that the Adamses had no other daughters. No evidence shows that Adams visited the Douglasses that summer. *Massachusetts Vital Records: Springfield, 1640–1894*, 4: 60; 1860 U.S. Census, Massachusetts, Hampden County, Springfield, 205.

54. OA to LA[G], 26 March 1874 VC, BJK; OA to FD, Hoboken, N.J., 14 April 1870, Rome, Italy, 5 January 1877, Boston, 21 August, 6 September 1878, Stamford, Conn., 18 November 1878, Hoboken, N.J., 8, 18 December 1878, 15 January, 24 February 1879, FDP, DLC; OA to LA[G], 29 January 1874, VC, BJK.

55. The only evidence that Assing visited that summer is her 20 July 1860 declaration of intent to become a US citizen filed at the Monroe County courthouse and naming Rochester as her residence. She did not become a citizen until 1871. Diedrich, who confused the declaration of intent with naturalization, interpreted this act as a gift to Douglass. That would be a strange gift indeed since the Supreme Court had declared Douglass and his family not to be federal citizens in the 1857 *Dred Scott* decision. Diedrich asserted that his gift to her in return was a kitten named Fox. If true, then Fox would have been eight years old by the time Assing first mentioned the feline in 1868 and ten when she mentioned it in 1870. Another kitten, Ray, appeared in an 1868 letter, but both cats belonged to the Douglasses and there was no evidence of them being presents to Assing. Diedrich also believed Assing introduced Frederick to the work of atheist Ludwig Feuerbach, citing an 1871 letter from Assing to Feurbach. The letter most clearly demonstrates Assing's unreliability as a narrator. In it, she wrote that Douglass

had embraced Feurbach's ideology, a demonstrably false claim. While Assing described herself and Douglass as encountering Mary Ann Evans's (a.k.a George Eliot) 1854 English translation of Feurbach's work together, she said nothing about the moment taking place in 1860. Diedrich rested her argument on the bibliography of the Cedar Hill library, which mistakenly identified the publication date of this translation as 1859. The volume itself does not contain an inscription. Ottilie Assing, Naturalization Record, Petition No. A252, New York, 1865-1875, NARA; OA to SRK, Rochester, 8 September 1868, SRKP, DCAWR; OA to LA, Rochester, 16 July 1868, 17 August 1870, VC, BJK; OA to Ludwig Feuerback, New York, 15 May 1871 translated in Diedrich, *LACL* , 227, 259–60; Petrie and Stover, *Bibliography*, 354, 266.

56. OA, *Radical Passions*,190; *DM*, August 1860. The most comprehensive recent history of the 1860 election is Douglas R. Egerton, *Year of Meteors: Stephen Douglas, Abraham Lincoln, and the Election that Brought on the Civil War* (New York: Bloomsbury Press, 2010). For a detailed and nuanced discussion of Douglass's responses to the campaign and election, see Blight, *Frederick Douglass' Civil War*.

57. OA, *Radical Passions*, 188; *DM*, July, September 1860.

58. FD to GS, Rochester, 2 July 1860, GSP, NSyU; FD to ECS, Rochester, 25 August 1860, in *L&WFD*, 2:497–8; Sterling, *Ahead of Her Time*, 326–30; SBA to ECS, Worcester, 25 August 1860, in *ECS/SBAP*, 1:439–41; *DM*, October 1860.

59. *DM*, November 1860; *NYT*, 21 May 1860; *ECS/SBAP* , 1:407–08n2.

60. *DM*, December 1860; OA, *Radical Passions*, 204; *DM*, April 1861.

61. *DM*, May 1861; Coffee, "Lest We Forget," AMH, NSH; "Adams' Escape," *Norfolk Weekly News*, 7 March 1894; OA, *Radical Passions*, 207. Maria Diedrich speculated that "It is possible that they now hoped that Haiti might be a place for a radical new beginning for both of them together." She suggested that, in spite of bringing Rosetta along on the trip, he would entirely abandon his family in America to pursue a political career with Assing at his side in Haiti. No evidence indicates that this was the case. Diedrich, *LACL*, 235–36. Harriet Adams and her family, sailing on the same ship as Douglass, did continue on to Port-au-Prince, where they lived through the Civil War. Perry Sr. survived the epidemic of typhoid fever that nearly obliterated their settlement, but the illness so weakened him that he died in 1865 after their return to Springfield. Neither Perry Jr. nor their adopted son, Samuel Hall, were with them by that time. Joseph Carvalho III, *Black Families in Hampden County, Massachusetts, 1650-1855* (Westfield: Institute for Massachusetts Studies, 1984), 25; Cornelius M. Abbe, *Springfield: Map, Street Guide, Introduction, Ads, City Directory* (Springfield, Mass., 1866–67), 36, 44; "Adams' Escape," *Norfolk Weekly News*, 7 March 1894; 1865 Massachusetts State Census, Springfield, Ward 5, 476.

62. OA, *Radical Passions*, 207; *DM*, May 1861.

Chapter 7

1. *DM*, May 1861; *L&WFD*, 3:95–7; FD, *L&T*, 367; SBA to Wendell Phillips, Seneca Falls, 29 April 1861, *ECS/SBAP*, 1:464–65. For further discussion of northern women in the Civil War and Reconstruction, see Catherine Clinton and Nina Silber, eds., *Divided Houses: Gender and the Civil War* (New York: Oxford University Press, 1992) and *Battle Scars: Gender and Sexuality in the American Civil War* (New York: Oxford University Press, 2006); Dudden, *Fighting Chance*; Nina Silber, *Daughters of the Union: Northern Women Fight the Civil War* (Cambridge, Mass.: Harvard University Press , 2005), 10–12, 224–26.

2. P. Dolores Brewington Perry, "Frederick Douglass: Editor and Journalist" (doctoral diss., University of North Carolina, Chapel Hill, 1972), 93–102; FD to Gerrit Smith, Rochester, 2 July 1860, GSP, NSyU; *Rochester City Directory* (Rochester, 1861), 123; CRD, "Some Incidents," FDjr, "In brief, 1842–90," (notation in Scrapbook), Evans Collection; *DM*, August 1860.

3. Jones, *All Bound Up Together*, 133–35; Nancy Hewitt, *Women's Activism*, 192–94; Silber, *Daughters of the Union*, 232–35.

4. RD[S] to FD, Rochester, 2 February 1859 [filed in 1858], FDP, DLC; FD, *Speeches*, 3:435–45; RD[S] to FD, Philadelphia, Penn., 4 April 1862, FDP, DLC; *DM*, February 1862.

5. RD[S] to FD, Philadelphia, 4 April 1862, Salem, N.J., 9 October 1862, FDP, DLC; 1870 U.S. Census, Pennsylvania, Philadelphia, 8th Ward, 26.

6. RD[S] to FD, Philadelphia, 4 April 1862, FDP, DLC. Octavius Catto became one of black Philadelphia's leaders against discrimination after the Civil War. Lewis Douglass covered his 1871 assassination in the *National Era*. Douglas R. Egerton, *Wars of Reconstruction: The Brief, Violent History of America's Most Progressive Era* (New York: Bloomsbury, 2014), 168–72.

7. RD[S] to FD, Philadelphia, 4 April 1862, FDP, DLC; 1860 U.S. Census, Pennsylvania, Philadelphia, 8th Ward, 210.

8. RD[S] to FD, Philadelphia, 4 April 1862, Salem, N.J., 31 August 1862, FDP, DLC; 1860 U.S. Census, New Jersey, Salem County, Salem City, 44. William McFeely believed that Rosetta had first applied to a school in Washington, DC, run by Myrtilla Miner and then enrolled in Salem Normal School. Miner's school had closed in 1861 and did not reopen until after the Civil War, and Rosetta makes no mention of it in her letters. The Salem Normal School was not located in New Jersey. McFeely, *Frederick Douglass*, 220–21; G. Smith Wormley, "Myrtilla Miner," *Journal of Negro History* 4, 1 (January 1920): 448–57.

9. RD[S] to FD, Philadelphia, 4 April 1862, Salem, N.J., 31 August, 24 September 1862, FDP, DLC.

10. RD[S] to FD, Philadelphia, 4 April 1862, Salem, N.J., 31 August, 24 September 1862, FDP, DLC.

11. Ezra Greenspan, *William Wells Brown: An African American Life* (New York: W. W. Norton, 2014), 342–45; Yee, *Black Women Abolitionists*, 28–32.

12. RD[S] to FD, Philadelphia, 4 April 1862, Salem, N.J., 31 August, 24 September 1862, FDP, DLC.

13. RD[S] to FD, Philadelphia, 4 April 1862, Salem, N.J., 31 August, 24 September 1862, FDP, DLC.

14. RD[S] to FD and A[M]D, Salem, N.J., 31 August 1862, FDP, DLC.

15. RD[S] to FD, Salem, N.J., 31 August, 9 October 1862, FDP, DLC; 1860 U.S. Census, Pennsylvania, Philadelphia, 10th Ward, 141.

16. RD[S] to FD, Salem, N.J., 31 August, 24 September 1862, FDP, DLC.

17. RD[S] to FD, Salem, N.J., 31 August, 9 October 1862, FDP, DLC.

18. RD[S] to FD, Salem, N.J., 9 October, 24, September, 31 August, 13 October 1862, FDP, DLC; 1860 U.S. Census, New Jersey, Salem County, Pilesgrove Township, 126.

19. RD[S] to FD, Salem, N.J., 9 October 1862, FDP, DLC; LHD to Amelia Loguen, Rochester, 8 December 1861, Evans Collection; P. J. Straudenraus, *The African Colonization Movement* (1961; repr. New York: Octagon, 1980), 247; Blight, *Frederick Douglass' Civil War*, 135–43; *DM*, November 1862; LHD to Amelia Loguen, Salem, N.J., 20 November, 29 December 1862, Evans Collection; RD[S] to FD, Salem, N.J., 13 October 1862, FDP, DLC. As to Lewis's divergence from his father's position on Central American colonization, Douglass explained, "My son is of age, forms his own opinions, pursues his own plans," as any young man would. *DM*, October 1862.

20. *L&WFD*, 3: 306.

21. FD, *Speeches*, 3: 435–45.

22. *DM*, March 1863; Blight, *Frederick Douglass's Civil War*, 169–72.

23. *L&WFD*, 3:317–19. For a detailed and engaging history of the Massachusetts 54th, 55th, and 5th Cavalry, including the roles of Charles and Lewis Douglass, see Douglas Egerton, *Thunder at the Gates: The Black Civil War Regiments that Redeemed America* (New York: Basic Books, 2016).

24. CRD, Company Regimental Description Book, 8 April 1863, Compiled Military Service Records of Volunteer Union Soldiers, U.S. Colored Troops, 54th Massachusetts Infantry, NARA; LHD, Company Regimental Description Book, 1 April 1863, Compiled Military Service Records of Volunteer Union Soldiers, U.S. Colored Troops, 54th Massachusetts Infantry, NARA; Blight, *Frederick Douglass's Civil War*, 157–74; JGC to FD, Leeds, England, 3 April 1863, FDP, DLC. William McFeely characterized the Douglass sons as "vulnerable to their father's newest great cause," but their subsequent correspondence indicated that they embraced the opportunity to fight. McFeely, *Frederick Douglass*, 223.

25. LHD to Amelia Loguen, Readville, Mass., 20 May 1863, Evans Collection.

26. Egerton, *Thunder*, 107–8; Blight, *Frederick Douglass' Civil War*, 161–72.

27. Blight, *Frederick Douglass' Civil War*, 161–72; *DM*, August 1860.

28. LHD to FD, Morris Island, S.C., 20 July [1863], Addition I, FDP, DLC; Egerton, *Thunder*, 139; LHD to Amelia Loguen, Morris Island, S.C., 20 July 1863, Carter G. Woodson Papers, DLC; LHD to Amelia Loguen, Readville, Mass., 15, 27 August 1863, Evans Collection; LHD, Company Regimental Description Book, 1 April 1863, Compiled Military Service Records of Volunteer Union Soldiers, U.S. Colored Troops, 54th Massachusetts Infantry, NARA; CRD to FD, Boston, 18 September 1863, FDP, DLC. Using significant dramatic license, Maria Diedrich depicted Anna as a recluse and absent from her son's bedside, while Ottilie Assing accompanied Douglass on daily visits to Lewis in a military hospital for three weeks. Absolutely no evidence supports any of this beyond Lewis being wounded, in New York, and visited by his father, all of which is documented in the single source that she cites. Indeed, Lewis most likely stayed at the exclusive black Brooks House near McCune Smith's residence. Diedrich omits the more pertinent information of Lewis being wounded in the line of duty in a battle that Assing herself covered for the *Morgenblatt*. As in many of her columns, Assing's report about Fort Wagner contained no information that did not also appear in other newspaper accounts, indicating that she did not have daily access to one of its veterans. Anna's visit to Camp Meigs earlier in the year undercuts Diedrich's depiction of her as a shut-in unwilling to visit her wounded, oldest son during his recuperation. Diedrich, *LACL*, 253–54; OA, "Colored Troops," in *Radical Passions*, 269–70.

29. LHD, Company Book, NARA; LHD to Amelia Loguen, Rochester, 31 January 1864, Evans Collection.

30. FD to Thomas Webster, Rochester, 19 August 1863, *L&WFD*, 3:377; LHD, Company Book, NARA; CRD, Company Book, NARA; CRD to FD, Boston, 20 December 1863, CRD to FD and AD, Point Lookout, S.C., 15 September 1864, FDP, DLC; Account books, RLAS.

31. Hewitt, *Women's Activism*, 196; SBA to AKP, N.Y., 13 April 1863; Dudden, *Fighting Chance*, 51–55; ECS, SBA, MJG, *History of Woman Suffrage* 2:57; *ECS/SBAP*, 1:481–501.

32. Julia A. Wilbur to Anna M. C. Barnes, Washington, DC, 24 October[1862], RLASSP, MiU-C; JGC to FD, Leeds, England, 5 December 1862, FDP, DLC; Carol Faulkner, *Women's Radical Reconstruction: The Freedmen's Aid Movement* (Philadelphia: University of Pennsylvania Press, 2004), 15–26; Sterling, *We Are Your Sisters*, 294–305. The RLAS asked Julia Griffiths Croft for a recommendation for Rosetta. Although Croft told Douglass that she gave a positive assessment of Rosetta, her actual response was noncommittal, telling the society that she was "*unable to judge of her* [Rosetta's] *fitness*" having not seen her since she was a girl. JGC to FD, Leeds, England, 5 December, 1862, 9 January [1864], FDP, DLC; JGC to Anna M.C. Barnes, Leeds, England, 20 February 1863, RLASSP, MiU-C.

33. RD[S] to FD, Philadelphia, 24 September, 4 April, 9 October 1862, FDP, DLC.

34. General Affidavit, Nathan Sprague, 28 June 1905, Civil War Pension Records, NARA; RDS to FD, Rochester, 24 April 1867, FDP, DLC; Nathan Sprague, Company Regimental Description Book, 13 September 1864, Compiled Military Service Records of Volunteer Union Soldiers, U.S. Colored Troops, 54th Massachusetts Infantry, NARA; FD to Samuel Porter, Washington, DC, 18 June 1873, FDP, DLC. Nathan Sprague's great-granddaughter told a family story that he had run away when he was about sixteen years old, only to be caught and jailed. The escape allegedly took place 1848, but that would have made him a small child at the time and did not fit with the details of the rest of the story. The more likely date was 1858, twenty years after Frederick Bailey's escape from Baltimore. Such documentable inconsistencies in those recollections suggest that the family story may have evolved to combine some of Douglass's story with Sprague's, thus drawing parallels between the two men. Genealogical Notes, Addition I, FDP, DLC. Amelia Loguen, Lewis's wife, was the daughter of the Reverend Jermain Loguen and his free-born, wealthy wife, Caroline. Virginia Hewlett, Frederick Jr.'s wife, was the daughter of the first black faculty member at Harvard and the sister of a Shakespearean actor. Charles's wives were slight exceptions, Mary Elizabeth "Libbie" Murphy's father was a whitewasher, and Amelia and Virginia tended to comment unfavorably on her origins, "making fun of her dress and her education," according to Charles. His second wife, Laura Antoinette Haley, from Canandaigua, New York, had worked as a hairdresser before her marriage. Her father was involved in various aspects of small-scale textile

manufacturing throughout her life. None, however, were former slaves and all had some basic education. 1860 U.S. Census, New York, Onondaga, Syracuse, Ward 8, 39; Cambridge *Press*, 7 August 1869 California *Elevator*, 7 July 1877, Scrapbooks, Evans Collection; 1865 Massachusetts State Census, Middlesex, Cambridge; CRD to FD, Washington, DC, 13 May 1873, FDP, DLC; 1860 U.S. Census, New York, Monroe, Rochester, Ward 3, 176; 1855 New York State Census, Ontario, Canandaigua, E.D. 1, 21; 1875 New York State Census, Ontario, Canandaigua, E.D. 1, 46.

35. FD to HB/RCA, London, 18 August 1846, Addition II, FDP, DLC; FD quoted in Holland, *Frederick Douglass*, 279–80.

36. San Francisco *Pacific Appeal*, 20 February 1864; RDS, General Affidavit, 20 February 1905, CRD, General Affidavit, 17 September 1906, Civil War Pension Records, NARA; LHD to Amelia Loguen, Rochester, 31 January 1864, Evans Collection; Ball, *To Live an Antislavery Life*, 85–97, 106–8; Tess Chakkalakal, *Novel Bondage Slavery, Marriage, and Freedom in Nineteenth-Century America* (Urbana: University of Illinois Press, 2011), 69–74; Doriani, "Black Womanhood," 199–22; Anne duCille, *The Coupling Convention: Sex, Text, and Tradition in Black Women's Fiction* (New York: Oxford University Press, 1993), 51–65; Yee, *Black Women Abolitionists*, 4.

37. *Pacific Appeal* (San Francisco), 20 February 1864; LHD to Amelia Loguen, Rochester, 31 January 1864, Evans Collection; LHD, Company Regimental Description Book, 1 April 1863, Compiled Military Service Records of Volunteer Union Soldiers, U.S. Colored Troops, 54th Massachusetts Infantry, NARA; CRD, Company Regimental Description Book, 8 April 1863, Compiled Military Service Records of Volunteer Union Soldiers, U.S. Colored Troops, 54th Massachusetts Infantry, NARA; FDjr, "In brief, 1842–90" (notation in Scrapbook), Evans Collection; Nathan Sprague, Company Regimental Description Book, 13 September 1864, Compiled Military Service Records of Volunteer Union Soldiers, U.S. Colored Troops, 54th Massachusetts Infantry, NARA; JGC to FD, Staffordshire, 23 November 1864, FDP, DLC.

38. The sutler was Mark R. De Mortie, a Boston abolitionist, who was probably the brother of Louisa De Mortie and the son of Frances De Mortie, all originally from Norfolk, Virginia. Louisa billed herself as "Mrs. De Mortie" in order to pursue a career as a dramatic reader, and she or her mother hosted Anna and Rosetta Douglass when they arrived in Boston in May 1863 to see the Massachusetts Fifty-Fourth off. When Mark De Mortie sold his business, after asking Lewis if he wanted a partnership, Lewis went to work for another sutler, "Mr. Whitfield," also in South Carolina. Egerton, *Thunder*, 242, 392n61; LHD to Amelia Loguen, Mitchellville, S.C., 28 September 1864, Camp Meigs, Mass., 20 May 1863, Evans Collection; LHD to Frederick Douglass, Morris Island, S.C., August 22, 1864, FDP, DLC; Caroline M. Jones, "Louisa De Mortie (1833–1867): Lecturer, Missionary, Fund-Raiser," *Notable Black American Women*, ed. Jessie Carney Smith (Detroit: Gale Research, 1996) 2:173–76; 1850 U.S. Census, Virginia, Norfolk City, Norfolk, 94.

39. "Proceedings of the National Convention of Colored Men," Syracuse (Boston, 1864); Jones, *All Bound Up Together*, 137–38; FD, *Speeches*, 3:483; Egerton, *Wars*, 186–87.

40. "Proceedings of the National Convention of Colored Men," Syracuse (Boston, 1864); Highgate quoted in Sterling, *We Are Your Sisters*, 296.

41. "Proceedings of the National Convention of Colored Men," Syracuse (Boston, 1864), 13; Yee, *Black Women Abolitionists*, 145–49; Jones, *All Bound Up Together*, 130–38.

42. James Brewer Stewart, *Wendell Phillips: Liberty's Hero* (Baton Rouge: Louisiana State University Press, 1986), 244–56; Dudden, *Fighting Chance*, 61–64; [New York] *National Anti-Slavery Standard*, 13 May 1865; Appeal, 26 December 1865, ECS/SBAP, 1:566.

43. Eric Foner, *Short History of Reconstruction, 1863-1877* (New York: Harper & Row, 1990), 114–17; ECS to GS, New York, 1 January[1866], Eleventh National Woman's Rights Convention, [10 May 1860], ECS/SBAP, 1:568–69, 584–90.

44. This argument is taken up most extensively by Dudden in *Fighting Chance*. For the subsequent battles among activists over the 14th and 15th Amendments, see also Ellen Carol DuBois, *Feminism and Suffrage* (Ithaca, N.Y.: Cornell University Press, 1978); Washington, *Sojourner Truth's America*, 334–54; Ginzberg, *Elizabeth Cady Stanton*, 108–31; Hoffert, *When Hens Crow*; McMillen, *Seneca Falls*, 149–84; Tetrault, *Myth of Seneca Falls*, 19–37.

45. ECS, SBA, and MJG, *History*, 2:917; *FDWR*, 79, 78, 81–8; SBA, ECS, and MJG, *History*, 2: 310–12, 382–84, 391–92; Yee, *Black Women Abolitionists*, 146–50.
46. *FDWR*, 79; *ECS/SBAP*, 1:600–601; *NYTrib*, 21 December 1866; FD, *Speeches*, 4:146–48; *ECS/SBAP*, 2:54.
47. ECS to *National Anti-Slavery Standard*, [N.Y.], [c. 17 February 1866], *ECS/SBAP*, 1:576–78; Egerton, *Wars*, 192–94; "Ichabod" to FDjr., [Washington, DC],16 February 1866, Evans Collection; Henry O. Waggoner to FD, Denver, 27 August 1866, LHD to FD, Denver, 29 October 1866, FDP, DLC; LHD to Amelia Loguen, Denver, 30 September 1866, Ferry Neck, Md., 7 January 1866, Evans Collection; Nathan Sprague to FD, Rochester, 26 March 1867, RDS to FD, Rochester, 11 April 1867, FDP, DLC; Perry Downs to FD, Millican, Brazos Co., Tx., 21 February 1867, FDC, DHU-MS; "Found", *Colorado Tribune*, [n.d.], Walter O. Evans Collection; OA to SRK, Rochester, 29 August 1867, SRKP, Archives of American Art; FD to Theodore Tilton, Rochester, [September 1867], in *L&WFD*, 4:205–6; *FDWR*, 79, 84; *ECS/SBAP*, 1:600–601; *NYTrib*, 21 December 1866; FD, *Speeches*, 4:146–48.
48. ECS to Ellen D. Eaton, New York, 17 December 1867, *ECS/SBAP*, 2:117.
49. Article by ECS, [14 January 1869], *ECS/SBAP*, 2:201–3.
50. Meeting of the Illinois Woman Suffrage Association in Chicago, [12 February 1869], *ECS/SBAP*, 2:215.
51. SBA article, 7 October 1869, SBA remarks, [12 May 1869], *ECS/SBAP*, 2:272–73, 238–41; ECS, SBA, and MJG, *History*, 2:382–4, 391–93; *FDWR*, 86–90; *NYT*, 15 May 1869.
52. Hannah Rosen, *Terror in the Heart of Freedom: Citizenship, Sexual Violence, and the Meaning of Race in the Postemancipation South* (Chapel Hill: University of North Carolina Press, 2009), 3–9, 76–81; Truth, quoted in Washington, *Sojourner Truth's America*, 337; ECS, SBA, and MJG, *History*, 2:392; Boyd, *Discarded Legacy*, 130; Forret, *Slave Against Slave*, 259–71; Yee, *Black Women Abolitionists*, 1, 148–51.
53. ECS quoted in Dudden, *Fighting Chance*, 3; Meeting of the Illinois Woman Suffrage Association, Chicago, [12 February 1869], *ECS/SBAP*, 2:215; Ida B. Wells-Barnett, *Crusade for Justice: The Autobiography of Ida B. Wells*, ed. Alfreda M. Duster (Urbana: University of Illinois Press, 1970), 69–72; ECS Editorial Correspondence, *ECS/SBAP*, 2: 222–45.
54. SBA to *NYT*, New York, 4 June 1869, *ECS/SBAP*, 2:247–48; N.Y. State Equal Rights Convention, 20 November 1866, ECS to GS, New York, 29 January 186[9], *ECS/SBAP*, 1:599–604, 2:212; ECS Editorial Correspondence, *ECS/SBAP*, 2:226–29; SBA to *NYT*, New York, 4 June 1869, *ECS/SBAP*, 2:247–8.
55. FD, *MBMF*, 229; [Washington, DC] *New National Era*, 23 January 1873; ECS Editorial Correspondence, *ECS/SBAP*, 2:222–45; FD quoted in *ECS/SBAP*, 1:573n.
56. SBA to ECS, Washington, DC, 27 January 1884, *ECS/SBAP*, 4:323–38; Harper, *Life and Work*, 1:59.
57. SBA remarks, Western Woman Suffrage Association, Chicago, 10 September 1869, Article by ECS, 23 September 1869, *ECS/SBAP*, 2:265–70; Tetrault, *Myth of Seneca Falls*, 27; [Washington, DC] *New National Era*, 24 November 1870; SBA remarks, AWSA, Cleveland, [23 November 1870], *ECS/SBAP*, 2:376–79; Sally G. McMillan, *Lucy Stone: An Unapologetic Life* (New York: Oxford University Press, 2015), 181–87.
58. Allison Sneider, *Suffragists in an Imperial Age: U.S. Expansion and the Woman Question, 1870-1929* (New York: Oxford University Press, 2008), 72.
59. The number of conventions Douglass attended may have actually been five. He was supposed to have shared the stage with Victoria Woodhull at the 1871 NWSA convention, but his travel journal from his third European trip indicated that he did not meet Woodhull until she introduced herself to him in Rome in 1887. See FD, *Speeches*, 4:xxvii–xxxvii, 184, 395–96; ECS, SBA, and MJG, *History*, 3:149, 188–89, 264, 269, 315, 340, 349–50, 370, 442, 593; *NYT*, 20 July 1870; [Washington, DC] *New National Era*, 20 October 1870, 23 January 1873; *NYT*, 28 January 1876; SBA to Marietta Holley, Rochester, 26 June 1878, "Third Decade Celebration at Rochester, New York," *ECS/SBAP*, 3:382–84, 386–402, 480; FD, Diary, FDP, DLC.
60. SBA to FD, Washington, 13 January 1873, FDP, DLC; ECS, SBA, and MJG, *History*, 2:858–60; Memorial for Lucretia Mott, Washington, DC, 18 January 1888, ECS to the Editor, *National Citizen and Ballot Box*, New York, January 1881, *ECS/SBAP*, 4:26–39; Tetrault,

Myth of Seneca Falls, 113–14, 128–35, 151–52. Carol Faulkner makes a similar argument about the NWSA leaders' use of Lucretia Mott. Faulkner, *Lucretia Mott's Heresy*, 215–16.

61. FD, *L&T*, 369–71. Tetrault makes a slightly different argument that "Douglass implicitly endorsed Stanton and Anthony's historical interpretations of the movement, acknowledging them as 'eminent,' and even preeminent." Tetrault, *Myth of Seneca Falls*, 152.

62. ECS to FD, Tenafly, N.J., 29 January, 4 February 1882, FD to ECS, Washington, 6 February 1882, FDP, DLC; FD to ECs, Washington, 31 January 1882, *ECS/SBAP*, 5:150; FD, *L&T*, 310–11, 438; Gallman, *America's Joan of Arc*, 83–89.

Chapter 8

1. FD to Sarah Loguen, Washington, DC, 12 August 1882, quoted in *FDWR*, 22; RDS to SBA, Takoma Park, DC, 27 January 1896, FDP, DHU-MS; RDS, *MMAIRH*, 24.

2. RDS, *MMAIRH*, 24.

3. RDS to SBA, Takoma Park, DC, 27 January 1896, FDP, DHU-MS; SBA to Antoinette Brown Blackwell, Rochester, 22 April 1858, *ECS/SBAP*, 1: 360–61; Baker, *Sisters*, 65–66; Ginzberg, *Elizabeth Cady Stanton*, 92–93; McMillan, *Seneca Falls*, 143–45.

4. LHD to Amelia Loguen, Rochester, 31 January 1864, Evans Collection; Genealogical information from Scrapbook, Evans Collection; Harriette Bailey Sprague, "List of Descendants," FDC, DHU-MS; RDS to FD, Rochester, 21 February 1865, Mary Carpenter to FD, Bridgeport, England, 9 October 1866, CRD to FD, Rochester, 24 February 1867, Nathan Sprague to FD, Rochester, 26 March 1867, RDS to FD, Rochester, 11 April 1867, 4 February 1868, FDP, DLC; *Daily Iowa State Register*, 3 May 1867.

5. FD, *Speeches*, 4:146–48; 1865 N.Y. State Census, Monroe, Rochester, Ward 7, 45; Perry Downs to FD, Millican, Tx., 21 February 1867, LHD to FD, Ferry Neck, Md., 9 June 1865, FDC, DHU-MS; "Found," *Colorado Tribune*, [n.d.], Clipping, *Chicago Tribune* [c. 1867], Scrapbooks, Evans Collection; OA to SRK, Rochester, 29 August 1867, SRKP, Archives of American Art; FD to Theodore Tilton, Rochester, [September 1867], in *L&WFD*, 4:205–6; *FDWR*, 79, 84; *ECS/SBAP*, 1:600–601; *NYTrib*, 21 December 1866; CRD to FD, Washington, 14 July 1867, FDP, DLC. Louisa Keys may have been Eliza Mitchell's second daughter, born in 1835. Preston, *YFD*, 206–7.

6. CRD to FD, Washington, 16 August 1867, FDP, DLC; OA to SRK, Rochester, 29 August 1867, OA to SRK, Rochester, 29 August 1867, 8 September 1868, SRKP, AAA.

7. OA to SRK, Rochester, 29 August 1867, OA to SRK, Rochester, 8 September 1868, SRKP, AAA.

8. RDS to FD, Rochester, 24 April 1867, FDP, DLC; 1870 U.S. Census, New York, Monroe, Rochester, Ward 7, 70; 1871 Rochester City Directory (Rochester, 1861), 238; RDS to FD, Rochester, 4, 18 February 1868, FDP, DLC. Louisa may have been Nathan's half-sister. When Frank Sprague visited Rochester, Rosetta referred to him as "Nathan's or at least Alfred's brother." Louisa was a year younger than Alfred Sprague, so if Alfred and Nathan did not share two parents, then she may have had a different mother or father than Nathan. RDS to FD, Rochester, 8 December 1869, FDP, DLC.

9. RDS to FD, Rochester, 21 February 1865, 26 March 1867, 25 April 1869, 11, 19, 24 April 1867, 21 February 1865, Rochester, 4 February 1868, 25 April 1869, 11, 19, 24 April 1867, 21 February 1865, FDP, DLC.

10. OA to SRK, Hoboken, N.J., 20 May 1870, SRKP, AAA; Coontz, *Way We Never Were*, 68–73; Doriani, "Black Womanhood," 199–22.

11. CRD to FD, Washington, DC, 11, 18 September 1868, 26 February 1869, RDS to FD, Rochester, 18 February 1869, FDP, DLC. Charles may have projected a little of his own guilt onto Nathan, since he himself owed Frederick the full $1800 he had borrowed to purchase land and build a house in Washington, and constantly insisted to his father that his seemingly extravagant financial choices were the more economical options in an expensive city.

12. CRD to FD, Washington, DC, 26 February 1869, RDS to FD, Rochester, 15 March, 25 February, 25 April 1868, FDP, DLC; Paula Marantz Cohen, *Daughter's Dilemma: Family Process and the Nineteenth-Century Domestic Novel* (Ann Arbor: University of Michigan Press, 1991), 27, 35–39.

13. CRD to FD, Washington, DC, 26 February 1869, RDS to FD, Rochester, 15 March, 18 February 1869, FDP, DLC.

14. RDS to FD, Rochester, 15 March, FDP, DLC; Cohen, *Daughter's Dilemma*, 27, 35–39.

15. RDS to FD, Rochester, 25 April 1868, 8, 23 December 1869, FDP, DLC; OA to SRK, Hoboken, N.J., 20 May 1870, SRKP, DCAWR; Genealogical information from Scrapbook, Evans Collection; Harriette Bailey Sprague, "List of Descendants," FDC, DHU-MS.

16. New York *Cable News*, 3 June 1872; Albany *Evening Journal*, 4 June 1872; Worcester *Massachusetts Spy*, 7 June 1872; Portland [Maine] *Daily Press*, 10 June 1872; FD, *L&T*, 207; "Lou Douglass" [Louisa Sprague] to FD, Washington, DC, 31 January 1873, FDP, DLC; OA to LA[G], Washington, DC, 15 August 1872, VC, BJK.

17. New York *Cable News*, 3 June 1872; Albany *Evening Journal*, 4 June 1872; Worcester *Massachusetts Spy*, 7 June 1872; Portland [Maine] *Daily Press*, 10 June 1872; FD, *L&T*, 207; "Lou Douglass" [Louisa Sprague] to FD, Washington, DC, 31 January 1873, FDP, DLC; OA to LA[G], Washington, DC, 15 August 1872, VC, BJK. The loss of Douglass's newspapers contines to affect historians today. No repository or database possesses a full run, and a composite of issues from all known sources would probably not yield a complete set, either.

18. [Washington, DC] *New National Era*, 1 September 1870; Blight, *Frederick Douglass' Civil War*, 203; John Muller, *Frederick Douglass in Washington, D.C.: The Lion of Anacostia* (Charleston, S.C.: History Press, 2012), 46–61.

19. FDjr to AKP, Washington, DC, 14 February 1872, IAKPFP, NRU; Petition quoted in Rosalyn Terborg-Penn, *African American Women in the Struggle for the Vote* (Bloomington: Indiana University Press, 1998), 46–47; Muller, *Frederick Douglass in Washington*, 46–61; Nancy Hewitt, "Amy Kirby Post: 'Of whom it was said, 'being dead, yet speaketh,'" *University of Rochester Library Bulletin* 37 (1984): http://rbscp.lib.rochester.edu/4018 [accessed 15 July 2016]; Rhodes, *Mary Ann Shadd Cary*, 177–81.

20. Douglas, "Cherished Friendship," 265–74; OA to LA[G], Rochester, 24 August 1871, 16 April 1872, VC, BJK; Hewitt, "Amy Kirby Post," web: http://rbscp.lib.rochester.edu/4018 [accessed 15 July 2016]; *ECS/SBAP*, 2:653; Jones, *All Bound Up Together*, 151–71.

21. Lillie Buffum Chace Wyman and Arthur Crawford Wyman, *Elizabeth Buffum Chace, 1806-1899* (Boston: W. B. Clarke co., 1914), 2:110; OA to LA[G], Washington, 15 August, 30 December 1872, VC, BJK.

22. OA to LA[G], Hoboken, 15 August, 30 December 1872, VC, BJK; RDS to FD, Rochester, 4 February 1868, FDP, DLC; RDS, *MMAIRH*, 9; OA to FD, Rome, 5 January 1877, FDP, DLC; OA to LAG, 29 January, 26 March 1874, VC, BJK. The translation in which Assing refers to Anna Douglass as a "monster" appears in the 29 January 1874 letter as interpreted by Katherina Schmidt, who noted that an alternate translation would be "beast" and that Assing used a neutral form of the noun (*das*) rather than feminine (*die*), there by stripping Anna of her gender. Heike Polster translated the passage as "a real monster that is not able to give love itself nor knows how to protect it," Maria Diedrich rendered it as "a true monster, who herself can neither give love nor appreciate it," while Terry Pickett quoted it as "a being incapable of valuing or giving love." The original German is "ein wahres Ungethüm, das selbst weder Liebe zu geben hat noch zu schätyen weißö." Diedrich, *LACL*, 313; Pickett, "Friendship of Frederick Douglass," 99.

23. "Lou Douglass" [Louisa Sprague] to FD, Washington, DC, 31 January 1873, Louisa Sprague to FD, Washington, DC, 22 January 1874, 15 July 1883, FD to RDS, Washington, DC, 25 May [1875, DLC dated as 1878], FDP, DLC; FD to RDS, Washington, DC, 30 June 1875, Addition I, FDP, DLC. The date of Louisa Sprague's arrival at the A Street house comes from a lawsuit she filed against Douglass in 1884. *National Republican*, 8 February 1884; *Philadelphia Press*, 6 February 1884; *Boston Daily Globe*, 8 February 1884; *Washington Star*, 7 February 1884.

24. FD to RDS, 28 August 1873, Washington, DC, Addition I, FDP, DLC; OA to LAG, Washington, DC 26 March 1874, VC, BJK; OA to SRK, Washington, DC, 4 July, 3 November 1874, SRKP, AAA.

25. FD to RDS, Washington, D.C., 2 August 1875, FDP, DLC; OA to LA[G], Rochester, 24 August 1868, VC, BJK; OA to FD, Hoboken, N.J., 19 March 1879, FDP, DLC.

26. OA to SRK, Hoboken, 10 October, 13 November, 19 December 1880, 22 February 1881, SRKP, AAA; Notes in scrapbook, Evans Collection.

27. FD to RDS, Washington, D.C., 2 August 1875, FDP, DLC; Sarah Luria, *Capital Speculations: Writing and Building Washington, D.C.* (Durham, N.H.: University Press of New England, 2006), 75–87; Fredericka Perry, Recollections, FDC, DHU-MS.

28. OA to FD, Stamford, Conn., 18 November 1878, Hoboken, N.J., 14 April 1870, FDP, DLC. I am grateful to the insights provided by German translator Katharina Schmidt for her nuanced and sympathetic insight into Assing's perspective, to which I have not done proper justice.

29. OA to LAG, Hoboken, N.J., 26 March 1874, VC, BJK.

30. OA to LA[G], Rochester, 10 October 1868, VC, BJK.

31. FD to RDS, Washington, 30 June 1875, Addition I, FDP, DLC; Helene von Racowitza, *Princess Helene von Racowitza: An Autobiography*, trans. Cecil Mar (London, 1910), 368–73; Behmer, "From German Cultural," in Fluck and Sollors, *German? American? Literature?*, 147–55. Racowitza paints a highly romanticized portrait of the friendship between Douglass and Assing, much of which is demonstrably inaccurate.

32. RDS to FD, Rochester, n.d. [c. 1869], "Lou Douglass" [Louisa Sprague] to FD, Washington, DC, 31 January 1873, FDP, DLC; FD to RDS, Washington, DC, 25 May 1873, Addition I, FDP, DLC; Perry, Recollections, FDC, DHU-MS.

33. FD to RDS, Washington, 13 April 1875, 25 May 1878 [more likely 1875, since Herbert was the only son, born 17 May 1875], 2 June 1875, Addition I, FDP, DLC.

34. *Ohio Plain Dealer*, 3 December 1875; *New York Commercial Advertiser*, 3 December 1875; *Alexandria Gazette*, 3 December 1875; RDS to FD, Rochester, 17 September 1876, OA to FD, Rome, 5 January 1877, FDP, DCL; Ginzberg, *Elizabeth Cady Stanton*, 97–101; McMillan, *Seneca Falls*, 21–23, 27–30; Isenberg, *Sex and Citizenship*, 161–67; Genealogical information from Scrapbook, Evans Collection; Harriette Bailey Sprague, "List of Descendants," FDC, DHU-MS.

Most middle-class families, both black and white, limited their number of children, but the second generation of Douglasses did not. With the exception of Amelia [Loguen] Douglass, Lewis's wife, and Laura [Haley] Douglass, Charles's second wife, the wives of Rosetta's brothers followed the same pattern of frequent childbearing. Frederick Jr. and his wife Virginia had seven children, ending with Virginia's death of tuberculosis in 1889 at the age of forty. Charles's first wife, Mary Elizabeth "Libbie," gave birth to six children. He and his second wife had only one. Lewis and Amelia had no children due to his war wounds. Unlike Rosetta's family, however, theirs experienced high rates of mortality; only two children lived into the twentieth century. Mintz and Kellogg, *Domestic Revolutions*, 51. Genealogical information from Scrapbook, Evans Collection; Harriette Bailey Sprague, "List of Descendants," FDC, DHU-MS.

For all of Nathan's other failings, over the years he seemed to enjoy not only his own children but also his nieces and nephews. His younger sister preferred to live with him because he was kind to her, and he liked that his five-year-old daughter Alice "thinks it grand to sleep with me" when her mother was away. When Frederick, Jr.'s wife lay dying, he and Rosetta took in their baby, Robbie, and another of Frederick, Jr.'s sons, Charlie, repeatedly ran away to the Sprague house. Whatever his adult in-laws thought of him, the children seemed to find him affectionate.

35. Muller, *Frederick Douglass in Washington*, 89–109; Luria, *Capital Speculations*, 87–98; Fredericka Perry, Recollections, FDC, DHU-MS; Washington, DC *Republic*, 23 October 1883, *Atchison Daily Champion*, 1 January 1881, Evans Collection. The current interpretation of the home does not necessarily reflect the Douglasses' living arrangements. Anna may have arranged the home one way, but her choices were likely revised after her death by Frederick's second wife, Helen, who occupied the house for nearly twenty years after Anna. She also lived there for eight of those years as a widow, with boarders and with an eye to maintaining the house as a museum featuring items from her husband's career.

36. Pamela Barnes Craig, "Married Women's Property Laws," American Memory, Law Library of Congress, c. 2001, accessed 7 July 2015, http://memory.loc.gov/ammem/awhhtml/awlaw3/property_law.html; NS, 21 April 1848; SBA, ECS, and MJG, *History*, 1:587; SBA, ECS, and MJG, *History*, 1:587; SBA, ECS, and MJG, *History*, 1:587; Dudden, *Fighting Chance*, 28; *NYT*, 21 March 1860 Deeds, 1843, 1851–59, 1871–79, 1897, Abstracts of Titles, Legal

File, FDP, DLC. The editors of *The Selected Papers of ECS and SBA* interpret his remark at the 1853 convention as opposition to joint ownership of property within marriage. *ECS/SBAP*, 1:85n10.

37. Muller, *Frederick Douglass in Washington*, 45–46; FD, *L&T*, 386–87; Silber, *Daughters of the Union*, 78–82; Account Book, 1881–1883, Addition I, FDP, DLC.

38. FD, *L&T*, 387–9; Doriani, "Black Womanhood in Nineteenth-Century America," 199–222.

39. Notations in scrapbooks, Evans Collection; OA to SRK, Washington, DC, 12 November 1878, SRKP, DCAWR.

40. *Easton Gazette*, 30 November 1878; FD, *L&T*, 31.

41. LHD to FD, 1870 U.S. Census, New York, Monroe, Rochester, Ward 12, 15; LHD to FD, Ferry Neck, Md., 9 June 1865, FDC, DHU-MS; 1870 U.S. Census, Maryland, Talbot, District 2, 54; 1880 U.S. Census, Maryland, Talbot, District 2, 30; 1880 U.S. Census, Washington, DC, 7th District, 143; MSS on scrapbook page, Evans Collection; RDS to FD, Washington, DC, 20 November 1889, FDP, DLC; OA to SRK, Hoboken, NJ, 13 November 1880, SRKP, AAA; Providence [R.I.] *Journal*, 15 January 1881; Washington, DC, *People's Advocate*, 8 March 1884.

42. Providence [R.I.] *Journal*, 15 January 1881; *Washington Star*, 7 February 1884.

43. FD to RDS, Washington, 2 August 1875, Addition I, FDP, DLC; Fredericka Perry, Recollections, FDC, DHU-MS; RDS, *MMAIRH*, 18; "Stories of Douglass," [no source, Rochester?], [n.d., c. February 1895, after FD death], Evans Collection; Julia D. Lucas to FD, New York, 10 August 1882, JGC to FD, Gateshead-on-Tyne, England, 28 November [c. 1868], Addition I, FDP, DLC.

44. Notes in scrapbook, Evans Collection; RDS, *MMAIRH*, 22; Fredericka Perry, Recollections, FDC, DHU-MS; *NYTrib*, 5 August 1881; Washington, DC *Evening Critic*, 4 August 1882; *Washington Post*, 5 August 1882; *Denver Star*, 12 August 1882; *New York Globe*, 12 August 1882; RDS to SBA, Takoma Park, DC, 27 January 1896, FDC, DHU-MS; William P. Frye to FD, Washington, DC, 1 August 1882, FDP, DLC.

45. Fredericka Perry, Recollections, FDC, DHU-MS.

46. *New York Globe*, 12 August 1882; *Denver Star*, 12 August 1882.

47. RDS to FD, Rochester, [n.d., c. 1869], FDP, DLC; FD, *L&T*, 159.

48. FD to Sarah Loguen, Washington, DC, 12 August 1882, quoted in *FDWR*, 22; *Cincinnati Commercial*, 27 August 1882.

49. FD, *L&T*, 372; RDS to FD, Cedar Hill, 13 July 1883, Annie Sprague to FD, Washington, DC, 15 July 1883, Louisa Sprague to FD, Washington, DC, 15 July 1883, LHD to FD, Washington, DC, 19 July 1883, Annie Sprague to FD, Washington, DC, 19 July 1883, RDS to FD, Cedar Hill, Washington, DC, 20 July 1883, LHD to FD, Washington, DC, 19 July 1883, Louisa Sprague to FD, Washington, DC, 25 July 1883, RDS to FD, Cedar Hill, Washington, DC, 26 July 1883, FDP, DLC; *Washington Star*, 7 February 1884.

50. Henry O. Waggoner to FD, Denver, 7 August 1882, FDP, DLC.

Chapter 9

1. Grimké, "The Second Marriage of Frederick Douglass," *Journal of Negro History*, 324–25; *Rochester Democrat*, 26 January 1884; *New York Globe*, 2 February 1884; FD to Oliver Johnson, Washington, DC, [24 January] 1885, FDP, DLC. Helen did not return to work at the Recorder of Deeds office after the wedding, receiving her last paycheck on 23 January 1884. Account Books, 1883–1886, Addition I, FDP, DLC. A story in the *National Republican* gave a slightly different account, describing Frederick's "furtive" visit to the city clerk's office to secure a license, followed by a meeting with his children to inform them of the wedding. The reporter was supposed to have badgered Helen, as well, until she confessed the pending nuptials. *National Republican*, 25 January 1884.

2. For the range of Helen's ages, see *NYTrib, National Republican, Washington Post*, 25 January 1884; *People's Advocate*, 26 January 1884; *PennYan Express*, 30 January 1884; *Cleveland Gazette, New York Globe*, 2 February 1884; *Boston Daily Globe*, 8 February 1884; *Raleigh Banner-Enterprise* and *Pittsburg Weekly* in *New York Globe, Louisiana Standard*, 9 February 1884.

3. *Washington Grit*, 16 February 1884; *People's Advocate*, 9 February 1884.

4. Quarles, *Frederick Douglass*, 298–300; P. Foner, ed. *FDWR*, 41; Martin, *Mind of Frederick Douglass*, 98–100; McFeely, *Frederick Douglass*, 319–23; James O. Horton, "'What Business Has the World with the Color of My Wife?': A Letter from FD," *OAH Magazine of History* 19, 1 (January 2005): 52–55; Stauffer, *Giants*, 313–14. Maria Diedrich makes less of Pitts's age than her youth in contrast to Ottilia Assing, and suggests that Douglass's marriage to Pitts was a betrayal of Assing. Diedrich, *LACL*, 366–69. Julie Nelson, a master of arts student at Shippensburg University, however, did explore Helen Pitts in depth in her thesis, pointing out valuable information for future researchers. Nelson, "'Have We a Cause': The Life of Helen Pitts Douglass, 1838-1903" (MA thesis, Shippensburg University, 1995).

5. FD, *Speeches*, 1:359–86; Senior Citizens' Bicentennial Committee, comp., *An Informal History of Richmond, New York* (Honeoye, N.Y., 2002), 1–4; Edie Badger and Peggy Treble, comp., *Looking Back, Richmond, 1789-1989: A Collection of Fact and Folklore* (Honeoye, N.Y., 1989), n.p.

6. Florence Short Ellis, "Short-Pitts History," "Typescript of Tombstone Inscriptions, Lakeview Cemetery," "Gideon Pitts Family Births & Deaths," Gideon Pitts obituary, Helen Pitts Douglass files, Town of Richmond; Nelson, "Have We a Cause,'" 181.

7. [Maria G. Frost and Lavinia Goodell], *In Memoriam: William Goodell* (Chicago, 1879), 26–31, 41. At the time the Richmond church hired him, Goodell edited the *Christian Investigator* in Whitesboro, New York.

8. See Helen Pitts Douglass files, Town of Richmond; Badger and Treble, comp., "Pitts-Douglass Marriage," *Looking Back*, n.p.

9. Lib., 2 September 1842, 25 August, 8 September 1843; FD, *Speeches*, 2:xxx–xxxi.

10. Nelson, "'Have We a Cause,'" 25–28, 33–34, 182; "Frederick Douglass-Helen Pitts: The Honeoye Connection," [n.p.] *Courier*, 8 March 1984; Margaret Treble to Jean Czerkas, [Richmond, N.Y.], 19 May 2004 [e-mail]; "Frederick Douglass at Honeoye," *Livonia Gazette*, 26 July 1879, County Clerk's Office, Town of Richmond; FD, *Speeches*, 2:xxx; 1850 US Census, New York, Ontario, Richmond, 94, 100.

11. *Ten-Year Book of Cornell University, 1868-88* (Ithaca, N.Y., 1888), 158; *Catalog of Officers and Students of Genesee College* (Lima, N.Y., 1855–56), 31, 37–9, 41, Genesee College Collection, NSyU.

12. *Finding Aid, Class of 1861 Photograph Composite, Catalog of Officers and Students of Genesee College* (Lima, N.Y., 1855–56), 31, 37–39, 41, Genesee College Collection, NSyU.

13. Mount Holyoke Female Seminary, *Memorial: Twenty-fifth Anniversary of the Mount Holyoke Female Seminary* (Springfield, Mass., 1862), 27–35; Cole, *Hundred Years of Mount Holyoke College*, 145–46. Helen Pitts did not, as asserted by William McFeely, attend Hampton Institute, nor did she teach there, as Maria Diedrich claimed. The school did not open until 1868, and the university archive reports no record of her as either student or instructor. The confusion probably results from her Civil War experiences in nearby Norfolk, Virginia, on the shores of Hampton Roads, or from the year that her sister Eva taught at the Peace Institute in Raleigh, North Carolina, in 1880–81. McFeely, *Frederick Douglass*, 310; Diedrich, *LACL*, 350; *Cornell University, Ten-Year Book of Cornell University II, 1868-88* (Ithaca, N.Y., 1888), 158.

14. Helen Pitts diploma, 28 July 1859, Memorabilia, Family Papers, FDP, DLC; 1860 U.S. Census, New York, Ontario, Richmond, 30; Class of 1861 Photograph Composite, *Catalog of Genesee College* (Rochester, 1861), 9, Genesee College Collection, NSyU; 1870 U.S. Census, New York, Ontario, Richmond, 1; 1860 U.S. Census, Illinois, Rock Island, Moline, 328–29; *Twin Cities Directory* (Davenport, Iowa, 1861), 19; Mount Holyoke College Alumni Association, *One Hundred Year Biographical Directory of Mount Holyoke College, 1837-1937* (South Hadley, Mass.: Mount Holyoke College Alumnae Association, 1937), 95; *Photocopies, Third Class Letter of the Lulasti* (Northampton, Mass., 1866), 16; *Seventh Class Letter of the Lulasti* (Holyoke, 1899), 34; Helen Pitts Douglass Alumni File, Mount Holyoke College Archives. Ten-year-old Eva and eight-year-old Gideon were still at home with their parents, but Lorinda had followed her older sisters to Genesee College. After her graduation in 1861, she promptly married a Honeoye farmer, Spencer Short, and began what became a large family. Two of their father's brothers, Hiram and Cyrus, had moved their families to Moline,

Illinois. In 1863, Jennie followed them, taking a teaching job at a school in Davenport, Iowa, just across the Mississippi River. Although Jennie had reported herself as teaching in Iowa, the Seventh Class Letter confused the two sisters, listing Helen as having taught for a year in Davenport and Jennie as not teaching at all.

15. 1860 U.S. Census, New York, Ontario, Richmond, 30; Helen Pitts to S. S. Jocelyn, Honeoye, N.Y., 16 March 1863, AMAA, LDA. For more on northern white women's responses to the war and Reconstruction, see Faulkner, *Women's Radical Reconstruction*; Silber, *Daughters of the Union*. The American Missionary Association was formed through the union of three organizations that had protested the lack of antislavery conviction among other missionary societies and churches. While the society's initial interest lay in foreign missions, its attention turned to slaveholding regions in the United States through the 1850s. Missionaries held many prejudiced assumptions about the objects of their benevolence, but they also offered education, which became a central part of their activities through the next three decades. Douglass criticized missionary organizations, but he had alliances with the Missionary Association's known abolitionists and supported the effort to teach slaves to read and write, so he printed notices of their meetings and debates between their members in his paper. Helen's association with the organization likely came through her old minister, William Goodell, who was a leading member and wrote her a recommendation. [American Missionary Association] *History of the American Missionary Association* (New York, 1874), 3–11; Richardson, *Christian Reconstruction*, vii–viii; *National Era*, 14 October 1852; 3 January 1856; Hiram Pitts to Lewis Tappan, Honeoye, N.Y., 21 December 1841, William Goodell to Lewis Tappan, Honeoye, N.Y., 29 April 1848, William Goodell to George Whipple, Honeoye, N.Y., 11 March 1851, AMAA, LDA; *NS*, 5 January 1849; *FDP*, 9 September 1853, 30 June 1854; FD to S. S. Jocelyn, Rochester, 15 December 1855, AMAA, LDA.

16. William S. Bell to S. S. Jocelyn, Norfolk, Va., 17 August 1863, AMAA, LDA.

17. L. P. Jackson, "The Origin of Hampton Institute," *Journal of Negro History*, 10, 2 (April 1925): 131–49; Richardson, *Christian Reconstruction*, 4–5.

18. Charles Reed to [John Reed], Portsmouth, Va., 4 May 1863 [typescript], Helen Pitts Douglass Files, Town of Richmond; George N. Greene to S. S. Jocelyn, Norfolk, Va., 21 April 1863, AMAA, LDA.

19. George N. Greene to S. S. Jocelyn, Norfolk, Va., 11 July 1863; Henry M. Naglee, *Report of Brigadier General Henry M. Naglee, of the Command of the District of Virginia* (Philadelphia, 1863).

20. John Oliver to S. S. Jocelyn, Norfolk, Va., 14 January 1863, AMAA, LDA.

21. William Coan to S. S. Jocelyn, Norfolk, Va., 7 May 1863, AMAA, LDA.

22. Helen Pitts to George Whipple, Norfolk, Va., 22 May 1863.

23. George N. to S. S. Jocelyn, Norfolk, Va., 6 May 1863; "Mission House Expenses for December 1863," Norfolk, Va., 1 January 1864; "Mission House Expenses, February 1864," Norfolk, Va., [February 1864]; George N. Greene to S. S. Jocelyn, Norfolk, Va., 23 July 1863, AMAA, LDA; Judith Weisenfeld, "'Who is Sufficient for These Things?': Sara G. Stanley and the American Missionary Association," *Church History* 60, 4 (December 1991): 493–507. Pitts's service overlapped only slightly with the arrival of the first black teachers in Norfolk. Not much evidence exists to determine her place in some of the discrimination that they faced, but racism within the association's missions plagued African American workers.

24. Charles Reed to [John Reed], Portsmouth, Va., 11 May 1863 [typescript], Helen Pitts Douglass Files, Town of Richmond.

25. George N. Greene to S. S. Jocelyn, Norfolk, Va., 6 May 1863, William Coan to S. S. Jocelyn, Norfolk, Va., 7, 12 May 1863, AMAA, LDA.

26. George N. Green to S. S. Jocelyn, Norfolk, Va., 16 May 1863, AMAA, LDA.

27. George N. Greene to S. S. Jocelyn, Norfolk, Va., 21 July 1863; Helen Pitts to George Whipple, Norfolk, Va., 22 May 1863, AAMA, LDA.

28. Richardson, *Christian Reconstruction*, 189–209.

29. George N. Greene to S. S. Jocelyn, Norfolk, Va., 28 April 1863, AMAA, LDA.

30. Blanche Harris to George Whipple, Norfolk, Va., 30 March 1864, AMAA, LDA.

31. George N. Green to S. S. Jocelyn, Norfolk, Va., 16 May 1863, AMAA, LDA.

32. George N. Green to S. S. Jocelyn, Norfolk, Va., 27 May 1863, AMAA, LDA.

33. George N. Greene to S. S. Jocelyn, Norfolk, Va., 13 May 1863, AMAA, LDA.
34. Richardson, *Christian Reconstruction*, 7-10.
35. William Woodbury to George Whipple, Norfolk, Va., 7 November 1863, AMAA, LDA.
36. William Woodbury to S. S. Jocelyn, Norfolk, Va., 2 October, 4 November, 8 December 1863, AMAA, LDA.
37. HP[D] to George Whipple, Norfolk, Va., 10 November 1863, AMAA, LDA.
38. William Woodbury to George Whipple, Norfolk, Va., 7 November 1863, AMAA, LDA.
39. William Coan to S. S. Jocelyn, Norfolk, Va., 28 July 1863, William Woodbury to S. S. Jocelyn, Norfolk, Va., 2, 20, 29 October, and 7 December 1863, HP[D] to S. S. Jocelyn, Mission House, Norfolk, Va., 1 August 1863, Lydia Woodbury to George Whipple, Norfolk, Va., 22 December 1863, AMAA, LDA.
40. HP[D] to George Whipple, Norfolk, Va., 10 November 1863, AMAA, LDA.
41. HP[D] to S. S. Jocelyn, Norfolk, Va., 15 April 1863, AMAA, LDA.
42. HP[D] to S. S. Jocelyn, Honeoye, N.Y., 7 September 1863, AMAA, LDA.
43. Mrs. Gideon [Jane Wells] Pitts to George Whipple, Honeoye, N.Y., 15 February 1864, AMAA, LDA.
44. William Coan to S. S. Jocelyn, Norfolk, Va., 12 May 1863, George N. Greene to S. S. Jocelyn, Norfolk, Va., 11 July 1863, AMAA, LDA.
45. Oliver Brown to S. S. Jocelyn, Norfolk, Va., 11 July 1863, AMAA, LDA. For public health conditions postemancipation, see Jim Downs, *Sick from Freedom African-American Illness and Suffering during the Civil War and Reconstruction* (New York: Oxford University Press, 2012).
46. George N. Greene to S. S. Jocelyn, Norfolk, Va., 27 May 1863, AMAA, LDA.
47. HP[D] to George Whipple, Norfolk, Va., 22 May 1863, AMAA, LDA.
48. Mrs. Gideon [Jane Wells] Pitts to George Whipple, Honeoye, N.Y., 15 February 1864, William Woodbury to George Whipple, Norfolk, Va., 8 March 1864, AMAA, LDA.
49. HP[D] to George Whipple, Honeoye, N.Y., 20 April, 16 June 1864, William Woodbury to George Whipple, Norfolk, Va., 17 February 1864, William Coan to George Whipple, Norfolk, Va., 26 March 1864, AMAA, LDA.
50. Louise Woodbury to George Whipple, Norfolk, Va., 5 April 1864, Blanche Harris to George Whipple, Norfolk, Va., 8 April 1864, William Woodbury to George Whipple, Norfolk, Va., 6 April 1864, AMAA, LDA.
51. HP[D] to George Whipple, Honeoye, N.Y., 20 April 1864, AMAA, LDA.
52. HP[D] to George Whipple, Honeoye, N.Y., 16 June 1864, AMAA, LDA.
53. HP[D] to George Whipple, Honeoye, N.Y., 8 December 1864, AMAA, LDA.
54. Jane W. Pitts, Class of 1859, Alumnae File, Archive, Mount Holyoke College.
55. 1870 U.S. Census, N.Y., Ontario, Richmond, 13. An April 1989 clipping from the Huntingdon *Herald Press* in Helen's alumni file at Mount Holyoke asserted that Helen was a teacher in Seneca Falls, New York, in 1875, where she was also a member of the Union Woman's Suffrage Society. According to the article, she secured a job in Washington, DC, after taking the civil service exam. The civil service exam, however, was not implemented until the Pendleton Act of 1883, the Union Woman's Suffrage Society existed only between 1871 and 1872, and the Seneca Falls Historical Society has no record of Helen teaching in the city. Helen Pitts Alumni File, Archives, Mount Holyoke College.
56. *Neighbor's Home Mail*, 1 November 1876.
57. *Alpha*, February 1877; 1865 Washington DC City Directory, 220. In 1903, Pitts's death certificate identified her as having lived in Washington for twenty-five years, placing her arrival at the capital in 1878. Her work in the Moral Education Society contradicts this, and her residence was not continual. Helen Pitts Douglass, Certificate of Death, 1 December 1903, Death Certificates, Legal File, FDP, DLC.
58. OA to FD, Hoboken, N.J., 10 December 1878, FDP, DLC.
59. MWG to FD, Fall River, Mass., 8 December 1878, 3 July 1880, FDP, DLC.
60. *Alpha*, September 1875, August 1876, December 1881, May 1882.
61. *Alpha*, October 1875, October, November 1881, 1 February 1882. For a list of the women who, along with Winslow, attempted to register and vote in Washington, DC, in 1871, see *ECS/SBAP*, 2:649-70.

62. *Alpha*, October 1875, June 1888; OA to FD, Hoboken, 10 December 1878, FDP, DLC.

63. *Alpha*, August 1876.

64. *Washington Post*, 26 January 1884.

65. Mrs. George S. Puffin to FD, Boston, 25 March 1884, FDP, DLC. In an effort to make something out of the little evidence surrounding Helen Pitts's life before her marriage, scholars have inflated this episode of her life, leading to a consensus that she was deeply involved in radical feminism and the publication of *The Alpha*. According to William McFeely, who usually serves as the source for other scholars, Pitts was "active in the women's rights movement in Washington, and collaborated with Caroline Winslow in the publication of a radical feminist newspaper, *The Alpha*." Maria Diedrich asserted that Pitts "quickly became involved with the local feminists around Caroline B. Winslow" and misdated Pitts's arrival in Washington to 1878. She also misidentified Frances Pitts, Hiram's wife, as Helen in an 1878 letter in which Assing referred disparagingly to a "Mrs. Pitts" associated with *The Alpha*. The contents of the letter, however, indicate that Assing was referring to Frances Pitts, who was also a member of the Moral Education Society, serving as its recording secretary from 1882 to1884. This mistake undercuts Diedrich's argument that Assing was intimidated by Helen, but Assing's disgust at the *Alpha*'s content belies Diedich's premise that Assing was sexually liberated. The only evidence of Helen's connection with the Moral Education Society was her service there as secretary in 1877, her relation to Frances, and a handful of newspaper reports, riddled with other inaccuracies, that also attempted to say something about a little-known woman. As for the sobriquet "radical," while the Moral Education Society did provoke strong reactions in some people because it promoted sex education and woman's suffrage, the term is both imprecise and does not take into account the complexities of the women's reform movements of this period. McFeely, *Frederick Douglass*, 311; Diedrich, *LACL*, 350, 356; OA to FD, Hoboken, N.J., 10 December 1878, FDP, DLC; *Alpha*, February 1876, August 1876, February 1877, 1882, 1883, 1884; *New York Globe, Cleveland Gazette*, 2 February 1884. See also April Haynes, *Riotous Flesh: Women, Physiology, and the Solitary Vice in Nineteenth-Century America* (Chicago: University of Chicago Press, 2015) for more on the antebellum moral reform movement and the antecedents of the Moral Education Society.

66. *Ten-Year Book of Cornell University, 1868-88* (Ithaca, N.Y., 1881), 158; [FD] to HP[D], Washington, DC, 19 February [1879]; *Huntington Herald Press*, April 1989, clippings in Helen Pitts, Class of 1858, Alumni File, Mount Holyoke College Archives.

67. 1880 U.S. Census, Connecticut, Fairfield, Darien, 39; [MWG] to HP[D], Washington, DC, 19 March 1880, FDP, DLC.

68. Helen received her first paycheck on 29 September 1881. Annie's pay started after Helen had departed the office, suggesting that she replaced Helen, who stopped working there after she married Frederick. Account Books, 1881–1883, 1883–1886, Addition I, FDP, DLC.

69. Maria Diedrich believed that Pitts "took a spontaneous liking to Douglass and he to her," and that Ottilie Assing "could not overlook the eroticism in the air," so much so that "the more she saw of the younger woman, the more she feared her." The only evidence to support these assertions was the letter in which Diedrich misidentified Frances Pitts as Helen. Diedrich further speculated that two undated "love songs," for which she provided no citations, were written by Douglass to Helen. Diedrich, *LACL*, 350, 360–61. The "love songs" are actually unsigned poems filed as "Poems Written by Frederick Douglass" in Speech, Article, and Book File, FDP, DLC.

70. FD to Frances Pitts, Washington, DC, [c. 1882–1883], FDP, DLC. This letter appears to have been written sometime after the publication of *Life and Times* and before his marriage to Helen.

71. Grimké, "Second Marriage," 324.

72. *Washington Star*, 9 February 1884.

73. Elizabeth Thompson to FD, N.Y., 29 November 1882, FDP, DLC.

74. Mary Ann Pierson to FD, Mowbray Cottage [Lockport], N.Y., 8 December 1882, FDP, DLC.

75. MWG to FD, Fair Haven, Mass., 14, 22 October 1882, FDP, DLC.

76. *Augusta (Ga.) Baptist* in *New York Globe*, 9 February 1884.

77. *National Republican*, 16 April 1883, in Scrapbooks, Evans Collection.

78. Two years and ten months after the death of his first wife, Charles married Laura Antoinette Haley, who became step-mother to his four surviving children, aged six, seven, eleven, and thirteen. "Hymenial" (clipping), [c. April 1880], Scrapbook, Evans Collection.

79. Grimké, "Second Marriage," 325.

80. *Washington Grit*, 26 January 1884.

81. *Washington Pilot* in *Washington People's Advocate*, 9 February 1884.

82. *Springfield Weekly Review* in *New York Globe*, 9 February 1884.

83. *Raleigh Banner-Enterprise* in *New York Globe*, 9 February 1884.

84. Grimké, "Second Marriage," 325; Washington, DC, *Grit*, 26 January 1884; Pittsburgh *Weekly News*; Birmingham *Pilot*; Springfield, Ohio, *Weekly Review*, quoted in *New York Globe*, 9 February 1884; *American Baptist*, *People's Defense* and *Virginia Baptist Companion* quoted in *People's Advocate*, 9 February 1884; *Cleveland Gazette*, 16 February 1884.

85. IBW-B, *Crusade for Justice*, 73.

86. Clipping, [n.p.], [c. 1884], Scrapbooks, Evans Collection.

87. *Cleveland Gazette*, 21 August 1886.

88. *Washington Bee*, 17 April 1886.

89. MWG to FD, Greenwich, R.I., 4 June 1885, FDP, DLC.

90. *Washington Bee*, 17 April 1886. Copy of Gideon Pitts's will, Helen Pitts Douglass File, Town of Richmond.

91. FD to H[P]D, Carlisle, England, 28 June 1887, FDP, DLC.

92. Esther Short Boyd memoir, [n.d.], Helen Pitts File, Town of Richmond.

93. FD to H[P]D, Carlisle, England, 28 June 1887, and Bridport, England, 12 July 1887, FDP, DLC. Helen's brother Gideon appears not to have registered a strong opinion, but his daughter, Etta Pitts, invited the Douglasses to her wedding in January 1885. Invitation File, 1882–85, FDP, DLC.

94. *Washington Star*, 7, 8, 9 February 1884.

95. RDS to FD, Rochester, 4 February 1868, 18 February 1869, FDP, DLC; FD to RDS, Port-au-Prince, Haiti, 6, 30 March, 9 April 1891, Addition I, FDP, DLC.

96. *Chicago Tribune*, 7 August 1884; "Samuel Lathan, Chester County, South Carolina Genealogy Trails," *Genealogy Trails*, accessed 3 July 2014, http://genealogytrails.com/scar/chester/bio_lathan_sam.htm.

97. *National Republican*, 8 February 1884; *Philadelphia Press*, 6 February 1884; *Boston Daily Globe*, 8 February 1884; *Washington Star*, 7 February 1884.

98. *Washington Star*, 8, 9, 12, 14 February 1884; *Harrisburg State Journal*, 16 February 1884.

99. *Philadelphia Press*, 6 February 1884; *Cleveland Gazette*, 16 February 1884; *Washington Star*, 9 February 1884.

100. *Washington Star*, 7 February 1884.

101. CRD to FD, Washington, DC, 17 February 1884, FDP, DLC. Charles also believed that Nathan fed gossip to Richard Greener, one of Frederick's black adversaries in the debate over black migration out of the South.

102. *Washington Star*, 9 February 1884.

103. John S. Gillies to FD, Angelica, N.Y., 6 August 1884, FD to Nathan Sprague, [Washington], [c. 1886], FDP, DLC.

104. *Washington Star*, 14 February 1884.

105. *Washington Star*, 14 February 1884.

106. *Washington Star*, 8, 9 February 1884.

107. "Helen L. Sprague v. Frederick Douglass, No. 25112," Legal File, Lawsuits, FDP, DLC.

108. *City Directories for Washington D.C.* (1885), 772.

109. MWG to FD, Fall River, Mass., 9 April 1884, FDP, DLC.

110. *Washington Post*, 30 May 1897.

111. *Washington* (DC) *Grit*, 16 February 1884.

112. *Cleveland Gazette*, 10 May 1884.

113. *Charleston and Wheeling News & Courier*, 18 May 1885; *Baltimore Sun*, 19 May 1885.

114. *Washington Critic*, 13 February 1886; *Baltimore Sun*, 13 February 1886; *Jamestown Weekly Alert* [N.D.], *Whapeton Times* [N.D.], 18 February 1886; *Little Falls Transcript* [Minn.], 19 February 1886.

115. Invitation File, undated, FDP, DLC; *Columbus Daily Enquirer* [Ga.], 9 April 1886.

116. *Leader* (Washington, DC), 22 December 1888.

117. *Shenandoah Herald,* (Woodstock, Va.), 12 March 1884; *Washington National Republican,* 6 March 1884.

118. ECS to FD, 27 January 1884, Addition I, FDP, DLC.

119. SBA to ECS, [Washington, DC], 27 January 1884, *ECS/SBAP,* 4:323–28. The editors of *ECS/SBAP* believe that this letter had many emendations by Anthony's biographer Ida Husted Harper. The version appearing in their volume is what they could discern of SBA's intention. The incident did not appear in Anthony's biography or *History of Woman Suffrage.*

120. ECS to FD, Johnstown, N.Y., 27 May 1884, FDP, DLC; ECS to SBA, Johnstown, N.Y., 23 February 1884, *ECS/SBAP,* 4:339–40; FD to ECS, Washington, DC, 30 May 1884, *ECS/ SBAP,* 4:356–57.

121. Invitation Files, Miscellany, FDP, DLC. These included invitations to the opening of the Washington Monument, memorial services for President U.S. Grant, the centennial celebration of George Washington's inauguration, the semicentennial of Rochester's founding, and a memorial for poet John Greenleaf Whittier, among many others.

122. RDS, *MMAIRH,* 20; Autographs, 1885–1892, Addition I, FDP, DLC; *Washington Leader,* 23 March 1889.

123. Autographs, 1885–1892, Addition I, FDP, DLC.

124. *New York Globe,* 31 May 1884; FD, *Speeches,* 5:xxi; Invitation File, 1882–1885, Miscellany, FDP, DLC; *New York Freeman,* 12 June 1886.

125. *New York Freeman,* 12 June 1886. They intended to host the meeting the following year, but instead extended their tour of Europe through the summer 1887.

126. Ella Barrier to FD, Brockport, N.Y., 2 July 1889, FDP, DLC.

127. *New York Globe,* 31 May 1884.

128. Henry O. Wagoner to FD, Denver, 19 April 1886, FDP, DLC.

129. *Bennington Banner* (Vt.), 29 January 1885.

130. Peter N. Stearns, "Modern Patterns in Emotions History," *Doing Emotions History,* ed. Susan J. Matt and Peter N. Sterns (Urbana: University of Illinois Press, 2014), 25–27.

131. FD, *Speeches,* 5:viii.

132. *Harrisburg State Journal,* 10 April 1884.

133. *New York Globe,* 19 July, 2 August 1884; *Cleveland Gazette,* 9 August, 11 October 1884; FD, *Speeches,* 5:viii, xx.

134. *Bennington Banner,* 29 January 1885; FD, *Speeches,* 5:xxi, 192–211; *Nantucket Journal,* 20 August 1885, *Nantucket Inquirer and Mirror,* 29 August 1885, *Inquirer and Mirror,* 22 August 1885 in scrapbooks, Evans Collection.

135. "Hayti," Subject Files, FDP, DLC; RDS, *MMAIRH,* 10.

136. *New York Freeman,* 6 March 1886.

137. *Washington Leader,* 22 December 1888.

138. *Colored American,* 26 October 1901; *Manning Times* (S.C.), 20 April 1904; *Marlboro Democrat* (S.C.), 22 April 1904; *Broad Ax* (Salt Lake City), 6 November 1904; 27 June 1908, 24 October 1908.

139. FD, *L&T,* 408–9.

140. Grover Cleveland to FD, Washington, DC, 4 January 1886, FD to Grover Cleveland, Washington, DC, 5 January 1886 [misdated 1885], FDP, DLC; *Washington Bee,* 11 September 1886. The Douglasses left Charles Douglass in charge of Cedar Hill while they were gone, with "Mr. And Mrs. Clark" as caretakers. Frederick gave power of attorney to Lewis. FDjr to FD, Washington, DC, 10 April 1887, FDP, DLC.

141. FD, Diary, FDP, DLC; FD to RDS, Paris, France, 25 October 1886, FDMHA, DLC. Both Helen and Frederick kept diaries of this journey. Hers broke off once they arrived in England, but his continued as he took notes to use in later speeches. Mark Emerson, a public history graduate student at Indiana University, completed an annotated version for his master's thesis that has not been published. Mark G. Emerson, ed., "Scholarly Edition of the Grand Tour Diaries of Frederick Douglass and Helen Pitts Douglass" (MA thesis, Indiana University, 2003). Frederick also described their journey in the last edition of *Life*

and Times and in a two-part speech, "My Trip Abroad." FD, L&T, 408-95; FD, Speeches, 5:315-16.

142. FD, Diary, FDP, DLC; FD, Speeches, 5:332-38; Benevolent Banner [Topeka, Kans.], 4 June 1887.

143. Cleveland Gazette, 20 August 1887. Frederick, still unaware that his birth year was 1818, believed that he had just turned seventy. FD, Diary, FDP, DLC.

144. Cleveland Gazette, 20 August 1887; Travels, Subject Files, FDP, DLC.

145. FD, Diary, FDP, DLC; Travels, Subject Files, FDP, DLC.

146. FD, Diary, FDP, DLC.

147. In Rome, Frederick ran into Victoria Woodhull, now an expatriate and married to John Biddulph Martin. "I am not sure that I quite concealed my surprise, but a train of events flashed upon me, the impression of which was difficult to drive from my face and manner," he confessed. "I however soon began to think, what do I know of this lady, that I should think her otherwise than merely holding strange, and erroneous opinion." FD, Diary, FDP, DLC.

148. FD, Diary, FDP, DLC. Wilhemina Webb to FD, Dublin, Ireland, 24 June 1887, FDP, DLC. Frederick's correspondence through summer 1887 show the pace of his travel and the requests from old acquaintances that he visit, and they include the last letters he received from Isabel Jennings and Rosine Ami-Droz. Isabel Jennings to FD, Cork, Ireland, 31 July 1887, Rosine Ami-Droz to FD, Zurich, Switzerland, 29 July, 1887, FDP, DLC.

149. FD to H[P]D, Carlisle, England, 28 June 1887, Bridport, England, 12 July 1887, FDP, DLC.

150. FD to H[P]D, Carlisle, England, 28 June 1887, Bridport, England, 12 July 1887, H[P] D to FD, Honeoye, N.Y., 19 July 1887, Ellen Richardson to FD, Newcastle, England, 14 September 1887, FDP, DLC; FD, Speeches, 5:xxii.

151. FD, Speeches, 5:279, 280. Mark G. Emerson referred to Maria Diedrich's insistence that Frederick had intended to join Ottilia Assing on her 1876 visit to Paris. Emerson postulated that Frederick also made "a journey that would remind him of a former lover and unfulfilled promises." This now seems unlikely in light of challenges to Diedrich's premise throughout this volume. Frederick made no reference to Assing, although Helen did recount a conversation about her with Herman Kudlich just before their departure. Nor did Frederick seem to seek her grave in Paris or betray a desire to visit Germany, although he did search for Ludmilla Assing's villa in Florence. Emerson, "Scholarly Edition," 4; H[P]D, Diary, Family Papers, FDP, DLC.

152. Emerson, "Scholarly Edition," 12; Cleveland Gazette, 25 December 1886.

153. Mary Barlow to FD, Carlisle, England, 5 July 1887, FD to H[P]D, Bridport, England, 12 July 1887, FDP, DLC.

154. For an analysis of the typical American on the Grand Tour, see James Buzard, "A Continent of Pictures: Reflections on the 'Europe' of Nineteenth-Century Tourists," PMLA 108, 1 (January 1993): 30-44; Jeffrey Steinbrink, "Why the Innocents Went Abroad: Mark Twain and American Tourism in the Late Nineteenth Century," American Literary Realism, 1870-1910 16, 2 (Autumn 1983): 278-66; Jeffrey Alan Melton, "Touring the Old World," Mark Twain, Travel Books, and Tourism: The Tide of a Great Popular Movement (Tuscaloosa, Ala., 2002), 59-94; Foster Rhea Dulles, Americans Abroad: Two Centuries of European Travel (Ann Arbor: University of Michigan Press, 1964); William W. Stowe, Going Abroad: European Travel in Nineteenth-Century American Culture (Princeton, N.J.: Princeton University Press, 1994).

155. FD, Diary, FDP, DLC.

156. Clipping, Travels, Subject Files, FDP, DLC.

157. FD, Diary, FDP, DLC; Kalamazoo Daily Gazette, 27 January 1884.

158. FD, L&T, 413; FD, "My Trip Abroad," in Speeches, 5:294-308.

159. FD, Diary, FDP, DLC; Sterling, We Are Your Sisters, 96, 147, 175-80; Yee, Black Women Abolitionists, 15-16.

160. FD, Diary, FDP, DLC.

161. Kirstin Pai Buick, Child of the Fire: Mary Edmonia Lewis and the Problem of Art History's Black and Indian Subject (Durham, N.C.: Duke University Press, 2010), 27-8; Melissa Debakis, A Sisterhood of Sculptors: American Artists in Nineteenth-Century Rome (University Park: Pennsylvania State University Press, 2014), 155-57, 166-75.

162. H[P]D to Jennie Pitts, Rome, Italy, 25 April 1887, FDP, DLC.

163. *San Francisco Daily Evening Bulletin*, 15 October 1886.
164. Chicago *Daily Inter-Ocean*, 14 December 1886.
165. *Kansas City Times*, 22 August 1887.
166. *Cleveland Gazette*, 25 December 1885.
167. FD to LHD, Paris, France, 29 November [1886, misdated as 1885], FDP, DLC.
168. FD to RDS, Port-au-Prince, Haiti, 25 April 1891, Addition I, FDP, DLC.
169. Isaiah Mitchell to FD, Jackson, Miss., 1 July 1889, FDP, DLC.
170. FD to RDS, Port-au-Prince, Haiti, 12 April 1890, Addition I, FDP, DLC.
171. *New York Herald*, 3 October 1889, Scrapbooks, folder 2, Addition I, FDP, DLC.
172. *Washington Bee*, 28 June 1890.
173. FD to RDS, Port-au-Prince, Haiti, 5 February 1890, Addition I, FDP, DLC.
174. [*New York Age*], 4 January 1890, Hayti, Subject File, FDP, DLC.
175. *New York Herald*, 3 October 1889, Scrapbooks, folder 2, Addition I, FDP, DLC.
176. Hayti, Subject File, FDP, DLC.
177. FD, *L&T*, 443.
178. L. Diane Barnes, *Frederick Douglass: Reformer and Statesman* (New York: Routledge, 2013), 127–33; Hayti, Subject File, FDP, DLC.
179. *Washington Bee*, 5 April 1890.

Chapter 10

1. FD to RDS, Port-au-Prince, Haiti, 13 December 1889, Addition I, FDP, DLC.
2. FD to RDS, Port-au-Prince, Haiti, 22 March 1890, Addition I, FDP, DLC.
3. FD to RDS, Port-au-Prince, Haiti, 12 April 1890, Addition I, FDP, DLC.
4. FD to RDS, Chicago, 20 June 1893, Addition I, FDP, DLC.
5. FD to RDS, Port-au-Prince, Haiti, 18 April 1891, Addition I, FDP, DLC.
6. FD to RDS, Port-au-Prince, Haiti, 21 February 1891, FDP, DHU-MS.
7. FD to RDS, Port-au-Prince, Haiti, 5 February 1890, Addition I, FDP, DLC.
8. Chambers, *Weston Sisters*, 175–86.
9. Rochester Genealogical Society, comp. *Mount Hope Cemetery, Rochester, New York, Interment Index* (Rochester: Rochester Genealogical Society, 2005–2006), 2: 9. Of the Porters, only Maria outlived Douglass, surviving until December 1896.
10. Isabel Jennings to FD, Cork, Ireland, 31 July 1887, FDP, DLC.
11. Rochester Genealogical Society, comp. *Mount Hope Cemetery, Rochester, New York, Interment Index* (Rochester: Rochester Genealogical Society, 2005–2006), 3: 11.
12. Robert Arnowitz, *Unnatural History: Breast Cancer and American Society* (New York, 2007), 50–88; OA to SRK, Hamburg, Germany, 22 August 1881, SRKP, DCAWR; Frederick Douglass (General, folder 8 of 9), Subject Files, Rinaldo Kuntzel to Henry Bergh, Florence, Italy, 27 October 1884, Addition I, FDP, DLC; *NYTrib*, 27 October 1884; *National Republican*, 28 January 1885; Vanessa Schwartz, *Spectacular Realities: Early Mass Culture in Fin-de-Siecle Paris* (Berkley: University of California Press, 1998), 45–88; Herman C. Kudlich to FD, New York, N.Y., 18 July, 5 August 1885, FDP, DLC; [FD] to Henry Berg, 7 November 1884, FDP, DHU-MS; "Miss Assing's Will," 9 November 1971, Legal File, FD to [MWG], Anacostia, [n.d.], Addition I, FDP, DLC.
   A 2012 study found that cancer patients are five times more likely to commit suicide in the first twelve weeks after a diagnosis, and three times more likely within a year after a diagnosis. On 24 June 1884, Assing wrote one of the last letters in which she made plans, expecting to go from Florence to Paris, and then on to Spain by 1 September. Thus, her diagnosis possibly came sometime in the two months that followed her letter. "Suicide Risk Spikes in Week after Cancer Diagnosis, Study Finds," 4 April 2012, NBC News (http://vitals.nbc-news.com/_news/2012/04/04/11022340-suicide-risk-spikes-in-week-after-cancer-diagnosis-study-finds, accessed 26 June 2014); Renee Twombly, "Decades after Cancer, Suicide Risk Remains High," *Journal of the National Cancer Institute* (http://jnci.oxfordjournals.org/content/98/19/1356.full, accessed 27 July 2015). Bertha Hirschfeld to FD, Hamburg, 15 November 1884, FDP, DLC.

The timing of Assing's suicide, seven months after Douglass's marriage to Helen Pitts in January 1884, has proved a tempting morsel for romantic imaginations. Both William McFeely and Maria Diedrich all but blame Douglass for Assing's death because of this correlation, although she had probably learned of the marriage long before August. Pointing to Assing's alleged history of depression, then juxtaposing Helen's happiness at becoming the new Mrs. Douglass with Assing's suicide, William McFeely insisted that "Douglass seems not to have taken into account how demanding his own sense of his rightness was, or how vulnerable was the seemingly most sophisticated of his friends, Ottilie Assing." Although Assing had made a public display of her intention to harm herself in Germany thirty years earlier, McFeely's only source for her mental state is an 1873 letter concerning an auditory condition and Assing's tendency to overwork herself. Diedrich portrayed Douglass as facing a choice between marrying Helen for love and happiness or fulfilling an obligation to Assing, although their union would be "for the sake of pity and gratitude, for the sake of moral obligation, for the sake of friendship—the only feelings he apparently could still muster for Ottilie Assing." His marriage to Pitts, in Diedrich's interpretation, was a betrayal not only in itself but also because Douglass turned to a minister to perform the ceremony. "It was as if she never happened," Diedrich concluded, going so far as to dismiss the diagnosis of cancer as "an invention" and "a final gesture of love and generosity to Douglass, to protect him against the charge of being responsible for her death, or a gentle lie, a parting kiss of absolution for the man she still loved, or an invention she needed to maintain her pride and integrity, and act of defiance against the man who had betrayed her." Diedrich's is a fanciful perversion of the evidence. The information about Assing's cancer was confirmed by Kuntzel, who received the news from the coroner at the morgue. Assing was simply another unidentified body on the mortuary table, one who had died from poisoning, as evidenced by the vial found on her body, and one with a misshapen breast indicating her condition. He had no reason to fabricate a story to protect anyone. Indeed, there is more evidence for Assing's breast cancer than there is for a sexual liaison with Douglass. McFeely, *Frederick Douglass*, 321–22; Diedrich, *LACL*, 368–74; Gustav Frauenstein to FD, New York, 4 May 1873, Rinaldo Kuntzel to Henry Bergh, Florence, Italy, 27 October 1884, Addition I, FDP, DCL.

Assing had ordered that all of her correspondence be burned. This naturally leaves much room for speculation as to the contents of the destroyed documents, especially those from Douglass. If, however, Assing was involved in a romantic and sexual liaison with Douglass, and if she grounded her sense of self and her importance as a muse in her role as his alleged soul mate, which McFeely and Diedrich argue, she would likely have asked that he keep his letters or that their correspondence be preserved as proof of their bond.

13. 1880 U.S. Census, Maryland, Talbot, St. Michaels, 30; Notation in Scrapbook, Evans Collection.
14. *People's Advocate*, 8 March 1884.
15. FD to RDS, Port-au-Prince, Haiti, 18 April 1891, Addition I, FDP, DLC.
16. FD to RDS, Port-au-Prince, Haiti, 24 June 1890, Addition I, FDP, DLC.
17. FD to RDS, [Santo Domingo], [30 January 1890], Addition I, FDP, DLC.
18. Rosetta and Nathan took in the youngest, three-year-old Robert Smalls, but the elder, Charles Paul, coped with the misery at home by repeatedly running away. Scrapbooks, Evans Collection; RDS to FD, Washington, DC, 20 November 1889, 6 February 1890, Nathan Sprague to FD, Washington, DC, 29 November 1889, FDP, DLC.
19. No obituaries appeared in the Washington papers; only the *Washington Bee* briefly noted his funeral, nor did his brothers include any clippings about his death in their scrapbooks. Correspondence and condolences mentioned no illness or accident. *Washington Bee*, 30 July 1892.
20. Genealogical information compiled from Scrapbooks, Evans Collection; List of Descendents of Frederick Douglass prepared by Harriet Bailey Sprague [19 January 1936], News Articles about Members of the Douglass Family, FDP, DHU-MS; FD to RDS, Port-au-Prince, Haiti, 8 November [1889, filed in 1890], 5 February 1890, 22 March 1890, Santo Domingo, [30 January 1890], Addition I, FDP, DLC.

21. RDS to FD, Washington, DC, 6 February 1890, FDP, DLC.
22. FD to RDS, Port-au-Prince, Haiti, 21 February 1891, FDP, DHU-MS.
23. FD to RDS, Port-au-Prince, Haiti, 6 March 1891, Addition I, FDP, DLC.
24. FD to RDS, Port-au-Prince, Haiti, 12, 20 February, 6, 12 March 1891, Addition I, FDP, DLC.
25. FD to Fredericka Sprague, Port-au-Prince, Haiti, 20 February 1891, FDP, DLC.
26. Rosetta Douglass Sprague, [n.p.] February 21, 1891, DHU-MS; FD to RDS, Port-au-Prince, Haiti, 21 February 1891; FD to Fredericka Sprague, Port-au-Prince, Haiti, 20 February 1891, FDP, DLC; FD to RDS, Port-au-Prince, Haiti, 6 March 1891, FD to RDS, Port-au-Prince, Haiti, 12 March 1891, FD to RDS, Port-au-Prince, Haiti, 25 March 1891, FD to RDS, Port-au-Prince, Haiti, 28 March [1891], Addition I, FDP, DLC.
27. FD to RDS, Port-au-Prince, Haiti, 12, 20 February, 6, 12 March, 8, 18 April 1891, Addition I, FD to LHD, Port-au-Prince, Haiti, 30 March 1891, FDP, DLC; FD to CRD, Port-au-Prince, Haiti, [April 1891], Evans Collection.
28. Fredericka Douglass Perry, Recollections, FDP, DHU-MU.
29. 1880 U.S. Census, District of Columbia, Washington, 7th District, 3, Washington, 52; IBW-B, Crusade for Justice, 73.
30. Estelle Sprague to FD, Cappahosic, Va., 21 March, 3 April 1893, FDP, DLC; Fredericka Sprague to CHJ Taylor, Anacostia, DC, 29 June 1894, FDP, DLC.
31. FD to RDS, Washington, DC, 2 August 1875, Addition I, FDP, DLC.
32. Lawrence Otis Graham, *The Senator and the Socialite: The True Story of America's First Black Dynasty* (New York: HarperCollins, 2006), 90.
33. Wanda A. Hendricks, *Fannie Barrier Williams: Crossing the Borders of Region and Race* (Urbana: University of Illinois Press, 20014), 26.
34. Fredericka Douglass Perry, Recollections, FDP, DHU-MU. Fredericka misidentified Fannie as "Jessie." The names of the Barriers' three children were Ella, Fannie, and George. Hendricks, *Fannie Barrier Williams*, 26–31. Fannie Barrier returned the favor in 1892 when she opened her Chicago home to Frederick for several months during the Columbia World's Exposition. Fannie Barrier Williams to FD, Chicago, 14 January 1893, FDP, DLC.
35. Angela F. Murphy, *The Jerry Rescue: The Fugitive Slave Law, Northern Rights, and the American Sectional Crisis* (New York: Oxford University Press, 2016), 80–83.
36. RDS to FD, Rochester, 17 September 1876, FDP, DCL.
37. Eric Luft, "Sarah Loguen Fraser, MD: The Fourth African-American Woman Physician," *Medical History* 92, 3 (March 2000): 149–53.
38. FD to RDS, Washington, DC, [316 A St. N.E.], 23 August 1875, Addition I, FDP, DLC.
39. Fredericka Douglass Perry, Recollections, FDP, DHU-MS.
40. RDS to FD, Rochester, 19 February 1869, FDP, DLC; *City Directories for Washington, D.C.* (Wm. H. Boyd, 1883), 774; MWG to FD, 8 December 1878, FDP, DLC; Notes in Scrapbook, Evans Collection; Account Books, 1881–83, 1883–86 Addition I, FDP, DLC.
41. Eliza Pierson to FD, Mowbray Cottage [Lockport], N.Y., 6 May 1885, FDP, DLC.
42. RDS to FD, Washington, DC, 6 February 1890, FDP, DLC; *New York Age*, 5 April 1890; *Cleveland Gazette*, 18 July 1891.
43. *City Directories for Washington, D.C.* (1881) 681, (1883) 774, (1884), 775, (1885) 772, (1886) 767; John S. Gillies to FD, Angelica, N.Y., 6 August 1884, [FD] to Nathan Sprague, Washington, DC, [c. September 1885; filed in 1886], FDP, DLC.
44. CRD to FD, Washington, DC, 17 February 1884, John S. Gillies to FD, Angelica, N.Y., 6 August 1884, [FD] to Nathan Sprague, [Washington, DC], [filed in 1886], Nathan Sprague to FD, Washington, DC, 29 September, 31 December 1885, FD to Nathan Sprague, Washington, DC, 31 December. [1885; filed in 1886], Nathan Sprague to FD, Washington, DC, 16 June 1886, Katherine Chase Sprague to FD, Edgewood, DC, 11 May 1882, FD to George Arnold, Anacostia, DC, 26 April 1888, FDP, DLC; *Cleveland Plaindealer*, 20 October 1886.
45. John S. Gillies to FD, Angelica, N.Y., 6 August 1884, Eliza Pierson to FD, Mowbray Cottage [Lockport], N.Y., 6 May 1885, FDP, DLC.
46. Elizabeth Pierson to FD, Mowbray Cottage [Lockport], N.Y., 27 February 1889, FDP, DLC.
47. *Washington Bee*, 12 January 1889; *Washington Leader*, 27 April 1889.
48. *Washington Bee*, 28 February 1891. Unfortunately, no known copies of this paper survive and WorldCat has recorded its existence only as a "black publication" with N. Sprague as

editor. OCLC, *The Pilot*, WorldCat, (http://www.worldcat.org/oclc/17434592, accessed 27 May 2014).

49. FD to RDS, Port-au-Prince, Haiti, 12 March, 8 April 1891, 12 April 1890, Addition I, FDP, DLC.

50. FD to Nathan Sprague, Port-au-Prince, Haiti, [14 May 1891], Addition I, FDP, DLC.

51. *Washington Bee*, 4 April 1891, 16 May 1891; *Cleveland Gazette*, 5 September 1891; *Washington Bee*, 14 March 1891, 19 September 1891; *Detroit Plaindealer*, 25 September 1891.

52. *Washington Bee*, 16 May 1891; *Cleveland Gazette*, 5 September 1891; *Detroit Plaindealer*, 25 September, 7 November 1891.

53. *Cleveland Gazette*, 5 September 1891.

54. *Washington Bee*, 19 September, 5 December 1891.

55. FD to Nathan Sprague, Port-au-Prince, Haiti, 23 May 1891, FDP, DLC.

56. *Detroit Plaindealer*, 7 November 1891.

57. *Indianapolis Freeman*, 28 November 1891.

58. *Detroit Plaindealer*, 22 January 1892.

59. *Detroit Plaindealer*, 25 September 1891.

60. "Editor Sprague Fined of Assault," *Washington Post*, 9 June 1892, in Scrapbooks, Evans Collection.

61. *Baltimore Sun*, 21 February 1893.

62. James Hallock to FD, Rusk, Tx., 18 September 1891, John S. Pole to FD, Takoma Park, DC, 5 January 1894, FDP, DLC; *Trenton Evening Times*, 8 October 1896.

63. RDS to FD, Washington, DC, 20 November 1889, Nathan Sprague to RDS, Rochester, 7 April 1873, FDP, DLC; Nathan Sprague to FD, Washington, DC, 29 November 1889, FDP, DLC; Notes in scrapbooks, Evans Collection.

64. *City Directories for Washington, D.C.* (Wm H Boyd, 1892), 884.

65. RDS to FD, Washington, DC, 20 November 1889, Nathan Sprague to RDS, Rochester, 7 April 1873, Nathan Sprague to FD, Washington, DC, 29 November 1889, FDP, DLC; Notes in scrapbooks, Evans Collection.

66. FD to RDS, Washington, DC, 25 May 1873, Addition I, FDP, DLC.

67. FD to RDS, Port-au-Prince, Haiti, 6 March 1890, 12 February 1891, Addition I, FDP, DLC.

68. Fredericka Sprague to FD ["Grandpa"], Washington, DC, 11 December 1886, FDP, DLC.

69. RDS to FD, Washington, DC, 20 November 1889

70. FD to RDS, Port-au-Prince, Haiti, 13 December 1889, Addition I, FDP, DLC.

71. FD to Fredericka Sprague, Port-au-Prince, Haiti, 20 February 1891.

72. FD to CRD, Port-au-Prince, Haiti, 26 February [1891? n.y.], Evans Collection.

73. Account book, 1883–86, Addition I, FDP, DLC.

74. FD to LHD, Paris, France, 29 November 1885 [misdated, 1886], FDP, DLC.

75. *Washington Bee*, 8 September 1888, 4 August 1894; FD to RDS, Port-au-Prince, Haiti, 12 April 1890, Addition I, FDP, DLC; City Directories for Washington, DC, (1892) 884, (1893) 870.

76. *Washington Critic, Baltimore Sun, New York Freeman*, 6 March 1886; *Washington Bee*, 22 October 1904, 3, 17 September 1887, 14 April 1888, 13 June 1891; *New York Freeman*, 12 June 1886; *New York Age*, 3 October 1891.

77. *Washington Bee*, 14 March, 31 October 1891; *Cleveland Gazette*, 25 March 1893; Annie Sprague to FD, Hampton, Va., 8 April 1893, FDP, DLC.

78. FD to RDS, Port-au-Prince, Haiti, 23 January 1891, Addition I, FDP, DLC.

79. FD to RDS, Port-au-Prince, Haiti, 6 March 1891, Addition I, FDP, DLC.

80. *Washington Bee*, 13 July 1889; *Indianapolis Freeman*, 1 November 1890.

81. *Washington Bee*, 16 May 1891.

82. RDS to FD, Rochester, 15 March 1869, FDP, DLC.

83. FD to RDS, Port-au-Prince, Haiti, 7 May 1891, Addition I, FDP, DLC.

84. Mary Ann Pierson to FD, 23 Oliver St. [Lockport?], N.Y. 16 December 1893, FDP, DLC.

85. U.S. Register, 1891, 1:38, 42; *Cleveland Gazette*, 25 March 1893; *Washington Bee*, 31 October 1891; McMurry, *Keep the Waters Troubled*, 348. The *Washington Bee* speculated that Blanche K. Bruce, now the Recorder of Deeds, had rejected him for a position in that office but secured him one as a "first-class messenger" who "is wrestling with spittoons in the Treasury department." The U.S. Register listed him as being a clerk.

86. Annie Sprague to FD, Hampton, Va., 8 April 1893, FDP, DLC.
87. Annie Sprague Morris to FD, Harpers Ferry, W.Va., 13 June 1893, FDP, DLC. The timing of the birth seven months after the marriage, the length of the engagement, and the wedding occurring before Charles entered law school all could suggest that Annie could have been pregnant before she married. Rosetta, however, had planned to join Annie for her confinement. The news of Annie's death shocked her not simply because of the tragedy but also because she seemed not to have expected labor until later in the winter, suggesting that Annie had conceived early in the marriage and that her complications were, indeed, severe. RDS to FD, Takoma Park, DC, 27 November 1893, FDP, DLC.
88. RDS to FD, Takoma Park, DC, 27 November 1893, FDP, DLC.
89. RDS to FD, Washington, DC, 11 November 1893, FDP, DLC.
90. Fredericka Sprague to C. H. J. Taylor [Recorder of Deeds office], Anacostia, DC, 29 Jun 1894, Estelle Sprague to FD, Capahoosic, Va, 15 November 1894, FDP, DLC; Official Register of the United States, Containing a List of the Officers and Employees in the Civil, Military, and Naval Service Together with a List of Vessels Belonging to the United States (1895), 1:1034. City Directories for Washington, DC (1895) 857.
91. FD to RDS, Port-au-Prince, Haiti, 14 December 1890, Chicago, 20 June 1893, Addition I, FDP, DLC.
92. FD to RDS, Port-au-Prince, Haiti, 23 January 1891, Addition I, FDP, DLC.
93. FD to RDS, Port-au-Prince, Haiti, 7 May 1891, Chicago, 20 June 1893, Addition I, Harriet Sprague to FD, Jacksonville, Fla., 25 February, 4 March 1894, RDS to FD, Takoma Park, DC, 27 November 1893, FDP, DLC; Florida Baptist Academy Catalog 19 (1910–11): 56–57; Kevin M. McCarthy, African American Sites in Florida (Sarasota: Pineapple Press, 2007), 60, 170. Harriet's first job in Florida was abbreviated when she fell ill and had to return to Washington.
94. George F. Bagby, "William G. Price and the Gloucester Agricultural and Industrial School," Virginia Magazine of History and Biography 108, 1 (2000): 45–84.
95. FD to RDS, Port-au-Prince, Haiti, 6 March 1891, Addition I, FDP, DLC. Her first foray into teaching in 1891 was abbreviated by a long sickness, which was when Douglass made this observation. She sought "medical treatment" in Rochester in 1902, which may have been a cause for her return to Washington two years earlier. She also complained of "a year of sickness and consequent idleness" preceding her tenure at the Conroe Normal School. Washington Bee, 14 August 1909; Hattie [Sprague] to Amelia [Loguen] Douglass, Normal and Industrial College, Conroe, Texas, 3 December 1916, Evans Collection.
96. Hattie [Sprague] to Amelia [Loguen] Douglass, Conroe, Texas, 3 December 1916, Evans Collection.
97. 1920 U.S. Census, Texas, McClennan, Waco, 14. At least four of Estelle's children were too young to fend for themselves at this point. Other than her son William, who at age eighteen lived with Fredericka and Harriet in 1930, and an undated postcard from her oldest daughter, Annie Weaver [Teabeau] to Fredericka, they do not appear in association with any of her family. Presumably the Weaver family took them in. In 1964, Teabeau donated many of the papers in the Douglass Collection to the Moorland-Spingarn Research Center at Howard University. 1930 U.S. Census, Missouri, Jackson, Kansas City, 8; Annie Weaver to Fredericka Sprague Perry, n.p., n.d., Addition I, FDP, DLC; Finding Aid, FDP, DHU-MS.
98. "Douglass Kin Passes On! Miss Harriette Sprague, Former Rochesterian," The Voice, 8 November 1940, in news articles about members of the Douglass Family, FDP, DHU-MS. Sprague worked at Tuskegee from 1917 to 1918. Daniel T. Williams, comp., "Positions at Tuskegee Institute, Names and Tenure," (Tuskegee Institute, 1974), 17.
99. Fredericka Sprague to FD, Culpeper Co., Va., 9 February 1893, FDP, DLC.
100. RDS to FD, Takoma Park, DC, 27 November 1893, FDP, DLC; Sarah [Blackall] to FD, Rochester, 6 May 1894, Addition I, FDP, DLC; Fredericka Sprague to CHJ Taylor, Anacostia, DC, 29 Jun 1894, FDP, DLC; Official Register of the United States, (1895), 1:1034; Washington Bee, 4 August 1894.
101. Washington Bee, 4 August 1894; RDS to FD, Takoma Park, DC, 27 November 1893, FDP, DLC; City Directories for Washington, DC (1896), 855; US, Register of Civil, Military, and Naval Service, 1897, 1:826; Washington Post, 9 June 1897. Although the 1900 U.S. Census

lists Fredericka, Harriet, and Rosebelle as teachers, neither Harriet nor Fredericka appear in the U.S. Register for the surrounding years.

102. 1920 U.S. Census, Missouri, Jackson, Kansas City, Ward 11, 8, Ward 10, 5; "News Articles About Members of the Douglass Family," FDP, DHU-MS. Thomas Perry Jones became one of the few black men with a pilot's license, but died in a plane crash in 1931. Poet Langston Hughes composed a poem, "Beyond the Fog," to his memory. Thomas Perry Jones, "Beyond the Fog" by Langston Hughes, FDP, DHU-MS.

103. Alma Coles, "Mrs. Perry Dead," *Rochester Voice*, 9, 17 (29 October 1943), in News articles about members of the Douglass Family, FDP, DHU-MS.

104. Egerton, *Wars*, 284–320; Hodes, *White Women, Black Men*, 165–75; Hannah Rosen, *Terror in the Heart of Freedom*, 181–83.

105. Hodes, *White Women, Black Men*, 176–78; Diane Miller Sommerville, *Rape and Race in the Nineteenth-Century South* (Chapel Hill: University of North Carolina Press, 2004), 237–43.

106. IBW[-B], *Southern Horrors and Other Writings: The Anti-Lynching Campaign of Ida B. Wells, 1892-1900*, ed. Jacqueline Jones Royster (Boston: Bedford Books, 1997), 61.

107. IBW-B, *Crusade*, 72.

108. IBW-B, *Crusade*, 64.

109. IBW-B, *Crusade*, 64.

110. IBW[-B], *Southern Horrors*, 52.

111. IBW-B, *Crusade*, 58–63.

112. IBW[-B] to FD, New York, 17 October 1892, FDP, DLC.

113. FD to IBW[-B], Anacostia, DC, 25 October 1892, in IBW[-B], *Southern Horrors*, 50.

114. IBW[-B] to FD, London, 3 June 1894, FDP, DLC.

115. IBW-B, *Crusade*, 82.

116. Benjamin Harrison to FD, Washington, DC, 3 February 1893, FDP, DLC.

117. IBW[-B] to FD, Brooklyn, NY 14 November 1894, FDP, DLC.

118. IBW-B, *Crusade*, 83.

119. IBW-B, *Crusade*, 85–86.

120. IBW[-B] to FD, Liverpool, England, 18 March 1894, FDP, DLC.

121. FD to C.F. Aked, Anacostia, DC, 27 March 1894, FDP.

122. FD to IBW[-B], Anacostia, DC, 27 March 1894, FDP, DLC.

123. FD to CRD, Port-au-Prince, Haiti, 26 February [1891] Evans Collection; FD to RDS, Port-au-Prince, Haiti, 23 January 1891, Addition I, FDP, DLC.

124. IBW[-B] to FD, Manchester, England, 6 April 1894, FDP, DLC.

125. IBW[-B] to FD, London, 6 May 1894, FDP, DLC.

126. IBW[-B] to H[P]D, London, 26 April 1894, FD to Helen P. Bright Clark, Anacostia, 19 July 1894, FDP, DLC.

127. Quoted in IBW[-B] to FD, Chicago, 20 December 1893, FDP, DLC.

128. IBW[-B] to FD, Chicago, 20 December 1893, FDP, DLC.

129. Willietta Johnson to FD, Boston, 20 February 1893, FDP, DLC.

130. Joseph Banneker Adger to FD, Lowell, Mass., 24 February 1893. FDP, DLC.

131. Trumbull White and William Igleheart, *The World's Columbian Exposition* (Chicago, 1893), 510.

132. *The Historical World's Columbian Exposition and Chicago Guide* (St. Louis, 1892), 4–5.

133. FD, IBW[-B], et al., *The Reason Why the Colored American Is Not in the World's Columbian Exposition* (Chicago, 1893), 12.

134. IBW-B, *Crusade*, 116.

135. *Cleveland Gazette*, 16 September 1893.

136. IBW-B, *Crusade*, 207.

137. Isabel Somerset to FD, Reigate, England, 28 May 1894, FDP, DLC.

138. IBW[-B], to FD, London, 3 June 1894, FDP, DLC.

139. FD to Helen P. Bright Clark, Anacostia, DC, 19 July 1894, FDP, DLC.

140. Quoted in FD, "Lynching Black People Because They Are Black," *Christian Educator* 5, 3 (April 1894): 98. Willard also repeated the second part of the quote in an interview with Lady Somerset. IBW-B, *Crusade*, 207. Willard had a fondness for comparing African Americans to locusts, as well. IBW[-B], *Red Record*, in *Southern Horrors*, 120.

141. Frances Willard to H[P]D, Evanston, Ill, 26 July 1894, FD to Helen P. Bright Clark, Anacostia, DC, 19 July 1894, FDP, DLC.

142. Frances Willard, *Let Something Good Be Said: Speeches and Writings of Frances E. Willard,* ed. Carolyn De Swarte Gifford and Amy R. Slagell (Urbana: University of Illinois Press), 193, 203–4.

143. FD to R.A. Armstrong, Anacostia, DC, 22 May 1894, FD to Helen P. Bright Clark, Anacostia, DC, 19 July 1894, FDP, DLC.

144. IBW[-B] to FD, London, 3 June 1894, FDP, DLC.

145. FD to R.A. Armstrong, Anacostia, DC, 22 May 1894, FDP, DLC.

146. FD to R.A. Armstrong, Anacostia, DC, 22 May 1894, FDP, DLC.

147. IBW[-B] to FD, Brooklyn, 14 November 1894, FDP, DLC.

148. FD, *Speeches,* 5:587–58, 581.

149. IBW[-B], *Red Record,* 78.

150. FD, *Speeches,* 5:581.

151. IBW[-B], *Southern Horrors,* 58.

152. IBW[-B], *Southern Horrors,* 66.

153. FD, *Speeches,* 5:584. Technically, Douglass's statement was not true and rape did occur. As after the war, however, they were isolated instances rather than the epidemic that southern propagandists would have had their audiences believe, and the rape of black women by white men was far more prevalent. Hodes, *White Women, Black Men,* 176–78; Sommerville, *Rape and Race,* 237–43.

154. FD, *Speeches,* 5:586.

155. FD, *Speeches,* 5:586.

156. FD, *Speeches,* 5:586–7; IBW[-B], *Southern Horrors,* 65; FD, *Speeches,* 5:588.

157. IBW[-B], *Red Record,* 75.

158. FD, *Speeches,* 5:588.

159. IBW[-B], *Southern Horrors,* 53–54, 57.

160. IBW[-B], *Southern Horrors,* 58–59.

161. FD to RDS, Port-au-Prince, Haiti, 25 March 1891, Addition I, FDP, DLC.

162. *New York Times,* 20 February 1895.

Epilogue

1. The *Boston Herald* as quoted in Nelson, "Have We a Cause," 146.

2. *NYT,* 7 March 1895; *NYTrib,* 7 March 1895.

3. *Washington Post,* 8 March 1895.

4. *Boston Journal,* 27 March 1895.

5. FD Will, Legal File, FDP, DLC.

6. *Washington Post,* 5 April, 4 October 1895. Robert, age eleven, and his uncles Lewis and Charles acting as his legal representatives, challenged Charles Paul's will later that year. They cited Charles Paul's incapacitation due to illness. *Washington Post,* 9 November 1895.

7. *Boston Journal,* 27 March 1895; *NYTrib,* 14 June 1895; *New York Herald,* 14 June 1895; *Philadelphia Inquirer,* 16 June 1895.

8. William H. H. Hart to H[P]D, Washington, DC, 13 March 1895, FDP, DLC; *Washington Post,* 30 March 1895.

9. *Washington Post,* 27, 30, 31 March, 4, 14 April, 9 July, 29 August 1895; *Cleveland Gazette,* 6 April 1895.

10. Gordon-Reed, *Hemingses of Monticello,* 243–48; Nancy Isenberg, *Fallen Founder: The Life of Aaron Burr* (New York: Viking, 2007), vii–ix; Franklin B. Sanborn, *Life and Letters of John Brown* (Boston, 1885); Wendell Phillips Garrison, et al., *William Lloyd Garrison: The Story of His Life,* 4 vols. (New York, 1885–1889); Chambers, *Weston Sisters,* 175–86. John Brown's wife and daughters had difficulty controlling his legacy due to their poverty. See Laughlin-Schulz, *Tie That Bound Us.*

11. Blight, *Race and Reunion,* 231–37; FD Will, Legal File, Jobel Forster and John C. Yorston to H[P]D, Philadelphia, 30 April, 7 May 1895, DeWolfe, Fiske, & Co. to H[P]D, Boston, 26 March 1895, FDP, DLC; H[P]D to Amanda Franklin, Anacostia, DC, 22 April 1898, FDC, DHU-MS.

12. *Washington Post,* 4 March 1895; H[P]D Will, 10 March 1895, Legal File, FDP, DLC.
13. As late as the 1950s, the Department of the Interior did not consider Cedar Hill a site of national importance and rejected it for inclusion in the National Parks system. Patricia West, *Domesticating History: The Political Origins of America's House Museums* (Washington, 1999), 2–5, 35–37, 39–50, 153–54.
14. Grimké, "Second Marriage,"327.
15. *Colored American,* 13 August 1898.
16. Grimké, "Second Marriage," 327.
17. H[P]D Will, 21 November 1896, Legal File, FDP, DLC.
18. The court ruled that they were a "specific legacy," and therefore could only be claimed as bonds, not as a monetary value. Since the bonds had been sold between the writing of the will and before Douglass's death, she was not entitled to the cash. *Washington Post,* 24 June, 2, 11 July 1896, 24 January, 6 February, 23 April, 11 December 1897; *Cleveland Gazette,* 11 July 1896, 11 June 1898; *Douglass v. Douglass,* 9 May 1898, 13 App. DC 21, 1898, WL 15542 (App. DC); *Washington Bee,* 21 May 1898; William H. H. Hart to Helen Douglass, Washington, DC, 24 June 1896, B. F. Leighton to Helen Douglass, Washington DC, 22 April 1897; Charles S. Baker to Helen Douglass, Rochester, N.Y., 15 May, 3, 11, 18 June 1897, FDP, DLC.
19. Jobel Forster and John C. Yorston to H[P]D, Philadelphia, 30 April, 7 May 1895, DeWolfe, Fiske, & Co. to H[P]D, Boston, 26 March 1895, FDP, DLC; Parsons *Weekly Blade* (Kans.), 7 March 1896.
20. *Indianapolis Freeman,* 1 August 1896; *Colored American,* 8 February 1902; "Popular Lectures Given by Mrs. Frederick Douglass," [c. 1898], Helen Pitts, Class of 1859, Alumnae Files, Mount Holyoke College.
21. MWG to RDS, Lawrence, Mass., 11 April 1898, Addition I, FDP, DLC.
22. *Indianapolis Freeman,* 1 August 1896.
23. *Washington Bee,* 25 July 1896.
24. *Indianapolis Freeman,* 1 August 1896, *Washington Post,* 19 July 1896.
25. Grimké, "Second Marriage," 327.
26. IBW-B, *Crusade,* 75.
27. *Washington Post,* 30 May 1897.
28. *Colored American,* 6 August 1898.
29. *Cleveland Gazette,* 6 August 1898.
30. *Colored American,* 13 August 1898.
31. *Colored American,* 13 August 1898.
32. "A Bill to Incorporate the Frederick Douglass Memorial and Historical Association," S4832, 1 July 1898, Legal Files, FDP, DLC; *Cleveland Gazette,* 13 August 1898.
33. *Colored American,* 13 August 1898; *Washington Post,* 30 September 1898.
34. Agreement, September 1897, Miscellany, David Z. Morris to H[P]D, Rochester, 4, 11 August 1898, FDP, DLC.
35. Rochester Genealogical Society, comp. *Mount Hope Cemetery, Rochester, New York, Interment Index,* 2: 170.
36. David Z. Morris to H[P]D, Rochester, 11 August 1898, H[P]D Will, 28 September 1900, Legal File, FDP, DLC. One of her obituaries reported that "It is Mrs. Douglass's wish that she be buried at Cedar Hill" and that Frederick's body be removed to join hers. That report appeared in a Kansas may have recycled old news without verifying the information. *Topeka Plaindealer,* 11 December 1903.
37. Grimké, "Second Marriage," 329.
38. Essay by LHD, n.d., Addition II, FDP, DLC.
39. Joan Johnson, "'Ye Gave Them a Stone': African American Women's Clubs, the Frederick Douglass Home, and the Black Mammy Monument," *Journal of Women's History,* 17, 1 (Spring 2005):62–86.
40. H[P]D to Editors of the *Transcript,* Washington, DC, 5 September 1900, Alumnae File, Mount Holyoke College.
41. H[P]D Wills, Legal File, FDP, DLC.
42. *Colored American,* 13 August 1898.
43. Essay by LHD, [n.d.], Addition II, FDP, DLC.
44. CRD, "Some Incidents," 13 February 1917, Evans Collection.

45. Essay by LHD, [n.d.], Addition II, FDP, DLC.
46. CRD, "Some Incidents," 13 February 1917, Evans Collection.
47. IBW-B, *Crusade*, 74–75. Wells-Barnett reiterated that "Cedar Hill was the home of Helen Pitts Douglass" and considered Jackson's statements a "deliberate insult," and a breach of "Christianity and good breeding."
48. *Washington Evening Star*, 20 July 1895.
49. RDS, *MMAIRH*, FDP, DLC. Rosetta's daughter, Fredericka, had the speech published as a pamphlet in February 1923, in honor of her mother, grandmother, and grandfather, and dedicated to the NACW.
50. Fredericka D. S. Perry, Notes on Travels, [n.d.], FDC, DHU-MS. The same brooch also appeared on a portrait of Rosetta from the turn of the century. The portrait of Anna currently hangs in the formal parlor of the house.
51. *Washington Post*, 30 September 1898.
52. H[P]D, Certificate of Death, 1 December 1903, District of Columbia Archives; *NYT*, 2 December 1903; *Washington Post*, 4 December 1903; *Colored American*, 5, 19 December 1903; *Topeka Plaindealer*, 11 December 1903; *Broad Axe*, 12 December 1903; *Cleveland Gazette*, 26 December 1903; *Indianapolis Freeman*, 19 December 1903; *Washington Post*, 4 December 1903; CRD to Archibald Grimké, Washington, DC, 15 December 1903, 2 January 1904, Haley Douglass to Archibald Grimké, Washington, DC, 1 January 1904, FDP, DLC. The cemetery in Honeoye where the Pitts family is buried also contains a tombstone for Helen.
53. Johnson, " 'Ye Gave Them a Stone,' " 65–68; James R. Hinds, *Cedar Hill Historic Structures Report*, part 2 (Washington, DC, 1968), 22; Fredericka D. S. Perry, Notes on Travels, [n.d.], FDC, DHU-MS; Sallie W. Stewart, pres. to Trustee [Fredericka D. S. Perry] Evansville, Indiana, 4 December 1943, FDMHA to Robert Hutchins, [n.p.], [n.d.], FDMHAR, DLC.
54. Johnson, " 'Ye Gave Them a Stone,' " 65–68; James R. Hinds, *Cedar Hill Historic Structures Report*, part 2 (Washington, DC, 1968), 22; West, *Domesticating History*, 153–54; "Establishment of the Frederick Douglass Home as a Part of the Park System in the National Capital," 13 July 1962, FDMHAR, DLC; Finding Aid, Addition II, FDP, DLC; *Washington Post*, 8 August 1972, FDMHA, DLC.
55. General Affidavit, RDS, 20 February 1905, Pension File, NARA; Certificates of death, District of Columbia Archives; Frederick Douglass Family Initiatives, (http://www.fdfi.org/, accessed 1 August 2015).
56. Robert Schnacky to Mary Gregory, Rochester, 7 January 1972, FDMHAR, DLC; Inscriptions on gravestones, Mount Hope Cemetery, Rochester, N.Y.

INDEX